Diary of a Disgru

Vernon Coleman

Dedication

To Donna Antoinette, The Princess

Always in my heart, always on my mind
I will always be by your side
And always on your side
You will never be alone
Because we will always be together

Boring Bit For Lawyers

These days, most books include disclaimers in which the authors apologetically warn readers that they should not rely on any information their books contain, and nor should they follow any of the advice they may find within. I certainly do not recommend that any reader makes any decisions of any kind based on any of the absurd ramblings in this book.

Disclaimers invariably go on to insist that readers who rely on anything in the book they are reading do so at their own risk. These warnings are included because the world is now full of lawyers and litigants who, under the often misguided impression that there might be money to be made, will leap at every opportunity to gouge lolly out of anyone who can be blamed for fate's little tricks. And so, as author and publisher, I feel that I must follow fashion and warn readers that if they act on any of the facts in this book, or decide to follow any of the advice, they do so entirely at their own risk. I advise readers to treat facts with disdain. I recommend that advice and opinions should be disregarded or treated with great suspicion. Any reader who believes the facts in this book, or follows advice the book contains, does so entirely at their own risk. Moreover, I would also like to make it clear that books can be dangerous objects and should not be dropped, thrown or otherwise projected into areas where people or delicate objects might be damaged. In other words, dear reader, drop your reading device onto your toes and you're on your own.

Preface

Welcome to my life, my world; the good and the bad; the ups and the downs; one year's supply of the inside of my head; my joys and my sadnesses; my everything.

There are two types of diary: the one you keep to tell you where you are due to be and when, together with a brief summary of whom you met and what you did. This is the sort of diary produced by authors who want to tell the reader about all the celebrities they've met. You know the sort I mean. `I met A at the Ivy. He ordered the pickled lobster and told me about his experiences duck shooting at Lord B's place in Norfolk. We waved to C and D who were sitting at the next table and afterwards had drinkies at the Groucho Club.'

Any controversy is carefully designed to titillate but not to annoy people in power and such diaries generally consist of long lists of dates, lunches, dinners and parties. `I met Simon Cowell at the studios today. We compared notes on cars and I found out that his new Bentley is equipped with a gym and an Olympic sized swimming pool.' If they contain enough gossipy bits, are indiscreet, and give away enough secrets, they get serialised in the popular papers. I think these diaries are tedious, though they sell well and are clearly popular with large numbers of readers. And then there is the diary in which the writer keeps a private note of what he thought and felt as life alternately treated him and then kicked him in the goolies, as it does with relentless efficiency. Why? Well, why did Pepys keep his diary? Why did Kilvert make the effort? It seemed a good idea at the time is probably the best explanation.

This is the second sort of diary. It would be disingenuous to claim that this book was written for me alone. I am, after all, a professional writer. But it was started for my own benefit. I wanted to assess my life at what was clearly a professional crossroads; and to obtain some insight into my own life as a publisher and author. The book is about real incidents. This is my life. As I wrote it, I gradually realised that it might be of interest to those readers who are kind enough to read my books.

When Rousseau wrote his Confessions he argued that a writer should tell the truth all the time. If people are upset then so be it. Hemingway believed that to write well all you had to do was to write truthfully. Mark Twain and Charles Dickens wrote with rare honesty about their travels, adventures, successes and failures.

It is only an adventure to read someone's diary if it was not written (self-consciously) to be read by others. This wasn't. I started writing it because I realised I was starting to forget where I'd been and what I'd done. And why. I continued writing it because I found it cathartic and enjoyable. The book contains events, thoughts, accidents, appreciations, incidents, disasters and consequences.

What follows is a sometimes painfully sad, always honest account of one year in my life. I hope to heaven that bits of it are funny. It's an autobiography, a social commentary on life in the 21st century, a commonplace book, a guidebook describing one man's battle to survive in a world where he invariably feels like a stranger. It's a book about publishing and about staying alive in the 21st century. It's a book full of opinions (some of which doubtless mature into rants).

I hope that some people will find some of it amusing. Others may find it comforting. And a few may, I hope, find it offers inspiration. It's an account of what happens in a world where genuinely threatening iconoclastic writing results in genuinely effective bans.

Many diarists, like many travel writers, go out of their way to create incidents and excitement. I have had no need to do that. The incidents and excitements seem to queue up at my door each morning, waiting to pounce. `Let's go round to Vernon Coleman's,' they say to one another. `We can always have some fun there.'

This book has taken more out of me than anything else I've ever written. Maybe that's because I've put more into it.

Vernon Coleman
April 2011

Note 1. Any proceeds from the sale of this book will go to the author.

5

Note 2. Many thousands of verbs, nouns, pronouns, adverbs, adjectives, etc. were used in the preparation of this book. All were acquired without any damage being done to the environment. They are used with permission of the appropriate authorities.

January

1
11.50 a.m.
A few months ago I saw an advertisement from MI5. They were looking for a new Chief Scientific Advisor. I couldn't resist it. I obtained an application form and filled it in. It was all terribly casual though they did tell me I shouldn't tell anyone I'd applied. I sent in an e-mail request for a form and it occurred to me afterwards that the people at MI5 who routinely read my e-mails must have had something close to a fit when they saw it.

When I told The Princess I had applied for a job at MI5 she misheard and wanted to know why I'd applied for a job with a furniture superstore. `There are two things I don't understand,' she said. `Why do you want a job with MFI and why can't I tell anyone?' I told her I couldn't answer either question.

When the form arrived I filled it in very neatly. I gave them the Post Box address, of course. Either they know where we really live (in which case they don't need to be told) or they don't (in which case I'm not going to tell them and they're so incompetent that they don't deserve to know anyway). On the form they seemed more concerned about whether I had any disabilities than anything else. They asked three times and in the end, because I felt that I wasn't likely to be taken seriously unless I could tell them about some disablement, I made something up. I can't remember what it was now so if anyone ever finds the form and asks me about it I'll be in a tricky position.

Going through my accumulated e-mails I see that I haven't got the job.

I wasn't terribly disappointed or surprised.

The Princess said she wondered if it was because they thought I was too old and asked if I thought I should take them to an industrial tribunal. The thought did appeal but somehow I expect I'll forget about it and never get round to doing anything. It would be a jolly wheeze, though.

It did occur to me this afternoon that if they had any sense they would have hired me. A bit of imagination and lateral thinking wouldn't have done them any harm.

2.35 p.m.

One of the biggest advantages of self-publishing is that I have direct contact with my readers.

When I first started out as a writer I quickly realised that although I really only wanted to write books that I wanted to write I would then have to `sell' those books to a whole host of people who might want entirely different books.

First, an agent has to be convinced that a publisher might like a book. Then a publisher has to be convinced that wholesalers will like the book. Then wholesalers have to be convinced that bookshops will like the book. And then bookshops have to be convinced that members of the public will like the book. Finally, book-buyers have to be persuaded that they might like to read the book.

That's an awful lot of convincing that has to be done. And it means that there are a lot of barriers between what the author wants to write and what the reader wants to read. Agents don't really care about readers. They only care about what publishers want. And publishers want what their marketing people think will sell to the wholesalers. The whole chain is littered with faults because most of the people with the power to say `yes' or `no' to a book don't know anything much about books or readers. It is a simple fact that most of the people with the power to decide what books will be published never buy books at all. Most of them never actually *read* any books.

I've always followed a simple philosophy for writing books. I don't believe it is possible to know what readers will really like. And even if I did know what readers wanted I don't think I could write like that. I have to make my books true to my dreams, I have to be able to write with passion and purpose. I believe that my system gives me as good a chance of producing a commercially successful book as any other. And I know that whatever happens at least I will like the book. If I write a book just to please a marketing team there's a real chance that no one at all will like the result. Books are best when they are written because the author wanted (needed) to write them rather than because some marketing man, after consulting a committee of supermarket buyers, advised some editorial pimp to commission a book.

My first agent, one of the most powerful and successful agents in London, constantly told me that I had to prepare outlines for publishers' eyes and that I had to think of the marketing department rather than the editorial department. What she perhaps didn't realise was that marketing departments are totally unimaginative. They only ever look for books that are similar to books that have already been successful.

I felt that I was being separated from my readers by masses of people - mostly parasites - who didn't understand anything about books and who certainly didn't know what people wanted to read.

Self-publishing enables the author to cut out all these parasitic middlemen.

2

09.55 a.m.

I am thoroughly fed up with Amazon. Months after the book was published our webshop, which is run by Amazon, is still offering *Cat Tales* with no picture and no availability. Other dealers are offering second-hand copies of the book at £38.50 and £32.25 but we don't earn a penny out of that. I have racks of the book stocked up in the Publishing House warehouse which I would be delighted to sell for £12.99. I despair of Amazon. Lots of my books are listed as unavailable when there are plentiful stocks just sitting on shelves waiting to go to good homes. We are going to have to abandon webshop sales and go back to good old-fashioned cheques through the post.

12.25 p.m.

A mailing company we have used for some time this morning returned several boxes of catalogues which were left unused from a 2008 mailing. I am appalled that a mailing house should keep over 6,000 time sensitive catalogues sitting in a warehouse. The catalogues are, of course, now entirely useless and have to be thrown away.

3

23.15 p.m.

The Princess and I don't go to parties, dinners or social events of any type but today we went to a neighbours' home for drinks. We got suckered into it in such a way that it was impossible to say `no' without being rude. While The Princess talked to an elderly lady, who is an expert on compost, I met a man who, when he had asked me what I did for a living, said that it is his intention to write books when he retires in three years time. He was well oiled but not quite at the falling over stage. He said he thought he might write novels and biographies and that it didn't matter whether he earned any money from it because he had a good pension to look forward to. I asked him what he did for a living. He said he ran a gas appliance showroom. I said wasn't it funny but it was my intention to run a gas appliance showroom in my spare time when I retire. He indignantly said it would not be possible because his job requires a good deal of knowledge and training and skill and other things he didn't go into but expressed with an airy wave of the hand. I said I felt sure I could do it and that I thought it would actually be very easy. I said I might manage several showrooms and would be happy to do it for very little money. He got very red faced, spluttered and said that if I did I would be putting trained men out of work. He then stalked off in a huff. A few moments later The Princess came over, told me I'd upset one of the other guests and said that she thought we should leave so we left.

4

22.45 p.m.

The Princess and I took down the Christmas decorations and found ourselves with a dozen superfluous balloons. We didn't want to burst them so we waited until dark, tied the balloons to a long piece of string and then fastened the whole lot to an ornament in a nearby garden which we felt would benefit from a touch of colour. Afterwards, as we skipped home vainly hoping that no one had noticed us, we felt like kids.

Tying balloons to a neighbours' garden sculpture undoubtedly contravenes the Public Balloon Act (1999) but it gave us a few moments of laughter and fun. And these are qualities that are far too rare these days.

The male owner is a rather stern and humourless fellow who does something very important at the local town hall.

5

9.22 a.m.

Another television licence fee reminder came today. I loathe the rancid licence fee collection people almost as much as I loathe the BBC, our State media monolith.

Most folk in the media live in a world where reality and truth are merely occasional visitors but those working for the BBC inhabit a world where these two are complete strangers; the BBC is an organisation which doesn't even reach the heights of telling half-truths. It is a home for hypocritical media masses who live by their own corporate code of political correctness but do nothing about the corporation's suppression of the truth. The BBC appears to be a safe haven for aggressive women and chippy homosexuals; it seems dominated by self-serving, complacent, snooty, unimaginative individuals whose religion is multiculturalism and political correctness and whose daily lives are spent sucking up to the establishment which feeds them riches. The BBC is so far to the left that if the world were flat it would have long ago toppled over the edge; it is a loathsome imperial organisation where vulgarity, ignorance and prejudice are regarded as employment requirements and worn as badges of honour.

The BBC used to be gutsy and used to employ people who cared, who had courage and integrity; today its employees have become so accustomed to politicising news reports that I don't think they are aware that they are doing it. Vast numbers of people who work for the BBC are foreign, in origin or temperament, and have no interest at all in England or its history. Many (both imported and home-grown) are England-haters and regard England and its history as offensive. They sneer at England, Englishness and English virtues. (They dare not sneer at Scotland or Wales, of course.)

The BBC has bred interviewers who are like school prefects; they are establishment through and through, careful never to venture into areas which might cause distress in high places. They have no sympathy for, or understanding of, the principles of free speech or free enterprise; they despise genuine entrepreneurs and real heroes.

I confess I find it amusing when BBC interviewers are occasionally described as `iconoclasts'. The BBC would not employ an iconoclast if they received an EU grant to take him in. The BBC is staffed with establishment lackeys. In my quite extensive experience the people who work for the BBC are, by and large, a bunch of unoriginal, sanctimonious, hypocritical, self-righteous nonentities who wallow in the security of each other's company but couldn't really do anything creative or useful outside the safety of the corporation. The BBC is the ultimate mother corporation.

It is no exaggeration to say that the BBC is packed with racists (anti-English) fascists (pro-EU) and statists (supporters of the Government). The important issues are carefully avoided. To my knowledge the BBC has never investigated, researched, discussed or made programmes questioning the European Union, the value of genetic engineering, the truth about climate change, the safety and effectiveness of vaccination or the usefulness (or otherwise) of vivisection. There is an in-house determination to take sides in advance and an inbuilt refusal to allow licence payers to discuss important issues openly and fairly. Many of the people working for, or appearing on, the BBC are bigoted fools; as ideologically bent as paperclips. As a result, most editorial decisions are bent and, since we don't know which programmes are a direct result of prejudice, we have to assume that the whole damned service is bent. Like most people in the media, BBC staff seems to disapprove of anyone who stirs things up, asks difficult questions of important people, or threatens the status quo. Most BBC employees are reactionary and unquestioning people who don't like anyone who does anything different or unusual unless whatever they do can be ignored or laughed off as harmless eccentricity.

Instead of using its vast wealth, gouged from unwilling taxpayers, to make useful programmes, the sponsored BBC uses its money to make *Eastenders*, arguably the greatest cause of misery, violence and elementary dissatisfaction in the country. And their attempts to make programmes about business or finance result in such superficial claptrap as *The Apprentice* and *Dragons' Den*. (We caught both these programmes once each. The first, we both found utterly appalling and little more than a master class in greed and deceit. The second we found even more disappointing since it consists of smug, self-important, excruciatingly rude people who want to touch the fringes of fame being smug, self-important and excruciatingly rude to decent, hard-working people who are often talented and ambitious but whose only fault was their bad taste and desperation in agreeing to go onto such an appalling programme.)

The real insult is that we are all forced to subsidise this deceitful organisation which bends or suppresses the truth about many of the things we take seriously. Anyone who wants to listen to the radio or watch television in Britain, is forced to pay a licence fee. The fee entitles us all to watch the output of scores of different broadcasters but the Government then gives all the money it collects to the state-owned, state-run broadcaster. To be honest, I suppose we can, therefore, hardly be surprised if the BBC provides a biased view of every issue it touches, although the real problem is perhaps the fact not so much that there is a bias, but that a large percentage of the population does not realise that there is a bias. The BBC has sold itself to us as the broadcasting organisation we can trust most when in fact it is the broadcasting organisation we can trust least. It is alarming that anyone in the country still does believe anything they hear or see on the BBC. Still, I suppose there were people in the USSR who thought Pravda a reliable source of information

The money given to the BBC is collected by a menacing, threatening private organisation which will, if you don't pay up, send people round to your home. The organisation actually has no more right to come into your home than you have to walk into the BBC and sit in the director general's undoubtedly expensive and overstuffed chair but most people don't realise that. If you tell the BBC's debt collectors that you don't have a TV set they will tell you that they are going to come round and check; bluntly calling you a liar.

A friend of mine who is a professional broadcaster for a commercial organisation, and who has never paid the licence fee, long ago advised me not to let the licence fee thugs into my home. `Don't even answer the door. You do not have to let the BBC's representatives into your house. They can only come in if they have managed to persuade a magistrate to give them a court order and if they are then accompanied by a policeman. And they can only get a court order if they can convince the magistrate that you have a television set which is connected to an aerial and being used and that you don't have a licence and that you are watching programmes live and not just watching recordings.'

My guess is that the vast majority of hapless souls who do get fined are tricked or bullied by people collecting money for the State's official mouthpiece. Prosecutions of licence fee evaders undertaken by the courts on behalf of the BBC represent at least 10% of all prosecutions of all kinds.

Occasionally, brave souls make a public stand against the BBC arguing, not unreasonably in my view, that the BBC is in breach of its charter. This never works, however, because there is no justice in Britain these days and the courts always side with the official Government broadcaster.

When a viewer who didn't want to pay the licence fee complained that the BBC had repeatedly supported the European Union in its broadcasts, had failed to investigate the lack of EU audited accounts for over a decade and had taken £141 million from the EU and suggested that the organisation had broken its contract under the Royal Charter, he was taken to court and fined £240 plus £60 costs and £15 victims' surcharge (presumably the BBC felt hurt and needed the money to put towards a bottle of celebratory champagne).

The authors of the American constitution understood that letting the Government choose what (and what not) to publish is a very bad idea and unacceptable in a democracy. I believe that Benjamin Franklin and Thomas Jefferson got this right: any public funding of the media is a bad thing because it is the middleman (the Government) and not the cheque writer (the public) who plays the part of piper and therefore calls the tune. (It is the same with the health service.) A state broadcasting organisation which is sustained by a tax on the citizens but which gives its loyalty not to its employers (the licence payers) but to the Government and is, inevitably, staffed by government whores, is not to be relied upon.

I regularly receive letters complaining about the BBC. A growing number of people are fed up with being forced to pay a licence fee to the Bent Broadcasting Corporation, a propaganda organisation which many now consider to be a major threat to our freedom and democracy. P.G. Wodehouse, who knew a good deal about such things, and had a great sense of taste, described the BBC as a loathsome institution. Since his day things have got considerably worse. We have been betrayed by the BBC. In my view, the single biggest crime of this statist broadcaster has been to support the EU so enthusiastically and uncritically.

Still, the good news is that the television licence is an outdated and absurd concept. The BBC is going to find it increasingly difficult to work in a world where many people watch and listen on computers and mobile telephones.

I tossed my television licence fee reminder onto the fire where it burnt nicely and helped keep us warm for 0.17 seconds.

15.57 p.m.

Our balloons have, sadly, disappeared already from our neighbours' house. The Princess was coming back from the postbox this afternoon when she saw a council truck parked outside the house where we had left the balloons attached to an ornament. The owner of the house had clearly sent two council workmen round to untie the string and take the balloons away. It was, presumably, far too complicated and dangerous a task for an executive to perform. Mind you, he and his wife do manage to cut their lawn by themselves so they aren't entirely useless. Last summer we could not believe our eyes when we walked past and saw Mrs Council Official on her hands and knees. She was cutting a particularly tricky piece of lawn edging with a pair of kitchen scissors. She was wearing yellow rubber gloves. Her husband was standing next to her giving her instructions. If I hadn't seen it myself, I don't think I would have believed it. If it snows The Princess and I are going to go out in the middle of the night to build a huge snow wall across the end of their drive.

18.32 p.m.

The nation has come to a grinding halt because of snow. Our chances of making any profit this month are devastated because the Royal Mail is unable to move post around the country. We have become a very wimpy nation. When I was small I remember my father leaning out of our bathroom window and pouring hot water from a kettle onto the downpipes so that we could have a morning wash. I remember seeing beautiful Jack Frost ice patterns on our windowpanes. On the inside! These days, even asylum seekers and the homeless demand central heating as a right. When I was at medical school I lived in a flat where the only heat came from a tiny gas fire. It was frequently colder indoors than outdoors. In the winter of my final year, when I had to go to different hospitals all over Birmingham, I remember brushing a foot of snow off the saddle of my moped before riding from one hospital to another.

20.10 p.m.

Publishing is in a gloomy state. I spent much of today taking a cold, hard look at the economics of the business I seem to be in.

Bookshops and wholesalers want up to 45% of the retail price. So, assume a book sells for £10. And assume you've allowed the wholesaler or shop to take the 45% they want. (Big publishers frequently give more than that to get the business.) The wholesaler or retailer will pay £5.50. But the £5.50 isn't normally paid straight away. Shops and wholesalers expect 60 or 90 days credit and so it may be paid two or three months down the line. Or it may never be paid at all. The increasing number of bad debts which result from bookshops going broke mean that the £5.50 becomes £5 at best. And having to send regular statements in order to gouge the money out of the shop costs more money.

Shops and wholesalers expect books to be sent out post free. It costs on average between £2 and £3 to post a single book. Say £2.50 as an average. Larger quantities are slightly cheaper to post but still expensive now that Royal Mail is trying to turn itself into a profitable giant. The cost of packing materials (cardboard and padded bags) adds at least another 50 pence to the cost. The cost of having someone to turn the book into a parcel, prepare a label and stick the label onto the parcel has to be accounted for but is at least another 50 pence a book. So it's not unreasonable to assume that the overall posting cost is £3.50 per book. And remember, the bookshop or wholesaler expects the publisher to pay the cost of postage. Ordinary book buyers expect to pay extra towards the cost of postage and packing. Bookshops and wholesalers do not. When books are damaged or go missing (much commoner than you might imagine) Royal Mail will only refund the cost of printing the book - which is not, of course, the true cost to the publisher.

Attempts to make them understand the economics of publishing have failed miserably. This policy, and the resultant losses, means that the overall posting cost is closer to £4 per book.

So, for a £10 book the shop will take £4.50 and posting will take £4. The average hardback book, with a print run of at least 1,000, costs around £4 to print. Jackets cost more. Transporting huge piles of books around the country costs a small fortune. Large or illustrated books cost considerably more to print. And the soaring price of paper means that printing costs are rising almost daily. And on top of all this must be added the cost of maintaining and heating premises, paying staff and allowing them to have holidays, maternity leave and so on. Paying the local authority, having rubbish taken away, having fire extinguishers serviced, having electrical appliances checked annually, paying insurance - oh, boy, the expenses all mount up.

In the old, sensible days, publishers would price their books at five times the cost of actually making the book. And so a book that cost £2 to make would cost £10 in the shops and a book that cost £5 to make would cost £25 in the shops. Those were the sort of prices that were charged a decade ago. (My book *Alice's Diary* has been on sale for over 20 years. When it was first published in 1990 the price was £8.99. Today the price is £9.99.) But competition from supermarkets and the Internet has resulted in book prices being slashed. Margins are wafer thin; sustainable only by big publishers who can publish international co-editions.

Just to make all this even crazier, bookshops and wholesalers will often return books if they don't sell them in a month or so. So, unless sales are `firm' there's a risk that the books will come bounding back unsold and the bookseller or wholesaler will demand a credit. Bookshop returns can be devastating. You think your stock levels are down to 100 and then suddenly, without any warning, 500 books which you think you had sold, come back and so now you have 600 books in stock and the extra 1,000 that you have just ordered aren't necessary. Returns can destroy a small publishing business.

Where does this leave Publishing House?

Well, it leaves us with £10 coming in and £12.50 going out before the costs of staff and premises have been paid for.

Naturally, there are no royalties for the author or profits for the publisher.

In other words, selling books through bookshops and wholesalers is a disaster unless you can persuade the shop or wholesaler to take a much smaller cut of the price. Or unless you can charge more for the book. If the book retails for £20 then things work tolerably well because the cost of postage (which is, today, the deadly catch as far as small publishers are concerned) is a much smaller percentage of the total. If you can sell enough books (and judge your print run carefully so that there aren't masses of books remaining unsold) there may even be some money left out of which to pay taxes to the Government, royalties to the author, bonuses to staff and (speak it softly) profits for the publisher.

I am going to have to spend some time this year restructuring my publishing business. Many publishers are now, like big newspapers, `vanity publishers' in everything but name. They lose money on book sales but hope to make some profit out of the serialisations, the film rights, the overseas translation rights and so on. Book publishers have become conglomerates, with subsidiaries all over the world, so that they can cut costs through making deals. There are very, very few small independent publishers making a profit these days. Many of those who do make a profit do so because they have been lucky with a single, often unexpected, bestseller. I doubt if there are many (if any) other authors making a living out of publishing their own work. I am determined to continue writing, publishing and making a living.

6
10.34 a.m.
I don't read newspapers much any more. They are full of nonsense and frippery, prejudice and bigotry and are mostly composed of press releases. This morning I succumbed and spent half an hour skimming a bundle of daily papers. The American Government now thinks that Osama bin Laden is in Pakistan. It is good to know that after eight years of hunting, bombing and killing they are getting closer to knowing which country he is in. Years ago I seem to remember that they and we invaded Afghanistan because he was

supposed to be there. Now they know he's not there. And we're still at war.

I see that enterprising thieves have stolen £1 million from HMRC by hacking into the taxman's computer and granting themselves tax rebates. I know I should frown at this but it's difficult not to be amused by it.

And there is news that Americans are excitedly buying a popular new computer game in which players must either convert or kill non-Christians. (The implication seems to be that the non-Christians are Muslims.) I wonder if Americans will be so thrilled when Muslims produce a computer game in which players must either convert or kill non-Muslims. I suspect not. And I can't even begin to imagine the response of the pro-Zionism lobby when someone produces a computer game in which players must either convert or kill Jews.

Through ill-based arrogance, the Americans have broken all the elements of any code of civilised conduct just as they have broken all the rules of war. There is no code and there are no rules. Obama, the former hope of liberal America but now, predictably, a constant source of deceits and disappointments, has continued in the modern American tradition of broken down imperialism, driven by nothing more glorious than self-interest and greed.

Finally, I read an obituary of Franco Corelli the tenor. What a wonderful man he was. When someone booed him during a performance of *Il Trovatore* in Naples he leapt off the stage and ran up three flights of stairs to throw himself on his tormentor. An appearance in *Don Carlos* with Boris Christoff ended prematurely when the two men, using stage swords, actually tried to kill each other in the auto da fe scene. Corelli was one of the world's leading tenors in the 1960s and 1970s. He was, however, a man constantly in need of reassurance. After performing, he listened to a tape of his entire performance just to make sure that his voice was still there.

18.45 p.m.

I watched a little television news this afternoon and spotted a good example of news manipulation and bias that most viewers would probably never notice (not least because most people watch only one channel). Sky news ran a 20-minute item on the leadership challenge to Gordon Brown and then ran a small item on the snow. The BBC, by contrast, ran 20 minutes on the weather and then a short item on the Gordon Brown challenge. The item about Brown started with him having a rare good moment against David Cameron in that day centre for thieves, the House of Commons.

There is an argument that `real' history is what we remember and what influences our lives; it may or may not be true in reality, in terms of facts, but in real life facts in themselves are of far less significance than myths, and perception is more important than reality. The problem today is that what we think of as news is too often nothing more than propaganda because it has been changed - both factually and in emphasis - by people who have a vested interest to protect. Everyone knows that it is terribly easy to alter photographs and tape recordings but the real danger comes from far more subtle changes. Television companies present as news only those items for which they have film footage, and therefore what we see on television tends to be what someone wants us to see. Interviews on TV can be edited to give a view that fits the prejudices of the editor or his bosses. And the same thing is true of newspapers. I remember a friend of mine, who worked as an editor on a national newspaper, telling me that he was in a `story conference' (where the editors sit and discuss what items will be where in the following morning's paper) when a news story about a vicar came up. One of the other editors wanted to make the vicar a hero. (I can't remember what he had done and it doesn't really matter.) But the paper's editor-in-chief wasn't interested. `We already have a hero story,' he said, drawing attention to another story planned for the paper. `We need a villain piece. Write it that way.' And so the vicar, who had so nearly become a hero, became a villain and instead of receiving applause and medals his life was ruined. What he had done hadn't changed at all. It was the perception, not the reality, that changed. But as far as the readers were concerned the perception became the reality. He was turned from a would-be hero to tomorrow morning's villain. In our news-rich society, truth and facts are ultimately of far less significance than widely appreciated myths, images and perceived truths. A widely believed falsehood is more powerful and relevant than a little known truth. Many of these myths affect our lives in numerous, significant ways. Sometimes journalists propagate myths through ignorance and gullibility rather than wickedness or carelessness. For example, science and medicine have given us many false beliefs. Usually there is a reason (the doctors or scientists promoting the myth have a hidden agenda or represent someone who has a hidden agenda) but the myth is reproduced and publicised by journalists who don't have enough knowledge to tell the truth, who trust too much and who have no incentive to work hard and attempt to find the truth. Everything is propaganda. Perhaps it was always thus.

23.15 p.m.
We have built a snow wall across our neighbours' driveway.

7
11.05 a.m.
I have a serious book buying problem. I can hardly leave the house without returning with an armful of books. On average, I buy 20 to 30 books each week, every week. I buy new books, I buy rare books and I buy old, scuffed second-hand books. I live in a world dominated by books. I write them, I read them and I collect them. I have several thousand books on my 'to read' bookcases. Trying to sort through a pile of books today I found that I have recently bought three copies of Colin Wilson's *The Outsider* (which I have been meaning to re-read for 30 years), two copies of the same Joyce Carey novel and no less than four copies of Hesketh Pearson's *Smith of Smiths*. If I live a long time and don't buy any more books I might just read the ones I have already bought. Nothing in the world gives so much sustained delight, for so little outlay, as a book. I find books in the most unlikely places. Today, I found a collection of old hardbacks and paperbacks for sale in a local corner shop which specialises in selling an eclectic mixture of bread, milk, sweets, cigarettes and kindling. The owners buy their food stock from their local Tesco supermarket. They shop at night, when the supermarket is quietest, and fill the boot and back seat of their car with groceries. Most of the books they had for sale were Mills and Boon romances which I would read if I were stuck in a country house hotel with nothing else to amuse me but would not buy from choice, but I did find a copy of Elliot Paul's classic *Springtime in Paris* which I bought for 20 pence. I don't think there

was anything else in the shop so modestly priced. It was a first edition but I didn't buy it because of that.

I don't go to high street bookshops such as Waterstones much any more. This is, I confess, mainly because they won't carry stock of my books and I find it painful to look around and see shelf upon shelf of books by television celebrities. Neither they nor W.H.Smith carry many books I want to read. The chain stores seem to specialise in selling cookery books or books by or about reality television participants (I find it hard to call them celebrities). There isn't much chance of finding anything by Evelyn Waugh, Hilaire Belloc, Charles McCarry, Ross Thomas or Lawrence Block or even Charles Dickens, P.G.Wodehouse or Graham Greene. I like hunting for old books that I missed the first time round (or that were published long before I started reading). Given a choice I prefer the old small format orange Penguins and Tauchnitz editions because they fit more comfortably into a jacket pocket. Why are the new Penguin classic novels issued in editions that seem nearly twice the size of the old ones? They cost more to print. They cost more to post. And they don't fit easily into hand or pocket. And I buy smaller format old hardbacks for the same reason.

12.21 p.m.
We were standing at a kerb waiting to cross the road in very heavy traffic. The Princess always freezes in situations like this - and the moment is then lost - so I usually grab her hand and yell `Go!'. When I did this today nine other people all waiting to cross the road ran with us. Two laughed, one looked peeved that she had obeyed so quickly and two said thank you.

16.10 p.m.
We have been trying for some time to decide what to do with my parents' ashes. We looked at one or two cemeteries but decided that they were soulless and depressing. Last night, at last, we decided what to do. We mixed their ashes together in a stout paper bag and took them to the beach at Budleigh Salterton where they lived for many happy years. I made a large hole in the bottom of the paper bag and then walked about at the water line, spreading the ashes on the beach. When the paper bag was nearly empty, I

put some stones into it and threw it into the sea. There were still some ashes left in it and I wasn't going to put them into a rubbish bin. The wind was coming off the sea and some of the ashes flew back into my hair and face. I didn't mind the ashen embrace. I got closer to my parents in death than I had in life. I did think of asking the council's Sprinkling Human Ashes on the Beach Department for permission to sprinkle ashes on the beach but decided not to bother. I was worried that they would probably say 'no' even though there are really no rules about distributing ashes in places where they aren't going to get into the food chain. Come to think of it, I suppose there's a vague risk that a millionth part of my parents might end up in a fish.

21.18 p.m.

I see that company directors at 100 of the biggest companies in the UK each spend an average of 25 days a year doing work for the companies which pay them, often handsomely. It is nice of them to spare so much time from grouse shooting, Wimbledon, Twickenham, the Polo and their annual trip to Davos. Talking of Davos I see that there are the usual calls for more women at Davos for the World Economic Forum. I assume this is because local shops have put pressure on the organisers because not enough spending is being done. The whole damned shindig is just an excuse for a bunch of self-important yahoos to have a good time at our expense. I wonder if any of the people attending pay their own airfares and their own hotel bills. I wouldn't bet on it.

8

11.22 a.m.

This morning I had this conversation in a shoe shop.

'I'm looking for a pair of brown brogues in size 11.' I would have liked to ask for wide fitting shoes, the way I used to be able to do, but I knew that the chances of my being able to walk into a shoe shop and buy size 11 shoes off the shelf with a choice of widths were about as good as finding Tony Blair in a truth telling mood.

The assistant looked like a man overlooked for promotion, years of bitterness had lined his face and left him with a turned down mouth and sulky, resentful eyes. He duly brought a pair of brown brogues in size 11. I tried them on. They were too tight. The assistant, like his colleagues, was wearing headphones and the sort of microphone used by rock and roll singers. I have no idea why. When they wanted to speak to one another they just yelled. Because they were wearing headphones they had to yell quite loudly.

`These are too small,' I protested. `Are you sure they're a size 11?'

`Oh yes,' said the assistant. `But we changed to American sizes recently. Our old size 11 has become a size 12.'

`Fine,' I said, resisting the temptation to ask why he hadn't mentioned this before. `Have you a 12 then please?'

`Oh no, we don't stock 12s. They're not normal.'

`Not normal?'

`No. Sizes 12 and above aren't normal?'

`No.'

`But 11s were normal?'

`Yes.'

`But what was an 11 is now a 12?'

`Yes, that's right. We moved over to American sizes, so our old 11 is now a 12.'

`But 12 is not normal?'

`No.'

`So my feet were big but normal but because you've gone over to American sizes they are now big and abnormal?'

`Yes, that's correct.'

I left.

I will take my old shoes to a cobbler to be repaired.

13.07 p.m.

People who want to have private conversations should have them in private places. Very few do. Most people seem to regard privacy as an optional extra they can do without. Maybe they've just given up. Maybe it's bravado. Maybe they just don't care. Like most writers I always listen to other people's conversations when they talk loudly enough for me to do so without making any obvious effort. I find I pick up a good deal of material I can use in books. You can learn so much about people by hearing what they say and how they say it. It's eavesdropping, I suppose. But it never makes me feel guilty.

I was standing in the bra section of the lingerie department of a large store. Two elderly women were shopping together. One had picked up and was examining two bras. She had a chest like a pouter pigeon and was the sort of woman for whom the word `embonpoint' was invented. The other woman looked bored and clearly wanted to be somewhere else.

`Why don't you just buy one of those?' asked the bored woman.

`I wanted something a little prettier,' said the one holding the bras. She looked disappointed.

`Why?' asked the bored woman. `No one's going to see it!'

`I'm going to see it,' said the woman with the bras. And the emphasis on the first word was full of pathos and pride and sadness.

15.16 p.m.

My book *Gordon is a Moron* has been banned just about everywhere. Although the book was listed in the *Independent* as one of the top ten political books it was not reviewed anywhere. And adverts have been banned everywhere. It is not considered appropriate to be rude about a Prime Minister who has destroyed England. (He has done very well for Scotland.)

I sent the following letter to all bookshops and ran the letter as a full-page advertisement in *The Bookseller* (described, rather sweetly, as the organ of the book trade).

`One or two of you still don't have copies of Gordon is a Moron on your shelves.

This may be because you disapprove of the title. And if that's the case then I respect your willingness to put your feelings above your desire to make a profit. The title is based on an old Jilted John record but several morons have written to me objecting to the use of the word in relation to Gordon Brown; presumably they feel aggrieved at being linked with the architect of our economic disaster. I understand and, in a way, sympathise with their point of view although I did not mean to disparage morons as a group or intend to compare them to Gordon Brown. I'd probably be pissed off if someone wrote a book called Gordon is a White Male Englishman. Still, it's too late to change the title.

The book may not be on your shelves because the author (me) isn't a celebrity. And that's an inescapable truth. I was the TV AM doctor back in the 80s and I made a series of appalling daytime shows for the BBC when most of you were still at school. The highlight of my career was telling the viewers of The Afternoon Show how much semen the average man produces when he ejaculates. (Not one person complained incidentally but the producer is still in therapy.) Since then I've steadfastly refused to appear on television at all. Of course, you could argue that Gordon Brown is something of a celebrity himself. And the `credit crunch' gets nearly as many column inches as Jordan which presumably gives it some sort of celebrity status. But the plain fact is that this book doesn't fit into the celebrity book genre.

You may not have stocked Gordon is a Moron because you haven't heard of it. And though that's clearly our fault we do have some damned good excuses. Advertisements for the book have been banned by most national newspapers and magazines. Even young Milksop at Private Eye has banned ads for it. As has his predecessor old Ingram at The Oldie. I can understand their point. Gordon hands out the MBEs and I don't. And for much the same reason there haven't been any reviews or promotional interviews and I'm pretty sure there won't be.

The fact is, however, that an awful lot of people in Britain are angry and want to know the truth about the economic crisis. They want to know why and how it happened. And since they don't get any answers from their newspapers or from the TV, they buy Gordon is a Moron. And when they've read it they tell their friends. It's one of those books. Readers tell us they love it because it tells them the truth about what has happened (and is going to happen).

Compared to the latest work from Jordan we haven't sold many but 20,000 at £9.99 isn't bad for a paperback selling entirely by word of mouth. And sales are rising. I know this not because we have computers and things but because the interval between 2,000 print runs is getting shorter and shorter. Small, truly independent publishers notice things like that.

We'd do a hell of a lot better, of course, if a few bookshops actually had the book on display. And I know this isn't the sort of gentlemanly thing to mention but we'd all make tons more money if people wanting to buy the book didn't have to order it or peer inside a friend's copy to find the publisher's address.

So, there you go. Why not go mad and order half a dozen for shelf stock and see what happens?

If you want to stock a book you can be proud to sell and that you won't have to send back in three months, order an armful of Gordon is a Moron by Vernon Coleman.

Yours sincerely

Vernon Coleman

P.S. The title is Gordon is a Moron. The author is Vernon Coleman. The publisher is Blue Books. The price is £9.99. And the ISBN is listed. The wholesalers have stock. P.P.S. I bet if you order some you don't send them back.'

I've now worked out how many copies of *Gordon is a Moron* we sold to bookshops as a result of that letter and advertisement.

None.

Not one.

I should not, I suppose, be surprised. In the only year for which I can find records (2004) our trade sales value was £254,220. But this meant supplying books to 1,840 individual bookshops and wholesalers around the world. Every single order was a result of a customer going into a shop and asking for a book. Not one book was sold from the shelf because no shops carried any of our books on their shelves.

9

11.34 a.m.

The Royal Mail strikes are still having an effect. I had to cancel advertisements during the last lot of strikes. My publishing business is basically a mail order business. When there is no mail the orders cannot come in and the books cannot go out. But the costs continue to mount. No orders in and no books out mean no cheques in. But the staff still have to be paid, the building heated and lit, the council tax paid, the insurance paid, the boiler serviced and so on and so on. It costs around £75 an hour to run Publishing House. And the damage done by a Royal Mail strike lasts for weeks, if not months. The total cost runs into many thousands of pounds. The last set of strikes destroyed our Christmas season and mean that we will make no profit this year. I don't suppose anyone working for Royal Mail gives a damn about this; they are too stupid to realise that destroying the customers is a bad thing for the future of their business.

The problem is that the damage lasts a long time. Advertisements have to be booked weeks, sometimes months, ahead. Whenever there is a strike I have to cancel adverts and mailshots and the effect lasts for months afterwards.

For the postmen the strike itself is quite short-lived. A day here, a day there. (And isn't it odd how many of their strikes result in their having a nice long weekend off work?) Striking probably doesn't cost them much, if anything at all. Some probably claim tax refunds and benefits to cover their losses.

For my business the losses are very real and long lasting. Last autumn I had to cancel £100,000 worth of planned advertisements. I also abandoned a plan to print 500,000 inserts and extra catalogues. Those are lost advertisements and lost sales. The cost to the economy as a whole will be small but when all the similar losses are added together the cost must be significant.

Last October my bill for one week's postage was £18,276.04. I will not be spending that much on postage for quite a while. I now have 50,000 books worth around £750,000 which are just sitting on shelves in the warehouse. And I have thousands of catalogues which are going out of date and will have to be dumped. I also have staff with nothing to do.

10
14.29 p.m.
I have stopped using direct debits and in future will pay as many bills as possible by cheque. Four times in the last three months, large organisations have used the direct debit system to take five figure sums that they weren't owed out of my accounts. Whenever they do this it is, of course, always a `mistake' but, like MPs doing their expenses, the `mistake' always seems to benefit them. On each occasion it has taken the thieves ages to put the money back.

When the Royal Mail (not content with attempting to destroy my business with strikes) took around £22,000 too much from my account (I gather a Royal Mail employee took the money out by altering a docket - though no one ever explained why) it took ten days and a lot of threatening from me for them to put it back. They took money they weren't owed not once but three times. It took a lot of effort to get the money back, even though Royal Mail admitted that the money was taken without authority or justification and was an 'unacceptable error'. When confronted with the evidence that they had taken money not owed they agreed to put the money back into my account but said it was normal practice to take five working days to do this. 'We're very busy,' my staff were told when I protested. So, since these things always manage to cover a weekend, it turned out to be longer than five days even when they'd agreed to give me back my money. The fraudulent theft of my money meant that I didn't buy advertisements I might have bought because I thought we were losing money when we weren't. The opportunity cost was enormous.

11
12.08 p.m.
I went to buy railway tickets this morning. 'Have you a railcard?' asked the clerk. I showed him the card through the grill. He just glanced at it. When he'd finished I told him I wanted to buy a second ticket. (I have found that if you ask for too much at once it confuses them.) 'Have you a railcard?' the clerk asked. 'Yes, you saw it about a minute and a half ago.' 'I need to see it before I can book a ticket,' he said, officiously.

The country is in safe hands.

14.15 p.m.
The Princess said today that it is a real pity that we can't all have a sleep bank. 'We could,' she said, 'sleep a lot when there isn't much going on and the weather is bad and then store up the sleep so that when the fine evenings come we can stay up late for a month without feeling tired.'

12
11.34 a.m.
I see that my book *Oral Sex: Bad Taste and Hard to Swallow* is for sale on Amazon at £160.86. *Why is Pubic Hair Curly?* is being sold for £161.74. This reminds me that I have a couple of boxes of each somewhere.

12.19 p.m.

A national magazine's advertising department has offered us three quarter page adverts for £500 but told us that we can have six advertisements for £1,200. When I was a small boy I remember seeing a woman at a jumble sale selling raffle tickets at a rate of half a crown each and six for a pound. I remember my mother telling me not to laugh because the seller was a little simple-minded.

13

15.12 p.m.

I see that the circulation of *The People* newspaper is down to half a million. When I resigned because the editor (I can't remember his name; I suspect he was just another corporate lickspittle) refused to publish a column criticising the illegal invasion of Iraq, the circulation was comfortably over a million and had been rising steadily for some time. Since then it has halved. I suspect that the circulation might have stayed higher if the editors had had the guts to publish a newspaper, instead of a propaganda sheet for an unpopular Government. Leaving *The People* cost me around £150,000 a year but I have never had a moment's regret.

14

18.12 p.m.

I received an e-mail telling me that a financial newsletter has been awarded a prize as the best newsletter of the year. The newsletter writer concerned had, during that year, made recommendations which would have led to his subscribers losing over 76% of their money. And over the previous decade anyone who had followed the advice in the prize-winning newsletter would have made an annual loss of 8.7%. The price of this newsletter is phenomenal. I couldn't help wondering how badly the other newsletters had done for this one to have won a prize. I know of one newsletter writer who uses the Delphic Oracle principle of saying stuff that can be interpreted in more than one way (so that later he can always say he was right) and some, more simplistic, who just print opposing views in the same newsletter so that whatever happens they can say: `There you are, we were right!' The financial newsletter business is, I fear, full of confidence tricksters. But many of them do very well for themselves, if not for their readers. Of course, if they were really good at picking good investments they would become very rich and wouldn't need to sell newsletters.

15
10.12 a.m.

As I had breakfast I heard something drop through the letterbox. This is a strange event because we receive hardly any mail at the house. On the mat was a small piece of card telling me that someone had tried, and failed, to deliver a parcel. I opened the door, saw a commercial delivery man just 20 yards away. I chased after him. He hadn't rung the bell or knocked on the door. `I can't give you the parcel unless you have the delivery number,' he said. `What delivery number?' `The delivery number on the package.' `I don't have the delivery number because I don't have the package. You have it in your van. You left a card.' `Where's the card?' `Back at the house. I shot off after you when I saw it and stupidly I left the card on the shelf just inside the door while I put on some shoes.' `I can't give you the parcel without the card.' `But you'd give me the parcel without the card if you had rung the bell because I wouldn't have had the card.' `But I'd know you belonged at that house.' `Well, I'll pop back and get the card.' `I can't wait around while you do that.' `It will take me a minute at the most.' By now he was climbing into his van. He started it up. I reached into my pocket and produced evidence that I lived at the address to which he'd tried to deliver the packet. `You could have stolen that,' said the deliveryman. `If I had the card I could have stolen that too.' `Yes. But you'd know the delivery number, wouldn't you?' And off he drove. I went back to the house and threw the card into the log basket to be burnt. I never did find out what the parcel was.

14.15 p.m.

A television company wants me to allow them to film me for a sixty-minute profile programme. I tell them I am not interested but ask if they would like to make a programme about the perils of modern medicine. They aren't interested in my idea. They just want to follow me around with a camera. I tell them I'm not interested in their idea.

16.12 p.m.

I have discovered that Noddy is called Oui Oui in France. Fair enough. We used to call General de Gaulle `Non Non'.

16

11.47 a.m.

The utility companies which supplied my father's home have at long last given up threatening to sue me. After my Dad died I had lengthy and increasingly acrimonious rows with the gas, electricity and water suppliers. All of these utilities had been turned off but all continued to send bills and then demand money they weren't owed. It took nearly two years to deal with all the claims and threats. Most threatened to sue me. One lot of idiots said they would have to send me bills for £0.00 to clear their books. I said that if they did I would send them a cheque for this amount. They did and I did. Even the local council got in on the act. They threatened to send the bailiffs in to an empty house, though what they would have raised by selling the doors and skirting boards would not have been much. Eventually, they all backed down but it was a tiring and upsetting business and I rather imagine that most bereaved relatives just pay up to get the corporate leeches off their backs. It seems to me that gouging unowed money out of relatives is probably a profitable sideline for the utilities. (I suppose they might claim that everyone makes mistakes. But how strange that the utility companies concerned, like MPs doing their expenses, all made mistakes that favoured themselves.) In order not to pay the water rates people I had to fill in a complex form which I confess I didn't really understand. The council eventually sent me a form to claim back some of the money they thugged me into paying. All gave in eventually. HMRC and the television licence people both got in on the act and took a good deal of persuading to go away. But British Gas took all the biscuits. At one point a British Gas buffoon claimed that I was being sent bills to pay for the pilot light and for gas leakage. I pointed out that the boiler had no pilot light and that I thought the leakage was their problem and that if they thought hundreds of pounds worth of gas were leaking out they really ought to do something about it.

In my experience, no company in Britain deserves its bad reputation more than British Gas. On one single day, nearly 18 months after my father had died, I received eight letters from them, including a variety of different final demands, two cheques and a letter of apology. I received a letter from a firm of solicitors telling me that on behalf of British Gas they were going to commence legal proceedings against me (with the usual warnings about the damage this was likely to do to my credit status) but on the same day the company agreed that I had paid all their bills, that they had, in fact, sent me cheques for overpayments and that I didn't owe them anything. They finally e-mailed to say that they had been making big mistakes.

15.14 p.m.

Another magazine has refused one of our adverts on the grounds that it contains too many words and doesn't look pretty enough. This is a common complaint not just about our adverts but about all mail order advertisements.

Adverts designed to sell products off the page never win prizes. But they work. The only people who can measure the success of their advertising are mail order advertisers. We can measure the effectiveness of an advert very accurately. Within a day or two we can tell whether a particular advert is going to work or not. We can compare the success of an advert in one publication with the same advert in another publication. We can make modest changes to an advert and see whether the response rate goes up or down. We know that the headline on an advert is crucial. We know that lots of words are more effective than a few words and a lot of pictures. We know that simple black on white adverts usually work best. Big companies pay their advertising agencies a fortune for design that won't attract any readers because although they know what looks pretty they don't know what works and what doesn't work. Nothing beats a clever headline and a mass of text. Adverts that really work well are invariably much better written than the editorial in a publication.

I know that if I am buying an advertisement in a magazine or newspaper I want to be on a page in the front half and I know that I must be on a right hand page. If my advert is smaller than a page in size then I want it to be on the outside edge and not near the staples (or `gutter'). If I am buying an advert in a newspaper then I want to be `above the fold' (i.e. on the top half of the page). I know that newspapers and magazines don't understand any of this because they don't charge more for prime positions. The key to buying advertising is the same as the key to buying property: location, location, location.

16.45 p.m.

I telephoned the tax office to see if they had received a letter I'd sent them over a month ago. I was told that they are so busy that there is a delay of six weeks in opening mail. So since my letter was sent only five weeks ago they do not yet know whether they have received it.

17

11.34 a.m.

My Public Lending Right statement has come in. It is very disappointing. I sell more books than ever and have more readers than ever but my PLR income goes lower every year. It has now dipped under £1,000 for the year. A few years ago my PLR income put me among the top 200 authors in the country. But since I've been self-publishing my books, my income from the libraries has fallen. There's one good reason for this: public libraries won't buy books published by small publishers. And they are especially reluctant to buy books which are self-published. I receive a constant stream of letters from readers complaining that they have been unable to borrow my books from their local library. All have been told (quite incorrectly) that my books are `unavailable'. And yet whenever I have managed to find my books in public libraries they have been falling apart and full of stamps showing that they have been heavily borrowed.

15.12 p.m.

The whole climate change debate is now so one-sided that it is embarrassing. Scientists have long forgotten their basic obligation to tell the truth - however inconvenient it might be. Too many scientists want to lead the debate (and acquire vast grants) by fiddling their results. Like politicians and journalists they have learned that if they present their findings in the correct way they can win friends and power and money. And they're enjoying their new-found power enormously. There is no evidence proving that global warming is man-made. I used to believe the lies that are told, until I really studied the evidence. I then became a firm disbeliever. I am now utterly convinced that the global warming threat is a ruthlessly efficient scam, introduced to accustom us to the fact that the oil is running out and to give bureaucrats and politicians a constant excuse to introduce repressive new regulations which enable them to introduce an endless stream of new taxes. (Several readers wrote criticising me for changing my mind. I asked them what their policy was when they found new evidence.) Modern scientists decide on a commercially acceptable solution and then select the facts which support the solution they have selected. That's not science: it's propaganda. Churches have recently been ringing bells to draw attention to the global warming problem. I would be more impressed if they rang bells to draw attention to the pointless killing in Afghanistan. Global warming is a scam. The killing is very real.

If the EU and the Government really believed that climate change is a man-made problem they could easily do lots of things to save energy (and protect the environment). They could, for a start, promote vegetarianism and provide subsidies for vegetarian foods. Rearing animals for meat production requires vast quantities of grain and is one of the major reasons why so many people around the world are starving. Growing all the grain to give to animals creates havoc for the environment and uses up massive amounts of water. It takes a million gallons of water to grow just one acre of corn. As the water trickles into streams and rivers it carries with it the remains of the fertilisers the farmers used. The fertiliser chemicals then pollute the water we drink (because, as I reported over a quarter of a century ago, it is impossible to get chemicals out of the water). The fertiliser also increases the growth of algae in rivers. As the algae decomposes it uses up oxygen in the water, killing fish. In America there is an 8,000 square mile dead zone below Louisiana and Texas, thanks to American agriculture. And, of course the 100 million cows in the USA are all belching out methane - which is much more potent as a greenhouse gas than carbon dioxide. It enrages me that so many ardent campaigners against global warming aren't vegetarian. You can't

35

campaign for the environment, and against hunger, if you aren't vegetarian without immediately branding yourself a hypocrite.

There are tons of other things the authorities could do, of course. They could provide subsidies to help village shops stay in business. (They don't actually have to hand out money. Just removing the VAT on products sold in village stores would be enough to keep many village shops open.) They could tell the police to clear traffic jams more speedily (instead of allowing 20 mile tailbacks to develop). They could remove VAT from all materials used in the repair of equipment that would otherwise be thrown away. They could provide better, and cheaper, train services. They should get tough with companies which overpackage their products. They could insist that brochures for electrical equipment are printed in just one language (instead of being printed in every language imaginable). They could cut back on the number of wars we're fighting. (All those planes and bombs don't help the environment.) They could arrange the VAT rules so that people are encouraged to repair and restore old buildings. (Bizarrely, there is no VAT on new buildings but there is VAT to pay if you want to restore a building.) If governments cared about the environment they would be encouraging restoration. After all, older buildings are invariably better to look at and far more functional than new ones. (The worst Italian earthquake for 30 years destroyed modern buildings that were supposed to conform to quake-proof building regulations but centuries old churches and palaces remained intact and undamaged. Why am I not surprised?)

The current tax system encourages people to knock down perfectly good buildings and build brand new ones. They could introduce taxes designed to limit households to one car. They could subsidise buses and ensure that better services are provided. They could put a stop to the huge lorries which, having been designed to cruise along European motorways, now blast their way through tiny English towns. They could encourage the use of the canal system but that would make sense so they won't.

I have been campaigning against pollution, waste and so on for far longer than most of the current batch of campaigners have been alive. There are many issues that need urgent attention: our seas are overfished, our drinking water is polluted with drugs and chemicals, our air is polluted, our food contains more carcinogens than vitamins and so on. The whole global warming fraud (designed to distract our attention from peak oil and to help the bureaucrats and statists gain more control over us) has taken attention away from these vital issues and has damaged interest in real environmental problems.

This is not a world for worriers or for those who believe in honesty and justice.

18

13.14 p.m.

The Princess and I were sitting in a pub. She had a pot of Earl Grey tea. I was drinking coffee. I doubt if even an analytical chemist would have been able to find a difference. A couple approached the bar, ordered two meals and two half pints of shandy. They were both dressed in black and had clearly been to a funeral. When they'd ordered they came across and sat at our table. `Do you mind?' asked the man. `Not at all,' said The Princess. When he'd sat down the man undid his tie, took it off and put it in his pocket. `We've been to a funeral,' he explained, unnecessarily. `Best friend of ours.' The Princess and I made sympathetic noises and faces. `We've known him 40 years.' The man looked suitably funereal. I nodded. He held the funereal expression for a minute or so and then brightened unexpectedly. `It's a long trip,' he continued, `so we thought we'd make a weekend of it.' His wife nodded. `Do a little walking and relax a bit,' she said. `We love this part of the world,' said the man. `I got the day off work for the funeral so we thought it a pity to waste the opportunity.'

It is amazing what one hears in pubs and cafés. Later on that day The Princess and I were sitting in one of those rather delightful English cafés that abound in market towns; one of those places where they serve home-made cakes and tea so strong that it eats through the spoons; the sort of place where any woman who has a chest bigger than her waist is regarded as having a `good figure'. An elderly woman and her middle aged son sat at the table next to us. She wore a coat with a fur collar and the sort of hat women wear to 'occasions'. He wore an expensive but wrinkled suit and a shirt that looked as if it had been ironed by someone with a serious neurological problem. There was a small burn mark on the collar. They ordered tea for two and a selection of cakes.

`She's far too young,' said mother, when she'd selected a cream horn and put it onto her plate. She looked as if she were the sort of person who sends a card to say thank you for the birthday card she's been sent.

`But she seems very willing,' said her son. `And she says she'll do everything. The other one won't do certain things.' He looked an exceptionally naive man; the sort of person who goes on holiday with his home address and telephone number (landline and mobile) clearly visible on his luggage label, together with the numbers and dates of his flights, and then shows genuine surprise when he gets back from his fortnight in Marbella to discover that he has been burgled.

The Princess, who hadn't been listening to this, asked me a question. I put a hand on her wrist and flicked my eyes towards the table where the mother and son are sitting. I had to hear the rest of this conversation.

`I think she's too flighty,' said mother. `She'll up and leave you. You want someone steady and reliable.'

Now The Princess was listening too. She looked at me and frowned slightly. I shrugged my shoulders almost imperceptibly to show that I didn't know what was going on either. It sounded as if mother and son were discussing possible new girlfriends. Or maybe a prospective new wife. Or maybe a mistress.

`My friend Nigel had her for six months,' said the son. `He said she was very, very good.'

`So why did she leave him?'

`He got married,' said the son. `He said he didn't need her any more. But I don't think his wife approved of her.'

`I'm not surprised!' said mother with a snort. `The older one would be much better for you. More experienced. She'll do you nicely.'

The son sighed. `You're probably right,' he said. He was clearly disappointed. He sipped at his tea, unwrapped another sugar cube and dropped in two more lumps. `How much do you think I should give her?'

`I pay mine £6.50 an hour and her bus fare,' said mother. `It's the going rate for cleaners.'

19

12.12 p.m.

'Breast screening benefits are a myth', says a new review. 'Thousands of women are having cancer misdiagnosed and being treated unnecessarily.' I got into terrible trouble when I said this in a book a couple of decades ago.

15.20 p.m.

The publishers who are admired in the industry and by investors these days are those who are willing to embrace digital technology. Those, in my view, are the publishers with absolutely no future at all. The publishers who will survive and thrive are the ones prepared to eschew all digital publishing and to concentrate on producing printed books that people really want to read, making sure that the books are available only as proper printed books and never turned into digital books of any description.

20

14.34 p.m.

My trusty mountain bike has died at last. I took it to a local shop for repairs and was shown a number of deep cracks in the framework. I shouldn't have been surprised. The bike has done sterling service and over the years I've ridden many miles on it - mainly over rough tracks. Various parts of it have had to be replaced (buckled wheels and so on) but up until now the frame had survived. I left the poor old thing at the bicycle shop, doubtless to be sold as scrap, and bought a replacement. But this time I haven't bought a mountain bike. Instead, I rode home on a brand new road bike with mudguards, sit up and beg handlebars and a wicker basket attached to the front. It cost about £200 and looks perfectly suitable for an elderly gentleman. 'At least there's one thing,' said The Princess when she saw it. 'You won't have to worry about it being stolen.' 'But it's brand new and shiny!' I said. 'No bicycle thief is going to want to be seen riding away on that!' said The Princess. I think she's probably right. I feel sad that my mountain biking days are over.

16.12 p.m.

There is a review on Amazon complaining that my *Bloodless Revolution* is too small and cheap. I published the book as a mass-market paperback hoping that shops would take copies. I really wanted the book to make a difference. But despite all our best efforts no shops would stock the book and the mass market price was a disaster for a mail order book.

21

08.00 a.m.

The Princess woke me up in the middle of the night to see if I was still alive. She gave me quite a thwack on the head and I thought at first that a piece of ceiling had fallen down. After having satisfied herself that I was, indeed, alive and well, she told me rather sternly that she would be very grateful if I could look less dead when I'm sleeping.

22

09.49 a.m.

The gas company is investigating a leak. A man digging a hole in the road managed to ignore a stopcock entrance valve and sliced through our lead water pipe with a pneumatic drill. I was surprised for two reasons. First, it was pretty obvious even to me where the water pipe lay. I would have thought that a professional hole-digger might make it his business to watch out for pipes. Second, I was surprised to see that our water travels through lead piping. I suspect that if we wanted to put lead pipes into our home we might find ourselves facing an army of interfering bureaucrats. When I rang the water board to see when they would be able to repair the damage I was told we would have to wait our turn. `There are lots of other people with no water in your area,' said a sanctimonious, supercilious woman who was obviously not concerned about flushing her lavatory or finding the wherewithal to make a cup of tea. The inspector who came to look at the damage and authorise the visit of a team of water board pipe-menders was much kinder. He told us that as residential customers we had priority over such second rate customers as drinking fountains and horse troughs. It felt good to know that we were regarded as important and that our sliced pipe would be mended with haste. It looked such a simple job that I would have thought a half-trained plumber could have sorted it out with a Basic Plumbing Kit in twenty minutes. We are, however, prepared for a weekend without water. The Princess said she was glad it had happened to us and not to the family across the road because they have a lot of small children. I thought that was both sweet and noble of her. And also typical.

12.11 p.m.
The water people called and a nice man brought us two bottles of water for flushing the loo and making tea. Then the gas man called to say that they had found the leak (the good news) but that there were two not one (the bad news). One in the gas main and one in the pipe leading to our house. He has, he said, mended the main leak but not the leak to the house. He has however wrapped a rag around the leaky pipe and will leave it because it is late and hopefully someone will be back to mend it in a day or two. When I asked if it is safe he pulled a face, rocked his head from side to side, and then nodded. He has promised a visit on Saturday but somehow I doubt if this will happen. There are traffic lights to keep cars and lorries out of the huge hole they have left in the road. We have to stay in until they turn up so that they can turn off our gas and mess with the pipes.

23
10.18 a.m.
In the past `good news' newspapers have never worked. People haven't wanted to buy them. But I sometimes wonder if one might not do well today. Personally, I often wake up feeling I simply haven't any more room for bad news. And The Princess is the same. `I am full up with bad news. If you want to give me news you must give me good news first. It's good news or no news at all,' she said this morning. I know what she means. I sometimes worry that if I see one more bent news bulletin I will be driven sane with rage.

The danger is that we all become immune to bad news because we see and hear so much of it. The toxic stress around us is so all encompassing and so invasive that it affects our lives. We are exposed to it all the time.

Part of the problem is that news has to be created to fill all the space that is available. Twenty four hour news programmes need an endless supply of news. And they like it to be exciting and frightening. The news programmes even put rolling banners along the bottom of the screen so that while viewers listen to one piece of bad news they can read about another. The result is that many people are suffering from news-overload.

Of course, most so-called news isn't news at all. It is propaganda; distorted and manipulated truths brought to us by biased news organisations which have been bought and pressured by lobbyists and public relations experts. Nothing is ever questioned if the questioning will upset people with power and money. Distorted truths are used to take away our basic freedom and our hard-won rights. We are subjected to a constant barrage of political and industrial propaganda; press releases become news and I am constantly aware that there is a lot of difference between what they want to tell me and what I want to know. TV companies are the worst; they lead their news programmes with their own little scoops rather than the real news. They only report the news for which they have pictures and so if a camera crew wasn't there it isn't news. News is celebrity led and viewers are fed trivia while important truths are suppressed.

14.22 p.m.

On the M5 going south, just after the turn off for Taunton, on the right hand side of the road, there are more trees with more mistletoe than I have ever seen before. If we are ever short of money I intend to buy a pair of long handled pruners, cut the mistletoe and sell it on the market. I tell The Princess that it is my pension fund and she says she thinks it is probably safer than anything else we have.

24

10.11 a.m.

The men who came to mend the leak in the water pipe outside our house arrived equipped with pneumatic drills. Unfortunately, in mending the water pipe they drilled through a gas pipe which now has another leak. It was all very reminiscent of Flanders and Swann. The man from the gas company told us that he has discovered that the gas pipes running underneath our house do not satisfy current EU standards. What does? The gasman says that he might have to re-lay all the pipes and that this will involve digging up the floors. He tells us not to worry because we will not have to pay for the new pipes to be laid. We worry, nevertheless, because they will still have to dig up our floor to put down their new EU-approved piping. In the end they manage to put the new pipe inside the old pipe and pull it through. The new pipe is made of plastic but is apparently impregnated with poison to stop rats eating it. I wonder how long it will be before the rats can eat the plastic piping without any ill effects but I do not mention this because the gasman seems a pleasant fellow and I do not want to worry him. There is still a leak in the road but he tells us that this is not a major problem. When he and his colleagues have finished re-laying the pipes underneath our house I ask him to check on a nasty smell that has developed in our back garden. The gasman diagnoses a petrol leak and, indeed, he is absolutely right. Petrol is leaking from the tank in our now quite elderly 7 series BMW. I call the AA and a polite man arrives, checks the car and says that the petrol tank is leaking and that I should not drive the car anywhere except to a garage. This I do. The garage tells me that a new petrol tank will have to be imported from Germany and will cost more than £700 plus VAT. This is almost as much as the car is worth and I think that if I sell the car for scrap I will be able to claim back tax relief on the capital loss. However, we have had the car since new and feel affection for it. Apart from the leaky petrol tank and a dent in the side where our gate blew inwards just as I was reversing into the driveway, the car is in excellent condition. It certainly doesn't seem right to take advantage of the Government's absurd 'scrappage' scheme. (If I allow the Government to destroy the car I will receive £2,000 for it - which is more than it is worth.) So I tell my local garage to order the platinum and gold petrol tank and to fit it to the BMW. At the garage a bright mechanic suggests that I nearly empty the petrol tank (so that it doesn't leak) and sell the car on eBay. I smile and thank him for the suggestion but instruct him to install the petrol tank anyway. One of the reasons why our elderly BMW is worth so little is that the Government has put a very high road tax on large, old cars. Naturally, this means that such cars are frequently dumped for scrap because no one can afford to run them. On the other hand, I suspect that the cost of second-hand cars will rocket when the scrappage scheme stops. This will mean that poorer people wanting to buy vehicles won't be able to. I loathe the smug, sanctimonious environmentalists who promote the car scrappage scheme and claim it will help the environment. These are the idiots who live off Government handouts and EU grants and spend all day on their computers, blissfully unaware of the energy they are consuming as they do so.

15.46 p.m.
The weather has been so horrid that we haven't been shopping for ages. And the supermarket hasn't delivered. `We've run out of food,' said The Princess. `Don't be silly,' I replied. I opened the cupboard and took out a tin and a jar. `There must be some sort of meal you can make with custard and olives.'

19.14 p.m.
I am reading the autobiography of film director Roger Corman. His wife is quoted as saying that when she met him he told her he was always on overload but planning to get it under control within two weeks. She says that forty years later nothing has changed. I read this to The Princess who laughed out loud and nodded vigorously. She is always reminding me that when we first met I promised to get the chaos under control.

25
14.14 p.m.
Selling through Amazon is particularly bad for the environment. When they sell a book they have to order it from the wholesaler who orders it from us. We post the book to the wholesaler who posts it to Amazon who posts it to the customer. When the customer buys direct from us there is only one journey involved. This is cheaper, quicker and far more efficient. And more profitable for us, of course.

14.57 p.m.
No one has been to mend our still leaking gas pipe. I rang the emergency number for the gas people but they said that our leak was no longer an emergency leak because it had been found some time ago and their man had wrapped a rag around it to stop it leaking. They gave me another number to ring. I rang that and the person who answered said that they were a secondary sort of emergency number and I had to get off the line for people who had

nearly emergencies that were quite new and so they gave me a third number. When I rang that a message told me that the offices were closed but to hang on if I had an emergency. I hung on and while I was waiting my mobile rang and a man presumably triggered by the first call said they had been too busy to deal with our leak but might come tomorrow or another day. The Princess pointed out that if there were a gas explosion and the house was destroyed no one in world would know who was in it because everything in the house is in other names. We use different pen names for paying for groceries, rates, water rates, electricity and so on.

26
11.27 a.m.
We have our BMW back. It purred with delight when I drove it back from the garage. We are both pleased that we saved it from a crushing end.

15.04 p.m.
The gas people are here. I e-mailed The Princess who is in her study downstairs. `Shall we tiptoe out of the back and just run away?'

27
11.35 a.m.
I bought a first edition in Oxfam today. The word Oxfam was written beside the price on the flyleaf. Fair enough. I suppose they might forget who they are. But the inscription was in ink. In a first edition. Surely this should be a serious offence?

28
14.58 p.m.
I now spend around £100,000 a year on postage. (It used to be much more.) Between 5% and 10% of the parcels we send out do not reach their destination. They are lost or stolen. (I suspect that more are stolen than mislaid.) We have to send out replacement books. Technically, we then claim the cost of the lost book. I recently discovered, however, that my staff have been told by Royal Mail that we can only claim the print costs for lost or stolen

books. This is absurd. Producing a book costs far more than printing it. In a fair world we should be able to claim the retail costs plus the postage and packing costs. Those are our real losses.

But although Royal Mail will only refund part of my losses the EU's direct selling directive (a book in itself which is packed with blood curdling laws which almost every large mail order company ignores) says that I am responsible for goods which get lost in the mail, even though I have no control over them. So, I have to accept the Royal Mail's part compensation.

I sent a note to the Royal Mail pointing out that when a book that we have given to them goes missing we lose:

1. The book.

2. Our postage cost for sending it out (including the specialist packaging) and the packing time.

3. Time for dealing with the problem (including resending the book, apologising to customer, etc.).

4. Our packaging for sending out the replacement.

5. Opportunity cost because we have to pay those costs before we get compensation from Royal Mail.

Most important of all is the fact that the book value to us is not the print cost. The book is worth more than the print cost. (If it weren't, there would be no point in printing any books at all.) If we print 1,000 books and they cost £2 each to manufacture then our advertising and so on will be designed to sell 1,000 books. We print 1,000 because that is what we expect to sell and need to sell. But if Royal Mail loses 100 of those books then we have lost the ability to sell those 100 books. We have lost the profit on the books that Royal Mail lost. And if we need the extra 100 books - to replace the books they lost - we have to reprint. Reprinting small quantities costs far more. By reducing our stock, Royal Mail is reducing our profit. The profit on the last 100 books we sell is the greatest part of our profit. The major profit in any retail business is always in selling the last few items of stock.

If a thief breaks into a bookshop and steals 100 books that each retail at £10 then a court will describe the theft as having a value of £1,000. The `legal' value of the books is not the print cost. But when Royal Mail loses a book (or the book is stolen by a Royal Mail employee) the book is not on the shelf. It has been sold. The book has been stolen from the customer but we have to replace it.

Royal Mail loses an indecent number of books and we carry the cost of the incompetence or dishonesty of their staff. They have no incentive to improve.

It seems to me that most State employees fail totally to understand how business works.

16.17 p.m.

Our gas pipes have been repaired and the piece of rag which lay between us and a major explosion has been taken away, doubtless to be used elsewhere.

29

16.15 p.m.

The Government has announced a new stern clampdown on rebellious people who question the sanctity of the State. I mentioned this to The Princess who said `Oh' in a rather bored voice. Then, a few moments later, she laughed and said `Oh, that's you isn't it!'

Sadly, I fear that she is right. Once the Government has you in its sights they never forgive, forget or give up. They already listen to my phones, read my e-mails and tap into my fax machines. I'm not sure what else they can do but I'm sure they will try.

I have always been honest in my dealings with the Government, but I think it is fair to say that the Government has always been dishonest in its dealings with me. They have created a world in which it is seen as weak to be well-intentioned, passionate, caring, honest or sensitive. All they want us to do is to obey, conform and consume. And they treat all the information they demand we give with a cavalier disregard for our rights. I find that many people don't believe it but the Government actually sells the information they take from us. For example, if I put my car registration number into a commercial website, up will come a picture of my car. And all the details I gave in confidence have been sold. Nothing you tell the Government (or a State employee such as a policeman, tax inspector, local council employee, doctor, nurse or social worker) will be treated as confidential. The Government will either sell the information or lose it.

And the Government constantly lies to us. They make promises they have no intention of keeping. And official Government figures (for everything from unemployment to crime) are about as reliable as the weather forecast. Sometimes the information is false because the people collecting it are incompetent. Often the information is deliberately misleading because the people handing it out want to disguise the truth.

I long ago realised that the only way to deal with the representatives of the State is to be prepared to complain. Never explain, just complain. Take their names, write things down and complain, complain, complain. The incompetent, jackbooted representatives of the State are terrified of breaking a rule. Those who live by the rulebook also die by it. The Human Rights Act and the Data Protection Act do at least offer a little protection.

30
11.58 a.m.
I bought some rather fine serrated grapefruit spoons. These will save me preparing each half of a grapefruit by cutting around the edge of the pulp and then making preparatory cuts between segments. I reckon the new spoons will save me 10 hours a year. This means that they will pay for themselves in a matter of days. They are the most cost effective purchase I've made for years.

31
14.10 p.m.
A reader e-mails to let me know that there is yet another malicious and nasty attack on me on a website. This one, like many others, seems to concern my book *Oil Apocalypse*. My predictions about the oil running out (and the resulting changes which will have to be made to our society) have all been proven to be absolutely accurate but naturally that doesn't stop the nutters from having their say. The Internet is home for a good many lost, lonely people who allow their lives to be directed by a bunch of nerdy youths whose own lives have, since childhood, been spent staring at computer screens and whose vision is constrained and controlled by the breadth and depth allowed by a monitor. It is, I suppose, hardly surprising that the Internet is tailor-made for nutters and bigots and I suspect there are more of them using the Web than there are pornographers and confidence tricksters. I used to wonder sometimes about the people who attack me on the Web. I don't any

more. I had always thought that the sort of people who use the Web a great deal often lead sad lives. A year or two ago I proved this by chasing down a nutter who had been sending me abusive e-mails. This particular fellow was mad with me because I couldn't get him a job with a national newspaper. He rang Publishing House regularly with offensive messages and over one weekend used his primitive computer skills to send my website 90,000 pornographic e-mails. Naturally, the police weren't interested so I hired private detectives who traced him. It turned out that he was a really sad bastard living in a broken down flat on a Scottish council estate. He was laughed at by the local children whenever he went outside and was regarded as a pervert by his neighbours. He was just tough and threatening at the other end of the computer. I left him alone and eventually he went away and presumably found another target. But he did a lot of harm and wasted a lot of time.

February

1
12.48 p.m.
I never bother buying travellers' cheques but always carry cash. It's far more convenient and as long you don't put all your cash into one wallet or one pocket I can't see that the risk is unduly high. If in trouble abroad it is far easier to solve problems with cash than it is to try to solve them with a credit card. Cash talks. Credit cards don't say anything. I called at the bank and asked for £1,000 worth of euros. The teller wanted to know why I wanted the money. A year or two ago I would have asked what it had to do with her, the bank, the Government of anyone else. I no longer bother to argue. I told her that I needed the cash to bribe corrupt border guards. She dutifully wrote this down on the form she had in front of her.

15.18 p.m.
We have had to put up our prices for postage and packing. Since 1988 we have charged £1 per book. I have had to put up the charge to £2. And I suspect it will have to rise again very soon because £2 doesn't cover the cost of postage (let alone packing) for most of our books. The constantly rising prices from the Royal Mail monopoly are eating deeper and deeper into our profits. Amazon's usual charge for books is £2.75 and I know quite a few booksellers who charge nearer £5 per book. I can understand why. We now charge £2 towards postage and packing but we still lose money on just about every book we send out. And many readers send £1 instead of £2. Others just send £1 to cover the postage for three or four books. We send out the books but lose money because of this.

It cost 1d to post a letter in the 1840s and it cost 1d in the 1930s. In recent years, however, postage costs have soared as the post office has becoming increasingly incompetent and inefficient and as it has struggled to pay off its huge pension debts. Despite the fact that we are officially in a low inflation era the Royal Mail has pushed its prices up dramatically. It cost 83p to post a copy of *Bodypower* in 2006. It now costs approximately twice as much.

If the Royal Mail had deliberately set out to screw up independent publishers and mail order companies they could not have made a better job of it. It is absurd that Royal Mail should be allowed to have a postage monopoly.

16.22 p.m.
A reader writes to tell me that a restaurant she visited recently listed Spotted Richard pudding on its menu. When questioned, the waitress told the diners that the original was considered too offensive. My reader wants to know if Stalin could best be described as a richardtator.

2
10.03 a.m.
We are planning to move home. North Devon is a wonderful place to live but there are two unavoidable problems. First, it is a long way from most of the rest of the country. Journeys to London or Paris are exhausting and time consuming. Second, the only realistic way to reach Barnstaple and the surrounding villages is by road. The rail service to Barnstaple is poor to say the least. It's a lovely journey for a day out to Exeter. But too slow, frustrating and infrequent to be of any practical use. And to reach North Devon by road you really have no choice but to use the awful A361. In the summer the road is clogged with tractors and caravans and it's an easy road on which to acquire points for your licence. Knowing that they can make good money out of both locals and tourists the police often park speed cameras in the various lay-bys and sometimes in specially built little nooks hidden behind hedges. They put the damned things on the only bits of road that are safe for overtaking, apparently unconcerned that this seems to prove that the aim is to make money. Hedge and verge trimming and road works are a commoner cause of blockages on this road than anywhere else I've ever known. All things considered, the A361 is probably the worst road in the country. In the winter the road has been cut off for the last two years. For a mail order company this is disastrous - especially when added to the postal strikes which occur and which are now going to be commoner. Whoever designed the road deserves to be tarred and feathered. Although the road is busier than some motorways it switches from two to three

lanes in a dangerously whimsical way. On the long stretches of road which are single carriage way, a large lorry can produce a tailback several miles long. And since every supermarket or business in North Devon is supplied via this route there are always lots of lorries blocking the way.

11.02 a.m.

A reader complains that I seem to spend much of my life digging out facts and then charging people a fee for the books I write. I think it was the fact that I charge people a fee for my books that she objected to, rather than the digging out of facts, though I could be wrong about that. This isn't the first complaint of this type I've had. Two readers wrote recently claiming that my books are so important that I should give copies away to everyone in the country. The snag with this wonderful thought is, of course, that printers insist on being paid for their work, the council wants taxes, the gas company and electricity companies demand cheques every couple of months, staff want paying even more often, and occasionally my wife and I need to eat a little something to keep up our strength and to banish the hunger pangs. This is, remember, how I earn a living. We do always try to keep books as cheap as possible. I would rather sell a million copies and make £1 profit than sell 100 copies and make £2 profit, but I have no backer, patron or sponsor and we accept no advertising of any kind either for my books or my website.

3

22.39 p.m.

We were invited to drinks with people whom we certainly do not know well enough to call friends and hardly enough to refer to as acquaintances. Neither The Princess nor I can remember where we met them. When we received the invitation we were asked to take a bottle of wine with us. He is a mean man who liked to look generous. Every October he wears a British Legion poppy he bought in 1983. He takes it out of the drawer, wipes it with a damp cloth and carefully pins it to his jacket. And the day after Remembrance Day the poppy goes back into the drawer where he keeps flags and badges for such things as Life Boat Day. I know all this because he has told me about it and has even shown me the drawer where he keeps the poppy. When he found out that I am a doctor he asked me if I thought it might be possible to buy a new hip on eBay. I told him I thought it probably would be but that I thought he might have to hire someone to fit it.

His wife loves sunbathing and as a result she has skin like old leather luggage. She moves in an almost tangible, almost visible, cloud of lavender. She too is mean and a mutual acquaintance once said that if you were drowning and held out an arm she would take your watch off your arm before letting let you drown. She must have the world's largest collection of cushions (The Princess and I refer to her as the Queen of Cushions) and must have spent more on soft furnishings than America spent saving its banks.

We were astonished when, at the end of the evening, the hostess asked us (and the other guests) for £10 per head for the cost of the evening. I'm told that asking guests to pay for hospitality is the latest fashion in *Guardian* reading parts of London. I'm surprised, however, that it has reached this part of the world. It is a charmless habit which will, I predict, soon die an unmourned death. If I were invited out for dinner by impecunious hosts I would rather have a slice of bread and jam than be given a bill at the end of the meal. Do you tip? Do you complain if the food wasn't very good?

`I think we should spend more time in Bilbury,' said The Princess, when we got home.

I agreed.

In *The Last Tycoon*, F Scott Fitzgerald wrote that we all live in the present but that when there is no present that is congenial to us, we invent one. Our invented present is the village of Bilbury in Devon. I sometimes think that The Princess and I spend as much time living in Bilbury as we do in the world that most people call `real'. Certainly, the fictional characters I invented for my Bilbury series of novels, and who share our lives in Bilbury, seem more real than most people we meet. When I am asked for my address I invariably put `Bilbury Grange, Bilbury, Devon'. It's the address I give journalists, nosy parkers from the Government and hotels. As the days go by The Princess and I slide ever deeper into our private world of Bilbury, books and old films as we struggle to escape from a hostile and alien world; a world which seems, increasingly often, to be just a little too much for anyone who is sensitive, caring and thoughtful. The Princess was carefully crafted by God from an exclusive mixture of butterflies, kittens and orchids and I sometimes think that together we are like two gentle butterflies, struggling to stay aloft in a stormy world. Bilbury is the petal upon which we rest from time to time. Or are we just barking? Who knows? I certainly don't give a damn.

The strange thing is that I think that the sort of world we have invented for ourselves (a world of pedestrians, cyclists, log fires and peaceful communities cut off from what used to be known as the `civilised' world) will soon become the real world. As the oil runs out (and becomes increasingly expensive) so the world around us, the world we know, will change. Canals and horse drawn barges will come back. Aeroplanes and buses will be seen only in old movies. And log fires will be the only way to keep warm.

4

11.02 a.m.

If history is all about perception then day to day politics is all about misconception. We live in strange times. By forcing taxpayers to fund illegal wars consecutive governments have turned us all into war criminals. (I look forward to the day when Blair, Brown and a thousand other politicians find themselves in the dock at the War Crimes Tribunal.) Temporary security legislation is always permanent. It is never repealed. Honesty, loyalty, courage, patience, respect, selflessness, caring and generosity are forgotten virtues. The Princess and I tried to name 10 modern politicians who exhibited three of these qualities but failed miserably. (Mind you, when we tried to name ten celebrities under 40 who exhibited any of these qualities we failed at that too.) In a country where convictions lead to convictions, it is dangerous to hold an opinion that does not fit neatly in with the establishment's guidelines. Anarchy is the only sensible credo for a thinking person to follow at the moment. The fact that it is dangerous to say this out loud is proof that it is true.

5

22.51 p.m.

On the news tonight I watched in astonishment as a bunch of environmental protestors drove slowly along the motorway. They claim that they were doing this to save the planet. A huge queue of traffic was lined up behind the protestors. Every vehicle was, of course, burning up twice as much fuel as would normally be used. The world is now controlled by interfering do-gooders who are misinformed, misguided and often crooked.

22.58 p.m.

In America a woman on a flight has got into trouble for spanking her two children who were squabbling. Homeland security special agents arrested the woman for committing an act of terrorism. She has been sent to jail for three months and has lost custody of her children. Confiscating children because their mother tries to make them behave doesn't seem like the rational behaviour of a balanced society so it must be the irrational behaviour of an unbalanced society.

It's about time all security guards at airports and railway stations were found more productive work. The nail file confiscation industry has lasted long enough. During the last few years millions of travellers have been inconvenienced and abused by Nazi style guards pretending to be protecting our aeroplanes and our nations from terrorists. It is time to abandon the pretence. Airport security has been a total failure. The obnoxious guards who so enjoy their power have so far failed to find a single terrorist or a single money launderer. In the USA the Department of Homeland Security has conducted three billion airport inspections looking for terrorists. Travellers have been patted down so thoroughly that many didn't know whether to complain or tip. But they did not catch one terrorist. Were there ever any in the first place?

23.06 p.m.

I loathe DVDs. They're an excellent example of the myth that the latest technology is always an improvement on the old stuff. DVDs were sold to us as an improvement in much the same way that CDs were sold to us as an improvement over cassette tapes which were sold to as an improvement over vinyl. Cassettes are in many ways far more convenient than CDs (particularly for audiotapes) and vinyl provides a much better sound than anything else. If they really want to introduce useful technology why don't they produce a player that knows what sound level I want? This would prevent me having to reset the sound level every time I watch a new DVD.

I hate DVD players. (On our DVD player the light goes on when it's off and off when it's on. How mad is that?). But I hate DVDs even more. Here are my top ten reasons for hating them:

1. You have to press lots of different 'play' buttons to make the damned thing start playing. I recently had to press the play button 11 times to move from one instalment to the next on a BBC series that had been turned into a DVD. And why could no one be bothered to get rid of the unnecessary 'top and tailing' at the beginning and end of each programme?

2. It's impossible to spin through the boring anti-piracy threats and the film of the little person stoking the fires of hell. It's not nice to be threatened, and damned near accused of being a handbag thief, before you watch something you have paid a lot of money for. Have these people not yet worked out that the people they are threatening are the people they shouldn't be threatening because they are the ones who have bought the DVD? (I suspect that crooks, not wanting to worry or annoy their customers, rub that bit off when making fake DVDs. If I knew where to buy bootleg DVDs I would, just to avoid having to watch the little blacksmith yet again.) It's even impossible to spin through the advertisements on some DVDs.

3. With a video it is easy to stop, turn off the machine, go away for a week and then resume viewing at the point where you stopped. With a DVD you have to spin through and find the scene. It can take ages. If you want to re-watch a scene it is much easier with a videotape than it is with a DVD.

4. DVDs are far more troublesome than videos ever were. They stick and jump and suddenly stop working for no apparent reason. Sometimes they don't work at all. And once you've removed the shrink-wrap you can't return them. We have far more trouble with DVDs than we ever had with videotapes.

5. With some DVDs it is difficult to find the starting point. Clever, clever producers hide the 'play' icon and put it in a point size that can only be read by six-year-olds with perfect eyesight.

6. With many DVDs the default condition is for the subtitles to be 'on'. And it can be terribly difficult to work out whether they are on or off until you start watching.

7. The sound quality with DVDs is generally appalling, though we have noticed that free DVDs, the sort given away with

newspapers are not only far more sensibly packaged but also have better sound quality. On some DVDs the sound is set so low that no more than two people, crouched close to the television screen, can hear it. This is presumably done to prevent people watching the DVDs in hospitals or on oil rigs.

8. The packaging of DVDs is frequently awful. We recently bought an expensive set of Poirot DVDs. There is no clue as to what each episode is about. There isn't even a leaflet with details in the box. Why is there no cast list (and sometimes even no running time) printed somewhere inside the box? And why are DVDs so expensive? They must be far, far cheaper to produce than videos. And yet they cost a great deal more. It's claimed that DVDs are smaller and easier to store than tapes. Well, they would be if the damned manufacturers didn't insist on putting them in cases that are three times as thick as they need to be. DVDs are desperately overpackaged. With some sets of films or TV episodes the makers could get all the films onto one disk in one thin box. Instead they put them all into over-complicated, easily broken packaging, put six separate disks into six separate boxes, put the whole into a large cardboard slip case and then shrink wrap it and put a cardboard sleeve on the outside. They then charge a fortune. This is a waste of space, money and time. It is also bad for the environment and is obviously done simply so that the manufacturers can charge more.

9. To give them an excuse to sell the package at an ever higher price they usually include a copy of the theatrical trailer (wow), some still photographs (wow again), a boring interview with the executive producer's agent's brother's best friend, who has always wanted to be a star but is, it is now clear, far better at being the executive producer's agent's brother's best friend than appearing in front of the camera. And they include long, tedious interviews with the man in charge of props, the make-up lady and one of the actors you've never heard of. We no longer watch any of this rubbish, though we have to pay for it.

10. With a DVD it is impossible to see how much of a film is left. On several occasions we have gone to bed and, the next day, spent fifteen minutes finding out where we were when we stopped only to discover that we had stopped the programme with two

minutes to go. With a video you could tell at a glance how much of a film was left.

Today, a leaflet fell out of a new DVD case. The leaflet was all about something called 'Blu-ray'. This is what the leaflet says: 'What equipment do I need to watch Blu-ray? First, check that your television is HD ready (it should say so in the manual or on the box). Almost all new flat screen TVs are now HD ready. Then all you need is a dedicated Blu-ray player or a Playstation 3 and you are ready to watch your favourite movies, television and music on Blu-ray disk in high definition quality. A surround sound system will also make the most of Blu-ray's groundbreaking audio quality.' So, now they want me to buy a new television set, a new player, a new cable and an entirely new collection of disks. I hope Blu-ray is a total failure. We won't be swapping our DVDs at all. Ever. We have already gone a step too far. I desperately wish we had bought a pile of video players and stuck to our old video collection. Many of my favourite videos simply aren't available on DVD.

6

12.09 p.m.

The pope has criticised our equality laws. Just what it has to do with him is beyond me. And how can a man who has a job for which only a male Catholic can be considered, find the nerve to comment publicly about equality?

14.30 p.m.

I spent some time trying to find out why American writers use the word 'gotten' so much. Even the best American writers seem to use it quite frequently. I came across it last night in *Christopher's Ghosts* by Charles McCarry. This is one of the best novels I've read for a long time but McCarry, who writes like a prince, uses the word 'gotten' so it must mean something. The first three dictionaries I look at don't include 'gotten' but I eventually track it down and discover that it is just another past participle of 'get'. Although it's not used in English, and is used widely by Americans, it dates back to the Middle Ages and is very Olde Englishe.

15.38 p.m.

A reader has returned a book he asked me to sign complaining that my signature is a disgrace. He says it looks like a scribble and he wants a fresh, unsigned book. I was a GP for ten years and the signature I use for signing books is infinitely more readable than the signature I used for signing prescriptions. I was tempted to send him a note telling him to take the book to the chemist to have it made up. But before I could do this someone at Publishing House had sent him another book.

7

10.52 a.m.

Sorting through a drawer this morning I found a copy of an old article I'd written in the early 1980s for a Sunday tabloid. It was called The X Factor and in it I tried to define the extra factor that makes a star a star. Suggesting that Jack Nicholson had it whereas Terry Wogan didn't I concluded that the X factor is the air of danger that some stars project. It isn't the air of confidence or arrogance often mistaken for star quality. It's never knowing what is coming next; never quite knowing what they're going to do or how they're going to respond to a particular situation. Robert Mitchum and Humphrey Bogart had it in spades. In my view, Tom Cruise, bless his heart for trying, doesn't have an ounce of it.

12.48 p.m.

I hear that a GP with whom I worked when I was young has died. He must have been close to celebrating his century. I often think of him. He was completely ignorant about modern medical practices and knew next to nothing about laboratories, X-ray investigations or pharmacology. But he was the best diagnostician I ever saw. And probably the best doctor too. He knew instinctively when a patient was ill and when he was not. And he had a fierce independence and determination to practice medicine his way. He didn't much care for rules and regulations either. The first time I met him I had arrived at his surgery to collect the addresses of some patients who needed home visits. His car, a huge old-fashioned beast, was parked outside on yellow lines. It was, in truth, parked so badly that it was difficult to tell which side of the road it was parked on. As I passed by I noticed his black doctor's bag was sitting on the back seat of the car. It was open. When I had picked up the addresses I needed I popped into his surgery. `I'm sorry to bother you, sir,' I said. `But your car is open and your bag of drugs is on the back seat.' `Oh, that's nothing to worry about,' he replied with an airy wave of a hand. `But the law...,' I began, with all the moral rectitude of a youth who has studied the regulations. `If you can touch my bag I'll come out and lock the car,' he said. I thought this was silly but when I got outside I stopped at his car and started to reach in. A microsecond later I leapt back as though the hounds of hell were at my throat. Two huge Dobermans, who had been lying, unseen, on the floor at the back of the car, leapt at the window, barking and snarling. No one was going to steal that drug bag. As I walked away I turned and glanced back at the surgery. The old man (and he seemed very old to me back then) was standing at his window looking out towards the car. He smiled and nodded. I smiled and waved. They don't make doctors like him anymore, and I doubt they ever will.

8

11.25 a.m.

The Stanley Gibbons stamp catalogue arrived this morning and I purchased a mint £5 Queen Victoria stamp. I buy a few stamps occasionally and bung them into a box in the bank. One thing puzzles me. A second class stamp now costs 32 pence. Back in Queen Victoria's days it cost 1d to post a letter. This means that the £5 stamp was worth around £400 in postage terms. What on earth did people post that cost so much money? Why did they have £5 stamps? I suspect I will never know the answer to this but it is good to have some unresolved puzzles in life.

9

18.16 p.m.

I bought a beautiful hardback edition of a book called *Peep Show* by Walter Wilkinson in the public library in Wells. It has no dust wrapper but apart from having an ugly `Somerset County Library Cancelled' stamp on the flyleaf in red it is in what an antiquarian bookseller would describe as `very good' condition. I paid 50 pence for it. I read several pages while walking around the city. It is a marvellous book. Wilkinson describes how he toured Devon and the Cotswolds with a puppet show strapped to his bicycle. It is an utterly brilliant book which I had never heard of before. Public libraries are a good place to buy unusual, out of print books. Sadly (for their patrons) they are also an excellent place to buy classic books in excellent condition and at giveaway prices. Within the last few weeks I've bought copies of books by Graham Greene, Evelyn Waugh, Joseph Conrad and P.G.Wodehouse. All in excellent condition and all for 50 pence each at most. Most public libraries sell their unwanted books at £1 or less and I find that if I am quick I can prevent the librarian stamping something nasty, such as `Discarded', on the title page. I have no idea why librarians feel the need to do this but they do it even on quite valuable first editions. When you ask them not to do it they seem surprised, puzzled that you would not want the discarded stamp - as though they were George Whitman at Shakespeare and Co in Paris offering to stamp your purchases with the shop's famous stamp. And if you remove the plastic wrapper carefully, the underlying dust wrapper is often in excellent condition. I honestly fear that most librarians know very little about books - and care even less. Like most people in the book trade they'd be just as happy selling tins of dog food or pots of mustard. Sadly, almost every time I enter a public library I am reminded that there is hefty evidence that the one thing that stops people reading books is the snootiness of bookshop assistants and librarians. Just why these people feel snooty is beyond me.

10

17.12 p.m.

A small, independent bookshop has ordered copies of *Alice's Diary* daily for a week. We eventually pointed out, rather timidly and without much hope, that if they took the book they had ordered and a spare then they could put one book on the shelf and they would get a bigger discount. We even said that if they didn't sell the spare book they could send it back for a full refund. `Oh, no thank you,' they said. `We will order as and when we need copies.' And so the lunacy continues. I'm not surprised that small bookshops go bust all the time. (Many bookshops have to be chased for payment so often that there is no profit left in the sale.)

19.21 p.m.

A foreign publisher wants me to fly out to speak to sales representatives. Sadly, I have to refuse. I no longer fly and travelling overland would take too long. I explain that I stopped flying a dozen years ago. The reasons are simple. Airlines have crammed so many seats into their aeroplanes that I get cramp even when sitting in business class. And if travelling alone I always find myself sitting next to a really fat American. The last time I flew I sat next to an American woman with buttocks like twin neighbouring continents and an overhanging stomach which seemed to have such an individual presence that it should have been allocated a separate seat, or, preferably, a separate aircraft, or at least put in the hold with the baggage. She spent the entire flight complaining about the lack of space. I spent it trying to sit on the armrest furthest away from her. It was the only seating space she left me. After that flight I also decided that when you fly it isn't the major bits of travelling which are exhausting but the twiddly bits, the bus, train or taxi from civilisation to the airport, the bus from the airport terminus to the plane, and the same at the other end. Even a dozen years ago the security had reached absurd levels. My luggage was X-rayed so much that I worried about it getting cancer. My Swiss Army Knife spent hours sitting in the hold in a sealed brown paper envelope. (I wonder if they still say: `Have an enjoyable flight'? Why did they say that? Has anyone ever had an enjoyable flight?) These days, if I can't get there by train I don't go.

11

10.18 a.m.

Disappointment always comes in inverse proportion to expectations. One of the sad things about getting older and more experienced is that expectations are kept low. A film company tells me that it wants to make a film of my novel *The Man Who Inherited A Golf Course*. I think this is the fourth or fifth such suggestion and I'll believe it when I see it. My disappointment will be light when nothing happens. Sadly, however, this means that I didn't whoop with joy when the news came in this morning. I can always get properly excited if something does happen and the film is made. On the other hand I never stop trying. Those who try sometimes fail but those who don't try never succeed. And if I keep trying then I suppose that deep down I must still be hoping. I think maybe I'll write a book of aphorisms and call it *Snacks for Thought.*

12

11.38 a.m.

I received a sad letter from a reader who said: `I have a job cleaning people's houses and in one very dirty house I caught head lice. I can't seem to get rid of them. I would be willing to pay you whatever you ask. I am desperate. Please, Vernon Coleman, help me. I will pay good money for results.' I also received a letter from a Sri Lankan asking me if I could offer some advice on how to solve the ethnic problem in Sri Lanka, a letter from India asking for my advice on the building of a new hospital and a letter from a reader who said: `I would like to say something about your book *What Happens Next?,* though I have not read it. The reader, from Staffordshire, then went on to discuss the book, which he has heard of but not seen. He criticises me for writing a book I didn't write, and says the book should contain exactly what it does contain. And I have an invitation to speak at the Conservative Monday Club: `Your sentiments most certainly coincide with those of the Conservative Monday Club and we would be delighted to invite you to address the Club, particularly on Gordon Brown's responsibility for our financial disaster or indeed on any other political subject of your choosing. Naturally we would offer you an excellent meal afterwards.' There is no mention of rail fare or a fee. A reader of my Bilbury novels has sent me a coat of arms which he has created, together with a Bilbury ID card. There is a Latin motto which he assures me is translated as `Billbury (sic) Always Remembered'. He hopes the coat of arms would be incorporated into the Bilbury Cricket Team sweaters or used on blazer badges. A kind reader says he has just read *Bloodless Revolution* and thinks it is the best book he has read since 1955. He says that if I get imprisoned he will dress up in appropriate clothing and effect my release. He says he is going to photocopy selected pages and distribute them.

12.49 p.m.

I have received an e-mail (marked urgent) from someone wanting me to sign a petition. Their pet kitten has been eaten by their pet python and they want legislation introducing to prevent this happening to anyone else.

14.56 p.m.

I have for some time now been puzzled by the fact that whenever I go into a shop to buy something I have to use a note. I never have any change. I have found out why. I have a large hole in the back pocket where I keep my wallet and loose change. The hole isn't big enough to let the wallet fall through but it is big enough to allow my change to disappear. I have no idea how long the hole has been there, how much money I have redistributed or how many beggars I have made happy.

13

12.03 p.m.

I've been sent a cutting from the *Frome and Somerset Standard* (not a publication which I see regularly). It seems that the EU is keeping a very close eye on things. The newspaper must have published a letter or review of one of my books about the EU because it has now published a letter from a defender of the European Union. The writer says: `Mr Coleman is known in France because he writes nonsense. Dear friend in Frome, please do not listen to this man.' But all is not lost. I have also received a letter from Guernsey's housing minister who writes: `I am at present reading your book *OFPIS*. It's a great title and a fantastic account of what is rotten in British politics and the fraudulent, unelected EU.' He wants to meet for lunch to discuss Guernsey's constitutional position.

14

09.23 a.m.

It is St Valentine's Day.

I wrote a 'pome' for The Princess:
    `We will always be together
    As long as I shall live
    And whatever I shall have
    To you I'll gladly give.'

11.16 a.m.

I've decided to write another book about the European Union and to call it *Hitler's Bastard Love Child: The Real inside Story of the European Union.*

12.10 p.m.

In London, in a taxi on the way to St Pancras, we stopped at traffic lights and I watched a policeman photographing a red barrier which lay on the pavement. He was using something that looked like a mobile telephone but might have been some sort of sophisticated police equipment. The barrier was one of three which had been erected around a small hole in the ground. This one had fallen or been knocked over. When he'd finished taking pictures and had sent them off he walked away. He could have lifted the barrier back into position with one hand. It would have taken far less time than taking pictures of it. Instead, he had clearly telephoned for workmen to be sent out to put the barrier back into position. I wondered if it was laziness or some sort of misguided respect for union boundaries. The Princess and I saw something similar in the Wye Valley not long ago. A rock had fallen onto the road. Three men were looking at it and taking measurements. The rock was by itself, not part of a landslide, and any one of the men could have lifted it up and moved it off the road. Instead, it was clear that they were merely assessing the situation and planning a report. I felt confident that men would be sent out in a truck to move the rock off the road. When we returned on the same route about six hours later the rock was still there, though it now had barriers around it. `At least they haven't erected traffic lights,' said The Princess. These incidents reminded me of something that happened in a television studio in Birmingham many years ago. I was making a programme about tranquillisers and had taken to the studio a variety of bottles, all containing benzodiazepines. When I sat down behind the table on which the bottles were arrayed I picked up one of the bottles to turn it round so that the label would be picked up by the cameras. Suddenly there was a commotion. Someone called the presenter of the programme away from his position next to me. A man in jeans and a T-shirt came over to the table and moved the bottle to the position it had been in before I'd moved it. Moments later the presenter returned. `The chief props man saw you move the bottle,' he said. `You mustn't do that. If you want any of them moving you must ask the director to send a props man onto the set.' He shrugged, as though disclaiming responsibility for this bit of nonsense. `These are all prescription drugs,' I told him. `Since I'm the only qualified doctor here I'm the only person allowed to touch them.' I don't think I've ever seen a presenter grin so broadly. He hurried back across to the director and relayed the message. A couple of minutes later the chief props man came across to tell me that I could move the pills wherever and whenever I wanted. He wasn't being funny, just respectful to another union man.

Generally speaking, today's trade unions are well past their sell-by date. Rather pointless and outdated they have become thuggish; the problem rather than the solution. They exist to preserve their power, and the inequalities and privileges their members enjoy over other members of society. It's not quite what the Tolpuddle martyrs were all about. It was the unions which destroyed Britain's car industry (in particular) and manufacturing industry (in general). Modern unions don't seem to care a stuff about anything but themselves. In the US, the United Steelworkers' Union has filed a complaint with the American Government, claiming that China is giving subsidies to companies producing wind turbines, solar energy products and other things designed to help the country reduce its pollution levels. They seem to think that is a bad thing.

12.35 p.m.
We arrived at St Pancras in good time for our train to Paris. As always I am wearing my MCC tie and a very English hat. Whenever we go to London I wear the most recognisable tie in the world and either a tweed fishing hat, a Grosvenor hat or, in the summer, a Panama hat. I wear these because I believe they reduce my chances of being shot by the police. It is surprising how many people passing through London railway stations still wear jeans and rucksacks. (The other advantage of wearing an MCC tie is that I can get into a cab and know that the driver will take me where I want to go the quickest way. Most cabbies are honest but without the tie I have sometimes been taken on what The Princess calls `sightseeing tours' of London.) It isn't only when travelling abroad

that one has to dress carefully these days. In big cities everywhere the trick is to look scruffy enough to be left alone by con men, touristy enough to be left alone by customs men, dull enough to be of no interest to kidnappers and terrorists, poor enough and local enough to be left alone by casual thieves, rich enough to impress hoteliers and restaurateurs, etc. and important enough for the police to think at least once and preferably twice before shooting you.

`Why have you got so much money with you?' asked an impertinent man at the customs. `To buy things with,' I replied, having absolutely no other answer to offer. And that was that. Daft question. Daft answer.

I actually like St Pancras. It has quite an air about it and is infinitely cleaner and smarter than Waterloo ever was. I particularly like the area where we wait after having gone through customs but before going up onto the Eurostar platforms. It is a pleasant no man's land; we are travelling but not travelling.

I am, predictably, less enamoured of the customs area.

I realised that `they' had either gone stark raving mad, or more likely were deliberately exaggerating the fears on the day when a gang of over-muscled airport psychos confiscated my mother's nail file on the grounds that with it she was a threat to the aircraft's safety and security. (If hoodies were to take a nail file that did not belong them it would be called stealing. When government thugs take a nail file that does not belong to them it is called confiscating.) Two minutes after they'd confiscated the nail file my mother bought an identical replacement at the airport shop (conveniently situated on the other side of the check-in desk) and carried it onto the aeroplane with her. She was 83 at the time. My father, who had had his small penknife confiscated, bought a replacement (bigger than the one they'd taken - it was all they had for sale) and took that onto the plane with him too.

As I say, it was then that I realised that the people who are in charge of these things were either just plain stupid or weren't taking the threat as seriously as they pretended to be but were, on the contrary, merely using the so-called threat to try to frighten us.

These days every minor half-hearted terrorist attempt is used as an excuse to tighten security and introduce more intrusive laws. Utterly inept security services on both sides of the Atlantic, and elsewhere, miss every opportunity to catch real terrorists and take every opportunity to frighten, threaten and harass entirely innocent taxpayers. So we travel on trains rather than aeroplanes. Since neither the American Government nor the Israelis have yet flown a train into a skyscraper the security is slightly, just slightly, less intrusive. Anyone who travels within Europe by aeroplane is certifiable. Customs officials are relentlessly rude, deliberately obstructive and unendingly officious. When our fascist Government follows Nazi Germany and modern America and starts building concentration camps they won't have to look far to find recruits to work as guards. The people who man (and woman) the X-ray machines and baggage check-in counters at airports and international railway stations will fit the profile quite nicely, thank you very much; they are the raw material from which concentration camp guards can easily be created. When my travelling bag was last examined at a customs post in England the cretin who was doing the searching called his friend over so that they could go through my things and laugh together. They were picking through my stuff like eager buyers at a jumble sale. When they ordered me to stand back and I asked them, politely, to say `please' they looked at me as if I had suddenly gone stark raving mad. Sometimes, when going through the metal detector at railway stations I go ping. At other times, carrying exactly the same items, I do not. Since explosives and guns are available in plastics the metal detectors are entirely useless anyway.

It is now illegal to make jokes when going through customs. Indeed, travellers have become too frightened to say anything in their own defence. `This isn't a changing room. Get on out of here and take your clothes with you,' shouted a guard as people struggled to put clothes back on after undressing to be searched. Everyone except The Princess and I picked up their clothes and hobbled away obediently. We stood still and quietly continued dressing. No one shot us. No one said anything else. When we'd finished I wandered over to the guard and whispered in his ear: `In two hours' time I will be sitting in Deux Magots with a glass of hot wine. You will still be here frisking sweaty tourists.' There is an air of incompetence that is often palpable. At Ashford station I recently went through a customs check point with two large tins of paint and a fireproof safe in my luggage. I saw the X-ray pictures.

No one could have possibly worked out what was there. But no one stopped me. The whole process is devised by people whose reactions make it clear that they are merely using past incidents as an excuse to complicate our lives - and to frighten us all. When a man was found to have potentially exploding shoes the idiots that be responded by instructing all travellers to remove their shoes. What are they going to do when a woman is found with a bomb in her bra? What if someone is found with an explosive suppository? What if a woman packs a bomb into her vagina? Are they really going to start performing rectal and vaginal examinations on all travellers? Actually, it wouldn't surprise me if they did. Sadly, most people would let them. Customs officials have only very recently started to bother asking me to remove my hat during a search. And most of the time they still don't bother.

There is a Caffé Nero in St Pancras station which serves excellent coffee. While we were sitting relaxing, sipping and flicking through magazines, our peace was disturbed by an urgent security tannoy announcement. `A red suitcase has been found abandoned,' said the voice. `Will the owner urgently report to the Eurostar desk.'

`How can someone lose a suitcase?' I asked The Princess. `It's probably one of those people moving house. Ten suitcases piled high on a trolley. They'd never notice if two or three fell off.'

`Do you think they'll blow it up?' asked The Princess.

`If they do then I hope whoever owned it was going away and not going back,' I said. `At least their underwear will be clean.' And I'm afraid we laughed. Oh, how we laughed at the idiots who'd lost a suitcase.

`I think they'll probably take it outside to blow it up,' said The Princess.

`I hope they don't close the station and make us all go out into the street,' I said. `They do that sometimes. I'm sure it's just out of spite.'

`People are stupid,' said The Princess. `Why can't they look after their luggage properly?'

I sipped at my coffee and The Princess reached down and patted her small suitcase as though it were a faithful dog. Because we have clothes and so on in Paris we travel very light. One very small overnight bag each is enough for a few books for the journey and maybe one or two things that we want to take over to the apartment in Paris. `Where's your case?' The Princess asked me, looking around.

I reached down to touch it for reassurance. I looked at the small blue suitcase. `Isn't that mine?'

`No, the blue one is mine. Yours is red.'

`I had it a moment ago when I fetched the coffees.'

`Did you take it with you to the counter?'

`Yes, I just went straight there while you got the seats.' I could feel myself going slightly red as it came back to me. `But I remember now...I couldn't manage the case as well as the drinks. I meant to go back for it.'

`It's definitely red isn't it?'

`Yes I think so. Red.'

The people at the Eurostar counter were very patient and understanding. They asked me what was in it, of course and I then had to open it to prove that it was mine. But they said nothing rude about me losing my case. And nor did they comment about the fact that it contained nothing but books and a well-wrapped painting which The Princess had bought and thought would look rather good in the kitchen of our apartment.

18.38 p.m.

When we arrived in Paris I was sad to see that the mattress maker who occupied a shop two doors away from our building has gone. His shop was empty. He used to stand sewing mattresses, with his door wide open whatever the weather so that he could more easily watch the world go by. I suppose there isn't much of a market these days for hand-made mattresses.

15

11.38 a.m.

A brass band is playing near the Eiffel Tower this morning. It consists of three trombones, three trumpets, three saxophones, three French horns and three drummers. There are also a dozen dancers. Pick up bands are enormously popular in Paris and can be regularly found in the parks around the city. The best usually play in the Tuileries Gardens, in the Place des Vosges, near the fountain in the Place St Michel and on the steps below Sacre Coeur. This is one of the best bands we've seen for a while. We stood and listened for a while before throwing money into the suitably positioned open instrument case and wandering off through the park.

14.23 p.m.

I have postponed old age for as long as I can; putting it off as one puts off having luncheon with someone one suspects one will have to meet eventually but hope that somehow something will come up and make it no longer necessary. But old age is creeping up on me unbidden, unwanted and unexpected but always, damnit, unmistakeable. It started with the eyes. Then the joints. And the stamina. Our apartment is the sixth floor of a building that was erected in around 1860. The lift looks as though it was put in very shortly afterwards. Ten years ago I used to be able to run up the stairs and beat the lift. It was my party piece. When we had visitors I would put them into the lift with The Princess and tell them I had to do something. I would then run up the stairs and be there on the top landing when the lift doors opened. It always produced puzzled looks and exclamations. But slowly the lift has got faster. I cheated for a while by asking The Princess to delay the lift for a minute or so, fumbling with the button in order to give me a flight's start. But the party piece is no more. Today, I am creaking and wheezing while half way up the stairs. So I use the lift.

16.12 p.m.

One of the two phones in our apartment is not working. I called into a telephone shop to ask for a replacement fixed line telephone. The shop is empty of customers (which is unusual for a mobile phone shop in the last year or two) and to my delight they have one or two fixed line phones for sale. The assistant is shocked and even distressed that I want to buy a simple, cheap phone that just plugs in and doesn't allow me to wander around without a cord, doesn't have enough memory to capture the telephone numbers of everyone in France and doesn't stop working when the electricity supply is interrupted (and involve yet another lead). He looks shifty and unreliable; the sort of person who steals coat hooks from public lavatories. Eventually, he goes into a back office and emerges, five minutes later, with a box which he is dusting off. He hands it to me. I buy it and take it home. Inside is a phone which still has an extensive memory but which takes batteries. There are three batteries heat sealed in a packet. The phone takes four batteries. And the little compartment won't open. My screwdriver destroys the screw. So I have to break open the compartment with a penknife. (I have taken to throwing away these silly little plastic doors anyway). The phone itself is made of cheap plastic and if I drop it then it will break. (I know this is true because when I threw it at the wall a little later it broke.) The little compartment is made of the indestructible stuff they use when making the black box to put in an aeroplane. Eventually, I plug it all in. There is a manual the size of the Bible. It doesn't work. There's a problem with the line not the telephone. Fortunately we have a fax line which we can use for making calls. Exhausted I decide to take the easy option. I ring the telephone company and cancel the line that doesn't work.

18.29 p.m.

An Australian who lives in our street in Paris says he is learning French. His problem, however, is that he is learning it from a course designed for travellers and so the vocabulary he has acquired is more suited for tourists staying in hotels than for residents dealing with unruly plumbing. He says he is constantly fighting the urge to match his lifestyle to fit the bits of French he has learned. So, when going into an ironmonger's shop the other day he found himself wanting to ask the owner's wife for a pillow and a bar of soap because those were the only words he knew. He really wanted a screwdriver and a roll of insulation tape and ended up wandering around the shop until he found what he wanted. He tried doing some mime to explain to the owner's wife that he needed a screwdriver but stopped when the owner turned up and glowered at him. The ironmonger, unlike most Frenchmen, is well over six feet tall and built like a prop forward. He is also very possessive.

16
10.29 a.m.

Down in the cellars of our building we have a small room or `cave' where we can store stuff we don't need but don't want to throw away. We have learned from one of our neighbours that we are using the wrong 'cave'. Wondering if the notaire made a mistake when the papers were drawn up I take a look at the deeds to the apartment. To my surprise I discover that we are indeed using the wrong 'cave'. We agree to swap and since we aren't using our 'cave' at the moment we hand over our key to the neighbour. He agrees to clear out his 'cave' and let us have his key before he leaves for his home in the country.

13.12 p.m.

I needed to send an urgent e-mail to an American friend who lives in Thailand but runs a Web-based business from his American home in New Hampshire. I couldn't receive any e-mails from him in Paris because my iPhone had turned into a paperweight. He doesn't have a fax machine in Thailand, so earlier today I sent a fax to his office in America asking his staff there to scan in my fax and e-mail it to him. Now, my iPhone has suddenly started working again. I have just found an e-mail from him. At the top it says: `I am sending this emboldened and in larger type and capital letters so that you may be able to read it.' I rather like this. It is, I suppose, the technological equivalent of shouting at a foreigner.

14.07 p.m.

We have to take a short trip out to St Germain en Laye. A group of rather frightening looking youths got onto the train and start to chat up The Princess who is much younger than I am, and looks younger than she is. They were about 18 or 19-years-old and heavily tattooed. One was carrying and swinging a long, heavy metal chain. I knew that The Princess was frightened. Wisely she did not let this show. I have long known that you cannot be brave unless you are first afraid. It follows that only the weak, nervous and afraid know how to be really strong. I have never known anyone more nervous than The Princess and I have never known anyone braver. In her heart she is like a nervous kitten but in a tough situation I have never known anyone stronger. I pointed out politely in halting French that they were chatting up my wife. To my astonishment the youth with the chain looked genuinely embarrassed and ashamed. He apologised profusely then bowed his head slightly. His friends then all apologised in turn and moved away down the train. I cannot imagine that the situation could possibly have been dealt with so easily in Britain. When it becomes clear that the energy is running out in Britain (as it will within a year or two), France will be high on the list of places to live.

17
12.55 p.m.
An English friend of The Princess's arrives for lunch. Vanda has a job in the fashion industry and like many almost but not quite famous people wears dark glasses even in cloudy weather and indoors in the hope that people will stare at her, wonder who she is and suspect that she might perhaps be someone really famous. She speaks French with what she believes is a very posh accent. I don't speak much French at all. (Like most Englishmen I am frozen by the fear of sounding like a foreigner when I speak another language. I want to get things right and am terrified of sounding like Poirot speaking English. The French make this fear worse by correcting every second word I say. I have found that it is much more satisfactory to make them speak English. I then take great delight in correcting their pronunciation and grammar. Since all French people believe they are brilliant linguists this annoys them enormously.) I once made Vanda very angry by telling her that she spoke French with an Algerian accent.

Vanda says that she has attended a first aid course and been taught that it is wrong to put a tourniquet on a bleeding limb. When I show surprise Vanda tells me that I am out of date and that tourniquets have been banished to that deep dark place where leeches are kept. She says that the way to stop bleeding is to apply firm pressure with a clean pad. I tell her that hospitals have started using leeches again, agree that firm pressure is an excellent way to stop bleeding but suggest that there are times when a tourniquet is the only way to save a patient's life. `You arrive at a road accident,' I say. `You are the only person there. The driver is alone. He is bleeding from a severed radial artery and is unconscious. You suspect a serious internal injury. Your mobile telephone doesn't work because you are in a valley in the countryside. You need to stop the bleeding from his arm but you need help. It is a quiet day and there is no other traffic on the road. What do you do?' This proves to be an insoluble dilemma for Vanda. If she relies on applying pressure then she may have to wait there for hours and the driver could die. If she leaves him to fetch help then he will bleed to death. Vanda doesn't know what she would, or should, do. 'The answer,' I tell her, 'is to apply a forbidden tourniquet and run for help.'

18
10.19 a.m.
I find the key to our new 'cave' in our mailbox and trot down to the cellars to check that the key works and that the 'cave' is empty. To my horror I find that the 'cave' is nearly full of rubbish. There is an old mattress, a bedstead, several pieces of broken furniture, an empty suitcase with a broken lock and all sorts of other bits of rubbish in there. I go back upstairs and knock on the neighbours' door. His wife opens the door and when I protest she shrugs, tells me that her husband has a bad back and slams the door in my face. It takes us much of the day to clear the rubbish. Fortunately, all we have to do is drag it up the cellar stairs, through the hallway and out onto the pavement. The dustmen will take it all away. In Paris it isn't even necessary to pay or to telephone anyone to arrange this. Put out your rubbish and it just disappears. While we are clearing out someone else's rubbish the couple to whom it previously belonged walk past us. Monsieur is carrying two large suitcases and a bag of golf clubs and doesn't seem to be troubled too much by his back. His wife scowls and snarls something incomprehensible as she has to clamber over their old mattress which is still in the hallway. Monsieur turns round and pauses and shrugs. 'You are much younger,' he says.

This is the second time I've felt slightly cheated by people in the building. When we bought the apartment we had to meet the previous owner in the offices of the notaire so that we could all sign the relevant documents. I asked the widow from whom we were buying if she would be leaving the fixtures and fittings - bathroom cabinets, light fittings and so on. The notaire and the woman selling the apartment looked at me as if I were mad. 'Of course!' they both said. 'Do people in England take these things?' I admitted that they sometimes did and that it wasn't unknown for doors, television aerials, skirting boards and lawns to disappear with the removal van. Everyone laughed at this and thought it a huge joke. I was assured that the woman selling was a very wealthy and successful and a well-known Parisian businesswoman who could be relied upon entirely. When we finally obtained the keys we found that the wretched woman had taken all the cabinets and light fittings and had even removed the toilet roll holder. She'd left behind her rubbish, too. Classy.

14.15 p.m.

While The Princess was busy in the kitchen I popped to the supermarket to buy groceries. There were boy scouts at the check-out helping to pack customers' food, whether they were asked to or not. The scout who packed my purchases put all the soft, vulnerable foods (tomatoes, eggs, yoghurt and so on) at the bottom of my bag and all the heavy stuff (tins) on the top. I gave him a tip for this. Next time I will give him some money before he starts packing and tell him to go and buy himself an ice cream.

16.17 p.m.

I receive a message to say that a friend of mine has died. K was a surgeon and he was special for a number of reasons. He was unusual in that he smoked 60 cigarettes a day. But he was special because he cared desperately about his patients. Everyone who worked with him loved him and his patients loved him too. He did not suffer fools gladly and was constantly in trouble with the authorities. I remember that when he was a registrar in Birmingham he was instructed to attend court. I can't remember what it was about but K's part in the case was fairly insignificant. He stayed there all morning, sitting on a bench in a hallway, and by lunchtime he'd had enough of waiting so he went back to the hospital to start his operating list. At just after 3 p.m. in the afternoon a policeman came to arrest him and take him to court. The policeman didn't even allow K to stop and change out of his surgical greens. When K arrived in court, with blood stains all over his arms and chest and with his boots spattered with blood, the judge went apoplectic. `What have you been doing?' demanded the officious judge. `I was operating on a patient,' replied K. `Where is the patient now?' asked the judge. `Still on the operating table,' replied K. `Bleeding to death.' The judge went very red and told the police to take K straight back to his operating theatre. They never did call him back to give evidence.

19
17.19 p.m.
We met an American acquaintance and took him by bus to Notre Dame. He had never been in Paris before and does not speak any French at all. He is the only fat person in the world who doesn't have problems with his genes, his hormones or his glands. `I'm fat because I eat too much,' he admits, though it is more of a reckless boast than an admission. `I'm greedy.' On the bus he pointed to a sign which says `Ne laissez pas votre bras depasser a l'exterieur' and asked me what it meant. I told him it means: `Don't dangle your bra outside the bus'. `Wow,' he said with a grin. `These French really are something else aren't they? I can't wait to tell the guys back home about that one.' Thus are myths started.

20
19.10 p.m.
We meet a man I know who is travelling through Paris. He lives in Spain where he works as a doctor. He has a private practice and specialises in providing medical care for expatriates and tourists. He is the only person I know to have cut himself while putting a plaster onto someone else. He was trying to cut a piece from a strip of sticking plaster and cut himself with the scissors. When he lived in England he once lacerated his scalp trying to pick apples in his own small orchard. Unable to reach the highest apples he put a children's trampoline under the tree and tried bouncing up and down on it so that he could grab at the apples and toss them to his wife. He became increasingly angry at the fact that his wife kept dropping the apples he threw (and therefore bruising them just as much as they had fallen naturally from the tree), lost concentration and hit his head hard on a stout branch. He needed six stitches for that one and was so embarrassed that he told everyone at the hospital that he had hit his head on a low doorway in his local pub. I also remember that for several months he used an aftershave which smelt of chemicals. It was only when his wife insisted on examining the aerosol can he was using that she found out that he was using insecticide. `It says perfumed on the can,' he pointed

out. `In big letters.' His wife, who was an emotionally blowsy woman, left him three years ago and he moved to Spain. The Princess and I agreed that we had never seen him looking happier. We asked him if he had a girlfriend and he said that he hadn't but that he had bought a Great Dane puppy and that he loved it very much.

21
10.12 a.m.
Back in England, I'm having bank trouble again. Do they deliberately employ the most stupid people they can find (running, perhaps, inverse intelligence tests before making appointments) or do the people who work for the banks *become* stupid? One of our banks insists on taking money twice when I buy shares. This causes not inconsiderable problems and I am currently refusing to pay the overdraft charges they are threatening me with since the account in question only became overdrawn through their stupidity. Still, my problems are as nothing compared to those my poor Dad endured after my mother died. He had endless problems with the banks and building societies with whom they had joint accounts and more than one stupid youth wrote him patronising letters telling him that if they were to take my mum's name off the account they would need her signature. It was, they explained, all for his own protection and to protect the country from money laundering and terrorism. When I sorted through his desk, I saw several letters my Dad had written in which he had enclosed copies of his diminishing pile of death certificates only to be told that the bank wouldn't accept a death certificate. They insisted that they needed my Mum's signature even though they knew she was dead. In the end my Dad, who was the most law-abiding citizen you could ever hope to find, was reduced to forging my Mum's signature on their damned forms. He got quite good at it, he confessed. (If the banks or police want to interview him about this he is currently sprinkled on Budleigh Salterton beach and if they want to interview anyone about that they are welcome.) I was also shocked to see how many threatening letters he had received. There were threats from the Government, the council, the police, the television licensing people and just about everyone else you can think of. I am so accustomed to receiving threatening letters

from pompous, self-important people that I don't take all that much notice of them. But it was depressing to see what awful mail my elderly father had received in his final months.

In 1939 my Dad was told he could not join the Navy because he was in a protected occupation. So he resigned from his job and joined the Navy as a regular sailor. He signed up for 12 years to fight for his country.

22

12.14 p.m.

An acquaintance who can't obtain gainful employment and therefore works for the BBC has confirmed to me that the State broadcasting organisation erased numerous great radio and television programmes because a nameless, and presumably brainless, accountant thought the organisation would save money by reusing the tapes for other programmes. And so much of *Hancock* and *Dr Who* was rubbed out to provide space for more episodes of *Eastenders*. *Paul Temple*, *The Goons* and great sporting events were wiped clean to save pennies. In years of vandalism inspired by parsimony, the BBC destroyed heaven knows how many television and radio classics. Irreplaceable live recordings were destroyed simply so that the tape could be reused to record something else. Vast quantities of the nation's cultural heritage were deliberately destroyed by the same penny pinching executives whose extravagance knows no bounds and who waste millions of our money on champagne and taxis. Sending a handful of executives on unpaid holiday for a month or two would have saved enough to have secured the future of television and radio recordings that would, over the years, have probably earned enough money to cut the licence fee in half. Taxpayers have lost much joy and vast amounts of money because of the stupidity of one minor bureaucrat. And yet these days the organisation is constantly thinking up new ways to waste vast quantities of public money.

23

14.45 p.m.

We bought some electronic voice operated software made in Japan. We tried for ages to make it work. And then The Princess had a brilliant idea. She spoke into it with a silly faux Japanese accent. It understood every word. I don't think I would believe this if someone told me it had happened to them. But it's true. We didn't know whether to laugh or to cry. So we laughed.

24
13.50 p.m.
I was talking to a person at a bank today. The conversation went like this:

Bank: `For security reasons can you give me your mother's maiden name?'

Me: `Yes. But for security reasons I don't want to give you the whole name over the phone. Please ask me letters from it.'

Bank: `I don't understand.'

Me: `Rather than me giving you the whole name, you ask me to give you, say, the first and last letters in the name.'

Bank (after much thought): `OK. What are the letters in your mother's maiden name.'

15.16 p.m.
The Chinese have executed a man who abused his position of responsibility in their equivalent of the civil service. This seems to me to be a splendid idea.

25
12.11 p.m.
I received a letter from a doctor in India who is preparing to perform a delicate brain operation. He wants my advice on how best to proceed. He says he is using textbooks to guide him but that they are rather out of date. The letter is typed on hospital notepaper and it appears to be genuine. A newspaper journalist has sent me a list of questions which start with `Why is Michael Moore famous and you are not?' And a reader from Wales who says `I have read widely on the subject of politics and international affairs. I must take issue with you over your occasional description of the regime which operates this multicultural, liberty denying, drugs inducing, Negro apotheosizing, homosexual promoting, miscegenation encouraging, anti-Royal and morally degenerate society as fascist. No, Dr Coleman, you are decidedly incorrect to use the term

'fascist' which falls readily from the lips of our liberal/Marxist ruling 'elite' to describe whomsoever they deem to be opponents or hostile to their governance and policies.' I write back pointing out that I have always taken my definition of fascism from Mussolini and that since he invented fascism his is the only definition which counts. Yah boo sucks.

15.16 p.m.
'Youth and ethnicity can be an author's most valuable assets these days,' said the *Financial Times* recently. Looking good on camera and being prepared to do anything to promote a book are also high on the list of essentials. The Princess suggests that I hire an out of work, 25-year-old, foreign actor to take my next MSS to a publisher and to pretend to be me. I think she's joking but it isn't a bad idea.

26
15.11 p.m.
I spent another four hours replying to reader mail. One reader has sent me a huge typescript. I can hardly lift it. I have to wrap it up and send it back with a note explaining that like a lot of authors I never look at unpublished manuscripts (scared that something might seep into the brain and then come out again 10 years later) though I always read published stuff people send me and don't need returning. Another reader sent me a letter telling me how much she loves my books. She adds in a P.S. 'Please don't tell anyone about this letter.' A reader from Middlesbrough says she enjoyed Mrs Caldicot's adventures and wants to know if she lived happily ever after. I write and explain that there is a follow-up book called *Mrs Caldicot's Knickerbocker Glory*. I have a feeling that this reader doesn't realise that Mrs Caldicot is a figment of my imagination but believes her to be real. In a way she is. I had other plans for Mrs Caldicot when I started to write the first book. But Thelma took over and insisted on doing things her way. Quite right too. A kind reader sent me an article of mine from 1968. She found it among her husband's papers. A reader from Coventry says she is defeated by all the dishonesty and crookery and the fact that those responsible never seem to be punished. And a very generous reader, who knows of my affection for the work of Henry David

Thoreau, has sent The Princess and I a sumptuous edition of Thoreau's *Walden*. I am not sure it quite fits in with Thoreau's love of simple things but bugger that, it's a beautiful book. It is without a doubt the best Folio Edition book I have ever seen. I also received three letters which all started with the same words: `I know you don't reply to personal mail but...'. The first, a teenage schoolboy, wanted me to tell him how best he can stop vivisection. The second, a woman, wanted me to tell her whether or not to have her cat vaccinated. And the third (hiding behind an e-mail address that looks like one of the passwords the tax people hand out) wants me to become a trustee of a charity which has aims which don't seem entirely clear even though I read them twice. I tell the second that I am afraid I don't give clinical advice to animals or humans and the first that the best advice I can give him is in my four books on vivisection which should be in his school library because I sent copies to every school library in the country and I tell the third that I am afraid I never accept positions of responsibility.

21.12 p.m.

I've been reading an excellent biography of Jacques Tati, one of my film heroes. In the film world an auteur is someone who writes, shoots, directs, edits, produces and distributes his own movies. Auteurs are the cream of the film profession. Directors such as Tati, Roger Corman, Jean-Luc Godard and Russ Meyer realised that if they controlled everything themselves then they would have complete artistic freedom. Lots of actors now produce, direct in and star in their own films and television programmes. It's considered a brilliant thing to do. It's nothing new. Chaplin, Pickford and Fairbanks started United Artists a million years ago. Musicians who start their own music label are praised. Racing drivers who run their own teams are revered. In every walk of life artists and sportsmen who take control over production as well as creation are applauded. But in the snobby world of publishing an author who also publishes and distributes is regarded as a failure; someone to be ignored and sneered at as self-indulgent. I hope this changes one day (and I have a suspicion that it will) because most modern publishing is controlled by faceless bureaucrats working for industrialised conglomerates. I've sold several million books around the world since I began self-publishing but I'm confident that although I had a successful career with `official' publishers in my previous publishing life, many of my recent, successful books would have never been published by any of the conglomerates. I don't believe any `proper' British publisher would have brought out books such as *OFPIS*, *Living in a Fascist Country* or *Gordon is a Moron*. The men and women in grey suits would, quite simply, have been too scared to have such books on their lists. When I first began self-publishing my books were quite widely reviewed - accepted as an oddity. But when it became clear that my books were actually out-selling many of the books produced by `big' publishers the reviews dried up. And when I started buying large quantities of advertisements for my books the publishers banned my adverts from their newspapers and magazines. The establishment looks after itself very carefully and the publishing establishment doesn't like the idea of anyone threatening the status quo. (Though editors at big publishers seem happy enough to nick our book ideas.) Journalists and others protect the system because the system works well for them too. They get armfuls of free books and eventually they may be rewarded by having their own slim volume brought out. Writing is the loneliest business there is. But self-publishing is the loneliest form of writing. The Princess has a solution. She said that `privately printed' sounded better than self-published. And I think she's probably right. Either that or `independently published'.

22.01 p.m.
The Princess is writing a book about Wales and has discovered that the traditional Welsh costume (tall black hats, red shawls and plenty of petticoats) was actually invented in the 19th century by a woman who was born Augusta Waddington to English parents (and who later became Lady Llanover). Add this to the fact that David Lloyd George was born in Manchester and Welsh Nationalism looks very insipid. Mind you, as we discovered when we were writing our books on English history, Lawrence of Arabia was born in Wales. I wonder how many people know that?

27
11.56 a.m.

Many online bookshops allow customers to post reviews online and to give the books they sell star ratings. This is utterly absurd. Many of the reviews which are written are prejudiced. Some are written by people who admit, quite openly, that they have never even read a copy of the book they are `reviewing' but are either making assumptions about it or are using the opportunity to express their views on the subject of the book. Here's a real review I spotted on Amazon: `I haven't read this book but I don't like the subject or the author so I don't think I'll like it.' (This wasn't about one of my books - though I've suffered equally damaging but pointless remarks.) The writer of the review gave the book one star (the lowest possible) thereby knocking down the book's overall rating. Casual browsers would see the rating but probably not the review behind it. I find it difficult to see just how this sort of prejudiced nonsense helps authors, readers, publishers or Amazon.

Amazon is also destroying authorship as a profession by allowing private individuals (such as journalists who have been sent books to review) and small, professional booksellers to sell brand new, newly published books online for as little as a penny each. (The sellers make their money by charging considerably more for postage and packing than that service actually costs.) This practice destroys the author's chances of making any money because when even brand new books are available second-hand for pennies publishers are not going to be able to sell many books at full price (or, even, at a discounted price).

The problem, I suspect, is that most of the people involved in the bookselling business these days don't give a fig about books. They would be just as happy selling cat food or hairdryers. A few decades ago people went into publishing, bookselling and librarianship because they loved books. No more. Publishing and book selling are now simply trades. The people involved would be selling beans or socks if the profit margins were better. I care desperately about books because they have been my life. Most writers are not professionals. They have other jobs (as journalists, editors, teachers and reviewers to pay their bills) and their earnings as writers are often modest and often well below the national minimum wage. I have been a professional, freelance writer for 30 years since I gave up practising medicine and for 20 years I've published my own books. Throughout that time I have earned my living entirely by my pen, my typewriter and my computer. I care passionately about books.

17.12 p.m.

I have been invited to give a lecture in Scotland. `We only want 45 minutes of your time,' says the letter of invitation. But it isn't just 45 minutes, of course. It will take me a day to travel to Scotland and a day to travel back. It will take me more than a day to prepare a 45-minute lecture. There will be travel expenses and hotel expenses. And all the time Publishing House will be running up the costs at £75 an hour. Naturally, the invitation doesn't mention a fee or any expenses. Meanwhile, if I don't write something new to sell there will be nothing to put in the next catalogue. Self-publishing has grown into something of a treadmill. If I give the lecture I will have to find some more hours for working and I'm already working about twice the number of legal hours every week. If I ever decide to report myself to the EU I will be in serious trouble. I send the usual `I'm sorry I cannot come' reply to the invitation and as usual feel bad about it. It occurs to me that many of the people who invite me to speak are academics or civil servants or corporate employees who will be paid their salaries when travelling or speaking at public meetings. I have never earned a salary (and have never wanted to) but there are times when it puts me at a disadvantage. The problem, I suspect, is that people with salaries simply don't understand how my world works.

18.01 p.m.

House prices are still absurd. Greed has been rewarded and sustained by the absurdly low interest rates introduced because Gordon the Moron wanted to save the housing market to minimise his losses at the election. His last present to the nation was, therefore, an accelerating and enduring depression. House prices are going to do one of three things: they are going to crash by 50% or so, they are going to drift downwards over the next few years or they are going to remain stable while inflation eats away at their value. I firmly believe that there aren't going to be many house owners making a real capital gain out of their homes in the next decade. We discuss the possibility of waiting for a possible crash before buying a new house but decide that we can afford to miss the crash but cannot afford to risk missing another summer. We have to find a new house, with a decent sized garden before next spring. To make things easier for ourselves we aren't going to sell our current UK home until we've moved. We'll then decide whether to sell it, rent it out or keep it for storing books.

The two most important things in life are time and space. You can buy some of the former by reducing your workload and cutting your expenditure on non-essentials. But the only way you can buy more space (and the privacy that goes with it) is by spending more money or moving to an area where the same amount of money buys you more.

We want a detached, period house with a little space and plenty of quiet. We want to live where there is no hamburger restaurant, where there are no pit bulls pulling along tattooed hoodies and where the nearest parlour advertising tattooing and genital piercings is a long train ride away. And we want a house not a flat. In a building occupied by twelve families there is always going to be one cooking curry, one on night duty coming in at daybreak, one woman who is a screamer when she has an orgasm and one bastard who does DIY with an electric drill at 3 in the morning. We don't want to live near a town which has more charity shops than regular stores.

One of our few specific requirements is that our new home has at least one and preferably two working fireplaces. As the oil runs out and energy supplies become intermittent so it will be increasingly important to be able to heat a home, and to cook, without outside help. For similar reasons we also want a few trees so that we can at least pick up our own kindling, and enough land to be able to grow a little food. And we would like a private water supply too. If there is no spring or borehole then a small stream passing through would be a bonus. We want a house to look after us. We don't want to buy a house which is going to need us to look after it all the time.

I have always argued that I do things for three reasons: to try to change the world, for fun and to make money. The money is for buying freedom (and for having fun and trying to change the world). But it is also for buying time and space and in the new cruel and dangerous world that means buying a little freedom from the authorities. For example, we now need to buy a garden big enough to have a decent bonfire and, if necessary, to bury our rubbish. The increasingly absurd rules about rubbish disposal make it essential that we find a place where we can gain independent control over what happens to our waste paper, unwanted magazines and redundant bits of packaging. So, one of the priorities for our house search is that there be enough space for a bonfire.

We are getting weary of the pointless, time-wasting little tricks estate agents try. They take photographs of a house that makes it look detached and it's only when you get there, or have spent 20 minutes finding a map of the area on an Internet search, that you realise that it's connected to its next door neighbour. Or they send details of a marvellous looking house and then, when you scour the details you discover that you're being offered a small part of the house and that the rest of it belongs to someone who runs a kennels and a nursery and a motor cycle repair shop.

They don't tell you about the petrol station, sewage works, campsite, school or pig farm next door. Indeed, they actually try to hide the existence of something you will see the moment you visit. This is stupid and I cannot believe anyone is ever deceived by such simple trickery into buying a property.

This morning, an estate agent sent us particulars for a new property by e-mail. It was a two bedroom terraced cottage for which they were asking £1,000,000. I sent an e-mail suggesting that even by their standards this seemed a trifle overpriced. I received a reply apologising and explaining that they had sent the particulars for the wrong property. I'm not entirely sure that I believe them. I suspect they might have been simply trying it on.

Moving house is one of the most stressful things any of us do. It's especially stressful when you want to buy, rather than rent. Everyone - estate agents, bankers, etc. - seem determined to make the whole thing as stressful and as complicated as they possibly can. Moving house is like childbirth. If people could remember just how painful it is they would never do it twice. And it isn't just the technical business of buying that is tiring; the looking is a miserable business too.

The world is full of people such as undertakers, divorce lawyers and emergency plumbers who earn their living out of charging huge fees from people too consumed by sadness or distress to notice the price until it is too late (and who deliberately overcomplicate everything they touch in order to maximise their profits). But estate agents still come top of everyone's hate list. I'm not surprised. They well deserve to be the most hated trades people on the planet. We travelled 50 miles to see yet another house whose owners had greedily sold a big chunk of their garden for development. A once smart Edwardian house, sitting neatly on its land, is now sharing its plot with a hideous building which looks as if it must have been designed by someone who usually designs council buildings or multi-storey car parks.

The Princess said that we should sue the agents for wasting our time.

We saw a decent enough house two days ago. It wasn't perfect but it was reasonably well built and had a decent garden. But the asking price was absurd. It was so overpriced that even the estate agent seemed embarrassed. We made an offer. They turned it down. `The people living there want enough money to buy a smaller house and a villa in Spain,' he said. `They think they need another £100,000 for this house to buy what they need.'

He made us feel bad about our offer but we didn't like the house enough to go any higher. We then successfully talked ourselves out of liking it. The agent rang back today. He says his clients will now take our offer. We told him that we were very sorry but that we no longer wanted to buy it.

28
09.12 a.m.
My father was an inventor, company director and World War II naval veteran. He died on February 28th 2008. He was 87-years-old. The inquest into his death was held on 16th November 2009 in Exeter. Although the inquest was held at my request I did not attend. I am still haunted by his death.

On the morning of 5th February 2008 my father telephoned Dr Benjamin Hallmark at Budleigh Salterton Medical centre. My father was, according to Dr Hallmark, complaining of excruciating pain. But instead of visiting my father, Dr Hallmark simply told him to call 999.

I believe that if Dr Hallmark had visited, my father might have still been alive today. I believe that a GP has a duty to visit patients who call for help. (Even if an ambulance is also considered necessary.) If Dr Hallmark had visited he might have decided that my father did not need to go to hospital.

My father was taken to Royal Devon and Exeter Hospital where he was given extensive tests. No serious or new problems were found and the admitting consultant considered sending my father home again. He decided, however, to keep him in overnight. I know this because I was standing by my father's bedside at the time. My father was quite well. The pain was caused by a long-standing back problem. My father was sitting up in bed taking a very active interest in what was happening.

Unfortunately, the ward to which my father was sent had an outbreak of gastroenteritis. The ward was put in quarantine and no one could leave. My father caught the bug at least twice. He also contracted a chest infection and a urinary infection while in the Royal Devon and Exeter hospital. He naturally became weaker and frail. I rang him and the hospital staff several times a day and eventually managed to arrange for my father's release. Because two weeks in hospital (and a number of hospital infections) had made him too ill to go home I arranged for him to spend a week or so convalescing in the Cranford Nursing Home (close to his home in Exmouth). He went to the nursing home on 22nd February. The hospital had prescribed a regime to control his pain and given him an outpatient appointment for further investigations of his long-term respiratory problem. I was told that after admission to the nursing home my father was walking about and laughing and joking with the nurses.

On 25th February the nursing home staff called for my father's doctor. My father was again complaining of pain.

The doctor who called on Dr Hallmark's behalf, was a GP registrar, Dr Stuart Livingston. He prescribed Oramorph (morphine) for my father. The manufacturers of Oramorph state clearly that the drug should not be given to patients with severe respiratory problems. Dr Livingston stated in his report to the coroner, in support of his action, that he believed that the contraindication was relative rather than an absolute one. The manufacturer of the drug, however, made it clear that the contradiction is absolute. The company making Oramorph wrote to me on 16th June 2008 and told me: `...the use of Oramorph is contraindicated in any patients with respiratory depression or obstructive airways disease regardless of age.' My father had chronic obstructive pulmonary disease - a serious respiratory problem.

Dr Livingston suggested that prescribing Oramorph is acceptable in `end stage' respiratory disease. But my father was not `end stage' anything. I don't believe that Dr Livingston had met my father before he prescribed Oramorph for him.

I hadn't been able to visit my father for a couple of days (I had a bad cold and didn't want him to catch it) but I rang him regularly in the nursing home.

When I rang him on the morning of 27th February my father was having great difficulty in breathing. He also kept falling asleep. Suspecting that my father's drug regime had been changed I spoke to a nursing home employee called Martin and discovered that my father had been given morphine (Oramorph). I was horrified. I have spent much of my professional life investigating the dangers of prescription drugs. I discussed the situation and the person I spoke to (Martin) agreed with my opinion that if my father had another dose of the morphine it would kill him. I asked Martin to make sure my father was not given any more morphine and said I would take full responsibility for this.

I rang my father in the afternoon. The morphine had worn off and my father was much better. He was alert and not breathless. He was talking and breathing as well as he had been for some while. I said I would visit him the following morning. We discussed the morphine. I told him that I would take him some scientific papers showing that the drug was not safe for him to take. We were planning a trip to one of his favourite hotels to celebrate his birthday the following week. But at around 8pm that evening someone at the nursing home gave my father another dose of Oramorph (morphine) as prescribed by Dr Livingston.

At about 8.15 p.m. to 8.30 p.m. a nurse rang me on my mobile phone to tell me that my father was a bad colour and was having difficulty in breathing. (The nursing home telephone records should prove this call was made). The nurse asked when I was visiting. I said I would be there the next day. I asked if I needed to visit immediately. (It would have taken me a couple of hours to get there). The nurse said she thought the next morning would be all right. She was wrong.

On my way to the nursing home the following day I was telephoned to say that my father had died.

I believe that my father would not have died if he had not been prescribed Oramorph by Dr Livingston. The drug was clearly contraindicated. And my father, an elderly man, was especially vulnerable.

And I also believe that if Dr Hallmark had visited, instead of simply telling my father to ring for an ambulance, my father might not have needed to be admitted either to the hospital or, as a result of the hospital admission, to the Cranford Nursing Home.

I decided that there was no point in attending the inquest because the coroner, Dr Earland, had informed me that she had already decided (before the inquest) that Oramorph did not cause my father's death. She also decided not to have witnesses whom I considered vital at the inquest. (The two members of the nursing home staff to whom I had spoken about the Oramorph.)

As a registered GP and the author of numerous books on prescription drug toxicity, I firmly believe that my father's death was caused by Oramorph, and could have been avoided.

Prescription drugs are one of the top killers in Britain today. The wrong drug can kill a patient - particularly an elderly patient - as surely as a bullet. The medical profession as a whole still underestimates the problem - even though doctor-induced illness is now the third biggest killer in Britain. One in six patients in hospital is there because he or she has been made ill by a doctor.

I made a formal complaint to the General Medical Council about Dr Hallmark and Dr Livingston. To my dismay the GMC agreed with my father's GPs that any contradiction for the use of Oramorph in COPD patients is relative rather than absolute. They apparently ignored the fact that the drug company which makes Oramorph has an absolute ban on the use of the drug with COPD patients. The drug company stated that Oramorph is contraindicated in any patients with obstructive airways disease. I asked the GMC to explain why the defending GPs' views were considered more relevant than the manufacturer's advice. They refused to answer. And they refused to consider evidence from the professional witnesses who observed the effect of the Oramorph on my father.

If I was astonished by that judgement I was utterly dumbstruck by their decision that it is standard practice for GPs to advise patients living alone, and in excruciating pain, to be advised to call an ambulance and wait for the ambulance to arrive. That's medical care in Britain in the 21st century. I think it stinks. I don't know what my Dad thinks about it. He's dead.

Some months ago I started writing a book about my father's death. But the book has grown and changed (as my books always seem to do). It is becoming a different book: a book explaining what is wrong with the health service and why doctors and nurses no longer care for their patients in the way they should. It occurred to me this morning that there is one massive reason for the current problems: doctors working for the health service have changed their allegiance. A doctor who works for the Government is a civil servant, his obligations and responsibilities are split. A doctor who works as a freelance medical adviser is bought and paid for by his patients. They give him money to look after them. The relationship is simple. But a doctor who is paid by the Government has two masters: the patient and the people who pay him (the Government). I believe it is because of this that doctors now promote unsafe vaccines and withhold treatments they know are necessary. The Government (through its administrators) now controls all doctors working for it. And so patients get a raw deal. As the gospel of St Matthew reminds us, no man can serve two masters. That includes doctors. GPs have attempted to retain their independence by remaining self-employed. But it's an accounting independence not a primary independence.

Hardly anyone will buy this book. But I have to write it. And I will then publish it. Because no one else will.

10.02 a.m.

I received a letter from a reader who describes herself as a greying, middle class woman. She describes what happened to her as she was driving home in the middle of the night. `A car with three people in it came up behind, too close. They were harassing me, trying to make me go faster. Then blue lights flashed. It was a police car. I was not going to stop for anyone miles from anywhere and drove five miles on to my town and stopped outside the police station, pursued by the police car, by now blaring its siren in a built up area. On the pavement three of them accused me of not having stopped. They were aggressive and very rude. They had not asked me to stop. If they had wanted me to stop they would have passed me and flashed the `Stop Police' light on the back of their car. They accused me of speeding. I told them I was being chased and harassed. They gave me a speeding ticket. I will get a £60 fine and three points on my licence. One of them, probably half my age, said I probably shouldn't be driving. A friend said it was a common tactic of the police. They harass a lone driver to make him break the speed limit, then ticket him. I expect the police to have better things to do - three of them - than harass a greying, middle class woman in the middle of the night.'

11.50 a.m.

I read today that P.G. Wodehouse had published 11 novels in the UK before the sales of a single one of his novels reached 2,000 copies. (The first successful novel was *Piccadilly Jim*). I doubt if any modern commercial publisher would persevere with an author whose novels had taken so long to reach such a relatively modest landmark.

12.12 p.m.

When I first started to earn my living as a professional author I was frequently offered work for money. Newspapers and magazines and television stations and radio stations all employed writers. And paid them money. The Internet has changed that. Today, I am contacted just as frequently. But nearly all of the people who want me to do things want me to do them for free. No fee, no expenses. It is, not surprisingly, difficult to make a living. I feel sorry for young writers struggling to make a living.

12.35 p.m.

At Publishing House our mail arrives at midday. At least it does on the days when Royal Mail can be bothered to bring it round. Some days they don't bother to bring it at all. Our problem is that there is too much mail for a postman to carry and so the mail comes in a van. You might think that a business which is bringing in so much work would be treated with a little basic courtesy. Not a bit of it. If we want a reliable morning delivery we have to pay extra.

In Victorian and Edwardian times in England there were up to seven postal deliveries a day in urban areas. And if you posted a letter in the morning to an address in the same city, you could expect it to be delivered the same afternoon. Women would post an order to their grocer in the morning and receive the groceries in time for dinner the same day.

In the good old days, just a few years ago, we used to get mail twice a day: early in the morning and lunchtime. Mail was collected seven days a week from the local postbox - several times a day. Today, there are fewer postboxes and less collections. The service has deteriorated more rapidly than any other service I can think of.

When things go wrong it is like talking to shop window mannequins. I've given up expecting sense from Royal Mail. (Though, to be honest, most other big companies are little better.) And the wretched employees always say it's someone else's fault and not their responsibility. That's not an argument that held much water at Nuremberg and it doesn't hold much water today. Nothing will improve until the half-wits on the other end of the phone are prepared to take some responsibility and to try to put things right.

But I'm too tired to fight them anymore. The `little people who disclaim responsibility' will between them doubtless destroy what the Government doesn't manage to destroy. And they'll shrug aside blame with: `Well it wasn't my fault, I was just doing my job'. So be it.

I estimate that I've spent over £2,000,000 with Royal Mail since I started self-publishing. I can't wait for the day when their damned pension fund sinks them and their monopoly is removed.

18.19 p.m.
The Princess and I went to visit a friend in hospital in Wales. There was a sign in the hospital that read: 'Please put bag's in bin's'.

While waiting for The Princess, I looked at a daily paper and saw that a woman whose daughter had been accused of bullying had defended her daughter rather aggressively. `She wasn't doing

94

anything,' the mother said. `She was just watching.' And that's the problem isn't it. People just stand by and do nothing and think they're innocent if they don't actually strike any blows. In France, thanks to Napoleon, it is illegal to offer no help to a fellow citizen in trouble. In modern day Britain everyone thinks it is fine to stand and gawp.

A bathukolpian and callipygian woman who was clearly one of those people who only feels really comfortable when wearing a label, and who had one of those plastic covered identity cards dangling on a cord around her neck, told us off for standing in the corridor. We were standing there while I took a photograph of the sign about the 'bin's'. `You would be a hazard if someone wanted to move a trolley along here in an emergency,' she said. She actually wagged a finger at us. I promised her that we would move out of the way if such a thing were to happen. Since the corridor was at least twelve feet wide they could have driven a tank down it without endangering our tootsies. She then said she was going to seek higher authority to force us to move. I said that I thought this an excellent notion and recommended that she not waste any time in putting this thought into action. She hurried off, her heels click-clacking on the hard floor of the corridor with purposeful certainty. We waited a few minutes to see if she returned but, sadly, she didn't and eventually we got bored and left.

22.04 p.m.
An angry reader has written to complain that he can no longer pay for my books with a credit card. He wants to know what on earth I think I am playing at and claims that the Government is planning to do away with cheques next year. He says I shouldn't be running a business since I clearly don't know what I am doing and that not taking credit cards over the phone is ridiculous. He says that cheques are going to be phased out and that he intends to consult his solicitor and take legal action against me. With tongue planted firmly in my cheek I sent him a polite but firm letter telling him that he was banned from buying any more of my books. (Ten days later I received a rather apologetic letter from his wife asking if she was allowed to borrow my books from her public library.)

This is by no means the only such complaint. Indeed, they come in regularly. Occasionally, readers become extremely aggressive and rude. I had to ban one immensely aggressive cat book reader from ever buying any of my books again. He claimed to be an extremely important ex Marks and Spencer manager and he too wrongly insisted that cheques were soon to be outlawed. The fact is that although cheque guarantee cards are disappearing in 2011, cheques won't disappear before the end of 2018 at the very earliest. My guess is that although banks hate them (because they are not as profitable as electronic banking) they won't disappear then. (My business model will collapse in a heap if they do.)

I started taking credit cards soon after I started Publishing House. Everyone working in mail order claimed that taking orders by telephone (and allowing buyers to pay with a credit card) dramatically increased sales. The assumption was that if you increase sales then you increase profits. I was told that the politicians and the banks would like to get rid of money and cheques (in the false name of preventing terrorism and money laundering they have already imposed limits on the amount of cash that can be used in a single transaction). I understood that when people use debit and credit cards to make purchases it is much easier for the banks and governments to keep track of where money is going and of who is buying what. When people pay with cash or by cheque it is almost impossible to track people in the same way. And so the authorities were conspiring to convince people that they should be able to pay by credit card for anything they wanted to buy.

I quickly found that taking orders by credit card was an expensive option. We had to pay to rent special machines on lengthy contracts in order to take credit cards, we had to pay the bank to process credit card sales, we had responsibility for errors and I was personally responsible for any illegal use of information obtained by people working on my behalf. This meant that I had unlimited personal liability for financial losses resulting from the illegal use of information by my staff and by people who weren't my staff. This liability was not covered by my insurance. I also had to buy special software to put the credit card orders into our system (naturally, there are laws covering how and when we could do that). I had to pay set up fees, cancellation fees and annual fees for everything you can think of and some things no sensible person could possibly imagine. One credit card company wanted us to pay service charges for three years in advance and seemed to put up their charges dramatically every time the sun came out. The problems caused by the fact that the bankers had screwed up the world's economy naturally meant that all these charges were ratcheted yet higher.

There were other problems with credit cards. For example, at one point I tried offering books at low prices. The cost of taking credit cards meant that this was only viable if I took payment by cheque. However, when I tried this some would-be purchasers complained that the law did not allow me to do this. Nasty little men and women in cheap suits said that if I offered books at a low price I had to make them available to those using credit cards as well as cheques.

And, added to all this was the fact that since I deliberately don't have a credit rating and, therefore, no bank can check me out, I was finding it increasingly difficult to be allowed to operate a credit card scheme.

Apart from being an additional complication in an already over-complicated world, and one requiring extra equipment and imposing massive obligations, I quickly realised that credit cards looked weak from a strategic, business point of view. It cost us at least £3 more to process a credit card order than to process an order by cheque. That's a huge cost. And credit cards are more complicated and troublesome in many ways. I just didn't make any money by selling over the telephone and accepting credit card orders. And it wasn't difficult to work out why.

I was relieved to see that I wasn't the only one to notice that credit cards are expensive things to use. Taxpayers have to pay extra if they pay their tax bill with a credit card and quite a number of councils add a 3% surcharge if citizens want to pay their council tax by credit card. (The authorities want us to do as much of our financial business (including our buying) online so they can get information and control. It is, of course, also cheaper for them. There is no little irony in the fact that they then charge us extra for doing what they are forcing us to do.) The charges, the paperwork and the onerous regulations mean that more and more companies are now charging a fee for the use of credit cards. One day I went into three shops (one after the other) which all displayed signs announcing that they did not take credit cards for sales under £10.

Since a good many of our books cost around £10 this cheered me and gave me heart in the decision to abandon credit cards.

When we sold a book for a fiver or so the costs became impossible. So, for example, we sold *Bloodless Revolution* for £4.99 plus £1 towards postage and packing. If I sold a book by telephone, with the purchaser paying by credit card, I would lose money on every single sale. (And that doesn't count the number of times that a credit card payment doesn't go through because the card has been used dishonestly or fraudulently. This problem is much worse with credit cards than with cheques. The book, of course, has been posted out and so the loss is the cost of the book, the postage and the administration.) I believe it is actually impossible for a small business to make money by selling something by mail order for less than £5 and accepting payment by credit card.

So that I could concentrate on what I think I do best (writing and publishing books) I decided to think about the unthinkable: not accepting credit/debit cards at Publishing House.

Constant new rules from the EU and the Government and the banks meant that the administrative costs kept rocketing and the red tape became mind numbing. Not taking credit cards meant that I wouldn't have staff spending hours taking credit card orders.

For several years I even paid for an outside company to take telephone calls 24 hours a day, seven days a week. This was enormously expensive because the company charged by the minute. When callers rambled on for a minute or two or wandered off to search for their credit card the bill for taking the call sometimes exceeded the price of the book they were buying. The answering machine service took on average four minutes to take an order - at 50 pence per minute or £30 an hour that's an average of £2 to take an order. But some people stayed on the phone for ages to report books that had gone missing or simply to have a chat with someone and leave a long rambling message for me. The costs quickly mounted up. And, of course, many of these callers had to be telephoned back the following day. Cutting out telephone orders cut costs dramatically because it meant I could do away with the phone answering service and some of the complicated telephone equipment I'd had installed.

In the world of mail order it is relatively easy to test things. You can, for example, create two promotional leaflets and send each one to 500 potential buyers. As long as the two sets of 500 are identical then the result will tell you which leaflet is most effective. The staff at Publishing House were insistent that readers preferred to pay by credit card. I didn't believe this. And so last year I decided to test cheques against credit cards. I did two mailshots of regular readers. In one mailshot I allowed readers to choose between paying by cheque or credit card. In the other mailshot I gave them only the option of paying by cheque. The test proved without doubt that readers preferred paying by cheque and suggested that readers positively disliked having a choice between paying by cheque or paying by credit card. When the extra costs associated with credit cards were taken into consideration it was clear that cheques were better for readers and much better for us. I then repeated the test in *Moneyweek* magazine. I split the leaflets I put in the magazine into two groups. Half of the leaflets offered the readers the opportunity to buy *Gordon is a Moron* by cheque alone. The other half offered the readers the choice to pay by cheque or by ringing up and paying by credit card. Once again, the test proved that readers vastly prefer paying by cheque. We made more than twice as much money from the leaflet selling books by cheque alone as we did from the leaflet offering a choice. Why the difference? It may be due to the fact that offering cheques only is simpler than making a choice. Or maybe people don't trust credit cards.

I realised that if we stopped taking credit cards completely we could still sell on the Web by selling through websites run by organisations such as Amazon, Waterstones, WH Smith and Tesco. So, readers still had two easy ways to buy books. First, they could send a cheque or postal order (payable to Publishing House) to the Publishing House address. Second, they could buy via one of the website shops such as the one run by Amazon for www.vernoncoleman.com. Customers could still pay by credit card if they chose to purchase books that way.

And so, in May 2009 I decided to abandon selling books by credit card. The administrative costs had rocketed, the red tape had become now mind numbing and most readers had told us they prefer to buy books by cheque. I gave instructions that if anyone wanted to know why we were no longer taking credit cards it should be explained that we had abandoned cards because of the increased cost, the paperwork and the EU regulations. The savings on credit card costs and telephone answering service costs far exceeded any loss of orders.

To get around the snag of selling through commercial websites such as Amazon (rather than directly ourselves) I decided that we would include details of my other books in every new book we printed.

I do find that it is always better to keep life as simple as possible.

The fact is that 37 million people in Britain still write cheques. Take out children, prisoners and the illiterate who can't write their own name and that's just about everyone. At Christmas around seven million people give cheques as Christmas presents. Every month around 24 million people write at least one cheque.

And the banks might be surprised to know that some people still regard cheques as rather an unpleasant new innovation. The owner of a garage we use thinks cheques are rather new fangled and untrustworthy. He will take one if he has to but prefers cash. He would not, I'm delighted to say, know what to do with a credit card if you showed him one.

March

1
11.02 a.m.

I find that it doesn't take me long to read the newspapers these days. Most of them are full of badly written columns which don't seem to do anything other than air the columnists' prejudices. Many editors seem to assume that any journalist can write a column. This is nonsense. Real journalists are trained to stand back from the things they write about, not to get involved or to allow their personal views to interfere. Columnists do the opposite. Writing a column is like writing a tightrope and the editor's main job is to give the columnist a nudge occasionally if he seems likely to fall. I have, over the years, written columns for dozens of magazines and newspapers. At one point I was writing a column for *The Sun*, a column for *The Star* and a column for *The Sunday People*. I was also writing a column for a Scottish paper, a magazine column and a column that was syndicated to around 40 local papers. (Not all were under the same name.) I started writing columns while I was at medical school. I wrote two weekly columns (for both of which I masqueraded as a doctor). Heaven knows how I found the time but I also reviewed plays several nights a week for the *Birmingham Post,* (for which I also wrote book reviews) wrote theatre reviews for the *Times Educational Supplement*, wrote regular articles for a variety of magazines and newspapers, ran a night club masquerading as a youth club, sat on several committees (for the first and last time in my life) and used the money I earned writing to begin an investment portfolio which I managed on a daily basis. I feel exhausted just thinking about it.

I learned that columns need humour, passion, irreverence and pace. Most of all the columnist needs to establish a relationship with his readers. And he needs to snag their attention so that they occasionally look up and say: `Hey, listen to this!' I treasured a letter from a reader who told me that he always used to read out chunks of my *People* column in his pub on a Sunday morning. A columnist who isn't in more or less constant conflict with his editor isn't doing his job properly. I wrote agony columns for over a decade and all the questions I published were made up to match the pre-written answers I wanted to give. I could never be rude to real people, nor would I have ever given personal advice to strangers. In my opinion, a lot of agony columnists make up at least some of the letters they print - if only because the vast majority of letters which come in are too rambling and imprecise to use.

2

12.16 p.m.

A friend of ours who runs a small stationery business is always moaning that he can't sell his house. It has now been on the market for 18 months and it is his sole topic of conversation. Both The Princess and I think his property is absurdly overpriced.

`You can always sell anything if the price is right,' I told him.

`No you can't,' he moaned. He pulled a face. If he'd been in the movies he would have made a good living out of playing scary bad men in horror movies. Producers would have loved him because they wouldn't have had to spend extra money on makeup.

`I'll buy your house,' I told him.

His face lit up. 'For the asking price?'

`No, I'll give you a quid for it.'

`Don't be stupid,' he snapped.

`Fair enough. You've turned down my offer. But you could have sold. All you have to do now is find a spot between my offer - the one you turned down - and the price you think it's worth.'

15.13 p.m.

When we were writing our two books on England the Princess and I discovered that Tommy Cooper, the funniest comedian of both our lifetimes, was born in Wales, though he was brought up in England. The Princess is, therefore, writing a few pages on him for her book about Welsh heroes. Cooper was a fascinating character. I, like many others, have spent much time trying to analyse his success. Part of his success was obviously down to his timing, which was brilliant, but there was clearly more to it than that. I suspect it was his almost palpable fear of failure which audiences felt. They wanted him to be successful, and shared every moment of anxiety and delight. In that he was similar to my snooker hero

Alex `Hurricane' Higgins. Audiences felt sympathetic and warm towards him. Most modern comedians are aggressive and battle against their audiences; they never bother to build a relationship. Cooper's relationship was built on the rock of his insecurity. Why, I wonder, do the Welsh always promote Catherine Zeta Jones (in my opinion an absurdly overrated actress), Tom Jones (who seems to me to be a painfully embarrassing singer) and Dylan Thomas (the talentless overhyped son of a mixed marriage between a culturally blind BBC and wildly prejudiced and obsessed Welsh nationalists) as the most famous Welsh heroes. They always forget Lawrence of Arabia and Tommy Cooper.

3
13.11 p.m.
I spent the entire morning replying to reader mail. One reader has invited me to contribute a chapter to a book he is preparing. There is, of course, no mention of a fee or any suggestion that I will be paid royalties. I thank him for inviting me to contribute to his new book but point out that I'm rather up to my ears (with several new books in various stages of work). I add that since I write for a living (and have ever-growing overheads, including staff salaries) I have to give priority to writing work which will earn me money to pay the bills!

A second reader has sent me three articles which he has written. `Please edit them for me before I send them off to newspapers' he says. There is, of course, no stamped addressed envelope. I sent the articles back with a note wishing him good luck in finding homes for them. A third reader wants me to find the address of a magazine she used to subscribe to and send it on to her. I have never heard of the magazine and have no idea why she has written to me. I cannot read her name or her address and so I cut out both from her letter and stick them onto the envelope in the hope that the postman will have more luck. A fourth reader wants me to give him advice about the book he has written. He tells me that I can download a copy to read for just £5. At the end of the morning I counted the envelopes and found that I had written 27 replies. Even at 32 pence per letter this meant that my morning's work cost me £8.64 plus the cost of the paper, ink and envelopes.

15.16 p.m.

If my father hadn't died when he did he would have been celebrating his birthday today. I remember that when he reached the age of 87 my father started to complain of breathlessness on walking uphill. He made an appointment to see a consultant cardiologist. I accompanied him. When the doctor had examined my father, and found relatively little wrong, he said to him: `What can I do for you?'

My father stared at him for a moment and thought about it. `I can't walk uphill as quickly as I used to be able to,' he said. `What are you going to do about it?'

The consultant, clearly startled, looked at me.

`It's OK,' I said. `You can tell him.'

The consultant smiled at me gratefully. `I didn't want to appear ageist,' he whispered, having realised that my father was rather deaf.

`I'm afraid it's your age!' he said to my father.

My father was terribly disappointed and turned to me. `Let's go, then,' he said. He was never a man to waste time on unnecessary chit chat.

18.12 p.m.

There is a suggestion from an estate agent in this morning's *Financial Times* that `the basic rule these days is to offer half the asking price.' Judging by the response we have had when suggesting that a property might be 10% overpriced we would be killed if we tried that. Most vendors (and most estate agents) seem to think that knocking off 1% counts as a `significant price reduction'. We were sent particulars two days ago of a three quarters of a million pound house which had been reduced by £500.

19.24 p.m.

A huge American computer company has invited me to give a lecture. They will, they say, be absolutely thrilled if I speak to their employees and guests in London. As usual these days there is no mention of a fee. There is not even any mention of expenses. When I mention these two things the company suddenly becomes less thrilled. I don't know why they think I would want to travel to

London, stay in a hotel and speak at their function at my own expense. I assume it is because they are in the world of computers where copyright is regarded as theft, unless it is their copyright of course when stealing is still stealing. I told them that I was too thrilled by their invitation to be able to accept it. The corporate idiots were so gullible, and so susceptible to flattery that I expect they believed me. They do not understand irony at all. Poor America is a nation whose two greatest achievements are Mickey Mouse and barbed wire. When it has gone America will be remembered for greed, obesity, purposeless violence, a complete lack of good taste or style and a child-like sense of humour.

20.12 p.m.

I tried to sort out my books today. I decided that I would take books off my shelves if I did not think I would read or consult them again. I added two riders to this. First, I would keep books which were of value. Second, I would keep books which I knew I wouldn't read again but which had some sentimental value because they had touched my heart or mind in some way. I then spent several hours going through a few of the bookcases in my study. After three hours I had decided to throw out just two books: an out-of-date copy of the *Writers And Artists Yearbook* and a copy of a novel by Georges Simenon of which I had found I had a first edition and two reading copies. I felt so bad about throwing out these two books that I put them back on the shelves.

21.16 p.m.

A staff member who left told me that he wanted shorter hours, fixed breaks, no responsibility, longer holidays, no need to think and little work. I've discovered that he has gone to work for the local council and he will, I suspect, be well suited there.

4

12.39 p.m.

The house search continues. We now realise that you can't trust anyone when you are looking for a house to buy. You can almost certainly trust some people but it's difficult to know who the trustworthy people are. And if you can't tell who you can trust and who you can't then the only sensible solution is to make sure that you don't trust anyone.

We drove for two and a half hours to see a house we were interested in. When we got there the agent told us that we couldn't see inside the annex because it was let to visitors. `You can only go in there between visitors on Saturday at lunchtimes,' she said. I asked if we could look in the garage. `I don't have keys for that.' `The summerhouse? The garden sheds?' `They're all locked. And I don't have the key.' Inside the house it was a similar story. `I can't show you this room I'm afraid,' she said, passing a locked door. `It's let to someone and they don't like people looking round.'

We left.

After that we went to see a house we thought looked really attractive. When we got there we found that it was a quarter of what we thought we were buying. `It says in the brochure that it forms a part of the whole property,' sniffed the agent. Not having read the brochure with a magnifying glass I'd missed this. The property in the picture was a large detached house. The property he was selling was a flat. Actually, it was a flat on two floors so technically speaking it was, I suppose, a maisonette.

Finally, we saw a splendid looking house with a large garden but it had no less than 14 immediate neighbours. When there are so many neighbours it is inevitable that whenever it is sunny one of them will be cutting the lawn, one will have a children's party in the garden, one will be washing the car with the radio on full blast and one set of small boys will be knocking on the door wanting their ball back. You will never have a peaceful moment in the garden of such a house. So we said `no' to that one.

14.15 p.m.

We called into a café to discuss some brochures we had collected from estate agents. A group of young mothers were having coffee together. Their children were behaving like wild animals. They were running around, screaming and climbing onto chairs and tables. The mothers didn't seem in the slightest bit embarrassed or even interested. I was about to say something when The Princess wisely stopped me. Even a mild rebuke would, I suspect, have led to serious trouble. The majority of British parents no longer seem to make any effort to control their children. When children are seen behaving badly abroad we always know that they will be British children.

16.17 p.m.

We were in a charity shop looking at the shelves of books when two women came in and one of them led the way over to where we were standing. The women were both in their 40s. One was simply fat, the other was obese. `I'm looking for a book,' said the fat one. `What sort?' asked the obese one. `Dunno. Jack wants another one. He's read the one he had.` `Who was it by?' `Dunno.' `What about this?' asked the obese woman. She prodded the author's picture on the front of the book. `I've heard of him. He's on the telly. He does that programme.' `Oh yes,' agreed the fat woman. `I've seen him on the telly. I'll get that one.' And she did.

5
11.12 a.m.

We met two of our neighbours this morning. They live just a few hundred yards away but we have hardly seen them for several months. They were both very angry. They borrowed far more than they could afford and are deep in negative equity territory. They owe more than Ireland. She is extremely neat and in the days before we were issued with EU-approved plastic dustbins was famous locally for plumping up their black rubbish bags and arranging the ties at the top very neatly, in such a way that they looked like Christmas parcels. `We've just been to the bank,' she said, rich in indignation. `A spotty youth told us that we should stop our Sky Television subscription! Can you believe it?' `We have to have our Sky!' insisted her husband. `The bank actually wanted us to cancel it!' He used to work in `financial services' but lost his job recently. After he was made redundant his wife came round with a letter she was planning to send to his boss. She wanted me to rewrite the letter for her. `You're a writer,' she said. `You know how to use words.' The letter she'd written was a mixture of angry accusations and pitiful begging. It was the sort of letter an overbearing mother might send to her son's schoolteacher to complain about him not being picked for the school cricket team. `I don't think sending this is going to help,' I told her. She was very cross with me and has hardly spoken to me since. They are now both unemployed spendaholics. `They say we have to cut back on our spending,' she said. `It's their fault we're in this mess. They lent us the money.' I suspect they aren't the only people in the country who feel this way.

15.16 p.m.
I spotted two pieces of news today that go together rather well. First, there are now 140 million people writing blogs on the Internet; each one the technological equivalent of a wild-haired madman shouting in the street. Second, computer servers use 5% of the USA's entire energy consumption. I wonder how many of those bloggers, busily using up the world's disappearing energy supplies, are pontificating about energy conservation.

6
12.14 p.m.
When I was a medical student I travelled by train through France and Italy and while visiting the Island of Elba I bought a copy of the leaflet Napoleon distributed to the soldiers sent to arrest him. I've been collecting Napoleana ever since and have an extraordinary collection of books and documents (including the originals of some documents written and signed by him). There are reputed to be 60,000 to 70,000 biographies now published. On the train this morning I read Napoleon's own account of his escape from Elba and the subsequent trip to Paris. It is surely one of the most dramatic pieces of history. I also read his book about Waterloo which is equally fascinating (though rather self-serving, since he blames the loss of the battle on his generals and the weather) but it nevertheless shows his strategic genius. He was a surprising general. He describes, for example, how he wandered off from his army and, with just a couple of aides, climbed neighbouring windmills in order to examine the position of the enemy army. Waterloo was the 50th major battle he had fought in just a few years. He was outnumbered two to one and damn near won. He attacked Blucher's army first because he thought Wellington was likely to move more slowly in response. He suspected that if he had attacked Wellington first then Blucher would have moved more speedily to counter the attack. Napoleon was undoubtedly the most brilliant military strategist ever to have

lived, though the Moscow enterprise was not impressive. He also created many things the French still give thanks for. He was the creator of modern Paris and gave France its legal, administrative and moral guidelines. By all accounts he was a workaholic with a power fixation. Psychiatrists would probably say the fellow suffered from a Napoleon Complex.

15.16 p.m.

I met an old newspaper friend in London this afternoon at the National Liberal Club. The Princess had never met him before and was intrigued to meet a real old-time newspaperman. He entertained us both with extraordinary stories of his life in Fleet Street. He and his father were both journalists working for national newspapers back in the days when a scoop was the Holy Grail for men who wrote their stories on Reporter's Notebooks and filed their copy via public telephone boxes. They were stringers, covering a huge area in the West Country and both paid by the line. The bigger the story the bigger the pay day. The two were competitive in that way that fathers and sons sometimes are and because they worked for competitive newspapers they never gave each other an inch. The son told us a story which illustrated the intensity and serious nature of the relationship. The pair of them were sitting having their supper one Sunday evening when the telephone rang (this was, of course, long before mobile telephones had been dreamt of). The call was for the father and the son could tell by the fact that his dad had shut the hall door that it was business. It was; it was the news editor of the paper for which he worked. A much sought after criminal had been arrested in a town just a few miles away. The news editor wanted a few facts to give strength to his front page splash. Without saying `goodbye' or explaining where he was going the father left. All the mother and son heard was the slam of the front door. The son immediately got up from the table. `Where are you going, son?' asked the mother. `You don't know where he's gone and you'll never be in time to follow him.' `I'm going to put the phone back on the hook,' said the son, who knew that if the story was a big one his own news editor would be trying to get through. And knew that his father would have left the receiver off the hook. As soon as the son had put the receiver back the phone rang. Sure enough it was his own news editor with the same story and the same urgent need for facts. The son grabbed his coat and hat, shouted goodbye to his mother and ran to his car, which was parked outside in the road. (His father's car had been parked in the driveway). As soon as he tried to drive away the son realised that something was wrong. He got out of the car. He had two flat tyres. His father had stabbed them both with a penknife. `What did you do?' asked The Princess, horrified. `I had to borrow a car from a mate. I got there late, missed the first edition and had a bollocking from the news editor.' `What did you say to your Dad?' `Nothing much,' grinned my friend. `He just said something about it being business and not personal. It was just a lesson to let me know not to expect any favours. Journalism was a tough business in those days.' He paused, and took two sips from his coffee. Then he grinned broadly. `It was fun, though,' he said. `Not like the namby-pamby business it is these days. They're all wussies.'

On the walk back to Paddington we passed a large government building. Outside, standing on the pavement, there was the usual knot of office workers that you see outside all large buildings these days. They were grabbing a quick puff or three on their cigarettes. None of them was wearing coats. The men were in shirtsleeves. The women were in skirts and blouses. They were all shivering and stamping their feet to try to keep warm. I sometimes wonder if the EU forces smokers to stand outside in the cold and rain so that they get pneumonia and die quickly rather than dying slowly and expensively of lung cancer. It's the sort of thing a cruel and fascist organisation would think up so it's probably not as absurd as it sounds.

Closer to Paddington, we saw a motorcycle carefully padlocked to a lamppost. The owner had put chains through both wheels to prevent them being stolen. Sadly, the engine was missing and had clearly been removed by a thief.

At the station a busker, outside the station, was blowing into a penny whistle and making noises. The Princess gave him money. She always gives money to buskers. (She gives money to beggars, but only if they look old and worn out.) `If we're ever broke I'm going to play my violin in the street,' she said. `By my feet I'll have a sign that says `Money needed for lessons please'.'

7

12.48 p.m.

I have just found a letter inviting me to the Citizens Commission on Human Rights annual Human Rights Awards Banquet in East Grinstead. The letter says: 'We celebrate CCHRs 40th anniversary and we would like to invite you to accept the CCHR Human Rights Award on this special occasion. This is being offered to you in recognition of your courage and tireless conviction in exposing the harmful effects of psychiatric drugs and practices in the field of mental health. There are over 300 people attending the awards banquet. Among these there will be many mayors and dignitaries from local areas, ambassadors from several countries, academics, doctors, educators, lawyers, allied members of the media, mental health campaigners and even psychiatrists. I would ask that you would be present at the banquet to receive this award.' I couldn't go and I desperately hope I remembered to say I wouldn't be there. I hardly ever go anywhere these days. Because I didn't go, I didn't get the award. I assume someone else got it instead. I did see what I think was a photo of it though and it looked the ugliest thing I've ever seen. Now that the council are so difficult about taking away rubbish I'm glad they didn't send it to me.

15.10 p.m.

We sent a copy of *Bloodless Revolution* to every bookshop buyer in the country, together with a letter giving sales of other relevant (political) books. As far as I can tell not one bookshop bought any stock. We pointed out that *Gordon is a Moron* had sold over 20,000 copies at £9.99, *England our England* had sold over 41,000 at £8.99, *Living in a Fascist Country* had sold over 10,000 at £15.99, *Oil Apocalypse* over 11,000 at £12.99, *Rogue Nation* over 9,000 at £9.99 and so on. Not one bookshop took one copy of shelf stock of *Bloodless Revolution*.

I see that on the Web *Bloodless Revolution* has so far garnered nine reviews. Eight of the reviews give the book five stars. One reviewer has given the book just one star, complaining that the book is too cheap and the print size too small. (I had the book printed as a standard mass market paperback in order to keep the price as low as possible.)

I am seriously considering writing books but not bothering to try to sell them.

8
17.55 p.m.

We bought a new Acer netbook. It was the most expensive one we could find and is pretty well unusable. The minute we turn it on the popups start to appear. Advertisements, warnings, threats and more advertisements. And they keep on coming. Every time one appears it has to be manually dispatched. But then, like one of those dolls that never tips over, it comes back again. We have done everything we can to stop them but nothing works. I hate the World Wide Web. It is an annoying, intrusive and utterly obstructive invention. The world would be an infinitely better place if it could be uninvented. It has, I firmly believe, done more to damage our standard and quality of living than any other invention in man's history. The only people who benefit from its existence are those tedious souls who earn their living creating and selling computers and software.

9
13.12 p.m.

Back in the simple days when petty bureaucrats had not yet been fitted for jackboots and shiny peaked caps, I used to throw away old insurance policies on the grounds that an out of date insurance policy was probably as much use as last year's calendar. No more. The bureaucrats from the EU have introduced a new law which means that at Publishing House we have to keep old insurance policy documents for ten years in case someone remembers that they were hit by a falling book in 1999. The paperwork mounts up. There was, of course, no warning for this retrospective legislation and so we had to scramble around, and spend much time and money, obtaining copies of old policies. Now I keep old copies of personal home and car policies too because it won't be long before the EU tells us that we have to keep those for ten years. The tax people have also got into the retrospective record keeping too. It used to be enough to keep records for six years. Now they've announced that they have the right to demand to see financial, accounting and banking records going back ten or even 20 years. I like the use of the word 'or', which in this context clearly means '20'. We already have a room designated for storing old accounts. We now clearly need more space for storing old paperwork. We may just be able to manage if we convert the space currently used for storing the books we used to sell when we weren't spending all our time collecting and storing paperwork.

10
18.01 p.m.
Yet another reader has written and asked why I am not on Facebook, Twitter and YouTube. There are several reasons. First, I write books and don't find the idea of communicating one sentence at a time either entrancing or potentially profitable. Second, unless someone at the EU creates days with more hours I don't have time. I honestly don't understand how people whose lives are already full of texts and telephone messages can find time for twittering. Third, I think there is a real security problem with Facebook. I never put valuable or confidential information on any computer connected to the Internet. Indeed, I never put anything on a net-connected computer that I wouldn't happily see painted on my garden wall or printed in my local newspaper. I will never put private information on a website and to be honest I think anyone who does is barking. I actually believe that sites such as Facebook are not only making people ever lonelier and inward looking but are exposing the vulnerable to exploitation by fraudsters and tricksters. Fourth, I don't think either Facebook or Twitter is likely to last. Fifth, I suspect that there is enough drivel on these sites without me adding to the energy waste. And, finally, I confess that all these websites sound rather sad and nerdy. They are rather cheesy and seem designed to glorify the vanities of publicity seeking megalomaniacs. (From what I've heard about it YouTube ought, perhaps, to be renamed Me Me Me Tube.) If these sites are going to change the world they aren't going to change it in a way I find attractive. I've never even visited any of these websites and I have no inclination to do so.

The Internet has devalued information, knowledge and communication. I find it just as frightening that people apparently take seriously a communication system which relies on messages of a maximum of 140 characters as it is that students apparently trust an encyclopaedia that can be rewritten by anyone, controlled by lobbyists and those with a vested interest in publishing misinformation and which is as reliable a source of information as graffiti scrawled on a lavatory wall. Now I hear that there are services where people can ask questions and rely on anonymous strangers for the answers. And, of course, there are naive simpletons who spend huge parts of their lives putting private and personal information onto Web based services over which they have absolutely no control. These are, I suspect, the same individuals who then complain bitterly when their identities are stolen. I wasn't in the slightest bit surprised when photographs of one of Britain's senior spies and his children appeared on Facebook, put there by his wife.

Apparently important business people, and politicians who ought to have better things to do, now twitter constantly, responding to one another's logorrheic outpourings. Minor celebrities twitter away every time their bowels open or they put the kettle on. `Had wonderful movement this a.m. Great joy.' This is a medium for the self-obsessed for whom nothing about themselves is too trivial for sharing. *Time Magazine* recently reported `....Twitter turns out to have unsuspected depth. In part this is because hearing about what your friends had for breakfast is actually more interesting than it sounds.' Really? In my world, tweeting on Twitter is an occupation for twats.

11
11.22 a.m.
I received an abusive and threatening letter from a reader who objected to the title of my book *Gordon is a Moron*. He ended his letter with the words `I bet you don't reply to this'. He was right; though I would have done so if he'd had the courage to give a name and an address. Gordon Brown wrecked the economy for generations to come. He is responsible for heaven knows how many deaths in the wars he helped take us into. The dictionary definition of a moron is someone who is stupid or foolish. On reflection, the title was an understatement. When *Gordon is a Moron* first came out I received quite a number of letters complaining about the title (which was, of course, taken from a popular song). I remember one newspaper sent along a whole

bundle of complaining letters. The editor responded by banning all future advertisements for all my books, including my books about cats. But the bottom line is that largely thanks to Gordon Brown, Britain is stuffed and is likely to remain so for a long, long time.

14.12 p.m.
We had a book delivery today. A pallet loaded with 1,000 books was left on the pavement outside Publishing House. It was raining.

15.16 p.m.
A production company has left a message offering me £150 to travel half way across the country and spend a day filming a programme for them. They also want me to ring the researcher and do some preliminary planning work for them. I get out of this by telling them (truthfully) that, if they employ me, their programme will never be aired.

12
11.01 a.m.
I had another letter today asking me how I got started in self-publishing. As I confessed in an afterword I wrote for *Alice and Other Friends*, it was a cat called Alice (aka Her Royal Fluffiness) who was responsible for my starting to publish my own books. My career as an author was going quite well (with books regularly hitting the top ten bestseller lists) until I wrote *Alice's Diary* and was forced into the world of self-publishing.

By the mid 1980s, I felt that I knew my cat Alice well enough to write a book with her. (She usually sat with me when I worked. At the time I was using an IBM electric typewriter. She liked the hum it made and the fact that it became warm after a few minutes and she learned to switch it on herself. I would often go into my study and find her sprawled across it, warming herself.) And so together we produced *Alice's Diary* - the memoirs of a cat. At the time it was unusual for me to write a book without having found a publisher and my agent usually arranged a contract before I started to write, but this book was different: I felt I had to write it, but since I wasn't quite sure how it was going to turn out I didn't think there was much point in trying to find a publisher to commission it.

When I'd finished the book I felt it needed illustrating. I knew exactly what sort of drawings I wanted but I didn't know an illustrator I could trust to draw Alice and Thomasina. So I did the drawings myself.

When the book was finished the typescript started a long and fruitless journey around London. Publisher after publisher turned it down.

`This isn't the sort of book Vernon usually writes' `Is it intended for children or adults?' `Who is going to buy it?' `I don't understand it' and (my favourite) `Vernon doesn't write cat books' were just some of the comments.

After a year or two it was clear that no one wanted to publish *Alice's Diary*.

I felt certain that there was a market. And so I published it myself.

Within a very short time we had sold over 10,000 hardback copies of *Alice's Diary* - big enough sales to have put the book into the bestseller lists for many weeks if we had been a `proper' publishing company.

At the beginning, a publishing company's sales representatives helped to sell the book but we also put small advertisements in magazines and quickly decided that this was the most successful way to promote and sell the book.

Despite the misgivings of the professional publishers in London there clearly were people who wanted to read a book written by a cat. At the time I remember being rather pleasantly surprised that we were right and they were all wrong. These days I so expect the `professionals' to be completely out of touch with what the reading public really wants that I would be worried if I thought I had written a book which any London publisher wanted to put on his or her list.

Readers started buying additional copies for friends (I remember that quite early on one reader ordered 11 copies to give away as presents) and Alice started to receive fan mail. Bookshop staff started to ring up about the book. Whenever they wanted to know the identity of the author I always just said that the book had been written by a cat called Alice. No one ever questioned this.

After the success of *Alice's Diary* I self-published several more books. All sold well. A novel about cricket called *The Village*

Cricket Tour proved enormously successful. And so when I wrote my next serious medical book, *Betrayal of Trust*, I published that myself too. In truth I didn't have much choice. No one was prepared to publish it. Some said the style was too `popular'. Other publishers used the excuse that the book was too `academic'. I rather suspected that no one wanted to publish the book because they were frightened that it might annoy the medical and scientific establishment too much. And they were probably worried that they'd be sued.

When I published *Betrayal of Trust* I didn't care whether or not it made money. I just felt that the message it contained was so important that the book had to be published. The commercial and financial success of *Alice's Diary* made it much easier to take this decision and so once again Alice had affected my life. If I hadn't published *Alice's Diary* I doubt if *Betrayal of Trust* would have ever been published so I was following the old tradition of being prepared to allow a bestselling book to subsidise the rest of the list.

Modern publishers and agents won't look at books which are a challenge to the establishment because they are themselves representatives of the corporate establishment and are themselves usually politically correct folk, left inclined, and believing fervently in such modern nonsenses as multiculturalism. (Multicultural means that outside cultures are promoted and ours is suppressed. The world is of course inescapably, and by definition, multicultural but to force individual societies to become multicultural is absurd and doomed to failure).

Sadly, the `traditional' publishers hate self-publishers and do everything they can to stop such a threat to their control of publishing. I've always felt that enormously hypocritical, given that many who work in publishing like to pretend to be liberal free-thinkers.

Editors commission what they are told to commission by the marketing people (who know what the world wants just as much as 19-year-old management consultants know how to run a factory) and agents, who knowing which side their bread is buttered, loyally feed the system. The people I have met in publishing are in general not particularly bright or innovative. They're too insensitive to be in the business of producing (or caring about) books. Unlike their predecessors a generation or two ago, they are largely corporate voices, empty suits, schooled in mediocrity; banal hacks who distrust anything daring, original and iconoclastic. To them `original' means risk and makes them shudder. It means the possibility of losing money. They are at their happiest when publishing the autobiographies of television celebrities and cookery books written by television chefs. Occasionally they even go mad, right to the edge, and publish a vegetarian cookery book (as long as it has been written by someone with a television show).

In my view, anyone who suppresses points of view they don't agree with is a bigot. And in my experience most publishers are bigoted, prejudiced propagandists. They think they are the good guys but I think they are the bad guys; their stupidity and ignorance suppresses honest debate and encourages extreme attitudes - such as racism.

Betrayal of Trust proved to be commercially successful and from then on things just went on and on. I had just written a book called *Food for Thought* for a big London publisher. It was originally one of a series of books I had agreed to write for one of the world's largest publishers but the publishers and I disagreed about the content. They felt that the book was too controversial, too opinionated and contained too much of an attack on meat. This, they felt, would damage the book's sales in Germany. They wanted me to change the text. I disagreed with them and wanted to keep the book as it was. In the end I asked them if I could keep the book and abandon the contract. They agreed. I gave them back their money and kept my book.

Food for Thought reprinted five times in the first 12 months and was my first real self-published `bestseller'.

When I was a boy I frequently read with admiration about the relationship between authors and publishers. An author and a publisher would stay together for life in what was more like a marriage than a commercial partnership. But by the time I started writing books the world of publishing had changed irrevocably. The first big change was that editors started moving about between publishing houses. Authors found themselves having a book commissioned by one enthusiastic editor and aided through the editorial production process by a second editor. The book would then be brought into the world by a third editor who might, or might not, like the author or his work. The old-fashioned, cosy relationship between publisher and author had changed for ever.

The second big change was that the salesmen and the marketing directors took over the world of publishing. Today, editors no longer have control over which books they will publish. The traditional publishing image of a wise, well-read man in a tweed jacket helping an author to turn his raw pages into a good book - and then helping to create an oeuvre - has been out of date for decades. Publishing is now controlled by marketing men in smart suits. They want more of what is already selling and then they panic when they realise that the market is saturated with more of the same. The marketing men tell the editors what to commission. The editors then find an author and tell him to write a book he doesn't particularly want to write. The result, inevitably, is a book without passion which fails to excite the readers. Most of the people in the publishing industry are scared stiff by the very thought of innovation. They prefer to imitate.

I am now convinced that self-publishing is now the purest form of publishing available to an author. The large publishing houses which traditionally and currently dominate the literary world simply produce books which the marketing men believe will sell in the largest quantities. In the future real books - written from the heart, with passion and with no thought of commercial purpose - will have no place in the large publishing house. Only authors who are prepared to publish their own work will see truly original work in print. Self-publishing is the only way for an author to be truly creative and imaginative and to take the chances that are (or should be) an integral element in book publishing.

The great beauty of having my own publishing business is that I can write the books I want to write - and then worry later about how to sell them. Most of the books I have chosen to write would not have been published by a modern publishing conglomerate. And yet most of the books I have chosen to write and publish have been reprinted (some of them many times) and have sold well. Many of our books would have been on the best-seller lists if we had sold more through the bookshops (where the official best-seller lists are created) and less through the post direct to readers.

When I used to write for big publishers just about every book I ever published involved a battle. It took years to find someone brave enough to publish *Bodypower*. Publisher after publisher insisted that there was no market for such a book. And yet *Bodypower* went straight into the *Sunday Times* Top Ten and the *Bookseller* bestseller list and has never been out of print since. It has been translated into over a dozen languages, and extracts from it have appeared in scores of newspapers and magazines around the world. I have made several television series and a radio series based on it.

When the original paperback version of *Bodypower* went out of print a mass-market paperback house bought the rights. Their edition went out of print before it was even published. I took the rights back and sold the book to another publisher. When they, in turn, remaindered their version I bought up all their stock (around 2,000 copies), gave them away and published my own *European Medical Journal* version. Within 18 months of taking back the rights to *Bodypower* I'd sold 10,000 copies of my new edition and without any effort I'd sold foreign rights to several more publishers abroad.

When I first wanted to write a book about tranquilliser addiction just about every publisher in London told my agent that there was no market for such a book. When a publisher eventually commissioned *Life Without Tranquillisers* they wanted major changes making. I refused to make the changes and so we took the book away and eventually sold it to another publisher. The book went straight into the *Sunday Times* Top Ten the minute it came out. I remember that someone from the publishers rang the *Sunday Times* to find out why the book had gone into the bestseller list. `Because it is selling so quickly,' was the logical reply.

I could fill a book with stories like this. I have very little respect for modern editors and publishers. They live in an enclosed world in London and seem to me to have very little idea of what the world wants to read. Literary editors are, it seems to me, even worse!

I have published dozens of my own books and I have found it far more enjoyable than writing books for traditional publishing companies. I can write exactly what I want to write with no interference. I use the profits I make from the current books to pay for new books. A traditional publisher will usually take between 12 and 24 months to turn a manuscript into a published book. Books which are likely to annoy the establishment or attract legal opposition are often unpublished. I don't have those problems.

Because bookshops wouldn't take books from a small publisher I spent a fortune on advertising (in my first proper year of publishing I bought around between £200,000 and £300,000 worth of advertising space in newspapers and magazines) and sold direct by mail.

I run my publishing imprints rather in the way that I believe old-fashioned publishers used to operate. I write books which I want to write (rather than books which I know will be commercially successful). Once the book is written I then worry about how to sell it. And at the end of the financial year I hope that the books which sell well will earn enough to subsidise the books for which there is not such a clear market.

I believe that there are only three reasons to do anything: to try to change the world, to have fun and to make money. Sometimes it is possible to do things which satisfy all these three objectives. More often the success of one objective means that one is more capable of pursuing another objective. (So, for example, making money doing something which is dull may enable you to enjoy an experience which is fun.) Only very occasionally is it really possible to combine these reasons. When I first started producing my own books, publishing fitted the bill perfectly.

15.20 p.m.

A friend of mine received a copy of the *Playfair Cricket Annual* today. The book isn't in the shops yet. `I bought it for £3.49 post free,' he told me. The shop price is £6.99. I have been involved in publishing all my life and have spent over 20 years as a publisher. I have no idea how anyone made any money out of that transaction.

13

11.58 a.m.

I woke feeling tired; weary, dispirited, whingey, self-pitying. But during the morning I was working on a book about great English revolutionary writers and reading about Defoe, Paine, Cobbett et al and I gradually began to feel ashamed and embarrassed. What giants they were. What an inspiration. Compared to them, today's journalists (particularly all those working for the BBC and the nation's broadsheets) arc lily-livered, fearful, obedient and hollow; mincing in the footsteps of the great.

Today Henry David Thoreau would be in an orange jump suit in Guantanamo. Thomas Paine (the English architect of the French Revolution and the American constitution) would have been extradited and water boarded.

14

14.12 p.m.

In a charity shop I bought a complete set of John Buchan's novels (hardback, beautifully bound editions) for £10 and discovered that I had not read (or certainly could not remember) his novel called *The Free Fishers*. This is a delight. Buchan is largely forgotten today though he produced a huge number of excellent novels.

Not many writers produce more than one great classic. Jane Austen (*Pride and Prejudice*), Thackerary (*Vanity Fair*), Emily Brontë (*Wuthering Heights*) all had one each. Bram Stoker is remembered only for *Dracula* and Mary Shelley for *Frankenstein*. Victor Hugo is remembered only for *The Hunchback of Notre Dame* and Flaubert for *Madame Bovary*. John Bunyan produced a whole library of books but is rightly remembered mainly for *Pilgrims Progress*. Jerome K Jerome is remembered only for his speedily written potboiler *Three Men in A Boat*. There are great exceptions. Dickens, of course, produced a classic every time he sharpened a new quill. (Dickens was, perhaps, the first true multimedia star. He wrote stories, edited and ran a newspaper, wrote bestselling books and gave lectures and theatrical performances. There has never been an author who had such a reach - or one who had such influence.) And Conan Doyle, Dumas and Simenon produced great stories with such frightening regularity that it is difficult to believe they could have ever produced anything unreadable. Robert Louis Stevenson produced at least three classics (*Treasure Island, Kidnapped* and *Dr Jekyll and Mr Hyde*). And P.G.Wodehouse wrote more great books than is decent.

Sometimes an author is famous for a book that may not best represent his skill. So, John Buchan is remembered mainly for *The Thirty Nine Steps* (because of the Hitchcock film starring Robert Donat and Madeleine Carroll) when he wrote at least half a dozen better novels. His best book is surely *John McNab*, the story of three eminent men who decide to liven up their dull lives by doing a little poaching in Scotland.

These days it's largely forgotten that Buchan also wrote some splendid non-fiction. He was the author of a number of history books and biographies (among them lives of Cromwell and Sir Walter Scott). Himself a successful politician. Buchan spent his final years as Governor-General of Canada where he was known as Lord Tweedsmuir. And I suspect that as small bookshops disappear so will Buchan. The Web is all very well for finding books when you know what you are looking for, but it is a soulless and dispiriting place for browsing. Nothing beats getting down on your hands and knees in the dusty corner of a second-hand bookshop or junk shop. I pity book lovers of the future. Browsing among computer files just isn't half as much fun.

Buchan has been pushed aside these days because of the efforts of the politically correct Nazi style literary police. In the same way that Mark Twain is accused of being a racist because he attended minstrel concerts in the mid 19th century so John Buchan is regarded by some as anti-Semitic because he made mildly rude remarks about Jews in some of his novels.

Attempting to pass judgements on important figures like these because of things that happened years ago, when ethics and expectations were different, is bizarre, hypocritical and sanctimonious. But the power of the politically correct movement is so great that books by Twain and Buchan are now rarely seen and future generations will be deprived of two of the greatest and most innovative authors of all time because present day politically correct bigots are too unimaginative to realise that the day to day behaviour of people must, to a great extent, be judged by the mores and standards of their time and not by the mores and standards of our time.

Still, the bright side is that if his books were more popular I wouldn't have been able to buy a beautifully bound, collected edition of Buchan's novels for a tenner.

15
13.54 p.m.

I am invited to speak at a conference in Blackpool. I say no. The organisers send back a message offering even more money. I don't care how much they are offering or what they want me to speak about. I will never visit Blackpool again. The Princess and I went there once. It is hell on earth.

16.12 p.m.

We saw a house which the local authority had besieged with planning regulations. `You can't use that piece of land at the front or that piece at the side. The planning people have decided that they are a buffer zone which you own but can't fence or do anything with. And that big tree which is falling over is protected. And the windows of the bedroom there are made of frosted glass because they overlook next door's garden.' We left quickly.

19.18 p.m.

Yet another industrialist is giving a big chunk of money to one of the political parties. The impression is given that he's doing this for ideological reasons. What balderdash. People don't give vast amounts of money to politicians and political parties because they think they are helping the democratic process. They give money because they are buying power, influence and commercial benefit. The donations are an investment and they want a return. And corporate donations are given so that the Chief Executive or Chairman can buy a peerage, a knighthood or some other bauble at shareholders' expense.

16

11.29 a.m.

I saw figures today which show that thieves stand a better chance of getting away with their crime than entrepreneurs have of succeeding with a new business. The man who works hard to start a business is more likely to go bankrupt and end up in prison for debt than a burglar has of going to prison for stealing.

15.14 p.m.

We have a large elderly car which has not been taxed. It was due to have a new tax disk at the end of February but we aren't using the vehicle at the moment and I simply haven't bothered to renew the tax disk (though the car does have a valid MOT and insurance certificate). Today I received a letter from the Head of Vehicle Licensing Products and Services at DVLA who seems terribly upset about the fact that I haven't renewed my tax disk or sent him something called a SORN. Instead of writing politely and asking me if I've forgotten, and telling me about the SORN option, he gets straight into threatening mode. It's a typically heavy-handed piece of thuggery from an arrogant Government functionary who thinks that citizens have nothing better to do than fill in forms and who delights in cowing the innocent with rank belligerence. In his letter about my untaxed car he tells me that I could be fined £80 or more. `Even worse,' he adds ominously, `we may impound and crush it!'. I particularly liked the exclamation mark. Here is my fanciful reply: `*Thank you for the letter in which you are kind enough to say that you may impound and crush my car because it has been untaxed for two weeks. I am sure that crushing two tons of perfectly serviceable vehicle will help the environment enormously. You could round things off nicely by dumping the crushed remains in a river of your choice. I haven't taxed the vehicle because I'm not using it at the moment. Thanks to the endless barrage of red tape and time wasting directives from London and Brussels there hasn't been any opportunity for me to do any work and earn any money. And so the car which you would like to crush is sitting behind locked gates on private land awaiting better times. I don't honestly see what this sad story has to do with you but maybe life at your office is dull at the moment and my little piece of news will add something to your joie de vivre. I've never heard of a SORN before and my local Post Office doesn't have a suitable form. If it would make your life infinitely better if I were to fill in a SORN do send one along and I will put it on the vast pile of government paperwork awaiting my attention. Sadly, this will delay the point at which I can afford to tax the car. But every silver lining has a cloud behind it.*'

16.29 p.m.
A reader from Newcastle writes to tell me that every week, thanks to the whim of a faceless, brainless bureaucrat in Brussels, she and her family have to sort their rubbish into nine separate plastic bins for recycling. Nine. There's a newspaper report today with a

125

picture of a woman with ten recycling boxes. `Do the people who think this up imagine we have nothing else to do with our lives?' my reader asks. `It's probably no problem for the unemployed - and for those working for the council who have little enough to do, and who think of themselves as hard done by if they have to type one envelope in a day - but for those of us with proper jobs and family responsibilities the time this sort of nonsense consumes is just too much. The rubbish has to be sorted, compacted and packed tightly into the always too small containers. My husband has to squeeze some of our rubbish bags (yes, we wrap it in plastic to stop it blowing about) before we can cram them into the containers. The air has to be squeezed out. We live in dread that the binmen (are we allowed to call them that?) won't be able to get the bags out of the boxes.'

I remember when I was a kid the dustmen used to walk down the drive and collect our dustbin from near the back door. They would take it to the lorry, empty it and bring it back. Streets looked neat and tidy. Sorting out the rubbish took no time at all. You just threw what you didn't want into the galvanised bin. The council took the rubbish away in a cart. Once a year you would wash out the bin. Every ten years you would buy a new one. The rubbish was used to fill up old pits and mines and quarries and so served a useful purpose.

I reckon The Princess and I spend a minimum of half an hour a week sorting out our rubbish, putting it outside on the pavement and then going out to fetch in the empty plastic containers. Half an hour a week may not sound much but it adds up to 26 hours a year. That's the equivalent of three normal working days. It is time wasted because although I am forced by law to sort my rubbish the council, having avoided an EU fine by forcing its citizens to sort their rubbish for `recycling', just tips the carefully sorted rubbish into one big pile. (I know this isn't a myth because I've seen them do it.) The resultant mess is packed up and sent off to China on the boats that brought television sets, bras and trainers for us to buy. And we're supposed to believe that by sorting our rubbish we are saving the planet.

Most people's lives are now blighted and complicated by this nonsense but few realise that the rubbish collecting isn't really about the environment. It's about pretending to sort it so as not to be fined by the EU. The cause of the rubbish (the manufacturers who triple wrap indestructible DVDs in shrink-wrap, cardboard and plastic) are, of course, untouched by the bureaucrats.

We still produce the same amount of rubbish as before, of course, but these days we spend ages stamping on things, bending things and compressing things so that they will fit into the appropriate plastic bins. We put much time and effort into this though I confess I haven't yet worked out precisely how it saves the environment. All it does is cut the cost of the landfill taxes the local council has to pay to the EU. Was there ever a more arbitrary, unreasonable, unfounded tax than this?

The best and most convenient, cheapest and most efficient and most environmentally sound way of dealing with rubbish was in black bags. They were put outside once a week, taken away and dumped into landfill (of which there is unlikely to be any shortage for the foreseeable future). The streets were not scarred by vast numbers of plastic containers constantly littering gardens and pavements. And to cut down waste it would be easy to tax the manufacturers who overpackage.

The EU's recycling programme is, like just about everything else it does, badly planned and executed. As an organisation the EU comes across as self-satisfied, arrogant and wasteful. It is an extraordinarily incompetent and corrupt organisation which wastes money by the lorry load. And money they have in abundance. It is surely no coincidence that the EU has chosen for its anthem the very same piece of Beethoven music that accompanies the thuggish footwork of Malcolm McDowell and his chums in the film *Clockwork Orange*. We pay billions for annual membership of the EU and we then pay billions more in fines because our bureaucrats can't quite keep ahead of the rules their bureaucrats keep introducing. I suspect that more crooks have grown rich through the EU than through any other organisation in history. The EU's policies on the environment fit this master plan precisely.

Smaller recycling containers are often kept in the kitchen so that food and empty bottles can be put straight into them. Are these containers sterilised each week? I very much doubt it. So, via the garbage sorters and collectors, every household in every town will soon be contaminated with one another's bugs. Incidentally, why do big families get more rubbish containers? They pay the same council tax as everyone else. And it was big families who complained about the poll tax being unfair. People who live and work at home - the elderly and the self-employed - need more rubbish space but don't get it.

17
17.11 p.m.
I managed to buy another Dickens' letter at auction. It was the Great Man's habit to burn all his correspondence so that it could not ever be reproduced but gems do occasionally appear on the market. I managed to buy a cheque signed by him not long ago. He couldn't burn those. He had the very best signature in the history of the world – though Napoleon's unmistakable signature makes the hairs on the back of my neck stand up when I touch it.

18
11.19 a.m.
A neighbour, a schoolteacher who retired at the age of 50 and who receives an enormous pension, called in with a copy of a history book he has written and which has been published by a well-known major publisher. We congratulated him and opened a bottle to help him celebrate. `I won't be getting rich on it,' he told us. `But I didn't write it for the money so it doesn't matter.' He tells us that the publisher gave him £250 for the copyright. When he'd gone I felt gloomy. Retired public sector employees are, it seems, all busy writing books. They don't need the money and are happy to accept derisory terms from publishers. No professional author could possibly write a book for £250 and still manage to buy food. The problem is that this huge reservoir of amateur authors is weakening still further the already perilous position of the professional author. Journalists are in much the same boat. A friend who has worked for the national newspapers all his life has given up and is thinking of opening a café somewhere. Papers which used to pay hundreds of pounds for a story that `led' a page now pay just a tenner - and for that they expect a photograph too. The papers, like magazines, are filling their pages with material provided by retired amateurs who don't expect or need to make a profit from their work. `I wonder how some of these teachers would have felt if I had walked

into their schools and offered to teach their pupils for the joy of it,' said my pal.

19
12.40 p.m.
We are in London, at the hotel we always use. (It is next door to the National Liberal Club.) This afternoon I was standing near the reception desk waiting for someone when a new visitor arrived. 'What's your name?' asked the receptionist, rather rudely I thought. 'My name is on the bag,' replied the man, equally brusquely. 'Where is your lavatory?' he demanded. The receptionist told him and the newcomer hurried off, obviously eager to take advantage of the facilities. When he returned to the desk I was still there. 'How long will you be staying, Mr Vuitton?' asked the receptionist.

At the Club, I met a pal with whom I worked when I was a GP. He looks old and when I was tactless enough to mention this he said it was not surprising because he *is* old. He believes that the world started to fall apart when women put a leg on each side when they were riding horses, went out of control when fish and chip shops started putting meals in little polystyrene boxes, instead of wrapping them in old newspaper, and disintegrated completely when the authorities at Lords started to allow advertisers to paint slogans on the grass. I agree with him. I have decided to become an irritable old man. I think I will start drinking port so that I can develop gout.

12.45 p.m.
The Princess has just looked at the piece I wrote a few minutes ago. She says that I fulfilled my ambition to become an irritable old man some time ago.

22.11 p.m.
We bought a new kettle today. (We bought it at Paddington Station which says something uncomfortable about the modern railway station.) Here's an extract from the instructions: 'The appliance is not intended for use by persons (including children) with reduced physical, sensory or mental capabilities, or lack of experience and knowledge, unless they have been given supervision or instruction

concerning use of the appliance by a person responsible for their safety.' So, there you go. Courses in Kettle Management will doubtless be starting soon at a nearby University.

23.15 p.m.
'I love eating,' I said this evening. 'If someone told me I had to give up eating I wouldn't want to live.'

20
15.16 p.m.
Our refrigerator has broken down. The man who came to repair it tells us that it will cost more to put it right than to buy another one. Moreover, the part he needs, a compressor, will take weeks to obtain. So, for the sake of a relatively small item a massive refrigerator must now join the nation's fridge mountain. If the EU really gave a damn about the environment it would force manufacturers to make spare parts for kitchen equipment more readily available. And they would insist that such products carried no VAT. Two weeks ago our shower broke. We were told that it simply needs a new thermostat but that since it was impossible to buy a thermostat we had to buy a new shower. There is, presumably, a shower mountain too.

16.58 p.m.
A journalist called Tony Edwards sent me an e-mail asking what I feel when I write the words 'the end' at the completion of a novel. 'Relief? Despair? Do I mourn the parting from characters?' I replied: 'All the characters I have ever written about are alive and kicking in my head. Sometimes, I don't hear from them for a while (just like ordinary earthly folk) but the ones I have written about a lot are as real as real people. Sometimes I feel bad about the fact that I don't send them Christmas cards. The places I invent exist too and are often much more pleasant than the ones I didn't invent.' This is true. The Princess and I spend much of our time 'living' in Bilbury and talking about what the characters who live are doing. This doesn't feel in the slightest bit odd to either of us.

21
13.11 p.m.

`You look like an English gentleman,' I said to a German publisher who arrived for a meeting dressed in a smart blue blazer and cream trousers. I thought he'd be pleased. `A German gentleman!' he said, pulling himself up to his full five feet five inches and very nearly clicking his heels. It had honestly never occurred to me that being called `an English Gentleman' would not be an incomparable compliment or that anyone (even a German) would consider being described as a `German Gentleman' a compliment. In fact, of course, he didn't look at all like an English gentleman. He was trying far too hard. He had a handkerchief in the breast pocket of his jacket. And, horror of horrors, it matched his tie. If he resembled anything English it was a second-hand car salesman.

18.11 p.m.

In China a car park has been built with spaces three feet wider for women drivers to allow `for their different sense of space'. I have written to ask if the Government will instruct car park owners to introduce something similar here. It sounds a splendid idea.

19.16 p.m.

The VAT people at Her Majesty's Revenue and Customs insist that to save the planet I must fill in my quarterly VAT report online. (They don't seem to have realised yet that computers are massive users of electricity.) This is now the law and means that they will no longer post out a form for me to fill in. But every quarter they send me a stern reminder (through the post) reminding me to fill in the form online so that we can save the planet together by not sending stuff through the post. It is comforting to know that the planet and the future are in the hands of such people.

22

14.15 p.m.

I've been re-reading John Osborne's two volumes of autobiography. According to Osborne the three great lies are: 1) I hate money, 2) I'm glad I'm a Jew, 3) I'll only put it a little way in.

15.16 p.m.

On the way to Minehead we passed a road sign which said, simply: `Falling rocks'. The Princess and I spent some time trying to decide whether it would be better to slow down or to speed up. We couldn't decide.

23

11.18 a.m.

As a result of the Inland Revenue losing the personal details of 25 million citizens the Government is bringing in new controls and punishments for small businesses which haven't lost any data. From April 1st (and as far as I know the Government has not yet started playing April Fool jokes) companies and sole traders can be fined up to £500,000 (not a misprint) for not looking after data properly and for not having a satisfactory system of protection. I understand that this refers to the physical protection of computers and disks. If Government departments lose data then taxpayers will presumably pay the fine. If companies lose data then shareholders or directors will pay the fine. If anyone working for me (and that includes the Royal Mail) loses the data then I pay the fine. Another reason not to be in business.

14.16 p.m.

The Princess has been looking for a new mobile telephone. It is incredibly difficult to buy a telephone that doesn't take photographs, play games, do the ironing and whistle 9,327 different tunes. Most of the things we buy are far more complicated than we need them to be. Cars, telephones, television sets and computers can all do a zillion things we don't want them to be able to do. These extra facilities make things more difficult to operate and get in the things we really want to be able to do. Not surprisingly, because they are more complicated they break down more often. And when they break down they have to be thrown away.

16.12 p.m.

For the first decade or two of my publishing life, publishers used to make much of their money out of selling `serial' rights to newspapers and magazines. Newspapers in particular used to pay a lot of money for serial rights. I frequently sold first, second or even third serial rights for five figure sums. Payments for serial rights were always higher than payments for features and I don't expect I was the only author to sell serial rights in books that didn't exist. I would send a `chapter' from an MSS (for which I knew there was no market as a book) to a newspaper editor and sell him the serial rights in material that was never going to be a book. Instead of receiving a fee of £2,000 for an article I would be paid £20,000 for serial rights. This form of mild deception was distinctly profitable.

Sadly, this small bonanza has disappeared because publishers have lost what brains they once had and now give away serial rights. I was astonished when I discovered this. A feature editor from the *Daily Herald* in Scotland offered a derisory sum for the serial rights in a book that The Princess and I had written together. When I protested I was told to take it or leave it because the `big' publishers in London don't expect any money at all in return for serial rights. This, of course, is utter madness.

24
14.38 p.m.

The Internet is a festival for spammers and crooks, pornographers and terrorists, lobbyists, propagandists, liars, deceivers and those with a grudge. It is an electronic heaven for those with a vested interest to promote. As a source of unbiased, factually based information it is about as useful as a pot of strawberry yoghurt. Pitiful excrescences such as Wikipedia look like caviar but turn out to be horseshit. In my experience the Internet's best known information site is unbalanced, vindictive and prejudiced. Anyone can write anything about anyone. Knowledge is not a prerequisite. Facts are optional. As is truth. One editor I identified turned out to be a 15-year-old, who proudly described himself as 'an authority on literature, music and politics' and other things that I am interested in'. An expert. The damned site seems to me to be written by anonymous failures sniping from the safety of the sidelines of life.

Wikipaedia reminds me of Spain in the days of the inquisition. Instead of secret messages dropped furtively in little boxes, today's evil little worms do their dirty work without even having to leave their bedrooms.

Much of the site is, I suspect, written by people with vested interests; lobbyists (professional or merely obsessed) with more prejudice than information. Biographers and would-be historians who cannot sell their work offer it free of charge. Wikipaedia has, I discovered, a strange rule that people who are alive are the only people on the planet not allowed to interfere with their own entry.

I suspect there are people who think Wikipaedia is an independent encyclopaedia; but as an encyclopaedia it is built on a firm foundation of mud. To describe Wikipaedia as an encyclopaedia is like describing the BBC as an independent broadcaster. The basic concept is so flawed as to make the result entirely worthless. To me, Wikipaedia exemplifies everything that is wrong with the World Wide Web; it is a potent mixture of ignorance and prejudice masquerading as an impartial source of accurate information. Contributors mix their lies and libels and deceits and half-truths into a poisonous pot of rumour, innuendo and falsehood. No wonder many celebrities and politicians employ people to check their Wikipedia entries and to comb the Internet daily for inaccuracies and libels. Wikipaedia is an utterly pointless and dangerous invention. I would ask anyone who approves of it one simple question: How would you like to be the subject of a Wikipaedia profile, knowing that you cannot correct any errors but that all your enemies can put on whatever they like and libel you freely and without concern?

The sad truth is that there is no innocent fun online. The Internet is a meeting place for intellectual vandals, for terrorists and for pornographers and paedophiles. Bloggers may not be paid (most of the 140 million tapping away do so without pay) but they are competing for popularity and the only way they know to achieve that is not through wisdom but through verbal violence and shock.

25

11.40 a.m.

Another company wants to buy advertising space on vernoncoleman.com. I turn them down as usual. But it is becoming increasingly difficult to say `no' to people who offer me money for doing absolutely nothing.

And I'm not entirely sure why I am turning them down. The entire world seems to be built on advertising. Why won't I allow anyone to sponsor items or put adverts on the site? I suppose it's because although I know damned well that I would never alter anything to please an advertiser I am worried that readers might think that I would. Without adverts there can be no suspicion.

26
15.10 p.m.
The new phrase in the investment world is `black swan event'. It's as popular now as `elephant in the room' was a year or two ago. The idea is that black swan incidents are rare and unpredictable and improbable and, because they are unexpected, can therefore cause chaos in the financial markets. The fact is, however, that black swans aren't particularly rare. I have just developed some photographs I took in Dawlish of a black swan sitting on her nest. The small river running through the town is full of black swans. There isn't a single white swan to be seen.

27
12.17 p.m.
Three letters today from readers wanting me to write another book on politics. I believe that my last book on politics (*The Bloodless Revolution*) contains the best answer I can give and there seems little point in continuing to redefine the problem when I have already defined the answer. So, no more books on politics. Unless I change my mind.

15.16 p.m.
A fellow I know who runs a printing company has just bought a new press. He has paid a vast sum of money for this machine and I fear he may regret the expenditure. These days we are all accustomed to the idea of equipment going out of date before we've worked out how to use it. That's now the norm. But the danger in the world of printing is that the industry may well disappear before the down payment has cleared through the bank. The whole publishing industry is going to be turned upside down and inside out by e-books and the Internet. Authors, publishers, agents, bookshops and wholesalers are all going to be badly hurt. Printers could well be mortally wounded.

28
15.43 p.m.

I am well accustomed to constant technology changes. At primary school I learned to write using a piece of slate and a scratching stone. When I wanted to rub out what I'd written I used a damp cloth. At grammar school I dipped a nib pen into an inkwell. Blotting paper played a large part in my early life, though mainly because strips of it could be made into pellets, soaked in ink and fired with great accuracy with the aid of a rubber band stretched between thumb and forefinger.

I was selling computer software in the early 1980s. A piece of medical software which I wrote with a friend sold in 26 countries and was widely praised. (It was written for something called the Sinclair ZX computer.)

I do not object to new technology because I don't understand it or because it threatens my life in some way. I happily accept and use and enjoy new technology which improves my life. But most new technology doesn't make things easier or better and doesn't save time or energy or effort. Most new technology is crap.

One member of my staff used to accuse me of being something of a Luddite because I insist on writing in DOS rather than Windows but I was the first person I know to have an Internet website, to use a computer, to have a hand-held computer (a Psion - still the best) and to have a mobile phone (it was the size and weight of two bricks, it filled a decent sized briefcase and had a proper phone with a curly wire attached to the handset). I was the first person I know to have a Blackberry and the first to have an iPhone. I had a fax machine when only one person I knew had one. (We faxed one another constantly.)

I choose to use new technology when it helps me and not because it's there or fashionable and I have to admit that these days most new technology doesn't make my life better in any way. Most seems absurdly over complicated, badly designed, badly made and unreliable. And, for a wordsmith, DOS is much better than Windows.

21.19 p.m.

The Princess pointed out today that I am, in different ways, like both of my parents. I am like my father in that I am remarkably trusting and often sadly naive. When a garage mechanic tells me that something needs changing I trust him. And I am like my mother in that when I (or someone I love) is tricked or cheated, or treated unfairly, I am likely to fight like a demon. This is an uncomfortable combination. The first trait leads me into confrontational circumstances. The second trait means that the confrontations are often explosive, and may cause considerable collateral damage.

29
14.02 p.m.
We drove to Hereford. We are still searching for a new home for us and a new home for Publishing House. Most of the journey was up the glorious Wye Valley but the first part of it involved a tedious strip of motorway. I'd never really noticed before just how fed up people seem to look when they're driving up and down motorways. I couldn't help but notice that all the drivers and the passengers in the various vehicles seemed to have the same fixed look on their faces. The drivers were all white-faced and rather angry looking while the passengers were all rather pale too but they just looked thoroughly miserable and bored stiff.

When I was a boy, we always used to look forward to a spin out on a Sunday afternoon. My parents and I would pile into the car and we would pick up any aunts, uncles and miscellaneous grandparents that we could find. Going on a proper holiday would always be looked on as a real adventure and I would set off with *I Spy* books and notepads for collecting car numbers. We didn't really mind how long it took to get to wherever it was that we were going to and the journey itself was a genuine part of the pleasure; to be enjoyed rather than endured. We got a tremendous amount of fun from waving at people, spotting thatched cottages and searching for fluted pillar-boxes.

When my father joined the RAC and we started to get saluted by RAC men travelling because *very* special. RAC men used to ride around on super little three wheeled motorcycle combinations in those days. They wore enormous leather gauntlets and old-fashioned goggles and carried all their tools and spare parts in brightly painted little sidecars.

I remember once, when my Dad was driving us to the seaside for the day, we passed an RAC man parked by the side of a roundabout on the Welsh borders. I made my father drive round two or three times just to see if the RAC man would keep saluting us every time. He did.

We used to spot all sorts of fascinating things from the car in those days and we'd stop and have cups of tea and platefuls of buttered scones in lovely out of the way places. Everything was fairly leisurely and we were quite happy to average 30 miles an hour.

Now that there are motorways criss crossing the countryside everything is very different. The emphasis is all on speed and everyone seems determined to get from their point of departure to their destination in as short a time as possible. A minute spent travelling is a wasted minute. No one seems interested in looking at the countryside or the strange bits and pieces of rural architecture any more. People don't make unscheduled stops now just because they've seen an odd looking building, a herd of wild deer or a rather jolly looking café. Motoring is about red and white rubber cones, roadworks and motorway police.

At the motorway service areas you can see the effect that all this is having on people. Cars and coaches hurtle into the car parks, and screech to a halt. The people inside leap out and rush around as quickly as they can so that they can get back on the road without losing too much time. If there is a queue for the lavatories, a queue for food or a queue for petrol people get very upset and bad-tempered. It is hardly surprising that the staff working in these out of the way service stations invariably become as edgy as the people they serve, as they struggle to provide a speedy service at the cost of all friendliness. The price for all this haste is a high one. Instead of arriving fresh, rested, full of fascinating little titbits of knowledge and ready for fun the modern traveller arrives sweaty, stressed and so uptight that it takes him hours to recover. Progress.

16.47 p.m.
I went into a shop to try to put £30 into my mobile phone. `It won't do £30,' said the assistant. I looked at her and waited. `It will do £10 and £20 but not £30,' she explained.

18.28 p.m.
One third of British companies face a regulatory procedure each year. In any one year 50% of British companies are sued at least

once. These problems destroy many small companies. Big companies, protected by regiments of lawyers, welcome these problems because they know that they cause serious damage to their small competitors.

30
14.10 p.m.

I've been thinking a lot about progress recently. We are taught, and encouraged to believe, that progress is always good. The corollary is, of course, that anyone who tries to stand in the way of progress must be bad. There is an erroneous assumption that this year's doodah is inevitably better than last year's doodah, simply because it is new. It's the same with books. Publishers abandon their backlists and sell only what is new, new, new (and preferably from a new author too). Knowing that manufacturers invariably stop making good things and replace them with things which are never as good - that's almost a definition of progress - The Princess and I buy lots of it when we find something decent in the shops.

The simple truth is that many of the things invented, and described as progress, are bad for us and make our lives worse. Progress isn't always a good thing. Cigarettes, modern farming methods, vaccinations, the Internet and genetic engineering are just a few of the things described as `progress' but which I could argue are damaging our lives. I believe that just about all progress in sport is bad. There has not been a development in half a century that has improved cricket or football or rugby or motor racing in any way. Similarly, much so-called progress in medicine actually results in patients being worse off - not better off. It is generally assumed that `change' is a synonym for progress but this patently isn't true.

Most worrying of all, perhaps, is the fact that an increasing number of broadsheet commentators and politicians, now assume (and accept, apparently unquestioningly) that `progress ' must always be synonymous with a larger State. Anything which reduces the power and size of the state is `recessive' and `bad'. All those who support the EU (and that is the BBC and most of the rest of the media, and almost all politicians in the doomed House of Commons) are in favour of statism and increased state spending.

A few years ago I took our BMW into the garage to have something repaired. A salesman at the garage tried to sell me a new 7 series and part of his sales pitch included the extraordinary claim that there was a device in the car which, through manipulating a mouse on a small pad, enabled me to change over 700 functions. He insisted that the car had more computing power than the early devices NASA sent into space. His pitch actually put me off the car completely and I found myself physically backing away from it. Who on earth wants to be able to control 700 different functions while driving a car? I drove a BMW for ten years and there were so many knobs and dials that at the end of that time I still couldn't remember how to make the fog lights work. Whenever the car came back from the garage with settings altered it took me half a morning to reset them. When a bulb needed replacing it took skilled men at the garage half a day to do it.

Of course, some progress is good. The man who invented a brush suitable for cleaning chimneys put a lot of small boys out of work. That was a good thing for it freed them up to play conkers and go scrumping for apples while people's sooty chimneys still got swept. But much change isn't progress because it isn't an improvement on the way things were done before; it's just good for the people initiating or promoting the change (and profiting from it in some way). How many houses built today will still be standing in 30, 50 years' time, let alone be still fit to inhabit in 100 years' time? The Princess and I always prefer to buy and live in old houses simply because they are much better made. The building industry may have found cheaper, faster ways to do things. But cheaper and faster aren't necessarily good when the end result is something shoddy and temporary. All real progress is made as a result of steady observation and careful deduction but these skills are not valued today. Just about all great discoveries in history have been made by people who weren't recognised by their peers before they made their discoveries and often weren't recognised for years afterwards either. Their discoveries made members of the establishment feel uncomfortable because their acceptance imposed `change' on a society which really didn't like change. For millennia advantageous changes to society happened only through the work of unreasonable men. Great things happened only when enough unreasonable men were brave enough to be unreasonable in public. Today, things are reversed. Anyone who opposes change is regarded as an unreasonable backwoodsman; someone to be pitied and avoided.

I'm often described as a Luddite but I'm not. I'm a realist: someone who understands that progress is more often bad than good and that progress for the sake of progress is no progress at all. Very little change is change for the better. I am not against change. I am against change without purpose because progress for the sake of change is not progress.

31
21.08 p.m.
I discovered today that in Victorian times there were 500 varieties of apple tree and over 1,000 varieties of pear in England. I rather doubt if there are that many varieties on sale in today's shops. Where did they all go? Progress took them I suppose. The same progress that took the small farms and the greengrocery shops.

April

1

09.52 a.m

The Princess sent this letter to a friend who lives in Wales:

Dear Ms D,

Owing to the shortage of housing provision in the Carmarthenshire area combined with the high influx of workers from central, southeastern and northeastern European countries, we have been called upon to make the most of the region's existing resources. We have done this by devising a plan called the 'Habitat Share Scheme'. Through the use of relevant data we have carefully selected candidates for our scheme who have fulfilled our criteria, and we are pleased to inform you that you have been selected. Congratulations! Your membership reference number for our Habitat Share Scheme is: 784333VX28PO914550CD (Please quote this number in all correspondence).

In order to help us appoint a suitable Habitat Share Scheme partner for you, please fill in the details below. Your chosen partner will remain resident with you for a minimum of 12-18 months because research confirms that this is the average time scale when 50% of workers decide to return to their country of origin.

Please specify your preference of the nationality of your Habitat Share Scheme partner:

(Please place a tick alongside the country of your choice)

Lithuanian

Polish

Romanian

Please specify your preference of the sex of your Habitat Share Scheme partner:

(Please place a tick alongside the sex of your choice)

Male

Female

(Please note: you can either opt for male or female)

Please specify your preference of the age range of your Habitat Share Scheme partner:

(Please place a tick alongside the age of your choice)
18-25 years
25-35 years
35-45 years
45-60 years (Knowledge of first aid will be required for this age category)

As soon as we have processed your details, we will send you the dates of when your Habitat Share Scheme partner will be despatched to you. This is expected to be four weeks from the date shown on the top of this letter. In the meantime, we shall forward onto you the language phrasebook of your choice. This will be provided to you free, however, there will be a charge of £10.99 for postage and packaging. We strongly suggest that you opt for the Polish language as many linguists agree that it is less challenging to master than Lithuanian or Romanian. Added to this, it will make shopping for your Habitat Share Scheme partner easier because records show that Polish food is more easily obtainable from the supermarkets in your area.

Congratulations again on being selected as a member of our elite scheme. We look forward to processing your details and despatching to you your new Habitat Share Scheme partner.

Yours sincerely,
Palo Frilo
Executive Advisor

15.14 p.m.
I've received a request to speak at a fringe event at a small book festival held in a place I'd never previously even heard of. The organisers offered to let me have the use of a hall for £15 plus 25% of my ticket take and suggested I charged £4 to £5 for tickets. `We price tickets at £7 for the Big Guns, so that should be fine for you,' an organiser told me, as though in training for a Gold Medal at the Patronising Olympics. The too important to be named Big Guns would not, of course, be expected to hire their own hall, arrange their own sales or share the proceeds. They would arrive later, met by chauffeur driven limousines no doubt.

I was so annoyed by what seemed to me to be a carefully calculated insult that I sent a childish note back saying that I didn't do little festivals. It wasn't so much the insult that rankled (I really should be used to it by now) but the fact that the woman who sent the e-mail felt so comfortable about insulting me that she didn't even seem to be aware that she was doing it. It was as though she thought that I would accept being second-rate as obvious and inevitable. It was the easy assumption that I would accept my lesser standing which seemed so damned insulting.

Looking around the other literary festivals I see that the big name author speakers at the Hay on Wye Festival include author Chris Evans, author Bianca Jagger and author Jerry Hall (one can only assume that Evans has some connection with Mick Jagger but I can't imagine what it is). I can't help wondering if the organisers could be prosecuted under the Trades Description Act for using the word `literary' to describe their festival.

Literary festivals are springing up all over the place these days. At most of them television personalities and politicians are treated as the superstars. Some of these shindigs are sponsored and I assume someone must be making bundles of loot out of them.

I used to receive regular invitations to speak at the damned things. But either my star has waned or word has got around that I always say `no'. I don't think I have ever received an invitation that has included an offer of a fee or any expenses. I think the idea is that I will be thrilled to be in the same town as such literary luminarics as Gordon Brown. The organisers of these events love minor television celebrities, topless models and authors who are young and sassy and preferably black and female. If they can find a speaker who is leprotic and in a wheelchair they are over the moon. I doubt if the people who run them, speak at them or go to them know or care anything much about books or writing.

2
16.17 p.m.
I went to meet someone called Bill Bonner in London. Bonner is a publisher of financial magazines such as *Moneyweek* and a wide variety of newsletters. He is something of a publishing phenomenon and seems to have enough energy to light up a small town. He wants me to write a newsletter for him. Knowing that he lives part of the time in Paris I had arranged for him to be sent a copy of my book *Secrets of Paris*. His first words to me were: `I bet I know more about Paris than you do.' He then proceeded to

tell me that he had an apartment there and was, therefore, far more knowledgeable about the city. It was immediately clear that he hadn't even looked at the book because in it I refer to the fact that we live part of the year there and have an apartment in the city. He offered me £10,000 a year and 7.5% of the take, to write and edit a newsletter for him. Even if the money had been good I would have turned him down. Although he is thin I think he is American.

19.18 p.m.

As usual we made our own sandwiches before travelling home. We bought bread, cheese and other essentials in Sainsbury's at Paddington station. We hardly ever eat out these days. Not even sandwiches are safe. The average sandwich is stuffed with e coli - simply because the people who make them don't bother to wash their hands properly. Eating out these days is like letting strangers put their fingers into your mouth after they've just been to the loo and not bothered to wash their hands. Television chefs set a terrible example. They are always dipping their hands into the food they are preparing.

I am constantly surprised at the way that people in restaurants eat food which has been prepared and fondled by the bare hands of complete strangers. Would any of them, I wonder, let complete strangers put their bare fingers into their mouths? On the odd occasion when I've found myself watching a television chef I've always been appalled to see him (or her) mixing salads or whatever with bare hands. No television chef seems to understand anything about nutrition or hygiene.

The only television chef who was worth watching was oenophile Keith Floyd but I damned well wouldn't have wanted his fingers in my mouth either.

3
15.16 p.m.

In Gloucestershire today I saw a van which had the words `Monet - house painter' painted on the side. How wonderful to be able to say that your front door had been painted by Monet.

17.16 p.m.

The Financial Times is proud of its model for charging people who use its online website. The newspaper sends out flurries of daily e-mails (each just a few sentences long) and allows readers to look at the articles upon which these e-mails are based just ten times a month. The idea is that once a Web user has used up his allowance he will pay to access the other articles he wants to read. This system may well work for *The Financial Times* (where the people paying are almost certainly doing so with someone else's money) but it won't work with ordinary punters who are paying with their own money. It won't work for three reasons. First, the short pieces of news (intended as tasters) are long enough to tell most people everything they want to know on the subject. If Goldman Sachs has done something terrible all I want to know is that they've done something terrible. I'm not interested in the rest of the article quoting people saying how shocked they are and I'm certainly not interested in whingeing excuses dreamt up by the Goldman Sachs publicity people. Second, if there is something about which I want to know more, all I have to do is put the key words into a search engine and then read the full story on someone else's website. Third, even if *The Financial Times* tries to cut down the amount of information it includes on its teasers or tasters, there will be someone (probably the publicly funded BBC) prepared to provide a similar service for free. And readers who want to know more simply have to press on the link to visit the relevant site.

I'm as sorry as anyone else is that the pay-for-information model won't work. Towards the end of the 20th century, I was one of the first people to set up a series of websites designed to sell information. Although I was sceptical (because I was aware that most of the people using the Internet expect to get everything they want for free) it was something I had to try. It failed.

4

12.14 p.m.

I was standing in a queue in Lloyd's bank today and overheard this. A man in a tweed jacket and corduroy trousers turned to the man standing beside him. `I'm worried about this place going bust.' he said. `But I have a plan. I'm going to diversify.' You mean divide it between different banks?' `No. I'm getting it all out. I'm going to keep some under the mattress and some in the teapot and I'm going to bury some in an old biscuit tin in the garden.'

15.16 p.m.

Why do solicitors stop cheques when people who have ordered books die? It seems so sad. Moreover, although they stop the cheques the solicitors always keep the books which have been sent. Since quite a number of our readers are elderly this happens frequently. This has happened again today. It happened two weeks ago. The customer who died most recently had ordered four books she wanted to read. But her solicitor stopped her cheque. He did not, of course, return the books and ignored my letter asking him to do so. So, thanks to him, the last thing the old lady did was steal four books posthumously.

5

16.17 p.m.

I bought a lovely edition of *Some People* by Harold Nicholson at a charity shop today. When I got the book home I spent ages trying to pick off the sticky price label that the shop had affixed to the cover. The label was one of those immoveable ones that really needs removing with a blowtorch. After picking away for several minutes I eventually managed to remove most of the label. But there was, inevitably, a nasty rectangular mark left behind to show where the label had been. Why do charity shops always allow their books to be handled by people who know nothing and care less about the items for which they are responsible? Most charity shops overcharge for anything remotely interesting but still ruin their books (and indeed everything else they sell) by slamming on sticky labels that were never intended for use on books (or indeed anything else that isn't packaged in military thickness plastic). A few months ago I bought a beautifully crafted brass shoehorn from a charity shop. Even that still bears the mark showing where the price label had been.

6

18.17 p.m.

One of the problems with being old is that I really cannot blame anyone else for the stupid things I do. There comes a point in life where we all have to take responsibility for our errors - even the egregious ones. The snag with knowing this, of course, is that one can become overly cautious; weighing all the pros and cons before making a decision and eventually finding it almost impossible actually to reach any sort of decision.

19.12 p.m.

A reader has written suggesting that I must adapt to Internet selling. How on earth can I? Amazon won't carry any stock unless I pay them extra. I'm told that they will guarantee to stock our books in our webshop if we pay them a fee, give them 60% discount on the books and pay to post the books to them. Oh, and if they decide they don't want the books they will send them back and we will have to pay the postage on the returns. This isn't business - it's commercial suicide. Just to add to the bewilderment I feel, one bookseller told me that he wouldn't stock my books because they are too widely available on the Internet. I sometimes wonder if I am perhaps living in some sort of lunatic asylum. I am often described as `controversial', `iconoclastic' and `eccentric' but I am beginning to feel that I am the only sane and sensible person on Planet Publishing.

7

21.14 p.m.

A policeman has advised members of the public who are arrested to avoid saying anything except to complain about everything and everyone. I think that this is probably excellent advice for anyone dealing with any civil servant.

22.10 p.m.

Our search for a new home is not going well. I'd forgotten just how stupid and deceitful estate agents are. They ask us what we want and we tell them. We give them enough detail to help them select something suitable from what they have for sale but not enough detail to make it impossible for them to find suitable properties. They write all this down on a large pad. And then they hand us a pile of brochures for houses which match none of our requirements. `This isn't quite what you're looking for,' they say, offering a one bedroomed flat in the middle of a city 50 miles away from our chosen area, `but the owner has recently decorated the bathroom and there's a nice view of the park from the spare bedroom window.'

Part of the problem, of course, is that there really isn't much property on the market. By deliberately keeping interest rates low to protect the millions who greedily bought houses they couldn't afford (and to prevent the housing crash which the market needs but the Government doesn't want for political reasons) the Government has enabled people to stay in houses they should have never bought in the first place. And so, despite the fact that we are in what should be a buyers' market, sellers are reluctant to drop their prices. Some of the houses on the market are priced at an absurdly high level and have been on the market for two years now. They haven't sold because they were too expensive when they were first put on the market. They are now even more absurdly overpriced.

One estate agent told us that house prices, particularly at the higher end of the market, are derived not from any sense of what is the right price but from what the seller wants. `Everyone becomes a property dealer and when they come to sell they view their house as their pension, an investment. Moreover their expectation of price is dictated by what they want rather than by the market or by logic.'

22.57 p.m.

Yet another journalist has jumped on the overloaded bandwagon and attacked me for publishing my own books. I am, apparently, not a `proper' publisher. London publishers (the ones who are usually described as `proper' publishers) specialise in printing books by footballers, women who have had sex with footballers, men who have gone out (or stayed in) with women who have had sex with footballers and women who have had breast enlargement surgery. These `proper' publishers pay the biggest advances for women who can satisfy more than one category (they have had sex with a footballer *and* have had breast enhancement). I'm happy to stick with improper publishing designed to change the world.

Most big, well-known London publishers no longer publish books which are important in any real sense (in that they have educational or literary value or even offer real entertainment).

149

They prefer to publish superficial, exploitative trash because that is easier and safer than rocking the establishment boat. And so publishing houses which used to be brave trend setters now produce row after row of books by nonentities; materialistic, egocentric fame whores who seek notoriety for its own sake, rather than as an offshoot of achievement. Most of these `authors' don't write books because they have something to say but because it is the next thing to do - another part of the multimedia celebrity experience. A ghostwriter will produce the words. The putative authors are merely writing books as another way of capitalising on their transient, transparent fame. Their eccentricity is about as genuine as a Cherie Blair smile.

Most publishers are now solely in business to make money. The sad thing is that they aren't even very good at that. (Making money is on my list of reasons for writing. If I don't make money then I won't eat. But it is not my main reason.

Because the books they produce have such a limited shelf life (today's reality celebrity will be tomorrow's forgotten person) modern publishers have become exceedingly short termist. They don't bother about their backlists. Once a book has sold they forget about it. They don't bother to reprint.

And so I will stick to self-publishing, thank you.

8
14.15 p.m.
The co-editor of a small magazine called *Resurgence* has written to say that they won't take any more advertisements for my book *Oil Apocalypse* because their readers think it is `alarmist fear-mongering'. The editor goes on to say that `in future we are not prepared to accept any material in *Resurgence* relating to any work by Vernon Coleman' and ends `It may be an idea for you to revisit your publicity regarding this book, because if this is the response from *Resurgence* readers...then I'm not sure it will be successful.' I wrote back and pointed out that we had received a better response from the advert in *Resurgence* than from any other advertisement in any other magazine. I also pointed out that when I wrote *Oil Apocalypse* the oil price was under 50 dollars a barrel.

I am always surprised by the number of editors who are prepared to ban books, and even authors, on the basis of letters from a few disgruntled readers (many of whom usually have a particular axe to grind).

9

11.26 a.m.

A letter has arrived from a reader who complains that my book *Alice's Diary* is out of print and I should not be advertising a book that I know is unavailable. He has been told this both by his local bookshop and by his local library. I write back and assure him that we have nearly 3,000 copies of *Alice's Diary* in stock, sitting patiently on the shelves at Publishing House. Why do bookshops and libraries lie so often about our books being out of print? I know that many readers are reluctant to take my books out of their local public library in case they are put on an official `blacklist' but it seems unlikely that librarians have the same concern. To my knowledge this business of denying that my books exist has happened several times a week for the last twenty years. I suspect it happens much more often than that. How many books would we have sold if bookshops and libraries had shown a little interest? Since I started self-publishing in 1989, I have begged bookshops to take stock (on a sale or return basis). I have bought advertisements aimed at pushing buyers into bookshops. I have bought advertisements in trade journals politely suggesting that bookshops might like to stock my books. I have sent bookshops free copies of new books. But they have, by and large, only ever bought what has been ordered. They have never taken books to put on their shelves. Browsers cannot go into a bookshop and find my books (as they used to be able to do when I was published by London publishing houses).

10

10.15 a.m.

The Government has pledged to move everyone online and to force every businessman to pay his tax as well as his VAT online. It seems absurd that we are now forced to do the taxman's work for him. Every small businessman is now a tax collector; spending days every month sorting out problems that are rightly the province of HMRC. Maybe I could send some of my work round to their offices. I wonder how long it will be before we are all forced to conduct all our business (and probably non-business) affairs online. From today, I must fill in my VAT forms on the Internet. This means that I am forced to put at least some of my financial information online where it will, of course, be vulnerable and insecure. If I refuse to do this then small spotty youths in uniforms will come round and do terrible things to me in the name of the State. They are, of course, doing this partly because it saves them money but also because it enables them to keep track of everything I do. It is now also the law that I have to pay the VAT I collect for the Government electronically. Cheques may still be legal tender but they're not legal tender as far as the Government is concerned. `It's...just as secure as doing it on paper,' claims a HMRC advertisement. No it's not. I would complain to the ASA about this blatant lie but the chances of the ASA criticising HMRC are about as great as the Royal Mail providing a decent service or Gordon Brown flying a St George's flag from No 10. When I wrote to protest about this, and said that I would have to close my business if they forced me to do financial reporting online, the official line, shorn of bureauspeak, was: `Go ahead, punk, we don't give a stuff if you do'.

11

12.34 p.m.

On the train to London this morning I overheard this snatch of conversation:

   `I don't get paid enough. And they won't pay me more.'
   `So why not leave?'
   `I can't. I will never get another job as good as this one.'

13.22 p.m.

At St Pancras station I put my jacket into a tray with my coat, and the small chap sitting in front of the X-ray machine said there was something in the pockets so another small fellow (who seemed Eastern European in origin and who spoke a little English) told me to empty my jacket pockets. I could understand most of what he said but I found it strangely irritating that our national security was in the hands of people who weren't of our nation and could not be expected to give a damn about it. I could accept rudeness and high-handedness far more easily from a British citizen who thought that

152

he or she was defending their country. The irony is that there is a large sign warning travellers: `Do not abuse or attempt to intimidate our staff.' (These ubiquitous signs are, of course, a consequence of EU policy which mean that employers are responsible if one of their employees is subject to rudeness.) There really should be a sign warning staff members: `Do not abuse or attempt to intimidate our customers.' Fat chance.

Emptying my pockets took some time. I am a writer and I always carry tons of stuff in my pockets. Indeed, I deliberately buy coats with lots of pockets and if there aren't enough I have extra pockets added. They invariably become baggy with all the stuff I carry.

From the breast pocket I took half a dozen train and metro tickets, three cards advertising three different taxi services in Paris, two pencil stubs, a flat torch slightly thicker than a credit card and a device which also looks like a credit card but which contains a pair of scissors, a screwdriver and a small knife. (I carry this as a substitute for my Swiss Army penknife).

The rest of my pockets contained: a spare pair of folding spectacles, another torch (one that winds up), a metal tape measure, a Psion pocket computer, a mobile telephone, a small electronic Encyclopaedia Britannica, two passports, two train tickets, a piece of card on which was written the access code for our apartment building in Paris, two brand new notebooks, the notebook I was using, four pens, two propelling pencils, a small pencil sharpener, a rubber, a conker, a spare shoelace, a packet of sweets that had congealed, a small book to help me identify trees, a wallet, a small copy of Hazlitt's essays, a copy of an Evelyn Waugh novel, another wallet, an empty spectacle case (my spectacles were perched on the tip of my nose), a small metal car, a tiny model of the Little Prince and a variety of loose change in two currencies.

The customs official examined all these items suspiciously and then tested my pockets with a dirty swab which looked as though it had been used on at least 10,000 other travellers. He also did the drug test on my mobile telephone.

When he'd finished I put my jacket back on, then added my overcoat. No one had inspected my overcoat (or asked me to empty its many pockets). No one had looked at my hat or my scarf. And no one had looked inside any of the electronic devices I had removed from my pockets. They also missed four pockets in my waistcoat and didn't ask me to empty the six pockets in my trousers. The whole damned system is pointless and pathetic. I invariably travel with the same things in my pockets. Sometimes they trigger the beeper. Sometimes they don't. On one occasion I was told by an idiot who should have found work as a comedian's straight man that the metal eyelet holes in my shoes had set off their alarm. Curiously, I never beep coming from Paris to London but I beep 50% of the time travelling from London to Paris.

After a short wait and a quick cup of coffee, we then got on the train.

`Look at all those daft people getting on that train,' I said to The Princess, as we boarded a completely empty Eurostar train. `I'm glad we're not on that one. It seems crowded.' There was another train on the other side of our platform and it was filling up very quickly. We found our carriage, found our reserved seats and sat down. There was no one in the compartment.

`Do you think we're on the right train?' asked The Princess, who is always very gentle about these things.

I stood up and looked out of the window.

We then got on the right train.

18.01 p.m.

Journeys through Paris are usually exciting and rather nerve wracking. Parisians regard traffic laws as guidelines, starting points for discussion. They think of themselves as adults, and capable of making better judgements than bureaucrats who aren't there are at the time. But, arriving in Paris today we found ourselves being driven by the only timid taxi driver in Paris. He stopped for everything and even waited while a car driver and a motorcyclist (the former male and the latter female) chatted each other up. `There are a lot of Germans here,' said The Princess, while we waited. `How do you know?' I asked. `I've seen a lot of fat, badly-dressed people around,' she explained. We sat behind the flirting pair until the car driver wrote something on a piece of paper and gave it to the motorcyclist. The Princess pointed out that in the taxi driving business it makes good financial sense to be

154

timid. As usual she was right. The bill was 10 euros higher than usual.

There was the usual thick wodge of mail in our mailbox. The local magazine reported that there was a murder in the 7th arrondissement a few weeks ago. This had, apparently, happened after a late night fight. The mayor immediately called in senior police officers to discuss ways to make sure that nothing similar happens again. The 7th is one of those areas of Paris where unpleasant things are not allowed to happen.

19.03 p.m.

When we had arrived at our apartment we discover that there had been a fire in the Channel Tunnel just after we'd got through. This is the second time that we have just avoided a serious problem. And on two occasions we've been on the last train to get through before snow closed the tunnel. We must remember this good fortune when something does go wrong and we end up spending ten hours sitting on a cold train. It's all rather reminiscent of my novel *Tunnel*. And that was just too scary.

19.14 p.m.

While The Princess prepared dinner, I popped out to the supermarket to buy bread and other necessities. As I left the supermarket I overheard an English tourist complaining to his wife. 'These French handkerchiefs are very odd,' he said, examining the item upon which he had attempted to blow his nose. His wife looked at what he had bought. 'That's because you bought sanitary towels,' she explained wearily. Outside the supermarket I picked up a leaflet for local mobile phones. The screen measurements for the phones are given in inches.

22.01 p.m.

Although we have a DVD player in Paris we hardly ever use it. This evening we listened to a CD of P.G. Wodehouse chatting away. Called *Speaking Personally* the CD consists of a wonderful evening of him chatting when he was 93. He talks about writing musicals with the Gershwins and Jerome Kern and working in Hollywood, surviving prisoner of war camp and writing books. 'I started writing at five,' the Master begins. 'I don't know what I was doing before that. Loafing, I suppose.' It all sounds very off the cuff but I am convinced that it was scripted. P.G. Wodehouse was far too much of a professional to sit down before a microphone without knowing exactly what he was going to say. P.G. mentioned that early in his career he had enough rejection slips to paper a large ballroom. This reminds me that when I was a medical student I actually did paper my room with the damned things.

12
11.11 a.m.
My iPhone has, as a communications tool proved to be about as much use as a carrot. There is a good reason for this. A few months ago the owners of all the apartments in our building were offered a substantial amount of money to allow a telecommunications company to put a mobile phone mast on our roof.

We unanimously turned down the offer and it seems as though everyone else in the street has rejected the offer too. Actually, I don't think they would have been able to put up a mast anyway. We live close enough to the Eiffel Tower for the building to be `protected'. The Parisians may have wanted to tear the Tower down again as quickly as possible when it was first erected but today the area around The Eiffel Tower is a protected area; a sort of grade 1 listed arca around a building of national importance. We cannot wave out of the window without first obtaining permission from nine government departments. The mast would have had to have been put in our loft apartment and there is no way that was ever going to happen.

To get any reception I had to lean out of the window and wave the darned thing in the air (nearly dropping it five storeys). A pigeon came and landed a foot away. It looked as though it wanted to eat the phone. It then occurred to me that I would be better off tying a message to the pigeon's leg. So I have tossed the wretched iPhone into my case where it can sit until we return to the land of the bankrupt, the feckless and the millions with their heads in the sand. At least in France they regard corruption as an inevitable, nay necessary, part of public life. The last time Mitterand stood for President his opponent was a well-known fascist and Mitterand himself was facing corruption charges. His supporters ran advertisements which read `Better to be a crook than a fascist'. The crook won.

13.14 p.m.

It was a beautiful clear morning and so we walked up to the second floor of The Eiffel Tower. That's around 700 steps going up and, not surprisingly, roughly the same number coming back down again. When you're climbing that many stairs you can get into quite a pleasant rhythm. The lifts which go up the Eiffel Tower are invariably horribly overcrowded (the attendants tend to cram in as many people as possible) and when you climb up the stairs you get a chance to enjoy the view from a variety of different angles. There were, not surprisingly, no fat Germans to be seen and no rubbish at all.

During the climb I remembered a doctor I knew who was worried about his heart. He had been getting chest pains which he'd dismissed as muscular and then one day he decided to check himself out by running up the stairs at the hospital where he worked. Tragically, he had a heart attack and died on the staircase.

On our way back a tall extremely well-dressed woman walked past. The Princess gave her a big smile. `Transvestite,' she whispered, when the stranger had gone by. `How on earth did you know?' I asked. `She smiled at me when I smiled at her,' said The Princess. `Most real women don't.' `But how did you know to smile at her?' I persisted. `She was looking at me,' explained The Princess. `And so I just knew.' The Princess has a sixth and seventh sense that I often find miraculously incomprehensible. There are a lot of transvestites in Paris. Most dress extremely well; far better than the majority of foreign women and far, far better than all tourists. I have no doubt that the transvestites in the city keep the lingerie shops in business. Women don't wear twin sets; they wear suits. They don't wear camisoles and knickers; they wear vests and pants. They don't wear stockings and suspenders; they wear socks. When buying for themselves younger women tend to choose functional rather than pretty. The majority of women are now fervent, committed crossdressers.

The average woman apparently thinks she is being rash if she buys a new bra every six months. The average transvestite buys a new one every week. Since a reliable survey showed that one in ten men is a transvestite this rather suggests that men buy considerably more bras than women. But the twist is, they are buying the bras to wear themselves. The corsetry industry is almost entirely dependent upon male crossdressers.

We stopped off at the American Library which had a trolley of free books outside on the pavement. They do this from time to time and I have, over the years, picked up some marvellous books there and discovered many new authors. It was through a biography picked up free from their `discarded' trolley that I first discovered Preston Sturges; a film director whose work I had not heard of until then. It was Sturges who said: `Dialogue consists of the bright things you would have liked to have said, except you didn't think of them in time.' Having stuffed our pockets with free books (including two first editions and a good variety of paperbacks) we wandered back home for tea and crumpets.

One of the things that makes a walk through Paris a delight is the relative absence of those wretched motorised scooters which now endanger pedestrians on British pavements. The French are, on the whole, far too proud to use such contrivances and the only people we've ever seen using them in Paris were fat tourists. Today, for example, we saw two fat women travelling the streets on golf carts. They weren't disabled, just too fat to walk. They both had white poodlcs sitting where the golf clubs might normally go. At a café they stopped, got out and lumbered over to a table to order vast ice creams. Two waiters asked if they could try out the golf carts and then spent several minutes zooming up and down the pavement.

15.27 p.m.

The people living in the apartment below have complained that there is water coming into their flat. The service company which looks after the building has sent round a man to take a look to see if he can find signs of a leak. We have no sign of water coming in and since their flat is below ours I find this strange but we are in France and funny things happen here. The workman begins by climbing out of a window, up a drainpipe and onto the roof. He is clearly a cat burglar with a day job. We have a couple of skylights and he pulls on these as though trying to tear them open. Eventually he comes back in and announces that everything is fine because the roof is galvanised and painted and entirely waterproof. A duck would be proud of it. I realised that he thought *we* had a leak and so I tried to interrupt to explain that we don't but he held up a hand, looked at me sternly and told me to let him finish. French workmen, like French waiters, can be very serious about their work. So I let him finish. When he had finished telling me that we didn't have a problem he stopped and raised an eyebrow in a 'so what do you think of that then?' way. I explained that the problem was with the flat below and we were providing only access to the roof so that he could deal with their leak. Without a flicker of embarrassment he left, went downstairs and was back in what seemed two minutes, though it may have been three, to report that the problem below was condensation on the inside of their windows, caused by the fact that they had their heating up very high and there was a fault with the double glazing (which I suspect they should not have anyway because of our proximity to the Eiffel Tower). The workman seemed frustrated by having found nothing to do so he decided to clean out the gutters around the front and back of the building. He announced that he was going back to his lorry to collect the necessary equipment. Five minutes later he returned, carrying a bucket, a trowel and a brush. He climbed out of the window, onto a ledge about three inches wide and, bending over, cleaned all the gutters as though sweeping the floor. He does this like a tightrope walker, without hanging onto anything. His bottom and back were hanging over a six storey drop and it did not seem possible that he would not fall. He seemed completely unconcerned by the drop to the street below. When he had finished clearing the gutters on one side of the building he walked up and over the roof and then dealt with the other side. I couldn't watch. I was convinced that he was going to plunge to a messy death. The ledge at the back of the building is narrower and only provides space for toes. Britain is awash with health and safety regulations which come from Brussels. They affect every aspect of our life. Just before we came here I was told that postmen are no longer allowed to ride bicycles when delivering mail. Apparently there is a risk that they might fall off and hurt themselves. But the French take notice of regulations only when they are convenient or profitable. When the workman had finished doing far more than he was originally asked to do he climbed back in through the window.

159

I breathed a huge sigh of relief. He shook hands firmly, collected together all his tools, and the debris he had removed from the gutters, and left.

21.19 p.m.
We decided to watch a DVD. I put on the Alfred Hitchcock version of John Buchan's *The Thirty Nine Steps*. It's one of my favourite movies. `Do you mind if we watch something else?' asked The Princess. `I've had enough steps for one day.' We watched a Woody Allen film instead.

13
11.10 a.m.
There is a strike today and everything is supposed to be closed. We walked across the 7th, 6th and 5th arrondissements to visit Shakespeare and Co, George Whitman's legendary bookshop opposite Notre Dame. We passed one shop which was closed but the shop outfitters were busy inside so I don't think the closure had anything to do with the general strike. We stood for a while and watched two cats walking along a narrow ledge. One was helping the other, constantly looking behind and making helpful miaowing noises. When the two cats finally came down to earth it became clear that the sccmingly nervous cat, the one which had been following, was blind in both eyes. As Shakespeare and Co, George, who has an eye for a pretty lady and once waved, smiled and posed flirtatiously for The Princess's camera, wasn't around.

14.17 p.m.
We received a money laundering form from our bank in Paris. The last time we were in France I put 10,000 euros into the account because, as a result of new EU laws, we had to pay a fairly hefty sum towards the cost of fiddling with the perfectly good lift in our building. Putting in 10,000 euros has obviously triggered alarm bells and so the bank wants all sorts of silly questions answered. I gather that if I'd put in 9,999 euros everything would have been fine. One euro more and I become a suspected money laundering terrorist.

They want details of my job, my earnings (in euros) separated into a number of different sources, including different types of pensions, earnings salaried or entrepreneurial, investments and so on. They also want to know if I have, in the course of my profession, ever visited Cuba, Iran, Syria, Myanmar, Soudan or Coree du Nord. They are, they say, asking these intrusive, pointless, unimaginative and stupid, impertinent questions in order to comply with the 3rd directive of the EU as part of their money laundering laws. (They don't actually describe the questions as intrusive, of course.) At least they admit it's because of the EU. The hidden irony here is that the two countries most favoured by money launderers are the UK and the USA. It occurs to me that I do have a small problem. My books sell around the world and I have no doubt some of them have sold in some of those countries on their list. I dare not tell the authorities this because they will become over-excited. I have struggled against this suspicion but I am increasingly convinced that all this inquisitorial nonsense is designed to make us lose trust in every institution (and every individual), to make us all feel lonely and afraid and to give the State more power over us. It's a world conspiracy.

The Princess suggests that I ring my pal David Icke and fix a meeting. We've known each other for years (I was his GP and then interviewed him for a TV series I was making based on my book *Bodypower*). If nothing else it will give MI5 something to do.

The bank in Paris tells me that any failure to provide the information by a date five weeks ago will affect my relationship with the bank. I scribbled all over the form in doctor writing (in English) in thick felt pen (which makes it impossible to fit anything neatly into the little boxes on the form) and posted it back.

17.11 p.m.

After posting the 'blanchissement' form I got chilly feet and thought I'd better ring the bank and explain that I couldn't fill in the section about my income because I am self-employed and my income varies from day to day.

'Did you send back the 'blanchissement' form?' asked the woman at the bank. I told her that I had filled the form in and that it was in the post. She sounded very relieved. 'Oh, well that's fine then,' she said.

`Does it not matter that I haven't filled in the whole of the form?'

`Oh no,' she said, seemingly puzzled by the question. `As long as you signed it. Just send it back.' She laughed at my concern. `It is not `grave',' she said dismissively.

I am greatly reassured by this. It seems that I have once again escaped the guillotine.

I have noticed before that as long as they have a piece of paper to file the French don't much care what you put on it.

22.11 p.m.

In the evening we walked to the Champs Elysee to watch a recent Johnny Hallyday film. We walked along the Avenue Montaigne where all the fashion houses are. It's fun looking in the windows to try to find the most absurdly overpriced item. The Princess found an unwired see-through orange bra and see-through knickers for 500 euros but I found a green handbag that would have stayed on the shelf for ever at your local charity shop and was on sale for 2000 euros.

Hallyday is hardly known in Britain but in France and much of the rest of Europe he is a major star. It is difficult, most weeks, to travel across Paris without seeing posters and magazine covers promoting his latest record, film, book, concert or television show. He has been making hit records since 1423. At the cinema The Princess gently shepherded me to a seat near the front and on the left. When I asked her why she had chosen those seats she pointed out that the latecomers who always wander into French cinemas would not wander in front of us because the only aisle goes down the right hand side of the cinema. She's a clever girl, my wife. Unfortunately, the French mounted a counter attack. A couple sitting on our right brought with them a large hamper containing sustenance to see them through the two hour show. When the French picnic they are never content with a bag of sandwiches and a flask of coffee; they take tables, chairs, cut glass drinking vessels, three types of wine and enough food to have sustained Napoleon's army throughout the snowy Moscow winter. Apparently, this routine is maintained when food is taken into the cinema. Our temporary neighbours brought with them every conceivable type of food that makes a noise. They had crunchy foods, fizzy foods, squelchy foods and creamy foods. And naturally they did a lot of lip and finger licking too. We crept out half way through and walked back home in a fine, drizzly rain which fitted our mood perfectly.

14

12.01 p.m.

The Princess wanted to clean and tidy the apartment and so I tottered out alone to do the shopping this morning. I had a bad hour or so. The first supermarket I went to was packed with people. I eventually got everything we needed and then went to the checkout. I was feeling very English and terribly polite. Two checkouts were open and there was a long line at each one. The woman at the head of the queue I chose was putting things on the conveyor belt one at a time and not putting down the next item until the first had reached its destination, been scanned and handed to her companion at the other end of the process. I reckoned that it was going to take the woman around four hours to empty her trolley, and that the items in my basket would have all passed their sell-by-date by the time I got to the head of the queue. The other queue wasn't moving any faster. So I put down my basket and went to a second supermarket. The seventh arrondissement in Paris is stuffed with supermarkets. I didn't know this shop quite as well but I eventually found everything on my list except for tomatoes. By now I was getting a little fed up. At the greengrocery counter a pack of people were grabbing stuff as though the end of food shopping had just been announced. Very politely, I asked if I could just grab a few tomatoes but it quickly became apparent that politeness was outside the rules and barging was definitely de rigueur. When pushed I can barge with the best, and certainly just as well as any French shopper. Indeed, I quite like barging rules because I'm far bigger than most French folk. So I got my tomatoes and once again went to the checkout section. At this shop there were four tills open. All had long queues so naturally I chose the one with the shortest queue. The housewives of Paris seemed to be buying food in preparation for a siege. All had trolleys packed with stuff. I waited there for a few minutes and then the check-out clerk looked up, said 'termine' and disappeared to have her lunch. So I put down my basket, stormed out and went to a third supermarket.

As I entered I noticed that there was one till with no queue so I rushed round and grabbed the stuff I wanted to buy and then returned to that till. Naturally, by time I got back there were six people in the queue. I have no idea where they came from because I swear the shop was empty when I entered. Naturally, every one of them paid with a credit card. Even the two who just bought a bottle of wine and a loaf of bread paid with a card. When it was my turn the idiot American family behind me put their stuff on the conveyor belt together with mine. This caused great confusion as their purchases got mixed up with mine. After that I popped into a pharmacy to buy a bottle of `après shampooing' for the Princess. The woman behind the counter looked as though I had asked to buy a nuclear submarine and shook her head and muttered sharp comments in untranslatable French. Outside, on the pavement, there was a healthy young fellow begging. He was in his twenties and had a nauseatingly ingratiating, simpering smile. He waved a paper cup under my nose. `Get a bloody job!' I snarled at him, and stormed off along the pavement, leaving in my wake a wreckage of pedestrians hopping and skipping aside. I then started shouting at inanimate objects which got in my way. This, I realised, is how those people who walk around muttering and cursing got the way they are.

15.14 p.m.
I cooled off after lunch and we went for a walk around the Eiffel Tower and spotted a beautiful example of French pragmatism. In the park near the tower there is a large notice warning visitors that no alcohol is to be drunk in the area. But next to the sign there are three large rubbish bins, one for general rubbish, one for plastic containers and one for glass bottles that have contained alcohol. On our walk back to the apartment we passed the American Library in Paris which had one of its irregular book sales. The Library was selling books by size and weight, which seemed to me to be a unique way of doing it. Small books cost one euro each. Big books cost two euros apiece. I bought eight small ones and seven large ones.

When we got back there was a letter from the Mayor of the 7th Arrondissement, where we live, asking when we would like to have our rubbish collected. They collect daily of course but the

Mayor wanted to know whether we would prefer to have the rubbish collected in the morning or in the evening. Our views are solicited on all sorts of issues. Two months ago we were asked our views on the suggestion that our street be turned into a pedestrian precinct and before that we were asked to comment on a proposed change in bus routes. Paris is a magnificently well-run city. Well-devised local taxes mean that there are loads of small shops selling essentials such as ironmongery and stationery, and public transport is cheap and reliable. It's just a pity there are so many French people living in the city.

The only thing I couldn't buy today was a newspaper. My friend at the newspaper kiosk told me that it was because of yesterday's strike. So I couldn't read about yesterday's strike and find out how successful it was. How clever of the strikers to ensure that the only thing they affected was the method of telling the world how successful they had been.

A friend once told us that women aren't allowed to wear trousers in Paris and this may well be true. The French, like the English, still have a number of strange laws on their statute books. But I remembered this today and noticed that the policewomen now always wear trousers, presumably so that when things are quiet they can arrest one another, or even themselves, just to keep things ticking over. The same friend told me that at Heathrow he once overheard an elderly gentleman reply to the standard question `Have you packed your bag yourself?' with: `Of course not. Do I look like the sort of person who packs his own bag?'

22.14 p.m.

When I tried to listen to the sports news on BBC radio 4 (I don't ever rely on the BBC for real news but they can manage sports news fairly competently) I found myself listening to a BBC programme in which participants were suggesting that Britain should have all-black, segregated schools. At first I assumed this was a satirical programme but it wasn't. No one suggested that we had all white schools which would of course have been racist and was, I seem to remember, one of the reasons for the race riots in America many years ago.

15

14.01 p.m.

We sat in the Palais Royale watching the sparrows. I had a copy of *The Open Air*, a collection of essays by Richard Jefferies on my lap. We ate eating apples we had bought from a greengrocer nearby. They were delicious and tasted just as good as they looked. This made a more than agreeable change from the apples sold in England, most of which are made for display and not for eating. They look perfect but are waxy and inedible. Even when the pesticides and protective coating have been peeled off they still taste nothing like fruit.

I bought the book I am reading from a second-hand bookshop (having seen it recommended by Henry Williamson). I read an essay in the book called *Nature on the Roof* and found this passage about sparrows, written a century earlier: 'They are easily tamed. The Parisians are fond of taming them. A certain hour in the Tuileries Gardens, you may see a man perfectly surrounded with a crowd of sparrows - some perching on his shoulder; some fluttering in the air immediately before his face; some on the ground like a tribe of followers; and others on the marble seats. He jerks a crumb of bread into the air - a sparrow dextrously seizes it as he would a flying insect; he puts a crumb between his lips - a sparrow takes it out and feeds from his mouth. Meantime they keep up a constant chirping; those that are satisfied still stay by and adjust their feathers. He walks on, giving a little chirp with his mouth, and they follow him along the path - a cloud about his shoulders, and the rest flying from shrub to shrub, perching and following again. They are all perfectly clean - a contrast to the London sparrow. I came across one of these sparrow-tamers by chance, and was much amused by the scene, which, to any one not acquainted with birds, appears marvellous; but it is really as simple as possible, and you can repeat it for yourself if you have the patience, for they are so sharp that they soon understand you.'

I have seen this exact scene played out so often, exactly as Jefferies describes it, that it could be the same man. Sure enough, within half an hour of my reading this passage a man arrives in the Palais Royale and starts feeding the sparrows. Is it life imitating art or art imitating life?

In most of Paris's great gardens (particularly the Palais de Royale, the Tuileries and the Luxembourg) there are people, usually old men, who regularly turn up to feed the birds crumbs of bread. The birds always turn up in advance, congregating and waiting noisily. The birds don't turn up because the man with the food has appeared; they turn up 15 minutes before the man appears and wait for him. They do this summer and winter and always arrive on time.

16
22.04 p.m.

In an attempt to find an American distributor for our books I went again to the London Book Fair. I also wanted to have a look around to see what the `big boys' were doing. While I was there I was rather depressed. Everywhere I looked publishers seemed to be doing exactly the same things. There was a `follow the leader' air to the whole dismal business. I remembered why I had lost faith and interest in traditional publishing companies, and had been inspired to start publishing my own books. When we are young we all think we can change the world. My problem is that I never grew out of this impossible, impractical, destructive dream.

When we left the book fair, we walked back to Paddington Station, through Kensington Gardens. By the time we reached the station I had cheered up. I had realised that the fact that most big publishing companies are still playing `follow the leader' (without really knowing who the leader is, or where they are heading) was excellent news for any small, innovative and daring publishing company.

On the way back from London our train stopped at Chippenham. After a few minutes delay there was an announcement that a passenger had reported a knocking sound underneath a carriage and so the train was being inspected. So we parked at the station while a man in railway uniform walked down the train. As he passed our carriage he kicked the carriage, seemed satisfied and walked on. It didn't seem terribly reassuring but the train got us home without any further excitement.

17
10.14 a.m.

Why do so many people use the word `profit' in the same way that they use words such as `paedophile' or `terrorist'. Profits are regarded as a dirty concept, obscene and unacceptable by the functionaries who work for the State or the executive saloon driving quasi communists who represent trade unions. (Curiously, the functionaries always change their mind when they get involved in management buy-outs and privatisations, when they suddenly regard profits as wonderful and desirable.)

What these idiots don't seem to realise is that profits are the oil which enables our society to survive. Without profits there would be no businesses (small or large), no service industries, no sole traders and no self-employed. Without profits big companies would pay no dividends, pensioners would starve to death and rich unions would make no profit out of their investments. Profit pays for innovation and without it there would be no employment at all. Profit pays for the fat salaries and bonuses of civil servants and union officials. Governments are wildly enthusiastic about minimum wage levels but these have been proven to damage developing businesses and everyone (especially the poor and the unemployed) would be much better off if governments encouraged profitability. It is only by making profits that businesses expand and hire more people. Governments love to print money these days but the money they create that way isn't real. The only solid way to create wealth is by improving profitability.

11.45 a.m.

The postman put a card through our door this morning telling us that they were holding a letter addressed to us. They have kidnapped it and will not release it until we pay a ransom of £1, in addition to the postage which, they say, had not been pre-paid by the sender. I suspect that the envelope has missed a franking machine and we have no intention of collecting it. If it's an important piece of mail the sender will re-send it. It's not the money I object to but the time it will take to go to the sorting office, find somewhere to park, queue, pay and pick up a letter that I almost certainly don't want. I don't think the postman bothered to ring the doorbell and I'm pretty sure he didn't even bother to put the letter into his bag. In the bad old days he would have brought the letter, knocked on the door and asked us to pay the postage. Presumably, the Royal Mail no longer trusts its postmen to collect small sums of money from its customers. Given the number of parcels they `lose', that's probably not unwise.

18
11.12 a.m.
A reader has complained about the fact that the prices of many of my books end with 99 pence. He said he was going to leave me £270,000 in his will but decided not to because I sold him a book for £12.99. He also sent me extensive details explaining how I could bury myself cheaply, using a mini JCB to dig the hole and having myself placed inside a home-made coffin. He offered to do my probate for £600. I replied, and pointed out that I have spent most of my life fighting the entire establishment and had succumbed to the habit of pricing books with a 99 pence on the end because it is an industry standard and, compared to everything else, it really didn't seem to matter. I also thanked him for his advice about how to die cheaply.

12.04 p.m.
Details of a house came today together with a letter announcing that there had been a price reduction. We peeled the label off the particulars and found that the house had been reduced in price from £699,000 to £697,000.

Residential property has been kept artificially high by government support and low interest rates. Time after time we have seen houses where the vendors claimed they were selling so that they could move to a place nearer their children. Time after time we didn't believe them. They were mostly selling because they knew that they had bitten off more than they could chew and that a modest rise in interest rates, and a notable fall in values, would leave them wallowing up to their ears in a stormy ocean of negative equity.

We saw an honest estate agent today. He seemed very tired of the whole business. `Everyone has gone mad,' he said. `Vendors are living in cloud cuckoo land. They have a price fixed in their heads and they won't budge from it. They want to sell their house and buy a bungalow by the sea, a boat and a new car. They think their house is worth a certain sum because that's what a friend or another estate agent told them it was worth. They don't understand that the real worth is the price someone will actually pay for it in hard cash. If you find something you like offer 25% less than the asking price. You'll still be overpaying.'

16.17 p.m.
I was in a long queue today to buy a newspaper. When the woman in front of me arrived at the counter she put down her two magazines and a bar of chocolate. The assistant waved the bar codes at her machine and told the woman how much she owed. `Oh,' said the woman, as though surprised by the fact that she was going to have to pay for her purchases. Only then did she delve into her handbag, find her purse and decide which of her 12 credit cards she had might contain enough credit to pay her bill. It took her forever and the queue behind us started to stretch out through the door. A man behind me, frustrated by the woman's interminable rummaging, put down the newspaper he had intended to buy, and stormed out. I hate people who seem surprised when they buy something and the assistant wants money. It's a female thing. Men nearly always have their wallet ready. Women never do. While standing in the queue I worked out that if women had their money (or wretched credit card) ready when they got to the front of the queue I would save nine hours a year.

19
11.56 a.m.
A reviewer sneers at my book *Living in a Fascist Country* and says that the title alone is absurd. He hasn't bothered to read the book that explains and supports the title and is apparently clever enough to review the book without bothering to read it. This is, apparently, the new way with reviewers. It must save them a lot of time and effort.
The fact is that in many countries which we regard as being run by dictators the people have the power to demonstrate and even force change through by persistent people power. That couldn't possibly happen in the UK because if several thousand demonstrators collected in Trafalgar Square and tried to occupy it they would be beaten up, bottled up and locked up by thuggish policemen hired to suppress and oppress dissent. We have lost our freedom without most people being aware of what has happened. That's the whole

point of the book. (The police have taken quite a critical bashing recently and I have a suspicion that they may soon change tactics. If they are Machiavellian enough they will realise that if they allow a few demonstrators to cause a good deal of property damage in London there will be calls by people whose voices matter for all demonstrations to be banned.)

16.46 p.m.

A pen pusher who works for the council has written to tell me that bin men are no longer called bin men. Apparently I must now refer to them as waste removal engineers. We are talking about blokes in orange overalls who empty plastic containers into a lorry. This is one of the most pretentious job descriptions around but this sort of nonsense is now commonplace and a quarter of all adults have an occupation with an absurd job title. Here are some of the other (genuine) job titles I've come across:

1. Chimney sweep - flueologist
2. Receptionst - head of verbal communications
3. Petrol station assistant - petroleum transfer engineer supervisor
4. Chiropodist - foot health gain facilitator
5. Teacher - knowledge navigator
6. Masseuse - leisure services administrator
7. Postal worker - despatch services facilitator
8. Shelf stacker - stock replenishment adviser
9. Dinner lady - education centre nourishment production assistant
10. Window cleaner - vision clearance engineer

20
11.45 a.m.

`I'm on a website which won't let me do anything until I give them a telephone number,' said The Princess. `Have you a number for one of your old unused mobiles that I could give them?' We rarely use telephones and certainly don't give any of our numbers to anyone.

I told her that it is far more fun to give the company their own telephone number. This has the added advantage that when they try to ring the number you've given it will be constantly engaged. So in the red starred box demanding a telephone number she put the company's own number. My favourite variation on this trick is to put in the private office number of the Chief Executive or Chairman.

16.17 p.m.

The Government has spent £500,000 on a study of overcrowding and punctuality on trains. The report has concluded that commuters want trains to run on time. Well worth the money. How else would we have known? And I am also delighted to see that the Government has set up a quango to look into the number of quangos. I guarantee the result will be more, not less, quangos. I have decided that the word `quango' stands for Queer Useless And Nasty Government Organisation. What would we do without all these people? More to the point, perhaps, what would they do without us? There are so many of them now that there is always going to be one on my back. Am I the only person who is fed up with being threatened by bureaucrats and quangocrats? No one working for the State is ever polite any more. They all threaten first and talk later. Standard letters from HMRC talk about legal action and all the awful consequences and then, as an afterthought, add: `If you have already paid please disregard this letter'. But when they owe me money it takes months, even years, to get a refund. And as for interest! Ha.

17.05 p.m.

The papers are full of how our brave police, avoiding the temptation to catch murderers, muggers and thieves, have managed to arrest a couple of pornographers whose crime appears to have been making a few bob out of selling photographs of willing models to willing customers and then sharing the profits with HMRC. There is one thing I have never understood about pornography. In order to decide that a book or film is pornographic, policemen and judges must read or view it. Occasionally, members of the public must sit on a jury and read or view it. When they choose to ban something considered pornographic it is on the grounds that if it is not banned then the people who see or read it will be corrupted. Now, if the judges and policemen and jurors are right then they must, by definition, have been corrupted themselves. Consequently, their views are of no value and they must, therefore, be removed from public office immediately. To allow corrupted individuals to remain in any position of authority would be a nonsense.

21
10.09 a.m.

An acquaintance of mine rang to tell me that he has been appointed to a committee of the Arts Council. From the way he burbled it must be one of the 1,000 most important committees they have. He is a rather nerdy, half-witted sort of fellow; the sort of sad bastard who listens to U2 and believes that Bob Geldoff is a saint. He seemed delighted by his appointment, poor soul, though I suspect that this may be because he hopes that if an Arts Council appointment comes then the knighthood or even the peerage cannot be far behind.

I really don't see the point of the Arts Council. It seems to me to be a pompous and expensive quango which subsidises and supports artists who aren't good enough at what they do to make a living but who are good at filling in government forms. Why not be honest and create a department which provides money to the citizens who are the most skilled at filling in forms?

I can't think of one great book, film, play, poem, painting or sculpture which has been produced with the aid of taxpayers' money that wouldn't have been produced without it. I can, however, produce an impressive portfolio of pseudoartistic rubbish that has been produced with the aid of taxpayers' money. People apply for grants because they aren't good enough at what they do to make a living at it. There is something lunatic about subsidised art. It is absurd that the Government should hand over vast skipfuls of taxpayers' hard earned money to the artistically challenged, who insist that the State must subsidise what they call art because it is so bad that no one wants to pay them for it.

22
18.11 p.m.

We went to Birmingham. I hadn't been back there for years. It was deteriorating a decade ago. Someone could film a science fiction horror movie there without any set dressing. In cities and towns everywhere bureaucrats have wilfully destroyed quaint streets and buildings because they were of no commercial value to the State but stood in the way of what the State saw as progress. Narrow streets and steps all added to the complications of running a town or city. It is easier to manage an urban environment (as the planners think of cities and towns), and to get people to and from work efficiently, if streets are straight and the buildings functional. And so the bureaucrats have standardised our towns and cities, eradicating history and imagination and colour. Birmingham is the perfect example of this attitude. Government planned developments are appallingly badly sited and, despite all the red tape, pay little or no intention to the needs and wishes of local residents. There is no soul or character in our towns and cities these days and the planners and architects are clearly all devoid of imagination. What a dull environment we have created for ourselves. Ugly concrete and glass decorated only with a plethora of signs telling us to go here, go there, do this and don't do that. Out of town shopping centres have helped ensure that town centres have become miserable, grey places. Most provincial cities look identical now, and all small county towns look the same too. Faded, dilapidated, run down and depressed. There will be an incredibly ugly post office, the old grand town hall now derelict or converted into a branch of a chain store or pub, the old library covered in plywood and offered for sale. There will be three mobile telephone shops (the variety depending on the strength of the local coverage), a shoe shop, a pet shop and the only memory of olden days will be, if you're lucky, an ironmongers kept alive by farmers who haven't yet discovered that there is an out of town DIY store selling everything at a quarter of the price.

You only have to spend an hour in almost any French town to see just how badly we've messed up our world. Their towns have squares and street markets and eccentricities. They celebrate their architecture and decorate everything with their national flag. Our towns have shopping malls, heaven help us, and office blocks and town halls that look like multi-story car parks. If there is a flag it is that of our conquerors, the EU.

21.10 p.m.

Back in 1997, as the Labour party came to power, a big survey showed that most people agreed that looking after the community's interests was the best way to improve the quality of life for us all as individuals. A dozen years of Labour Governments have encouraged us to be far more selfish. A survey published recently showed that people now believe that they should simply look after themselves, and their own interests, and should be concerned only with what they can get out of their work or the community, rather than what they can put into it. This is worrying. Many years ago, the Iks, a tribe of former hunters and gatherers in Uganda, were displaced from their traditional terrain by the formation of a new national park. The Iks were forced to become farmers on poor hillside soil. The dismantling of their traditional culture, coupled with the meagreness of their new existence, stripped them of any sense of community and they became stingy and sullen. They started stealing one another's food and defecating on one another's doorsteps. They repelled one another through every means available.

When our sense of community is destroyed there is not much left. It is ironic that as the State has grown so our sense of community has collapsed and for this I blame the European Union; an organisation that is devotedly fascist and favours a brand of corporate socialism that rivals Soviet communism in the way its main proponents gather all the goodies unto themselves while pressurising the workers with seemingly endless varieties of restrictive but purposeless legislation. Whenever I look around these days I see people behaving towards one another with greed, cruelty, heartlessness, irresponsibility and no sense of caring. Even bees and ants are much better at community than our post-Labour society manages to be.

23
12.34 p.m.

I have received a letter from someone who says: `The inflammatory ranting against doctors and medical practice in *Coleman's Laws* (which I have not read) was most unjust. Having worked in the nursing profession all my life, and having been saved from whooping cough and pneumonia at the age of four by antibiotic drugs, I feel most insulted.' Since she admits that she has never read my book, this seemed a trifle unfair.

24

16.16 p.m.

A female acquaintance of The Princess came to lunch today. She believes in equality and the liberation of women and is a huge fan of Harriet Harman which I personally believe probably makes her certifiable. She complained bitterly that her new boyfriend always leaves the toilet seat up. She asked why men do this. I told her that men are equally upset by the fact that many women leave the toilet seat down. She tried to comment on this but failed to find anything to say and managed only to give an excellent impression of a goldfish singing in a church choir. As she was leaving she asked if I'd written any new books. The Princess said we'd just published *England's Glory* which we had written together. `Oh good, I'll take one off your hands,' she said, as though doing us a favour. `If I don't like it I can always give it as a birthday present to someone.'

17.19 p.m.

While browsing in a bookshop I met a bloke who had two fingers missing from his left hand. He had a huge German Shepherd dog with him. The fingers had obviously been removed quite recently. I asked him how he lost them. `I cut them off with a circular saw,' he said, quite proudly. `Why didn't they sew them back on?' I asked. `They're quite good at that sort of stuff these days.' The man looked down at the dog and then back at me. `They couldn't,' he said. He nodded towards the huge creature by his side. `The dog ate them.'

25

15.16 p.m.

A woman The Princess has known for some years rang her today in a terrible state. She sold her first novel two years ago but has never met her publishers. She told them that she suffers from agoraphobia and is unable to leave her home. She did this because when she was asked to send a photograph of herself she sent, instead, a photograph of a young, beautiful black girl whom she knows. (The Princess's friend is in her fifties and readily admits that she is not photogenic.) She not unreasonably surmised that this would prove more commercially advantageous than a photograph of a plain looking woman with bottle glass spectacles and a slightly hairy chin. Now the publishers have been approached by a magazine journalist who wants to conduct an interview. The Princess's friend is terrified that she will be found out and that her blossoming career will collapse around her ears. The Princess told her that she had two choices: she could either persuade her young, beautiful friend to conduct the interview or she could refuse and claim that she does not ever want to be interviewed or photographed because, in addition to suffering from agoraphobia she also suffers from chronic shyness and she feels that the fear of being recognised would make her condition worse. The Princess points out that this policy worked very well for J. D. Salinger. Her friend agrees this is the line to follow.

17.22 p.m.

The estate agent who is selling my father's former home sent me a message demanding a copy of my passport and driving licence and a home utility bill. He says that they need all these before they can sell the house. It is, he says, a money laundering requirement. He suggested that I post the documents, or take them into one of their branches where someone will make copies and then fax them on. He said that it is quite impossible to sell the house without these documents. I point out that since they will not be handling any money there cannot be any need for them to have any of this paperwork. He then sent a sharp rather threatening note insisting that under the law he was entitled to demand these documents. I sent back an equally sharp note telling the rather snotty estate agent that the firm's compliance officer is mistaken for there is no legal requirement for them to ask for copies of personal documents and there is no law requiring me to provide them. I pointed out that since they do not handle any money their chances of being involved in money laundering are not as high as the couple who run our corner shop and told him that it would make as much sense for me to demand a copy of his passport and his gas bill. I suspect that this is merely an attempt by this agency to appear important and quasi-professional. Even those who do have a right to see documents don't understand the rules properly. Those who are entitled to see documents are entitled to just that - a chance to `see' them. Not even banks or solicitors are entitled to have copies of documents. I feel strongly about this. The more copies of private documents there are lying around the world the greater the chance of identity theft. Early in the afternoon I received another e-mail from the wretched agent telling me that `sight of an entry in a telephone book' would be sufficient. I ignored this. Late in the day I received a rather poor apology in which the estate agent said that he had consulted the firm's compliance officer who had told him that I was right.

20.18 p.m.

Hubert, an elderly friend of ours, tells us that he is thinking of applying to join the army, with a special request that he be sent to Afghanistan. We are surprised at this since we attended his 85th birthday just two months ago. He explained that he has applied because he has discovered something called the `killed in war' tax exemption which entitles an estate of any size to be exempt from inheritance tax. Apparently, the `killed in war' exemption applies to anyone whose death is caused by injury or disease received or aggravated while on active service in the armed forces. Hubert tells us that the family of the 4th Duke of Westminster successfully argued that his death in 1967 from cancer was hastened by septicaemia from a war wound he received in 1944. His estate therefore attracted no inheritance tax. I tell Hubert that he deserves a medal for ingenuity but that it is probably the only one medal he is going to receive. He winks at me and smiles. Hubert is a wise fellow. Many years ago he taught me two things that I will never forget. First, he said, always be patient, especially when you are in a hurry. And, second, never tell anyone everything you know. He said that if you keep something back, and people suspect that you know more than you are telling, you will seem both wise and mysterious.

26

12.50 p.m.

Between 2005 and 2008 the Government spent £221,726 on buying 2,515 games consoles for prisons. That's nice of me. Sadly, I haven't had any thank you notes from the lucky recipients. But then I guess they're probably not the sort of people who write thank you notes for stuff they haven't had to pay for.

14.16 p.m.

Although I have always done my best to make it known that I cannot offer medical advice through the mail, I constantly receive letters asking or demanding my opinion on personal health matters. Sometimes I can go for a week without receiving any such enquiries. But on other days the demands arrive like buses. This morning I received a letter from a reader in Scotland who sent me 34 pages of medical notes and doctors' reports, asking for my medical opinion. The letter came with a list of 17 specific medical queries and a note, on expensive, headed notepaper, saying `I do not expect this for free, I want to pay the going rate'. There was a £5 note pinned to the package which I worked out meant that my professional views were being valued at just under 30 pence each. Another lengthy letter came together with laboratory results and X-ray reports and again wanted my opinion. This time there was no £5 note and no mention of money. I also received an e-mail which, I was told, contained a 6,000 word medical summary, a collection of X-ray photographs and a wide variety of hospital reports. The letter accompanying this mass of information included the words: `I know you don't usually offer clinical advice but if you have a minute or two please send me your opinion on the enclosed.'

20.19 p.m.

Some days I wake up, head for my desk and wonder: should I retire, start again or give up. The big disappointment of my writing life has probably been Bilbury. Years ago, when I wrote the first Bilbury novel, I dreamt of creating a new, parallel world. I wanted a place where people relied upon one another and where there was very little contact with the outside world. Scripts were written for a television series. But nothing came of that. TV production companies which had shown interest drifted off when promised commissions turned, as television promises so often do, into dust. Back in the very early 1990s I dreamt of creating an imaginary computer world where refugees from the real world could live village lives, interacting with the characters they knew from the books. I could, I thought, fund it by allowing the new villagers to

179

buy property in the village. My thought was that readers could develop secondary, imaginary lives in Bilbury and thus escape the real world which I know so many find so difficult. It was, however, too daunting a task for any of the computer people I met. They just wanted to do something quick and profitable - to sell me a new piece of addressing software or to design a new website for a fee. (I tried many new websites in the 1990s. But in the 1990s and the early part of the 21st century people weren't prepared to pay for information they culled from the Internet and so, without funding, the sites died.) And I wanted to set up a regular Bilbury magazine, complete with fake advertisements for the village pub and the village shop. Maybe it's not too late.

21.09 p.m.

I received an anonymous e-mail which said: `If you expect to be successful communicating your message you should offer people a less confrontational view of the issues you discuss.' The writer is correct, of course, but I fear this well-intentioned advice has arrived several decades too late.

27

15.17 p.m.

I found a review of the autobiography by H.E. Bates on Amazon in which the author dismisses the book as `a typical writer's book - all about himself'. I wonder what the reviewer thinks an autobiography should be about? In general the quality of reviewing on the World Wide Web is third form quality. Most of the reviewers are semi-literate. Many of the rest are merely baring their prejudices to the world. Some will write reviews of anything and everything. (I have even seen reviews of batteries.)

There is a review of my book *Alice's Diary* on Amazon in which the reviewer complains that his (or her) cats don't have conversations with one another and so the book (which is, as the title suggests, the diary of a cat) is unrealistic. Books (and therefore authors) are given stars on Amazon so why aren't reviewers rated to show the value of their contributions? Naturally, only authors should be allowed to rate the reviewers. I can think of no reason to oppose this other than that the reviewers wouldn't like it and that is no reason at all.

17.18 p.m.

An advertising agent wants me to buy an advert in the *Big Issue* magazine. I tell him 'no thanks'. When I last bought advertising in the *Big Issue* it failed almost totally. I couldn't understand why until one day I was sitting in a café in London and noticed that there was a *Big Issue* seller outside. I watched in amazement and horror as buyer after buyer bought a magazine and then just dumped what they had bought into a nearby bin. Most didn't even glance at the magazine before throwing it away. I've always wondered if, at the end of the day, the seller picked the magazines out of the bin and resold them. None of his buyers would have known or cared.

19.18 p.m.

A marketing consultant writes offering to help me make my business grow. Why? I don't want it to grow.

28

14.19 p.m.

Every few months a story will appear in the national press with a headline something like this: 'Sheep not as stupid as we think say scientists' or this 'Sheep are a lot smarter than we think, says top scientist'.

I read an old cutting today which described how Professor Keith Kendrick of the Babraham Institute for agricultural research, based near Cambridge, told the British Association Annual Science Festival that sheep have far better powers of recall than experts used to think, are far better at telling the difference between humans than humans are at distinguishing between sheep and share similar thought patterns to those of people.

When shown pictures of human faces sheep could tell the difference between them and could remember at least ten human faces for more than two years. They recognised and remembered friends from a flock, using the same visual cues that we use when identifying people, and could distinguish between at least 50 different sheeps' faces.

Professor Kendrick found that sheep learn new faces very quickly and use part of the brain's temporal lobe to do this (just as people do). He found that showing a sheep a picture of a friendly face made the sheep feel happy.

Like humans sheep can have difficulty in recognising faces when they are presented to them upside down but sheep have no trouble recognising upside down objects. `We may have underestimated the complexity of a sheep's social environment, and, indeed, their intelligence,' said Professor Kendrick. `Sheep have developed the same kind of sophisticated social recognition skills normally only thought to exist in man and other higher primates. The presence of such skills raises questions as to whether we have underestimated the importance and complexity of their social needs and intelligence.' Absobloodylutely right! Sheep are *very* intelligent creatures. After I wrote about them in *Alice and Other Friends* I received many letters of approval and agreement.

18.09 p.m.

Not having a credit rating makes it difficult to run a business. I long ago found a way around small daily problems (such as not being able to buy a mobile telephone) but it seems it's impossible for me to set up a Pay Pal account so that customers can pay for books that way. I don't much mind. Apart from cash (which is impractical for buying books through the mail) cheques are still much better than anything else. And, contrary to the rumours, they are not going to be banned for a long time yet. If I had a credit rating I would deliberately trash it. I don't want to borrow money and with a trashed credit rating no one is going to bother to steal my identity.

Life running a business is also made rather difficult by my reluctance to use the telephone. I keep a mobile telephone for emergency use but I use the telephone about as often as I send telegrams.

20.03 p.m.

A publisher in London has written offering me a fee of £5,000 to write a medical book for them. I get the impression they think they are being generous. I estimate that the book will take me six months to write. I send a polite letter thanking them for their offer which I decline on the grounds that I have acquired a severe addiction to food and warmth and that in order to fulfil their commission I would have to abandon both.

29

11.19 a.m.

I received a letter complaining that because I disapprove of the war against Iraq I must be anti-Semitic. The writer of the letter says that the media have lied about the Israelis doing terrible things to Palestinian children and that since I am clearly anti-Semitic he is going to write to all the newspapers and tell them not to review my books or accept advertisements for them. In the same post I received a letter saying: `I loved your book *Bloodless Revolution.* But what control have we since the Zionist impact and takeover? Your one weakness is that you do not take a strong enough line on the Zionists and I suspect that this is because you are a Zionist supporter and sympathiser.'

17.18 p.m.

A neighbour has a very noisy motorbike which he starts up at about 6.30 a.m. every morning. He doesn't just start the thing, he revs the engine for at least five minutes. As I walked back from the postbox today I saw him tinkering with the machine. `What time do you go to bed?' I asked. He glared at me, belligerently. `Why do you want to know that?' he demanded. `So that I know what time to start the car up,' I told him. `We go to bed rather late so I could give it a really good revving up at, say, two o'clock if that would wake you up.' He frowned and clearly didn't understand.

As I approached our gate I noticed that cowboy workmen employed by our local council have been repairing the road outside our house. I call them cowboys because they didn't even both to sweep the road clear before pouring their tarmac. They laid the stuff on top of leaves and an empty drink can, in a paper-thin layer that covered everything in its path. It was the sort of job confidence tricksters do for little old ladies. The layer they laid was so thin that the leaves were poking through before they had gone. Later on some men came by to paint yellow lines on top of the tarmac. They did it by hand and I suspect they must have had a very good three bottle lunch before they did the painting. The road is now decorated with very wavy yellow lines. Maybe the council will submit it as an entry for the Turner prize.

30
15.20 p.m.
We are in the Lake District for a few days, staying in a hotel which seems to have stars. This morning, our first, I asked for lemon tea with my breakfast. When the tea came there was no lemon so I caught a passing waiter and asked again if I could have some lemon. `You have lemon,' he said. `It's in the teapot.' I took the lid off the teapot and looked inside. Sure enough there was a whole lemon floating alongside two teabags. A whole, uncut and quite probably unwashed lemon. Our room, though expensive, is so small that if The Princess wants to open her suitcase I have to leave, and vice versa. Late this morning the hotel lounge was filled with a convention of what looked and sounded like social workers. (Whenever you see an army of shouty women and weedy men gathered together there's a pretty good bet it will be a congregation of social workers.) It's a beautiful spot but we are finding it difficult to relax.

17.15 p.m.
A report suggests that the majority of parents in the UK would be happy if their daughter chose to earn her living working as a prostitute. The world has become a mystery to me and there are now many things I don't understand or, to be honest, really want to understand. Still, I find myself constantly besieged by questions not even Google can answer satisfactorily. (Come to think of it, in my experience Google, though it always provides thousands of answers, actually answers very few questions satisfactorily unless you happen to be a complete idiot.). Here are some of the questions to which I cannot even begin to imagine the answers. Why do religious fanatics who believe in an all-powerful god, believe that their god's work won't get done unless they do it for him? Why does toast taste better when made on an open fire? Why do you have to walk all the way to the back of the chemist to get a prescription if you are ill, while people wanting to buy stuff that is bad for them can buy as much as they want at the front of the shop? Why do people who eat burgers bother to buy diet cokes?

Why do banks always only have one person on the counter at lunchtime with the result that there are huge queues of people spending their lunchtime standing in line? Why do people who do sign language on television always look as though they got dressed in the dark at a party and put on someone else's clothes? Why does the cap not stick to the tube of glue when the packaging tells you that the glue will stick anything to anything? Why don't slugs eat weeds? Why is it that most men are bald but most celebrities have a full head of hair? In films, why do women running away from the baddies always go up onto the roof or down into the cellar when anyone with half a brain would know that they will be trapped? Why are council, post office and BT offices always the ugliest in any town? Why is it that the only building materials British architects seem to know of are concrete and glass? (They invariably favour functionality and economy over style and aesthetic delight. Whimsy is a mystery to them. The buildings that win prizes look as if they were put up without any plans by bottom cleavage baring builders using whatever materials may have fallen off the back of a lorry.) Why are 93% of pharmacists so bloody snotty when all they do is count out pills? (And why do you have to go to university to have a licence to count out pills?) What would happen if the heir to the throne were a Downs syndrome sufferer? Would it be politically incorrect to say he couldn't be King? Why do socialists insist on free education and free health care but never insist on free food? Do Germans take `bad dressing lessons' or is something that comes naturally? These worries come to me as fast as snowflakes in a snowstorm but the answers never seem to come with them.

May

1
11.59 a.m.

A reader who is an accountant has written to complain that he has been told that he must, in future, keep records proving the identity of all his clients. He is worried about this because he thinks it is intrusive and unnecessary. I replied telling him that I have, in the past, succeeded in forcing solicitors to acknowledge that it is only necessary for them to see (or 'have sight of') identity documents. They do not need to keep copies. I do not believe that there is any law requiring anyone to keep records of identity. There are laws requiring people to satisfy themselves as to an individual's identity but that is an entirely different things. I have won this argument several times with compliance officers who have, in the end, always agreed that they must only satisfy themselves that X is who he claims to be. It is utterly absurd that so much confidential information is being stored all over the country. And hardly surprising that ID theft is so common. Curiously, the Government never bothers to ask for identification. It is possible to buy National Savings products without sending off birth certificates or passports. And HMRC never seem concerned about my proving that I am who they say I am.

I've had endless battles about this over recent years. Most of the time I've won. One finance organisation gave in and said they would accept my signature as proof that I am who I say I am. Another, requiring proof through the post, accepted a photocopy of my driving licence which had 'Only Valid for XYZ Bank Until (a date a week ahead)' printed across it in large black lettering.

The only time I've failed was with an idiot at the Royal Bank of Scotland, back in the days when staff at Publishing House were keen for me to set up a scheme for accepting payment without cheques.

I sent this letter: *'Thank you for your letter asking for copies of documents. If you check with your compliance officer you will find that the FSA does not require you to take and store photocopies of sensitive documents. You only need to check the existence of such documents in order to verify my status. I am not prepared to allow you to have and store copies of sensitive documents. To do so would expose me to the risk of identity theft and greatly increase the risk of the nation being put at risk by terrorists or moneylaunderers. Once documents are copied and distributed the risks increase dramatically. I am happy to take documents from Table 1 and Table 2 into a local branch of RSB so that these can be viewed. This would enable the bank to satisfy FSA requirements and help ensure that I and the nation are protected from identity thieves, money launderers and terrorists. Are you prepared to accept this safer alternative in order to help protect your nation from money launderers and terrorists? Or do you prefer to stick with the bank's present system (requiring copies to be made, distributed and stored unnecessarily) which endangers your country's security?'*

I never heard from them again. The civil servants who run the State-owned bank were probably all too busy counting their £1 million bonuses, celebrating their losses and laughing at daft taxpayers like me.

Actually, it's probably just as well I didn't hear from them. I really don't want to have anything to do with such an egregiously inept organisation. Who wants to have financial dealings with a bankrupt bank? It would be as daft as hiring a solicitor who is in prison for fraud.

2

15.14 p.m.

We went to see a former approved school today. The local authority had ripped the soul out of the house and is now offering it for sale. It had once been beautiful. It is now completely dead and I suspect that no amount of work, money or love could ever bring it back to life. It would have been cheaper for the authority to build a new property rather than destroy this once proud and beautiful house. And I really cannot bear the thought of all the work that would have to be done. When I was restoring a big country house many years ago I had 17 workmen beavering away in it all at once. They were driving me mad. They wouldn't do what I wanted them to do but would insist on doing things they wanted to do and I didn't want them to do. They merrily tore down old panelling and then put up false ceilings that I'd said I didn't want. It became a huge battle of wills and I simply could not get them to see that I was paying for the work and was, therefore, entitled to at least have a say in what was or was not done. I arrived one day and found that one had left a note to another nailed to the front door with a nine-inch nail. Another had emptied gallons of diesel waste into a sewer leading to the septic tank. I fired all 17 of them there and then. It felt good. And although I had to find new workmen my stress levels halved instantly. Later I met two of the guys I had fired. `We were taking the mickey', one of them admitted. `We really respected you for firing us,' said the other. If you are nice to people to start with and you then have to be tough, they will hate you. But if you are nasty from the start they get used to it and say `he is tough but fair'. We know this place required too much work to turn it into a house but we persevered with the tour. The smartly dressed woman who was taking us round told us that the local shopping centre is very good. `There are some excellent charity shops there,' she confided. So, that is now how people judge a town's shopping centre; by the quality of the charity shops.

16.34 p.m.
While out on our house search we stopped for tea. The cups were so thick you could drop them and they wouldn't break. I suspect that someone had tested my cup by throwing it at the wall. But despite two large chips and a wide crack, the cup was still in service. At the next table a woman talked incessantly about how busy she was and how she had so much to do that she didn't get any time to herself. I wanted to tell her to get off her bum and do some of the things she needed doing.

`Was everything satisfactory?' asked the waitress, as we left. `No, I'm afraid not. It was terrible,' I replied. I explained why. She stared at me for a moment. `That will be £15.45,' she said. I paid.

As we walked away a small portly man accompanied by a taller but proportionately even more portly woman stopped me in the street. `Are you Vernon Coleman?' he demanded. Reluctantly, and involuntarily backing away a step, I smiled nervously and admitted that if there were a prize to be won he would have won it. He turned to his wife. `There you are,' he said. He walked on a pace or two and then turned back. `We had a job recognising you,' he told

188

me, as an afterthought. 'You look a lot older than your photograph.'

Afterwards we walked around the town to check things out. We are unlikely to make an offer on the house we saw today. But there are other houses on the market in the area so we decide to take a look. The Princess and I have devised a good way to check out a town. We start by looking at the newspapers and magazines on sale in the main newsagent. In a decent town there will be plenty of copies of the *Financial Times* and *Country Life*. In a rough town, which is going downhill, there will be very few newspapers but a huge pile of magazines on tattooing and hairdressing. And there will, of course, be a large number of what The Princess describes as 'Pot Noodle newspapers'. I have written columns and thousands of articles for most of the tabloids but these days I am ashamed when I see what they are printing. They really should not be allowed to call themselves 'newspapers'. Sleazepapers would be more accurate.

This time there were a lot of magazines on tattooing and hairdressing. Although she is still a young thing, The Princess prefers to find (and read) the sort of magazines which carry advertisements for stairlifts, incontinence products and walk-in baths.

There's another way to spot a naff town. In a naff town virtually all the small greasy spoon cafés will have tables and chairs on the pavement outside. The proprietors of these establishments are not aping the Café de la Paix or Deux Magots but are, rather, catering for those customers who want to enjoy a cigarette with their coffee.

21.14 p.m.

I've spent much of the past week filling in my tax return. The problem is that they've simplified it. Last year it took my office a week or two to prepare the basic stuff for the form and me a week to fill in the form. Now that they've simplified it the whole thing looks as though it's going to take a month. I doubt if I'll get my bit of it done in under ten days. Ten whole productive days gone. That's two working weeks for a bureaucrat. Actually, given their working hours and mine it's probably four working weeks for them. I had to ring up the tax advice line twice. Sadly, their technical advisers couldn't answer simple queries with any confidence at all. The whole form, and the notes that accompany it, seem to have been written by Kafka with a little help from the Marx Brothers. Unlike instruction manuals for Japanese DVD players (which are written by illiterate pea-brained morons) tax regulations are deliberately written to be incomprehensible so as to create an endless sea of work for lawyers and to give the system an edge over the rest of us.

22.19 p.m.

A reader has written asking me to remove his prostate gland. His letter is headed `urgent' and he describes his problem as `life threatening'. Oh dear. I have no clinical practice and no access to an operating theatre and it must be nearly 40 years since I last performed an operation of any kind. An operation on our kitchen table, with my shaking hands holding our second best kitchen knife as I struggle to navigate my way around his nether regions, would truly not be in his best interest. It is slightly alarming to realise that I am legally entitled to perform any surgical operation I fancy trying my hand at. Maybe I could offer our Prime Minister some free brain surgery.

3

12.04 p.m.

The manager of a café where The Princess and I have drinks occasionally, offered me a free meal if I wrote a brochure for them. `It won't take you more than an afternoon,' said the cafe owner. A meal in his café costs at the most £20 so he is valuing my time as a writer at £40 a day. This is the third time this has happened to me. I must look very poorly paid. Maybe I need a new coat.

While sitting in the café I was rereading *The Great Crash 1929* by John Kenneth Galbraith. Our political leaders like to give the impression that the financial crash which started in 2007 and accelerated throughout 2008 was an exceptional event. It wasn't. It bore many similarities to previous financial crashes which took place in 1929 and the 1930s and in the 1970s and if our overpaid leaders had spent any of their expenses money on the book they would have known what was coming. Galbraith concludes that `five weaknesses seem to have had an especially intimate bearing on the ensuing disaster'.

The five weaknesses he defined were:

1. `The bad distribution of income.' The rich were very rich and had far too much of the available wealth. The problem is that the rich don't buy more bread or socks The situation was exactly the same at the beginning of the 21st century.

2. `The bad corporate structure.' American enterprise in the 1920s had, in Galbraith's words, `opened its hospitable arms to an exceptional number of promoters, grafters, swindlers, imposters and frauds'. Who would dispute that America (and Britain) had been even more hospitable to fraudsters in the run up to the 21st century crash?

3. `The bad banking structure'.

4. `The dubious state of the foreign balance.' In the 1920s America had a surplus of exports over imports and the United States of America was a massive international creditor. By the end of the 20th century the situation was reversed. The USA had become a massive international debtor. The end result was the same.

5. `The poor state of economic intelligence'. Anyone who has studied the words of Gordon Brown, the Bank of England or the nation's economists will be forced to conclude that the problem had recurred. In the 1920s the Government failed to act wisely because it didn't understand the extent (or the cause of) the problem. The same situation prevailed throughout Gordon Brown's tenure as Chancellor of the Exchequer. Everything Brown did made things worse.

In the run up to the recent crash, all Galbraith's five reasons existed but were not recognised. The problems were global (globalisation had seen to that) but, thanks to Brown, they were worse in England than in any other country.

14.15 p.m.

I saw a group of hoodies slouching along the street. They were shuffling and I could see why. They hadn't tied their shoelaces and they were all wearing trousers which hung precariously on their hips. Grey underpants are, it seems, part of their uniform. It occurred to me that if I shouted rude comments at them, and then ran away, they would not be able to catch me because they would not be able to run without tripping up over their shoelaces or their trousers. This knowledge gives me strange comfort. I did not tell The Princess because she knows me well and would worry that I might do it.

19.10 p.m.

I'm writing a novel set in Paris and I have quite a lot of the plot sorted out. The problem is that the characters keep changing. It's normal for characters to take over once they've been defined but these characters just won't take any shape. And until I have characters I have no book. I like to know more about my characters than I tell the reader. I want to know something about their lives before they appeared in the book. And I want to have an idea of what will happen to them afterwards. I often leave the way open for another book, or even a series, at the end of a novel. I did this with *The Bilbury Chronicles* and *Mrs Caldicot's Cabbage War*. And I also did it with *Second Innings*, *Deadline* and *Tunnel* (though I haven't written those sequels yet). I did it with the series of novels I wrote as Edward Vernon. Sometimes I think it's fun to give the reader a note explaining what happened to the characters after the book had ended. It's good to know that the characters carry on their lives. It's not for nothing that writers of fiction often put 'based on a true story' at the front of the book, even if the link to the true story is fairly tenuous. (I confess that *Mr Henry Mulligan* was based on a three line news story.) At the end of one novel, *Paris in My Springtime*, I invented an entire epilogue to describe what happened to all the characters. My father was so convinced by this that he really believed that the book was autobiographical.

4

15.12 p.m.

I received a message from someone who wants to check my credit rating for me so that I can see if anyone has been trying to steal my identity. If I pay them money every month they will tell me how my rating is doing. This is a waste of time because I have no credit rating at all. This means that I cannot buy anything which cannot be purchased with cash. But it also means that it is rather tricky for crooks to steal my identity and buy expensive toys with my money.

I don't see why people are so desperate to have a good credit rating. You only need one if you intend to borrow money.

I admit that having no credit rating can be a little bit inconvenient at times but there is usually a way around the problem. Not having a rating means, for example, that I cannot buy a mobile telephone on a contract. That's fine by me.

When I wanted to buy a couple of iPhones the man in the shop wanted £30 per month as a rental. But since I don't have a credit rating I couldn't do that. So, instead, I bought two phones and paid £360 each for them. Since we use them exclusively for business they were, of course, a tax-deductible expense. I got free Internet access for the first year but now have to pay £10 a month for unlimited e-mails and Web use. The salesman in the shop thought I was mad to buy phones which I could have had `free of charge' if I'd signed a contract.

Since we've now been using the iPhones for well over two years I am in profit on the deal. If I'd signed the contracts I would have paid over a total of £1,440. But because I bought the phones they have cost me £360 plus £360 (the cost of two iPhones) plus £120 plus £120 plus £120 plus £120 (the cost of buying e-mail and Web services for two phones for two years). And that comes to £1,200. If my iPhones last another year I will save even more money. And there is no paperwork to bother with.

5
16.17 p.m.

A man in a cheap suit (doubtless representing the European Union) has apparently told us that the front door at Publishing House must be widened so that people in wheelchairs can enter. We have, so I'm told, sold two books to customers who turned up at the door. And so we must knock down the front of the building and rebuild with a wider doorway. Even if this is possible it will cost tens of thousands of pounds. I have given instructions that in future we do not, under any circumstances, sell any books to callers who turn up and knock on the door. Progress.

17.19 p.m.

My long-standing campaign encouraging voters to support independent candidates has borne fruit in recent years. At the 2005 election there were 166 independent candidates and two were elected. At the 2010 election several hundred independent candidates stood (despite the fact that the costs of standing have risen dramatically, as the authorities do their best to discourage independent candidates) and more independent candidates were elected. This is, it seems, a universal theme that has found its time. In America thousands of people are leaving the two big parties and becoming independent voters, choosing to select candidates according to the issues and the real personalities of the people involved. There are now more declared `Independents' in America than either Republicans or Democrats.

If Britain must be run by a political party then it needs a party which believes in the supremacy of the individual, which believes in protecting personal freedoms, which believes that government must be wary of taking on too much but which must limit itself to providing a basic physical, administrative and legal infrastructure, which believes that when capitalists take risks they must take personal responsibility for their losses as well as their gains, which believes that individuals are entitled to protect their identity and their privacy and which believes that the welfare state should be a safety-net and not a smothering blanket. We need a party which is proud of, and prepared to defend, the nation's culture, history and integrity.

At present we have three parties which are indistinguishable and notable only for their complete lack of ethics.

And we need politicians with a little gravitas. The modern political leader has little or no experience of real life. David Cameron, for example, was 39-years-old when he became Tory leader. He'd had four years in the House of Commons and before that had worked in public relations. Compare and contrast David Cameron's personal history with that of Winston Churchill. Indeed, compare and contrast the personal history of any modern politician with that of any politician of Churchill's generation.

We need politicians who are separated from the machinery of the State. Politicians should not be part of the State apparatus, receiving expenses and allowances as if they were Inland Revenue officers on assignment. MPs should represent us, and as such they should be above the State, not part of it. How can you rule and control a system of which you are but a small part?

19.18 p.m.

I spoke to a London publisher today who asked me what market research I did before writing and publishing books. I told him that I never do any market research. If I want to write a book I write it and then work out how to sell it afterwards. Just about every book I've ever written has sold out and had to be reprinted. 'You really ought to do market research,' he insisted and went on to argue that his firm would never commission a book without having first established a demand for it by putting the proposed project to a 'focus group'. I didn't have the heart to tell him that I knew of a major electronics company which had organised a focus group to find their views on a new CD player they were launching. One of the questions they asked the focus group was: 'Would you buy a black or a yellow player if both colours were available?' Over 90% of the respondents said they would buy the yellow player. At the end of the meeting the focus group members were given a free player as a 'thank you' for their help. They were allowed to choose between a black player and a yellow one. They all, without exception, chose the black players - proving that there is often a huge divide between what people say they want and what they really want. I prefer to stick to my system which does at least mean that when I write a book I know there will be one person who will be interested in it - me. (It also means that I get to write books about subjects which interest me. I cannot imagine anything more soul destroying than writing a book on a subject that had been chosen for me by a focus group.)

6

11.17 a.m.

In a Marks and Spencer store today I noticed that they have a huge cardboard box for recycling bras. How do they do that? Do they melt them down? Or do they just take them to Africa and give them to all those women who used to model for National Geographic magazine?

14.15 p.m.

I bought a Graham Greene first edition today for £1. I found it, inevitably, in a cardboard box at the back of a shop. If the owner of the shop had been nicer I would have given him more than the £1 he asked for it.

16.17 p.m.

After the Blair and Brown years we desperately need someone to inspire us. We need someone we can follow. We need someone we can trust. We need someone who will lead. We need someone who understands the meaning of integrity and honour. We have Cameron and Clegg. What did we do wrong? History will show that this pair are incompetent buffoons. Neither of them could lead a bunch of boy scouts on a country ramble.

17.35 p.m.

A few months ago The Princess found a pair of slipper boots which she really liked. They are already wearing out. I have persuaded her to buy another six pairs. In days gone by only obsessive compulsives bought items they liked in bulk. Today, any sensible person does. I have been doing it for years. Manufacturers and retailers frequently stop selling popular items when they run out. (Book publishers do it too, of course). I have found that the only sensible way to avoid this recurring frustration is to stock up whenever I find something I like. I recently found a notebook I particularly liked in the stationery store called Ryman. It's pocket-sized and is designed for artists but the paper is thick and the cover stout. There is a bookmark and an elasticated band, with a metal clip, to keep the notebook closed in the pocket. Wonderful. I bought all the stock I could in several branches of Ryman and then simply rang the head office and ordered 250. They should last me six months or so. Maybe I should have bought more. I've been using notebooks since the age of 5 and must have got through two or three a week at least. That's probably nearly 10,000 notebooks so far. I clearly have an obsessive compulsive disorder (glued on top of my hypersensitivity, chronic shyness, self-consciousness and constant feeling of failure). I used to worry about this a little. But writers have always carried notebooks. Aubrey's *Brief Lives* includes this about Thomas Hobbes, who in 1651 published the *Leviathan*. `He walked much and contemplated, and he had in the head of his Staffe a pen and inke-horne, carried always a notebook in his pocket, and as soon as a notion darted, he presently entred it into his Booke, or els he should perhaps have lost it. He had drawne the Designe of the Booke into Chapters, etc. so he knew whereabout it would come in. Thus that booke was made.' And numerous writers have published their notebooks. Somerset Maugham's published notebooks are a revelation. (Mine, the world will be relieved to know, have all been burned as soon as they have been filled.)

18.54 p.m.

Late this afternoon a neighbour who knows that I collect books came round to ask me to view his collection. When I got there I found that he had a large, glass-fronted bookcase stuffed with book club editions. Every single book was brand new and unread. And, although they were behind glass, every book had been carefully wrapped in protective film. 'What do you think of that?' he asked me. 'They're my pension. I don't put my money into stocks and shares like all the idiots. These are going to go up and up.' I didn't know what to say. I didn't have the heart to tell him that his entire collection was pretty near worthless. I made appreciative noises and he smiled and nodded and cooed. It isn't surprising, I suppose. Even auctioneers sometimes think that book club editions are worth money. Not long ago I attended an auction because the catalogue had included a number of James Bond books by Ian Fleming. Sadly, although the prices they were expecting were high the books were all book club editions. I could have bought every single one in a charity bookshop for less than a quid.

7

16.48 p.m.

I recently bought a letter written by Orson Welles. It arrived today. Although the letter is signed by Welles it was clearly typed by him on a rather cranky portable typewriter. It was written to the composer of music for a film he was making.

19.12 p.m.

Dress shops report that it is increasingly common for their customers to 'buy' goods, wear them for a special occasion and return the goods for a refund when they've finished with them. EU law gives customers extraordinary rights and shopkeepers have little choice but to provide the refund. This sort of behaviour can be absorbed by large companies (who are cutting corners in every conceivable way) but small businesses, struggling to cope with red tape and bureaucracy, cannot. The result will be that more and more small shops will go bust.

Publishing House often receives packages from customers who return books for a refund or an exchange. The books they return are well thumbed, the pages marked with coffee cup stains and cigarette ash. `You sent this in error,' they claim, when it's painfully obvious that they've read and re-read the volume. This morning we received a book which had pencil marks all over it. The spine was completely broken. The person who sent the book back claimed it wasn't wanted and hadn't been opened. There is a coffee mug ring stain on the cover and the book smells of cigarettes. I doubt if a second-hand bookshop would sell it. If I don't send a refund cheque I will undoubtedly be in breach of some EU regulation. Another reader complains that we sent a book to the addresses we were given. `But that isn't my address now, so please send a book to my new address.' (There is no mention of the old address, no mention of the book title and no offer to pay anything.) Last week a reader wrote saying: `I liked your book very much but gave my copy away to a friend. Please can I have another?'

I don't care what the rules and regulations might be. This nonsense is stopping. And it is stopping now. I am told by the staff at Publishing House that I cannot do this. Really?

8
11.12 a.m.
We needed new boilers in the UK and in France at the same time. We recently bought virtually the same combi boiler in both countries. (With a combi boiler there is no need for a hot water tank and therefore far less risk that many gallons of water will suddenly burst through the ceiling). In the UK our new boiler cost £2,000 and having it fitted took six weeks to arrange. Two men took a day to take out the old boiler and put in the new one. They made a great mess which they made no effort to clear up. They offered no service afterwards. Indeed, after they had gone we discovered that they had set up the boiler incorrectly and it had to be adjusted by a man from the manufacturers. He came this

morning and seemed to be shocked by their shoddy workmanship. In France the same boiler cost £1,000. We had to wait five days to have it fitted. Removing the old boiler and putting in the new one took one man two hours. He cleared up all his mess and took away all his rubbish. We were given a free annual service and a two year guarantee.

16.39 p.m.

I discover that several local councillors are unemployed. I do not approve. No one who isn't a taxpayer should be allowed to be a councillor. No one who does not contribute to the nation's purse should decide how public money is spent. That seems to me fair and commonsensical. But you will not hear any politician ever suggest it. Actually, I would go further: people on sickness benefits should not be allowed to campaign on behalf of political parties or to take political office and if they do then they should be arrested as cheats because if they are fit enough to campaign or take part in politics then they are fit enough to work.

17.59 p.m.

I ordered some Eurostar tickets over the telephone and asked for the tickets to be posted to me. 'We don't usually do this', said a very jolly Eurostar man. 'It's to save the environment. You're supposed to print out your own tickets.' I'm not sure how this saves the environment but I don't argue. 'I'd be grateful if you would post them to me,' I say. 'I'm frail and I live a long way away. I panic if my train is late and I have to rush around at St Pancras.' The nice Eurostar man agrees to post them. I am constantly amazed at the way big companies now play the 'environment' card to save themselves money. It's a remarkably easy card to play. A friend of mine was stopped driving the wrong way down a one way street. He told the policeman that by so doing he cut a mile off his journey. 'It's quicker and uses less petrol and is therefore environmentally sound,' he said. The policeman was so confused by this that he merely helped my friend turn his car round and let him go on his way.

21.57 p.m.

Half wits who don't believe in `peak oil' are again suggesting that the oil price is high because of speculators. This is so silly. When one speculator buys another sells. That's the way it works. Only big countries (such as America) buy and hoard oil in vast underground caverns. Speculators are betting on the price and they have a neutral effect; they no more change the price of oil than tipsters or bookies change the outcome of a horse race. Horses don't run faster or slower because people bet on them. And the oil price doesn't go up or down because people bet on where the price will be in a day, a week or a month. The real worry about oil is the fact that the Saudis are, in my view, still claiming to have far more oil than is really there. Maybe the Saudi royal family need to pretend to have more oil than they have in order to convince the Americans that they are worth protecting.

9

11.38 a.m.

It's been some time since I had my eyes tested so instead of passing I called in at a branch of Vision Express and had my eyes tested. The optician told me she thought I had early signs of macular degeneration. This is not good news. It means that I'll effectively go blind in a few years. Meanwhile, I still need new spectacles. A kindly assistant took me to the cheapest rack of spectacles available. I must look poor as well as old. I picked up a leaflet which promised me that they could find any frames I wanted. `Do you have half-moon spectacles?' I asked. `Oh, no,' said the assistant. They could, it seems, find any frames they had in stock.

12.14 p.m.

The euro has collapsed as a result of waste and corruption in Greece. It couldn't have happened to a more deserving currency. The director of foreign relations at the Dutch finance ministry has proposed a special purpose vehicle with the right to raise funds backed by 440 billion of euro guarantees. The deal has allowed the European Central Bank to announce a government bond purchase programme to stabilise the markets and save the euro. Someone called Trichet, the president of the ECB, was quoted as saying `no politician is going to tell me what to do'. The UK has refused to pledge any money to the euro support fund on the grounds that the euro is nothing to do with us. `The British position was not very constructive,' said Anders Borg, the Swedish finance minister. `The British could pay a price for this for some time to come. At such a sensitive time, to make such a drastic statement was not very wise, and it will not be easily forgotten.' So the result of our being in the bloody EU is that the finance minister of Sweden feels fit to threaten us because we won't bail out a currency which has nothing whatsoever to do with us.

15.16 p.m.

We see cakes in a shop window and are tempted to buy one each. But then one of the assistants sneezes over them and we walk away. It is easy to resist temptation in such circumstances. We go out to eat very infrequently these days. Just as we all are, in a public lavatory, at the mercy of the cleanliness of the dirtiest person to have used the facility so, in a restaurant, our health is at the mercy of the dirtiest person in the kitchen.

16.17 p.m.

While wandering up the road I saw an absurdly fat man hit an absurdly fat child in the doorway to a store. I caught his eye. He stood and glared at me with the belligerence of a fighter, a body builder. But he was neither. Just an absurdly fat man. He wore a T-shirt with the arms cut off to show off the tattoos on his fat arms. It hadn't been much of a blow. More of a half-hearted slap. But he shouldn't have hit the little girl and it was obviously something he did often. If he had hit the child again I would have hit him. He was angry looking and gross but too fat to move easily. Afterwards I thought I should have telephoned the police. But the children would have probably been taken away by social workers. Would that have been a good thing?

19.40 p.m.

I have lost the Orson Welles letter I bought. I put it somewhere safe but now I can't remember where that was. I have been busy shredding a lot of old, unwanted correspondence and I am frightened that the Great Man's letter may have been shredded with junk correspondence between myself and the various utility companies. I feel incredibly guilty because the letter was a small piece of cinematic history. And Welles isn't writing any more letters.

21.34 p.m.

A DVD which I bought from a public library didn't work so I took it back today. `This DVD doesn't work,' I said. The librarian turned away from reading the online edition of the *Independent* newspaper, took the DVD, glanced at it and handed it back to me. `Yes,' he said. `That's why we took it off the shelf. We can't loan DVDs that don't work properly.' `But you can't sell DVDs that don't work!' I protested. The librarian shrugged and turned back to reading the newspaper on the Internet. I put the useless DVD on the counter and left.

10

21.25 p.m.

We went to Hay on Wye today. I always think of it as Richard Booth's town of books but it's now merely a ghost of its former self.

Hay is a peculiar place. The Welsh claim it but if the locals want letters to reach them they have to give their address as being in Herefordshire which is as English as you can get. The route up the Wye Valley, one of the most glorious stretches of road in the whole country, takes us to and fro across the border between the two nations. Every time we go into Wales there is a notice welcoming us but only rarely are there signs welcoming us to England. Presumably, the Welsh have more money for this sort of thing than the English who have given most of their money to Scotland and Wales. I like Wales very much, it's a beautiful country but it does annoy me that all the road signs are in two languages. This is expensive and dangerous and it's also a nonsense because only a tiny proportion of Welsh people actually speak the language. If they must put the road signs in two languages why not put them in two colours so that it's easier to spot the ones you need to see? There are no Welsh newspapers or magazines on sale and the television channel which broadcasts in Welsh exists only because it receives a massive subsidy. It would be cheaper for the presenters of programmes to go round to people's homes. If the Welsh used the money they waste on signs and notepaper they could provide jobs for thousands of unemployed Welsh folk, though maybe they'd rather have the useless and confusing road signs than the jobs. I was appalled to hear from a local that in order to satisfy the political activists many Welsh schools now teach basic subjects in Welsh. This is a particularly toxic form of child abuse which permanently damages the hopes and ambitions of Welsh children. I think it is a wonderful thing that the Welsh language survives but teaching children in a language which has very few textbooks and not enough words should be a crime. It's not surprising that it has been reported that Welsh unemployment is high because of poor education.

At Tintern we stopped at a bookshop called Stella's. As a collector I found it very disappointing. I couldn't find anything by Dickens, Conan Doyle, Fleming, Greene or Wodehouse. Rows of books but I walked out without buying anything (though I did purchase a couple of cheap paperbacks from a rack outside).

Hay on Wye itself seems to have lost its way and become a parody of its former self. It's difficult to get to and remarkably disappointing once you get there and manage to put a ticket on the car in the local car park. (I had to key my car registration number into the machine to make sure that I didn't give the ticket I bought to anyone else if there was time left on it when we departed. I think this is extraordinarily mean.)

The town is now rather tatty and very touristy. I haven't been there for years, though I have been invited to speak at the literary festival which is held there (I have always declined). The bookshops are overpriced and didn't contain much of interest. Most seem full of overpriced remainders. I bought an armful of interesting, rain soaked books from Richard Booth's honesty shelves (they had obviously been on shelves in the open air for days if not months) but even these seemed absurdly overpriced. A pound for a hardback and 50 pence for a paperback is rather over the top for books which have suffered badly from the weather. I did however find a first edition of James Agate's *Ego 3*. Agate's diaries are difficult to find and usually quite expensive. They are among the best of all 20th century diaries. I first came across them when I picked up one free from the American library in Paris. Miraculously this one hadn't been affected by water damage; it had survived by being protected under an old long out of date directory.

On the way back we stopped for petrol. The bill was £80.01. I hadn't got the penny so I had to give the assistant a fifth £20 note. In the change the assistant handed me there was a one penny piece. `I can give you the penny now,' I said, holding up the coin. `So if you give me back the £20 note we're all square.' He would have done so too if I hadn't refused it.

22.05 p.m.
I received a lovely e-mail from a reader of the German version of my book *How To Stop Your Doctor Killing You*. I sent back a thank you for the note. I love e-mails like this: cheering, simple and undemanding.

22.25 p.m.
I've had another e-mail from my German reader. This time he has sent a long letter asking for advice about his illness and the drugs he is taking. Clearly, the first e-mail was merely sent to soften me up.

11
12.04 p.m.
An interesting bag of mail this morning included an envelope which contained a whole page from the *Guardian*. This turned out to date from the 1970's and to be part of the serialisation of my book *The Medicine Men*. The reader wanted to know why I don't still work for the *Guardian*. Although I wrote for the *Guardian* when I was a teenager, and they bought the serial rights to my first book, I have never written for it since. Indeed, in the 1970s a *Guardian* editor who had read something of mine of which she disapproved (I can't remember now what it was and I am not entirely sure I knew at the time) wrote out of the blue to tell me that I was banned and that she would never use any of my work on her page and that I was to promise very faithfully not to send anything in because if I did it would be sent straight back to me and she had instructed all her staff about this in case I tried

sneaking something through by sending in something while she was on holiday. I was mildly flattered by this. I had never heard of her and nor had I ever submitted anything to her pages so it was a rather curious incident but I do remember the letter. I got the impression that she had been red with anger and hitting the keys particularly hard. At the time I remember wondering if the whole incident could have been triggered by some hormonal surge though I am now not sure that women at the *Guardian* allow such things to happen. Most, I suspect, have their hormone producing equipment surgically removed.

I also received a note from a reader in East Anglia. The note read, in its entirety: 'Pythagoras's theorem has 24 words. The Lord's Prayer has 66 words. Archimedes' Principle has 67 words. The Ten Commandments take up 179 words. The Gettysburg address has 286 words. The EU rules on the sale of cabbages runs to 26,253 words.' I've seen this many times but it always makes me smile.

22.14 p.m.

Among her many other talents The Princess is a healer. She has remarkable skills. My left knee had been causing considerable pain for some months. I was knocked off my bicycle when I was 12 and as a result I've now developed quite bad arthritis in the damaged joint. The Princess has been spending ten minutes a day healing the knee and today, for the first time the pain has disappeared. I've been a fan of healing for many years (I once made a television programme showing X-ray proof of the effectiveness of healing) and I feel very fortunate and privileged to have my own in-house healer.

22.56 p.m.

A friend asked why we buy so many DVDs and don't watch movies on television. The answer is simple: the films shown on the television are, most of the time, edited by blind people equipped with dressmaking scissors. I suspect that they cut three or four films at a time, arbitrarily chopping out a few frames so that what is left will fit neatly between the reality television programmes which make up the staple diet of their channels. Three out of five main channels also chop bits out to make room for the advertisements.

23.15 p.m.

A report shows that the unemployed are happier than people who have jobs. I am not surprised. The country is not going to recover from the mess it is in until this is reversed and people have a real incentive to work and earn their own keep.

23.48 p.m.

According to a smartly printed leaflet which has been put through our door the council won't take away shredded paper. But we are constantly told to shred everything private. So what do we do? The answer is to burn everything instead of shredding it. There are those who complain that bonfires are bad for the environment. My reply: shredders use electricity and taking the shredded paper to a dump uses petrol. And I like bonfires.

12

10.19 a.m.

I have received a letter complaining about the power and greed of Jewish bankers and asking me why I have not pointed out that most of the bankers who caused the current financial crisis were, or appeared to be, Jewish in origin. The writer asks if I am frightened of the Jews because they can cause so much trouble. I have always taken what I believe to be a reasonable view about Israel and Zionism. But I have been widely criticised by both sides. The criticisms from Jews have been particularly potent and unreasonable. Every time I have murmured even modest criticisms of Israel's policies with respect to the Palestinians I have been swamped with abusive letters from Zionists threatening all sorts of retributions. Moreover, a few of the most virulent Jewish agitators send furious letters to newspapers and magazines demanding that all advertisements for my books be banned for ever if not longer. They are often successful. When I wrote a 100 word comment about the barbaric practice of killing domestic animals by slitting their throats (a practice shared with Moslems, of course) in my column in *The People* newspaper I twice mentioned that this was a criticism made on the grounds of animal welfare, rather than religion. This didn't prevent high level Jews launching a violent attack on me and demanding apologies. Since then I have noticed that any mention of Israeli naughtiness immediately attracts violent opposition. Similarly any criticism of America always attracts venom not from Americans but from Jews. My criticism of the Iraq War (which began before the war started with my book *Rogue Nation* and continued when I resigned from *The People* because the editor refused to publish a column in which I questioned the validity of the war) has attracted a steady stream of abuse from Jewish correspondents who seem to support the killing of hundreds of thousands of innocent Iraqis. I have found that all attempts to reason with such correspondents simply make things worse and attract even more spitefulness. The final irony is that, despite all this, I regularly receive mail accusing me of promoting the Jewish cause.

15.16 p.m.
A friend living in the Far East reported two days ago that he has inoperable cancer with secondaries in his spine. He was told that he had months to live and that there was nothing that could be done for him. I told him to get a second opinion. He has now been told that an MRI scan shows no cancer but a ruptured disk that may not even need surgery.

16.43 p.m.
When television programmes have phone votes why do the presenters always give a cut-off time and then say: 'Votes received after this time will not be counted but may still be charged.'? Why don't they just turn off the machine – and thereby prevent callers being charged? Too easy and not profitable, I suppose.

19.34 p.m.
Small businesses make up a massive part of the British economy. No other major country in the world relies so heavily upon small businesses. And yet small British businesses are closing by the thousand. Almost to a man the owners say bluntly that they are giving up because of the paperwork and regulations generated by the European Union. Supporters of the EU sneer at small businessmen but they're sneering at the people who have for

decades kept Britain alive. And they forget that big businesses all started off as small ones. The businessmen who are closing up their factories, shops and offices and retiring are mostly emigrating. They've had enough of Britain. And where are they going? Most of them are going to France, Spain and Italy.

13
11.55 a.m.
I received a letter from a reader saying: `There is no point in buying your book *Bloodless Revolution* because books cannot change anything.' I think this is wrong. Books can and do change people's lives. I wrote back and pointed out that I have received hundreds, probably thousands, of letters from people who have given up eating meat after reading my book *Food for Thought.* I am as proud of that as I am of anything I have done in my life as a writer.

16.43 p.m.
HMRC has a `press one press two make a cup of coffee press three go for a walk press four' system which bedevils all their phone numbers. I find myself hurling abuse at the nameless voice (why do they all say `OK' before anything else?) and the longer the tape continues the more abusive I become. Suddenly, I realise that the toneless electronic gibberer has been replaced by a gentle and rather nervous voice. `Hello? Can I help you? I'm a person.' I pause. `Are you real?' I ask. `Yes,' she replies. I wonder how much of the abuse she heard and hope she didn't take any of it personally.

19.24 p.m.
`If it weren't for bad feet, chronic fatigue, deteriorating eyesight, rotten intestines and a weak stomach I would be in pretty good shape for a man of 93,' I told The Princess today. She said that I'm not looking too bad for such an age.

21.18 p.m.
According to a review, a famous female actress, being interviewed about her latest autobiography, describes her often disastrous off-

screen experiences with her leading men as 'one monumental cock up after another'.

14

11.11 a.m.

I see that businessmen going to Scotland on business are now able to hire interpreters to help them converse with the locals. This is an excellent idea. I pretty much gave up trying to understand what Scottish people say when I commuted to Scotland once a week to present a television programme in the 1980s. The programme was networked but for reasons best known to the BBC all the presenters and most of the guests had to fly up to Glasgow. Every week, for two years, I spent 45 minutes in a taxi going from the airport to the television studios in the heart of Glasgow and every week I had to put up with a monologue from a taxi driver who spoke a language I'd never heard before. I would grunt occasionally, to show that I was listening, but I never had the faintest idea what they were telling me. I don't think they ever wanted a response. As long as I made a noise which suggested that I was listening they were happy enough.

These days I find watching television programmes almost as difficult as sitting in those taxis. The English media has been infiltrated (overrun would perhaps be more accurate) by Scots and Americans. It's now perfectly possible to watch an entire news programme on television without seeing a single Englishman - either doing the interviewing or being interviewed. Most of the time I can't understand what these people are saying. I do not know what the Scots speak but it is definitely not English, nor any variation of it. Most Scottish broadcasters and actors are incomprehensible and should be given subtitles.

I wonder why so many Scots are allowed to work at the BBC in England. Whenever I worked in Scotland - and while on book tours I made many radio programmes and television series there - I don't think I ever heard a single English voice.

15

12.14 p.m.

One of last things Gordon Brown's wretched Government did was to order two hugely expensive aircraft carriers that Brown must have known the country could not possibly afford. These were to be built in Scotland, of course. The country cannot afford these expensive white elephants and cannot afford to buy any planes to put on them. There is talk that one of the aircraft carriers might be sold when it is completed though no one seems sure which Russian oligarch would buy one. Most of them seem to prefer buying football clubs. Maybe the new Government could advertise the damned thing on eBay. Or, perhaps, it could be moored ten miles off Great Yarmouth. Attractive bungalows could be built on the flight deck and sold to hedge fund managers who want to avoid paying British tax but can't bear to be away from the British climate.

14.12 p.m.
I really miss our former advertising agent. David was brilliant at finding advertising space at low rates. He specialised in buying what is called `short-term' space. He would ring me at 6.30 p.m. and tell me which of the national newspapers had advertising space left for the following morning. I would then buy the space at a rock bottom price. It worked brilliantly. David left in unhappy circumstances and was replaced by a seven-year-old who thought *The Sun* was a big round thing in the sky and the *Daily Mail* was his sister's ever changing boy friend rota. The advertising man we have now is just not working as well. He calls my books `product' and doesn't like my advertisements or my proposals. Not surprisingly I do not feel comfortable with him. I think he will have to go. I have tried to persuade David to come back and work for me exclusively but he has a job working for a council somewhere and cannot be tempted.

15.17 p.m.
At the bank I told a clerk that I want to move £10,000 from one account to another. `What is the purpose of this movement?' she asks. (She then apologises and tells me it is an essential security question). `It is to take money from one account and put it in another,' I told her. She wrote this down on the form and so, once again, the country is safe.

16

20.08 p.m.

We saw four houses today. The first house we saw came with an astonishing number of covenants. The vendor had decreed that he would retain the airspace three metres above the house, that the house must never be used other than as a single private residential dwelling, that no additional structure be erected on the land without the prior written consent of the vendor and that the name of the property must be changed within three months of completion. We were so busy trying to take in all this information (and wondering what was going to happen three metres above the land) that we didn't really look at the house.

The second house had a cement factory on one side of it and everything outside and inside was covered in a thin layer of cement dust. There was a quarry at the back of the house and a big sign warned of occasional blasting. As if all that wasn't enough there was a carpet showroom attached to the side of the house. A door connected the two.

The third house had a caravan park in the adjoining field. Looking over the low fence which separated the two properties we counted nine large dogs. Seven of them were tied up with thick chains. Five of the chained up dogs were barking. `The owners have planning permission for a bungalow to be erected in the garden so they're selling that separately,' murmured the estate agent who was showing us round. She said it quietly, as though hoping that we wouldn't notice. The garden was about the length of a cricket pitch. `They want another £100,000 for the garden,' she told us when asked. She sounded embarrassed as indeed she should have done. Something happens when people buy and sell houses. They all become greedy and expert in the business of property dealing.

I once bought a house from a man who took me on a final tour of the property to show me how the boiler worked and where the stop taps were. `I've just put up a new television aerial,' he said. `It cost me £250. Would you like to buy it?' I said I would and handed him £250 in cash. `I've just put in a new gas pipe,' he told me. I handed over more cash. `Would you like me to leave you the metal hay feeder in the barn?' Although I had no use for it I said that would be very nice of him. He asked for £100. I gave it to him. I am not good at these things. A week after I had moved in he came

211

back and I found him digging up plants and taking cuttings. `I knew you wouldn't mind,' he said. `But you were wrong,' I told him. `I do.' I threw him out. Even worms can turn.

The fourth house was a former vicarage which is now being sold. I liked it very much because it had a huge horse chestnut tree in the garden. I was attracted by the idea of having an endless supply of conkers. We were shown round by a woman from the local church. She clearly disapproved of the diocese selling the house and so was very careful to point out all the problems. She had got very good at it and every time we entered another room she would point out all the stains, dubious bits of piping or dodgy bits of floorboard. She told us in graphic detail about everyone who had died in the house. She explained why the central heating needed replacing, where all the leaks had been and about the ghosts which haunted the house. She told us about the marriages which had broken up in the house, about the child who died in the garden and about the problems with the neighbours. She told us that the parishioners have managed to insist that although the house is being sold, the parking space at the side will not go with it. The church is retaining that though it will consider allowing any new buyer to have access through the parking space in order to make a parking space within the garden at the back of the house. She tells us that the church will charge £150,000 for this permission and admits that because the original parking space will almost certainly be constantly occupied it will be nigh on impossible to get through to the new parking space at the back of the house. We thank her, say goodbye, wonder if the estate agent knows that their representative is putting the boot in so successfully and go to find a café for a pot of tea. The woman who serves us sees the brochure for the vicarage we've just seen. `You don't want to buy that place,' she whispers. `It's haunted.' We tell her that we don't think we'll buy it and we order two hot buttered cinnamon teacakes. When they arrive they are as big as dinner plates and taste as good as they smell which is magnificent.

When we got back home we found we had been sent details of a house which is advertised as having two gardens. Intrigued we look closer. There are indeed two gardens: one at the front of the house and one at the back. This does not seem to us remarkable but estate agents, searching for something to say about a property, can be extraordinarily creative.

17
09.01 a.m.

Tomorrow I am 64. I began claiming my NHS pension as a former GP four years ago (State employees are entitled to retire early) but in another year's time I can claim my official old age pension. It's a good job I don't need to live on my NHS pension. I practised as a doctor for more than a decade but receive around £5,000 a year. When I snuff it, The Princess will receive around £400 a year. The reason for the modest sum is simple. Like the Government, the NHS runs a Bernie Madoff style Ponzi scheme. The contributions I made to my pension were long ago used to pay some other doctor's pension. The money I paid in hasn't earned me a penny in interest or dividends. And so the pension I now get is the sort of pension I'd have received when I retired from general practice in the early 1980s.

I read recently that the former singer Nana Mouskouri is going to give her EU pension to the Greek Government to help rescue it from bankruptcy. Apparently, she receives £14,700 a year as a reward for being an MEP for five years in the 90s.

11.45 a.m.

A large piece of council owned tree has fallen onto the roof of the BMW and severely dented the roof. Other bits of the tree are clearly about to fall. It needs lopping and pruning and generally tidying up. I rang the council. `You need to speak to the tree preservation officer,' said a woman. `But he's gone on paternity leave.' `Well, could I speak to his replacement, please?' `The post is mandated as unfilled under the council's way forward scheme.' I ask what this means. She repeats it. I can get no more out of her. I move the car so that it is not in the line of fire.

15.16 p.m.

I don't feel like a pensioner (though I'm well aware that I probably look like one) but there are constant reminders that bits aren't functioning quite as well as they once did. I need to wear spectacles. My hearing isn't as sharp as it used to be. My joints creak. And if I walk too far too quickly I feel tired. Moreover, anyone who dies is another reminder that I'm on the downward slope. When I was young, illnesses were never associated with the organism wearing out and deaths of those around me were mostly accidents, choice or ill fortune. Mostly, death was just something that happened to old people.

18
09.38 a.m.
It's my birthday. I am old enough to remember when policemen addressed citizens as `sir' or `madam' and when politicians who lied resigned in disgrace. Gosh I am old. I don't feel 64 except physically and mentally. When I am 75 I can get a free television licence and have the right to reserve a seat in the pavilion at Lords for big match days. It's the second of these that I am really looking forward to but for years now they have been gradually increasing the age at which members can do this and I have a suspicion that if I struggle to 75 the magical age will be 80 and then if I creak to 80 the magical age will be 85. I'm also pretty sure that the free television licence will be an historical footnote. It occurs to me that although I am now 64 I have never had a plan; I have not yet really decided what to do with my life. I really must get on and do something about this.

21.34 p.m.
We drove to Sidmouth and called at the Riviera Hotel on the seafront for a mid-morning cup of tea. I made the mistake of ordering coffee. It was that dark, undrinkable fluid they sell in English provincial hotels. In addition to being undrinkable it was cold. The bill came to £7 for the two of us (£8 with tip). The drinks came with a couple of biscuits which I fed to a hungry seagull. A couple walking by stopped to tell me off. Afterwards, we stood on the front at Sidmouth by a stern sign saying `Do not feed the seagulls'. We accidentally fed them the remains of our picnic lunch and they seemed to enjoy it. None of them complained. It is the bureaucrats, the EU officials and the people who make these damned signs whom I object to feeding. They are the ones doing all the damage. Walking through the town I was run over by a youth on a bicycle. He didn't bother to stop or to see if he had done

any damage. It occurred to me that if I had been injured and the local paper had carried a story the headline would have been `Pensioner hit by cyclist'.

Later we sat on a bench overlooking the sea. There was a notice in front of us (partly obliterating the view). The notice told us that we were sitting in a `Designated Public Place'. The Princess said she was glad they had told us and that it made her feel better about sitting there.

On the way home we stopped several times and in a junk shop I bought a copy of a note signed by Hilaire Belloc. The note was framed. I paid £3 and the frame was worth more than that. An hour later, in another small shop, I found a first edition of Charles Dicken's *Cricket on the Hearth* for £1. I also bought a collection of 28 different books in the *Britain in Pictures* series for £1 each. All but two had their dustwrappers and all were in excellent condition. After I had struggled back to the car with all these books I returned to the shop and bought 15 first editions by Colin Dexter and Dick Francis. These were all jacketed and none looked as though they had been read. These cost £1 each too. I suspect that the Book God was looking down especially kindly on me today. I dropped a pen in the shop. An old lady stooped, picked it up and handed it to me. Oh dear. I must look my age.

19

12.14 p.m.
I bought a memory card for my camera from Jessops. Naturally the card does not work with my camera or my printer. I suspect this is because my camera is two years old and completely out of date. I have bought a selection of memory cards from an Internet site in the hope that one of them will be archaic enough to work. I have problems like this all the time. It is now apparently impossible to buy laptop computers that take floppy disks. It is even difficult to find laptops that will allow me to use my zip disks.

16.19 p.m.
I've been reading *The Truth Cautionary List for 1910* which I picked up from a junk shop (for the usual 50 pence). *The Truth* was an extraordinary little magazine, together with an annual book. It published warnings about confidence tricksters (both individual

and corporate) and gave the names and addresses of people it warned against. Among those listed is Margaret Wilkinson of 236 Vauxhall Bridge Rd, London SW. `Represents herself to be in search of a permanent home for an uncle who is willing to pay £100 quarterly in advance for accommodation, and asks for half her travelling expenses to be sent to enable her to call and inspect the home.' It's the Nigerian bank scam! I have, like thousands of others, received many letters in the last few years from Nigerians who have money `stuck' in a bank somewhere and need a British passport holder to help them liberate their wealth. In return for help they promise to pay a percentage. The sums involved are always astronomical. `There is $17,736,298 waiting for me. I will pay you 10% to help me obtain the money.'. `I am the widow of a Nigerian banker. My husband left me $100 million in a bank in Switzerland. I cannot liberate the money myself but need help from an EU citizen. I will give you half the money if you help me with this. Simply send me your bank details (so that I can ask the bank to put the money into your account) and send me a banker's draft for £10,000 to cover bribes and expenses. 'The scam is that they need my bank account details (so that I can receive the money on their behalf). But they usually also want a cheque for a modest sum (□£5,000 or so) to pay the lawyer to prepare the paperwork. The same scam is now sometimes also conducted by confidence tricksters claiming to be ex US army officers who have served in Iraq and have a suitcase full of valuable artefacts to dispose of. (At least I assume they are confidence tricksters.) Miss Wilkinson got there a lot earlier. *The Truth* is also full of the names and addresses of share pushers and bucket shops, money lenders and their touts, home employment tricksters and the tallyman trade. Sadly, I suspect that our libel laws put *The Truth* out of business some time ago.

19.12 p.m.
I asked The Princess to buy something for me by telephone and I gave her my credit card so that she could read out the numbers to the online store. Rather sensibly they wouldn't allow her to order anything until I had given my permission for her to use the card and so I had to speak to them to say I was allowing her to use the card. `Now, sir,' said the person at the other end of the telephone,

`for data protection reasons we have to confirm that you are who you say you are. Would you please give me your postcode.' I can never remember this. `You'll have to ask my wife,' I told him, handing the phone back to The Princess. She gave him the postcode and handed the phone back to me. `Thank you, sir,' he said. `That's fine.'

20
10.05 a.m.

How wonderful it would be if computer software designers and salesmen had to upload and use their own software and if MPs had to fill in their own tax returns. It comforts me no end to hope that the executives who work for DVD player manufacturers have to read their own manuals. (The directors probably have someone sent round from the factory to set the damned things up for them.)

21.46 p.m.

We stayed in a hotel in London for the night. While in our bedroom I wanted to ring a publisher I was due to meet. `I can't make my phone work,' I complained to The Princess. `I don't think there's any reception.' `You won't get to speak to anyone with that,' said The Princess. `Why not?' I demanded. `Because it's the remote control for the hotel television.'

21
09.54 a.m.

Delight and relief! I have found my Orson Welles letter. I found it when I was looking for a contract I signed with a Russian publisher. I'd lost that too. I found them both in a folder I had put on top of a bookcase for safe keeping.

12.34 p.m.

A man told me today that he has stopped buying a daily newspaper and that he and his wife have given up buying magazines. `You use the Internet, I suppose,' I said. `Oh no,' he said. `It's just that we don't have room in any of our plastic bins to put old newspapers and magazines so we don't know what to do with them when we've finished with them.'

22

11.18 a.m.

Someone today described me as eccentric. I find this as curious as `controversial', a tag which always used to be attached to my name and which I never really understood. Am I really eccentric? I don't think so. But then I don't suppose eccentrics ever do. I certainly never deliberately do anything that might make me appear eccentric - indeed, on the contrary, I try really hard to be inconspicuous.

It used to be said that eccentrics were loonies with money but I don't think it is true these days. I don't really think there are many genuine eccentrics around. The world is full of manufactured, self-conscious eccentrics who do things in order to make themselves look `different' and in order to attract attention. But *real* eccentrics never want attention.

The best eccentrics were always English, of course. The Princess and I have a list of some of our favourites in our book *England's Glory*. Only the English do eccentricity naturally. The French are, in contrast, exhibitionists rather than eccentrics. The sadness is that real eccentricity is dangerous today. Whenever the police are faced with a tricky murder, and a lot of criticism from the press, they simply rush out and arrest the nearest eccentric.

23

15.16 p.m.

Clearing out some old papers I found a letter from Jon Carpenter dated December 1994. When I first started self-publishing Jon helped enormously with turning typescripts into books. In this letter he wrote: `Just back from sales meeting. Interesting how everyone now agrees that you were right and the shops were wrong. Price is right, covers are right, there is customer demand and shops that take stock sell and reorder. Shops cannot understand where the demand comes from. The general conclusion (among the salesmen) is that the wholesalers and even Smiths will crack eventually.'

Well, after 16 years it now seems that they didn't crack and that I was wrong and the shops and the sales reps were right. It is today even more impossible for a small, independent publisher to crack the shops properly - especially if they are self-publishing. And as the wretched Internet gets stronger and shops get weaker and there is an exponential increase in the number of unemployed yahoos selling books for 1 penny and making their profit out of the postage charge so there will be less chance for small publishers, who rely so much on back list sales, to survive let alone prosper. Jon also made the valuable point that I should use phrases like `new edition' and `fifteenth printing' to reinforce the point that the books were already selling well. I did that. It didn't make a damn of difference. I even bought huge ads in the trade press telling bookshops of the sales we'd had. They still refused to budge. I have done everything I could possibly do. But all to no avail. And now bookshops and wholesalers are going bust - destroyed by the Internet and the supermarkets. Their only hope lies in selling books from small publishers who produce higher priced books in smaller quantities. But they still don't see that and most will, I suspect, simply go under.

I found this old letter enormously depressing.

24
18.19 p.m.

For some time The Princess has had painful muscle spasms, sensory loss, memory loss and a whole host of other symptoms. We went to hospital to see a neurologist. The consultant to whom The Princess had been referred was busy, or elsewhere being important, and so we saw a fairly young registrar. She thought The Princess might have a tumour on her spine and ordered an urgent MRI scan of The Princess's brain and spine. When we got back home I looked up the symptoms and signs in a neurology textbook. If The Princess had this condition she would probably have a loss of temperature sensation on her shoulders. This hasn't been tested so I checked The Princess's shoulders with a frozen vegetarian sausage. There is no loss of temperature sensation. I tell The Princess and we hold each other tight. She is 26 years younger than I am. I had always assumed that I would go first. Secretly I write this: `The most important thing in my life is to be with you; to share everything with you; to hope together; to journey day by day together; to fail together; to achieve together; to fight together; and to win together. Without you, nothing is worthwhile. With you everything is worthwhile.' I do not give it to The Princess because I think it might worry her. I have no idea what the diagnosis is. I'm terrified.

25
11.56 a.m.

Our gas bill arrived today. I now know how the Treasury must feel when they get a bill for a new aircraft carrier. I have no idea how to understand the bill but the sums involved seem huge.

But this was put into perspective later when, while looking for a letter I had put away somewhere safe and will probably not now see again until 2015, I found a typist's bill for £1,200. This may not sound a lot now but the bill was dated 1974 and it was for typing a new copy of my first book *The Medicine Men*. I remember that the lawyer's bill for libel reading the book was £750. And I also remember that the advance I received from the publisher for writing the book was £750. This was paid in three stages: £250 on signing the contract, £250 on delivery of the typescript and £250 on publication. The *Guardian* bought serial rights, a book club bought rights and Arrow bought paperback rights and there were one or two foreign sales so I probably just about made a profit. (I remember being terribly excited when told that an Italian publishing company had paid millions of lira for the right to publish the book there. And I remember being terribly disappointed when I checked the exchange rate.) The BBC made a programme about the book but I received no money at all for that.

15.14 p.m.

I was trapped in a shop aisle by two motorised scooters. One was heading one way down the aisle. The other was coming in the other direction. Neither of the drivers (both of whom looked fat rather than ill) could reverse their vehicles. I am convinced that 90% of the people using these things are just fat or lazy or both, rather than disabled. In the end I had to climb out through a gap in the greetings card rack. I left the two motorised scooters where they were. I have no idea what happened to them.

26
15.01 p.m.

A friend who works for a radio station rang today in quite a panic. He has the worst memory of anyone I know. He has always been absent-minded and rather dotty. He slipped from chronic adolescence into acute senility without bothering to trouble adulthood, nod hello to middle age or say a word of greeting to maturity as he passed them by. `It's me,' he said. `I know it's you.' I wasn't feeling very friendly towards him. Nor, I knew, was The Princess. But I wanted to hear what he had to say. `I met a lovely woman,' he told me. `I took her to the cinema last night.' I waited. It was obvious that something had gone terribly wrong. `We sat down and in the interval I went out to get some popcorn. While I was queuing I met a chap I know. I hadn't seen him for years. He was with his wife. We were talking about how awful the film was and he said why didn't we just miss the second half and go to the pub instead. So I went with them.' `Did you ask the woman you were with what she wanted to do?' I asked him. `I didn't,' confessed my friend quietly. `Actually, I forgot she was there.' `Let me get this straight, you took a woman to the cinema. You went out half way through and you abandoned her and left without her?' `Yes.' `That's the most stupid thing I've ever heard anyone do.' `Yes. I agree. What do I do?' `When did you realise that you'd forgotten her?' `About two hours later. I went back to the cinema but it was shut. No one there.' `Do you have her telephone number?' `I tried ringing her but her phone was switched off.' `I'm honestly not surprised. Do you know where she lives?' `No. It was our first date.' `Where did you meet her?' `She came into the radio station. She works for a record company. She seemed nice. I'd really like to see her again.' `Find out which one. Someone at the radio station must know. When you know where her office is send her more flowers and chocolates than you can afford. And send a note with them.' `Shall I be honest?' `Yes!' I said. `It's so awful that you have to. She probably won't ever want to see you again. But you owe her an apology and the truth.' `Is that all I can do?' `There's one other thing you can do,' I said. `You can include a note I'm going to give you.' `A sick note?' he asked. `Something saying I suffer from temporary amnesia?' `No,' I said. `I'll give you a note confirming that you're the most forgetful bastard I've ever known and that this isn't the first time you've done something like this.' `Isn't it?' `No,' I said. `You were supposed to have dinner with us last night. The Princess is sharpening her best kitchen knife. She's going to skin you alive when she sees you.'

22.04 p.m.
I saw a DVD on sale on the Amazon website. It was described as `mint'. There was a note with it saying `hardly used'.

27
12.06 p.m.
The Princess said that people who went to Eton sound as if they have nasal polyps. I have this vision of doctors checking out children to find out if they are suitable candidates for an Eton education. `I'm so sorry, Mrs Bigarse-Pompouspratt. I'm afraid your child can't come to our school. He has no polyps and won't ever be able to speak properly. Send him to `Arrow or one of those State places.'

28
10.18 a.m.
We went to the hospital for The Princess's MRI scan. Dr Peter Heywood, the consultant wasn't available (again). The Princess saw the same registrar as before. She was kind and gentle. The scan doesn't show anything. There is no tumour. The registrar examined The Princess again and found that she has brisk reflexes, fasciculation in her tongue and upgoing plantars. There is also muscle weakness. Another diagnosis is made. This time the doctor decides that The Princess may be suffering from motor neurone disease. I can't believe it. The Princess is far too young for this. And her symptoms don't really fit. But maybe I am just reluctant to accept the diagnosis. I am so sad for her. Selfishly, I am sad for me too. The Princess is the love of my life and without her I have no life. She is my everything. When her sky is blue my sky is blue. When her flowers bloom mine bloom too. When birds are singing in her world, they are singing in my world too. I will have to try to stay busy but I know I will find it difficult to do anything.

The only piece of good news we had was that the car wasn't clamped so we could leave the hospital without having to find someone to free us. There is a huge sign at the hospital warning that anyone who stays more than the maximum three hours may be clamped. This is ruthless and cruel. What were we supposed to do? There was nowhere else to park. We have enough to worry about without worrying about being clamped. Extra tests and a lengthy consultation meant that we were lucky to escape. I didn't dare leave the hospital in case The Princess came out and I wasn't there. Besides, there was nowhere else to leave the car. The people who run hospitals should be running prisons. Maybe they could make them profitable.

19.02 p.m.

While The Princess was having tests I wrote a rambling love 'pome' for her. Actually, I wrote it for me. To try to put my feelings into words.

`You are patience and kindness wrapped in a princess,
and given the heart and soul of an angel
I love you all ways and will do always
You are the light that brightens my life
You make the world's brightest diamond look dull
You make the world's deepest ocean look shallow
You make the world's highest mountain look tiny
You make the world's most beautiful flower look plain
Is it any wonder that I love you?
You are the Queen of my world
We are joined at the soul
You are the one for whom my heart beats
And the one for whom my soul exists.
When you are happy I am very happy
When you are sad I am very sad
You give me love, hope, spirit, faith, joy and purpose
You are, and always will be, the very centre of my universe
For you are the meaning of my life
We will always walk together wherever the path may take us
For it is the being together not the going nor the arriving which
is important
Without you there would be nothing
With you there is everything
You make days into dreams without which the world would be
cold and dark and pointless
You make my heart beat

When you smile I feel happy

I will always be with you, always be for you, always be by your side, always be on your side

We will fly free and high together

You are my everyone.

You will always be loved

Because I will always love you.'

Actually, it isn't a 'pome'. It's just a stream of consciousness from a heart which is tearing apart. I do not want her to know at the moment just how worried I have been. And so I do not give the words to her. My life started when we met and it will end if she is not here. With her there is everything, without her there would be nothing.

29

15.16 p.m.

We have to do something to cover our minds with images and thoughts and busyness. In a charity shop in Ross on Wye, I put my hand on The Princess's bottom and said: `What a lovely bottom!' I offer no defense for this inexcusable lapse in behaviour other than that it was an honest thing to say and do. Unfortunately, although I thought I had whispered I fear I may have spoken a little too loudly. Wc were standing outside a small changing cubicle at the time and moments later a woman emerged clutching the dress she had been trying on. She glowered at me and marched over to the assistant to complain that the curtain across the cubicle clearly didn't fit properly. I put down the book I was examining, grabbed The Princess's hand and left the shop before the police were called. We have enough to worry about.

21.11 p.m.

`Have you moved the scales?' asked The Princess. `Yes,' I admitted. `I moved them a couple of feet to one side. I kept tripping over them.' `I'm going to put them back,' she said. `I weigh less when they're where they were than I do when they're where you put them.' I did not argue.

22.06 p.m.

I received a lovely letter about Kirkby, near Liverpool which is mentioned in a story in my book *Cat Tales*. My reader wants to know if I ever lived there. I did. I was in Kirkby in the 1960s, working as a Community Service Volunteer. I remember that it was quite rough at the time. The buses from Liverpool were always escorted by police cars. There were very few shops and the ones which there were had their windows covered with thick wire mesh. But I very much enjoyed my time there. Apparently the town has changed and is now quite smart.

Another reader writes to congratulate me for not taking credit cards. He says: 'Credit cards were yet another lousy idea for real people. They immediately inflated the cost of everything, opened the floodgates to fraud and encouraged reckless spending by the financially naive. The prudent end up bailing out the profligate. What a brilliant con!'

22.59 p.m.

About three weeks ago I received a letter from a reader asking if I was a freemason. I wrote back to say that I was not. I then received another letter, from the same reader, repeating the question. I wrote back and again confirmed that I am not, and never have been, a freemason. I have now received a letter from him saying: 'Your denial proves that you are a freemason. Why are you lying about it?'

I also received a letter claiming that coal can be manufactured and that consequently my book about the coming energy crisis (*Oil Apocalypse*) is nonsense. He does not explain where he will obtain the energy to manufacture the coal.

And the police in the north of England tell me that they have arrested a man who has been sending threatening letters to celebrities. They say that his flat was papered with columns I had written and that he had a large file of cuttings about me. On days like this I am pleased that my address is secret and that hardly anyone knows where I live.

30

11.19 a.m.

Friends of ours who have been looking for a new home for even longer than we have gave up last month and just bought something.

I suspect that this is something that happens remarkably often. `We didn't fall in love with the house we bought,' they admitted. `We just bought it because we were tired of looking.' Much to their own surprise they bought a brand new house. They bought it from an award-winning builder. They have already prepared a long list of problems. Their staircase is coming away from the wall. Eight tiles have fallen off the roof. The walls are so thin that they can hang pictures in two rooms with but a single nail. Their so-called Devon bank is in reality a long, high pile of rubbish covered in weeds. The windows and front door are falling out of their frames. The bricks from which the house was built are already becoming discoloured. The white plastic window frames are turning pink. The garage is too narrow to fit in a motor car, though (as the builder's representative pointed out) it will take a motorcycle and sidecar. The roof is so poorly insulated that they can hear every drop when it rains. The taps have turned a strange colour and the entire plumbing system shakes and makes terrifying noises when any tap is turned on. A modest rainfall flooded the garden which turned out to be pretty well 100% clay. And, finally, when a large puddle appeared in the garage a builder found that the overflow pipe for the downstair's lavatory had been boxed in and could not be reached without knocking a hole in a wall.

Many houses which people buy with 30 year mortgages will fall down (or require demolition) just as the mortgage is paid off. We aren't going to buy a new house. The stairs in our friends' house are coming away from the wall because the award-winning builder had used green timber. In old houses some of the wood is salt cured oak from former English sailing ships; oak so tough you can't get a nail into it. That's for us.

15.17 p.m.

The Princess and I walked into town today to do what The Princess called 'a little light shopping'. (We wanted to buy more old-fashioned light bulbs before the EU ban on sensible lighting comes into operation.) On the way down the High Street we were stopped nine times by chuggers. These wretched people have become a terrible nuisance. Their incessant, ubiquitous, guilt-making questioning of pedestrians is close to menacing. They are as difficult to avoid, and just as annoying, as dog faeces. Most know little about the charities they promote, and care even less. They are driven not by goodwill but by the desire to make lots of commission.

31
13.15 p.m.
On a bookshelf in a charity shop The Princess found five of my novels. My books are more popular now than they have ever been, but whereas I used to be able to walk into any bookshop in the country (or any library) and find numerous books of mine on the shelves, today I only see my books in second-hand shops and charity shops.

17.01 p.m.
I popped into a mobile telephone shop to buy a new telephone. They did the usual checks. I can't buy a phone on a contract because I don't have a credit rating but the pay-as-you-go phones are still OK. And they're much cheaper too. I gave my real name which the man in the shop recognised. He was having difficulty setting the thing up so I said I'd pop out, do a bit more shopping and go back. When I returned three quarters of an hour later he had rung a friend in London to tell him I'd been in the shop. (They must be very low on excitement in that shop). He was terribly excited. `I know about you,' he whispered. `You work for MI5 don't you?' I stared at him in disbelief. `I mentioned your name, said I'd had you in the shop, and my friend - who works there - said they knew you.'

In the end I ended this bizarre conversation by swearing him to silence. I didn't like to tell him that his friend knew of me not because I work for them but because they've had me under constant surveillance for years.

My campaigning, though always entirely peaceful, has meant that my phone lines have been tapped for over 20 years. The clicking and beeping has been annoying at times. And although I no longer hear my own conversations played back to me (they're getting slightly better at it) it's pretty obvious what is going on. They don't just do the generic echelon surveillance (the sort which follows what everyone says or writes and picks up on key words) but they listen to everything.

They used to open the mail, too. But they've given up on that now. I think there's too much of it. The only troublesome thing is that our doorbell somehow gets triggered when they ring up to suck the faxes off the fax machine line. I haven't been able to sort it out so we took the batteries out of the doorbell and it doesn't disturb us any more. We never answer the front door anyway so it's no problem.

They have more files and cuttings about me than I have. I saw some of them once and believe me it's an impressive collection. If I ever change my mind about writing an autobiography I'll use the Freedom of Information Act to pick up my cuttings files and leaf through them.

I expect they will keep doing it until I die, though it is of course a complete waste of money. I know they're doing it. And if I were stupid enough to do anything bad would I be stupid enough to talk about it on the telephone? They know I know they're doing it so can't they work that out for themselves? I suspect they have done so but decide to carry on because it's what they do and they don't have enough knowledge or wisdom or authority not to do it.

My MI5 special branch file contains a note that I am no physical threat and never have been. Which makes it even dafter that they keep wasting the taxpayers' money listening to all my telephone calls and reading my faxes. The odd thing is that I bet they don't read my books and so they won't see this. And so they won't get round to wondering how I know what my highly secret file says about me. I wouldn't tell them anyway. It's secret and I wouldn't betray a source because he still works there and is quite high up now.

I first found out that they were tapping my phone when I dialled 1471 (when the service first started) and dialled a number which turned out to be a private, unregistered line inside Aldermaston Atomic Research Centre. The man who answered the phone was very surprised that I had the number because the 1471 thing had only been going for a couple of weeks, but after I'd spoken to him I slowly realised why my answering machine messages were disappearing, why my phone kept bleeping and why my fax machine started dialling out all by itself. A kind man at British Telecom checked out the Aldermaston number for me and became very excited. He'd been told that it was all top secret and that I wasn't to be told but he was too excited about it to keep it to himself. Suddenly I realised why there had been a yellow van parked outside the house for two days and why two men had spent hours repairing telephone wires that didn't have anything wrong with them.

Since then they've followed me around quite a lot. I used to speak at anti-vivisection rallies quite often and I always had my own film crew, photographer and special branch observers wandering around behind me. In later years I even had my own helicopter hovering overhead whenever I spoke. The officer in charge once asked me how long I was speaking for so that they'd know how long they needed the helicopter for. I think the idea was that the noise would drown me out but once everyone got used to the thub thub thub of the rotors it didn't make a lot of difference.

When I went to South Africa a few years ago one of the first people I met was a smart man in a suit who pretended to be running a local group called Lawyers Against Vivisection. He wanted to know if I knew a man called Alf and if I could introduce him. He was desperately keen but desperately obvious too. I think it was the BOSS suit that gave him away.

Over the years I've had some papers stolen (though the thieves are always very tidy) but they never take anything valuable so I've no real complaints. I always have copies of everything important so it doesn't matter very much. I put the copies in safe places where they aren't likely to be found by small children, petty thieves or anyone working for the security services.

When I left the phone shop the man who'd served me gave me a big, knowing wink. I think he was telling me that my secret is safe with him.

June

1
11.14 a.m.
The German president has resigned after having been caught
telling the truth. He said that there is fighting in Afghanistan to
protect commercial interests and secure trade. So he had to resign.
He was the only politician in the world to tell the truth so naturally
he had to go. It must have been a considerable embarrassment to
the others. Politicians hardly ever resign these days, though they
often should. I have resigned several times on principle and believe
people should do so more often. I stopped writing my column for
The People because a feeble minded editor wouldn't let me
criticise the invasion of Iraq (before it started). When I resigned
from *The People* I was earning around £150,000 a year from the
column (they paid me about £100,000 a year to write the column
but I also had an income from telephone advice lines and book
sales that were part of my contract). And when I was a GP I
resigned because the authorities insisted on fining me when I
refused to put specific diagnoses on sick notes. I suppose that was
a risky and adventurous resignation too but I really had no choice.

16.45 p.m.
I had to fill in my VAT form today. When I had worked my way
through the endlessly and unnecessarily complicated on-screen
forms I came to this: 'HMRC are waiting for notification that your
return has been successfully received by HMRC.' Wonderful.

2
15.17 p.m.
I was utterly astonished to see a branch of Waterstones selling one
of the new e-book readers. This seems to me to be utter madness.
But the madness seems widespread and Waterstones certainly
aren't the only corporate idiots in the retail book trade. I saw my
first e-book reader displayed, with great razzmatazz and pride, in
the branch of W.H.Smith in the Rue de Rivoli in Paris. E-books are
cheap and convenient and, boosted hard by webshops, they will

soon be selling more than paperbacks or hardbacks. Most of the people buying books this way won't read them, of course. They'll just have them tucked away safely on their e-book readers while they play games or text one another. The e-book will kill an entire industry within a couple of years. Bookshops, publishers, printers, librarians and professional authors are all at risk. And since books provide the principle vehicle for ideas, debate and all the basic principles of civilisation the result will be far more significant than the loss of an industry and another few million jobs around the world. Does anyone really imagine that websites, twitterings or vodcasts can possibly replace books? For bookshops to aid this process by promoting the damned things is as daft as a Ford motor car dealer promoting cheap railway tickets in his showroom.

I didn't buy anything in Waterstones, though The Princess bought some audiotapes and had a little fun with their stock. We neither of us likes Russell Brand, whom we consider to be an unpleasant oik who is about as funny as chronic irritable bowel syndrome (and has many of the same characteristics). He must hold the record for the most books seen heavily discounted in remaindered bookshops but there were apparently some of his books in Waterstones. The Princess said she had hidden them where no one could possibly find them.

`Where?' I asked, puzzled. `In the humour section,' she replied. I agreed with her that no one would ever think of looking for his books there.

As we left I overheard two boys talking. I don't know what they were talking about. `I don't know if it's true,' said one. `But I read it in Wikipaedia'.

I smiled at this. Maybe there is hope. I've never heard anyone say: `I don't know if it's true, but I read it in the Encyclopaedia Britannica.'

3
16.17 p.m.
`Drink up, it will put hairs on your chest,' said the man. `I'm not sure that's as great an incentive as you might imagine it to be,' said the woman he was talking to.

22.15 p.m.

This evening we watched *The Perfect Spy* again. It is the classiest piece of television drama ever made. We watch it every year and see something new in it every time we watch it. The two Smiley films (*Tinker Tailor, Soldier, Spy* and *Smiley's People* are brilliant too. I very much doubt if anything of such quality will ever be made again by any British television company. When I watch Ray McAnally's performance in *The Perfect Spy* I am reminded of the legendary actor John Barrymore who could, it was said, cry from either eye at will - according to the needs of the director. The Americans in *The Perfect Spy* are ridiculed with such scalpel sharp accuracy that I sometimes wonder if John Le Carré, undoubtedly one of the great novelists of the 20th century, might not have been hired by the Russians to discredit the Americans by turning them into a laughing stock.

4
13.12 p.m.
With some regret we have decided to abandon using inserts in magazines to sell our books. We only managed to make inserts work when The Princess started to write them. She has a natural talent for picking out the salient bits from a book and preparing an advertising leaflet that will make readers want to read more. Good promotional lcaflcts have to be chatty and friendly and informative and teasing and irresistible.

In addition to sending out leaflets to readers who have already bought books from us we have, for several years, been sending out inserts within magazines and newspapers. But inserts are a dangerous game. There are many pitfalls. The most obvious problem is that when inserts are placed inside a magazine which is sold on a bookstall there is a good chance that the insert will fall out and end up on the floor. Before I realised just how wasteful this is I often used to walk into a branch of W.H.Smith and look with horror at the carpet of expensive leaflets on the floor. Inserts cost money to print, of course, and the publisher has to pay the magazine a fee for every insert that is included. These fees can be massive. So if, out of 50,000 inserts, just 20% end up on the floor the cost can be huge. The easy way to get round this is to put inserts only into copies which are being sent to a subscriber at home. This means that even if the insert falls out it will fall onto the subscriber's table or floor and will stand a chance of being picked up and read.

For several years we did well with the inserts which The Princess wrote. But in recent years the problems have grown so fast, and are now so varied, that we are abandoning them.

Magazines throw inserts away by accident, they change their minds about whether or not to run them, they lose them, they damage them and then refuse to run them because they won't fit into their machinery, they put half in and lose the other half and they lie about their circulation so that we print far more inserts than are needed.

There are some magazines which claim huge print runs but which sell few copies. They make their money out of selling advertising space or taking inserts for a circulation which is much higher than they really have. So, a magazine may claim that it prints 50,000 copies but 40,000 of those may be returned and pulped. The magazine's advertising department will sell advertising space on the basis of a circulation of 50,000 when they are selling only a fifth of that. Advertisers who put inserts into the magazine will almost certainly lose money because they will have paid to print five times as many inserts as they really needed.

The equipment the printers use has become so sophisticated that even a slightly dented insert won't be accepted. And so if the inserts aren't packed very carefully, or the drivers of the delivery lorries which take the inserts to the magazine printer don't handle the boxes carefully, the inserts will be rejected. The rising cost of paper has meant that inserts have become enormously expensive to print. The increase in the cost of fuel means that they are also enormously expensive to deliver. The extra packaging that has to be used to protect the inserts means that the weight has gone up and the cost has increased still more. If the inserts are rejected we have to deal with them (another expense). We used to bring inserts back to Publishing House if they were rejected but after two journeys in lorries the leaflets became totally unusable and had to be disposed of (at our expense). And, of course, Royal Mail strikes can mean that magazines (and their inserts) are delayed or are delayed so much that people don't read them.

The final straw occurred last winter when an editorial note appeared in the magazine *Moneyweek* advising readers that, during troubles with the Royal Mail, readers could peruse their magazine online. It seemed that no one had thought about the advertisers. With readers studying the magazine online the chances of our inserts being read were clearly low. And that is exactly what happened. We had a far smaller response than we would have otherwise expected. When I protested and asked for a discount I was dismissed as `opportunistic'. The advertising agent I was using at the time didn't seem to understand why there was a problem.

And so we're abandoning outside inserts.

Thanks to The Princess's skilful writing, our inserts worked better than almost anyone else's. But I fear that their day is done. Pity.

16.15 p.m.

I rang my bank and after ignoring the usual litany of invitations to press this for that and that for this I eventually found myself talking to what sounded like a real person. `What's your name?' she asked. I told her. `Brilliant,' she said, as though I had just discovered gravity. `And your date of birth?'

I told her. `Fantastic,' she said. Now that the security checks were completed she happily told me everything I needed to know.

20.19 p.m.

I have for years made a point of never meeting my heroes. Sometimes I regret this. Sorting through a pile of old paperbacks I found a copy of Eric Ambler's autobiography *Here Lies Eric Ambler*. Flicking through I noticed that the title page contained a handwritten dedication from the greatest spy fiction writer the world has ever seen. `Dr Vernon Coleman from Eric Ambler, London '87.'

I remembered then that back in the days when the BBC didn't think I was too dangerous to broadcast, the World Service invited me to pick a favourite author to discuss on one of their book programmes. I chose Ambler. The BBC wanted me to interview the man himself as part of the programme but, although I was tempted, I funked it. I simply couldn't face the idea of meeting, let alone interviewing, one of my great heroes. And so a BBC employee interviewed Ambler and they stitched extracts from the interview into my programme. I sent Ambler a note explaining why I hadn't interviewed him myself and he kindly wrote the dedication and left the book for me. Ambler was a very clever writer who always allowed his readers to think as well as read. The author photograph on the back cover of his last novel was taken from the back. I used to buy every new novel as soon as it came out in hardback and I was sad when I saw the cover. I knew the instant I saw it that the book was Ambler's last novel.

5

12.38 p.m.

An acquaintance of The Princess's works for the local council. She goes to work for fun and has such a good time there that she is heartily miffed if she is expected to take a holiday. The most arduous task she and her pals have to undertake seems to be choosing brand new office furniture. This is something they do regularly and at enormous expense. Once the furniture has been chosen and is delivered it has to be changed. This takes two weeks, during which no work at all is done. The staff simply move into the canteen to do their gossiping. It isn't difficult to see why the country is in such a mess.

Talking to her makes me feel glum and hopeless. Civil morality in the UK has evaporated in recent years. The whole idea of public accountability is now oxymoronic. That is bad enough but what is worse is that this lack of morality has infected almost all other areas of public and private life. `They don't care so why should we?' and `They get away with everything so we should be entitled to get away with stuff too.' A lack of sense of any sense of morality seems to be an essential requirement for politicians. In countries around the world leaders are arrested for theft and corruption and for taking advantage of their position. No one blinks at it. Blair and Brown have paid no price at all for the terrible things they did to Britain. They have, indeed, been richly rewarded. In business, science, sport and medicine there is now an almost complete lack of morality. There isn't even any sense of shame. No one apologises. The standard response for those caught cheating is to threaten to sue and to blame someone else. Drug taking in sport is rife because no one is ever really punished.

Politicians no longer respect us. On the contrary they (and their servants) treat us as enemies. Their knowledge is vast, their power extensive but their resolve is stiffened with bureaucracy. The only things they fear are the unknown and that which they cannot control. Oh, and the light of exposure and truth. Like vampires they fear the light. Oh how they fear the light. They scurry from it like cockroaches disappearing under the cooker.

In days gone by, genuine achievement and success depended on hard work, practise, patience, dedication, honesty, loyalty and a willingness to put up with boredom and overcome disappointment in order to get where you want to go, knowing that despite everything you might never get there. These are virtues which are no longer respected or taught. The whole world of reality television and modern celebrity has changed things. People who have no skills can be famous overnight through some quirk of fate or a few flicks of the surgeon's knife.

And for the rest of us there is a great sense of powerlessness. People are no longer in control of their own lives. Even very small things (how we dispose of our empty yoghurt cartons and beer bottles) are regulated. There are rules for everything. No one can possibly know the full extent of the law. I have met specialist lawyers who can't even keep up with the laws being brought in that relate to their own special area. People cannot fight back against authority and so they fight against one another; irritable, edgy and impatient they take out their anger on one another.

`You write books, don't you?' said The Princess's acquaintance before she left. I admitted that this was true. `I'd do that if I had the time,' she said.

19.18 p.m.

A chum who knows we regularly visit Paris asked me today why we don't go there by aeroplane. He's an unusual fellow who has a daily newspaper delivered but deliberately reads them a week late so that he can ignore most of the bad stuff. He's always depressed about something but I've given up trying to cheer him up. `You must learn to be positive,' I once told him. `I am,' he replied instantly. `I'm positive my life is crap.' He says flying is cheaper, which it undoubtedly is. I told him we travel by train because it's quicker (which is true). But that isn't the whole story. I hate flying. I hate the smooth, neat, plastic, antiseptic, ever smiling, charmless, morons who work in today's smooth, neat, plastic, antiseptic, charmless airports. I hate the constant queuing, the overpriced lukewarm tea, the fact that the lavatories are always closed because they are being cleaned and the way they put your flight details up on the departures board and then, with five minutes to go, tell you that the incoming plane you are waiting for has been delayed indefinitely because of a hailstorm in Ohio or a puncture in Athens.

I hate the fact that airports are full of people who, judging by the amount of luggage with which they are surrounded, are emigrating and have decided to move the entire contents of their eight bedroomed house on a scheduled flight. They have huge, metal framed suitcases; massive, canvas and zip suitcases which threaten to explode and hurl sweaters, socks, kitchen sinks and spare lingerie all around the airport (they usually have one case which has clearly already made an attempt to do just this and which is therefore tied up with lots of stout looking string); rucksacks with every pocket bulging; two sets of matching overnight bags; handbags and toilet bags and a wasteland of plastic shopping bags full of whatever it is that people feel the need to cram into plastic shopping bags. How aeroplanes are expected to lurch into the air and defy gravity when they are crammed with so much junk I will never know.

I hate the fact that we have to arrive at the airport two or three hours before the flight is due to take off (thereby virtually doubling the flight time of just about any European flight). There are two reasons for this. First, we have to get there early because airports and airlines only allocate one member of ground staff for every 30,000 potential passengers. This means that unless you are prepared to pay the extra 1550% for a first class ticket you have to queue for half an hour before they deign to rip up your ticket and give you a seat number. (Why they can't save everyone's time by giving you the seat number when you buy your ticket I cannot imagine though I expect it has something to do with the unions. The people at airports who rip bits out of your ticket always remind me of the usherettes in cinemas who sullenly tear your ticket in half when you get to the top of the stairs. What's the point? You can't get up the stairs without buying a ticket. What sort of job satisfaction do these people get? Do they have to be trained? `This morning we're going to show you what to do with the half of the ticket you've kept.') Second, we have to get there early so that we are forced to hang around the airport shops and spend all our holiday money before the plane even takes off. In the old days they were content with allowing the waitresses on the planes to flog the duty free, the perfume and the watches. (Sorry. They are not called waitresses are they. They aren't even stewardesses any more. These days the handers out of meals and instructors in seat belt fastening all have wonderfully grand titles. My favourite is 'In Flight On Board Senior Executive Director of Passenger Cabin Services' - a job description which must surely deserve an award.) These days the airports have got greedy. And boy have they got greedy. I know a bar at one European airport where a can of fizzy drink costs about the price of a meal in a four star restaurant. Whenever I went there I used to hang around just to see travellers handing back the drinks they'd just ordered. Wander around your average modern airport and you'll find that they've turned the whole damned place into a massive shopping precinct.

I can understand them selling books and magazines. (I confess that I would rather read anything in preference to an in-flight magazine). I can understand them selling bottles of booze. (There are still mugs around who think it is worthwhile buying alcohol at the airport and lugging it around with them for hours afterwards). And I can understand them selling sweets and crisps. (Unreliable research has shown that compared to the plastic rubbish they serve up on aeroplanes a bag of crisps and a packet of sweets are packed with tasty goodness). But these days you can buy a suit or a dress at an airport.

Don't people pack enough?

What sort of people are just about to get on the plane when they remember they haven't packed enough suits?

I was at an airport once where I saw a shop selling whole dinner services. Who the hell is going to buy a dinner service while they're waiting for a plane?

'Oh, gosh Maureen! Look! That reminds me - we must buy a dinner service!'

'Golly Henry. You're right. Let's get one now. It'll be so much easier to carry it on the plane to Majorca, take it to the hotel, and bring it back again than it will to pop into town when we get back.'

Or maybe people buy the darned things as presents. `Oh, look George. Let's buy your mum a dinner service instead of that knitted toilet roll cover in the shape of a donkey.'

`Wonderful idea Brenda. We've never bought her a dinner service before. Shall we take the 82 piece or the 134 piece?'

You can even buy luggage at the airport.

Are they really hoping that you're going to buy so much stuff that you have to buy another case?

Or do they imagine that some poor idiot is going to turn up with an armful of socks, shirts and undies and make a beeline for the luggage shop as soon as he gets through customs?

`Oh, thank heavens! You won't believe this but I completely forgot to put my stuff into a case! Silly old me.'

I even know an airport where they sell cars.

Now, I too dislike those grotty buses they sometimes make you take even when the plane is only about twenty yards away but I can see a car being a real problem. For a start how the hell would you get it into the overhead locker?

I hate the fact that no one ever smiles at airports. And I hate the fact that the walls are covered with lists of things you can't do and can't take on the plane with you. At Johannesburg airport they have a three foot diameter landmine and a six foot long bazooka stuck on the wall. Below them there is a notice telling travellers that they are not allowed to take such objects on board with them. At Paris Charles de Gaulle airport they always took away my Swiss army penknife and put it in the hold. This used to distress me. What, I wondered, would I do if called upon to perform a tracheotomy or remove a stone from a horse's hoof? Later, when I got on the plane, they gave me a knife with a blade sharper and twice as long.

I hate the fact that the seats seem to get closer and closer together every time I fly. I am six foot three inches tall and I have to sit sideways on most flights. Do the people who design aeroplanes think that the only people who fly are stunted Japanese bonsai people?

I hate the way other people are allowed to struggle onto the plane carrying six plastic bags, a canvas shoulder holdall, a huge cardboard box, a wicker laundry basket, an electronic organ in the original box and an oversized teddy bear. When I try to get on with my regulation size shoulder bag I'm sternly told that it has to go into the hold because there isn't any space left. Of course there isn't any damned space left: that idiot with the six plastic bags, a canvas shoulder holdall, a cardboard box, a wicker laundry basket, an electronic organ in the original box and an oversized teddy bear has filled up all the overhead lockers.

I hate it when one of the waitresses shows off the toys on her demonstration life jacket. I must have watched all that at least a million times and I still haven't the faintest idea where the life jacket is kept. Have you ever even seen the life jacket they say is under your seat? I think they sold all the life jackets a million years ago.

I hate the way the waitresses sell booze to other travellers. I feel uncomfortable, knowing that I'm flying inside a huge Molotov cocktail. And I hate the idiots who buy booze on planes and in airports and then fill what is left of the overhead lockers with plastic bags full of gin and whisky. Do they really need to save 36 pence that badly?

I hate the fact that the meals they give you always taste so bad that it is impossible to tell whether you are eating the food or the packaging. I hate those in-flight magazines which are full of maps with coloured lines all over them, articles about how Portuguese peasants have mastered the art of sun drying tomatoes and photographs of luggage that is so expensive that no one would ever dare let it out of their sight.

I hate the way the pilot is always so damned calm when anything goes wrong. `We're losing height,' he drawls, `but it's nothing to worry about.' `We're just going to jettison 45,000 gallons of high octane fuel over Swindon but there is no need for concern. All this is purely routine.' They're dumping 45,000 gallons of expensive fuel over Swindon and it's purely routine? Who are they kidding? I don't believe them.

I hate it when they let kids go into the cockpit during a flight. Kids always want to fiddle with things. I don't want to plunge into the Atlantic because some snotty nosed brat has pulled a lever he wasn't supposed to touch.

I hate it when the waitress tells us all that the pilot will order a taxi for anyone who wants one when we land. I don't want the pilot messing around on the radio ordering taxis, pizzas or take away Chinese meals. And I don't want him or co-pilot Biffo booking hotels or telling us what the weather is like either. I want the radio kept free for emergencies. And I want him piloting. I want his eyes glued on all those dially things underneath the windscreen. I want him to have a headache from concentrating by the time we've landed.

I hate the fact that there is only ever one customs officer on duty when the airport officials know damned well that twenty seven zillion planes are due in.

I hate flying. To be honest I hate trains, boats and cars almost as much. Like good wine, I just don't travel well. But I hate trains least of all. It is, all things considered, the only civilised way to travel. I haven't been on an aeroplane for years. And I hope I never have to board one again.

Airports are disgusting, unfriendly places staffed by people who clearly think they are superior to travellers – the people who pay their wages. The security guards are hired to prepare us for the New World. They are there to get us accustomed to being docile, and being humiliated. And hiring the guards enables the authorities to select future concentration camp guards. Every day I discover more evidence that governments are desperate to humiliate us and make us afraid. Not content with making travellers remove their shoes or go through full-body scanners they have given guards the right to touch breasts and groins. This has, of course, given these minimum wage grope fiends enormous opportunities to enjoy their power. A bladder cancer survivor's urine bag burst during an over aggressive inspection. A breast cancer survivor was told to remove her prosthetic breast. The head of the American Federation of Government Employees announced that screeners `do not get any pleasure from the new measures'. The real problem is that although at least one screener has been punched in the face (bravo that man) most people put up with this entirely pointless and intrusive crap, convinced by government lies that it is keeping terrorism under control. On the other hand I read today that when Hillary Clinton, the US Secretary of State was asked if she would submit to a groping (sorry, pat-down) she said `Not if I could avoid it.' And in order to keep flights moving pilots and flight attendants are now excused groping.

And so The Princess and I travel by train. And if we can't get there by train we don't go there.

6

10.07 a.m.

I received a letter from a reader who said `I have read many of your books. The frightening thing is that I seem to agree with just about all your views.' I replied: `Please don't be frightened about agreeing with most of my views. I agree with most of yours and am not in the slightest bit frightened about it.'

15.22 p.m.

A growing number of businesses now charge a penalty if we want to pay by cheque or to receive an invoice or receipt through the post. They want to do everything online. The excuse, of course, is that they're saving the environment. This is nonsense. They are cutting their costs. In order to keep complete accounts to satisfy HMRC I have to print out the invoice anyway. So all that is happening is that I'm having to subsidise the company that is billing me.

7

14.15 p.m.

The BMW is still alive but we are conscious that it has now done over 100,000 miles. This may not be a great deal for a modern car but the car seems tired and we have decided to buy a truck. There are several reasons for this. First, I have never owned a truck. Actually, I have never owned a sports car or a truck but I am clearly too old to own a sports car (even if I could cram my legs into one) so a truck seems a much better bet. Second, the roads are increasingly angry places these days and a classless, tough-looking truck should give us something of an edge over motorists in ordinary cars. Third, although I realise that a four wheel drive in itself is of limited value we want a four wheel drive vehicle to help us cope with muddy tracks and unsalted, ungritted roads. And most of the four wheel drive cars are either poncy or flimsy or agricultural. Fourth, we want something with high ground clearance that will withstand pot holes and enable us to drive over kerbs, humps, bumps and all the other bits of decoration the highways people insist on scattering about these days. Fifth, we want something big enough to carry loads of books.

We were going to buy a Japanese truck. But one big manufacturer has, after several weeks, finally admitted that they have stopped making trucks. Another (the one which has brakes which don't always do what they are supposed to do) makes trucks which are too small for me to get into. `How do you put the seat back?' I asked the salesman. `It is back sir,' he replied. `They are not big people.'

We decided to look at Ford trucks since Ford is an American company and Americans are so big that they probably make their trucks big enough for tall people.

We went for a test drive. Oddly enough, no one asked me if I had a driving licence entitling me to drive a stick shift vehicle (though I do have). I cannot buy the truck until I have proved that I have insured it though if my licence weren't valid the insurance would be invalid. There is tons of space inside and the truck is packed with extras which come in with the price. It has a CD player which is far too complicated to understand, heated seats, windscreen wipers which have many choices of speed and clever little gauges which tell me if we are about to tip over. It also has by far the best heating system I have ever had (and I've owned two Bentleys, one Rolls Royce, a BMW and three Volvos). I particularly like it because it has massive ground clearance (great for driving over potholes, pavements and traffic islands) and The Princess likes it because it sits high up in the air and so she can see the animals in the fields as we drive past. We can also look down (literally) on other motorists. It is a sort of fully-grown Volvo Estate. The only snag is that the headlights seem to me to be only slightly better than having a man walk in front holding a candle. In all other respects it is just as good as most of the far more expensive cars I have driven. For example, I cannot find the switch for the fog lights. I can't remember ever owning a car where I could find the fog lights without stopping, or find out how to switch them on without finding the manual, so this is reassuring.

I know nothing about cars (I hate it when men from the RAC or the AA ask me to open the bonnet because I never know how to do it) but I talk knowingly to the salesman about payload.

`What do you think?' I asked The Princess.

`What colours do they do?'

We choose a dark green one.

We didn't like the red one, thought the blue rather sudden and agreed that the black one looked like a cross between a hearse and something gangsters might drive. Having a green one will enable us to tell anyone who asks that we have bought a 'green' vehicle.

8
14.39 p.m.
I bought a second-hand edition of *The Fiction Editor, the Novel, and the Novelist* by American publisher and super-editor Thomas McCormack. Tom helped edit my early Edward Vernon novels in days that promised much. He had just edited, published and made huge hits of the James Herriot books and he'd spotted my Edward Vernon novels (published by Macmillan and Pan in the UK) as a natural medical follow on. We met at the Connaught hotel in London and it seemed that I was about to become a gazillion selling author in the USA. Then all went quiet and my agent reported that Tom had gone skiing and had broken a leg. The books came out in the USA but without Tom guiding and pushing them they quietly disappeared.

9
20.19 p.m.
We spent the day watching cricket. Thanks to health and safety rules, kids are not allowed onto the pitch during intervals to have a little exercise and play cricket with tennis balls. This was often the best part of the day. The health and safety cretins would presumably rather children sat at home with the curtains drawn hunched in front of a computer screen playing `Deathwar 16'.

10
21.34 p.m.
We went to London where there was a tube strike. The staff apparently want a 5% pay rise and a guarantee of no redundancies (jobs for life). Only people working for the State could do this in the middle of the worst recession ever. The whole nature of striking has changed. Modern workers (especially those working for the State) don't go on strike to gain enough money to buy food, they go on strike because they want enough money for three foreign holidays and a second car. They also want free travel, free

health insurance and a non-contributory, index-linked pension at three quarters of their final salary. The result of this latest piece of underground lunacy was, inevitably, a taxi queue at Paddington Station that stretched into the station and into the distance along Platform 1. The Princess and I walked out of the station and caught a cab two hundred yards away in Praed Street. It took three minutes at the most. The cabbie was a nice fellow who had been driving for just 18 months. He said he had never seen anything like it and was worried about going to the England match at Wembley that evening His concern was that he might have to take a fare there and would then get mixed up in some nastiness. As he drives us to Harrods he complains about the regulations which mean that he can get fined for putting a wheel in the wrong place and about the mountainous speed bumps which have given him a bad back. He also complains about the fact that London has replaced its Routemaster buses with deadly bendy buses. He said that the disabled can get free taxis so there was never any need to have buses they could use as well. As we drive around there are heaps of roadworks. I counted 34 workmen, all doing nothing, unless you count drinking tea and chatting as work. Not one workman was doing anything remotely constructive. This was between 11.30 a.m. to 12.30 p.m. I noticed that London buses carry signs boasting that they are 18 metres long. How easily we hand over our imperial heritage. Aren't yards and feet good enough for London transport? In Harrods we called in at the pet store where kittens sell for £1,000 or more and are guaranteed lives of luxury.

When we left Knightsbridge the traffic was so bad that we abandoned our next taxi and walked to the National Liberal Club, slipping between the Foreign Office and the Treasury. I hadn't been there for years since as a boy I used to wander round London just for fun. I remember that I walked past these imposing buildings I felt full with pride and respect for the men and women working within them. Today, I walked past and felt nothing but contempt. That's sad. In our modern world commitment, dedication, responsibility and respect are all just `jargon' used, with cynicism, to spin the truth and escape the consequences of the greed and incompetence which are so commonplace in these buildings.

We had lunch with a foreign publisher who is in London. This was the reason for the trip to London. He is a pleasant fellow but has a slight thyrotoxic condition which gives him a slightly insane look. He reminds me of one of those men who used to parade up and down in the street carrying placards warning of the nighness of the end of the world. He has just come back from a trip to New York where he had lunch at one of those places where patrons stop by the fish tank to pick out their meals. He was sitting nearby and said he found it fascinating to watch the other patrons choosing their food.

`Which one do you like best?' a mother asked a small boy of around six or seven.

`That one with the orange patch,' said the boy, picking out an easily identifiable fish. The parents then said which fish they liked best. The man in charge of the fish tank nodded and the family group proceeded to their table.

After the family had eaten, on the way out of the restaurant, the boy stopped at the fish tank.

`Where's my fish?' he asked, after studying the contents of the tank.

`What do you mean, dear?' asked his mother.

`That fish I liked,' explained the boy. `It's gone.'

`You atc it, dear!' explained his insensitive and stupid mother.

The anecdote reminded me of a friend of ours who is in the restaurant business. He is fairly ruthless and single-minded and has skin a rhinoceros would envy. Against the advice of his wife, his accountant and just about everyone he knew he opened a `Pick your own Rabbit' restaurant, designed along the lines of the places where patrons are invited to choose a fish or a lobster. The experiment was a miserable failure. He never understood why.

The publisher buys a few books, choosing them (as most publishers do) on the titles rather than the content. I remember going to Lisbon some years ago. My Portuguese agent and I visited a publisher and showed him a dozen covers for new books I had written for my EMJ imprint. The publisher immediately leapt on one, grabbed it and said `I want to publish this immediately!' He bought it there and then, without having any idea what the book was about. The title was *How To Stop Your Doctor Killing You*. (He subsequently published 14 of my books in Portuguese.)

Newspapers are sold on their `splash' - the contents of the front page. That's why editors keep some headlines pretty well permanently set up. They know that 'Cancer Cure Found' and 'Who Killed Princess Diana? New Evidence!' will sell papers. Similarly, books sell by their title.

After lunch at the Royal Horseguards The Princess and I wandered up Charing Cross road, browsed in the bookshops in Cecil Court and in the coin shop nearby, made a detour through Covent Garden to see the street entertainers, visited the music shops in Denmark Street to buy some sheet music for The Princess and then walked up Shaftsbury Avenue to Piccadilly Circus via Gerard Street and Chinatown. We then went down to Jermyn Street because I wanted to buy a new Grosvenor style hat at Bates the Hatter. I have left my other one in Paris where it seems happy enough. The Grosvenor is a sort of Fedora but with a slightly narrower brim. I'm delighted to see that I am still a 7 and 3 eighths. The assistant at Bates steamed the hat for me but was clearly rather glum and preoccupied. He explains that their landlord, the Crown Estate, is redeveloping part of Jermyn Street and Bates the Hatter will go. I suspect it will be replaced by a store selling diet coke and sandwiches or overpriced plastic models of the London buses that no longer run. Maybe it will be another Tesco mini store. Bates the Hatter has been protecting the heads of Englishmen for over 100 years. It will no doubt emerge elsewhere but not, I suspect, in Jermyn Street. The Princess and I both feel very sad. I bought my first hat at Bates when I was a newly qualified junior hospital doctor. It cost about a month's salary. It was pouring outside and I remember asking the assistant if the hat I had purchased would cope satisfactory with getting wet. `Sir,' he said, clearly hurt by the question, and drawing himself up to his full five feet six inches, `We have been making hats for kings for over 100 years.' It wasn't until I got outside that I realised that kings don't walk about much in the rain. To revive our dampened spirits we took afternoon tea at Fortnum and Masons. The teacake was magnificent. I have always had a soft spot for teacakes and crumpets and other delights of English teatime. The Princess and I once stayed at Gidleigh Park hotel in Devon and I will never forget being told that the chef didn't approve of teacakes or crumpets and wouldn't have them in the hotel. We never went back. At Fortnum and Mason I was moved to overtip outrageously. The bill came to £25 for two teas and one teacake. We then walked up the Burlington Arcade (where I used to buy my bow ties when I was a medical student) and turned left into Bond Street where there is a magnificent sculpture of Churchill and Roosevelt sharing a bench together. It is raining but at the top end of Bond Street there are taxis galore and this is surely a sign of the times. From the lower end of Bond Street we can see a long string of yellow lights as several dozen empty taxis move slowly down towards us. We took one of the cabs to Paddington and then sat in the first class lounge after buying food for a picnic on the train. We agree that we like London better in the winter when it goes dark early and it's raining slightly. `And a bit foggy,' adds The Princess. `London really needs a little fog.' She's right, as usual.

As we sat in the lounge we realised that apart from the cabbies, my publisher and the man in Bates, we had not met one person for whom English was their first language. In the station branch of WH Smith the assistant had no idea what I meant when I asked for a receipt. I tried `bill', `invoice' and `ticket' before resorting to sign language. Her colleague eventually helped her understand. I'm not surprised to read in today's paper that three quarters of all London property is these days sold to foreigners. (Most of them crooks, though the paper doesn't say that, of course.) The Princess said she was going to learn a foreign language so that when we go to London she can communicate with shop assistants and waiters. The problem is: which language should she learn? I said I was surprised there wasn't a chain of clothes stores across London called Burkha King. The Princess said she thought that saying this was probably the sort of thing that could get me into trouble.

At the station we picked up a pile of magazines to read on the train. It occurred to me that editors, advertising copywriters (and film directors) all have the power to elevate society and to make the world a better place. Instead, most of them choose to take the cruel and vulgar route; creating a brutal and more selfish society. It's the easy and obviously more profitable route.

11
18.58 p.m.

We had a glum morning in Taunton. To begin with we went to the railway station to buy tickets for London. We buy them there rather than in the town where we live because the staff at our local station are horrid and cannot operate their computer. If you want to do anything complicated such as buy a ticket they go into meltdown. I joined what seemed to be the shortest queue and stood behind a woman who was at the window. Just as I joined this tiny queue the woman's telephone rang. Instead of ignoring it, which is what any normal, polite person would have done, the woman took her phone out of her bag and answered it. And then, instead of saying `I'm busy at the moment can I call you back' she carried on chatting. It clearly wasn't an important conversation. She was chatting with a friend about a relative's baby and she spoke loudly as though we should all be interested in her opinions on the matter. The ticket seller just folded her arms and waited. After a few minutes of this I tapped the woman on the shoulder. `Excuse me,' I said, as politely as I could, `there is a queue behind you.' The woman glowered at me and carried on with her conversation. She had that air of command that, in my experience, is only found among infant school teachers and receptionists at GPs surgeries, though I suppose army generals must have it too, though probably not so vividly. The mobile telephone seems to have destroyed what remained of polite behaviour. I once picked up my Dad from hospital and found that my car was blocked in by a man in a white van. My Dad was quite poorly at the time and I wanted to get him home as quickly as I could. I knocked on the driver's window to ask him if he would mind moving his vehicle. The man held out his mobile phone and yelled at me `Can't you see I'm on the phone?'

As usual I had trouble buying railway tickets because my request was a rather complicated one. I wanted to buy two return tickets to London. And I wanted the reserved seats to be next to one another in first class. This always throws the computer into hysterics.

Eventually, after about three quarters of an half an hour of discussion and confrontation, we got our tickets. We parked the car and then walked into the town past the cricket ground hoping to catch sight of the cricket. Unfortunately, it was spitting slightly and although spectators were sitting around in short-sleeved shirts reading their papers the cricketers were running for the pavilion as though they would melt if they stayed out. Cricketers really are wimps these days. They all want to get into the pavilion to text their agents.

The Princess and I then parted so that we could do our separate shopping chores. I called into Jessops, the photographic shop, to buy more ink for my printer. Since The Princess had bought me the printer from one of their shops it seemed fair to expect them to have the inks for it. They didn't. The only cartridge they had was magenta.

Next, I called at Lloyds Bank to liberate some of my money. Unfortunately, the automatic teller machine printed a slip saying that it had given me money but didn't give me anything. I went into the bank and complained. Eventually, a clerk admitted that the machine was faulty, reluctantly filled in a form and asked me to sign it. When I'd done this I asked him for a copy. He told me that it wasn't bank policy to allow customers to have copies of forms they'd signed. I told him it was my policy to demand copies of forms I'd signed and said that since I was the customer my protocol overruled the bank's protocol. He stalked off and after I stood around singing verses from *Sound of Music* songs he eventually came back and gave me a copy of the form I'd signed.

I then went to the opticians, hoping to have my eyes re-checked. I can't remember the name of the store but there was a large sign in the window advertising eye tests. `There's no optician here,' said two assistants in unison. They seemed really pleased by their inability to help and, to be honest, they seemed rather surprised by my request. It was as though I'd asked them to sole my shoes.

I then retired to a café and bought a cup of weak, unpleasant coffee while I waited for The Princess.

When we got back home I had an unfortunate meeting with a neighbour of ours. He's one of those people who is determined to be one up on everyone else and he talks incessantly about his boat. He suffers from short man disease and is obsessed with one upmanship. He has one of those straggly Che Guevara beards that look like wispy pubic hair and his favourite saying is `you come into the world with nothing so if you go out in debt you've made a profit'. When he found out that I write books he said it was something he'd always thought he would do one day. `I suppose anyone can write books if they want to,' he said. His wife has an irritating laugh that sounds like troubled plumbing and always ends in a particularly unpleasant snort that would attract curious looks in a farmyard. She is a distinctly unpleasant woman and I some time ago decided that she has pus not blood in her veins. Now that we have our rubbish collected once a fortnight he drives to the municipal tip every Saturday afternoon. This annoys me unreasonably partly because he constantly claims to be 'green' and 'environmentally aware' and driving a 15 mile round trip to the municipal dump can hardly be described as 'green' and partly because I feel that this is exactly what the council wants us to do. If they can force more of us to take our rubbish to the tip they will, eventually, be able to stop making collections completely. I suspect, however, that my neighbour actually enjoys his weekly trip to the dump. It is, I think, his idea of a good afternoon out. He is an immensely boastful fellow. Whenever I see him he tells me his latest boating story and, over the months, the boat seems to have increased in size and importance. Today, there was a rubber inflatable strapped onto a trailer which was parked outside his house. 'Is this the tender to your boat?' I asked him, honestly thinking he'd be pleased by my interest. He went red. 'This is my boat,' he said. I don't know which of us was most embarrassed. I felt bad for a few minutes but when The Princess told me that she'd bought some crumpets for tea I quickly got over it.

12
11.49 a.m.
'I hate it when things are going well,' said a fellow I know this morning. Surprised, I asked him why. 'Because then they can only get worse,' he explained. 'It's only a question of time before something goes wrong to spoil things.' He is older than the devil (and some would say twice as dangerous) so I fear he knows of what he speaks.

13
16.23 p.m.
A zip drive I had ordered through the Internet arrived today. It doesn't work. More and more people seem to be selling stuff that is completely broken or doesn't work properly. They rely upon the

fact that it is too much trouble for buyers to send products back. Sellers are (as with this one) often helped by the fact that the goods they send out are not accompanied by an earthly address. I have now lost count of the number of things I've bought that are oversold or misrepresented. Fraud, not pornography, is the mainstay of the Internet.

14
15.16 p.m.
A foreign film company asked for permission to bring a crew to Publishing House. They wanted to interview me. I say `No' very firmly. Last year a film crew sent by the scientologists did some filming at Publishing House. Despite my asking them not to do so they turned off all the computers (they apparently didn't like the modest humming noise they were making). Naturally, they didn't close down the programmes before doing this. They came to interview me because my views on psychiatry and on psychotropic drugs match theirs. But I will never again have anything to do with these people.

15
11.54 a.m.
`My husband bought this but he's dead now and I'd prefer something about dogs or cooking,' wrote a reader from Essex. `Please send me something suitable.' The unwanted copy of *The Man Who Inherited A Golf Course* was sent back without any postage on the parcel and there was no mention of postage for sending another book. The returned book had a large pan mark on the cover. It had obviously been used in the kitchen and is quite unsaleable.

16
12.03 p.m.
BP seems to me to have been painfully honest in dealing with America after the recent oil spill but the company has in return received nothing but playground style abuse. BP's shareholders would, I fear, have probably been much better off if the highly-paid executives had denied all responsibility and told American lawyers that they would make sure any court cases lasted at least a

century. This is standard drug and tobacco company policy and it works in America. BP style honesty is expensive and destructive. Compared to the Bhopal tragedy in India in 1984 the BP disaster was but an insect bite. I sold my BP shares at a modest profit as soon as the crisis started because it was clear that the whole thing was going to become a political game - with BP playing the part of the football. A lot of people in America (including a good many writ wranglers) are going to make a huge amount of money out of BP shareholders. British pensioners will suffer so that American lawyers can buy new planes and boats. Many of the people in the Gulf area will, I suspect, make more money out of their compensation than they would have ever made before the spill. The mock indignation, feigned concern and Olympic class hypocrisy of American politicians have astonished me. Writ wranglers, bureaucrats and campaigners got 19 out of every 20 dollars paid by tobacco companies and I suspect it will be the same for the billions due to be paid out by BP. Apparently the person responsible for dishing out money taken from (largely British) pensioners intends to 'err on the side of the claimant'. Very nice too. Union Carbide gave a one off means-tested ex gratia payment of 1,500 rupees to families affected in the 1984 Bhopal chemical disaster. Incidentally, I haven't seen any mention in the press that BP gave Obama $77,051 towards his presidential campaign. Americans use more oil than anyone, they dirty the planet, they ignore all calls for restraint and for protecting the environment and they demand (and get) the cheapest oil on the planet. They complain about China polluting the planet but there are five times as many Chinese as Americans and yet the Americans still produce darned near as much pollution and greenhouse gas emissions as the Chinese.

Everything that happens in America has to be the biggest, best, or most dramatic and so BP's mess was treated as though it was a gazillion times more damaging than the Bhopal disaster. That (a real disaster) killed several thousand people but they were all foreign and, therefore, nowhere near as important. The Americans mess up everyone else's country but get very pissed if anyone wears dirty shoes in their own godforsaken land. It is no wonder that their coming fall will be cheered by the world's citizens.

When BP started talking about blocking the leak with golf balls and old car tyres I felt that someone wasn't entirely sure of what they were doing. And the company's endless screw-ups in dealing with the crisis at every stage (including losing control of the story) seemed pathetic. I rather suspect that BP is the sort of company which doesn't allow its employees to walk up and down stairs while clutching a cup of coffee but will ignore the big health and safety issues because they aren't easily defined in an everyday manual.

Obama, the Great Betrayer, must surely be the most disappointing President of modern times. The man whom I predicted would let everyone down has stuffed British shareholders for political brownie points. Other American politicians and media personalities turned the whole thing into an overtly racist attack on Britain. It was a bit rich to see the nation which has built its wealth on theft and bombing complaining about a bit of oil getting into the wrong place.

Any Briton who has savings or who has invested in any sort of pension fund will have been made distinctly poorer by BP's incompetence and by the sneery, wolfish, Brit-hating American politicians who joined in the `hurl a brick at BP' campaign and demanded that the dividend be stopped.

I wonder if British politicians would have had the guts to insist on an American oil company stopping dividend payments to American shareholders if it had polluted British beaches. And would the American oil company have obeyed?

Stupid question.

Incidentally, Americans are always keen to bash Britain but they are also keen to come here. And when they get here they live off us. The rate of unemployment among Americans in Britain is among the highest of any group of immigrants and considerably higher than the rate of unemployment among indigenous Britons.

22.08 p.m.
In the bad old days I used to receive letters from publishers offering me money for the rights in my books. Today I had two letters inviting me to pay to turn my books into e-books or audio books. My world has been turned upside down.

17

`Oh, I wish I could buy this house,' said the estate agent when we visited a cottage last week. `Isn't it wonderful?' She looked so happy, so overwhelmed by delight and expectation, that I was worried that she was going to have an orgasm. She stood there, dreamily entranced by the beauty of it all. Estate agents remind me of the staff who woman the tills in the clothing department at Marks and Spencers. Every time I buy a blouse or a jumper or a skirt for The Princess the woman taking my money looks at the present I've bought admiringly, and says: `Oh, isn't this wonderful. I haven't seen this one. It must have just come in.' The estate agent, like the woman in Marks and Spencer, is telling me what good taste I have. And so, even though I know what is going on, I like it. But it is sometimes necessary, with estate agents at any rate, to bring some reality back into the proceedings. `Do you know if there is mains drainage?' I asked the estate agent, desperate to bring her back to reality. `Or is the property equipped with a septic tank?'

Of course, male agents do it too. They can, indeed, sometimes be even more outrageously enthusiastic. We were in an estate agency late this afternoon, looking at some brochures a nice young man was showing us, when suddenly his boss, a senior deceiver, waltzed into view. He wore a green and brown flecked Harris Tweed jacket, a pair of grey flannels with razor sharp creases, a shirt with a light green and yellow check and a club tie I didn't recognise. He introduced himself and asked what we were looking for. The young man explained. `I have just the thing!' said the man in the Harris Tweed jacket. `Perfect for you. Your dream home. Came on the market this morning. Just got the brochures in from the printers. What are you doing now? Can you come and see it?'

The Princess and I looked at each other. It was dark and getting late. We were hungry, tired and ready to go home. We had long ago eaten all our sandwiches. It had been a long and fruitless day. But this might be the one. The Holy Grail of houses. I muttered something about our not having any immediate plans or commitments.

`Splendid,' said Harris Tweed. `Come with me. I'll lead. You follow in your car.' He drove us, in his expensive Audi, round to the car park where we had left the truck. (In the same way that antique dealers drive Volvo estate cars so estate agents drive Audis. It is, I think, some sort of industry wide requirement.) We then followed him on a 20 mile drive through the dark. I had no idea where we were going but we went there very quickly.

When we arrived at our destination in the centre of a small village, the Harris Tweed signalled for us to stop. He pointed out a parking place for us, while he parked his Audi 50 yards up the lane in a gateway. He came back to us at a run and then took us to the front door of a small house.

Inside the house Harris Tweed took us on the usual tour. He knew the house very well and pointed out every virtue and every possibility. As we left the guest bedroom he stopped suddenly and turned towards us. `I love this house,' he said. `If my wife left me and I were homeless I'd buy this. It's a house to be happy in.'

We finished the tour, thanked him, promised to think it over and received instructions on how to find the motorway but we had both known from the moment we'd seen it that it wasn't the right house for us. It was far too small. There was no garden. It was overlooked by several other houses. There was no place to park a car. As soon as we got home The Princess made dinner while I sent an e-mail thanking Harris Tweed for his time and effort and telling him that we wouldn't be making an offer.

After dinner The Princess went onto the Internet to look for more properties. The search must go on. After 20 minutes she handed me the netbook she was using.

`Look at this one.'

I looked.

`Isn't it the house we looked at this afternoon?'

`Yes. Now look at the date it was put on the market.'

I looked. The house had been on the market for two years. The asking price had been gradually reduced from £850,000 to £830,000 to £810,000 to £799,950 to £775,000, and to its current price of £750,000.

22.02 p.m.

I am totally convinced that most publishing operations in the UK are now variations on the vanity-publishing theme. Big publishers are subsidised by their television company sales or by selling copies of books specially written for corporate buyers. Occasionally a huge international hit (such as the Harry Potter series) will completely alter a publisher's bottom line. But this is simply a matter of luck. No one in publishing knew that the Potter books were going to be a phenomenon. (If Bloomsbury had known they would have published more than a few hundred when they produced the first book. They didn't limit the initial print run simply to excite the second-hand and antiquarian book trade.)

18
16.17 p.m.
We received a letter telling us that the waste of heat loss through windows can cost as much as £25 a month and that we should buy new windows. The cost of the new windows will be £15,000. 'It would pay for itself in 50 years,' said The Princess. 'Assuming that the windows lasted that long.'

20.46 p.m.
In *National Geographic* magazine there is a photograph of workers wiping oil from grass on the coastline around the Gulf of Mexico. They were using diaper like clothes to wipe up seven billion blades of grass. I'm sure that helped the environment. I wonder how much oil was consumed, and how much carbon was produced, to manufacture all those cloths. Pensioners whose BP dividends were spent on this farcical endeavour may or may not take comfort from the fact that the degree of marsh grass contamination turned out to be 'small'.

19
10.02 a.m.
I needed to telephone an insurance company. As usual I got the message: 'We are experiencing a much higher than usual call volume and so there will be some delay...'. It occurred to me that whenever I telephone a bank or insurance company or Government department I always get this message. It is clearly their default message to excuse the fact that they do not have enough people answering their telephones. My time is clearly far less important than that of a call centre operator.

15.07 p.m.

I see that a woman has been fined £75 for feeding ducks in a public park. Now I know that our society has crumbled.

17.12 p.m.

I feel particularly creaky today. Several joints seem about to seize up. Old age is a shipwreck. Every moment is a crisis and I am constantly fighting to survive. As soon as I have overcome the sea, the wind has a go, then there's the sun, and the storms and the hunger and the sharks and the cannibals. Desert island life is just one damned thing after another. Those who think life is exciting when they are young should just wait until they are old. The one big advantage (for a man at least) is that hair care is neither time consuming nor expensive. Sadly, however, the time and money saved on maintaining the roof is needed tenfold for the preservation of the crumbling ramparts and the creaky drawbridge.

On top of all the inevitable physical trials and tribulations I fear that I feel distinctly uncomfortable in the company of people who are at home in the 21st century; computer people, derivatives traders and women who think dresses are only for weddings; people who think civil servants are entitled to bonuses if they turn up and do their jobs and those who are driven only by a sense of entitlement.

I suspect that I am beginning to find things to worry about so that I do not worry about The Princess. I find that if I am lucky trivial worries occupy my mind for a few minutes at a time.

21.14 p.m.

A reader has sent an e-mail complaining that I did not reply to a letter written two days ago. I do always reply to mail but it sometimes takes a while. So that I can concentrate on what I think I do best (writing books) we only pick up our mail every two weeks or so. Everything is kept by the Post Office for us to collect. We never answer the door unless we know who is there and want to let them in. And we hardly ever answer the telephone. My dislike of the telephone goes back a long way. When I was a GP the telephone ruled my life. For day after day I was at its beck and call. It would ring all day, all night and then all the next day. When I worked as a columnist and writer for *The Daily Star* and then *The*

Sun the phone rang just as determinedly. And it rang seven days a week. `Give us 750 words on what it is like to be crushed to death. You have 30 minutes.' `Do 500 words on what it is like to die in a plane crash. You can have an hour.' I honestly believe that the best practice for a writer is to work for one of the tabloids. Articles for the tabloids need to be sharp and tight with every word counting. It is widely recognised in what used to be called Fleet Street that by far the best writers work for the tabloids rather than the broadsheets - many have, indeed, graduated to the tabloids from the broadsheets. Writing books requires a completely different style, of course. But a felicity with words doesn't hurt. I've had a mobile telephone since around 1983 (it was the size and weight of two house bricks) and cannot understand what people find to say all the time these days. I turn mine on only when I need to use it or if The Princess and I are separated temporarily (because we are shopping, for example). If my phone has been accidentally left switched on I ignore any noises it makes partly because there is no one else I want to take phone calls from, partly because I have answered enough urgent phone calls to last anyone a lifetime, and partly because no one has the number and so if it rings it will be a wrong number.

23.56 p.m.

I have just found a note I made this morning. I spotted a notice in a small local shop. I rather liked it and wrote it down. `High quality, good service, low price. Pick two.'

20

11.49 a.m.

The default condition these days is to have junk mail bunged through your door every day by the postman. You have to ask not to get it. But asking makes no damned difference. We've tried. And it doesn't work. The junk keeps flowing and fills up our recycling bin every week, leaving little room for anything else.

14.19 p.m.

An advertising salesman for one of the national newspapers tells me that his business is in terrible trouble. Apparently, when the Labour Government was in power it was the single largest source of advertising revenue in the UK. No car company, no building society, no soap powder manufacturer came even close. I am not surprised.

21
14.04 p.m.
The Princess and I were in a pub today, drinking coffee and reading. We were sitting near to the bar where two men were sitting on bar stools. Both looked to be in their sixties, though I suspect they might have been younger than that. Both were hugely overweight, both were drinking pints of beer and both had nicotine stains on their fingers. Both were wearing jeans and checked shirts. One had long hair at the sides and the back but very little hair on top. The appearance of the hair at the sides and the back was his choice. The absence of hair on the top was God's choice. The other man had a shaved head but you could see where he would be bald if he had not chosen to shave. One had a small earring in his left ear. They were arguing, though not with any anger. To my surprise they were discussing the fact that they both have high blood pressure.

`I bet my blood pressure is higher than yours,' said the one with the earring. `My doctor says it's the highest he's ever seen.'

`My doctor brought in another partner to check mine,' said the second. `He couldn't believe it when he took it himself.

These two guys were competitive about their blood pressure problems. For a few minutes they discussed drugs. They knew all the latest information about drugs. They knew the options, the side effects and the advantages of different types of treatment. They could not have known more if they had just attended a symposium on hypertension. I was impressed.

`My doctor says I'll be lucky to live another six months if they don't manage to get my blood pressure down,' said the guy with the earring.

`Mine says I could drop down dead at any moment,' replied the other. He finished his pint and raised his glass to the barman. `Two more, please, Geoff,' he says.

18.37 p.m.

A reader has sent me a bad review for *Oil Apocalypse* which he found on the Internet. The review, by someone who spells author as Authur or Auther (he or she tries both, presumably in the vain hope that one might be close) doesn't seem to have bothered to read the book. The EU likes laws. Surely there should be one requiring those who review books (and thereby affect my livelihood) to be able to show that they have at least looked at the book they are writing about. (I realise that requiring them to have read it would probably be too much to ask). I wonder how many people realise that a large proportion of Web reviews are written and put online by people who have a vested interest in promoting a particular prejudice; many are written by competitors (eager to give their own book or Web presence a plug), by people with a grudge or by a lobbyists paid to grind a particular brand of axe.

22
10.22 a.m.
I happened to be looking out of the window when the binmen called. The council uses four different lorries these days because of the variety of types of rubbish the EU forces them to collect. The lorries are specially made and look very expensive. The whole process takes everyone much longer. The capital costs are higher and the running costs of these lorries must be huge. The lorry that collects plastics and paper and cardboard of the right thickness was parked outside in the street for seven minutes, blocking the road and chugging out diesel fumes. A long line of cars slowly collected behind it. They, of course, were also chugging out diesel and petrol fumes. When they finally rumbled on to the next house, where it would doubtless take them another seven minutes to sort out the rubbish, they left behind them a litter of debris on the roadway; bottles and cans and bits of paper that they'd dropped. Most people leave their bins outside permanently, of course. I don't blame them. People leave the unsightly bins on their front doorsteps or the pavement (creating another hazard for pedestrians) because who wants to wheel one of those huge, dirty beasts through their home? They are smelly and unsightly. And so, much of England is now permanently disfigured with green and black plastic bins. It's almost impossible to take a picture of a beautiful English village without the picture being spoilt by waste bins. Pretty villages and

261

dignified towns and cities everywhere are ruined by the inglorious sight of plastic refuse bins parked permanently on the pavement. And so it will be until we find a government wise enough to extricate us from the clutches of that arch fascist organisation the European Union. How long will it be before there is a massive spread of infections now that streets are for ever full of unsightly rubbish bins?

15.56 p.m.

The Princess and I were in a charity shop. `There's a thing here to put on your knob if it gets stuck,' shouted a woman to her husband. Everyone in the shop turned and stared. It turned out that she had found a device to help arthritis sufferers open sticking doors.

23

17.24 p.m.

For some months I have been trying to escape from a variety of mailing lists. Magazines which I don't want still arrive. Mailshots for services in which I have absolutely no interest still pour in. Now that we are strictly limited in how much rubbish we can get rid of I find these unwanted bits of paper even more annoying than before. I usually tear open the wrappers, burn the bits with my name on, and put the rest into a public waste bin. I don't understand why mailing companies find it so hard to stop sending out unwanted material. It is no advantage to them to send out expensive mailings which end up in the bin. After my mother died, my father spent a year writing letter after letter asking companies not to send material to my mother. But the letters kept arriving and he found it deeply depressing. Even after his death mailshots were still pouring in for them both. It really is not difficult for large companies to remove names from mailing lists. And it is discourteous and commercially stupid not to do so.

19.28 p.m.

A note from our printers is always horrifying. The price of paper never seems to stay the same for two weeks running. The cost of buying the paper on which to print a book has rocketed. But then other costs have soared too. The costs of setting and printing a book have gone up. The cost of producing a cover and binding the book into its cover have risen dramatically. The cost of providing a dustwrapper has soared. The cost of transporting a pile of books from one place to another has rocketed too. The cost of storage has risen. The result is that an ordinary sized trade paperback, with a modest print run of 1,000 or 2,000 can cost £2 to £3 to produce and an ordinary sized hardback can cost £4 or £5 when all the various costs have been added together. Those are prices before the costs of providing office space and warehousing and staff salaries and insurance and administration have been included.

Despite this dramatic rise in costs, books cost the readers less these days than they did a decade or so ago. Books are ridiculously underpriced these days. The result is that publishers make little or no profit and tend to be subsidised by other parts of their enterprises. Even when sensible prices are given these are smashed down by supermarket or Internet booksellers which have demanded, and received, a massive discount. So a £20 hardback book can usually be bought for a third of that the minute it is on sale. It's difficult to see where the profit lies, for out of what the publisher receives must be paid the cost of making and storing the book, the promotional costs, transport costs (most modern books are obscenely and unnecessarily large because that is what the trade has encouraged people to expect) and the cost of dealing with red tape and administration. The amount left for profit for the bookseller, the publisher, the various agents who are necessarily involved and the author is pitifully small.

Over the years I have learned that publishing involves a mass of costs. Some I had expected. Some I hadn't. Whether books are sold direct by mail order, or to bookshops or wholesalers, there are, above all, the costs of postage. These have risen dramatically in recent years. And the number of parcels being stolen is now higher than ever. (I refuse to describe these as `lost'. They are, in my view, mostly stolen.) Anyone who accepts payment by credit card has to pay massive credit card charges but even cheques can be problematical. Banks charge to cash them. And they can be lost too. Members of my staff once threw away £5,000 worth of cheques. There is the cost of damaged books, and the cost of refunding buyers who return books they have clearly read. And all that assumes you don't over order and end up with selling only half of the 2,000 books you printed.

24

11.49 a.m.

Two days ago I rang Eurostar to book some train tickets. When I'd finished explaining what I needed I asked if we could both have vegetarian meals. `Do you want that coming back too?' asked the clerk. I offer to pay to have the tickets posted to me and he agrees to do this for an additional £5 payment. When I gave my address the Eurostar employee was at first reluctant because I had given a PO Box address. He claimed that they couldn't send tickets to a PO Box for security reasons. I persuaded him by pointing out that PO Boxes are issued by Royal Mail which is 100% owned by the Government. The tickets arrived today and did so in an envelope which carries, on the reverse side, a return address. This is, of course, a Post Office Box address.

15.16 p.m.

My Dad became a little deaf in his later years and tended to speak quite loudly. When talking on the telephone he acquired a habit of repeating whatever the person at the other end of the telephone had said. He did this loudly too. I suppose he did it originally just to make sure that he'd heard properly but later on it just became a habit. When he was in hospital in Exeter I rang him several times a day to see how he was getting on. Naturally, he repeated everything I said, with the inevitable result that the people at the other end could hear every word I was saying as well as every word he was saying. I'm not sure why, but today I remembered one conversation we had. It went like this:

   `You have to get of there before they kill you.' I said.
   `I have to get out of here before they kill me?' shouted my Dad.
   `They're a bunch of ignorant bastards.'
   `They're a bunch of ignorant bastards?
   `Don't repeat everything I'm saying, Dad!'
   `Did you say: `Don't repeat everything I'm saying?'

25

16.37 p.m.

In despair at failing to find a house to buy The Princess and I drove 200 miles to see a house for rent in the Wye Valley. We had never thought about renting before but thought it might be interesting to see what we could find. It was awful. The owner, apparently a rich man with half a dozen houses on a large private estate, seemed to be keen to make a name for himself as a slum landlord. He wanted £1,500 a month for a house with fungus growing on one interior wall, unsafe electricity appliances (one socket was broken and hanging half off the wall), floorboards ripped up, skirting boards off, wallpaper peeling, roof leaking and carpets that would have been thrown out of a squat. The toilets were disgusting, several windows had broken sashes, the kitchen was indescribably awful and the whole house stank of urine. The previous tenant had left a vast number of confidential files relating to other people lying around. We decided it would take between £25,000 and £50,000 just to make it habitable. We decided not to take it and have given up the idea of renting. The landlord and the renting agent should both be in prison.

18.12 p.m.

On our way back home The Princess and I had coffee and a bowl of chips each in a pub. The pub was crowded with people eating and drinking. While everyone ate, a woman sitting at the next table, who had finished her meal, changed her baby's nappy on the table top. Knowing that the woman would doubtless by protected by some bizarre piece of EU legislation no one dared say a word in protest. The Princess and I hadn't finished our snack but we left. The smell was foul.

26

09.18 a.m.

I received a junk e-mail from BT and, because it was boring, sent back an e-mail asking to `unsubscribe'. BT then sent me another e-mail telling me that it might take 28 days to `unsubscribe' me. That's the wonder of the new instant messaging system. They can send messages in an instant but it takes them 28 days to stop sending them. Other firms are just as bad. They can start sending e-mails in a moment. But ask them to stop and they announce that it will take a week, two weeks or three weeks. When I tried to cancel an e-mail from the *Financial Times* I received an immediate response assuring me that this would be done within ten working days. *The Times* was no better. When I repeatedly tried to get them to stop sending me e-mails promoting their new paid service. I eventually received an e-mail telling me that they were in the process of deleting my e-mail address from *The Times* mailing list. `However, this procedure will take approximately five working days to complete,' said someone or something. How can it possibly take days to stop sending e-mails? I thought these things were supposed to be instant and automatic? I suppose they are only instant and automatic when the people sending them want them to be instant and automatic. How typical it is that BT, a firm supposed to be in the communications business, should take a whole month.

17.18 p.m.

A reader complains that my book *Living in a Fascist Country* is alarmist. I point out that according to every definition of `fascism' Britain is now very much a fascist country - and that the EU is the most fascist state ever invented. And I also point out that the police shoot people in the UK - and get away with it.

27

10.34 a.m.

I had to ring one of the utilities this morning. Inevitably, I was kept on hold with recorded music being played. I put the telephone receiver down on my desk so that I could carry on doing some work while I waited. But there was an announcement every 30 seconds. A voice said: `We apologise for the delay. Your call is important to us. We know you are waiting. We are doing everything we can to get to you as soon as possible. Our consultants are currently busy helping others but will be with you as soon as humanly possible.' Every time I heard the voice I grabbed the phone in case it was a person. So I couldn't work or read or do anything else. Why don't they just play the damned music until someone can be bothered to put down the newspaper and speak to me?

11.12 a.m.

A friend of ours e-mailed to say that he couldn't make lunch tomorrow because he has flu and is feeling really rough and doesn't want to give us his bug. `Is there anything we can do for you?' I e-mail back. He says there isn't anything and that he will pick up a few essentials while he's out. I ask him why on earth he is going out if he's ill. He says he's going to drag himself to the tax offices and the council offices because he has some bills to pay so he'll deliver the cheques in person. `Can't the cheques wait?' I ask. `I want to give them my bug,' he explains. `They want everything else I have so they can have this too.'

28
15.26 p.m.
The Princess and I were sitting in a café - a real, old-fashioned one rather than one of those modern ones where there's a blackboard twelve feet by six full of nothing but descriptions of different types of coffee. A fat, red-faced man accompanied by a tiny, timid, pale woman approached the counter. `Do you have any ham sandwiches?' he asked. `I'm afraid we only have beef,' said the counter assistant. `We don't eat beef, we're vegetarian,' said the man. `But you asked for ham,' said the puzzled assistant. `We're not that sort of vegetarian,' replied the fat man.

29
11.41 a.m.
This morning I read that in 1886 a man called Sors Hariezon, a gold prospector from Witwatersrand in the Transvaal sold his South African gold claim for $20. Over the next 100 years mines which were sunk on or near his claim produced over 1,000 tonnes of gold a year, that's 70% of the precious metal in the west. The discovery would have made him or his heirs the richest family in the world. They'd be trillionaires by now. I wonder if there are any Hariezons around who know this. I wonder if they feel upset about it at all.

15.52 p.m.
The newspapers are full of more scare stories about the dangers of statins. It is truly alarming that so many people take these damned drugs. I first warned about the dangers associated with their use nearly 20 years ago. There is an essay about the hazards of statins in *How to Stop Your Doctor Killing You*. The idea of giving

healthy people potentially dangerous drugs is one that scares me and yet it is one that drug companies (and the medical establishment) finds irresistible. Until I had published evidence showing the hazards of the drug tamoxifen, a vast number of eminent doctors were keen for every healthy woman in the world to take the damned stuff. I have no doubt that when the statins are finally withdrawn from use for healthy people the drug companies and their medical handmaidens will think of another way to make a few billion quid.

30
09.12 a.m.

We were about to view another house today when I spotted a few lines in the particulars reading `Please note that the existing side drive and double garage are not included in the sale - the latter is to be redeveloped.' That's the fourth house for which we have seen details where the vendors have separated the garage from the house in order to sell them separately. We cancel the viewing. Sheer, bloody greed. I hope they never sell the damned house. The agents add: `We understand that mains water, electricity and drainage are connected'. Don't they know? How hard is it to tell? What do estate agents do for their money? What a loathsome and useless bunch of cheating, conniving parasites they are.

15.41 p.m.

A friend of mine told me that since the tax people who operate the advice lines seem to give many different answers to the same question he now phones repeatedly until he gets the answer he thinks most useful - and most in his favour. He then makes a note of the time and the person he spoke to. I tell him that he should be ashamed of himself and he says he is.

21.42 p.m.

We had coffee in a motorway café. I was tired and needed a break. Motorway cafés are like another world. I have long suspected that there are people there who never go anywhere else. They are another race of people who just inhabit motorway service stations. The place was filthy. The Princess and I chose bottled drinks not because we want to drink them but because we need an excuse to sit at a table for ten minutes. A man and a woman were sitting at the next table. They were in their 40s. He wore three quarter length shorts decorated with a floral pattern and a plain grey sweater. She wore jeans and a pink jumper with a blue cardigan over it. She had her hair tightly permed in an old-fashioned way. He was reading the *Daily Mirror*. She was talking. She never stopped. Occasionally he murmured something anodyne and meaningless. It was clear that he wasn't listening to what she said. She talked loudly and became increasingly irritated at his lack of interest in what she had to say. Suddenly her tone changed, though the man with her, who was presumably her husband, didn't seem to notice. `I'm having an affair,' she said, though it was obvious she was saying this just to try to attract his attention. `That's nice, dear,' said her husband, studying his paper. `It's with someone you know,' she said. He grunted and nodded. `He wants me to go on the street for him. He's offered to be my pimp.' `That's good,' said her husband. He turned the final page, scans the back page which he didn't seem to find interesting, folded the paper and put it down on the table. For the first time he looked at his wife. `Have you finished your tea?' he asked. `Shall we go?' She tuts loudly. `It's like talking to a brick wall,' she complained. `You never, ever listen to me.' He stood up. `Yes, I do,' he says. `How much does he think you can make?'

July

1
09.22 a.m.
I started to write this diary for my own entertainment but as the weeks go by I'm beginning to think that I should consider publishing it. The thought has occurred to me on several occasions. If I do publish it I will have to make sure that no copies get into the hands of our friends, acquaintances or neighbours.

11.19 a.m.
We were in the greengrocer's this morning when The Princess noticed an old lady rummaging around in her purse to find coins to buy some vegetables. The Princess tapped her on the shoulder, handed her a fiver and said: `I found this on the floor. I think you must have dropped it.' The old lady, surprised, hesitated. The Princess insisted and the old lady accepted the note gratefully and gracefully. Beautifully done.

2
14.42 p.m.
Standing at the Post Office, waiting in the inevitable queue and wondering how one organisation manages to find and employ all the really rude people in the country, I wrote out 12 things I have learned in life:

1. When travelling never miss a chance to go to the loo (the first time you spend 90 minutes stuck in a taxi in a traffic jam you will remember this advice).

2. If there are two articles I want to rip out of a newspaper or magazine they will be on the two sides of the same page. (I'm not sure how helpful this is. But it's something I've learned.)

3. Never answer the door unless you know who is there and you are pleased about their coming.

4. Always buy several pairs of socks that are exactly the same colour. This helps avoid trying to pair them up and saves 15 minutes a week. That doesn't sound much but in an average lifetime it adds up to 910 hours.

5. If you really want to help friends who are broke just give them the money, write it off and don't expect it back.

6. There will never be enough bookshelves.

7. Life is like a luggage carousel. The same familiar old stuff keeps coming round and round and the stuff you're hoping for never seems to turn up.

8. It is always wise to praise your dentist and dental hygienist and indeed anyone likely to put their hands and steel instruments into any orifice.

9. People who say that their school days were the best days of their life are sad bastards. If life doesn't get better after school then your life is pretty damned disappointing.

10. There is no such thing as a stupid question, though there are lots of stupid answers.

11. Too many people who claim to know all the answers don't even know any of the right questions.

12. There is no place like home when you don't feel well - (particularly if you have diarrhoea or any sort of tummy upset). The truth is that we are more like animals than we think we are and when we are poorly most of us just want to curl up in a corner.

21.38 p.m.

I received an e-mail message from someone who wants to advertise electronic cat flaps on www.vernoncoleman.com. There have been quite a few approaches like this recently - most of them from companies offering real money to buy advertising space on the site. I had always refused to accept advertisements but maybe I should rethink. The money coming in from adverts would help me to buy adverts in the press to promote the site.

3

12.29 p.m.

As soon as I could read I used to go to jumble sales and buy armfuls of books. My parents genuinely couldn't understand why I wanted so many books. `Why do you want all these?' asked my Mum one day as I struggled out of yet another jumble sale laden with books. `You already have books at home.'

Rummaging in my favourite antique shop in Wells I found some wonderful books today. (It is called an antique shop but I

271

think of it as a junk shop with a good book corner.) I picked up a copy of H.V.Morton's *Atlantic Meeting*, which is an account of Winston Churchill's voyage in HMS Prince of Wales in August 1941. It was this journey, ending in a conference with President Roosevelt, which resulted in the Atlantic Charter. Churchill had to sail all the way to Newfoundland for the meeting (where Roosevelt happened to be cruising in his yacht). Morton, the best travel writer of his generation, reported that although Churchill's dangerous trip was kept secret in the UK, at 10.45 p.m. on August 6 1941, Cincinnati Radio in Ohio reported, in German, (there were 100,000 Germans living in Ohio) that: `According to a report from Washington rumours show that President Roosevelt will meet Prime Minister Winston Churchill in the Atlantic'. Swiss radio immediately took up the story and so the Germans knew where Churchill was before the meeting took place. And Churchill, of course, still had to get back. Morton also describes how, when Roosevelt was leaving the British battleship one of the ship's three cats, Blackie, started to follow the American President off the ship. All the sailors were at attention and could do nothing about it. But Churchill bent down and prevented the cat leaving, `saving Blackie for England by bending down and leading him from the gangway'. Brilliant stuff. Morton had an eye for the sort of detail that makes travel writing fascinating reading. The Morton, in a beautiful hardback edition, cost me 50 pence.

Charity bookshops often charge too much for the books they sell and the people who fix the prices seem to know very little about books. Today, in a hospice shop, I saw a battered book club reprint of *Three men in a Boat* priced at £10. The binding had gone and the pages were loose. Apart from offering a damned good read the book had no value. You can buy a brand new copy for less than that. Well-thumbed old paperbacks which cost 2/6 when they were first published now cost £2.95 in some shops. That's a massive rate of inflation and suggests that paperback books make a better investment than equities or property. My second gripe with charity shops is that many have taken the fun out of book hunting by skimming off the best books for dealers to sell on the Web. Still, this policy means that finding a first edition becomes even more exciting. (Before they started this nasty practice I often used to pay more than a book was priced at if I thought the difference was significant. I don't do this anymore.) My final worry about charity shops is that they are destroying junk and second-hand shops. I have, over the years, found thousands of wonderful books in junk shops and second-hand bookshops which are now closed. Most of the books have been out of print or exceedingly difficult to find. And I would have never found them on the Web because I didn't know they existed. Only browsing produces really valuable finds. I discovered Joseph Slocum (whom I had previously missed) and the Charles McCarry novels by browsing. And it was in a now defunct junk shop that I first came across books by John Fothergill, whose marvellous books about innkeeping in the early 20th century should be compulsory reading for all politically correct zealots.

Charity shops get so much help (reduced taxes, free stuff to sell, volunteer labour, an 80% reduction in business rates and so on) that small businesses have no chance of competing with them. (I suspect it is the 80% reduction in business rates which is partly responsible for the rapid rise in the number of charity shops. Now that property owners have to pay business rates on empty buildings I would be surprised if some property owners weren't offering their premises free of charge to charities. Instead of receiving rent the property owner saves 80% on his rates bill.) Charity shops may make a lot of money for their owners (and help pay the fat salaries of headquarters staff) but they are destroying local businesses and, by charging higher and higher prices, doing very little to help local communities by providing low-priced items.

Oxfam is the worst offender. It seems to me to feel no responsibility towards the communities on which it leeches (reduced rates, free stock, volunteer labour). And yet there are some well-paid executives at the top of the organisation and I suspect that as with most charities a big chunk of the income goes to paying salaries. I am probably the biggest giver of books to charity bookshops in the country but I no longer give to Oxfam. Even for ordinary paperbacks their prices are absurdly high and for anything rare or unusual the prices are often absurd. In *Book and Magazine Collector* recently I read with astonishment that an Oxfam spokesman was claiming that book buyers 'shouldn't be able to find any decent books priced 50 pence to £1 in any Oxfam shop'. Why on earth not? I regularly buy wonderful books, in excellent condition, for less than £1 each. Spines firm and the pages unmarked. Who the hell at Oxfam imagines they have the right to overcharge people who want to read books which are often unavailable in bookshops and public libraries? When our public libraries are closed (which they soon will be, in the name of `cutting costs') this policy of overcharging will mean that there will be nowhere for the young and the poor to obtain books.

In addition, I don't like the way Oxfam has built up a chain of bookshops which always seem to me to be situated in towns which are (or were) fairly well served by local second-hand bookshops and never seem to appear in places where there is no second-hand bookshop.

I'm not the only book lover who feels that Oxfam is destroying small, private second-hand bookshops and I really don't see how this helps anyone except Oxfam. My boycott of Oxfam bookshops will continue indefinitely.

18.17 p.m.
A few weeks ago I opened an Amazon account so that I could buy out of print books. The computer programme asked me for a name. I called myself `Your Highness Royal Emperor'. I am pleased to see that Amazon now address me by this title whenever they write to me. Parcels come addressed to `Mr Your Highness Royal Emperor' which isn't quite so submissive but is definitely funnier.

21.56 p.m.
A friend of mine who is a dentist now calls himself `doctor'. Foolishly I congratulated him, saying I didn't know he had been studying for a doctorate. He rather pompously announced that he was calling himself doctor because he is a dentist. When I thought about it I realised that quite a few dentists I know now insist on using the honorary title. I asked my friend why he'd suddenly decided to be a doctor and he told me that it has been all the rage in America for some time and he'd picked up on the idea after attending a conference of dentists in Las Vegas. He says that it is the best way to get a table when ringing a restaurant at short notice. I remembered that Doc Holliday, one of the heroes of The OK Corral was actually a dentist and not a medical man.

23.35 p.m.

I discovered another Englishman I should have considered for my book on the 100 greatest Englishmen. Thomas Stevens was the first man to cycle round the world. And he did it on a penny-farthing in the 19th century. His story is told in his book *Around the World on a Penny-farthing*. He started the adventure in America and so (as always) the Americans claim him as theirs. But he was as English as they come.

23.49 p.m.

There are now many British families in fourth generation unemployment. I know of one family where the patriarch has been unemployed for decades. He claims sickness benefit as a result of a bunion. The State has created a human zoo. People are given food and they are provided with the essentials for life but they are not living. They do not have the dignity that comes with self-reliance, but have been dehumanised by welfare.

4

09.56 a.m.

The bag for life which I recently bought from Marks and Spencer broke. The handle snapped. I have had give-away plastic bags which lasted longer.

11.45 a.m.

I read an article by a Muslim complaining that she didn't like living in England because the English do not respect her religion with sufficient fervour. She should try being a Christian in a Muslim country. Surely if you choose to live in someone else's country it is your responsibility to fit in with them, not the other way round. Westerners living in Muslim countries get into terrible trouble if they drink alcohol or sit on the beach in bikinis. And quite right too. It's their country and their rules. What a pity that so many Muslims living in our country don't see things the same way. Worse still, many seem to see our tolerance as weakness. The real problem is that although the extremists in any religion are likely to be the minority, they will always take control because they want it more. It will always be impossible to integrate different religions because the leaders will always want to retain, and extend, their power. You can't say stuff like this in public these days so if I do ever print this diary I must remember to remove this entry.

5
11.51 a.m.

I walked past a shop window (converted temporarily into a second-hand bookshop) and saw a Penguin copy of Elliot Paul's *A Narrow Street* on sale for 50 pence. I went in to buy it and came out with ten books. The Elliot Paul was a real find. It's the only one of his Paris books I hadn't been able to find. Not even the Internet had been able to find me a copy.

14.15 p.m.

We passed a black woman and a small black girl, about three or four-years-old. The girl was pulling a huge wooden duck on a piece of string. She looked up at me and smiled. I smiled back at the girl and was about to congratulate her on her wonderful toy when the mother grabbed the little girl's hand and pulled her away. What a sad world we have created for ourselves.

6
11.56 a.m.

Readers constantly want to know what we can do to repair our society. In truth, I fear we have lost. No one in authority cares about the truth. And I don't honestly think things are likely to improve in the foreseeable future. Our only practical objective now must really be to look after ourselves. My last few books have, indeed, been designed to help readers do just that. The days ahead are rugged. We all need to be roped together with trustworthy guides. All we can really do is try to predict what *they* will do next, how it will affect us and how best we can protect ourselves and those close to us.

The big problem today isn't collecting information. There is plenty of information around. The problem is analysing, interpreting and understanding it. And, most important of all, being able to differentiate between information which is objective, accurate and valuable and information which is none of those things - though it may well appear to be so.

In the end the system which has been created will implode. The European Union (the source of much that is bad in our world) will die. There will be rioting and revolution and things will change.

But for now all we can do is survive.

7
11.47 a.m.
A scruffy young man approached me in the street and waved a mobile phone under my nose. 'Have you any money for the phone?' he demanded. When I told him (as politely as I thought appropriate) that I did not he swore at me and wandered off to stop another passer-by. This is, presumably, the new begging.

13.22 p.m.
The Princess and I called into a café for teas. The customer in front of us did not speak English. This would not have been such a big problem except that the girl behind the counter didn't speak much English and didn't speak the language the customer spoke. The assistant then called the manager who had about six or eight words of English (though apparently not the same words that the other member of staff knew). Everything was taking so long that we left, bought two bottles of water and sat on a bench.

8
12.01 p.m.
I discovered that you cannot buy National Savings products by post with a debit or credit card. You have to use a cheque. The bit of the Government that runs National Savings doesn't want customers putting their card details into the post because it is too risky. This is, of course, the same Government that owns the Royal Mail.

14.27 p.m.
I received a copy of a new insurance policy. The policy includes these words: 'It is a condition of this policy that we may use your personal data in any way we deem appropriate.'
I thought it was nice of them to let me know.

17.16 p.m.

Like everyone buying a house we have learned to hate estate agents. It really isn't difficult to see why they are the most loathed and despised tradespeople in the country. Not even plumbers are hated as much. Estate agents are constitutionally deceitful. They take photographs designed to hide the truth. They say that a house has three bathrooms when it has one bathroom and two shower rooms. They don't seem to understand that a bathroom is a room with a bath in it and a bedroom is a room in which you can get a bed. A room in which I can touch all the walls without moving my feet is a cupboard. They use all sorts of little tricks to make the properties they are selling seem better or bigger. We have seen houses where the gross internal area included the garage and outbuildings and on one occasion we even saw a house where the internal area included the attic - even though it was not boarded and was therefore quite unusable. This meant that the house was actually a third smaller than we had thought it to be. I loathe estate agents. I can't understand why there aren't more estate agent-politicians.

Estate agents don't seem to understand the concept of `honesty'. They use language in their own deceitful way. `Needs updating' means that the house was, for the last 60 years lived in by a hermit who never moved out of one room and who kept warm with blankets and a onc bar electric fire. `Needs refurbishment' means that there is a hole in the roof so big that you could fit a radio telescope in the attic and that the only question to ask is `Will the woodworm in the roof eat through what remains of the beams before they are drowned by the rising damp?'. Finally, `needs modernisation' means that it doesn't have running water or electricity.

Estate agents use a whole lexicon of euphemisms. For example, if it's a living room that is hardly big enough for two chairs they call it a snug. If the kitchen is so small that you have to go out if you want to put on a pinafore then it's a `boutique culinary experience' or a `galley style food preparation zone'. They fill their brochures with details of the number of miles to the nearest golf course and talk of duck and grouse doors and Jack and Jill bathrooms but they do not bother to mention the presence of an electricity pylon just a few yards from the back door. When they talk about `needs some attention to bring it up to modern standards' what they really mean is that it has dry rot, wet rot and woodworm, no heating system, one very tired Belfast sink in the kitchen and a bathroom that contains a zinc tub.

We saw three houses today. The first, described as compact and easy to manage, was a cottage with rooms so small that we could, with arms outstretched, paint two walls at once. With a brush in your mouth it would be possible to paint three walls at once. Some people might think four possible. The second property lay a few yards from a dual carriageway. It was worrying that out of ten houses in a row, four of them were for sale. The house would have suited a deaf person down to the ground. The woman selling the house wore a deaf aid but we still had to shout to make ourselves heard. Inside the house, the noise wasn't too bad. But once you got into the garden the noise was horrendous. As The Princess pointed out, there is little point in living in the countryside if you can't hear the birds sing. It would have been like living on the central reservation of the M1. The third house had a public right of way running through the middle of the garden. `It isn't much used,' said the estate agent, though there were obvious signs that it had been used recently by people with dogs and by horse riders. `Plenty of free manure for the garden,' the agent added hopefully. I love walking and have probably walked more along cliff top paths and countryside paths than most ramblers but I have never wanted to walk on paths that take me through people's gardens and I suspect that the people who choose to do so deliberately are probably not the sort of people I want to meet. Some walkers will keep using a public footpath just because it is there and they want to preserve their right to walk along it. So, rather than have a million arguments, we walked away from that one.

9
11.52 a.m.
This morning's mail included a letter from a reader in Grimsby who said: `Please e-mail me all the information you have about vaccines. This will save me having to get hold of your books.' I received a letter from a reader in Hampshire who wanted me to e-mail all the information I have about government and local authority expenditure. And I received around 30 letters from

schoolchildren doing a `class project'. Each one enclosed the same questions and asked for a reply to be sent by post.

12.34 p.m.

A reader wants to know why I don't allow people to put comments on my website. The answer, I explain, is very simple. I am legally responsible for whatever appears on my website and I have enough enemies, and enough people trying to close me down, without my encouraging other people to do it for me. (Some would doubtless do it deliberately just for the fun of creating trouble.) The Internet is a global creation but the law varies from one country to another. Stuff that is legal in one country might well be punishable with a long prison sentence in another. Libel laws vary. And since Britons can now be extradited easily, and without evidence, to the USA and to anywhere within the EU I think I will stick to preserving my website for my own thoughts. Personally, I think that anyone who allows strangers to put comments on their website is a good 97% on the Barking Scale.

16.17 p.m.

I told an American visiting Britain to be careful about bathing in the sea because the water isn't always clean. I explained that water companies somctimes allow raw sewage to empty straight into the sea. `You British are appalling,' he cried. `You dump your sewage into the sea and then you bathe in it.' I agreed that it isn't a good habit. `Still,' I said, `we're not as bad as you Americans.' `What do you mean?' he demanded. `You feed your sewage to your farm animals,' I pointed out. `And then you eat the animals. So although we only bathe in our sewage, you eat yours.'

21.41 p.m.

David Ogilvy, the advertising guru, reckoned that he knew three things worth passing on. First, never lend money to friends. Second, always carry matches. Third, never complain in a restaurant before you have finished your meal. Good advice.

22.15 p.m.

An astonishing 89% of British homes are now equipped with CCTV cameras. I can't help wondering why. What are all these people filming? `The world has gone barking mad,' I said to The Princess. `We are the only sane ones left.' `In that case,' said The Princess, `the world is in very serious trouble.'

10
14.38 p.m.
While clearing out old files I found a bill for typing one of my first books. I apparently paid £1,500 to have the *Story of Medicine* typed up neatly. That was more than the advance I received from the publisher so I made a loss on the first edition. The reader for the first publisher who saw the typescript wrote silly remarks all over it - largely because she disagreed with my interpretation of history and partly because she clearly had a feminist view of everything. Fortunately, these absurdities were scribbled in pencil so I could rub them all out. It was a task which took me several hours. Fortunately, the second publisher bought the book and it was published without any silly editorial amendments.

21.32 p.m.
I've been re-reading J. B. Priestley's marvellous book *English Journey*. He writes about the Whitsun sport of shin kicking, which was popular in the Cotswolds some years ago. Two contestants would stand facing each other, with their hands on each other's shoulders and then, at a word from the referee, would start kicking each other's shins. Not a game for wimps.

11
11.47 a.m.
We took several hundreds pounds worth of DVDs and books to a local charity shop this morning. They were in six black plastic bags. In order to get even remotely close to the shop I had to park on double yellow lines. The shop was deserted. A man at the counter looked at us as we struggled through the door with the first two bags: `Take them through to the back,' he said sharply. `I'm afraid I'm parked on double yellow lines,' I apologised, rushing out to the truck for more bags. When we had finished bringing in all the bags we put them to one side, out of the way. The man didn't even look up from the book he was reading to say thank you.

14.56 p.m.

After the slightly sour experience at the charity shop we drove on to a local cricket ground where two village teams were playing. At the tea interval I overheard this conversation.

'Why did you declare?' demanded an angry player.

'I thought we had enough runs and need the time to bowl them out,' answered his captain, not unreasonably.

'You might have let me go on to my 100,' said the player.

'You'd only scored 24!' replied the captain.

'Yes, but I was batting so well'

12

10.31 a.m.

A reader tells me that her council is insisting that all tin cans are washed out before being put out for recycling. This takes half an hour a day, she complains. 'Do these people think I have nothing else to do? If I don't wash the cans they refuse to take my recycling. And if I put the cans into my ordinary rubbish, and they find them, they will refuse to take that too.' The world is running out of water and whereas we might just be able to manage without oil we won't survive without water. It takes around a gallon of water to wash out a soup tin. The lunatics who think they are saving the planct are, in fact, guaranteeing us all a scary, thirsty future.

15.02 p.m.

I went into a bank I have been using for 40 years. I have been using the same branch for 25 years. I wanted to move a relatively small amount of money from one of my accounts to another. Both accounts are in my name. 'Do you have any ID?' asked a clerk I have dealt with countless times before. How absurd that they are encouraged to put more faith in a piece of easily forged plastic than in their own knowledge and experience. When I said I had no ID she said that was fine.

16.17 p.m.

Sixty per cent of British authors earn less than £10,000 a year and their median earnings are less than a quarter of the average national wage. Thanks to the Internet, things are going to get worse. Much worse.

18.19 p.m.

We sent a copy of *Bilbury Village* to Arrow books in the vain hope that they might want to produce a paperback edition. I received a letter from them which said: `Although *Bilbury Village* was an interesting concept but I am afraid we are going to have to say no, I wasn't convinced that we could make a commercial success of it in today's market. It was a strange format for a non-fiction book and though the initial chapters were very exciting I had trouble picturing a readership for it.'

It says on the cover of the book that it is a novel. It's a pity that Arrow can't find staff who know the difference between fiction and non-fiction. I am tempted to send a note back telling the writer that fiction is the stuff that is all made up. But it doesn't really seem worth the price of the stamp. Arrow were my first paperback publishers many years ago.

19.18 p.m.

I've been invited to give a lecture in Brussels. I can't think of anywhere I would rather not visit. Brussels is famous for two things: the extraordinarily expensive and ugly EU building (full to the brim with vastly overpaid part-time employees) and a statue of a small boy pissing. One is a cultural icon. The other is a pointless embarrassment. One makes people smile. The other makes people angry.

13

11.23 a.m.

I received a letter from a reader who wrote to say he has been wearing a T-shirt with `I've read *Living in a Fascist Country* by Vernon Coleman' printed on it. He reports that he was made to remove the T-shirt before being allowed onto a flight to Crete from Glasgow. I received a letter from a man who wanted me to `put together a document in order for me to present to the people of Bexhill a case to change the way we house ourselves', a letter from a reader telling me that she has been told by her GP that if she won't accept the swine flu vaccination her doctors would not give her any prescriptions ever again (that one must have put my blood pressure up at least 40 points) and a letter from a reader offering to do `proper' drawings to illustrate my cat books and suggesting a straight 50:50 royalty split. A reader says he can tell from one of my books that I was with the allied forces for the Battle of the Bulge and sends me a long and fascinating letter about the Second World War. There is a wonderful letter from a kind man who says he enjoys the `outstandingly frank exposures coming from Publishing House' and adds `we have not been stimulated by such a refreshing wind of patriotism since 1945 after which we descended by degrees into the blinding fog of multiculturalism'. He sent a cheque for more than the cost of the books he ordered as a `donation'. There is a card from a reader saying that she is disappointed that my column isn't in *The People* newspaper and that she misses it.

Another reader says he has bought 11 of my books and likes the accurate predictions they contain. He says he looks forward to ticking off the predictions in *2020* as they come true. He adds that his son has just finished *Oil Apocalypse* and was so impressed with it that he decided not to bother taking his driving test. A reader says he is now a pensioner and is too old to read my books. A reader sends a lovely letter about my novel *Paris in My Springtime* (which he thinks is autobiographical). He says he went to Paris with his banjo for a week and stayed there busking for six months. A highlight of his trip was being given money by Brigitte Bardot and Roger Vadim. I once did a radio programme with Roger Vadim. It was *Start the Week* which began at 9.00 a.m. The rest of us were there at about 8.30 a.m. A rather pompous Richard Baker. David Attenborough in an anorak which looked as if it had come from an army surplus store. But no Vadim. And then, just as the newsreader was finishing off the 9 o'clock news, the door to the studio was flung open and in walked Vadim, followed by two statuesque assistants. He was immaculately dressed in a grey silk suit, sparkling white shirt and silk tie. He had a camel hair overcoat draped around his shoulders in the French way. One of the assistants removed the coat from his shoulders. Vadim walked over to the table, slid into the empty seat next to me and the ladies disappeared. What an entrance. Timed to perfection. I have done television and radio programmes with many much bigger stars but

I have never ever seen an entrance like that. I've never met B.B. but she once sent me a wonderful, handwritten postcard denouncing vivisection and supporting one of my campaigns. Finally, there are three small parcels which all contain books self-published by readers who have read my book *How To Publish Your Own Book*. I honestly believe I have the best and kindest readers in the world. I never fail to be amazed by their kind words.

14
11.26 a.m.
I received a letter from a reader in Cornwall who says: 'Why are you still writing books? If you haven't enough money by now you never will have.' An ex-army officer offers to obtain coloured diamonds for me as investments. He says he brings them back from Belgium two at a time and that he always travels by taxi, train and taxi so that there is no fear of being run over by a bus. A reader wants me to write and publish the story of her car which she says she has loved for 20 years. She encloses photographs. I regularly receive letters from people who want me to write the story of their cat or dog but this is the first time I've had a letter wanting a book about their car. There are two letters from readers who say: 'I know you cannot send personal clinical replies but...'. And a reader in Worcestershire who tells me that he is planning his own funeral. 'I have had a plywood coffin made, then soaked in old engine oil. Cost £60 including delivery. Tested for size. I have bought a ground fixing plaque on a stake for £55 in stainless steel. A local grave plot for £80. A man who will transport the body anywhere in the UK (so that if I die outside my area he can collect me) £450. A man to dig the hole and throw dirt on top of my coffin £150.' He kindly offers to make similar arrangements for me. He is the second of my readers to offer to help with my funeral. A reader from London who has read *Paris in my Springtime* wants to know why I didn't publish the book which is mentioned as having been written but never published by a character in the book. (Since the whole thing is fiction I'm not sure what to say to this.) A reader points out that the American flag, the Stars and Stripes, came from an English family called the Washingtons. When one of the family emigrated to the American colony in the 18th century he took his coat of arms with him. His descendant George Washington became

President of the USA and the family coat of arms became the American flag. And, finally, a reader of *Mrs Caldicot's Cabbage War* writes to say: `Having just finished reading *Mrs Caldicot's Cabbage War*, which I enjoyed very much, I did notice something. George and Thelma Caldicot are said to have been married for 33 years and have a son Derek who, although no age is given has a son who is said in the book to be 16 years of age. Are we to assume that Derek became a father at the age of 16?' I wrote back: `Derek was seduced when he was 16. He was very much the innocent party. Please don't tell anyone because Derek is still very embarrassed by it (although his mother doesn't give two hoots).'

15
11.22 a.m.
I picked up a copy of a 1948 Penguin edition of *The Journal of A Disappointed Man* in Charing Cross Road. It cost me 80 pence. Great title. Written by W. N. P. Barbellion (whose real name was Bruce Frederick Cummings) it's exactly what it says on the cover. Cummings, who was for a while a naturalist on the staff of the Natural History Museum in South Kensington, suffered from incurable and progressive paralysis and towards the end of his short life the physical work of writing the diary was done by his wife and his sister. He kept the diary from the age of 13 until his death at 30 and he wrote, honestly and mercilessly, about life, the world and, most crucially, himself. Cummings was born in Barnstaple, where his father worked as a reporter, and he was an extraordinary being. At the age of 14, he read and enjoyed *Origin of Species* and by the age of 15 he had discovered 232 birds' nests and identified them as belonging to 44 different types of bird. There's a telling quote in the book: `There is no fiercer hell than the failure of a great ambition'. If you're looking down Mr Cummings, you did not fail. His diary is infinitely more revealing, and therefore more readable and more informative, than those awful celebrity laden things that are published these days by people like Piers Morgan.

21.59 p.m.
We watched Clint Eastwood's movie *Gran Torino*. At the end of it Eastwood dies. The film reminded me of *The Shootist*, which was

John Wayne's last movie. Curiously, Don Siegel, who directed *The Shootist*, also directed Eastwood's 1972 classic *Dirty Harry*.

As part of a self-selected double bill we also watched a wonderful Australian film called *The World's Fastest Indian*. Starring Anthony Hopkins as motorcyclist Burt Munro, it's one of those wonderful real life personality films that Australian filmmakers do so well.

22.14 p.m.

I constantly receive mail promoting new computer products. The problem, of course, is that the price is only a tiny part of the problem. The bigger part of the problem is the effort required to learn how to use a new device (let alone new software). So often it simply isn't worth the effort. The Princess and I are very cautious about buying anything electrical. I still use a Psion hand-held computer and I bought another three this week. Old stock and reconditioned stock are available and there are, I gather, quite a few people who, like me, regard them as the peak of hand-held computer hardware. I suspect that Psion killed off their pocket computer business when they replaced the excellent 3 series models with the too-complex 5 series models. I didn't upgrade because I couldn't move information across from my 3 series to the new model without doing something very complicated. The old diskettes which had fitted the 3 series didn't fit the 5 series. And the Psion hand-held computers died an undeserved death. I work in Wordperfect 5.1 in DOS and in order to do this I buy very old laptops which still have floppy drives attached and which can be set up to avoid any piece of software devised since 1999. My spellchecker, bless its heart, doesn't recognise words such as `website', `Internet' or `e-mail'. I attack a separate keyboard to the laptop I am working on and put the laptop on a pile of books. It works well for me. No new computer system works as well or provides me with anything half as efficient or as easy to use or, indeed, as fast. (Graphic based packages are always slow for processing words.) As back up, I have a cupboard full of old laptops, old keyboards, old zip drives and old floppy disks. I am not the only writer to have decided to stand still and let the technology progress without me. Donald E.Westlake, one of the great American novelists of the 20th century, had a store of obsolete manual typewriters tucked away in a cupboard because he was frightened about how he would cope if the machine he was using broke down. When he did have a breakdown he cannibalised bits from one of the machines in his cupboard to keep the original machine working.

16

09.38 a.m.

In today's *Financial Times* HMRC staff are described as `always polite'. I assume this is a joke. In my experience, HMRC staff are universally aggressive, nasty and inhuman. Once you find the answer they want they change the question. I am never much impressed with the *Financial Times*. The share price lists are invariably useful. The news stories are passable. But the columns and features would be an embarrassment in a school magazine. The *FT* doesn't have writers; it just has people who want to be writers.

11.46 a.m.

To help my appalling French I am reading a 1950's French history textbook for 'middle school children'. It explains how the French won World War I and World War II pretty much by themselves. In the chapter dealing with World War II, England gets a brief mention for providing a base from which General de Gaulle could mastermind the defeat of the Germans.

14.01 p.m.

By cooperating with the manufacturers of e-book readers publishers have signed their own death warrants. They made exactly the same mistake as the film companies, which brought about their own demise by making films specifically for their main competitor - television. The television companies, having bought the cheaply made films, then showed them to their audiences free of charge. For the film companies it was commercial suicide. Instead of promoting the differences and advantages of their medium, and keeping their product special, the Hollywood studios, desperately frightened, made `Made for Television' movies. Authors and publishers and bookshops are, of course, making exactly the same mistake by selling e-books. Record companies didn't really have a choice - their product can be easily downloaded and passed around. Books are much more difficult to copy and if publishers had refused to play the game the e-book reader would have probably failed. I have long been opposed to the idea of e-books but I thought I should dip a toe in the water before I finally committed myself and so a few weeks ago I accepted an offer from an American e-book publisher for one of my books. My fear is that e-books will take over and replace 'proper' books and that because it will be the only way to make a living, sponsored authors and publishers will produce e-books that carry a particular message - in the same way that websites are sponsored. The price of e-books will follow gravity down to 1p or even 0p. How long before public libraries in the USA offer free e-book loans to British readers? And the result will be that publishers, wholesalers, bookshops, agents and professional authors will have no future. Wholesalers in particular are not viable and I am astonished to see that some are promoting their e-book selling divisions.

The American publishers who are producing an e-book of *How To Stop Your Doctor Killing You* have just sent me a copy of the copyright warning they want to put at the front of the book. I signed the contract for this book as a test - just to see what happens. The warning explains that purchasers can keep one copy of the book on their computer, or print out one copy for their own use, but that if they make additional copies they will be liable to a penalty of up to $100,000 per copy distributed. I think this is an excellent idea but I can't help wondering how effectively such a warning can be policed. This reminds me just how dangerous it is to sell e-books and just how much authors are risking by allowing publishers to produce e-books. I suspect that within a few months there will be so many free copies of my book available that the back list sales will be non-existent. I also suspect that the amount publishers will be able to charge for e-books will be limited. I noticed yesterday that Amazon or its affiliates are 'selling' e-books for £0.00. It really doesn't matter whether the author gets 30%, 40% or 50% of that. Still, I am hopeful. If the American e-book of *How To Stop Your Doctor Killing You* sells well (I get 50% of the gross which is around $7 a book) I may allow some more old books to be produced as e-books. But I will never allow *Alice's Diary* to be sold as an e-book. (Incidentally, the publishers of *How*

To Stop Your Doctor Killing You are pretty clever. To disguise the age of the book they asked permission to put the date inside the book in Roman numerals.) My first e-book goes on sale later today. I will be interested to see what happens. But I'm not expecting to get rich from it.

15.19 p.m.

A film producer wants to make a cartoon film of *Alice's Diary*. I'll believe it when I see it. It is sad but I have become very sceptical and unbelieving.

18.34 p.m.

I found an article by Robert Louis Stevenson that was published in the *British Weekly* in 1887. Here's an extract: `Not all men can read all books; it is only in a chosen few that any man will find his appointed food; and the fittest lessons are the most palatable, and make themselves welcome to the mind. A writer learns this early; and it is his chief support; he goes on unafraid, laying down the law; and he is sure at heart that most of what he says is demonstrably false, and much of a mingled strain, and some hurtful, and very little good for service; but he is sure besides that when his words fall into the hands of any genuine reader, they will be weighed and winnowcd, and only that which suits will be assimilated; and when they fall into the hands of one who cannot intelligently read, they come there quite silent and inarticulate, falling upon deaf ears, and his secret is kept as if he had not written.' What a sentence, and what beautiful use of the now almost forgotten semicolon.

20.49 p.m.

I heard a sportsman today talking about playing in his comfort zone. This is, apparently, a revived concept among the young who have rediscovered it. The theory is that when playing within the `comfort zone' the sportsman feels relaxed and comfortable. He can operate easily and comfortably. The concept isn't confined to sport players, of course. It is seeping into every aspect of human life. There is, however, another word for it: complacency. The really great sports players (and the really great entertainers, authors, painters, musicians, investors, anything you likers) are constantly stretching themselves, pushing back the boundaries (to use another modern cliché) and doing greater and greater things. No one ever did anything great while operating within a comfort zone.

17

22.47 p.m.

We watched *The Thin Man* again. We both think it's one of the funniest films ever made and adore the glorious William Powell, Myrna Loy and Asta; probably the most loveable on-screen dog ever. The dialogue is sparkling (and surprisingly risqué for 1934 - `What's that man doing in my drawers?' asks Ms Loy as a policeman searches through her lingerie in her dressing table.) Just why the film series was named after the Dashiell Hammett hero I have no idea. The films bear little or no resemblance to Hammett's classic novels. We then watched *My Darling Clementine* with Henry Fonda as Wyatt Earp. `Have you ever been in love?' Fonda asks a barman. `No, I've always been a bartender'. I remember being shocked when I was a boy to discover that Earp, like Davy Crockett, Bowie, Hickock, the James brothers and Billy the Kid were all real people and that they lived not all that long ago. (Not as astonished as I was, however, to discover that Lawrence of Arabia had been real and had died not all that long before I was born.)

23.11 p.m.

On the day after *How To Stop Your Doctor Killing You* was published as an e-book I looked on the Web and found that one website was offering the e-book version of my book free of charge. A website I have never heard of is giving away my book as a promotional item. It took less than 24 hours for the book to become worthless. In addition there is already an Arabic version which I haven't licensed and someone is selling a book called *Stop Your Doctor Killing You*, with promotional tags exactly the same as mine, for a chunky $47. They have stolen the promotional material and for all I know the entire contents of the book. I've had thousands of articles and book chapters stolen over the years. But e-books enable thieves to steal whole books in an instant.

18

11.23 a.m.

Running a small business these days isn't a simple thing like rocket science or brain surgery. The rules and regulations change almost hourly and I don't believe there is a small business owner in the country who isn't breaking one rule or another almost every day of his working life. I cannot imagine why anyone would want to start a new business today.

14.56 p.m.

We have seen a lot of listed houses. There are advantages and disadvantages. The advantage is that the previous owner will not have been able to destroy or even change the fabric of the building. The disadvantage is that every modification or repair has to be approved in advance by bureaucrats in cheap suits. And the people who make decisions about listed properties tend to do so according to whim rather than reason. There are no strict rules about what is and is not allowed and so the administrators who make the important, and often expensive, decisions do so according to how they feel on any particular day. Moreover, they will only say what you can't do, they won't give any guidance on what you can do.

We were sent details of a house which looked very promising. Indced, it looked spectacular.

'It's listed,' said The Princess

'Oh well,' I shrugged. 'We can live with that. It's a terrific looking house.'

'It's Grade 1,' said The Princess

We'd never come across a Grade 1 listed property before. Most Grade 1 listed properties are owned by the Government, the Queen or the National Trust.

'You probably have to ring up someone in London if you want permission to draw the curtains,' said The Princess

I quietly, and reverently, put the brochure down on the 'No thanks' pile that will go into the recycling bin.

16.17 p.m.

We tried to go to Ilminster to look at a house. We found the house and then followed all the appropriate signs to try to look at the town. We thought we might as well, since we were there.

However, the signs kept sending us round and round on some sort of ring road. Eventually we decided that there is no town called Ilminster. Or maybe they just don't want visitors. The local council presumably feels that if no one visits, there will be less wear and tear on the pavements and less rubbish in the street bins (if there are any). It does, however, seem a rather short-sighted attitude.

We managed to find Chard but we decided we had nothing to say about Chard.

`It's not been that bad a day,' I said, when we got home. I filled the kettle and switched it on. It blew up.

`Yes it has,' said The Princess. `We drove miles to see a house neither of us liked and we got cut up by a line painting lorry.' (I still hardly believe this but it is true). `We tried to go Ilminster and failed completely. And we drove through Chard.' The reminder about Chard convinced me that she was right. It had been a poor day.

The Princess then turned on her computer and found an e-mail from a friend. `Some twit on twitter has twatted something nasty about you,' she said. `I don't want to know,' I told her.

18.25 p.m.
Today, I finally managed to persuade a small bookshop to pay its bill. All the books had been ordered by customers and paid for in advance. It has taken me six letters to get paid. Years ago I would have fought for little bookshops and I would have refused to allow my books to be sold in supermarkets. Not today. Small bookshops have been no friends of ours. Today, if Tesco wants to carry my books they are welcome. (But not if they want a huge discount.)

23.14 p.m.
We watched *Mr Holland's Opus* for the umpteenth time. The fact that Richard Dreyfuss did not receive an Oscar for this film about a composer who becomes a schoolteacher and has a deaf son is proof, if it were ever needed, that the Oscar system is a nonsense. Dreyfuss is one of my favourite actors and this is his best work.

19
16.17 p.m.

We went to Prinknash Bird and Deer Park in Gloucestershire. It is a wonderful, peaceful place. The animals live in the grounds of the monastery. A real little bit of heaven.

21.28 p.m.

A reader wants me to take part in an online chat room event. I have no idea what this entails or why I have been invited. I only know I don't want to do it. I write back saying that I used the Internet a great deal in the 1990s but that I have rather lost faith in it as a medium. I suspect that she will simply consider me to be a Luddite. I no longer care.

20

16.17 p.m.

We went to Lacock Abbey in Wiltshire and saw the window of which Fox Talbot took the first recorded photograph. I took various pictures of the same window. None of mine were as good as his.

18.35 p.m.

The reader who wrote about Mrs Caldicot's son has written back thanking me for the confidential information regarding Derek's love life. `If he is aware of our correspondence, please reassure him that his secret is safe with me.'

19.10 p.m.

Amazon has announced that in the last three months it sold more e-books than hardback books. And China is now the world's biggest user of energy. It has overtaken America. It occurs to me to wonder what will happen to e-books, and their readers, when the electricity runs out.

21

14.47 p.m.

We had coffee at The Old Bell Hotel in Malmesbury. It has apparently been a hotel since 1220 and is the oldest hotel in England. It is a delightful place and the people running it certainly seem to have the hang of running a hotel. I don't suppose they are the original people but there are apparently ghosts there so you never know. The Princess is frightened of ghosts. When she went to the lavatory she asked me to go with her. 'Please stand outside,' she said. 'If anyone walks through the door without opening it, come and get me.'

The hotel is right next to the Abbey which is famous because a priest called Eilmer leapt from the Abbey tower and became the first man to fly. He did this in the year 1010. He made himself some wings, jumped off, travelled a furlong, crashed and broke both legs.

15.06 p.m.

In bookshops, junk shops and auctions I always rummage in the cardboard boxes that haven't been properly sorted. I bought so many books in a junk shop today that the proprietor asked me if I had a shop myself. I told him that I was a bookaholic and that although it was very sad I knew of no cure. He pointed out that my addiction didn't cost me much more than a cocaine habit and was probably not much worse for my health.

18.00 p.m.

Sitting in a branch of Caffé Nero (they sell the best crisps in the UK and serve probably the most reliably drinkable coffee on the High Street) The Princess and I started thinking of actors who have never played James Bond but who should have. We decided we were looking for elegance, power and a big name. Here's our list.

1. Patrick McGoohan
2. Peter O'Toole
3. Cary Grant
4. Clive Owen
5. Liam Neeson
6. Christopher Plummer
7. Dean Martin

McGoohan would have been the greatest, of course, though he turned the part down because he didn't get on with one of the senior crew members. It was McGoohan whose character in Dangerman originated the iconic phrase: 'My name is Bond, James Bond' though with McGoohan it was 'My name is Drake, John Drake.'

22

08.12 a.m.

I wanted to put the rubbish out this morning but couldn't find my door key. The Princess, who was in the kitchen, said she would find her key and started rummaging in her handbag. After waiting several minutes while she searched through the bag I went upstairs, found my keys, walked downstairs, opened the back door, took out the rubbish, came back, locked the door, took my key back upstairs and put it on my desk where it lives and went back downstairs 'Here it is!' she cried, with delight, holding up her key. 'I've found it.'

11.17 a.m.

David Cameron, the British Prime Minister, has insulted British ex-servicemen and heaven knows how many bereaved families by describing Britain as the junior partner to the USA in WWII. In fact, if Cameron knew anything about British history he would know that, as in World War I, the Americans sat on the sidelines for ages, watching to see who would get the upper hand, before selling us their services.

Shortly afterwards CBS News interviewed a random sample of adults across the USA, asking them what profession came to mind when they heard the name David Cameron. The answers were: Film director 27%; Foreign Head of State 14%; Professional soccer player 11%; American Idol winner 8%; Don't know 40%.

23

15.16 p.m.

I went to the optician for another eye test. I thought I should have a second opinion. I very nearly got into terrible trouble within minutes of entering the shop. When directed to the machine used to do the visual field tests I almost sat down on a chair with wheels at the end of its legs. 'Not on that chair!' shouted the assistant. I looked at him, puzzled. 'Not on the chair with wheels,' he explained. 'Health and safety?' I said. 'Exactly,' he nodded. At the end of the test the optician confirmed that I have early macular degeneration. This confirms that I am slowly going blind. With The Princess having been told that she may have motor neurone disease and me told I'm going blind the future is beginning to look bleak. How safe will I be, as a blind person, pushing her round in a wheelchair? The optician suggests that I take Omega 3 fish-oil capsules. These are apparently supposed to help slow the progress. Another dilemma for a vegetarian.

24
19.18 p.m.
A reader today has ordered eight different books - including two novels, two political books, three cat books and one medical book. When I first started publishing my own books I wrote books under one name but circulated details to readers in different mailshots. So the people who bought fiction were offered only fiction. And the people who bought medical books were offered only new medical books. After a year or two of this I decided to experiment with a little `cross-selling' and to my delight I found that the artificial barriers I had created were entirely unnecessary. The readers who bought one of my novels were just as likely to buy a medical book or a book on politics.

20.49 p.m.
I heard today about a woman who had a baby which refused to take milk from her right breast. The baby would only feed from the left breast. The woman wisely went to her doctor who found that she had a lump. Cancer was diagnosed and treated. This is a pure example of *bodypower* in action.

25
14.02 p.m.
`How will your furniture look in here?' asked an estate agent today as we looked over a large, Victorian mansion that was cold, dark and rather damp. I think she was just looking for something to say that would draw attention away from the fungus growing out of the skirting board. We said our furniture would be just fine.

It is surprising how many people look for a house that their furniture will fit. It is much more sensible, and far cheaper, to find a house that you like and then carefully buy furniture that will suit it.

When buying furniture we try to buy old stuff. Antique furniture, or elderly second-hand furniture as we are happy to call it, is invariably better made, far cheaper and a good deal more attractive than modern furniture. And, unlike modern furniture, it will retain its value. If you sell a bookcase that is 100 years old you will probably get what you paid for it. You may even make a profit. You will have had the use of the bookcase for some years at no cost. If you buy a brand new bookcase then it will probably be close to worthless when you come to sell it.

And, of course, we always try to follow William Morris's simple rule: everything we buy needs to be either functional or beautiful or, preferably, both.

20.12 p.m.

We spent 40 minutes trying to fit a new ink cartridge into one of our printers. Why are refills so impossible to fit to fax machines and printers? The only pieces of equipment we have which accept new cartridges easily are an old HP printer (it recently celebrated its 25th birthday) and a HP photographic printer. Everything else is a nightmare. (It has only just occurred to me that both the easy-to-refill devices are made by Hewlett Packard. Maybe we should buy more of their stuff.) In the end we throw away the refill and the printer. In the last two years I have thrown away three printers and one fax machine simply because I couldn't get the damned refills into them. The last time I tried to put a new cartridge into our fax machine I ruined the carpet and a perfectly good pair of trousers and had to throw away two cartridges because they had leaked.

26

21.28 p.m.

Self-publishing has over the years often been the only way to get important books published. Self-publishing gives authors independence, freedom to write the books they want to write, freedom from men in suits who decide that this book might not make a profit or that book might cause too much trouble with the establishment and freedom from girly editors who got their job because daddy knows someone in the conglomerate who owns the publishing company and wants a place to park her until she marries a banker and settles down to enjoy point to pointing and a position on an Arts Council committee or two. This is now more than ever true because commercial publishers are frightened of lawsuits and of upsetting some other part of the conglomerate which owns them. Self-publishing has a long history; there have been more great books self-published than published commercially. For example, if they hadn't self-published the world would have been deprived of books by: Thomas Malthus, Virginia Woolf, James Boswell, Dr Johnson, William Cobbett, Lewis Carroll, Edward Lear, Robert Lewis Stevenson, Enid Blyton, James Joyce, Evelyn Waugh, Norman Douglas, Balzac, T.E. Lawrence, Graham Greene, Beatrix Potter, Walter Scott, J. M. Barrie, T. S. Elliot, Mark Twain, Jane Austen, Frank Harris, Anais Nin, W. H. Davies, Walt Whitman and D. H. Lawrence. (That's just a tiny fragment, off the top of my head, of the authors who I know to have self published their books.)

I started publishing my own books because London publishers wouldn't publish my book *Alice's Diary*. I had a literary agent at a smart London agency (Anne McDermid at Curtis Brown) who was fed up with me `crying in the wilderness' and who wanted me to write the books the marketing people wanted (and were prepared to pay good money for) rather than the books I wanted to write. Another agent got huffy when I wanted to write a vegetarian diet book. She had already sold one diet book by another author and was so vain she thought she would be typecast as an agent who sold diet books. (To prove a point I did sell that book to a publisher and received a £20,000 advance for it.)

Self-publishing is very much despised within the world of publishing. And yet doing it yourself is considered quite wonderful in just about all other areas of life. Musicians and singers who publish themselves are considered innovative and are praised for taking control from the international music publishers. Artists who take control of their own work are considered wise and film directors who produce their own movies are deified as `independents'. Actors who start their own theatres are praised. Fashion designers who set up their own labels are regarded as innovative and imaginative. Sports stars who set up their own management companies are regarded as brave and sensible for having the courage to back their own convictions. But authors who self-publish are derided and attacked by the entire publishing industry; they are patronised and sneered at as beneath contempt. It doesn't matter how successful they might be. (This is largely a

British phenomenon and has to be put into perspective. If you do anything original or exceptional or not quite ordinary in the UK then you are sneered at. It is for that reason, perhaps, that so few people do anything original or creative and so many choose to work for the bureaucratic and safe BBC.) When Andrew Lloyd Webber, the composer becomes an impresario and theatre owner it's regarded as wonderful. When the film of *Mrs Caldicot's Cabbage War* was released not one journalist in Britain was interested in the fact that a £12 million film had been made of a self-published novel. In a way I can understand why the publishing industry is so dismissive of self-publishing; if it ever caught on in a big way a lot of overpaid, untalented parasites would find themselves out of work.

Self-publishing is sometimes deliberately confused with vanity publishing. The broadsheet newspapers are particularly likely to do this. And yet most broadsheet newspapers are themselves in the vanity publishing business. What else do you call a business which consistently loses money? Just before the paper was sold to an ex KGB officer, the Independent News and Media's investment in the *Independent* and the *Independent on Sunday* had failed to make a profit from 1998. Now, that's what I call vanity publishing. And *The Guardian* wouldn't exist if it weren't kept alive by a supporting charity.

Of course, if you self-publish on a small scale that's fine. It is considered quite sweet. But when self-publishing becomes a threat to the publishing establishment then it's regarded as dangerous - a threat to agents, publishers and the whole darned industry. If you sell mail order that's a threat to bookshops too. The industry will do everything it can to stamp on self-publishers who actually sell books.

I've thought a lot about this and today I have to admit that I would not recommend self-publishing to anyone. Indeed, I don't think I'd recommend authorship as a career. Authors need encouragement and I confess I have been battered by the sneers from the publishing professionals. Publishers, libraries and bookshops have done their level best to make life difficult.

I always made life difficult for myself by insisting that I make a profit. I have never wanted to be a vanity publisher - printing books and then storing them in the garage. But I also know that

I've made things more difficult for myself by being a maverick; by insisting on telling the truth (even when it has proved dangerous and expensive). I would say that I have done just about everything wrong from a career point of view. But then I've never thought of writing as a career. It's just what I do. When I get maudlin and introspective like this The Princess is under instructions to mention one word: Cobbett. Whenever I think I'm having a tough time I re-read my own essay on William Cobbett in my book *The 100 Greatest Englishmen and Englishwomen*. I then feel ashamed of my whinging.

23.32 p.m.

In Germany elderly citizens, pissed off with their losses, have kidnapped a local financial advisor, trussed him up with duct tape and locked him in their cellar. This is not the English way, perhaps, but thank heavens there are still people on the planet who have had enough of bankers and financial advisers.

23.58 p.m.

An acquaintance of ours tells us that he bought a hotel, intending to turn it into a private house. Unfortunately, he does not have planning permission for the change. Despite this he and his wife and their three children moved into the former hotel and started altering it to suit family life. Three weeks later a man from the local planning department came round.

'We *are* running a hotel,' said my friend. He showed the planning officer some leaflets he had wisely had printed.

The planning officer demanded to see the tariff. Our acquaintance produced a copy of the tariff. '£10,000 a night!' exclaimed the man from the planning department.

'We only want special people to stay here,' said our acquaintance. And. he insists, there is nothing the planning department can do about it. The planning department is apparently not empowered to decide prices. This reminds me of a fellow I heard of who ran a window cleaning service. He carried his ladder on a Lamborghini instead of a bicycle and charged the costs. The taxman appealed but the window cleaner won. The judge decided that the taxman does not have the right to decide how a taxpayer conducts his business.

27

14.28 p.m.

We went to the hospital for tests which should show whether or not The Princess is suffering from a variety of motor neurone disease known as ALS. This is not a pleasant disease. We are both utterly terrified.

We have visited the hospital four times and still not seen the consultant to whom The Princess was referred. Maybe he doesn't exist. Maybe he retired or left and the system has not yet registered that he has disappeared. Maybe he is just too busy.

While The Princess had the tests done I wrote this:

`To my darling wife, my sweetheart and best possible friend. I thank God for allowing me to share the journey with you, for allowing me to be by your side and to hold you in my heart. You are more to me than life itself; the journey, with you, is the everything. Without you the world would be cold and dark and pointless, but with you there is hope. I would give you all the flowers in the world if I could. Instead I give you all my love and loyalty and friendship. You are my sunshine and without you there would be no light in my life.*

God will decide how far we journey but you will always be with me, in every form, for as long as either of us shall continue onwards.'

I don't give her this. She will see it if and when she reads this diary. If The Princess goes then I know that I will go too. Without her there will be no purpose.

21.14 p.m.

An unnamed self-employed man had overpaid his tax by £3,000. When the HMRC discovered his error they fined him £1,400 for paying too much. I can believe it. The self-employed are the backbone of any country. They are the people who provide the energy, the commitment and the enterprise that keeps everything else going. And yet public sector employees always hate the self-employed - possibly because they hate what they see as their sense of freedom. And so the self-employed are constantly oppressed by reams of new legislation. The single greatest difference between the employed and the self-employed is that for the self-employed time really is money. If a man working for the Foreign Office wastes a day filling in a useless form he still gets paid. The same is true for the man working for British Petroleum. But the self-employed guy who wastes a day on form filling has lost a day's earning capacity and must either work late into the night or eat less.

22.12 p.m.
Corn based ethanol is subsidised by the American government at around £1 per gallon. When will the Americans realise that this is distorting the markets for oil and food. The grain needed to fill the tank of a fairly typical American car would feed one person for a whole year.

23.01 p.m.
Increasing numbers of people are clamouring to be bailed out because their houses aren't worth what they were when they bought them. Two things occur to me. Would these people have handed over part of their profits if their house values had risen? And will the Government start to reimburse investors whose stock market selections have proved unfortunate?

23.58 p.m.
We are trying to keep busy and pretend that the world is still going round on its axis. We bought a new printer at PC World. We now have nearly as many printers as books. (That is a wild exaggeration). The assistant insisted that it would work with our new netbook and, with shameful gullibility, we believed him. Although we paid cash for the printer he naturally wanted a mass of private information before allowing us to depart with the printer. He was confused when I said I didn't have a telephone number and alarmed when I insisted on giving him a Post Office Box address. (`What street is it on? Do you actually live there?') The new printer came with an 80-page instruction booklet. Just two of those pages are in English, the rest are in a wide variety of other languages, many of which I have never heard of. That's 78 pages wasted. How does that help the environment? Still, I suppose we should be grateful that we got anything in print. The last time I bought a camera we had to print out the instruction booklet ourselves. The

damned thing took up 280 pages of A4 paper and was the size of a decent length novel when it had finished printing. In the bad old days, before progress ruined everything, there would have been a neat little booklet that I could have stuffed into my pocket with the camera.

When we got the printer home we found that it would not work with the netbook. The reason is simple. Before we can use the printer we need to install the printer software on the netbook using the CD they have supplied. And the netbook, of course, has no CD drive.

28
11.46 a.m.
The Government has revealed that two families have between them cost the taxpayer £37,000,000 over three generations. A strong argument both for compulsory sterilisation and euthanasia.

12.14 p.m.
A sad and rather sorry soul is apparently telling Web users that he isn't going to buy my book *Oil Apocalypse*. I have no idea why he has decided he isn't going to buy it and I really don't give a fig since the book pretty well sold out some time ago and I don't have time to produce a new edition. One reader has so far made over £1,000,000 by following the investment advice the book contains. The correspondent who told me about the person who isn't going to buy my book reports that the non-buyer has written a book about peak oil himself. I suspect he had his tongue sticking out of the corner of his mouth throughout the creative process. What makes me think his sales aren't going too well?

Everyone has the right to speak but the Web has proved beyond doubt that not many people are worth listening to. The main problem is that bloggers are so desperate for attention that they follow the abusive ways of the worst television presenters in order to attract attention. To protect themselves from the consequences of their outbursts, and to avoid responsibility, they often use the Web's anonymity. When found out they usually run a mile, whimper and beg for forgiveness; they are Gollums of the new underworld. People who write on the Web should have to identify themselves - especially if they are commenting on someone else or someone else's work.

15.16 p.m.

I hate clichés. At my request The Princess has collected a list of my favourite phrases. These are, apparently, the ones I use daily.

1. I'm hungry.
2. I've eaten too much.
3. I shouldn't have eaten that.
4. Is there any more of that?
5. I'm tired.
6. I hate the BBC.
7. I'm getting old.
8. You won't believe what I saw someone do today.
9. Did you see that? (Usually spoken on a motorway.)
10. What did I come in here for?
11. Have you seen my pen/notebook/reading spectacles?
12. I've lost the keys. I really mean it this time.

She says that if these phrases were removed from my daily conversation I would be largely silent. The awful thing is that I suspect she is right. I am mortified.

29

11.57 a.m.

A leaked HMRC internal document reveals that 82% of tax office employees are not proud to work for the department and 86% would not recommend working for it. A staggering 87% agree that, as a whole, HMRC is not well managed. And 88% have no confidence in the decisions made by HMRC's senior managers. It seems that tax office employees are as distrusting of their bosses as the general public. I wonder what top management are doing about this? My guess is that they're putting all their energy into finding out where the leak came from. When I revealed evidence that the NHS was paying more for things like envelopes, pens and soap powder than I would pay if I were buying them one at a time in my local supermarket the NHS immediately launched an investigation. But the investigation was not designed to find out why an organisation which was buying these items by the million wasn't obtaining a discount but to find out how I obtained a secret computer printout proving the waste.

14.25 p.m.

Google really should put less effort into stealing books and more into providing a decent search engine. (I am still aggrieved that Google appears to have helped itself to 271 different editions of my books and that if I want any compensation I have to fill in forms to claim any money that might be on offer.)

I go cold inside when I think that schoolteachers train children to use the Internet as a source of information. Anyone who thinks they can find news or truth on the Web is deluded. I believe that big search engines may sometimes give priority to sites which pay the most. You have to be very good to spot the truth. Computers themselves are absurdly overcomplicated and are obviously designed by half-witted nerds who are obsessed with obsolescence. They have not reached Model T Ford quality or reliability. Buy the very latest creation and you will still find yourself struggling to make the damned thing work efficiently. If fridges worked as well as computers our food would all go bad. And can there have ever been a more environmentally unfriendly industry?

The Web is an underworld community controlled and dominated by nerds, thieves, liars, fraudsters, cheats and perverts. No invention has done more harm and less good.

The Internet has destroyed honour, honesty, respect and decency and all the other virtues, and replaced them with envy, resentment and rumour mongering. It has done this not by itself, of course, but by enabling people to do these things without punishment; by allowing them authority without responsibility. The Internet, dramatic and instant, global and universal, wastes far more than it saves, destroys every type of commerce from the root upwards and is destroying music and literature by taking away the ability and the freedom of artists to earn a living.

30

14.23 p.m.

Yet another policeman has been found not guilty of anything after a member of the public was killed. I wonder how many people are aware that no British police officer has yet been convicted of manslaughter committed while on duty, in spite of a series of high profile deaths. So far there have, of course, been no charges after the deaths of Blair Peach, Jean Charles de Menezes or Ian Tomlinson.

17.18 p.m.
A friend tells me that he download *Ulysses* by James Joyce and connected it up to a computerised grammar check. The computer broke down.

31
21.14 p.m.
We spent a whole day today driving to see a house near Hereford. It looked wonderful on the estate agent's brochure. The house, large rambling and Edwardian, had a few acres of land and a country cottage in the grounds. There was a long driveway, a pond and a swimming pool (which we could, we thought, easily turn into another duck pond) and a summerhouse. The garden, we were assured, was very private. It looked perfect. When we got there we found that the owner, or a previous owner, had sold off a piece of the garden and allowed another house to be built in the grounds. The new house was on a slightly higher level, staring right down into the garden and the back of the house. There was no privacy at all. The photographs they had taken had, of course, carefully excluded all sight of this excrescence. It was a day and a tankful of petrol wasted. Did the agents really think that we wouldn't see the neighbouring house built in the garden? Or did they just not understand the word `private'?

Afterwards we went into the town of Hereford which is an excellent small market town. Everyone we met, in every shop, smiled and was helpful. Even the staff in the chain stores were courteous and pleasant. I bought a lovely edition of William Blake's work and a first edition of Hilaire Belloc's biography of Cromwell. Total cost £1. Once again, two fingers raised (palm inwards) to Oxfam. It has been a relatively quiet week for book buying but I counted up the week's purchases and I have bought 26 books. If this isn't an addiction I don't know what is. Maybe I should start a society called Bibliophiles Anonymous and make myself honorary President, Secretary, Treasurer and sole member. Perhaps I could apply for charitable status and a European grant.

22.17 p.m.

A reader from Liverpool wants to know why I still write books (which he describes as 'rather old-fashioned') and don't simply confine myself to writing a 'blog'. He also wants to know which of my books have been banned – and why.

England Our England was, the first of my political books to be banned. It has never been reviewed anywhere and advertisements for it are widely banned. Even the British Legion refused to take any more advertisements in their magazine, claiming that they had received complaints from members who were unhappy with the attack on the European Union. Numerous magazines which promote English virtues and qualities banned the book for the same reason, suggesting to me that many people still don't realise exactly what the European Union does and aims to do.

Even radio stations got very excited about the idea of a book criticising the European Union. I did very few radio interviews for *England Our England* and most broadcasting companies refused even to mention the book. On one rare and memorable occasion when I was interviewed on a national radio station a presenter whose name I have long since forgotten became so irate in defence of the EU, so aghast that anyone could dare question its aims, and so furious that he could not disprove of the arguments in the book, that he suddenly cut the interview short and announced that he was going to refuse to mention the title of the book. He was, presumably, worried that his more curious listeners might find a copy of the book, read it and discover the truth.

More recently advertisements for other books of mine, such as *Gordon is a Moron* and *Oil Apocalypse* have been banned by virtually every national newspaper - even though several papers had run one or more of the advertisements without complaint. By an odd coincidence all the papers decided to ban the books at the same time. I try not to suspect conspiracies and powerful people making telephone calls but sometimes it's difficult to suppress the thought.

(Sometimes the bans are downright silly. For example, *Country Life* magazine refused to take an advert for *Gordon is a Moron* because someone at the magazine thought that the advert wasn't pretty enough.)

I was told that I couldn't put advertisements for *Oil Apocalypse* and *Gordon is a Moron* into the national press because both were expressing the author's opinion. I pointed out that since *Oil Apocalypse* was a book about the future it was inevitably my opinion. `When an author writes about the future,' I explained, `the book must be a forecast which is inevitably an opinion. An opinion based on fact. But an opinion. The weather forecast is an opinion.' I pointed out that I had never seen the words `This is an opinion' on a weather forecast. I offered to put the words `Warning: opinion' on the top of the advertisement for *Oil Apocalypse* but no one would take me up on the offer. *Gordon Is A Moron* is, I pointed out, an appraisal of a political career. `It is,' I pointed out, `a commentary on part of a politician's career, so it is, of course, an opinion.' I offered to add the following words to the advertisement: `This is a book and therefore contains the author's opinions. The Government and the editor of this newspaper do not agree with his opinions.' In the end, neither of my offers was accepted. And effectively adverts for the books were banned.

Why do so many publications refuse adverts for my books?

It is, I suppose, impossible to generalise. (Though it is worth making the point that not one publication has refused to carry advertisements because someone has found a factual error in a book.)

My non-fiction books do question Government policies, do pose a real threat to many parts of the Establishment and are a commercial threat to many multinationals. And that, it seems, is what frightens so many editors.

Time and time again I find that I am banned because I make people think.

Curious.

I always thought that was one of an author's main responsibilities.

I hope my books continue to make people think.

Magazines, newspapers and broadcasters may ban them.

But I'll continue to write them. And they will continue to be published until The Princess and I run out of breath or money.

Having written articles and columns for most national newspapers and magazines, and having broadcast on most major terrestrial and satellite television and radio stations, I am convinced that only book writers really have freedom to say what they think. (I should add that it is only authors working for small, independent presses who enjoy real freedom.)

The Internet seems to offer great opportunities but in reality the problems with it are legion. Not least is the fact that it is too easy for the fascists to close down or interfere with websites which carry material which displeases them. That has happened to me so often now that The Princess checks regularly to see whether my website is up or down. Books are the ideal medium for communicating genuinely iconoclastic ideas.

And besides, I don't much like doing things the way other people do them. Television and the Web are today widely regarded as the most important and powerful forms of communication. And so I write books. Books are out of fashion, difficult to sell and disliked by the young (the ones with the money) and so I stick with books. Moreover, I sell proper old-fashioned books, printed on paper and then bound between covers, rather than e-books which are circulated through the ether.

23.57 p.m.

The Princess came into my study this evening with a short list of instructions for her funeral and a detailed plan of how she was going to communicate with me if she did have this dreadful disease and eventually lost the ability to talk. We just held each other and cried.

August

1

11.45 a.m.

I have a new book out under a pen name and I think it is about time to start using more pen names. I have over the years used quite a number of them. My first literary agent, Anne McDermid at Curtis Brown, persuaded me that I should write novels and non-fiction under two different names. And so it was that I found myself in the bizarre situation of sitting down with an editor at Pan Books and having to confess that although she knew me as the author of *Stress Control* I was also Edward Vernon, the author of a novel entitled *Practice Makes Perfect*. She was not amused and I got the impression she rather thought she'd been tricked - which, of course, she had. I did media interviews as Edward Vernon and grew a beard for my new persona. I ended up on Central Television (where I was a regular presenter as Vernon Coleman). The interviewer's first question was: `Vernon Coleman, why are you now calling yourself Edward Vernon?'. When I wrote my first thriller, called *Tunnel*, my agent didn't want me to publish it, telling me that it wasn't what I did so I offered it to the publishers Robert Hale who bought it and published it under the name Marc Charbonnier. When my agent found out she was very sniffy about it. (When I recently published a paperback edition under my own name I managed to get the perfect picture for the cover. I was in Paris when there was a fire in the tunnel so I rushed to the station and took a photograph of the signs at the station warning of the fire.)

12.16 p.m.

The Princess was upset today. A cake she had made had gone squishy. I tried to explain that I prefer squishy cake (I do). But she was too upset for comforting. `I don't know why I put myself down so much,' she said finally, when I had eventually managed to reassure her. `Other people do it so much better.'

16.24 p.m.

At the bank a teller wanted to know why I was taking out £3,000 in cash. I said I was going to buy sweets. She wrote this on the form which will, presumably, be sent off to whichever Government department deals with money laundering and terrorism.

2

11.27 a.m.

Why don't you drive to Ashford, asked a friend who knows we use Eurostar to travel to Paris. `There is a multistorey car park built into the station.' There is indeed and we used it for several years. There are two reasons why we now catch the train at St Pancras. First, we would often get on at Ashford and find that our reserved seats were occupied. The staff could not be persuaded to help us throw out the interlopers so we ended up sitting wherever we could. Second, the guards they employed at Ashford to search baggage and clothing were, in my view, the rudest and most aggressive people in the business. Maybe they've improved but if someone told me they'd been trained at Dachau I'd believe it.

14.48 p.m.

We went to see an ex journalist I know. He wrote a number of stories about me in days of yore. When I stopped writing my column in *The Sun* he wrote a story reporting that I'd left and mentioned that I had been paid around £100,000 a year for the column. (Actually, they paid me a flat fee of £1,000 a week for a column and extra for everything else I wrote. To save having to work out a price every time I wrote something, I fixed a price with the news and features editors. They used to pay me £1,500 for a spread (a feature across two pages), £750 if an article was used as a page lead, £500 for anything else which appeared on the page and £250 if whatever I wrote wasn't used.) For several years I had at least one story in almost every day's paper. My pal was inundated with letters from general practitioners offering themselves as my replacement and was particularly amused to get one from his own GP.

19.18 p.m.

The Magna Carta, which was the original of much of the American constitution (the bits they didn't nick off the Native American

312

Indians) and the blueprint for democracies everywhere in the world, has been tossed aside by recent British Governments. The obnoxious Edward Heath (who sold Britain to the EU for a £35,000 fee) and the unctuous, pustulant Blair should be hung. One as a traitor and the other as a war criminal. We would have to dig up Heath, of course, but it would be worth it. I hope the bastard wasn't cremated. Compared with Ted Heath, Tony Blair and Gordon Brown and a thousand other leading British politicians, Adolf Hitler was a trustworthy patriot who loved his country.

23.02 p.m.

How did Adolf Hitler (a dark haired Austrian Jew) manage to sell the concept of a blond, Ayrian super-race so convincingly? I suppose it's a bit like politicians telling us that we must all tighten our belts while they dig their snouts still deeper into the trough.

3

08.12 a.m.

It is The Princess's birthday today! I wrote her a 'pome'.
> `My wife's the best that ever could be
> To all with a brain that's quite clear to see
> She's beautiful, generous, warm-hearted and kind
> The most loving wife I ever could find.'

15.28 p.m.

I was interrupted by a knock on the door this afternoon. I don't usually answer knocks on the door but as I suspected it was one of the men cutting the hedges and trimming the ivy around the house. He stood there looking rather sheepish. He was in his early 20s; a bright looking lad with intelligent eyes. He told me that one of his colleagues had cut through a television aerial cable. `But it's OK,' he said, `I've mended it. And I'm a qualified electrician.' He asked me to check that the television still worked. I checked. It did. I asked the inevitable question. `Why is a fully qualified electrician working as a gardener?'

   `There's no work for electricians,' he replied. `The building trades are dead.' He shrugged, sadly.

   `Things will pick up,' I told him. `It'll just take a bit of time for the mess to be cleared.'

`It's going to take a long time,' he said. `I think there's going to be a double dip recession. It'll come when VAT goes up in January. People are buying stuff now but when VAT is 20% they'll buy far less. It'll make a difference.'

I agreed with him. We talked a little more. When I shut the door I couldn't help reflecting on the fact that the bloke who does our garden almost certainly knows more about the British economy than the so-called experts working for the Bank of England.

17.23 p.m.

A reader reports that when he rang the police to report a break in he was asked for his date of birth and his ethnicity. I agree with him that it seems socially divisive to ask for a caller's colour. It is certainly not socially cohesive and non-racist, which is what the police are apparently supposed to be these days. The only reason for asking the race of someone is if it is going to influence your actions. So, in other words, anyone who asks for your race is racist.

4

16.36 p.m.

We drove to Dorchester today. A local council has put up a huge notice which reads `Most Accidents Happen On Bends'. The warning is accompanied by statistics showing details of the number of accidents which have occurred at that spot. Trying to read the notice I almost swung out into the path of an articulated lorry. `We should put up a sign of our own,' said The Princess. `It should read: `Most accidents happen when drivers are distracted by large pointless road signs.' On the way we amused ourselves by composing slogans for companies to put on the back of their lorries or vans. For a logistics company, endlessly moving stuff about the country, The Princess suggested: `We get most of your stuff to where you want it to go. Eventually.' And for a chimney sweep I suggested: `We clean your chimney cheaply and without using small children'.

In the car park in Dorchester a man approached us and offered to clean our car while we wandered round the town. This seemed a good idea. I paid him and we wandered off. When we got back two hours later the car was as dirty as it ever was. I found the man who took the money and point to the car. He hurried over and gave it a wash. We stood and waited. He didn't make a very good job of it and could see I was not very pleased. He offered to give us the money back but he had thrown water over it and he had done something so I told him to keep it.

Later we sat in a café in Taunton. A man with an extraordinarily loud and annoying laugh sat with his wife at the next table. He told a seemingly endless series of very loud jokes and laughed uproariously a quarter of the way through each joke, half way through and three quarters of the way through. When he'd finished he laughed and laughed and laughed. The jokes weren't in the slightest bit funny. His wife seemed to me to be suitable for sanctification. She smiled beatifically at him as he talked and laughed and whereas I wanted to brain him after being near him for just a quarter of an hour she seemed perfectly content. When the man stood up to go to the lavatory our chips arrived and The Princess leant across to ask the woman if we could borrow the salt on her table. To our astonishment the woman, who was reading a newspaper, ignored her. The Princess asked again, this time making a more deliberate attempt to catch the woman's attention. `I'm sorry,' said the woman in the unmistakeable tones of someone born deaf. She smiled and then pointed to her ears, one after the other. `If I don't see your lips I can't tell what you are saying.'

5

15.03 p.m.

The people who run the EU and the country really do want to control every aspect of our lives. According to a consultation document released today by HMRC the latest plan is for something called `centralised deductions'. Under this scheme employers will use the electronic payments system to send all their employees' gross earnings to a central computer where deductions will be made according to calculations done by HMRC. All this will happen automatically and the resulting net payments will then be sent to each individual's bank account, with the deductions having been paid directly to the Government. I can see one or two possible problems with this scheme. For example, could troublesome individuals be liable to coercion from the Government which will, after all, find it very easy to stop their pay? How secure will the system be? How many mistakes will be made and how long will it take for them to be corrected? I don't suppose any of these potential problems will worry HMRC too much.

16.17 p.m.
I spotted this wonderful notice in a bookshop window this morning: 'We No Longer Except Book Tokens'. The sign was very nicely printed and had clearly been produced by a professional. Or maybe it had been produced by a 'proffesional'.

17.43 p.m.
Am I the only one to have noticed that Britain is now full of people who are very good at finding ways not to do good things; finding ways to say 'no'; finding ways to defend the inequities of a broken system and of allowing only change (described as progress) which further defends the wicked. It used to be just senior civil servants who protected themselves by saying 'no' to every request for permission to do something. But these days the disease has spread all the way down to the lowest pencil pusher in the steaming pile. And the disease has spread sideways into corporations too. There are a good many million people in Britain today who would willingly work as concentration camp guards if they were promised an index-linked final salary pension scheme, a non-contributory health care programme and six weeks paid holiday. Too many people refuse to think for themselves. Too many people are unwilling to trust their own ability to make decisions. Too many people have lost all sight of the meaning of common sense.

6
14.01 p.m.
I was standing in a queue in the bank. 'I'm not going to say anything about her,' said a woman to her companion. She feigned an air of superior restraint. 'There are a lot of things I could say, mind you. But I am not going to say anything.'

There was a loud silence. It seemed louder than gunfire and it lasted for several lifetimes. Everyone knew that in saying nothing the woman had said more than if she had ranted and raged for an hour.

The silence was eventually broken by the woman who had vowed not to speak.

'Nothing,' she said, holding up a hand as though she was resisting unspoken entreaties to speak about the subject she herself had banned. 'Not a word.' She shook her head and scowled. 'Not one word.'

The silence resumed. It was the most impressive and most destructive speech of condemnation I had ever heard.

I went to a café while The Princess went shopping and while there I made up the following list of Coleman's Rules, simple rules of thumb which might help make life go more smoothly.

1. When you find a product which works efficiently, effectively and economically the manufacturer will stop making it. So buy a few extras.

2. Expensive pieces of equipment invariably break down the day after the guarantee runs out. So give them a good work-out as the final day of the guarantee approaches.

3. You never really need a second helping of anything - especially pudding.

4. When you are invited to give a speech and the person inviting you assures you that you will only be expected to talk for half an hour remember that it will invariably take at least half a day to get there and at least half a day to get home. And you will take 50 times as long to research and write your speech as the speech will last. (So the average half hour speech may take up five days of your life.)

5. Stop eating the moment you think you might have had enough to eat and you won't ever get fat.

6. Electrical equipment is coming down in price so fast that the old stuff isn't worth having repaired professionally. Take a deep breath, chuck it away and buy something new.

7. If you are self-employed then 20% of the work you do will be responsible for 80% of the money you earn.

8. Never buy a piece of kitchen equipment or a tool that doesn't have the maker's name permanently engraved upon it. If the maker isn't proud enough to identify himself he probably doesn't expect the item to last long enough for you to be satisfied with it.

9. A caller who dials the wrong number will always ring again two minutes later and will seem just as surprised to find that they have the wrong number as they were the first time.

317

10. When you get put on hold by a telephone call stacking system an automated voice will stop you concentrating on doing anything else by apologising every 30 seconds.

11. If you file it you'll never need it again. If you don't file it you'll never find it again.

12. If you want to get anything done you will have to make a nuisance of yourself - and become unpopular with at least three people.

13. When things go wrong the most obvious and best solution will be the one no one likes to suggest because everyone will assume that such an obvious solution can't possibly be any good.

14. People under 60 invariably arrive late. People over 60 invariably arrive early or not at all.

15. Something you didn't really need but bought anyway will always appear in the sale, at a heavily discounted price, within two weeks. But if you don't buy it then it will never appear in the sale.

16. The quickest way to check out a nursing home is to sniff the moment you walk through the door. If you can smell urine walk straight out again.

17. When you start a new job, or move to a new area, be wary of people who are very friendly and anxious to make you feel comfortable.

18. When you unwrap your shopping the waste packaging will not fit into the bag you used to bring the items home with you.

19. People who do nothing but criticise are like eunuchs. They know how it is done. They have seen it done. But they can't do it themselves.

20. Never fight a bureaucratic organisation. You can't beat a large organisation because it will always have more time, more patience and more money than you have. Organisations don't get tired, they don't feel guilty and they don't become embarrassed. Nor do they worry about losing their jobs. If you want to win, pick a fight with a specific individual within the organisation.

7

10.05 a.m.

When I had parked the car I walked to the ticket machine and found a ginger tom sitting on the ground looking up. It was clearly waiting for a stroke. I put my money into the machine, and then bent down and stroked the cat. It purred loudly. When the machine whirred to let me know that it had digested my money and done its business, I reached out and removed the ticket from the little slot where they appear. `Look,' I said to the cat, `I won!' The cat brushed against my hand and the ticket, clearly sharing my delight. I then stood up and turned to leave. There was a man standing behind me, waiting to put his money into the machine. He looked terrified.

12.08 p.m.

After attempting to buy train tickets I have decided that it is not stupidity which annoys me as much as gross incompetence. I always have difficulty buying train tickets. A task which should take no more than five minutes often takes half or three quarters of an hour. To try to speed things up I wrote down exactly what I wanted. I wrote down the time of the train I wanted to catch on the outward journey and the time and date of the train I wanted to catch on the return journey. I noted that I wanted first class tickets and that I wanted tickets for two passengers. I gave the station I wanted to leave from and the station I wanted to go to. Direct trains travel regularly between the two. The woman clerk got everything wrong. She gave me second class tickets. She gave me tickets for the wrong train. She gave me tickets for a train travelling at the wrong time. Every time she gave me the wrong tickets I pointed out the mistake and gave her the tickets back. By the time she had finished and had given me the correct tickets there was a mound of tickets in front of her. Then I reminded her that I had asked for a receipt. She demanded that I give her the tickets back. I did so and watched carefully as she mixed up the correct tickets with the mound of wrong ones. When I had finally got my tickets and my receipt she scowled at me. `I wish people wouldn't write things down,' she snarled. `It was all your fault that I got confused.'

17.52 p.m.

Time after time estate agents offer us houses which have a garden, or a field next door which is being sold separately. Sometimes the sellers have acquired planning permission and so they want a huge price for the piece of land they are selling. If you don't buy the

319

extra land then you stand the risk of living next to a building site for a year and then having a house with a neighbour just yards away. We saw a house where the owner wanted another £200,000 for a field no more than half an acre in size.

We have so far seen three houses where the garage was being sold separately. On two occasions the vendors had obtained planning permission to turn their garage into a house. So if we had bought the house we would have no garage but another house in our garden. We saw a house where the field beside it, a mess of scrubland, was being sold for another £75,000 even though it had no planning permission and was patently useless since it was almost vertical and would have proved quite a challenge to a gardener fitted with crampons.

8
11.38 a.m.
We travelled on a train, in a quiet carriage, with a friend who is a show business reporter. The first 20 minutes of the journey were disrupted by the noisy chatter of four minor television celebrities. They were gossiping nastily about one another and about people they had met. They were being particularly cruel about various producers they knew. Eventually, our friend had had enough. He got up and walked down the carriage, spoke quietly to the four minor celebrities and then walked back to our table. The celebrities had gone silent. 'How did you do that?' asked The Princess, impressed. 'I told them I'm a show business reporter,' he said. 'I warned them that I could hear everything they were saying and that if I heard another peep out of them I would print everything they said.' The Z listers were silent for the rest of the journey.

15.04 p.m.
A Bournemouth paper carried a review of a book *Animal Miscellany* which The Princess and I wrote together. The reviewer managed to spell my name incorrectly and went on to complain that the book contains 'a deluge of emotive language and opinion that serves to alienate potential readers'. The reviewer then adds 'however, such a flaw only pops up sporadically'. The Princess said she is very proud to have mastered the sporadic deluge at such an early stage in her career as a writer. The review isn't all bad.

The critic describes the book as `highly interesting and extremely useful' and gives it three stars. Which is better and slightly less patronising than one star and `see me after school'.

9
19.16 p.m.

An American visits and insists on going to a cricket match. We take him to Lords and into the Pavilion. The gateman, whom I don't think I have ever seen before, looks at my MCC pass smiles and says: `Lovely to see you, again, sir.' I'm pretty sure he's never seen me before either but I always love that sort of nonsense. Naturally, our guest has no idea what is going on. Eventually, he admits that he doesn't like sport very much. I am not surprised. The Americans are no good at sport. They play netball, rounders and an embarrassingly wimpy version of rugby in which players are dressed up in acres of protective padding. When the British Empire collapsed we left the world with cricket, football, rugby, tennis, golf and a hundred other sports. When America collapses it will be remembered for introducing Mickey Mouse, barbed wire and very little else.

21.45 p.m.

A reader complains that some of my books are written in a `bitty' style. The truth is that I find it harder to write books this way than to write them in the old-fashioned way. But many readers do like books that are written in chunks. I did this first with *England Our England* and I've used the style several times since. It isn't an original idea, of course. The world's biggest ever bestselling book, The Bible, is written in a bitty style.

10
15.19 p.m.

A friend who locked his keys in his car when he got to his office tells me that he solved the problem by ringing his wife (who was at home) and asking her to fetch the spare key, hold it next to the phone and press the remote unlock button. While she was doing this my friend held his phone next to his car. His car then dutifully unlocked itself. I was very impressed by this.

18.36 p.m.

Two days ago we were sent smart, steel and glass, squirrel proof bird feeders by a reader in America. Today, we found the bird feeders broken up into bits and distributed around the garden. Teeth marks show the identity of the culprits. The squirrels were, I swear, sitting in the trees laughing. English squirrels (even of North American origin) are clearly cleverer and more industrious than their cousins across the Atlantic.

11

11.36 a.m.

The Princess telephoned the hospital to see if they had the results of her tests yet. She spoke to a secretary who reported that the letter telling her whether or not she has motor neurone disease has yet to be typed. And when it has been typed it will still have to be signed. The Princess asked if the letter could be faxed. She was told it could not. Her symptoms are worse than ever. The muscle twitching is really bad. To add to her problems an entire tooth filling fell out (probably because of bruxism caused by the extra stress). The hospital (it is the Frenchay Hospital near Bristol) could teach the CIA a thing or two about torture techniques.

12

13.09 p.m.

To take our minds off the missing hospital test results the Princess and I went shopping and separated to buy presents (mainly for each other). We arranged to meet at a local café. I got there first and when I entered the couple in front of me were trying to pay for two coffees with a credit card. They were having all sorts of problems. First, they couldn't decide which card to use. Then the machine rejected one card. And on and on it went. I caught the assistant's eye, quietly asked for a coffee and put the money down on the counter. He served me and I was sitting down, sipping my coffee and reading a book of Graham Greene stories in French (I was struggling) while they were still working out how to pay for the cooling coffees on the counter. Why do people insist on paying small bills with credit cards? It wastes time and it's bad security too. Around 90% of all high street transactions are now done using credit and debit cards. Oh, how easily folk are led into bad habits.

Earlier in the day I had stood behind a woman taking for ever to pay £2.95 for a birthday card with a credit card. It was one of the platinum cards and she flashed it around a lot, making sure that everyone could see her using it. I said something about cash being quicker. `Oh, this is much safer than cash,' she said. `No, it's not,' I said. `There are eight of us standing behind you and we all saw you key in your pin number. We're probably all honest but have you heard of credit card fraud and identity theft?' She grabbed her card and rushed out of the shop. `Cash is so much classier, don't you think?' I said to the assistant, who beamed approval.

17.18 p.m.
A cricket match is being played between two teams made up of women. Women cricketers used to wear nice little white dresses and blouses. They looked like women playing cricket. These players are all dressed like men. Until they do something, and start playing, it is difficult to tell that they are not men. They seem to be enjoying themselves but I can only assume that the spectators are relatives or friends.

21.11 p.m.
Working on ways to promote books it occurs to me that perhaps we could offer free adverbs and adjectives with all our books. `You only pay for verbs and nouns.' Maybe we would give the punctuation away as an extra added bonus.

13
11.31 a.m.
I telephoned the hospital. The registrar is off sick. The letter telling The Princess whether or not she has motor neurone disease has been typed. But it is sitting there waiting to be signed. I told the secretary to whom I spoke that the inmates of Guantanamo are treated better. She said that the letter would be sent when ready. I then pointed out that we have been waiting nearly three weeks to find out whether or not The Princess has a fatal disease. Three weeks of sleeplessness. Three weeks of fears and tears. I also pointed out that we have not once met her consultant yet. I added that when we went for nerve conduction tests two other men (one of them not medically qualified) had been invited to watch. I told

the secretary that The Princess had been extremely embarrassed when told to remove her tights in front of three men. There was no screen and no nurse. I added that I have a medical degree, am a registered and licensed GP and am a Professor of Holistic Medical Sciences and finally I said that under all the circumstances it might be a good idea if they faxed the letter to us that afternoon. An hour or so later the fax machine purred into life and the fax came through. All the tests were negative. The Princess does not have motor neurone disease. The Princess says she is not going to the Frenchay again and that she would rather just wait to see what happens. I will write more about The Princess's treatment in the book I am writing about health care. Meanwhile, I will endeavour to make her well with love. Stress, anxiety and unlove can cause illness. I believe that love can cure it.

We are too drained to celebrate.

But not too exhausted to thank God.

14
11.18 a.m.

Jewish American Bernie Madoff is reputed to have stolen $65 billion from the people who trusted him with their money. He was, in truth, just a small time crook. The really big tricksters are governments and huge international industries. They are people who cheat and fiddle really successfully, taking advantage of trust and innocence to steal unimaginable amounts of money from the citizens of the world. Vaccination and vivisection are two of the best known, long established frauds but AIDS and genetic engineering have done very nicely for their enthusiastic supporters over the last decade or two. Now, the fastest rising fraud is climate change; a brand new industry built on innuendo, threats and the insane beliefs of a few well-connected lunatics and apparently independent experts. The planet may, or may not, be getting warmer but there's no evidence proving that any change is man-made. I would report the Government's latest climate change advertisements to the ASA but the chances of that wretched little organisation finding against the Government are approximately the same as the Government suddenly being overwhelmed by an irresistible urge to tell the truth. (The ASA, the Advertising Standards Authority, is a private body which has the power to put out press releases but it cannot ban advertising.) I have reluctantly come to the conclusion that it is now impossible to change things in Britain because the media is bent and there is no longer any real debate on big, important issues. The BBC, being a mouthpiece for the Government and the European Union is the worst offender but it is not the only one. I've yet to see a proper, honest debate about any of the significant issues facing us on any British television channel. And I don't have great hopes that I will.

14.40 p.m.

I was interviewed by a journalist who talked incessantly about herself, her plans, her career, her hopes, the book she was planning to write, the second book she was planning to write after she'd finished that one, the interesting people she'd interviewed and so on. Then she spent some time moaning about unfairness at work. She should have been promoted but hadn't been. After nearly an hour of this I looked at my watch and apologised for having to leave. `Oh you can't go,' she said. `This is such a useful interview!'

15

10.51 a.m.

There is much talk in the newspapers about the importance of DNA evidence. I wonder how many people realise that DNA residue can be transferred easily from one person to another simply by shaking hands. So if a bad person shakes hands with a good person and the bad person then goes off and commits a crime he might well leave some of the good person's DNA at the scene of the crime. And the police will then arrest the good person and be able to produce DNA evidence at the trial. I can see that the authorities might prefer this knowledge to remain with the few rather than be shared with the many.

14.46 p.m.

It is often said that self-publishers should only publish books that a `proper' publisher would have bought and published. I can understand why people say this but it isn't true any more. Many of my most successful books would, I feel confident, have been turned down by London publishing houses. No one would have published *Gordon is a Moron*, for example. And, of course, *Alice's*

Diary was turned down by just about every publisher in London. People who work for publishing companies these days are terrible at understanding which books will sell and which will not. This explains why there are so many successful remainder shops selling books that publishers can't get rid of in the normal way. And it explains why so few publishers actually make a profit.

16.01 p.m.
When I rang the bank to ask them to move some money from an account they asked a series of security questions including: `What's the overdraft facility on this account?'. Puzzled, I said I didn't know. The bank employee pushed. I said I wasn't aware there was one. `So what's your answer?' he asked. `There isn't one,' I replied. `That's the correct answer,' he said. The Princess said if they are going to ask trick questions they should allow us to phone a friend. `Actually, I failed anyway,' I said. `He then asked me for details of the last cheque to go through the account. Naturally I have no idea when cheques are presented. I had three attempts but failed and was disqualified. I didn't get to the third question.'

18.32 p.m.
An actress is recommending that people borrow books instead of buying them. `This is a great way to save the environment,' she is quoted as saying. And I think people should stop going to films and theatres because of all the pollution and oil usage. People should stay at home and read their library books.

19.01 p.m.
I've had an e-mail from someone offering to write free articles for my website on any subject of my choice. The only payment I have to make is to provide free links, embedded in the articles. I suspect there will be ads and plugs in the articles too. This is reason 827,373 why the Internet is totally unreliable as a source of information. I will close my website before I accept free articles from someone else. I've also made a policy decision not to accept links. I don't know why. I just have.

21.49 p.m.

I have decided to sort through my books. Throughout the sorting I will apply four criteria: Will I read it again?

Will I consult it? Is it valuable? Does it have sentimental value?

16
11.14 a.m.

Today's mail includes a long letter written on a length of wallpaper, a letter from a reader who complains that my books seem to tumble out of my head, a note from a sailor who asks to meet to discuss his new 250,000 word book, a letter from a woman demanding that I join her local campaign against incineration and waste disposal (I've already explained to her that the decisions about such matters are made by the EU and so there is no point in campaigning locally) and a lovely letter from a Bilbury reader who writes: 'I hope there will be a new one before or for the Christmas season. I always look forward to the next Bilbury novel. I wish there could be one every year, as I like them so much. They give me a feel good factor and leave me happy and smiling. So, Vernon, I hope you have good news for a grateful, long standing fan of Bilbury village life, and its great characters'.

14.53 p.m.

When I was writing *The 100 Greatest Englishmen and Englishwomen* I was initially astonished at the number of great people who spent at least part of their lives in prison. The explanation, of course, is that many great men and women are intrinsically rebellious and therefore especially likely to get into trouble with the authorities. And, after all, no one ever did great things by agreeing with the establishment; no one ever changed things for the better without having original ideas. And original ideas are always an anathema to the establishment.

17
14.47 p.m.

I was about to pay for fuel at a petrol station and was looking for sweets to buy. The place was deserted except for a couple who had clearly just been guests at a wedding. He had a white carnation in the buttonhole of his ill-fitting suit. She wore one of those outfits that women only wear to weddings. They had clearly been discussing something in the car. `Well,' said the woman, clearly putting an end to the conversation. `I still think that a wedding without an organ is a big disappointment.'

When I got back to the car I told The Princess what I'd heard. `I suspect it was a bigger disappointment to the bride than anyone else,' she said.

15.38 p.m.
We stopped for a coffee at a very pleasant café. It was surprisingly busy. The terrace at the front of the building was packed with people relaxing, smoking, drinking coffee and eating cakes. I asked a waiter I recognised if they had any free tables. `Only right at the back,' he said, apologetically. `These days we're always full with these damned people.' I raised an eyebrow, hoping for more. `They're mostly Romanians and Poles,' he explained. `They don't work but they have money to sit there all day drinking coffee and smoking. I rush around waiting on them for a pittance and I'm helping pay for them to sit there and have a pleasant time in the sunshine.' I suspect that he is not the only one to feel resentful. There is, as I pointed out many years ago, going to be an explosion against the immigration policies the EU has forced us to adopt. Those who advocate multicultural policies have no idea just how many problems they are creating.

18.21 p.m.
We spent the afternoon in Wells and had a picnic on a bench overlooking the moat around the Bishop's Palace. We decided to play a game of I Spy. 'I Spy something beginning with B,' said The Princess. After ten minutes spent naming the objects around me (bench, bird, book, bag, etc.), I finally gave up. 'You win. What's the answer?' The Princess looked at me incredulously, as if I should have had the word 'dunce' emblazoned on the front of the Panama hat I was wearing. 'The answer is bee,' she sighed. 'But there is no bee,' I exclaimed looking around. 'Well, there was one earlier but you took so long guessing that it flew away long ago.'

The picnic was rather spoilt by the fact that some idiot had painted green paint on one slat of the bench we chose. This wasn't an official painting - it was a practical joke. The Princess ruined a beautiful new skirt and I ruined my favourite pair of trousers.

22.04 p.m.

The Princess's father, who lives alone well over 100 miles away, telephoned to tell us that he has been diagnosed as having a deep vein thrombosis. His doctor told him to make his own way to the hospital tomorrow morning. This is utter, absolute lunacy. A deep vein thrombosis is a serious problem and needs to be taken seriously. It took some fancy work on the telephone (including a good many threats) to get him admitted to the local hospital. People who think the NHS is wonderful, and who defend it, are usually quite ignorant of just how bad things are.

18

10.09 a.m.

A disabled man has been given taxpayers' money to go to Amsterdam to have sex with a prostitute. His social worker says he is entitled to this because sex is a human right and to refuse would be a violation of his human rights (makes you wonder if rapists will ever be arrested if this becomes common policy). I don't pay tax so that men who don't pay tax can go to Amsterdam to have sex with prostitutes. Why can't they have sex with English prostitutes? Don't they need the work? Or is it somehow more acceptable if foreign women are sexploited? And what about people waiting months for tests or surgery? Or people losing their jobs because of EU red tape? Or people living in shop doorways because they have no home? Or soldiers dying without proper equipment in wars we are fighting so that Blair could get pally with the yanks and boost his fee earning capacity? Don't they have human rights? It is my human right to express my views and the only way this is available to me is through books. Maybe I should write to the council to ask them to let me know how many copies of my book they will be buying.

12.04 p.m.

The Princess confessed to me that when she was young and growing up in a part of Wales where there was a high level of unemployment among young men, her ambition was to marry someone with a job. With some sadness I pointed out to her that she had failed in this since I do not have, and never have had, a job.

18.46 p.m.

Campaigners want motorway speed limits reduced to 50 mph or even 40 mph in order to save oil. I wonder if they realise that reducing speed limits would result in cars using up more fuel. When fuel consumption and speed are plotted on a graph it is clear that 56 mph is the ideal speed and gives the lowest consumption of fuel per mile. High performance cars may give the best consumption figures at speeds of 70 to 80 mph. And, of course, there will undoubtedly be more accidents if speed limits are reduced to the point where drivers are regularly falling asleep through boredom.

20.12 p.m.

I've been reading *Bounder*, a wonderful biography of Terry-Thomas by Graham McCann. I found this wonderful quote from Terry-Thomas about someone he knew. 'There's a fellow called Telfer who makes more pork pies than anybody else in the bloody world, old boy. So the Americans went and asked him how he did it - incentive schemes, graduated bonuses, productivity scales, vacation benefits, you know the kind of thing. 'No,' he kept saying, 'no, I never do anything like that, no, I just let 'em turn the bloody things out the best they can. Oh, there is just one thing - every so often I goes down to the yard and I bawls, 'Faster you fuckers!'

22.13 p.m.

I beat my chess computer today after a hard game that has been going on for three days. Afterwards, I actually felt sorry for the computer. Sometimes I think I might be too sensitive for my own good.

19
15.33 p.m.

A 90-year-old war hero has been killed on his own doorstep by a mugger who stole £40 from him. Sadly, I doubt if anyone will take the killing seriously. No one cares much about old people in our society. Ageism is built into our world. When the film of my novel

Mrs Caldicot's Cabbage War came out, the *Sunday Times* dismissed the film in a way that could only be described as ageist. I wrote complaining that the review had dismissively and patronisingly described the movie's audience as `undemanding oldies'. I asked if the editor would have printed `undemanding women' or `undemanding gays' and pointed out that I had written the novel on which the film was based to draw attention to exactly this sort of rampant ageism.

17.06 p.m.
We went to a house today where the prospective sellers took us on what can only be described as a `tour' of their home.

It was all done very professionally.

They began together, and introduced us to their hallway as a twosome. And then he said: `My wife will now show you the drawing room.' He then disappeared and she gave us the five shilling tour of the drawing room. Since it consisted of a standard, rectangular, boxy room with French windows and a fake fireplace (fitted with a gas fire) it shouldn't have taken her more than a minute. She stretched it to five by pointing out all the electrical sockets and explaining how the radiators worked. These things are important but on a first visit they are not going to make a purchaser take out his pen and sign anything.

As we left the drawing room, she announced: `My husband will now show you the library.' And she melted away, though we did not know where she went. The library turned out to be a very small room that had been fitted with shelves and which contained a few paperbacks and a very large collection of glass models of elephants. I take more books with me when I go on a train journey that is likely to last more than an hour. It is a constant surprise to me how many houses contain very few books. I think The Princess and I probably push up the national average to a decent level but most of the houses we have looked at this year have contained very few books. There are usually a couple of cookery volumes, written by television chefs, in the kitchen and one or two curled up paperbacks in the bedroom. But that's it.

And so the tour continued. He and she alternated between rooms. And when we `did' the garden we `did' it in a foursome. He would point out one plant and she would give us the name of the next one. He opened the door to the shed and pointed out its virtues and she explained the unique qualities of the six foot by four foot greenhouse.

We left, exhausted.

As we drove away The Princess turned to me: `Do you think we should have left a tip?' she asked.

`I left a couple of quid in the souvenir ashtray by the front door,' I told her.

20
12.16 p.m.
I met a man in a bookstore today who started talking about things he had seen and heard about on the news. He had a definite view about everything but his most bitter complaint was about people who opposed his views. `I hate people who are dogmatic,' he said.

15.41 p.m.
Two days ago various industry bigwigs complained about the nonsensical and time wasting and expensive security rubbish at airports. Today, predictably, there is news of a bomb found at Heathrow. The bomb was actually found in a postal package being carried as cargo and a White House expert said al Qaeda was probably responsible. `They are very innovative and creative,' said the security expert. Damned right. No American would have thought of putting a bomb into a parcel and posting it.

17.55 p.m.
The Web is a mystery to me. Our books are often sold on the Web as `new' at less than half price. In some instances I can buy my own brand new books cheaper on the Web than they cost to print. Since we don't even sell them at that sort of discount to the wholesalers I can't help wondering where these books come from. Before the official publication date my book *Bloodless Revolution* was being sold, new, for £2 on Amazon. I had not started selling the book and no review copies had gone out. The only copies which had left Publishing House had been copies which I had sent to buyers for some of the larger bookshops. So, that is where those books could have come from. I'm still puzzled about the origin of all the other books. Whenever I have a new book in from the

printers there are brand new copies being offered on Amazon within days. The books are sold at prices that no bookshop could possibly match. And the books are on sale before any readers have bought copies.

18.03 p.m.
I feel like an idiot. I know where all the books that are being sold on Amazon come from. Whenever I send hardback books to paperback houses, offering them the opportunity to buy the rights, copies of those books appear on Amazon within days. The bastards don't bother to read or assess the book, they just bung it onto Amazon so that they can make a few quid. How utterly pathetic publishers are these days. And, of course, review copies also appear on Amazon within days of being sent out. These sellers are stealing money from me because they are dramatically affecting my ability to sell copies. I can, however, get round this by only sending out review copies a few months after I have offered the books to my readers and have sold most of the copies I expect to sell. The reviewers will still damage my backlist sales so I will keep that problem to a minimum by dramatically reducing the number of review copies I send out. I reckon that if we send out 200 review copies, around 50 will end up on Amazon. We lose the price of the book we send out, the postage and the profit on the book we don't sell because they sell their copy.

21.44 p.m.
I've made another decision. My early books were well reviewed but I've been getting fewer and fewer reviews in recent years. As my sales have gone up so my review coverage has gone down. I can deal with this by not sending out any more review copies. Simple.

21
11.01 a.m.
I have been sorting through books for several days now. So far I have thrown out 35 books and retained approximately 14,965. This isn't going well. I think I will abandon the exercise and just keep everything.

16.39 p.m.

I read the results of the interview I did a week or so ago. I know it is about me because it mentions my name but that is all I recognised. Women feature writers are the nastiest by far. Most of the rancid features are written by women; they are the rabid attack dogs of wherever Fleet Street is hiding these days.

18.07 p.m.

There is much talk about the EU forcing the Government to put VAT on books. I have a plan for this. I will give away the books free and charge £20 for p&p. There is no VAT on stamps.

19.01 p.m.

The authorities are constantly encouraging people to report neighbours, friends and relatives whom they think may have broken the law or be acting `suspiciously'. I received two letters from readers who were confused by the conflict between their desire to act responsibly and their perception of their civic duty. The first was from a reader in Lancashire who wrote: `A man has just moved into a house across the road from us. He lives on his own and hardly speaks to anyone. However, the other day I was watching when he had a computer delivered. Should I inform the police in case he may be a paedophile?' The second was from a reader in Leicestershire who wrote: `My neighbour regularly has underwear which is of two different sizes on her washing line. No woman could possibly wear bras which are of such different sizes. Only her and her husband live there. Do you think that her husband could be a transvestite and if so should I report them to the police?' I have for some time had no doubt at all that the Government is deliberately changing the way we think about one another, and encouraging suspicion and fear. Equally, I have no doubt that they are extremely successful in their aims.

22

09.24 a.m.

It is announced today that oil has been found in Afghanistan. Oh what a surprise this is. I remember writing that the invasion of Afghanistan was about oil right from the moment the damned war started. We spent some time wondering who was the last person to invade Afghanistan successfully. Our American friend Ed wonders if it was Alexander the Great. I think he's probably right. The Princess suggested that we should rename the Ministry of Defence the Ministry of War. And she's right, of course. It used to be called that until the Orwellian spin-doctors changed it. It is possible to argue that the last war we really had to fight for our own survival was probably the one against Napoleon.

15.16 p.m.

It occurred to me today that I find it harder to obtain accurate information now than I did before the Internet was invented. In the bad old days I could obtain journal articles with relative ease from libraries. These days everything is digital and the good, reliable, relatively honest stuff is mixed in with the bad, unreliable, completely dishonest stuff. Sorting the wheat from the chaff takes forever.

I also find it harder these days to find people prepared to do what they say they will do, and to do it when they say they will do it, than I did before the EU introduced approximately 250,000 laws to `protect' me from myself. I don't need protecting from myself; I need protecting from thieves, crooks, bankers and eurocrats.

18.08 p.m.

A reader wants to produce Hungarian editions of my books. He says that he is arranging for a translator and asks me if I would like to publish the Hungarian editions myself. Another reader wants to know if he can borrow a copy of my book *2020* for a week so that he can read it. He says he will send it back when he has read it.

23
09.05 a.m.

I received an e-mail from a reader who said that he has heard of a fellow who has received a cheque for £3,000 from the Rural Payments Agency for not rearing pigs. Apparently, the most money he ever made when he reared pigs for a living was slightly less than half this so the not rearing pigs business is clearly a great improvement on his original business plan. My correspondent says he rather fancies getting into this business, which is obviously another EU wheeze designed to help the bureaucrats get rid of some of the billions leftover when they've eaten and drunk as much as they can, and the French farmers have filled all their barns with euros. He said he intends to write to the Ministry with a number of questions. How does he keep a record of the pigs he hasn't kept? Can he get a bigger cheque if he increases the number of pigs he doesn't rear? Is there a limit? Can he claim tradable carbon credits as a reward for the fact that the pigs he isn't keeping aren't producing methane gases? And since the pigs he doesn't rear won't be eating any food how much can he claim for not growing cereals to feed the pigs he's not rearing.

It all sounds surreal. But the sad thing is that it isn't surreal at all. On the contrary, it is very real. It's what we have come to expect from the European Union. If I heard that the EU had decided that prisoners should be allowed six weeks holiday a year I would believe it. And so, I suspect, would everyone else.

24

16.54 p.m.

I see that in national newspapers and journals there were 3,700 references to `the elephant in the room' last year. The cliché is clearly fast becoming the one to beat. Just ten years ago it appeared a mere 175 times in the press. Indoor elephants are, it seems, now breeding like rabbits and I expect the Government will soon form a quango to look into the problem.

17.02 p.m.

I received a note to tell me that my father's sister has died. She was, I think, the last of my relatives. I rang her when my father died. I had only ever spoken to her once before - over half a century earlier - though before he died my father had spoken to her quite regularly.

The last conversation I had with her is permanently etched on my memory. `I'm afraid I have some bad news,' I said. `Your brother Ted has died.'

`Ted?'

`Your brother.'

`Oh. Can I have his wheelchair then?'

20.47 p.m.

A reader has sent me a copy of a remarkably inaccurate piece about me which he found on the Internet. I despair about the stuff that is found on the World Wide Web these days. When my book *Living in a Fascist Country* was published not long ago those journalists who dared to write about it made no attempt to hide their sneers and sniggers but the *Daily Telegraph* had a particularly good time making fun of me and the book (though the journalist who wrote the piece didn't speak to me and I have a strong suspicion that he didn't even read the book so he was writing from a pretty comprehensive level of ignorance). His article would have won prizes for inaccuracy. Some people die in vain. I suspect that this fellow will live in vain, which is far worse. I sent the following letter to the then editor of the *Telegraph*, someone called Will Lewis.

`I don't usually bother complaining about inaccurate articles about me but the piece on the Daily Telegraph website by John Sutherland is so bad that I have to say something.

1. Sutherland (the journalist who wrote the piece) claims I drive a Rolls Royce on the proceeds of bestsellers published by myself. Two mistakes here. First, I don't own a Rolls Royce. I once had a vintage Rolls but I sold it in the mid 1990s. Second, although I do publish UK editions of my books I have also been published in the UK by (among others) Sidgwick and Jackson, Macmillan, Thames and Hudson, RKP (in hardback) and Penguin, Pan, Arrow, Corgi in paperback.

2. Sutherland states that my latest book is How To Stop Your Doctor Killing You. Wrong. HTSYDKY was published in 1996. The date is published in all my books so I can only assume that Sutherland didn't bother to look at any of my books before writing his piece. The book still sells well, and has recently been published by publishers in China and Germany, but it's not my latest book by a long, long way.

3. Sutherland sneers at my comment that `Doctors are officially one of the big three killers'. Sutherland should do some research. He'd see that I'm right. Iatrogenesis is a major health problem and a significant cause of death.

4. It was representatives of the meat industry (not doctors) who complained about the meat ad Sutherland quotes.

5. Sutherland claims that I publish my books from my kitchen. Really? With around 60,000 books in stock and six in-house employees? This is the most commercially damaging remark in the piece. I have quite large contracts with printers, wholesalers, agents and others. Publishing House is, in fact, quite a large building and I could no more run my publishing business from my kitchen than you could edit the Telegraph from yours. Sutherland's comment suggests that I'm a dabbling amateur. I think that's pretty damaging, don't you?

6. Sutherland scoffs at my book Living in a Fascist Country. Pity he didn't bother to read that one before scoffing. If he had done so he might have understood what it is about.

7. Sutherland implies that I publish my own books because they are unpublishable. If he had bothered to ask anyone at Publishing House, or to read my website, he would know that my books have been published in 24 foreign languages (all by other publishers) and that large print, audio and serial rights are frequently sold to British publishers. A multi-million pound film starring Pauline Collins was made of one of my self-published novels. Three of my self-published novels have sold over 30,000 copies apiece in hardback (not counting large print and audio editions). Unpublishable? I bet your lawyers wouldn't like to try defending that one in court.

8. Sutherland claims that all my books have been distributed by myself. It's true that some are sold by mail order. But vast numbers of my books have been sold by quaint little places called bookshops. If Sutherland had bothered to do any research he would know that my books have been in the Sunday Times Top Ten and the Bookseller Top Ten (which, as far as I know, only measure bookshop sales).

9. Sutherland's piece is accompanied by a photograph which is, oddly enough, the picture used on my website. I don't suppose he just helped himself to it?

10. Sutherland claims that ads for my books will be found in `surprising respectable places'. Indeed, this is true. I only advertise in respectable places. To date a total of 290 display ads have appeared in the Daily and Sunday Telegraphs - producing revenue for the paper of over £500,000.

I don't know who John Sutherland is, and I don't know whether the Web version of the paper aspires to the same standards as the earthly edition, but in the days when I wrote for the Telegraph (both varieties and the magazine) I would have been fired for such sloppy journalism. The curious thing is that if I were a singer and produced my own records Mr Sutherland would probably think what I did exciting and praiseworthy. But choosing to self-publish and standing apart from the literary establishment is, for some reason, perennially unacceptable. I'm pretty much past caring about that. But I do object to the damaging inaccuracies. A questioning journalist might have wanted to know why so many people buy my books and why I sell more books than many middle sized publishing houses. But that would mean thinking up questions and then going to the trouble of asking them.

It would be nice if you could arrange for this letter to appear on the Telegraph website, alongside Mr Sutherland's piece, so that `our' readers (I would guess that, after 290 display ads, at least 50,000 of your readers are also my readers) can read the two together. What do you think?'

I didn't hear a word from the editor; neither a reply nor an acknowledgement. And as far as I know they did not print a correction or an apology. I wonder if they would have been so lackadaisical if the article had appeared in print rather than online.

Curiously, the *Telegraph* started to refuse accepting advertisements for my books after I sent my letter. I have no idea why the paper feels so much angst. I was a regular contributor to its pages a few decades ago when it had a reputation for reliability, respectability and honest journalism. But I suspect that some of the new young staff on many of the London dailies don't like the idea of an author making a living by self-publishing books. When I was interviewed by a journalist from the *Sunday Telegraph* she said to me: `So, you write whatever you like, and there is no one to tell you that you can't publish something?' I agreed with that. `And you make a living at this?' Again, I agreed. `And you enjoy it?' I said I did. She looked at me, with loathing all over her face. `Isn't that rather self-indulgent?' she said.

25
19.18 p.m.

We went to Wells today and wandered around the Cathedral again. What an amazing treat of a place it is. Everything is so old. The cathedral clock is 700 years old, there is a street of houses called Vicar's Close (21 houses on each side, all with tall chimneys) which is 500 years old. The cathedral itself was begun in the 12th century and finished in the 13th century. Many of the inhabitants of Wells seem old enough to have been there at the time to celebrate the completion. The Princess said she was a little worried by the fact that although the cathedral is only 900 years old it is, in places, already showing signs of wear. I said I thought it was just a sign of the sort of shoddy workmanship commonplace at the time.

We sat on one of our favourite benches overlooking the moat around the Bishop's Palace, put up our large MCC umbrella and ate our picnic in the rain. People hurrying past, with collars turned up, looked at us in astonishment but we were cosy and dry. We ate cheese and cucumber sandwiches, completed an enormous crossword in a woman's magazine I had bought for The Princess and watched the ducks who were sheltering under a tree. I had never seen ducks sheltering from the rain before. In addition to a number of ducks there were four cygnets, one swan, some moorhens and a great many pigeons.

I sent an e-mail picture of the Palace from my iPhone to an American friend who lives in Thailand. He replied that he liked buildings like that and that they had lots of old buildings back home in America. I didn't tell him but the oldest building in America is actually a fort in Florida which dates back to the 16th century. I'm pretty sure that I have socks older than that.

Afterwards we very nearly bought a house. Neither of us was particularly taken with the house but it had a vast, spreading, horse chestnut tree in the garden and it was clearly preparing itself for a bumper season. I thought that if we worked quickly we might be able to complete the sale before all the conkers had fallen. I've always wanted my own conker tree. I have only ever once envied someone. I was at junior school with a boy whose father worked for British European Airways (now part of British Airways, of course) as a navigator. Each autumn the boy's father used to come back from France with several carrier bags full of conkers. To small boys in the 1950s conkers were better than sovereigns. They were the only truly acceptable currency and in addition to playing with them you could buy toy cars, marbles, string and even penknives. There was virtually no television in those days and our games were dictated by the seasons.

We made an offer for the house but were quickly gazumped by a couple who were borrowing virtually all of the money they were prepared to spend. Reluctantly, almost unhappily, we raised our offer but were quickly outbid again. It seems bizarre that `real' money should be so easily outbid by `Monopoly' money. I don't think the money seems as real when it is borrowed as it does when it has already been earned and saved. We retired from the bidding process and then both admitted that we were pleased we hadn't bought the house. `We'll get back to you if the deal falls through because of a problem with the bank lending the money,' said the estate agent. I told her not to bother.

We had tea in a hotel and listened to a conversation between a short, stout woman in a tweed suit and a short stout man in corduroy trousers and a well-worn tweed jacket. He had several maps and a guidebook on the table in front of him. They were talking about his plans to retire from his teaching post, take his pension and then take additional work as a supply teacher. `I'll earn more than I do now and work half the hours,' he said. `We'll still have the long holidays and we can take long weekends whenever we like.' She agreed that it all sounded pretty good. She then started talking about her friend, Doreen. She said that Doreen's husband, Philip, who works for the Post Office, is retiring at 50 and plans to do wedding photography. `He has one of those digital cameras,' she said. `And he can do it cheaper than anyone else because he gets a good pension and doesn't need to earn all that much. It's just a nice hobby really. Doreen says it'll keep him out of her hair for a couple of days a week. And the bit of money it brings in will help with John.'

I felt quite angry when I heard this. We have a reader who is a professional photographer. He is struggling to survive. Fewer people are getting married these days and the rise in the number of photographers offering a cut price service has devastated his business.

And then I realised that the woman's tone had changed. She was now talking about John, Doreen's son. `He's got a 2.1 in economics but can't get a job anywhere,' said the stout woman. `He's back home living with Doreen and Philip.'

`It's this recession,' said the stout man. `It's the bankers who are responsible for it all.'

It didn't occur to her or her husband that it isn't just the bankers who are responsible for the financial mess we are in. It didn't occur to them for a moment that by retiring early, on massive taxpayer funded pensions, they were a big part of the problem. And nor did it occur to them that by doing part-time jobs at cut price rates they were putting honest, hard working people out of work.

21.39 p.m.

My books are carefully and deliberately ignored. Newspapers and magazines won't print reviews. Bookshop chains won't stock my books. Major newspapers and magazines refuse to accept advertisements (even though they are desperate for advertising income). Television and radio stations refuse to do interviews even though they are bombarded with letters from my readers asking them to carry interviews. My books sell only by word of mouth.

Whingeing a little (as writers do better than most people), I asked The Princess why she thought I seemed to have so many important enemies. `I don't get any reviews these days,' I moaned. `And although they sell well round the rest of the world my books are banned everywhere in Britain.' The Princess said she thought it might be because I had annoyed so many members of the establishment. I said I couldn't have annoyed that many people. `I hardly ever speak to anyone,' I said. She thought for a moment and then asked if she could have a piece of paper and a pencil. I gave her both. Less than ten minutes later she gave me this list:

People Vernon has annoyed (a lot) with his books:

1. The entire medical establishment.
2. The entire publishing establishment (including publishers and agents).
3. The drugs industry.
4. The meat industry.
5. America.
6. The entire alternative medicine industry.
7. All social workers.
8. The tobacco industry.

9. Most of the national press and most broadcasters.

10. The vivisection industry.

11. HMRC.

12. Farmers and hunters.

'Gosh,' I said.

'I haven't included politicians,' said The Princess. 'Or the European Union. Or bureaucrats everywhere. Or civil servants.'

22.03 p.m.

A company called Zurich UK has been fined £2.275 million for losing the personal details of 46,000 customers. I was one of their customers and had huge rows with them. They seemed quite incompetent and I'm not surprised they managed to lose so much.

It would be nice if some of the money they've been fined were used to protect or compensate the customers. It would mean a nice little pay out of £49.45 for each customer. But it won't be, of course. It will, instead, simply be used to hire more quangocrats.

23.28 p.m.

A company has written offering me several hundred dollars to allow them to put a small advertisement on my website. This is by no means the first such offer. Making money out of the website (and using it to buy advertisements promoting the website) is an attractive idea. But it seems far too practical, logical and sensible. So I'm sticking to my decision not to take any advertisements for the website until it seems less rational.

23.56 p.m.

Although he died a couple of years ago I have still not finished sorting through my father's papers. Sorting through them today I found a huge pile of correspondence between my mother and the Department of Health and Social Security. She had worked most of her life, though some of her working life coincided with the Second World War and so she wandered about and lived in various ports where my father was stationed. (He was in the Royal Navy). Here's one of the letters selected at random, from the Exeter branch of the DHSS. I was particularly impressed with the final sentence.

Dear Madam,

I am writing with reference to your enquiry regarding your title to retirement pension. Your papers were referred to the `Pre 1948 Insurance Section' at the Central Pensions Branch and they have confirmed that you have no title to any basic pension. Perhaps it would help if I explain that the present National Insurance scheme did not start until 5 July 1948 and that contributions paid under the Contributory Pensions Act in force prior to that date, could only count for retirement pension purposes under the present National Insurance and Social Security Acts, if they were in payment at that date, if a person ceased to be insurably employed prior to that date, the insurance continued in a free insurance period for one and a half to two and a half years, which meant that if a person started to pay contributions again within that one and a half to two and a half year period the contributions paid prior to 5th July 1948 could be counted for retirement pension purposes under the present scheme. If however a person ceased to be insurably employed prior to 5 July 1948 and did not enter the new scheme within the one and a half to two and a half year period, pre 5 July 1948 insurance then terminated and could not count later. I hope this explanation clarifies the situation to you.'

The letter was signed `for Manager'.

I read this several times but however hard I tried I could not prevent my eyes from glazing over. After I had typed it into my computer I had to read each word to make sure I'd copied it in accurately. I have. My poor mother never did get the pension she'd paid for though they did eventually pay her a small pittance every week. Two months after she died they sent a letter claiming that they'd accidentally put an extra fortnight's money into her account and demanding it back forthwith. My father sent them a cheque. I would have told them to collect it.

Poor mother.

If I were psychoanalysing myself I would be much taken with the fact that my mother never told me that she loved me. I know this with certainty. I remember one evening visiting her in a hospital. She was lying in a private room in the BUPA hospital in Exeter. She had been diagnosed with breast cancer (which had spread) and she was due to have a mastectomy the following morning. We were alone in the room. I took her hand, looked her in the eye and said: 'I love you, Mum.' She looked back at me but said not a word. Not a word. I was living in Bideford at the time. I was devastated and drove back home from Exeter in under an hour. The tears were pouring down my cheeks so rapidly that on several occasions I switched on the windscreen wipers by mistake.

26
12.35 p.m.

A woman who saw a cat in the street, stroked it and the popped it into a wheelie bin is the subject of a great deal of anger. I suspect that there will be a lot more inexplicable behaviour in the months and years that come because of the stress we are all under. I hate what the woman did but I can't help feeling sorry for her. The curious thing is that most of the millions who attacked her neither think nor do anything about cruelty to animals. We claim to be a nation of animal lovers but we allow some pretty terrible things to take place on farms and in laboratories. I once sat in a pub where four people I'd never seen before sat at the next table. One of them was a vivisector who worked in a laboratory. He boasted about how he made rats unconscious. He said that instead of bothering to sedate them he picked them up by their tails, swung them round and hit their heads hard on the wooden top of his desk. He illustrated this claim with the appropriate hand movements. His companions laughed uproariously. I have long campaigned against animal experiments and my name is not unknown to those who favour vivisection. As I left I stopped at their table, looked into the eyes of the vivisector and thanked him for the insight. I then told him my name. The look on his face was a small comfort.

14.57 p.m.

I don't want to buy a house where the previous owners have obtained planning permission to turn the garage, the barn or the potting shed into another dwelling. I don't want to start a building company and I don't want someone else building in my new garden. And I know that the previous owner will want more for the house because he will believe that the planning permission has added value to the property.

Nor do I want to have paying guests or lodgers living in the annexe, the cottage at the bottom of the garden or the spare wing of the house. Today, for the umpteenth time, we were told that the current owners rent out part of their house and that by doing so they bring in a useful additional income. I suspect that their need to do this explains why they are selling but I try to grin and make suitable noises.

I once dabbled in property development. I bought a huge building in North Devon. I immediately sold off two cottages (one at each end of the main building) and so effectively acquired the large house in the middle for nothing. I paid a local builder to repair it, paint it and generally make it look good and then let it out to holiday-makers. I will never do this again. I remember receiving a telephone call one Sunday morning from the tenants complaining that the fridge wasn't working. I managed to find a replacement, took it round and installed it. Since it was a Sunday morning, in August, I was quite pleased with this. The tenants were not impressed. They simply moaned that they'd had to eat the ice cream they'd had stored in the freezer compartment and wanted to know if I was going to pay for it. Since they'd eaten the ice cream, rather than having to throw it away, I thought this rather a cheek but I paid them because it was easier. I don't want to be a landlord again.

27
15.15 p.m.
My life is being taken over by time consuming crap. There are rules governing absolutely everything we do. And for every rule there are at least 12 forms that have to be filled in. The tax forms used to be the bane of my life. But these days it is rules about the collection of rubbish which drive me mad. The council regards our time as of such little value that it now expects us to spend our days washing out tin cans and jam jars (have you ever tried to wash all the remaining bits of jam out of a jam jar?) and peeling the labels from all the bottles and cans we have finished with. The idiot who thought up these rules is obviously unaware that the world is desperately short of water. He or she is also obviously unaware that using hot water to wash out cans and bottles uses up vast quantities of energy. And the regulations about the disposal of many items are so absurd that if I am not careful I will soon spend my entire waking day trying to get rid of stuff I no longer need. It

is, for example, against the rules to put used torch batteries into the rubbish. Every time I have a couple of `dead' batteries I am supposed to ring the council to ask them for their latest disposal regulations and to then take the batteries to the `used battery disposal centre'. I've had enough. Today, I wrapped a broken shower unit and a used printer cartridge in a black bag, took them into town and put them into a rubbish bin. I've also broken up a cracked Belfast sink which the council refused to take away. I'm going to distribute the sink among waste bins all over the town.

21.53 p.m.

I long ago came to realise that the loudness of an individual's speech (for example in hotels and on trains) is in inverse proportion to their intelligence and the value of what is being said. The only conversations worth listening to are conducted in whispers.

On the train back from London today we sat in our usual seats in the quiet carriage but the peace was spoilt by a fat woman talking very loudly on her mobile telephone. After putting up with this for 50 miles or so I leant across and politely pointed out that we were all sitting in a carriage where the use of mobile telephones was prohibited.

`Do you know who I am?' demanded the woman, glowering at me. She had the look of a civil servant, self-important and pointless. I looked at her. I was tired, hungry and it had been a difficult day. I wanted to say: `You're a fat, loud woman in a dress four sizes too small for you who is annoying the hell out of me by talking very loudly in a quiet carriage.' But I said nothing and just glowered at her.

She went red, glared at me, picked up her bags. `I am not staying here with such rude people,' she said, and stalked out.

Unfortunately for her she headed into the second class carriage. And so two minutes later she came storming back through in search of the only other first class carriage.

Oh what fun.

28
11.02 a.m.

Something called the youth Olympics is apparently taking place. I can't imagine why. If the athletes are any good why aren't they competing in the real games? Why doesn't someone organise a Senior Olympics for people over 60. That would be worth watching and an inspiration to couch potatoes everywhere.

14.51 p.m.

I picked up a copy of a beautiful edition of *The Memories of Dean Hole* recently. (It cost me 50 pence in a second-hand bookshop. In my book buying world this still seems to be the default price.) It is hardback, beautifully bound and pocket-sized. Hole's book is a beautiful account of people he knew (both famous and not famous) and today I read of his meeting Charles Dickens for the first time. On his way to Gad's Hill, Hole met a man he knew who was on the staff of *The Times*. The reporter told Hole that President Lincoln had been assassinated and Hole duly passed on the news to the novelist, adding that the assassin had not been apprehended because the pursuers had taken the wrong turn when following him from the theatre. Dickens, writes Hole, smiled and there was a twinkle in his eye. `Ah yes,' he said, `when the man pursued turns to the right, and the men in pursuit to the left, the difficulties of capture are materially enhanced.' Beautiful. Hole also reports that there was a tiny grave, tombstone and epitaph in the garden at Gad's Hill and he adds that the inscription read: `This is the Grave of Dick, the best of birds, born at Broadstairs, Midsummer 1851, died at Gad's Hill Place, October 14th 1866.' That's a good age for a canary.

29

11.57 a.m.

A paperback publisher has sent back a copy of *Mr Henry Mulligan* (which was offered for paperback rights) with a note thanking us for the manuscript and saying: `If Mr Coleman wishes to be published he must first find himself an agent.' It is dispiriting to know that there are people working in publishing who cannot tell the difference between a hardback book and a manuscript.

12.45 p.m.

There seems to be some confusion about why fewer Britons are emigrating. Economists, politicians and commentators are all puzzled. The consensus seems to be that people are happier now and don't want to leave. When I read this I rolled around on the floor. The real answer is that people can't sell their bloody houses so they can't leave the bloody country. None of the economists spotted this, though it is probably painfully obvious to any half-wit with O level woodwork or a diploma in hairdressing.

We went to Taunton and The Princess waved to a pleasure boat on the river Tone. A dozen older citizens waved back enthusiastically, all smiling as people always do when they wave to or from a boat. `It's always old people and children who wave,' I said. `I'm 38,' The Princess reminded me.

21.34 p.m.

This evening our fourth and last digital radio suddenly stopped working. Over the last few years we have spent a small fortune buying digital radios. They all cost several hundred pounds each and none of them lasted more than a few months before stopping working. We agree that we were never impressed by the quality of the sound they produced and that we both found them no easier to use than old-fashioned analogue radios. We have dug out our old radios (the sort that used to receive the Light Programme and the Home Service and which now receive Radios 2, 3 and 4) and will use them until the Government puts a stop to broadcasting in the old-fashioned way. If our experience is anything to judge by it will, I suspect, be some time before the digital radio revolution becomes established.

30

14.05 p.m.

The Deputy Prime Minister (the awful Clegg) claims that high earners are tax dodgers, that anyone who uses an accountant to reduce their tax bill is morally wrong, that he will set up debt collecting agencies to collect tax money (as though the tax people don't have enough powers and enough nastiness) and that they will use lie detector tests on taxpayers. Oh how wonderful.

18.07 p.m.

`I finished my first book today,' The Princess told me. `It only took me four weeks to read it,' she added. I must have looked as puzzled as I felt. `It's a joke,' she explained. `I've just made it up.' She coughed and swallowed and rearranged her face to let me know that the joke was continuing. `I'm really pleased with myself,' she said. `On the back of the book it says 'Suitable for five to six years.'

I asked if I could steal the joke and use it in a book.

She said I couldn't.

31
11.24 a.m.

Search engines such as Google have enormous power. One senior Google employer is quoted as having written: `We won't (and shouldn't) try to stop the faceless scribes of drivel but we can move them to the back row of the arena.' So, who does Google decide are the `faceless scribes' and what do they define as `drivel'?

12.36 p.m.

In the back of a book from Faber & Faber I found a pre-paid postcard. On one side was the address of the firm. On the other side a section listed books which I could order. And underneath this section was an order form which asked: the type of credit card I wanted to use, my name, the card's expiry date, the card number, my address, my signature and the date. I wonder how many innocents fill in these cards and send their private details through the mail on a postcard. I am surprised only that Faber & Faber forgot to ask for the book buyer's date of birth. That would have made life even easier for identity thieves and credit card crooks.

15.18 p.m.

The next time we are stuck in one of those manufactured traffic jams (there's been a slight bump in the slow lane and so the police close off both carriageways and all nearby airports) I will try to remember to be grateful that we don't live and drive in China where they've just had the world's worst traffic jam. The line of cars and lorries was 60 miles long and some drivers were stuck for 20 days. Locals living near to the jam made quite a good living out of selling food and water.

September

1
10.48 a.m.

It has been announced that the ASA is going to police the UK's Web entries and online marketing. The announcement was made in a way that might encourage some people to believe that the ASA is a statutory, quasi-legal group with proper authority. It's none of these things. The ASA is a private organisation with no authority whatsoever. It is no more able to ban advertisements than I am. Its staff and costs are paid for by the ASBOF levy. Advertisers pay a percentage of what they pay for advertising to a bizarre little organisation called ASBOF which then hands great wodges of cash over to the ASA. I think the idea is that this somehow separates the ASA from the big, powerful advertisers and lobbyists - the drug companies, the meat industry and so on. When I first started advertising I had grave misgivings about the ASA but my advertising agent was aghast when I refused to pay the levy. He, like many others, thought the levy was compulsory and was astonished when he found out that it was not. I was so disgusted by the arrogant way the ASA operates that I stopped opening their letters years ago and warned them that if they contacted me again I would report them to the police for harassment. I've even reported them to the Office of Fair Trading. (The OFT accepted my complaint and told me they were keeping the ASA under surveillance.)

One of my many complaints about the way they operate is that the ASA allows anonymous complaints. This means that if a drug company wants to 'ban' a book it simply gets someone in the office to send in a complaint on plain notepaper.

Another reason to dislike and distrust these snivelling pawns of the establishment is that the organisation just isn't properly independent. One of the people who helped 'ban' an anti-vivisection advertisement of mine just happened to be employed by the cosmetics industry. The ASA said it didn't see anything wrong with this. In my view the ASA is (like the Press Complaints

Commission) effectively employed by big advertisers to police its industry and to ensure that no one else does it.

Curiously, I found that the only adverts of mine that aroused the interest of the ASA were ones which affected particular industries (such as the drug industry or the meat industry).

The ASA is widely thought to be an official body. Infuriatingly, *The Financial Times* describes it as a `regulator'. Even Michael O'Leary, boss of Ryan Air, who seems to hate the ASA almost as much as I do, wrongly thought it was a quango when he wrote to me about it in 2008. Because the ASA is a private organisation with no official authority it is impossible to protest about its decisions, which it promotes and publicises with great pomp. It has, over the years, managed to convince many journalists that it really has authority and can ban advertisements.

I don't take any notice of the ASA these days so I don't know whether they're still `banning' my advertisements or not. It doesn't really matter. The `bans' don't make much difference. *The Guardian* and *The Observer* were the only newspapers which refused to take adverts for my books because they were `banned' by the ASA. They pompously refused smaller advertisements on the grounds that they had been banned by the ASA. But they quickly changed their minds when I offered to buy a series of six full page advertisements in both newspapers. They then printed the `banned' adverts in return for around £60,000. All their reservations and protests disappeared overnight. I deliberately put in full page adverts for the three most contentious books we were promoting at the time: *How To Stop Your Doctor Killing You; Oil Apocalypse* and *Gordon is a Moron.*

The bottom line is that the ASA is a private body, largely funded by international corporations. Journalists help them by quoting their pompous official sounding pronouncements as though they were of legal significance. The ASA is one of the most arrogant, pompous organisations in the country and probably the very best at convincing the ignorant (among which must be numbered the vast majority of journalists and politicians) that it is an organisation which has the authority its name suggests. In my view the ASA is as independent and as authoritative as I am and a mauling from this wretched organisation is, if you know its background, about as effective as a mauling from any other lobby group.

2
12.35 p.m.
There are apparently great crowds in a nearby town today. A famous author called Jordan is here to sign copies of her book. Book signings only work for celebrities. Show me a professional author who does signings and I'll show you someone who knows how embarrassing it is to sit at a desk while everyone who walks in carefully avoids your eye and the only books you sign are the ones the manager invites you to sign and which you sign (even though you know he's doing it out of pity) because it means he can't send them back to the publisher. It is not uncommon at these signings for the manager to attempt to reduce the embarrassment by telling the staff to line up and ask for books to be signed.

14.15 p.m.
`You will be beaten upside the head with a truncheon. And that's it.' That's a quote from Russian Prime Minister, Vladimir Putin, threatening anti-government dissidents who continue to hold rallies. At least he was honest and at least he warns people. You have to admire those qualities in a politician.

3
11.36 a.m.
I see that a court has fined a man £200 for hitting a policeman. I am minded to write to the local Chief Constable to ask if I can arrange a bulk rate direct with him. Perhaps £1,000 for six? I remember when policemen called members of the public `sir' or `madam'. These days they beat you up and arrest you if you don't call them sir and get out of the way pretty damned smart when they're coming through. The police *should* call people `sir' or `madam'. You're less likely to beat someone up if you have to be polite and respectful. The police are, after all, our servants not our masters. I can't help thinking that things went downhill when police forces started hiring midgets. The policemen are not just younger, they are also much shorter. Who decided to let small people become policemen? It was bad enough allowing women to

become policemen. But midgets? The little bastards strut around looking as if they're auditioning for a part in the latest Rambo movie.

I find the police remarkably unhelpful these days. When over £10,000 worth of damage was done to my car no one could be bothered even to look at it. When Publishing House was damaged they were too busy to take a peep. When I reported my father's death as requiring police attention they ignored me. And when I reported that the Royal Mail had taken £22,000 that I didn't owe them from my account, and had then refused to give it back because they were too busy, the police metaphorically yawned and went back to sleep. There are bound to be exceptions but generally speaking the police these days are over-bearing, disinterested and rude. They mostly seem to have forgotten what their role is in society.

It isn't just the police who are rude, of course. The half-witted thugs who work for airport security arrest you for terrorism if they don't consider you to be sufficiently subservient. Take a little too long removing your shoes or emptying your pockets and they'll have you naked, blindfolded and on your knees before you can say `Tony Blair'.

4

17.32 p.m.

We went to Weston-super-Mare for the day. How the place has changed. The local council must take responsibility for turning a delightful seaside resort into a sad, depressing, characterless concrete embarrassment. Logistically there can be few better placed towns in England. There is a mainline railway station close to the town centre, a motorway just five minutes away and an airport within ten or fifteen minutes drive. Talking to a few locals we met explains what has happened. Instead of making an effort to attract wealthy commuters from Bristol and retired folk from the Midlands the council seemed to have made a real effort to attract drug addicts, unemployed hoodies and former criminals to the town. These people bring with them government money in the form of grants and dole payments. But the easy money comes at a high price, and when it runs out the town will be left with its seedy, underworld population of society's rejects. Today it is so cold that the only children in sight are bouncing on a trampoline on the beach to keep warm and even the donkeys are shivering).

We had a pot of tea in a café on the seafront. `I've learned one thing since we moved here,' said an elderly woman in a blue anorak who was sitting at the next table with a woman of a similar age. `Never look up with your mouth open.' Her companion looked puzzled. `Seagulls,' explained the woman in the blue anorak.

As we were leaving we passed a busker. I suppose she could be described a busker. She had a tape player by her side and a pile of tapes in front of her. She was playing music which I did not recognise. She had an open guitar case in front of her so that passers-by could throw in coins. She was reading a book.

5

15.27 p.m.

A quarter of junior doctors are giving up medicine because they find the training too arduous. They feel they have too many responsibilities. The sympathy seems to be with them. Ah, diddums. They are wimps. Thanks to the EU they have a 48 hour week. And that's part time work. When I was a junior doctor I shared my responsibilities with one other doctor. That's 168 hours shared between two. That's obviously a basic 84 week if we split it but we didn't because we both had to be present for consultants' rounds so effectively we did around 40 hours a week together and split the other 128 which made a basic 104 hour week unless one of us was ill in which case it was a 168 hour week. I have on many occasions worked 168 hour weeks, sleeping when I could wherever I happened to be when I nodded off. If other housemen were ill or on holiday we had to cover for them too.

6

11.25 a.m.

A reader was approached by a Romanian beggar in Paris and asked to write out a suitable note in English - to be handed to English tourists. My reader says that this is what he wrote: `I'm a lazy Romanian. If you are stupid enough to give me money I will spend it on expensive cakes and fine wine and I will curse you and your family.'

356

7

14.38 p.m.

The insurance agents who provide me with the policy for Publishing House write requesting the annual insurance premium of £1,282.76. They also enclose a standard employers' liability certificate and a note telling me that I should keep all such certificates and insurance documentation for 40 years. I am now forced to keep so many documents and accounts material that there will soon be no room left to store any of the books I hope to sell. Still, I will be 104 in 40 years time so one way or another I don't suppose I'll be much interested when the police come to take me away for not keeping my insurance documents for the correct duration.

8

15.50 p.m.

When yet another house hunting trip has proved fruitless The Princess and I often cheer ourselves up by making up fake Roy Brooks advertisements for the houses we have seen. Roy Brooks was a London estate agent in the 1960s who wrote brilliantly honest advertising copy. So after we had visited a house so close to a very busy road that when we stood in the garden we had to stand inches away from one another and shout to make ourselves heard we decided that a Roy Brooks advertisement would have promoted the house as `suitable for a deaf buyer'. And we decided that a house built on the side of a cliff would be `perfect for a mountaineer'. We remind ourselves of the houses we have seen by referring to idiosyncratic elements. For example, we talk together of the house `with the large, horrible spider in the bath' and the house `with that awful painting of a nude man in the bedroom'.

9

19.40 p.m.

We spent much of the day on trains. Our train to London this morning was delayed for an `engineering problem' which is about as meaningless as `comfortable' as applied to post-surgical patients. We had to endure endless repetitions of that most annoying sentence: `We thank you for your understanding and for your cooperation'. They don't ask if I am full of understanding and they assume that by not running up and down the train smashing windows I am cooperating. I don't understand and I don't want to cooperate but I don't have any choice. I really want to thump the complacent idiot making the announcement but I suspect that police marksmen will shoot me if I do. I would much rather feel resentful and angry and retain my self-respect than be patronised in this way.

At St Pancras there was a little light trouble over my penknife.

Penknives seem a particular target for men and women in uniforms. (What do you think they do with all the smart penknives they confiscate? Guess. And the correct answer is not `they throw them away'. Try: `Keep them or sell them' and you'll be closer to the truth.) Yesterday I read of a man who was fined for having a penknife in the glove compartment of his car. I don't understand the law about penknives. You can buy them openly, without a licence, in all sorts of shops. But if you carry one or use one or own one you are likely to find yourself in court. The law on the subject is clearly muddy.

I turned up at Eurostar with one in my pocket and a supervisor was called over to check that me and my small single bladed penknife were not likely to be a threat to the train's safety. It was a small, single bladed Laguiole, about three inches long; suitable for making sandwiches, sharpening pencils and performing tracheostomies. The supervisor inspected the knife and asked me, as a favour, to put it into my shoulder bag and not my pocket. This I happily did though I confess that I didn't quite see the point. For one thing it's difficult to force a train driver to take a train to Cuba with a small pocketknife and for another the shoulder bag was staying as close to me as my pocket. Still.

Within minutes of our sitting down on the train, the staff presented us with our luncheon trays which were, of course, complete with the usual pouch containing an array of stainless steel knives and forks. The blades on the knives were much longer than the blades of any knife I've ever owned and a fork is, of course, a pretty potent weapon.

This whole `let's ban penknives' movement is a real worry to me. There are so many uses for a penknife. And, of course, there is the question of horses' hooves. There will be thousands of horses struggling round with stones in their hooves.

If pointed knives really are considered too dangerous, why not stop manufacturers making pointy knives and make them produce knives which are sharp but which have a rounded end (like a butter knife). They would still be useful for slicing apples and sharpening pencils but it wouldn't be possible to stab with one. Slashing, which would still be possible, is messy but far less likely to be fatal.

I find all this very depressing.

It is sad to think that the current generation of schoolboys walk around with Nintendo computer games in their pockets instead of penknives, string, conkers and toy cars. What a sad, miserable world we have created for ourselves.

I wonder if I am the only person on the planet who objects to having the obviously innocent contents of his pockets perused, item by item, by a complete stranger? I do find myself becoming aggrieved when they ask `What's this for?' when they find something, obviously not toxic or explosive, which they find amusing or intriguing. Airports and railway stations are crammed with policemen and security guards harassing and prodding law-abiding citizens. Outside, on the streets, there is little or no protection and patrolling policemen are as rare as snowdrops in August. But then the streets are filled with a dangerous mixture of muggers, rapists, thieves and murderers and it's obviously much safer for the police to stay indoors, harassing harmless travellers. The result is that cautious law-abiding citizens don't go out much after dark. Many hardly dare leave their homes even in daylight. Town and city centres are controlled by feral youths of both sexes; drunks and drug users. They roam the streets in gangs, like extras in some futuristic science fiction movie. The police know well that nasty things happen on the streets - particularly after dark. There could even be money launderers and terrorists out there. The police and the security guards obviously don't want to be outside, in such hazardous, ungoverned territory where they might be threatened, attacked or spoken to rudely. It is safer, and cosier, to be inside, in the warm, harassing innocent travellers who are so terrified that they will remove their shoes, empty their pockets, explain where they're going and why (`What business is it of yours?' is the only sensible answer to that impertinent question) and suffer whatever indignities are foisted upon them without a murmur of protest. And so the various branches of the security services, consisting of State employees whose only concern is self-aggrandisement (it is what they are trained for) and who are empowered with the knowledge that they are acting with the power of the State behind them, concentrate their efforts in places where they know they aren't needed but where they know that they will feel comfortable, safe and warm and where they can be patronising, officious and pompous without having to endure a moment's fear that someone will talk back to them or bop them on the nose for being impertinent for if that were to happen, and the perpetrator were to escape unpunished, the spell would be broken and they would have to go back outside into the dark and cold real world and face the criminals who, knowing the way things are, have pretty well taken over the world.

When we finally arrived in Paris at around 5.30 p.m. (the worst time of day to try to find a taxi) we joined the queue for a taxi outside the Gare du Nord. On one occasion, while standing in this queue, we watched in astonishment as a tiny, neatly dressed man snuck under the barrier and took his place ahead of us.

I half lifted him off his feet and gently put him down behind us.

He protested loudly.

`You cheated!' I said, indignantly.

`But of course I cheated!' he replied, drawing himself up to his full height before announcing proudly and loudly: `I am French.' I was so delighted by this that I insisted on him retaking his place in front of us.

The wine on aeroplanes is invariably undrinkable but the stuff they serve on Eurostar is decent enough. Arriving in Paris after a couple of bottles I usually find that I can speak fluent French. Sadly, this miracle always coincides with the French natives losing their innate ability to understand their own language. So there I am, fluent. With no one to be fluent with.

As a result of my constant disappointments I have pretty well given up trying to speak French. Most people in Paris can understand English perfectly well and though they all think they speak English perfectly they all speak it appallingly. It's fun to turn the tables and laugh at them.

We have an American friend who has lived in France for 30 years. His main knowledge of French is the phrase `silver plate' which he seems to think means `please'. He offers this to anyone and everyone he meets as though they should be grateful that he is making the effort. He uses it as `hello', `thank you' and `goodbye'. It is, for him, the universal phrase. He is, however, enormously rich and so for him this works quite well. (Actually, I must admit that I once heard him add the phrase `mercy buckets' to his repertoire. Americans make me feel good about our language skills.) This friend is also rather deaf. He got this way smuggling gold in Asia after the Second World War. In the Hard Rock cafe in Paris he once asked the staff to turn down the volume of the music so that he could hear what I was saying. To my astonishment they did.

22.05 p.m.

The more time I have spent in France the less inclined I have become to bother to speak their language. First, they are impatient with foreigners and rude to those trying to speak their language. They pretend not to understand and they sneer a lot. And I have also discovered that French is different in real life to the stuff I've learned. For example, in real life I need to know the French for 'tap' and 'leak' rather than being able to buy two tickets for the opera and I need to able to understand workmen who come from Romania or Russia and who speak French with the French equivalent of a broad Somerset accent. So I now generally insist that they all speak English. And this gives me a chance to sneer at them. The ones who speak English always think they speak it better than they do. They make terribly wonderful mistakes. For example, at Orly Airport near Paris there is a sign: `Retarded Passengers Waiting Room'. Wonderful.

23.40 p.m.

We listened to John Le Carré reading his book *Single and Single* on an audiotape. Le Carré is the most passionate and caring and political sensitive novelist since Dickens and he is the best reader I have ever heard.

10
12.06 p.m.

I made the mistake of trying to speak French to a workman who came to service our central heating boiler. I asked him if he had swept the chimney - the `ramonage'. This is something that has to be done by law and it is in our contract that when the boiler is serviced the chimney must be swept. He then argued with me about my pronunciation of the word `ramonage' and said he had not done it because he had left his brushes in his van. I had previously decided that the next time a Frenchman told me off for pronouncing a word incorrectly I would argue the point with him and insist that I was right and he was wrong. This, I decided, would enrage him so much that he would explode and the problem would be solved. I was so cross at the sweep's attitude (which meant that we would have to ring the company and book another appointment for the ramonage to be done) that I simply stood right next to him and shouted at him in English. This worked very well. He looked absolutely terrified and rushed off, returning five minutes later with the missing brushes. Shouting at foreigners - particularly French people - often works well but you have to be very serious about it. Just getting cross won't do at all. You need to look slightly mad and rather dangerous.

15.02 p.m.

We bought a piano in an amazing shop at the bottom of Boulevard de Sebastopol. Buying the piano was the easy part. `Did you come with a van?' asked the salesman when I had paid. A colleague of his turned up with the piano wrapped up in thick cardboard. It now seemed twice as big as it had been when we'd chosen it. `No,' I told him. `We came on the bus.' He looked puzzled. We had told him that we wanted to take the piano back with us to the apartment. He telephoned for a taxi and asked for one that is shaped like a van. When it came the driver helped The Princess, the salesman and me to put the piano into the back. I suddenly started giggling. `What's the matter?' asked The Princess. I told her that I had suddenly remembered the daft Laurel and Hardy sequence when they try to deliver a piano to a house up about a thousand steps. She started giggling too. The taxi driver wasn't amused. In trying to create more space in the back of his vehicle he had broken something. When we got back to the apartment the driver helped us to manoeuvre the piano out of the back of his van but he wasn't interested in helping us get the thing into the lift. It was by now almost twice the size that it had been when we'd first seen it wrapped, and four times as big as it had been when we'd first seen it. The Princess and I had to try to squeeze it into the lift by ourselves. Try as we might it simply wouldn't go. We had to pull, push, carry and squeeze it up five flights of stairs. Two hours later, slumped in a chair with a cup of tea in one hand and a glass of whisky in the other, I looked at The Princess. `Why didn't you learn to play the flute?' I asked her.

11
15.45 p.m.
We walked round the first floor cloisters at Les Invalides. It is one of my favourite places in the world. Whenever we go there I always wonder why architects no longer design hospitals with covered walkways so that patients (and staff) can get a little fresh air even when it's hot or raining. The Hotel Dieu, near to Notre Dame, is one of the most beautiful hospitals in the world. It is built around a garden and has spectacular cloisters (though, sadly, they now seem to be used by members of staff taking a fag break).

17.39 p.m.
Someone called Hartnett, who is apparently some sort of senior taxman, has said that there is no need to apologise for the fact that HMRC got 1.4 million tax assessments wrong because tax reconciliation is a routine measure. If Hartnett thinks that making 1.4 mistakes is routine then it is a good job he doesn't work in the health service. This sort of arrogance is typical not just of HMRC but of the civil service zombies at large. Hartnett should be fired and put into the stocks for six weeks pour encourager les autres. But I expect he'll get a bonus, a knighthood and a bag of bones for Christmas.

12
14.25 p.m.
`Would you like a trip to Monaco?' our friend Marvin asked suddenly and utterly unexpectedly. We'd met them for coffee at Fouquets on the Champs Elysee. They live in Monaco but were in

Paris on a shopping expedition. 'There's so much more choice here,' said Sheila. 'And everything is so cheap,' said Marvin.

Marvin likes to think of himself as a rebel but he has always been a conformist. When he was young he was a punk and thought of himself as a revolutionary. However, like all his friends, he dyed his hair green and had it cut into a bizarre, spiky style. He had a safety pin through his nose and wore torn jeans and a T-shirt with holes in it. All the pals he went around with wore the same sort of clothes and they all had safety pins through their noses. They swore a good deal, picked their noses in public and spat on the pavement with unnecessary vigour and frequency. They were a sanctimonious little band; all desperate to fit into their own little group of neo-conservatives. One by one they got rid of their safety pins, acquired mortgages and bought semi-detached houses. Now they all wash their cars and cut their lawns on Sundays and watch television every evening. Marvin, who became rich out of selling mobile telephones, has become the most staid of them all. The one really odd thing about him is that he is a fervent conspiracy theorist. Just before the end of 1999 he and his wife bought a small farm in New Zealand. They equipped it with a diesel generator and enough tins of food to have fed Napoleon's army throughout a Russian winter.

His wife, Sheila, is old-fashioned and rather prim. On the bookshelves of their apartment in Monaco she keeps books by male authors on the right side of the fireplace and books by female authors on the left side of the fireplace. None of the books has ever been read. She buys them by the yard from a bookseller in Nice. Mischievously, I once took her a present of three books by James Morris, the author who had a sex change and became Jan Morris. When we went next I noticed that the books weren't on display.

'Stay a couple of weeks in our apartment free of charge,' said Marvin. He took the keys out of his pocket and put them onto the café table as though to seal the deal.

I stared at him as if he'd offered me a trip to the moon.

'All expenses paid,' said Marvin. 'And an extra $100 a day while you're there. All you have to do while you're there is make a couple of telephone calls and switch on the lights a few times,' said Sheila, his wife. Sheila, who was born in Barnsley, thinks we are desperately poor because we don't sell mobile telephones. Marvin thinks everyone he meets is poor.

'A couple of hours by plane,' said Marvin. 'Or you can get there by train on the night sleeper. Personally I prefer the train. I hate flying. All that waiting around at airports.'

'I keep telling him that if he bought an aeroplane we wouldn't have to wait around at airports,' said Sheila.

'I'm not buying an aeroplane,' insisted Marvin, rather sharply. 'If I buy a plane you'll be flying off all over the place and who will look after me?' He turned to me. 'Sheila loves travelling,' he explained. He turned to The Princess. 'Officially, I'm resident in Monaco,' he explained. 'And to maintain my residency I have to spend at least six months a year in the Principality. Otherwise the French authorities will leap on me and I have to pay French tax.'

'The trouble is that we prefer Paris,' said Sheila. 'But we don't want to pay French taxes.'

'We need someone we can trust to make it look as though we're there when we're actually here,' said Marvin.

'We just found out that the authorities are checking up on people by looking at phone bills and electricity bills,' explained Sheila. 'You'd be doing us a big favour.'

'So, what do you say?' asked Marvin.

I looked at The Princess. I could tell she was as unenthusiastic as I was. Neither of us wanted to go to Monaco. 'It is very tempting,' I told him. 'And very generous. But I'm not sure that I can leave Paris just at the moment. We have one or two things to do. They're painting the outside of our building and we need to be here to open the windows.'

'If we don't open them the painters will probably paint them all shut,' explained The Princess.

'That's OK,' said Marvin, with a wave of a hand.

'Maybe another time,' I suggested.

'Another time,' agreed Marvin, with a nod.

17.08 p.m.

Kind readers of my books recently sent me £50 worth of free SNCF vouchers which they'd received in compensation for some problems they had endured on a trip. They sent me the tickets because they know we spend a good deal of time in France.

Unfortunately, the vouchers are due to expire in a matter of days and we don't particularly want to go anywhere. We looked at the map and tried to get excited about a trip to Chartres or Fontainbleu but the weather was being kind to us and we really didn't want to leave Paris. We tried to think of friends to whom we could give the tickets but no one we knew was in Paris at the time apart from Marvin and Sheila and they are so rich that they wouldn't appreciate the gift at all. So, in the end we tied the vouchers to a large pink balloon (we always have balloons lying around) and threw the balloon, together with the attached vouchers, out of the window. I wrote `Servez-vous' with a felt tip pen on the balloon. The package landed on the pavement and was immediately picked up by two workmen from the embassy across the street. They examined the vouchers carefully and at first seemed confused. They kept looking up but didn't see The Princess or I because we deliberately kept out of sight. Eventually, with a shrug one workman took the vouchers and the other took the balloon.

13
17.34 p.m.
On the way back from a pilgrimage to Notre Dame (we didn't go in - the interior is always a melee of tourists - but just walked down through the wonderful little streets which lead there from St Germain) we stopped for a vin chaud and a hot chocolate at Deux Magots, still one of the most fashionable cafes in Paris. The terrace was packed so we went indoors, which was cooler and much quieter and sat in the corner where Jean-Paul Sartre and Simone de Beauvoir used to sit. It was here on the Left Bank, in the streets around the Sorbonne, that the 1968 riots took place in Paris. The indefatigable Sartre, the permanent rebel, was out there with the students and a friend of mine who was working at a Paris publisher's at the time saw him hurling cobblestones at the police barricades. My friend told me that Sartre clearly wasn't very strong and the cobbles weren't travelling very far but that he was definitely taking a very active part in the rioting. The police had been given strict instructions that they were not to arrest him whatever happened and so while students around him were gathered up and carted off the increasingly lonely Sartre was left to carry on with his cobble hurling. `Arrest me!' he demanded. But

the police were not stupid enough to want to turn him into a martyr and so they left him alone. `You are arresting those students!' said Sartre. `Yes, Monsieur Sartre,' replied a senior policeman. `We have to. They are throwing stones.' Sartre replied by picking up another cobblestone and hurling it as far as he could, which wasn't very far. `Please be careful that you do not hurt yourself, Monsieur Sartre,' said the policeman solicitously. After the riots were over the French ripped up all the cobbles and replaced them with boring tarmacadam which is far more difficult to turn into weapons.

The British police were never that bright. They arrested Bertrand Russell even when he was in his 90s and gave the peace protestors massive publicity. And the Americans weren't so bright either, during the demonstrations against the Vietnam War. The American police managed to avoid arresting Dr Benjamin Spock but they did make the horrendous mistake of arresting Norman Mailer who, when they eventually let him out, rushed home and wrote *The Armies of the Night*. I noticed the other day that the Russians do seem to have learned from the French. During recent demonstrations in Moscow they took care not to arrest Gary Kasparov, chess genius turned political campaigner. Putin may be a ruthless thug but he's bright enough to know that a bruised and battered Kasparov would be a public relations nightmare.

14

12.04 p.m.

It is apparently now official policy for the police in Britain not to chase motorcycle thieves who are not wearing helmets. It has been decided (though by whom I know not) that to do so would endanger the life of the thief. It will now presumably be police policy not to chase car thieves who are not wearing seat belts. The police however do chase cyclists who try to stay alive by avoiding busy roads. It has, for example, been revealed that in Manchester four brave officers swooped on an 84-year-old war veteran riding his bicycle on the pavement. The more innocent you are the more at danger you will be. After the police arrested a 59-year-old woman for sleeping in her car (apparently the police must have decided that this is a crime, even if Parliament hasn't) they claimed that she refused to give a breath sample and then flung her on the floor of a police cell with such violence that she sustained a nasty cut to her head. (The policeman who reported the authorised thug who did this was praised by his police force though I can't for the life of me see why he should be praised for behaving like an ordinarily decent citizen.) The police thug got six months in prison which seems absurdly light.

14.24 p.m.
Our bill from France Telecom arrived, accompanied as always by a leaflet encouraging me to do everything through the Web rather than by post. `Choisir la Facture sur le net pour utiliser moins de papier,' they advise me. No one seems to see the irony in sending me endless bits of paper telling me this. Every large company in the world wants me to do everything on the Web (the Government forces me to). They all claim it's to save the environment when it's really to save them money and trouble. Do they all think we are stupid? (Probably).

16.20 p.m.
This afternoon, at The Princess's suggestion, we threw a balloon out of the window with a ten euro note taped to it. It was picked up by a man on a tricycle. He rides around the arrondissement sharpening knives with an old-fashioned grindstone which he powers with the pedals of his cycle. He seemed delighted with his find. He put the note into his wallet and tied the balloon to the back of his bicycle.

The Princess loves making people happy. She has a habit of stopping people who look unhappy and poor, saying `I think you just dropped this' and then giving them a fiver.

17.38 p.m.
As we headed for the Gare du Nord the taxi driver took us on a round trip of Paris. Having done the journey several hundred times I know when someone is taking the mickey. When we finally arrived at the station and got out of the cab I swore at the driver in French until I ran out of suitable words and then reverted to English. I also told him that I wasn't giving him a tip because he was a crook. The people waiting for taxis in the queue outside the station were kind enough to applaud.

15

11.24 a.m.

Over the years I have known many people who have made the major part of their living out of buying and selling their own homes. The absence of any capital gains tax on the profits means that it is possible to become quite seriously rich this way.

I once employed a gardener who confessed that he only did a little grass cutting so that he had a small income he could declare to the taxman. He made his real money by buying houses, doing them up and selling them again. He was a professional property speculator but he paid no tax. I hope he is not still trying to work this very popular scam. I suspect that switching properties will, for the next ten years, lead to capital gains losses not gains.

The Princess and I have discovered a variation on this. We went to see house, where the owners had put up a new house in the garden. `We're going to move into the new house,' he told us, as he opened and closed the under the stairs cupboard. `So we're selling the old one.'

`We're going to stay in the new one for two years and then we're moving to France,' she said, as she showed us the kitchen cupboards.

At least they both told us the same story. We once viewed a house where the husband told us they were moving in order to be nearer their children and the wife told us they were moving because of a change of job.

The new house the couple had built was disgustingly ugly and very large.

`No tax to pay on this house and no tax to pay on the new one if we stay two years,' he explained, though that was pretty obvious. `I'm fed up with this country. I paid into Equitable Life for years and then the buggers screwed it all up. We built the new house as big as they'd let us so we'd get the maximum amount of profit out of it.'

You couldn't blame them.

But we didn't want to buy the house they were selling.

It had a huge, ugly house in the garden.

15.46 p.m.

369

Despite taking evasive action we saw one of our neighbours today. She always manages to say something unpleasant. As we headed back home The Princess leant close to me and whispered. `If we walked past their house and saw her husband putting something long and heavy into the car boot, and we never saw her again, I wouldn't tell anyone, would you?' I said I'd hold the boot lid open for him.

16
15.10 p.m.
One of Pope Benedict XV1's sidekicks, a certain Cardinal Kasper (who sounds like the baddie in a children's story) is reported as having said that Britain is a Third World country. Funny thing he's right. Young people in Britain grow up illiterate, innumerate and largely feral; a frighteningly large number are whingeing parasites. One in six kids grows up in a house where no one ever works and no one ever has worked. Most children in Britain are bastards, literally and possibly figuratively too. Politicians and bankers and business leaders who have power abuse it almost without thinking and the rest of us are subjected to a constant, dispiriting and distracting series of orders, requirements and demands. Thanks to well pensioned financial halfwits such as Gordon Brown and Fred Goodwin we are about to find ourselves living through seemingly endless decades of austerity. The people whose incompetence or greed created the crisis are all being well rewarded. I see that the executive members of the Bank of England have pensions of two thirds of their final salary and they are entitled to their pensions after just 20 years of service. They don't have to make any contributions themselves. The Governor, Mervyn King, has a pension pot worth £5.36 million which is nice for him. My pension pot consists of money I have saved myself. I am limited to a total sum of £1.5 million. The phrase `one law for them and one for us' springs to mind. If the Governor of the Bank of England is worth that much pension so are the nation's lavatory cleaners and lollipop ladies. They, at least, have been doing their jobs with some degree of competence. We boast of giving the world freedom, dignity and justice but we have none of those ourselves. Britain is awash with people who live their lives with little or no purpose; it now has the largest prison population in Europe (much of it unable to read or

write). Decency and respect have disappeared. Institutions that used to cherish values and traditions have been weakened to the point of breaking down. People who represent the law think they are the law. Most people smother the present with either hopes or memories. Millions are clueless, frequently apathetic and invariably in quiet denial.

The lawmakers have made a world in which people are so scared that they daren't cross the road even when there is no traffic for miles unless the little green man is visible. If the lights stop working no one will know what to do. Our last two Prime Ministers are waiting to see if they get arrested and taken before a War Crimes Tribunal. And, just like the sort of countries Blair liked to invade, we have an immensely rich and privileged oligarchy, who grab all the money for themselves, and a mass of impoverished workers who live on scraps and hope. We have no democracy: the mass of people want immigration stopped and want us to leave the European Union but have no chance at all of their wishes being obeyed. We have a parliament comprised almost exclusively of warmongers, fraudsters and thieves who want to make the world a better place - but only for them. This is all perfect Third World stuff.

In Britain today half a million more people are employed in retailing than in manufacturing. Napoleon described us as a nation of shopkeepers; now we are a nation of shoppers. We are permanent importers, doomed to deal with a constant balance of payments crisis.

Local councils everywhere are closing libraries so that former chief executives can continue to live in the sort of luxury they never deserved even when they were working. Every civilisation in history had public libraries. The final disappearance of ours will mark the end of our civilisation. It is worth remembering that most of our public libraries were built by the now often much reviled Victorians (who gave us most of our infrastructure and most of our most solid public buildings). Our public libraries are magnificent buildings which will, no doubt, be knocked down and turned into flats that no one wants to buy or into mobile phone shops. They will never be replaced. The public libraries which aren't closing are reducing their hours or concentrating solely on selling Internet access and renting out DVDs of violent and pornographic films. It's what sells, you see.

We have created a society which is driven by envy, deceit, resentment and violence. Whenever I ring the local council to complain that our rubbish has (again) not been collected, I speak to yet another bureaucrat. There must be thousands of them managing the deployment of a dozen bin men. Naturally, when cutbacks are made the bureaucrats never sack themselves. They cut the services rather than their own jobs.

Britain is a nation crammed full of people who expect free everything and take no responsibility for themselves. They expect everything but do nothing. They assume that society (the people who work) will provide them with all that they want (it goes without saying that society will provide them with everything they need). One fifth of the population have deep-rooted assumptions of entitlement. They believe, with frightening sincerity, that they are entitled to be looked after. It never occurs to them to wonder where the money comes from and it never occurs to them that in assuming the posture of servility they have become slaves. They may think that their arrogant demands give them the appearance of independence but in truth it gives them the reality of total dependence. `I can do whatever I want,' they say, and mean, `because it is someone else's responsibility to take care of me, just like they took care of mum and dad and just as they are taking care of my 11 brothers and sisters.'

We have a Government which is corrupt and deceitful, run by greedy self-serving cheats who will do anything, including murder, to protect their own interests. (The clumsy assassination of Dr David Kelly was, I suspect, merely the best known example of the State silencing an inconvenient voice. As a former police surgeon I am totally convinced that Dr David Kelly is the only person we can be absolutely sure didn't kill Dr David Kelly. I am not alone. A large number of other doctors share my view and my doubt that the truth will ever be published.) The Government wants to bully, exhaust and frighten us so that we don't believe that there is any hope that we can change things - even if we have the time and energy and it isn't illegal to complain. `What's the use, nothing is going to change?' is not just the only attitude today it is, for most people, the only way to survive without losing your sanity. I've fought for years about all sorts of things I believe in and where the evidence convinces me that I'm right - and it has been exhausting and largely pointless. The red tape becomes ever more impenetrable and most people don't care or have any fight left (or they have been brainwashed into believing the system is right and the politicians are doing their best and the bureaucrats are just doing their jobs). But the politicians, mendacious, malicious and mediocre, have betrayed everyone. Not even Profumo style disgrace finishes them. They take a few months out, write a book, make a few television programmes, do a few interviews, pose for photographs with poor children, visit somewhere foreign where there is a good deal of hunger and death (they don't need to do anything - just being there suggests that they are making amends). And then they're back. Redeemed. Forgiven by themselves.

Most people don't ask themselves if they are proud of what they do, or if they even enjoy what they do. Actually, most people don't think at all. They just do what they do and worry about the money they are making, the money they are spending and the consequences of whatever may be the difference between the two figures.

The Government is selling the infrastructure which taxpayers paid for (the bridges and the airports and the roads) and the people running them are naturally in it just for the profit.

The Cardinal is right. We are a Third World country. Suicide figures are soaring. Emigration figures are rocketing. Ambitious, hopeful people who earn and save and work are leaving in droves (when they can sell their houses). The consumption of tranquillisers, anti-depressants and alcohol is rocketing. The incidence of illegal drug use is rising and the authorities respond to this by giving drugs to those who want them. The Government lies about them but everyone knows that crime rates go up every year, every month and probably every day. Anti-social behaviour is rising. Mindless violence is becoming commoner with each new generation. Schoolchildren can't read or write but they are given happiness lessons so that they don't notice.

These are all symptoms of the basic problems caused by an inhumane, unrepresentative, oppressive government

The world used to be screwed up by lawyers and accountants and politicians and bureaucrats. But the bankers came out of nowhere and screwed up everyone (charging taxpayers for the fun of it). The bankers (largely but not exclusively American) are greedy beyond the comprehension of normal people.

The IQs of the average banker and politician (when added together) fall just between cretin and moron.

Anti-Englishness is everywhere. The Americans despise us. (The Americans laugh at us for thinking we have a special relationship with them.) Our former colonies loathe us. Our European neighbours despise our subservience to America. The Germans hate us because we beat them twice. The French hate us because we saved them twice. The Commonwealth countries hate us because we conquered them, seduced them and then threw them aside to conduct a liaison with America, France and Germany - countries which have all betrayed us so often that to the Commonwealth countries we look like battered wives, returning endlessly for more punishment.

Our world is built on fraud and sustained by greed. No one thinks much anymore: they just answer their e-mails and their texts and chatter away meaninglessly on their telephones. (What do people find to text and e-mail about?)

No one looks and sees. No one sits in a café and stares into space contemplating because no one has time to think any more. Very few people in Britain sit and read books. (They buy them as presents but they don't read them much. They're far too busy sending one another texts and e-mails which mean little and contribute nothing.)

In 2010, 9,000 public employees earned more than the Prime Minister. No less than 20,000 civil servants earned over £117,523 a year in basic salaries. On top of that they were paid bonuses they never earned and promised index-linked inflation-proofed non-contributory pensions paid for by taxpayers, as much holiday as they could stand, as much time off as they liked when feeling poorly and days at home in front of the television when the weather was inclement. A traffic warden working in Tower Hamlets in London earned £52,786 in 2010. Mind you, nasty little footballers are paid hundreds of thousands of pounds a week to kick a ball about. The heir to the heir to the throne decides to marry and an extra bank holiday is announced - regardless of the fact that it will cost the nation £5 billion at a time when we are struggling to pay off our massive Brown-induced debts.

First class train carriages are these days largely occupied by government employees, employees of Non-Governmental Organisation, charity employees, nuns and rail company staff and their relatives (zillions of whom get free first class travel). Just like any Third World country.

We are all being turned into sneaks. Even doctors, accountants and lawyers now have to sneak on their clients - without telling them they are doing it, of course. In our wonderful new EU world we can't trust anyone: neighbours, workmates, employees, employers, friends, relatives - they're all being seduced by the enemy; they're all turned into double agents.

We are importing armies of beggars and Big Issue sellers, many of them are young, fit and healthy. I am reminded of Talleyrand who turned his back on a beggar who approached him. `I must live!' said the beggar, though presumably in French. `I fail to see the necessity,' replied Talleyrand (also presumably in French). Elderly beggars are driven onto the streets by the vicissitudes of life. Many have worked hard and done everything right but have been betrayed and then ground down by a ruthless system. Young beggars are quite another thing; most have chosen to beg and for them it is a career option.

Ministers and judges have bodyguards and chauffeur-driven cars and have no idea what is happening in the real world. If they had to travel by train or bus they would see the real world and be terrified by it. It is not surprising that British politicians have failed to have much vision for the last few decades. Most of them have had their heads so far up the collective (and capacious) American backside that they have been rendered blind to anything but the next load of shit coming down their way. Now blind and firmly stuck in position, they welcome this as their reward and regard it as a proud proof of the special relationship.

Our leaders worry more about their personal legacies than our present or future. Every generation used to have a statesman. But we haven't had one of those for years. Statesmen make a few mistakes but they always learn from them. Politicians make a lot more mistakes but never admit to any of them and certainly don't learn from them.

People want low taxes and lots of benefits and haven't yet worked out that the two are incompatible. It's like wanting to drink 12 pints of beer a night and to remain sober and slim for ever. Those on benefits (and those who think that benefits are a right and a `good thing') don't realise that Beveridge, the well-meaning civil servant who introduced benefits, insisted on setting them at a subsistence level in order to prevent squalor without promoting idleness and wanted compulsory training camps for malingerers. Poor old Beveridge would die a thousand deaths if he could see what successive generations of politicians have done with what was, originally, a decent idea.

Greedy house buyers, who bought bigger and more expensive houses than they could afford, expect to be protected by zero interest rates. The greedy borrowers wanted houses twice as big as they could afford even though they must have known in their hearts that it would all go bad. Would they have offered to pay extra tax if their taxpayer protected gambles had paid off and they'd made a ton of money out of their extravagant purchases?

The planned Government cuts are still absurdly light. If the Cameron/Clegg coalition reaches its full term it will then be spending more than Brown was spending when he left Downing Street. That's not what I call austerity. (Incidentally, I see that the EU believes strongly in Britain making a dash for austerity. However, it does not believe that the cuts should affect its own budget. While encouraging member governments to sack workers and cut services the EU is demanding a large rise in its own income. You can always rely on the bureaucrats of the EU for a display of red-blooded hypocrisy.)

The sanctimonious Clegg and the smug Cameron, a coalition of professional indifference, are united only in their awesome failure even to begin to comprehend the problems of the society they profess to be fit to lead. These are political midgets, inconsequential misshapes, crumbs in the biscuit box of political arrogance.

But what can we expect?

We live in a country full of people who think pot noodle is food and the X-factor is entertainment.

All my life I have argued with pompous, overbearing representatives of the establishment. I'm doing it with increasing frequency these days and occasionally I wonder if I am becoming less tolerant. I honestly don't think I am. On the contrary, I rather suspect that I am mellowing with age and staying silent when I would previously have made a noise. The problem is that the establishment now employs more overbearing representatives than ever before; they are ever more intrusive and demanding and increasingly pompous.

Britain is a country run by people gorging themselves at the public trough because they aren't good enough to make a living themselves. Too much credit, too much debt, too much greed. We have battalions of incompetent regulators (themselves overpaid), politicians who had no experience of the real world but who have a staunch, unwavering commitment to feathering their own nests. Central bankers, finance regulators, bank officials and all others who describe themselves as bankers have proved themselves ingloriously incompetent. Better to exchange the letter b for a w.

In traditional Britain, the voters elected the legislature which made the rules. The executive ran things according to the rules. And the judiciary decided if rules had been broken. It's all just part of a largely forgotten history now. Today, if the State were a human being even those fervently opposed to capital punishment would vote to hang it.

Britain is full of people whose only aim in life is to avoid doing anything remotely resembling hard work and who regard themselves as having a right to be kept by others, not because of any infirmness or deficiency or awful luck but because of sheer bloody idleness. No vision, no vitality, no passion, no romance, no purpose.

Children think they cannot ever fail because they have never been allowed to experience failure and have been positively encouraged to feel superior. 'No fear', they say, and the sad, sorry idiots really believe it. They are unable to understand the meaning of words such as 'honour' and 'gratitude' and have a sense of entitlement that would embarrass royal princes.

None of the millions working for large organisations (and that includes Government departments and agencies) do what they are supposed to do any more but they all expect me to do whatever it is they think I ought to do and they want me to do it now, without waiting, without hesitation and without questioning. Isn't that a pretty good definition of slavery?

Civil servants such as tax inspectors and the thugs at airports assume that everyone is guilty until proved possibly (and surely temporarily) innocent.

We have a Parliament which is run by crooks and which ensures that hard work and thrift are punished while deceit and greed are rewarded. Local councils have bat officers working in planning departments and highly-paid pseudo specialists paid by taxpayers to teach residents how to wash their hands and how to eat fruit and vegetables. And there are, of course, thousands of overpaid, unelected terrorists paid to browbeat parents into allowing their children to be poisoned by unnecessary and dangerous vaccinations.

So scared are citizens of the forces of law and order that most people are careful to mind their own business these days. That's why there is so much violence and it's why our streets aren't safe and our politicians can't be trusted. Politics has become nothing more than propaganda.

Meanwhile, as the financial chaos continues the EU, Hitler's bastard love child, the great cause of our destruction, puts up its budget (including its own entertainment budget). As the euro collapses and the very foundations of the EU are threatened, so the bureaucrats continue their reckless, arrogant, spend spend spend policies. No one seems to understand that governments never create wealth. On the contrary they consume wealth. The more government there is the poorer the majority of people will be. That's the way it always works.

Today, anyone who supports or defends the EU is certifiably insane. (I say this as a licensed and registered physician rather than as a figure of speech). There are absolutely no good reasons for our membership of the EU but there are a thousand excellent reasons for our leaving this corrupt organisation. And yet, despite this, there is no major political party offering electors an opportunity to express their sanity through the ballot box. If you vote for one of the three big parties you are voting for the EU. Every bit of bad, confusing legislation comes from the EU, an accursed organisation which has made life infinitely worse by destroying our culture, our economy, our traditions and our quality of life. The EU is the most purely fascist organisation ever invented: anti-democracy, anti-freedom and anti-people. It exists to create and preserve itself and is, therefore, the ultimately statist organisation. I have absolutely no doubt that if one of the big three political parties promised to take us out of the EU (and promised nothing else) it would win the next election easily. Ironically, those who support the EU most enthusiastically are often the same people who complain most vociferously about the closure of local Post Offices, the closure of local schools and hospitals, the fact that GPs are no longer available at nights and weekends, the disappearance of centuries old regiments and the fact that many large employers now avoid EU legislation by hiring people on short-term contracts instead of giving them proper jobs. All these things are, of course, a consequence of our membership of the European Union. No one in public life dares criticise the EU for one very good reason: money. Prime Minister and traitor Edward Heath received £35,000 for taking Britain into the EU. And ever since then the EU's supporters have been swimming in money. Many organisations (such as the BBC) receive EU grants and loans.

Manners used to refer to moral aspects of our conduct. But nowadays, when people talk about 'manners' they are referring to not farting or spitting in a restaurant. Old time governments used to regard manners, the way of doing things, as being as important as the doing. No end was worth realising if one got there in an unmannered way. This remained our watchword for a long time. No cricketer before the Second World War would dream of cheating in order to win. Today sportsmen accept and expect cheating as part of the game.

People don't believe or trust anymore because our role models - the people we are supposed to look up to - aren't trustworthy or believable. And they don't even try to be.

Britain's young people have no passion, no beliefs, no respect for history, culture or tradition. They just have a me me me attitude, a fixation on self-glorification and attention and vast quantities of misplaced super-confidence. In the next Olympics they would win the 200 yard waddle to the unemployment office and the quarter mile dash by mobility scooter to the off-licence. They want money and know that to get it they must show silent obedience (because that is the way to get the money). They never rebel about important things. Just money.

State employees (as with employees of large organisations) have a lot of power but are frightened of making mistakes of commission. These are always regarded as being worse and less defendable than errors of omission. So they tend to say `no' as often as possible and so very little ever gets done. They say `no' because they won't get into trouble if they don't allow anything new to happen but they might if they do. Anyone with power abuses it. (They see politicians and bankers and industry leaders abusing their power so assume that power is there to be abused.)

People who work and pay tax are disenfranchised; second-class citizens; forgotten drones. All the political parties realise they can stay in power by pleasing the people who don't work and don't pay tax. The taxpayers are the main targets of the Government's storm of retrospective legislation.

Anyone who opposes the Government is demonised as an `undesirable political sympathiser' (undesirable to whom?). The public interest comes first. But what does that mean? The phrase is a gift for totalitarians. Dictators decide what they think is public interest.

Governments always hold the monopoly on the use of physical force. If we disobey we do so on pain of imprisonment or death (or death by a thousand investigations - and strangulation by red tape). These are powers we gave freely. But they have been abused.

Anyone who isn't angered by all that is happening should visit a doctor and check that they are still alive. Politicians, bankers, economists don't understand; they are so corrupt that they can't see the big picture. They are also wrong more than they are right. If a small businessman (or a doctor) made as many mistakes as they do they would go bust (or, in the case of a doctor, be struck off the medical register permanently). The enormously overpaid civil servants at the Bank of England, the FSA and the rest completely failed to protect the public because they simply didn't understand what was going on. Five words describe these idiots: hugely overpaid and massively incompetent. If the regulations ensured that bankers went to prison, or went bankrupt, if they destroyed a bank through greed, incompetence or any mixture of both there would be much more sensible behaviour.

In 1757, the Royal Navy executed Admiral Byng after a court martial decision that he had failed to show sufficient vigour in battle. Voltaire commented `It is a good thing to kill an admiral from time to time, to encourage the others'.

It occurs to me that if there were such a thing as a Fourth World country, Britain would be in the relegation zone.

22.32 p.m.

This evening, we watched the film of John Le Carré's book *The Constant Gardener*. It was our third time of watching and I don't think it merits a fourth watching so I fear the DVD is destined for the charity bag. During the film, two of the characters meet and have a splendid lunch in the National Liberal Club in London. I've been a member since around 1970 and although it is nowhere near as much fun these days (much of it had been sold off to the hotel next door and, bizarrely and inexplicably, the club now allows women to wander into all the rooms as and when they will) it was gloriously, magnificently stuffy and dusty when I knew it best.

Immediately after I'd qualified as a doctor, I used to spend one or two days a week living at the club while I worked in Wardour Street in Soho as editor of the *British Clinical Journal*. (The rest of the week I worked as an assistant in general practice in Leamington Spa. Some days I did both. Somehow managing to catch taxis and trains that enabled me to appear to be in two places at once. I also worked as the doctor on TV AM, the first commercial breakfast television show. I used to do the show live at around 8.30 a.m., jump into a waiting taxi to Euston, catch a train to Coventry and drive to Leamington Spa in time to do a morning surgery. This used to confuse patients who had seen me live on breakfast television almost as much as it confused me.)

The rooms and beds in the National Liberal Club were wonderful in those days, and the bathrooms, always it seemed, 100 yards from whichever bedroom you had (unless you managed to get the bedroom they usually kept for Jeremy Thorpe which had its own bathroom attached) were massive, with very high ceilings and baths big enough to swim in. The hot water system used to clank in the morning and an elderly maid would struggle in with a cup of tea. The high beds gave a wonderful view of the river and there was always a chamber pot under the bed. In the evenings I had dinner overlooking the Thames. They had the best sweet trolley I've ever seen. The staff never blinked when I said `and a slice of that too, please'; they merrily piled a huge portion of whatever it was I'd pointed to and waited for the third and fourth addition to the already overloaded plate. In the evenings I either sat and read the papers in the smoking room (it was a whipping offence if you sat in someone's favourite chair) or pretended I was Alex `Hurricane' Higgins playing shots in the magnificent subterranean snooker room. In the morning I breakfasted in the magnificent dining room, eating at a huge round table. When decimalisation was introduced there was much confusion among my fellow residents, some of whom were the wrong side of elderly. I remember one opening his paper and nearly collapsing when he couldn't understand what had happened to his share prices. The price for all this glory, back in 1972, was £3.25 a night for a room with a view of the river and as much breakfast as a man could eat. The price used to be three guineas before decimalisation killed off the dear old things. (Both as a doctor and an author I charged in guineas until they disappeared.)

23.10 p.m.
Copies of the world's most valuable book, Audubon's *Birds of America* sell for around £5 million (that is about five times the price of Shakespeare's first folio). It isn't widely known but Audubon published the book himself. He printed the book in the UK and sold it on a subscription basis to wealthy collectors.

17
14.05 p.m.
I don't suppose I am the only one who gets annoyed when hectored by rich pop stars, princes and politicians who fly around the world in private jets telling the rest of us that we should stay at home in order to save the planet. One well-known annoyance, who seems to have named himself after a brand of dog biscuit, appears to avoid tax by having his money tucked away in some offshore centre but tells governments and voters alike that they should be doing more to help save poor people.

But it isn't just the rich and noisy who are annoying. I am constantly annoyed by shop assistants tutting if they don't think I'm buying politically correct products (or, heaven forbid, asking for a plastic bag in which to carry the products back home). I find these self-righteous tutters particularly annoying because they don't understand that most of the products they think are `correct' are just a con. I find them annoying because I know most of them still eat meat (and are, therefore, choosing to condemn millions of people in poor countries to death from starvation). And I find them annoying because they don't understand that plastic bags are made from waste and that using them actually helps the planet and that cotton bags require vast amounts of water and energy to produce.

The people who make the biggest fuss about saving the planet and worrying about the environment are mostly selfish hypocrites. A team of Canadian researchers has studied people who buy green products and compared them with people who don't. They found that the people who buy supposedly ethical products are more likely to cheat and steal and less likely to take the chance to be kind than people who don't buy `ethical' products.

The explanation for this is, I suspect, that folk who make a big thing about buying `fairtrade' and who wear badges and T-shirts telling the rest of us what we should and should not do, proselyse as a substitute for being kind or nice.

Somehow I find it comforting to know that the people who boast about never using plastic bags and who are always going on about other people's carbon footprints are probably crooks and cheats. I find it reassuring to know that the people who buy fairtrade coffee probably don't leave a tip for their waitress. I find it enraging that people who adopt a child in some far-flung country then cheat on their taxes and complain to the police about the tramp trying to find a warm spot under the railway bridge they pass on their way home. I find it curiously unsurprising to know that the people who fly off to climate change conferences invest in companies that make landmines which are designed to blow the legs off small children. And I find it not in the slightest bit surprising to know that journalists who preach about the wonders of vaccination also promote drug using popsters who, by example, encourage teenagers to burn their brains and souls with illegal drugs.

I talk to The Princess and we decide that we must remember all this as the hypocrites become ever louder. As their voices seem to be ever more strident so we must give each other the strength to ignore their hysterical and ill-based abuse.

18
11.03 a.m.

There are plans to redevelop Lords cricket ground and as a member of the MCC I assume I'll have a vote in whether or not the plans go through. I suspect that members who object will be vilified as out of date and ruled by nostalgia. Change is always considered `good' these days.

I'm a non-believer and I don't see anything wrong with nostalgia. There was much about the past to be proud of. Children could play in the park or the street and were allowed to collect shiny, bright conkers, have snowball fights, make ice slides in the playground and make toast with a brass fork in front of an open fire. You didn't have to triple lock your bike when you popped into a shop or the library. For the first 30 years of my life I regularly rode bicycles and didn't even own a bicycle lock.

The past gave us Winston Churchill, Denis Compton, Stanley Matthews and Mike Hawthorn, it gave us the Campbells and Sir John Cobb, and England always held all the records that mattered. Men played cricket in whites, not pyjamas, and they played for counties not teams sounding like ice hockey franchises. It was a rarity for a professional football club to have players in the first team who weren't born in the county, let alone the country. In many clubs the majority of players were born locally. Today, there are professional football clubs which don't have a single player born in England.

Our modern world has given us John Prescott, Simon Cowell, platoons of unpleasant chefs and the Internet.

Corporate sport has destroyed the whole point of sport as entertainment. There are advertisements on the grass, and the players and there are flashing advertisements around the ground. The umpires are sponsored. It's all about money. Why? Admission fees are astronomical. Television stations pay a fortune for the rights. How much money do these people need? What's it all for?

Nostalgia is regarded as politically incorrect and verging on criminal behaviour. But it is a crucial and potent mixture of memories, culture, history, experience, learning and wisdom.

Nostalgia gives our lives a basis; it gives us terms of reference. And it's as daft to disregard it as it is to wallow in it. If more people enjoyed a little nostalgia maybe more would remember why respect and honesty are so important. Maybe the public would rediscover a sense of morality and honour and maybe, just maybe, these might leak into public life.

I shall, as always, be voting against anything I get a chance to vote against. But I have a feeling that it will all be in vain.

I voted against letting women into the MCC and eventually the authorities, in typical European Union style, wore us out by making us vote again until we gave them the answer they wanted.

19
15.37 p.m.

We see a house we quite like. It isn't perfect (what house is) but we both like it and we're getting tired of looking. The sellers want £750,000 but the house has been on the market for 18 months and in that time the market has fallen considerably. Having looked around we think that the house is overpriced. We offer £700,000. Oh dear. You'd think we were trying to steal the food from their table. Sellers always seem to think that their house is worth what their estate agent says it is worth. But in reality a house is worth what someone will pay for it. Not a penny more and not a penny less. People become crazed when selling houses. The problem is that many people don't see their house as a `home' but as an investment, a property deal or part of their pension fund. They become so overcome by avarice that although they think they are behaving like property dealers they are behaving like idiots. They want a profit but they don't behave like business people. People are told that their house is worth £750,000 and so they decide that they won't accept a penny less than £750,000. That, they decide, is what `it is worth' and anything less would be theft. They reject an offer of £700,000 as utterly unreasonable. If, in another two years they finally get a buyer who pays their price they will feel that they are vindicated. They will ignore the fact that during that period they will have lost vast amounts of interest, that the house they will themselves buy will probably cost them more and that inflation will have turned their £750,000 into £650,000. They would have been far better off to accept our £700,000 but they will never understand this.

As we drove home The Princess turned to me. `There was something odd about that house.' I agreed with her but couldn't explain what it was. Twenty miles down the road The Princess spoke again. `I know what it was,' she said. `No books.' She was right, of course. There were no books in the house. Not one.

20
21.09 p.m.

Infamous war criminal Tony Blair has been awarded the Liberty Medal from the National Constitution Centre in Philadelphia. The medal has been awarded `in recognition of his steadfast commitment to conflict resolution'. I assumed at first that this was a joke. But it wasn't. Still, both Obama and Kissinger got Nobel Peace Prizes so why shouldn't Blair receive a medal. Official figures seem to show that his invasion of Iraq led to 650,000 deaths - almost certainly more than would have died if Saddam had been left where he was.

21
19.00 p.m.

I bought several lots of assorted cigarette cards at an auction in Gloucestershire recently and spent much of this evening sorting through them. For a few hundred pounds I became the proud owner of a vast collection of cards. I had a small number of sets when I was a boy but these lots were an OCD sufferer's delight. Some were in complete sets but most were jumbled loosely together into a trunk and several large boxes. Sorting them and making up sets was strangely calming. Some cards are made of silk and many are quite exquisite. There are even some very early 3D cards - together with a viewer. It is amazing to see the subjects that were chosen. There are the obvious ones (wild flowers, footballers, cricketers and film stars for example) but in the 1920s one cigarette company produced cards showing pictures and details of cabinet ministers.

22.34 p.m.

I've been reading a disappointing book about Daniel Defoe called *Beyond Belief.* The author seems to me to suspect that because Defoe was a crossdresser he must have been a homosexual. Part of the evidence for this absurd notion seems to be that Defoe was a transvestite who spent some time with other transvestites. But homosexuality is rarer among transvestites than it is among the rest of the population. The ignorance about crossdressing doesn't seem to go away. In a newspaper recently I saw a transvestite being advised to see a psychiatrist. Since when have psychiatrists offered advice on selecting lingerie or putting on make-up?

22
11.56 a.m.
Once again I've seen a bookshop selling e-book readers. I also picked up a local paper carrying a promotion for a property website. Madness. When faced with such murderous competition these folk should promote their own advantages not support the opposition.

13.04 p.m.
A woman from Liverpool wrote to say that she had hit her husband with a mirror and that the mirror had broken. `Who gets the bad luck?' she asked. She added, as a postscript: `Do you know where I can buy Dolly Blue?'

15.16 p.m.
Another reader writes to say how much she enjoyed the film of *Mrs Caldicot's Cabbage War.* Her letter brings back happy memories. The Princess and I saw the film in a cinema in Exeter. At the end the entire audience stood up and gave the movie a standing ovation. I don't think I have ever seen this happen before or since. As people left the cinema they were all talking about what they had seen and were laughing and enormously happy. We stood outside and watched and enjoyed. Although the film won prestigious prizes the critics hated it, of course. It was about old people.

23
12.39 p.m.

The International Institute for Strategic Studies, apparently the world's leading think tank for military affairs, says that the threat from al Quaeda and the Taliban has been exaggerated and that the war in Afghanistan is a long drawn out disaster. I'm glad they agree with me. America's head of the CIA recently admitted that there are no more than 50 members of al Quaeda in Afghanistan. There are 120,000 American soldiers there fighting them. (And a good many Britons, of course.) Bush and Blair's criminal invasion of Iraq was based on lies and faked evidence. The evidence now shows that the Iraqis are worse off now than they were when Saddam Hussein was ruining the country. At least he was ruining his own country. The same is true of their war on Afghanistan. God knows how many innocent people have been killed. In both countries the wedding parties, the aid workers and the young soldiers (on both sides) are dying as part of the grab for oil (and oil pipelines).

24

11.05 a.m.

An advertising agent we sometimes use has suggested we buy advertising space in a magazine called *The Oldie*. I had to try to explain to him that the editor, Richard Ingrams, has banned all our advertisements from his magazine. It began when a reader sent me a cutting from *The Oldie's* letter page. The letter writer said: `I was surprised and dismayed to receive the advertisement for Vernon Coleman's book *The OFPIS File* with a copy of the latest *Oldie* magazine. It claims to tell the truth about the EU, when in fact it is full of half-truths and outright lies! I trust that there will be no repeat of these advertisements by Vernon Coleman in future editions of *The Oldie* otherwise I will be forced to cancel my subscription.' Naturally, neither the letter writer nor the magazine took the trouble to define any of the alleged half truths and outright lies. I honestly don't think anyone concerned had bothered to read the book. Not wanting to waste several years of my life fighting a libel action against a curious magazine with a tiny circulation I decided to deal with the matter more directly. First, through perfectly legal methods, The Princess obtained the EU supporter's home address. (She guessed that he would have written to other papers. And sure enough, there on the Internet, was a letter from him in the *Independent* - complete with his address.) She obtained his phone number and I rang and politely confirmed that he was the author of the letter in *The Oldie*. I then wrote to him, politely pointing out that I considered his letter to be an extremely serious libel and asking for an apology. I added that if he had actually read the book he would know that it is vigorously researched. I wrote a similar letter to Richard Ingrams, editor of *The Oldie* asking that he publish an apology. Ingrams was, of course, the previous editor of *Private Eye*. To my astonishment I then received a letter from Ingrams saying: `I have no intention of printing any letter which has been written under duress. If I find that you have threatened one of our readers with libel proceedings I shall see to it that *The Oldie* will no longer accept your advertising material. I have spoken to Ian Hislop at *Private Eye* about this matter and he is considering his position with regard to your material.'

I wrote back to Ingrams pointing out that there had never been any question of duress. `Indeed, I'm surprised that you used the word since it suggests `illegal constraint' and there certainly hasn't been any of that. I do hope you don't feel you were put under duress to agree to print my letter.' I went on to point out that threatening to ban my advertisements would make no difference whatsoever and added that I was very surprised that he thought it might. `Quite what Ian Hislop has to do with any of this I cannot imagine. I haven't advertised in his magazine for some considerable time and I hope he won't be disappointed to know that I have no current plans to do so.' (I didn't bother to tell him that *Private Eye*, a rather flaccid little organ these days, had already banned many advertisements for my books such as *Living in A Fascist Country*. I was told that Hislop refused an advertisement for my book *Food for Thought* because he thought the (entirely accurate headline) *Meat Causes Cancer* might upset his readers.) Despite his bluster Ingrams did publish a letter from me pointing out that everything in *The Ofpis File* is true. But my then advertising agent subsequently told me that I was banned from advertising in *The Oldie* magazine. When I relayed this to the advertising agent he did not believe me. He did believe me when he tried to place an advertisement for one of my cat books. I suppose I should not have been surprised that Ingrams should take such exception to my defending myself against a scurrilous libel that was clearly designed to damage my reputation and the sales of a book criticising the European Union. But I can't help feeling that Ingrams was behaving like a spiteful, childish prat.

25
10.00 a.m.
I see that a retired judge (almost certainly receiving a massive, inflation-linked taxpayer paid salary) has decided that Equitable Life pensioners whose savings were devastated by officially regulated incompetence should receive compensation of around 10 pence in the £1. Pensioners-to-be got hammered by the Equitable Life debacle. The staff of the company did themselves well and the regulators missed everything, patted themselves on the back and gave one another huge bonuses. And now some judge decides, arbitrarily, that the victims should pay the price for their destruction. There is no longer any such thing as a safe or sensible investment in Britain.

The judge has apparently decided that Equitable Life pensioners should be punished because of the nation's economic mess. I don't really see why innocent and trusting and prudent individuals should be singled out for punishment in this way. Are the courts going to charge only 10 pence in the £1 on fines because of the nation's economic condition? This absurd pontification about the public purse is not unexpected. Once again all the people who made the decisions which caused our national penury escape the responsibility. Overpaid, underworked, public servants retain their index-linked, inflation-proofed, non-contributory pensions and bankers still receive their obscene bonuses while the poor sods who paid the salaries, pensions and bonuses of government regulators have to pay the price. Civil servants joyfully devise schemes that destroy private pensions while making sure that their own remain obscenely generous (at someone else's expense). I no longer trust anything any State or corporate body tells me and I no longer trust anyone working for an organisation employing more than six people. They are all the enemies of the sane, hard-working citizen.

26
11.48 a.m.

A reader from Scotland writes: 'I have been told by my doctor that before I can receive treatment I must sign a 'counter fraud declaration'. What on earth is this?' I hadn't heard of this before but I was astonished to discover that patients registering at practices in Scotland are required to sign one of these documents (containing sensitive personal ID information) before they can receive treatment. The declaration entitles the doctor to share the patient's information with a variety of government agencies including the UK Border Agency, the Department for Work and Pensions and HM Revenue and Customs. I gather that doctors moaned a bit about the blatant breach of confidentiality, but accepted it.

27
14.05 p.m.

These days publishers won't look at books unless they come from an agent. We sent hardback copies of one of my novels to a variety of paperback publishers and have received back a number of letters advising me that if I ever want to be a published author I must first find a literary agent. I have a number of excellent agents around the world but although I have, over the years, had a number of agents in London I have never found one with whom I worked well. My first agent, who sold my first books for me and worked at a well-known agency called Curtis Brown, told me, just before I abandoned her, that I was 'a prophet crying in the wilderness'. I think she was probably right but I happen to think that society needs a few wild-haired prophets. The agents after that were even less successful. The last time I nearly hired an agent, I arranged a meeting with a chap at my club in London. He turned out to be a grubby, seedy little man who seemed keen only on negotiating newspaper columns for me so that he could help himself to 15% of a lot of money for not doing very much. He had no interest in anything requiring effort and leered at The Princess in a very unpleasant manner.

28
14.50 p.m.

I really have to decide what to do about the way we sell our books. We used to have our own webshop but had to abandon that when we stopped taking credit cards. For some time now we have sold books through a webshop which goes straight into the Amazon site and is run by them. Although our webshop takes readers direct to Amazon we have a problem: Amazon normally buys our books when they are ordered. They don't carry stock unless a book is selling. This is something of a Catch 22 problem and means that books which are in our catalogue don't appear in our shop on the Internet. We have had enormous difficulty persuading Amazon to carry books we are advertising. I would send out mailshots and buy adverts but Amazon would say `Not in stock'. Then, after they had received hundreds of enquiries and orders, they would order a huge supply. But, by then my mailshots and adverts would have finished. And so the number of people going to Amazon to buy the book would fall. And so Amazon would send back the books. This happened time and time again.

I'm told that Amazon will stock our books if we give them a 60% discount. These are not `firm' sales. Amazon can return books they don't sell. We are expected to pay the postage to send the books to them. And if they want to return books they haven't sold we pay the return postage. In addition, I must pay a fee for allowing Amazon to sell my books. So, if a book retails for £10, we will have to give at least £6 to Amazon and pay at least £2 to post the book to them. That leaves us with £2 to pay for the cost of printing the book and all the costs of running Publishing House. Since it is impossible to get anything but the smallest paperback printed for less than £2 (and even then only with a fairly large print run) it seems to me that this is a very quick way of going bankrupt.

29

16.03 p.m.

We found a perfect looking house in a pleasant village. The house had everything we wanted and the asking price was not entirely unreasonable. We offered a little below the price.

`Is that negotiable?' asked the estate agent.

Does anyone still fall for this, I wonder? If I say that the offer is negotiable then I am immediately making it clear that I will pay more. And so the vendors will demand a higher price. Only a fool says `yes' at this stage. I tell the agent that the price is fixed, firm and our final offer and that we have several other houses to see. If he comes back and rejects our offer we can always reconsider our position and say we've changed our minds.

When I said that our offer wasn't negotiable the agent said he thought the offer would be entirely acceptable and we drove off to the Snooty Fox in Tetbury, where they serve excellent coffee. We sat in front of a roaring log fire and The Princess did a little iPhone research. She wanted to find out about the community, to see what sort of clubs there were. `Maybe they'll have a cricket club,' she suggested. Moments later she handed me her iPhone. `Look at this,' she said. There was much sadness in her voice and in her eyes. I took the iPhone and read a story about the village which had recently appeared in the local newspaper. According to the story a huge number of local villagers were protesting about a request by a local farmer to have a caravan site on his land. Villagers were worried that the site would be used by travellers and gypsies and would have a huge impact on the tiny village's amenities. The planners have been inundated with objections from villagers who pointed out that the proposal could completely destroy the nature of the village, overwhelm the local school and destroy house prices in the area. There are apparently already two campsites for tourists in the village and neither is ever full. The planned site was less than half a mile from the house we were planning to buy. Our new home would be one of the first houses the campsite dwellers passed on their way to the village shop and pub. Our wonderful new home suddenly seemed like a disaster. If most of the villagers were worried about what was likely to happen we would surely be mad to move into the village. The chairman of the local Parish Council said that objections based on what the site might become in the future were not a planning consideration and would be ignored. `People need to understand,' said the chairman, `that devaluing your property or saying what it might become in future are not valid planning objections.' I found this extraordinary. For one thing local planners are hired by local people to protect their interests. And preserving the nature of a village is surely one of their responsibilities. For another, if planners aren't concerned with what might happen in the future why do they exist at all? If I draw up plans for something, the plans describe what I want to do in the future. You can't plan for the past or the present. You can only plan for the future. I went outside, telephoned the estate agent and withdrew our offer. It occurred to me as I did so that since the planning proposal had not been passed (though it seemed likely that it would) the usual sort of legal search might not have unearthed the details. We have now decided that whenever we find a possible new home we will put the name of the local village into a search engine. It's the quickest way to find out what local controversies there might be. Buying a house these days is a nightmare. I'm going to try to find out where all the local planners live. I am confident we'll be safer if we choose a village or town where they choose to live.

This is the second time this has happened to us. Just a few months ago we found a splendid looking house next to a river. The EU, via one of its wretched and unwanted Regional Assemblies, had put a gypsy encampment in the village, bang slap in the middle of a flood plain. The council reported that there was nothing it could do about the plan because it came with the official EU stamp on it.

It is difficult to avoid the thought that the EU's plan is to worry us endlessly about an endless series of lunatic new laws so that we don't have time to think about the source of the lunacy. Forcing us to provide land for gypsies and votes for prisoners are typical EU projects, designed to prevent us from concentrating on the big picture.

People argue that gypsies, travellers and others of that ilk take full advantage of the Human Rights Act and every other piece of legislation; it is said that they demand freedom and want to be left alone but they are happy to accept money from the State in the form of benefits and unemployment pay. Readers of mine have complained that such folk call themselves travellers but want permanent sites, equipped with electricity for their expensive television sets and garages for their expensive motor cars. `Isn't it a contradiction for travellers to want to live on permanent sites?' demanded a reader whose house had been burgled three times since gypsies had moved into his area. `In the old days, when travellers moved around their country they earned their living doing odd jobs and selling pegs and other bits and pieces. But when they settle in one area it is no longer possible for them to earn a living in the traditional ways. There are only so many clothes pegs a woman will want to buy. And when gypsies are given a permanent site in a small village the strain on the local facilities will be unbearable. A village school with a couple of dozen local children will suddenly find itself struggling to cope with twice as many pupils; many of them may be illiterate and require concentrated teaching attention.' None of this can be aired openly partly because it is against the law even to talk of such things and partly because people are too frightened of retribution to speak out openly.

As we ride home it occurs to us both how absurd it is that planning decisions are made by planning officers who do not live in an area. Sometimes the ultimate decisions are made by people who don't even live in the same country. Even when hundreds of villagers (often a vast majority of the local population) oppose some new development they can be overruled by a planning officer who makes a decision quite arbitrarily with or without a planning committee. (Not that planning committees are to be relied upon. Most committees have a collective IQ slightly lower than the IQ of the most stupid person on the committee. Most committees include one person who has the IQ of a walnut.) Increasing interference from Hitler's bastard love child in Brussels means that the ability of people to have any say over the control of their local environment is diminishing almost daily.

21.28 p.m.
`I don't like your books because they are all so very personal,' wrote a reader. `You always put your opinions into your books.' I wrote back: `Telephone directories, text books and dictionaries are the only books which should not be `personal'. Otherwise, all decent authors should make a personal statement in their work. And many good ones also offer a social statement or a political statement.'

30
11.47 a.m.
A few years ago people made an effort when selling their house to make it look attractive. They had the house painted and made the garden look neat and had the chimney swept and the septic tank emptied. Then about a decade ago people stopped bothering because house prices started rising inexorably and sellers assumed

that they didn't have to do anything at all to present their home attractively. Now things have changed and buyers have the upper hand but sellers still haven't changed back; they still think they are in a sellers' market; they try to sell dirty, scruffy houses which need a complete overhaul, if not complete refurbishment and renovation. Gardens are overgrown. And buyers who start worrying about these things are regarded by sellers and their estate agents as unreasonably fussy. Oh how things will change in the next five years.

Meanwhile, we see house after house that needs building work, complete redecoration and a good cleaning. Even well-presented houses have tiles missing and cracked window panes. Guttering is falling away from walls and window frames and soffits need painting. The front door doesn't shut properly in damp weather and the garden shed door is hanging on by one very rusty hinge.

We have been toying with the idea of making an offer for a house we saw. Earlier, the estate agent rang and told me that another buyer had come back and offered the asking price. He told me a mass of detail about the new buyers and even gave them a name which I recognised as the name of a local village. He gave me so much information that it was patently a trick to push us into making an offer. 'OK,' I said. 'They can have it at that price. It's too expensive.' There was silence for half a minute. A long, long silence. He left. Ten minutes later the phone went again. 'Great news!' said the agent, sounding excited. 'The other buyers suddenly decided they've changed their minds again. The house is back on the market.' We said we would continue to think about it. Estate agents have a store of these little tricks. They will tell you that there are loads of people about to make an offer. 'You must be quick and make an offer close to the asking price,' they will say.

15.45 p.m.
I found a story in this week's edition of the *Wilts and Gloucester Standard* which read: 'A desperate plea has gone out across the nation for mangolds, ahead of this weekend's annual hurl at Sherston'. The story, which dominates pages one and three, goes on to explain that 300 of these root vegetables are desperately needed for use as missiles in the traditional hurling event. The usual grower of mangolds, who lives at Wotton under Edge was ill

at the start of the planting season and then the dry summer caused the roots to split and shrink. Finally the remaining crop was hit by mangold fly. As a result of all these calamities, the Ancient Order of Sherston Mangold Hurlers, desperate to avoid the ignominy of using swedes, contacted the National Farmers' Union which agreed to ask farmers everywhere for supplies of mangold wurzels. The organisers are even considering importing from a supply from Ireland. The good news is that a total of 35 prize Yellow Eckendorf specimens have been grown. These are apparently the Normans, or target mangolds, and are due to be washed by Mangold Maids past and present at a special ceremony on the eve of the ceremonial hurl. I don't think I have ever seen a mangold wurzel but reading this story made me proud to be English.

16.05 p.m.

A workman across the street had his radio on very loudly. From our window I could see his van parked nearby and with the aid of a pair of binoculars I was able to read his mobile telephone number painted on the side of the van. I rang him, told him that his radio was far too loud and asked him to turn it down. He looked startled and looked around desperately trying to see who was making the call. But he didn't see me. He turned off the radio and the rest of the afternoon was delightfully peaceful.

October

1
11.40 a.m.
To use any sort of search engine successfully you really have to know what you are looking for. While searching Amazon for a book on the two ladies of Llangollen inevitably (and inaccurately) a variety of books on lesbian lovers came up on the search. But the most surprising book to come on the book list was a guidebook entitled *Offa's Dyke Path*. (Incidentally, when I then looked up Offa on Google I found, at the top, something called OFFA which turns out to be neither a dyke nor a footpath but the `Office for Fair Access'. This is, I assume, another bloody quango, possibly paying taxpayers' money to usurp the real Offa on a website search.)

12.37 p.m.
We keep our utility room (complete with washing machine and tumble drier) on the first floor. A visitor laughed out loud when she saw it. `Where do you keep your dirty clothes?' The Princess asked her. `In a wicker basket in the bathroom,' came the reply. `And where is the bathroom?' `On the first floor.' `Where do you keep your clean clothes?' `In the bedroom.' `And where do you have your washing machine?' The woman went slightly red with embarrassment before admitting that they kept their washing machine downstairs.

15.01 p.m.
An insurance company has written demanding that I give the name of a `designated person' at my address. This is because my address is a Post Office box. The company has used the address for around 20 years without ever wanting the name of a `designated person' before but I am now asking them to send me money and they are, presumably, looking for ways to slow things down. I pointed out that my bank uses my PO box address, the Inland Revenue use it and the Customs and Excise use it. I added that the mail travels through the Royal Mail and that the PO Box is owned and run by the Government. I pointed out that the money they owed me would

be going straight into my bank account and I ended by pointing out that their own address was a PO Box.

2

10.38 a.m.

My book *2020* (a series of predictions about how our world will change by the year 2020) has sold out in two weeks. I've already decided not to reprint it. I think it is fairer to my readers if the advice in the book (which I consider `sensitive') is shared only by a relatively small number of people. A reader wants to know if I am going to write a follow up. I've told him that I am already working on *3030*.

11.34 a.m.

A house brochure came today for a property that we looked at months ago. The estate agent announces with great delight that the price has been reduced by 0.6%. I honestly don't think we are on the same planet. The house was wildly overpriced when it was first offered and it is still wildly overpriced now.

The problem is that the Government is supporting the greedy and the indebted with low interest rates and special help and, at the same time, punishing savers and the cautious. The housing market would have been much healthier if the politicians had allowed house prices to fall to a more sensible level.

Regulating house prices can really be very simple.

Here's one scheme that would work.

First, the borrower who wants to buy a house has to find 20% of the price of the property. He can borrow only 80% of the value.

Second, the lender has to be responsible for the first 20% of the loan if things go bad.

That's it.

How do I know it would work?

Because it has been working very well in Denmark for ever. It is very simple to organise and police and it automatically gives a huge incentive to banks to behave responsibly.

The buyer who wants to buy a house costing £200,000 has to find £40,000 and can borrow £160,000. If the house value falls to £180,000 the bank loses £20,000 and the buyer is still ahead.

This system provides a very simple incentive to banks to behave and to lend money sensibly and so I doubt if it will ever be introduced in Britain.

15.16 p.m.
The Ryder Cup is being played. The European team has a sort of EU flag to fly. It is blue with yellow stars. The Ryder Cup used to be played between Great Britain and the USA. Then it was between Great Britain and Northern Ireland and the USA. Then it was between Great Britain and Europe and the USA. Then it was just between Europe and the USA. Now it's between the EU and the USA. I wonder if the EU has paid to adopt the tournament. Maybe next year they will rename it the Adolf Hitler Memorial Cup to celebrate the EU's spiritual guide.

I watch only a few minutes. The American players, WAGS and supporters are badly dressed, badly behaved, boorish, noisy, rude, brutish and unsubtle.

16.39 p.m.
It is 21 years since *Alice's Diary* was first published and still the book keeps selling. And the mail comes in regularly too. Barely a week goes by without our receiving a letter from a reader offering his or her own version of the diary for politicians. These packets of prose, poetry and photographs always come without any return postage, of course, and when a particularly large one arrives I sometimes begin to understand why large London publishers often refuse to return manuscripts which aren't accompanied by enough money to cover postage and packing. But sometimes the mail isn't so complimentary. A reader has written drawing my attention to a small literal in *Alice's Diary*. This has escaped everyone's attention for two decades. `Please do not send me details of any more of your books,' she wrote. She was not from Tunbridge Wells but was, nevertheless clearly disgusted. She added that she had enjoyed the book very much indeed.

20.41 p.m.
Science fiction writers have, in the past, often written about a future in which man loses power over his world because computers and robots have taken control.

That hasn't happened. But we have, unthinkingly, lost power in a quite different way. We have lost power and handed over control of our lives to an untouchable, nebulous, almost indefinable force.

When we are feeling angry or upset with the world we often blame `them'. When we feel that we are being forced to do things against our will we blame `them'. When we feel frustrated or cheated we blame `them'. When we are hampered by injustice or wounded by unfairness we say that it is `their' fault.

But there is no `them', of course.

The man who seems to represent injustice - and who may seem one minute to be one of `them' - will, the next minute, be standing shoulder to shoulder with you sharing your complaints. The man in a suit who, when sitting behind his desk, seems to be cruel, uncaring and utterly devoid of understanding, will, when he finds himself in a different situation become nervous and uncertain. The woman who works in a government office and treats supplicants with more contempt than compassion (and who seems to her victims to be one of `them') will find herself becoming a victim if she needs to visit a hospital as a patient. The customs officer who greets passengers with a sneer and a scowl (and therefore seems to be one of `them') will lose all his authority and power when he has to queue in his local post office to buy stamps.

The men and women who seem to be `them' aren't really `them' at all. They are each of them given their temporary `them' quality by the institutions for which they work. It is the institutions which have the real power. The man who sits behind the desk is merely borrowing or representing that power. When he steps out from behind his desk (either temporarily, to go home at night, or permanently, to retire) he loses all his `themness' and once again becomes an innocent in a cruel and distant world.

If you carefully examine the way the world is being run at the moment you could reasonably come to the conclusion that most multinational corporations and most governments are more or less exclusively controlled by ruthless, James Bond villain style psychopathic megalomaniacs.

What other explanation could there be for the fact that drug companies make and sell drugs which they know are both dangerous and ineffective? What other explanation could there be for the fact that food companies make and sell food which they must know causes cancer and contains very little of nutritional value? What other explanation could there be for the fact that arms companies sell products deliberately designed to blow the legs off small children? What other explanation could there for the fact that tobacco companies continue to make, promote and sell products which they know kill a high proportion of their customers?

And what other explanation could there possibly be for the fact that bureaucrats, civil servants and politicians allow all this to happen?

There is another explanation for all these things.

For the very first time in history the main opponents of justice and fair play, the proponents of abuse and tyranny, have no human form. We have created new monsters: new monsters which we cannot see or touch (we cannot see or touch them for the excellent reason that they do not exist in reality).

Much unhappiness and frustration is caused by the fact that in our society the law is commonly confused with justice, liberty, freedom and equality. The law no longer has anything to do with morality or right or wrong. It is obviously not morally right to invade countries which haven't threatened us or for the police to shoot innocent people. And yet the legal system of our country doesn't seem to see anything wrong with these things. (Am I the only citizen who believes that killing a policeman should be a lesser crime than killing an ordinary citizen? Soldiers are paid to risk their lives in war. Policemen, like soldiers, are paid to risk their lives to protect us. It's why they are paid so well. It's danger money. In motor racing the death of spectators is always considered `worse' than the deaths of drivers who are paid to take risks.) So our individual sense of morality is not the same as the morality of our legal and justice system. The law is a compromise and, sadly, it is influenced by lobbyists, pressure groups and corrupt politicians who regard it as their daily work to interfere with the truth and to ensure that justice remains well hidden. They do their job well. In our world individuals are innocent not until proven guilty but until they are accused by the State. At that point they pretty well lose all rights. Our state has given itself the right to torture, to confine without trial, to extradite and to do all sorts of terrible things. The State's representatives can kill us without much, if any, fear of retribution.

In truth the law has very little to do with fundamental moral principles. The law exists to help society defend itself; it is used by those who represent society as a weapon with which to dominate and discriminate against individual powers and freedoms. The law is man's inadequate attempt to turn justice - an abstract, theoretical concept - into practical reality. Sadly, it is invariably inspired more by the prejudices and self-interest of the law makers than by respect or concern for the rights of innocent individuals.

These misconceptions about the purpose of our law lead to much disappointment. And these misconceptions help to create a considerable amount of underlying stress.

No society has ever had as many laws as we have and yet few societies can have ever had less justice.

Many of the laws which exist today were created not to protect individuals or communities but to protect the system. It is because such crimes threaten the security and sanctity of the system that theft and fraud often attract harsher sentences than crimes such as rape and murder which affect individuals, whose rights are seen as less significant. And there are so many damned laws. The people who make them seem to concentrate on making laws about things that really don't matter while not making laws about things which do. It is difficult to avoid the conclusion that they regulate because they can. Anything which is fun or profitable will be prohibited. God managed with 10 commandments. Why do we need so many? When politicians introduce a new one they should have to get rid of an old one.

The irony is that although the law was originally introduced to protect individuals and to reduce their stresses the law has itself become a tyrant and a major cause of stress. Today few individuals can afford to take advantage of the protection offered by the law. The law oppresses the weak, the poor and the powerless and sustains itself and the powers which preserve it. The enormous costs of litigation mean that there is one law for the rich and no law at all for the poor. The result is that the law threatens and reduces the rights of the weak and strengthens and augments the rights of the powerful.

Things are made worse by the fact that the people employed by society to uphold and administer the law on behalf of the ordinary people too often take advantage of their positions to abuse their powers. The interpretation of the law is so often at the discretion of those who are paid to uphold it that those who have been hired by society become the law itself; neatly and effectively society protects itself against threat and bypasses the rights of individual citizens.

Too often society allows officers of the courts to abuse their power to satisfy their own personal ambitions, grievances and prejudices. In return society in its broadest and most undemocratic and domineering sense is protected by the people who benefit from its patronage. It is the worst sort of symbiotic relationship.

The final irony is that as respect for the law (and those hired to uphold it) diminishes so the divide between the law and justice grows ever wider.

When people who are given the power to protect society disapprove of something which threatens their status they introduce a new law. As political parties come and go so we accumulate layer after layer of new laws. It doesn't matter if the new laws conflict with the old laws as long as all the laws help to strengthen the status of the State.

Meanwhile, as the oppression of individuals continues, lawlessness (and disrespect for the law) grows among officials and those in power. Brutality, arrogance, corruption and hypocrisy have all damaged public faith in the law but the only response from society has been to create new laws to outlaw disapproval. Society's primary interest is to protect itself, and society is not concerned with justice, freedom or equality since those are values which are appreciated only by individuals. Those who have power are concerned only with their own survival and with perpetuating their power. The simple truth is that we live in a corrupt society which creates countless stresses for ordinary people.

When we complain about `them' we are really complaining about the world we have created for ourselves; we are complaining about unseen forces which structure and rule our society; we are complaining about forces which are now utterly out of our control.

3
22.06 p.m.
Our train spent 15 minutes in Bath station today. It is the best, and possibly only way to see the town these days and as near as I want

to get. It is certainly impossible to go there in a motor car. The last time we went there we drove round and round for an hour and a half and still couldn't find anywhere to park. At one point we found a space but it was a 30 minute walk away from the centre and we were informed by the ticket machine that we could only stay there for two hours. The whole town is full of misleading and confusing road signs, aggressive motorists and aggressive cyclists and pedestrians, all of whom seemed determined to make life unpleasant. The traffic system seemed to have been designed by a mad, game player. We did get into a car park at one point, and although the pricing seemed to make the short stay at Heathrow look cheap, the place turned out to be full. In the end we gave up. We couldn't find anywhere to park (though we did see spaces for rent at £2.90 an hour they were all full). We drove on to Bradford on Avon instead. It's a pleasant enough little place but without much soul or character. We vow that this will be the last time we ever try to visit Bath. It looks a miserable, rather squalid place. The new buildings are absurd. A few days after our last visit I received two fines through the post for driving in bus lanes. Since much of the town centre was dug up at the time there hadn't been much option. Perhaps they would have liked it better if I'd driven on the pavement. From what we saw of it the town of Bath seemed dirty, congested, unattractive and unwelcoming in every conceivable way. Fining visitors is, by the way, an excellent way for towns to discourage strangers and to keep their shops for themselves. I strongly suspect that some councils are short-sighted enough to discourage visitors quite deliberately. After all, visitors require public lavatories and fill up bins with litter.

Bath is in my view the ugliest town south of Birmingham and it is extraordinary that people still talk and write about it as though it were still beautiful. Local planners and architects obviously decided that anything would be acceptable if built out of traditional bath stone, or in something of the same colour. The result is what looks like an almost endless variety of warehouses with windows. Bath reminds me of Blackpool in that both were once marvellous in their own way but both have now become embarrassing parodies of their former selves. Both are deeply depressing places and although I suspect that I've probably been to worse places I cannot offhand remember their names.

As the train drew out of Bath I cheered myself up by thinking of some of the places which do delight me. Here's my top ten places to be with The Princess):

1. Walking from the National Liberal Club to Paddington Station on a dark, cold, slightly foggy winter's evening (but catching a cab at the Oxford Street end of Bond Street).

2. Sitting on the middle balcony at Lords during a county cricket match when there are few spectators on the ground.

3. Having teacakes and Earl Grey tea at Fortnum and Mason's in Piccadilly

4. Drinking a glass of vin chaud inside the Café de la Paix. Outside it is raining heavily and pedestrians are rushing to and fro under umbrellas. We don't have to go anywhere for an hour and I have a good book with me.

5. Having a picnic on a bench near to the Bishop's Palace in Wells and watching the swans, ducks and moorhens messing about on the moat.

6. Browsing in a second-hand bookshop I've never found before and asking the proprietor if it's OK if I put my first armful of purchases on his counter while I continue looking.

7. Sitting on a bench in the Palais Royale in Paris and enjoying an impromptu picnic with materials purchased from one of the little delicatessen shops nearby.

8. Visiting Shakespeare & Co's bookshop in Paris and finding a few books I've never heard of before.

9. Driving along the Wye Valley in autumn.

10. Walking along the River Lyn at Lynmouth and continuing after Watersmeet as far as Rockford. Best done in the rain because the path is quieter then.

The taxi queue in London was quite short, so instead of walking up the ramp and hailing a taxi in the street, we joined it. I'm glad we did because I overheard two women talking. They were standing in front of us and had clearly come to London to go shopping. `I love those shoes you bought to go with the dress you got last week,' said the first woman. `I love them too,' said the second woman. `But when I got them home I decided that they don't really go with the dress. So I'm going to have to find another dress to go with the shoes. And then I'll have to find some new shoes to go with the other dress.' They both sighed at the unfairness of fate and the difficulties of it all.

4

10.03 a.m.

The papers today are filled with bizarre news items. Someone (undoubtedly female) complains that there are not enough women running big companies. A coalition spokesman says that he doesn't understand the fuss about the number of people on benefits. The money they receive is, he says, no more than the average wage. Every year Americans throw away 206 million computer products and 140 million phones. The vast majority of these just go into landfill. The toxins such as lead and mercury and the rare metals used to make these devices (which are disappearing rapidly) all go into the landfill. Pension companies take fees and commissions worth 80% of the money paid into pension plans. Someone who pays £120,000 into an HSBC pension plan over 40 years will pay £99,000 of this to HSBC as fees. (HSBC said that their pension plan offered good value for money and was popular but it is hardly surprising that only 4 out of 10 individuals are saving anything for retirement.) There are now 420 million Chinese Internet users. A Nobel Prize has been given to someone who worked on infertility. (It would make as much sense to give a Nobel Prize to whoever invented breast enlargement surgery.) The BBC describes global warming as man-made, even though this is supposed to be a subject of debate. (In my opinion, the BBC doesn't do news. It only does propaganda.) In the Swindon area there were far less accidents in the year after the local police had given up speed cameras than there had been when they were using them. And in another part of the country the police have told residents who had erected dummy speed cameras that they must take them down because `the devices might make motorists brake too hard and cause accidents'. You couldn't make any of it up and expect anyone to believe you.

12.45 p.m.

Lloyds Bank is refusing to send me a new credit card because my address is a Post Office Box. We have been discussing this for several weeks now. Numerous people have promised to send me a card. But no card has yet arrived. Today I telephoned, made a cup of tea and a sandwich while various recorded voices wanted to know my waist measurement and my favourite ice cream, and eventually spoke to a person. She told me that my card had at last been authorised and sent to Lloyds Bank in Axminster.

`Why?' I asked. `I have never been to Axminster.'

The woman said she didn't know why it had gone to Axminster but that they would send a new one to my proper branch.

`Would you ring the bank in Axminster and ask them to destroy the one they've been sent?' I asked.

`I can't do that,' said Lloyds Bank. `They won't speak to me because it is your card.'

Eventually I persuaded her to ring Axminster. They hadn't seen the card. So my new card was floating around lost. Panic. So now all recent transactions had to be checked. I can never remember the exact sum I paid for whatever it was I bought three weeks ago. Presumably most people can.

`Where shall we send the replacement replacement card?'

I gave her the PO Box address.

`We can't send it there.'

I took a deep breath. I saw from the Financial Ombudsman Service's figures published today that far more complaints are made about Lloyds Bank than about any other financial institution. I'm not surprised. A staggering 22,420 complaints about Lloyds Bank got as far as the Ombudsman in the first 6/12 of the year. If I had complained about all the problems I've had, the figure would have reached 30,000. No other bank got anywhere near Lloyds.

`We don't accept PO Boxes as addresses.' The distaste was palpable.

`The tax people and the passport people and the driving licence people are all happy to use a PO Box.'

`We don't.' I swear she sniffed.

`You've been using it for 20 years. And you send my bank statements there.'

`We don't consider PO Boxes to be trustworthy.' Still defiant.

`Do you know who owns and runs PO Boxes?'

`No.'

`It's the same bunch of crooks who own 40% of Lloyds Bank.'

`I beg your pardon?'

`Who is your biggest shareholder?'

Pause. Silence.

`The Government?' I suggest. I am tempted to point out that they're the ones who bailed the bank out when it was going bankrupt.

`Er...yes, I think so.'

`Do you not trust the Government?'

`Of course I do. What's that got to do with your PO Box?'

`My PO Box is owned and run by the Government.'

They are going to send my card to my PO Box.

5

09.27 a.m.

I had an e-mail from a man in India who says he is a publisher. He wants to publish all my books in his country. He asks me to send him two copies of all my books. I wish all these `publishers' were real. Wearily, I send him half a dozen books. I live in hope. Maybe he really is a publisher. Experience tells me, however, that he is far more likely to be one of those absurd small-time confidence tricksters who pretends to be a publisher in order to get free books. This happens about once a month. I rarely hear from them again. I assume they just sell the books they've been sent.

Another similar scam is to pretend you are starting a new magazine and want books to review or for potential serialisation. I receive a lot of those requests too. The magazines never appear, of course. And I have no doubt that the books end up being sold on Amazon or eBay.

13.58 p.m.

I was in a publisher's office in London when a young assistant came in with a letter which needed signing urgently. `Because of who it's to I've put it on a nice piece of paper,' she said. `I found some really lovely cream paper in the stationery cupboard.' The man I was with signed the letter. `But you're faxing it,' said the man. `Yes,' said his assistant. `But I don't want Mr X to get a letter on that cheap copy paper we normally use.'

`Her name is Victoria,' said the man when the girl had left. He said it as though it were an explanation. `Her daddy is a director of something and she's engaged to someone in investment something. I have hopes that she won't be here long.'

6

12.46 p.m.

The current leaders of the Labour Party say that if they had known then what they know now they would not have supported the invasion of Iraq. Unfortunately, we all knew then what we know now so this argument doesn't hold a good deal of water.

Ed Miliband served in the Labour Government under war criminal leadership but says he is not guilty of anything because it was 'collective responsibility'. OK, so he had collective responsibility. I don't think that will be much of an argument when he is standing before a War Crimes Tribunal. It didn't do the Nazis much good. Collective responsibility just means that he can be hung alongside the others. Miliband, who does what I thought impossible and makes Gordon Brown seem charismatic, also admits that the Government of which he was a member destroyed the economy ('it was just an unfortunate mistake, honest guv; could have happened to anyone'), started two illegal wars and took away our civil liberties. So what the hell is he now doing in any sort of position of responsibility? The man isn't fit to confiscate nail files let alone run the country. Ed seems to me to be just as geeky and unpleasant as his banana-toting brother.

7

11.09 a.m.

A friend has an e-book reader. He says it is wonderful to be able to buy books for pennies and to store his entire library on a device that fits into a briefcase. Apart from the fact that you can't stuff it in your pocket, scribble on the margins and read it in the bath (too slippery) there are vast problems with these damned things and I will never use one. Books are friends, companions and memories. I sit surrounded by books; thousands of them. Their bindings and wrappers make a wonderful wall covering. I can remember where I was first introduced by my favourites, where I bought them and where I read them. I can see the notes I wrote on them. I can remember sharing them. Sometimes I write inside where I first read them. The next generation (the ones who will embrace e-readers and who will regard books as old-fashioned) will miss so much. And, of course, as e-books become more popular so publishers and authors will gradually disappear. Meanwhile, the e-book readers sell by the boatload and people who call themselves booksellers promote the e-book versions ahead of the old-fashioned hard copy editions. The end is coming fast. These days I often feel relieved that I am as old as I am.

8
14.00 p.m.
I see with some astonishment that an English swimmer has won a silver medal in the solo synchronised swimming event at the Commonwealth games. I spent some time trying to work out how this works. I even looked up synchronised. The dictionary defines it as things occurring at the same time or rate. How can one person be synchronised? To the music perhaps?

9
15.57 p.m.
We were sitting in the Palais Royale, one of our favourite parks in Paris, feeding the remains of our picnic lunch to the pigeons, and sparrows. Thirty birds had quickly gathered around our feet and we were, as usual, marvelling at the skill and agility of the sparrows. They can pluck a bread crumb out of the air with astonishing ease.

Suddenly the magic of the moment was broken by a boy, aged about 12, who ran straight at the birds, trying to catch them and kick them.

He wasn't trying to catch the birds because he was hungry. He was having fun. As the birds fluttered into the trees he grinned with delight.

Frightening, chasing and torturing is a uniquely human pleasure.

When other animals hunt they do so either because they are hungry or because their young are threatened.

Human beings are the only animals who get real pleasure out of terrorising, wounding and killing other beasts. (Cats play with mice to practise their hunting skills).

This perverted pleasure exists in many different ways: dog fighting, fox hunting, otter hunting, stag hunting, salmon fishing and grouse shooting. The arrogant hunter sitting proudly on his horse shows the same sort of malicious delight as the boy chasing pigeons.

Worst of all are the men and women who use animals for intellectual pleasure - vivisectors pointlessly torturing and killing millions of animals.

We claim to be a mature and imaginative race, increasingly aware of our awesome responsibilities to our planet and sensitive to the needs of the creatures with whom we share our world. But our treatment of other animals is crude and barbaric.

We should be ashamed of ourselves. We have a long way to go before we can hold up our heads and claim that we are truly the wisest, kindest and most responsible of God's creatures.

18.02 p.m.

According to the *Financial Times* there are worries about privacy and security on the Internet. I cannot imagine why. There is no privacy and security for users of the Web. None. Sadly, most people assume that anyone who wants to retain their privacy must have some dirty secret they wish to hide. Only when their identity is stolen or their bank account emptied or they find themselves being framed for something they didn't do or they have people they don't like and want to avoid banging on their door do they realise why we should all protect and preserve our privacy. But the erosion of privacy continues apace and although the UK wins (or loses) on most counts, countries around the world seem to vie with one another to be more authoritarian than one another. An American who lives in Switzerland sent me a relevant e-mail story this morning. According to a ruling from the US Court of Appeals for the Ninth Circuit in California and eight other western states, US Government agents can now sneak onto someone's property in the middle of the night and put a GPS device on the bottom of their car in order to track their movements. This is apparently legal as long as there is no gate or `no trespassing' sign. According to the court, if there is no sign or gate the owner of the property has no `reasonable expectation of privacy in their own driveway'. Effectively, it seems, any piece of your property which isn't gated or signed as `private' is public property.

20.07 p.m.

The Princess and I were sitting in the Rhumerie, one of Ernest Hemingway's favourite drinking places in Paris. The Princess was drinking Earl Grey tea and I was drinking a glass of hot rum. I overheard this. `She's self-righteous, pompous, patronising and hypocritical,' said a man in a blue blazer. `Yes, but apart from that, do you like her?' asked his slightly older male companion. `She's got decent legs,' replied the man in the blazer.

10

14.05 p.m.

When I resigned from general practice and became a full time writer I had a lot of trouble with the General Medical Council. Back in the 1970s and 1980s there were strict rules about advertising and even though I wasn't practising medicine or seeing patients the GMC received a steady string of complaints that my books, columns and television programmes were `advertising' and that I should, therefore, be struck off the medical register and have my stethoscope formally knotted. (The complaints invariably originated with the drug companies I was attacking.) After a while I got so fed up with this nonsense that I voluntarily took my name off the register. Naturally, my opponents used this as a new way to attack me: claiming that I wasn't a proper doctor at all. So I put my name back on the medical register and today I am both registered and licensed to practise as a GP principal. I don't actually practise but now that the NHS closes down at nights and weekends I do find it handy to be able to write out prescriptions so that we have a stock of essential drugs (antibiotics and so on) for emergency use. Since I'm not working within the NHS these have to be private prescriptions, scribbled on a piece of my notepaper. They work just as well as NHS prescriptions and one of these days I will have a little fun with the system by writing out a perfectly legal private prescription for a quarter of a ton of morphine. There aren't usually any problems with collecting medicines but today The Princess found a pharmacist who had been infected with the bureaucracy virus. She'd taken in a private prescription containing a list of six items but because the pharmacy didn't have one of the drugs in stock the officious pharmacist refused to let her have any of them. `I'll just cross off the one you don't have,' suggested The Princess.

`Oh no, you can't do that!' cried the pharmacist, clearly horrified at the very suggestion. `New rules,' he told her. `If we don't have one item on the prescription then you can't have any of them but must come back when we can fill the whole of the prescription.' Brilliant. This was a prescription for stock items but I wonder how many people will die as a result of this sort of nonsense. I don't need to guess twice to work out where this daft rule came from. Thank you, Brussels.

18.29 p.m.

It occurs to me that if, in future, we must have wars we should have `David and Goliath' style wars. But instead of having `champions' our leaders should fight it out live on television. We can have Cameron brawling with Obama or Putin or whoever. The Iraq war could have been Blair and Bush fighting Hussein and A.N.Other. In a mudpit, perhaps. A fight to the death would have been good.

11

11.32 a.m.

We put a few boxfuls of my book *Gordon is a Moron* outside the door of Publishing House with a note saying `Free books' written on a piece of cardboard. It will be difficult to sell the few books that are left now that Gordon has gone into well-paid semi-obscurity (at least, until the War Crimes Tribunal). I was standing in the hallway and heard one man say to another `This obviously didn't sell very well'. I watched as he picked up a book and took it. We sold around 20,000 copies of *Gordon is a Moron*. A few minutes later a young man in jeans and a leather jacket took a whole boxful. They will presumably appear at 1p each on Amazon or eBay.

14.20 p.m.

I have decided to do the accounts by hand, using a large notepad, a pen and a calculator. I have tried doing them with two different spreadsheets and two different accounting packages and it takes far too long. It is clear to me that it is quicker to do the accounts with a pen. Even using my own personal way of adding up (add up three times, divide by three and put that figure down as the total) it is

414

quick and easy. It will be even easier when VAT rises to 20%. When I told a friend that I was going to use a notebook for the accounts he thought I meant one of those things like a laptop and said that IBM make a good one. I explained that I meant the sort of notebook that you can buy in Poundland. Of course, my new accounting style does mean that if anyone from HMRC wants to check the accounts they will have to dig out a calculator. But I know of no law (yet) which forces me to keep my accounts on a computer.

17.50 p.m.

I wrote out six separate private prescriptions, one for each of the drugs I wanted to put into our home medicine cabinet. The Princess took the six prescriptions to a pharmacy in Barnstaple. `Why on earth has the doctor put these drugs on separate pieces of paper?' demanded the pharmacist. The Princess explained about yesterday's confrontation. `What utter nonsense,' snorted today's pharmacist. `Why didn't the idiot just cross off the item that he didn't have in stock?'

The Princess bought me a new pair of sunglasses made by someone called Ben Sherman. They had a tag attached. The writing on the tag said: 'Looking good isn't important. It's everything.' The frightening thing is that there are probably people who believe this crap.

20.00 p.m.

I bit into a Bounty bar and found a piece of broken tooth in my mouth. I was outraged, and ready to write a strong letter of complaint, until I realised that one of my own teeth had a bit missing. Damn.

21.34 p.m.

A nice cheque for £6,073.37 arrived today from my German publisher. It is a royalty cheque for the first six months of the year for the German edition of *Bodypower*. I wrote *Bodypower* back in 1983 but it still does well in various parts of the world, though I long ago gave up on British publishers who had produced editions of it. Corgi were the first paperback publishers in Britain. They bought the rights from Thames and Hudson who had a huge

415

bestseller with it in hardback. A couple of weeks before the Corgi edition was due out I rang asking if I could buy a couple of extra copies. I was told that the book had sold out and that they had no plans to reprint it. My agent at the time then immediately sold the rights to Sheldon Press who also took over the sale of foreign rights. Sheldon published their own paperback edition but after a year or two they seemed to get tired of the book. It was selling hardly any copies at all so I bought their entire stock to get the rights back. I then gave away all the books they had produced (which I didn't care for very much) and published my own edition. I sent off a few copies to foreign publishers and within a couple of weeks had managed to sell rights to several other countries. Since I took *Bodypower* back it has continually sold well, without any advertising or promotion. And the foreign editions still sell well too. An author's backlist can, if it is well-looked after, produce a pleasant little pension. Sadly, in my experience, most publishers take very little care of their backlists. The royalty cheque I received from the German publisher of Bodypower exceeds the annual value of the pension I receive for having been a GP for ten years.

23.57 p.m.

We were woken by a terrifying sound of screaming. It sounded as though a woman was wailing in agony. Convinced that someone was being murdered we rushed to the window and looked out to see if we could spot what was happening. At first we saw nothing. It was a still, quiet, peaceful night. And then, suddenly, The Princess pointed to a group of foxes. Two of them were fighting. The noise was coming from them. I heaved a sigh of relief at not having to confront a mad axe man.

12

11.02 a.m.

I've had an e-mail from a reader who claims to have read many of my books. He asks why I haven't written anything about the Regional Parliaments and the way the European Union is planning to take over our country. I despair. I have been writing about the EU (and Regional Parliaments) since 2002 when I published *England Our England*. I have been vilified, banned and oppressed for daring to expose these things. I don't think a day goes by when I don't get criticised for doing something or not doing something. But it's difficult to find any websites referring to the fact that I was the first writer to expose many of the now widely recognised truths in medicine and other areas of society. Two days ago I received an e-mail asking me to write something about benzodiazepine drugs. The writer, who claimed to have researched the subject, seemed unaware that I was campaigning about these drugs in the late 1970s and got into terrible trouble for doing so. This sort of thing now happens several times a week. I whinged a lot to The Princess about this and it really isn't fair of me. But I'm tired of sticking my head above the parapet on behalf of other people, being shot at and then being blamed for not doing enough campaigning. Worse still, I am then expected to sing out loudly in praise of writers who are regurgitating stuff I wrote ten or twenty years ago - stuff that caused terrible trouble when it was first published. When I've finished the book on health that I'm writing (the one triggered by the unbelievable things that happened to my father) I'm going to stop writing serious non-fiction books and return to writing more novels and books about Bilbury. I don't think I can stop writing books completely (though I have thought about just writing them and not publishing them) but I think it would make sense to stop `crying in the wilderness', `banging my head against brick walls' and `making people think'. I just feel so bloody tired, dispirited and downhearted. And I am beginning to feel ravaged by resentment and wracked by the guilt I feel at feeling resentful.

14.55 p.m.
I felt angry with myself for this morning's rant and self-pitying whining. But the worst thing is that deep down I still feel the same. My mood of despair is not lightened by a special delivery letter from a reader demanding that I take an interest in his pet peeve and ending with the usual sort of threat warning me that if I don't throw myself behind his campaign my failure to do so will prove that I am just a comfortable, hypocritical, uncaring old fart living in an ivory tower. This does not seem to me to be the best way to capture my attention or enthusiasm but maybe I am just too bloody tired. He also wants medical advice and encloses an envelope full of laboratory tests, X-ray reports and hospital letters. He says he

417

knows that I do not usually reply to letters requiring medical diagnoses but that he is sure that I will make an exception in his case. He does not, of course, enclose a stamped self-addressed envelope.

16.07 p.m.

For a decade or more I have suspected that companies which operate on the Internet use a different form of currency to the rest of us. They make losses and have no discernible way of ever making a profit but are nevertheless described as being worth billions. Today I encountered yet another example of Internet finance. Amazon is selling my book *Bloodless Revolution* for £4.29 post free. Now I can't post a book for less than £2 including the postage and the packaging. Let's assume (and this really is a stretch) that Amazon has overheads which are no greater than mine. (I have to assume that it pays the same as I do for stamps. The Royal Mail does special prices for mass mailings but I doubt if this makes all that much difference.)

Now, the book's retail price is £4.99 and the biggest discount I ever give is 45% which means that the wholesaler pays £2.74 for this book. Now I think it is fair to assume that the wholesaler takes a little profit. And, of course, they have to move the book from their warehouse to the warehouse used by Amazon. So, it is fair to assume that Amazon must pay at least £3 for each copy of *Bloodless Revolution* they buy. They then store it, pick it, wrap it and post it (an operation which must cost £2). And they sell the book for £4.29.

So my only conclusion is that Internet companies operate with a different currency.

21.30 p.m.

I see that the BBC has a new television series about a group of lesbians living in Glasgow. This is clearly just the sort of thing people pay the licence fee for. I have no idea whether it's a drama or a reality television programme and I will not, I fear, be finding out. The BBC led the way down with Eastenders, a smorgasbord of depression and violence. I remember writing, when it first started, that the programme would help encourage misery, violence and suicide. I think I was right. Moreover, dumbed down television in particular, and the media in general, help prevent people being aware of the real problems going on in the world around them. The BBC doesn't care, of course. It is an extraordinarily arrogant organisation run by extraordinarily arrogant people. When the BBC Trust was asked to provide information about how public money was spent, the Trust told the House of Commons public accounts committee that it would only provide the information if guaranteed that it would not be made public. 'The Trust seems to think it is acceptable,' said the committee, 'to negotiate the terms on which it will do business with parliament. This is unacceptable and a discourtesy.' The House of Commons concluded that the BBC has a track record of committing public money without fully analysing the costs and benefits. They drew attention to a redevelopment of Broadcasting House which saw project management failings cost the corporation more than £100 million and to the £576,000 bill for using a studio in the centre of Vienna for the coverage of the Euro 2008 football tournament in order to provide a 'backdrop'. The BBC should go. And go soon. There is no place for the organisation it has become in our society.

My father always told me to be nicer to the BBC. He was right. I should have been. But I can't. I have a painful and damaging inability to creep (and, I fear, a matching ability to alienate possible allies).

22.37 p.m.

There is much to do about the fact that frock salesman and Moss aficionado, Sir Philip Green has, after an investigation, discovered that civil servants waste lots of money when buying office paper and other essentials. I can guarantee that nothing much will happen. In the early 1980s I exposed much worse NHS waste in some articles in the *Daily Star* (where I was a columnist at the time). I wrote the exposé after I received a computer print out from a reader showing that the NHS was paying more for staples such as pens, paper and toilet rolls than I would pay if I bought them one at a time at the local Tesco. The editor told me that the Prime Minister was much excited by this and had given copies to every cabinet member. There was a great flurry of activity in Whitehall in general and in the NHS in particular. The NHS initiated an immediate enquiry. Unfortunately, the enquiry wasn't designed to find out why billions were being wasted but to find out how I had found out that billions were being wasted. The inquiry didn't find out anything which wasn't entirely surprising. I wouldn't have told them anything but they didn't even bother to ask me.

23.01 p.m.

There are rumours that the politicians are thinking about punishing people who don't recycle enough of their waste. Why on earth doesn't someone think of offering incentives? When I was small, shops would give money back on bottles that were returned to them. The system worked very well. Small boys would scavenge the neighbourhood, collecting bottles and taking them back to the shops.

23.51 p.m.

I hear that Claire Rayner, the nurse, has died. I found her to be an unpleasant, pompous and intensely jealous woman who took every opportunity to attack me because I dared to question the medical establishment. None of this would matter a damn if it were not for the fact that she constantly presented herself as a champion of British patients. In my view, she was nothing of the kind. In the 1980s, when I campaigned against the over-prescribing of benzodiazepine drugs, she opposed me vehemently – arguing that the drugs were useful and effective and that I should abandon my campaign. When I was working for TV AM I tried to establish a professional working relationship with her but she was having none of it. Rayner, who was probably best known for advertising sanitary towels on television, was, I think, particularly peeved about the success of my book *Bodypower* when it was serialised in the *Sunday Mirror*. The paper bought television adverts and put up posters all around the country to promote the serialisation. The book proved so popular that the serialisation was extended from two weeks to three weeks and finally to six weeks.

The highlight of the serialisation was a section in the book which described how women had successfully managed to increase the size of their breasts through self-hypnosis. The newspaper decided to conduct an experiment to see whether or not this worked. The features editor hired a group of Page Three models. A nurse then measured their breast size. Three weeks later the nurse measured them again. There was a considerable amount of excitement at the paper while they waited for the results and when the editors knew that the experiment had worked successfully everyone rushed across the road to a pub known to *Mirror* journalists as `The Stab in the Back'. Bottles of champagne were bought and consumed and we then went back to the offices to write the story. I remember I was photographed with the models and the picture was published across two pages in the paper. Rayner was working as the paper's agony aunt at the time and was furious about the attention my book was getting. She seemed very establishment-minded and since I have always been very critical of the close relationship between the pharmaceutical industry and the medical establishment she took every opportunity to write nasty things about me. Pity.

Another major Agony Aunt of the time, Marje Proops, was far more fun to know. Marje and I used to have lunches in Soho occasionally. Like most of the grande dames of Fleet Street she had a very well upholstered view of her own importance. At her insistence I visited her in Westminster hospital once where she was having a routine hip operation under an assumed name. It was all very secret. She seemed to think that the world's press would be hunting her down and ready to hold the presses in order to expose the story of her temporary incapacitation. I was still working as a GP at the time and went on my afternoon off. I picked a bunch of snowdrops from our garden as I dashed out of the house to catch the train to London. When I eventually got into her room it was packed with bouquets sent by the management. She was not, I fear, overly impressed with my small offering.

I did quite a lot of 'agony aunting' myself. I was the BBC's first agony aunt, I wrote an agony column for *Over 21* magazine and I wrote the agony column for *The People* for over a decade.

13
12.12 p.m.
The Princess and I were in a department store. She was looking at blouses. I was standing reading a Raymond Chandler novel I hadn't read for years. Two middle aged women were standing nearby. One was holding up a posh frock for the other to look at. `Oh, I don't know,' said the second, critically. `I like the colour but it's

very daring. I always think men rather look down on women who wear low cut dresses.' 'I think that's the idea,' replied her friend.

As we left I noticed that the cinema across the road was running a double bill. One film shows how the Americans won the English Civil War and the other shows how an American started the French Revolution.

14.51 p.m.

The Princess, a friend of hers and I found ourselves at the beginning of a narrow lane. There was a sign saying 'Light vehicles only.' 'We can't go down here,' said The Princess's friend, as I started past the sign. 'Why not?' I asked her. 'It's for light vehicles only,' she replied. 'And your truck is dark green.' When The Princess explained the meaning of the sign to her she looked embarrassed, but only for a brief moment. 'I thought it was something to do with making sure you could be seen,' she said. 'Why would we need to be seen?' I asked. 'Because of the other sign,' she said. 'What other sign?' I asked. I hadn't seen any other signs. 'The one that said 'Firing Range. Do Not Enter.' There wasn't room to turn round but I can reverse quite well when necessary.

17.24 p.m.

We travelled to Tintern Abbey and up through the glorious Wye Valley on our way to Ross on Wye. A shopkeeper tells us that business is very gloomy. There are, apparently very few hikers these days - and hardly any under the age of 50.

Driving up the Wye Valley at this time of year is like driving into and through a work of art.

20.42 p.m.

French schoolchildren are striking over their Government's plans to increase the retirement age from 60 to 62. The papers are full of pictures of fresh-faced 13-year-old girls waving banners demanding that the retirement age be kept at 60. Poor little sods. It's worrying that they care a toss about pensions at their age but don't they realise that if the changes aren't made then by the time they're 90 they will still be working. The money has already run out.

22.45 p.m.

We caught Newsnight by accident on BBC2 and heard an interviewer called Paxman ask a panel of two people who seemed to have been picked at random: 'Why are people so captivated by the story about the trapped Chilean miners?' The Princess said she thought the question said more about the interviewer than he would perhaps like us to know.

It occurred to me afterwards that no one in the media seems to have realised that one result of the Chilean mining disaster and BP's oil spill will be that there will be much stricter rules and regulations controlling the mining and oil industries. Quite rightly. But the side effect will be that commodity prices are going up, and so inflation will go up too.

We turned off the news and put on *Last Train from Gun Hill*, in which the honest Kirk Douglas triumphs over a powerful man played by Anthony Quinn, who is protecting his son; a rapist and a murderer. Like many great westerns it is a real morality play.

14

11.08 a.m.

In today's mail a reader who enjoyed my book *Bloodless Revolution* suggests that citizens should have one vote between the ages 18 to 25, two votes from 25 to 35 and four votes when they are over the age of 35. He wants to know if I think I will succeed in changing the system. I replied pointing out that the problem we have is that the establishment won't help us destroy itself. 'We sent out hundreds of review copies of *Bloodless Revolution*. Number of reviews? None. Not one.' But I added that many readers are buying copies to give away to friends and neighbours. Two lovely readers who are disabled and living on benefits because they have no choice write to say that they would like to buy 50 copies of *What Happens Next?* to give away as Christmas presents.

15.06 p.m.

My new novel set in Paris is going backwards and sideways rather than forwards. If the characters change their shape once more I will have them all killed by a mad assassin and start again. Playwright David Turner was a patient of mine when I was a GP and he was

423

writing scripts for the television series Crossroads I remember him telling me that he was so fed up with the existing characters that he was going to blow them all up.

15

11.35 a.m.

When I bought a spare charger at a phone shop today they demanded my full name and address. I pointed out that I was paying with cash. The rude and rather aggressive assistant said that they still had to have my name and address. When I asked him why he said it was because of money laundering and terrorism regulations. There is no point in arguing with people when they spout nonsense like this and so I told the silly man that my name was Bertie Wooster and when he asked for my address I gave him the address that was printed on an advertising leaflet about a foot from his hand. He keyed my name and address into the computerised till and seemed happy. He didn't notice that the address was the address of the store where he worked. If he had noticed and protested I would have given him the address of his company's head office which was on another leaflet nearby.

15.36 p.m.

It is now possible to buy a 3D Television though viewers still to have to wear silly spectacles to watch it. It was possible to watch 3D films in the cinema half a century ago when I was a boy.

21.45 p.m.

The new screening machines used at airports take photographs of travellers and cleverly 'remove' their clothing. This is, presumably, some sort of X-ray machine. (The sort of thing that schoolboys used to dream about owning.) How long will it before airport staff sell naked pics of travellers? They will, of course. And what will happen? There will be a rap over the knuckles for the pornographer and nothing will change because the same week there will, most conveniently, be a terrorist scare and we will be told that these useless, expensive, intrusive (and possibly dangerous) machines are the only things standing between us and Armageddon.

16

The Princess and I went to the railway station to buy tickets. I hate doing this because it is far more difficult than it should be. I told the clerk where we would like our journey to start and where it will, hopefully, end and I asked for first class return tickets. I gave him the dates and the carriage and seat numbers we would prefer (quiet carriage, table for two). He held up a hand and stopped me. I waited. After about an hour and three quarters he told me how much money he wanted. I pushed enough cash to buy a small car under the bulletproof, axeproof screen which protected us from each other. He, in turn, pushed the tickets under the screen. They were, inevitably, wrong. He had given us tickets for a shared table for four. I told him this. `Don't you dare tell me I'm wrong!' he screamed. `I hate people telling me I'm wrong.' I tried to reason with him but he started to twitch and sweat. I was, for once, glad of the bulletproof, axeproof screen. I couldn't see a gun or an axe but who knows what he had hidden behind his computer screen. I explained that I happened to know the way the numbering works in first class carriages. I know this sounds rather sad but I checked long ago so that we could always be sure of getting a little table for two and would not have to share our long journey to London with two fat businessmen eating bacon rolls and slurping lager. `Don't tell me I'm wrong,' he hissed. `I've done what you wanted.' I pointed out, as gently as I could, that he hasn't actually quite done precisely what I wanted and that if he had I would by now be half way back to my car happily clutching my clump of tickets. `I've given you window seats,' he spat. `That's very nice of you,' I said, `but I really wanted one of the little tables for two.' `I've given you one,' he insisted. `Do you have a seating plan of the carriage?' I asked. `No,' he said as though this were an absurd question; as though I had asked him if he had a knitting pattern for a pair of baby's bootees. `You can report me if you like.' `OK,' I said, though I knew this wouldn't get me anywhere. It certainly wouldn't get me the seats I wanted. `If you totter along to the platform and look at a train you'll see what I mean. Just check the seat numbers.' He stared at me as though I'd gone mad. There was spittle around his mouth and for the first time I realised I was more at risk of being bitten than being attacked with an axe. `I don't go on trains,' he snarled. With bad grace he fiddled with his computer again and after another hour and three quarters pushed a fresh set of tickets under the gun, axe and tooth proof screen. I looked at them. `You've given me a little table on the outward journey, but seats on a table for four for the return journey,' I told him. He stared at me as though I were mad. `You didn't say you wanted one of those tables *both* ways!' he said. The queue behind me was growing. There was much muttering and complaining. I feared that there might soon be a riot and if there were it would be on my side of the gun, axe and tooth proof screen. I took the tickets and thanked the clerk. It was half a victory. I knew from past experience that if I didn't take the tickets the screen would come down, the office would close and I wouldn't get any tickets at all. Railway clerks are temperamental divas, which I don't mind at all, but they are also incompetent buffoons and that doesn't seem right.

14.22 p.m.

The Princess was standing in a queue at the bank. There were two tellers serving a queue of a dozen people. The manager walked up and said: `Thank you for your patience and understanding.' The Princess said: `I have no choice do I?' The manager smiled but said nothing. No one else said a word, of course, though every single one of them had been complaining before the manager appeared.

20.10 p.m.

The BBC's decision to close its Asian Network radio station was greeted as great news by commercial Asian stations which will no longer have to cope with a tax-funded competitor. One radio station boss reckoned that the UK's 15 commercial Asian stations survive on £8 million a year in total revenue. The BBC Asian Network had a £12 million a year budget. The BBC was destroying the variety of commercial stations by providing free publicity to brands that might otherwise have advertised and by pushing up the salaries for presenters. It is well known that the BBC pays far more than commercial stations (it has vast amounts of taxpayers' money to play with and refuses to say where it all goes). One commercial station boss complained that the BBC hired all his presenters and doubled their salaries to over £50,000 a year.

23.15 p.m.

I bought a cheque for £5 which Charles Dickens wrote and signed. It arrived today. I paid £369 for the cheque from an auction at Bonhams in London.

23.47 p.m.

There is more talk about people of African origin claiming compensation for the fact that their ancestors were enslaved. I suggest to The Princess that since my great great great grandfather was a missionary who was eaten by cannibals I should be able to seek restitution and compensation from the descendants of the tribe who ate him. The Princess said she didn't know I had an ancestor who was a missionary. I tell her his name was Tobias Coleman and that I have been unreliably informed that he made a good meal for 11 cannibals.

23.58 p.m.

HM Revenue and Customs has issued a warning that the 2010 Employer CD ROM, which apparently contains most of the help guidance and calculators employees need to run their payrolls, should be updated immediately. This is news to me. I don't have a CD of any kind from HMRC though this doesn't matter a great deal since I have nothing to play one on anyway. (I do have a CD player on which I play opera, Led Zeppelin, AC/DC and lots of Beethoven and Mahler but I don't think their CD will work on it.) Just to make things worse, I'm told that many taxpayers have been prevented from completing their tax returns online because of a software bug which HMRC has not fixed for more than half a year. I'm not surprised, therefore, to also read today that most of British industry feels that the tax rules in this country are appalling. Big companies (of which Britain has very few these days, most of the ones we had having buggered off or gone bust or been bought up by Americans or Russians) deal with all the crap by hiring heaps of crap-monkeys (which is, I am reliably informed, the technical term for lawyers). Small businesses cannot possibly do this and are dealing with the problem by closing down and emigrating. Life was so much simpler before computers were invented.

17

11.12 a.m.

I persuaded a bookshop to take six copies of the *Village Cricket Tour*. They sold them all within ten days. 'Would you like some more?' I asked. 'Oh no thank you. Those went nicely.' 'Maybe you might like to take some for Christmas?' 'Oh no thank you. We will let you know if any customers ask us to order copies.' I give up.

14.15 p.m.

I have been reading Hank Poulson's autobiography *On the Brink* and it seems to me that though the American Government protected the bonuses of US bankers during the meltdown it did its best to screw British pensioners. The Americans even had the gall to be upset that the British Government wouldn't allow Barclays to take over Lehman's huge losses. (The American Government would not, of course, allow American taxpayers to take on this burden.) The Americans argued that bankers who had screwed the economy needed to be paid well because otherwise they would go elsewhere and do something else. No one ever explained where they would go or what they would do. Bankers' bonuses should be deferred ten years until it is clear that the bank has made a genuine long-term profit. And during that ten years the bonuses should be regarded as part of the bank's capital - vulnerable in case the bank goes bust. The management should be the first to suffer when a bank goes bust.

16.17 p.m.

I looked through the list of foreign publishers who owe me money. It's a depressing list. I have contracts and I know the books were published. But somehow the promised money never materialises.

17.12 p.m.

In his book *The Biology of Art,* Desmond Morris tells of an experiment in which apes were taught to be artists and to produce lovely work. Then they were paid (with peanuts) for their work. Under the reward system the art quickly deteriorated and the apes turned out scrawls just to get the peanuts. Commercialism destroyed their art. They were, literally, working for peanuts.

20.14 p.m.

The BBC has a clock which they claim is accurate to within a thousandth of a second every thousand years. `How do they know that?' asked The Princess. `What do they set it against?'

22.51 p.m.

We watched *Planes, Trains and Automobiles* yet again. Oh what a theft it was when John Candy was taken from us. He was one of the funniest, most charming and most graceful actors in the history of the cinema. If he had lost weight he would have probably lived longer. But would he have been as funny if he hadn't been so fat? The Princess and I tried afterwards to decide which other actors could have made the film. We decide that Jack Lemmon and Walter Matthau would have probably been even better than Candy and Steve Martin. Mr Martin has his moments but he has a tendency to overact. When the script is as good as this one the actors don't need to try to be funny; all they have to do is let the words be funny.

18

11.42 a.m.

An estate agent sent us a brochure for a rather decent looking house. It stood in five acres, had all the usual bits and pieces and costs just under £1,000,000 which is rather more than we wanted to pay but we decided to look at it. These are strange times and asking prices are often over-enthusiastic. But just before we fixed an appointment I noticed that it said on the brochure that the house was `attached' to another property. `Would you like to see it?' asked the agent when he rang later. `No thanks,' I replied. `Why not?' `We don't want a semi-detached,' I explained. He was rather upset, though I can't imagine why. A house fixed to its neighbour is semi-detached. It really doesn't matter how big or small it is.

15.32 p.m.

I noticed a woman shopping in Taunton. It was impossible to miss her. She was laden with bags. She had a shoulder bag on each shoulder and bags in each hand. The man with her was carrying nothing. Suddenly he stopped her and I thought he was going to take some of the bags. But he didn't. Instead, he lifted up one of the shoulder bags that was slipping. He stopped for a moment so that he could light a cigarette and then strode off. She hurried along behind him, like a good Arab woman. But this is in Taunton in Somerset. And they are both white.

17.22 p.m.

A man I know vaguely tells me that if he wanted to smuggle anything through customs he would hide it under his toupee. 'No one would ever dare ask me to remove it,' he said. He's probably right. I know a photographer who took pictures of the infamous Gibraltar shootings. He knew that the authorities were waiting for him at Heathrow so he put a roll of exposed film into his jacket pocket for them to find and confiscate and put the important roll of film under his hat. They didn't find it and the pictures appeared in every national newspaper.

19

10.40 a.m.

I see that a businessman is suing a bank for reporting transactions from his account as suspicious. Banks everywhere file thousands of suspicious transaction reports each year to the Serious Organised Crime Agency and this can be a real problem for honest folk moving money from one account to another. Even moving money about to buy a house is likely to result in your bank telling the authorities and then refusing to follow your instructions while they wait for some bureaucrat to decide whether to allow the transaction to take place or not. (By the time he does, of course, it will probably be too late to buy the house.) As far as I am aware not one terrorist or criminal has been caught by this intrusive system of spying.

17.01 p.m.

I bought our Christmas crackers today. I almost decided to buy fewer crackers because of the problem of dealing with all the rubbish that results afterwards. But then I realised that the wrappers are a mixture of paper and cardboard and will, therefore, burn perfectly well in the log burner. So I bought three dozen. It was all I could carry. I will buy more later. There are only the two of us for Christmas but crackers are good fun.

As we usually do when we are in Wells we had lunch at the Crown at Wells and afternoon coffee at the Swan Hotel. Both are splendid looking places though I don't much like the coffee they serve; I suspect that even the dining car attendants on old British Rail would have been embarrassed. I wonder what happened to those dining cars. I enjoyed being able to have breakfast on the train to London and dinner on the way back home. Despite the coffee, the food and service weren't at all bad.

I bought armfuls of books today. *Publisher* by Tom Maschler, S.N. Berhrman's book on Duveen, John Locke's *Second Treatise of Civil Government*, in a beautiful hardback edition, a lovely Everyman edition of Conrad's *Heart of Darkness* and Christopher Matthew's *A Nightingale Sang in Fernhurst Rd*. I also bought *More of Peter Simple* (I read both volumes of Michael Wharton's autobiography recently and am eager to be reunited with the utter madness of the Peter Simple column he wrote for so many years for the *Daily Telegraph*) and *Adventures with Impossible Figures* by Bruno Ernst. While not drinking my coffee I worked out these cost an average of 37 pence each.

In the local branch of W.H.Smith, The Princess moved all the copies of Tony Blair's biography that she could carry into the crime section, though I said she ought to have put them into the Tragic Lives section.

Wells is an unfriendly city and it was almost empty today, probably thanks to a new car parking system which prevents visitors parking in the centre of the city for more than three hours. I got round this nonsense by returning to the car after two and three quarter hours, moving the car and buying another ticket. I am sure this game of musical cars is illegal but it is not immoral. I fear that most visitors will not do this, however. Once people have gone round the Cathedral and the Bishop's Palace their three hours will be up and they will have no time left for spending money in shops or cafés. Wells will go into decline. Revolutionaries should be firing up their chainsaws and chopping down the car park signs and meters.

One thing that has always puzzled me is why such a long-established city should have no railway station. And is it the absence of a railway station which explains why the city never grew? Towns which refused railway stations (or which didn't use

431

them or fight hard enough when the relentless Beeching was swinging his axe) will die in future. It is extraordinary how many decent sized towns have no railway station.

20
11.50 a.m.
A letter from Lords announced that the MCC now wants control of the laws of cricket to be handed to a committee. One of the joys of being a member of the MCC has been the opportunity to vote on the laws of cricket. I suspect this is a trick to get rid of yards. If we allow a committee to make the decision a cricket pitch will soon be 20.1168 metres long, instead of 22 yards. Incidentally, I wonder why the Americans misspell a unit of measurement which they don't use.

15.01 p.m.
We went to Prinknash Abbey park to see the miniature goats (our favourite creatures there). The monks have installed a machine which dispenses pellets and The Princess had saved up every 20 pence piece she'd acquired for several weeks. She spent a fiver buying pellets to feed the goats. Money well spent. I noticed that the grass in their enclosure had been eaten billiard table smooth so I wandered off and found long, lush grass around some trees in the deer section of the park. I pulled an armful and went back to them. The goats saw, or smelt, the grass and leapt up and down in excitement. What a joyful visit it was. There was an auction at Chorley's in the grounds so we popped in, bought a catalogue and started to browse. Almost the first thing I saw was a pair of very large books. These turned out to be *Dr Johnson's Dictionary*, the 1755 second edition, listed on an amendments list as second to Richardson's two volume *Dictionary of the English Language* (1856). The four books were given an estimated price of £100 to £150. I couldn't believe it. The first volume of the Johnson had some work done on the binding but I don't think I've seen a book that is over 250 years old that hasn't had some work on it. I immediately filled in a commission bid form and put £250 down. We also bid on a few other things. I was terrified that if I put on too much it would draw attention to the lot. And I couldn't go because I had promised to be at Publishing House to pick up mail

and so on. A second edition of *Johnson's Dictionary* is worth up to £12,000, possibly even more. The one they had at Chorley's seemed to me to be in pretty good condition. The following morning I rang and increased my bid to £600. I wanted to put on £3,000 but I suspected that if I did the auctioneer might want to look more closely at the item and maybe even withdraw it for it to be assessed. Auctioneers do, after all, have a duty to the seller not the buyer. The woman who took the call seemed surprised at the extent of my increased offer and I worried that people might start wondering.

Book auctions can be fun. I once bought a row of books because I had spotted a first edition copy of *Brave New World*, by Aldous Huxley, sitting among a row of *Readers Digest* condensed books. I paid £9 for the lot and when a dealer saw me take out the book I really wanted he came across and asked me if he could buy the rest of the books for £9. I immediately agreed. He gave me £9, I gave him the row of *Readers Digest* condensed books and went home with a free first edition of *Brave New World*. It's difficult to beat that, though the other day I did find a first edition by Ian Fleming in the sort of box of assorted books that every junk shop has tucked away behind a mouldy armchair in the corner. That cost me 50 pence and the fellow selling it seemed keen to get rid of it though at a conservative estimate it's worth at least £300.

21.46 p.m.
We tried to watch a DVD of the `Mad Men' series which I bought yesterday. We gave up after three and a half episodes and dumped the DVD into our charity bag. The series is heavily praised but it's about as funny as scabies. Unlikeable characters and a slow and pointless plot which meanders from place to place without any sense of direction or purpose. This is Emperor's new clothes television. The programmes are so slow that several times I had to check that I hadn't accidentally pressed the pause button. I can see why critics working for the *Guardian* and *Independent* might like this rubbish but I suspect that humans disliked it as much as we did. Thumbs down after persevering for three and a half episodes.

21
09.18 a.m.

I received an e-mail from the auctioneers this morning. We have bought an 1879 oil painting by Wilson Harrison which we both liked, and which cost £100, and an assorted box of sundry plate, including three entrée dishes and a wonderful variety of other country house silver plate. We haven't the house yet but the house will now have to fit the silver plate. Tragically, I didn't get the Dr Johnson. The books went for £650. A bargain. My Bilbury friend Patchy Fogg would have written a note on the flyleaf in pencil `various pages missing' to deter other would-be buyers. Johnson's dictionary sold for over £4 when it first came out in the early half of the 18th century. With inflation that's probably what it costs now. Chorleys seem like good eggs. In the past I have usually found that if I have been successful at auctions I have invariably paid my top bid on all the lots I've bought as an absentee buyer. Not so with Chorleys. The two items I purchased were below my top bids. But I am gutted about the dictionary.

21.34 p.m.

I looked at a Tiger Woods golf game for Nintendo. Players can create their own characters who then play on selected golf courses. The software is skilfully done. But did they have to create characters who automatically kick the ball away, hurl the ball at the ground and break their clubs when they play bad shots? What sort of example is that? No one can possibly be surprised if young golfers behave badly in the future. It seems to me that sport has lost its way entirely. Even the people who run cricket have forgotten the meaning of the word `sportsmanship'. Players in Test Matches are now to be encouraged to question the umpire's decision. If the professionals do that then I guarantee that schoolboy players will start questioning umpires too. And once the umpires lose their authority the game will stop being a game.

22.05 p.m.

I suspect that the Olympic stadium which is being built in London at huge expense will probably be knocked down after a couple of weeks of use by drug soaked athletes. What the hell is anyone going to use it for? How many times a year will 100,000 people crowd into a stadium to watch fat Russians throwing hammers? The damned thing will be used for two weeks and then be a white elephant, leaving behind a carbon footprint the size of Norway. If Britons were asked: `Would you choose to have the Olympics in London for two weeks or to have your rubbish collected every week?' It wouldn't be difficult to guess the answer. The question will never be asked because celebrity politicians enjoy pretending to be on the world stage for two weeks and they adore the free trips to other Olympic games. I don't think the Olympics have had anything to do with sport for a long, long time. And the London Olympics won't do a thing for England or the English.

23.15 p.m.

I've just discovered that the Arts Council has held a competition to find artwork showcasing British culture in the months approaching the London Olympics. There are several winners. A wingless silver bird made from a recycled DC9 aeroplane will nest in various locations across Wales. A full size football pitch for amateur Scottish footballers is going to be created by chopping down a lot of trees in the Scottish borders. And three hand-crocheted 30 foot lions will be displayed in a taxidermy case in Nottingham. So, I feel guilty about saying that the Olympics will not add anything to our lives.

22

10.06 a.m.

A reader of mine put out his rubbish but the dustmen didn't come for two weeks. During that time cats, foxes and dogs tore the black plastic bags apart. The rubbish which was released then blew around in the street and when the dustmen finally arrived they refused to pick it up. My reader rang up the council and asked them to deal with it. They told him that it was his problem and that he had to pick up all the debris. `Oh no,' he told the council. `Once the rubbish is put out into the street it becomes your responsibility.' He pointed out that councils which send people round to rummage through the rubbish looking for names and addresses have (when sued for invasion of privacy) successfully argued that once rubbish is put out into the street for collection it no longer belongs to the person who put it there. `You can't have it both ways,' said my reader. Two hours later the council rang him back confirming that he was right. They sent men round to pick up the rubbish.

14.31 p.m.

A reader has returned a copy of *Mr Henry Mulligan* I had signed (with a special dedication) for her friend. `My friend doesn't read novels,' said the reader. `Would you please take this back and send me a cat book. Sign it again, put her name and write Happy Birthday.' What am I supposed to do with the book she has returned? I suppose I'll have to wait until someone else wants to buy a book for a friend called Doreen who is having a birthday. This is no way to run a business.

Another reader has written to complain that the Publishing House telephone number doesn't work. She said that she had wanted to ring to check that her cheque had arrived. I have hated the telephone ever since I spent ten years as a GP and lived with a phone which rang every time I sat down to eat, climbed into the bath or started watching a television programme. I am so delighted that the business no longer has a telephone.

17.29 p.m.

A major UK bank which managed to avoid a state bailout has apparently been letting employees go because it cannot match the wages being offered at a rival UK bank that was bailed out with taxpayers' money. Utter madness.

19.02 p.m.

I have decided to found the English Anarchy Party. I have made myself official founder, president, chairman, secretary and treasurer. My wife has founded the Welsh Anarchy Group and describes herself with great glee as a real WAG. There are few political systems on which chaos and anarchy would be an improvement, but the European Union is definitely one of them.

23

11.07 a.m.

Friends who are also trying to buy a house are gutted. They found their dream home and offered to pay the asking price. They have been outbid by a couple who have not yet sold their own home and are borrowing half of the money they need to complete the purchase. `We saved and scrimped for years,' said F. `But it seems to me that there are two sorts of money around these days. There's `real' money, for which people have worked hard, and there's `pretend' money, which is the stuff people borrow from the banks and which isn't at all like the real stuff.'

14.02 p.m.
When I telephoned HMRC I was asked two security questions. The first was my birthdate. The second security question was my office telephone number: the number which has, over the years, appeared in thousands of newspaper advertisements. Brilliant.

17.51 p.m.
Hardly a day goes by without the EU doing something else intrusive and intensely stupid. The European Court of Justice in Luxembourg has ruled that insurance companies cannot charge men and women different rates for different products. It's sexist and illegal. The newspaper commentators thought first about women. At the moment they get cheaper rates for car insurance because, statistically, they have fewer accidents. (Though they may well cause more). But it's men who will really suffer. UK pension annuity policies have traditionally offered men better annuity rates because men die sooner than women. No more. Thanks to the EU (which has already devastated pension payments) men will see their pension income cut again. It really isn't worthwhile putting money into a pension fund these days. Gold coins in a sock under the bed (or buried in a hole in the garden) make a much safer investment.

18.36 p.m.
There is news today that the Government is going to cut Public Lending Right (PLR) funding by 15% over the next four years. As far as I am aware no bankers or civil servants are having their pay cut by 15% but writers are easy prey so who cares? The closure of public libraries will also damage PLR income. And, as libraries go so will the demand for new books. Large print editions will doubtless disappear completely as will the production of unabridged audio versions of books. No one buys large print books or unabridged audio versions except libraries. I thought for a brief moment that subscription lending libraries might come back, along

the lines of the old Boots lending library, but they won't of course. The e-book will ensure that such an idea will never get off the ground.

I also read that the compensation money for equitable life policy holders who got shafted will be means-tested (the precise words are 'those whose need is greatest will be paid first' which probably means there won't be any left by the time they get to me). Since when was compensation means-tested? Still, I remember paying a huge chunk of tax on the compensation I received after the zero dividend preference share fiasco so the Government has form in this area.

I was still moaning about all this miserable news when people we know who live a couple of miles away telephoned to ask if they could come round. They were feeling glum for they have been notified by the council that their rates are going up because they have put in another bathroom.

They are decent, kindly people. He is a not terribly successful motivational speaker who looks as if he was put together by someone who hadn't bothered to read the instructions carefully. He has overgrown eyebrows, the sort politicians cultivate to give the newspaper cartoonists something to draw, and his hair can't quite decide whether to turn grey or disappear completely. K speaks in such a way that certain words begin with the oratorical equivalent of a capital letter. So, if he speaks about the Environment or Climate Change the words clearly begin with capitals. She used to work on local television but passed her view by date some time ago. She is the most hospitable person we know and it's impossible to enter their home without being served a large meal. The last time we went, intending to call round with a birthday present for their dog whom they adore and treat like a child, she insisted on serving us a snack. Her definition of a snack was a brown cottage loaf, warm, soft inside, crisp on the outside, a half pound of fresh butter, a hunk of cheddar and bowls of piccalilli, pickled walnuts, pickled eggs, pickled cucumber, red cabbage, radishes, lettuce, tomato and spring onions. Afterwards she produced three cakes, all home-made, and insisted that we had a large slice from each one.

They wanted to know why they should be punished for spending money on builders and improving their house. 'If we'd spent the money on booze and foreign holidays we wouldn't be punished,' they point out quite accurately. `And if we couldn't afford to pay our mortgage the Government would help us with a special grant or low interest rates.

24
10.09 a.m.
Looking at a copy of *Time* magazine I see that Norman Wisdom, who died recently, has the best part of a half page obituary (underneath a half page obituary of the very great Tony Curtis). Wisdom was a star when I was a child and I was appalled in later years to see him scoffed at by people who weren't fit to hold his cap. In the days when I occasionally watched television I watched in utter horror as a charmless, embarrassingly gauche, talentless, loathsome and cretinous interviewer sneered at a man who had been one of the nation's greatest and best loved film stars.

25
11.02 a.m.
The proof that civil servants have no idea how the real world operates outside their air-conditioned cages lies in the fact that they frequently send me forms asking how much my income will be for the current year. The honest answer is that I have absolutely no idea. If someone buys film rights or paperback rights to a book of mine my income could be in six figures. If I continue to spend most of my time filling in forms and too little of it writing books then I will probably make a loss. But forms are forms and without figures in the boxes they will not be accepted. So I make up a figure. Forms are just another work of fiction.

26
11.18 a.m.
A middle-aged woman held the door open for me today. I looked at myself in a shop window as I passed by and I could understand why. I feel knackered. Utterly exhausted and worn out.

14.48 p.m.
I spotted yet another bookshop selling e-book readers. Madness. When faced with such murderous competition bookshops should promote their own advantages not support the opposition.

20.01 p.m.

I have just worked out that I made approximately several thousand times as much money by following the financial advice in my book *Oil Apocalypse* as I made from the book itself. Numerous readers have written to let me know that they too have made a good deal of money by following the advice the book contained. Ironically, most of the comments about the book on the Web are negative and dismissive. Amazingly, writers on the Web don't seem to feel that there is anything odd about reviewing a book they haven't read. My favourite review was written by someone who accused me of deliberately pushing up the oil price simply to promote my book. Sales of the book were damaged not just by all this nonsense but also by the fact that Amazon ran out of copies just as my advertising reached a peak and visitors to the webshop were told that the book was not available.

22.19 p.m.

In *Motorsport* magazine I read an article about a man called Fitch who is 92 and who made an attempt on world land speed record when he was 88.

27

11.03 a.m.

I went into a shop which sells computer games. I wanted to buy a new chess game which I'd heard about. The shop was packed. 'Your customers all seem much the same age,' I said to the assistant. They were all men in their late teens and twenties. 'Ninety per cent of them are unemployed,' the assistant told me. 'They are the only people who can afford the games and the only people who have the time to play them.'

15.58 p.m.

I closed our own webshop (largely because of the costs and difficulties involved in taking credit card orders) and handed over the running of the webshop to Amazon. I had run some sort of webshop for well over 20 years so this was something of a wrench. And, sadly, it has been an utter disaster. I have given up trying to persuade Amazon to include our books in the webshop which they now manage for us. We begged and cajoled but all to no effect. For example, *Cat Tales* is only available through someone selling a second-hand copy for £38. I have thousands of copies in the warehouse but people who visit the shop on our website don't know they are there - and cannot buy them. Books of mine which have been out for a year are still not available through our shop. I have decided to sell books only by cheque. I am removing details of the webshop from advertisements, from inserts and from my website.

19.08 p.m.
Book sales are down everywhere. I'm not surprised. Even when e-books are included in the figures there are fewer books being sold these days. The problem is that publishers have, for years, allowed themselves to be led by their marketing departments. Too many of the books they produce are written by celebrities who care nothing about books. Many are written by ghostwriters who take a percentage of the royalties but have little passionate interest in the book's contents. Professional authors who write even a modestly successful book are encouraged to write the same book over and over again. Very few books published by the big publishers have a soul.

We live in a world where books are no longer an essential part of our culture. Schoolchildren use the Internet rather than books. If they are to succeed books must be exciting, dramatic and intellectually invigorating. But modern publishers prefer books which follow a safe, routine pattern and which are designed for profitable mediocrity. Editors don't like making people think. Modern publishing is all about making money and avoiding trouble; the words `methodical' and `plodding' describe most of the people in what used to be a craft but which has now become a rather grubby industry.

Making things worse is the fact that major imprints are now often part of large conglomerates with vast global interests. This means that they aren't keen on publishing books which might prove too controversial or which might threaten any part of their organisation or which might annoy some powerful person or lobby group with a view and interests to protect. Consequently, large publishers don't publish genuinely daring books. And too often the

441

editors themselves are far too politically correct to dare publish anything which might cause a ripple of controversy.

Today, the posh publishers specialise in printing books by footballers, by women who have had sex with footballers, by men who have gone out (or stayed in) with women who have had sex with footballers and by women who have had breast enlargement surgery. Any woman who crosses over two categories (has had sex with a footballer and has had breast enhancement surgery) can expect a huge advance payment.

Modern publishers are marketing led; hence the plethora of books linked to TV reality shows. Because these books have a very limited shelf life (they will die as soon as the reality celebrity fades from view) publishers have become exceedingly short-termist and tend to forget about their backlists.

Making things even worse is the fact that publishers' readers really aren't very bright. Every now and then a frustrated author will scan in or type in a classic book and send the result off to a publisher. It will invariably come back in a few weeks with a patronising rejection slip.

One author I heard of was given a huge amount of advice about how to improve her book. She didn't like any of the suggestions so she simply changed the font and then resubmitted the book to the same editor a couple of months later. The editor loved the book, and was delighted with the 'changes'.

Publishing is an unpredictable business. It is difficult to tell which books are going to be most successful. It is invariably the new and unexpected which make the big money - exactly the sort of thing that traditional publishers don't publish. It comes as no surprise to me that most really successful books are turned down by numerous publishers before they are finally published. It is only the persistence of their authors which eventually leads to their success. In my book *How to Publish Your Own Book* I produced a massive list of classic books which had been rejected by many publishers before eventually reaching the printing press and the bestseller lists.

Today's publishers don't publish books which are important. Instead, they produce a steady storm of superficial, exploitative trash. They produce row after row of books by non-entities, materialistic, egocentric fame whores who seek fame for its own sake, rather than as an offshoot of achievement, and whose sole reason for writing a book is not that they have something to say but because they have been contestants on television. Most have nothing to contribute. They don't even have a story to tell. They are merely writing books as another way of capitalising on their transient, transparent fame.

And most big publishers are in business just to make money.

I have never written a book because I think it will sell. I have only ever written books that I wanted to write, regardless of their commercial potential. I always write books I want to write, and work out how to sell them later.

Today, there aren't many small publishers left (the successful ones having frequently been bought up by the big ones). Bookshops and libraries won't take books produced by small publishers. Newspapers and television companies won't review books produced by small publishers. The whole business has become unhealthily incestuous.

The entire publishing industry (publishers, agents, printers, wholesalers, bookshops and libraries) is doomed, of course. The industry has embraced the e-book (they could have said `no') and so the industry will die. The curious thing is that I can see second-hand bookshops reappearing on our streets - if charity shops don't destroy them before they start. Seaside towns and holiday resorts should prove fertile ground for retailers prepared to sell cheap second-hand paperbacks to holidaymakers who haven't succumbed to the lure of the Kindle or the Ipad.

There will be people who want books for as long as I have left. But the publishing industry and I have nothing in common. So, that leaves self-publishing.

28
12.02 p.m.
EDF energy, the company which provide us with gas and electricity in England and in France, and whose bills in England are as utterly incomprehensible as they are clear and comprehensible in France, wrote to tell us that we have used so much less gas than expected and that we have built up a credit of £243.68. In view of this they are increasing our monthly direct debit from £90 to £110. Naturally, I don't understand. If I had three

days with nothing to do I would telephone the company to ask them why.

16.17 p.m.

I've been reading John Fothergill's book *An Inkeeper's Diary*. It's an utterly wonderful book. Published in 1931, the book itself is one of those beautifully bound, sensibly sized hardback books which just fit into a jacket pocket. Fothergill has filled his diary with anecdotes about friends he has loved, guests with whom he has argued, meals he has eaten, books he has read and wines he has drunk, enjoyed or regretted. Fothergill was an outrageous, shameless, glorious snob and, with the exception of the glorious John Mytton, probably the most politically incorrect Englishman of all time. He ran a series of upmarket inns with a largely upmarket clientele. Fothergill himself was both erudite and blunt (blunt enough to make Basil Fawlty seem positively benign). Innocent of the need for political correctness he makes it perfectly clear, both to his readers and his guests, that he doesn't approve of young men of breeding or scholarship bringing shop girls into his establishment.

His inns regularly imported food from Greece, France, Norway and Italy, To supply what he believed his customers should eat he forced local bakers to bake three different kinds of bread, made from flours he'd made them use. He had a cellar of thousands of bottles of rare wine.

I bought this book from a junk shop for 50 pence (Oxfam managers please note) and am delighted to have found two more of Fothergill's volumes of autobiography *My Three Inns* and *Confessions of an Innkeeper*. There's a photograph of Fothergill in *My Three Inns* and I admit he is the scariest looking bloke I've ever seen in my life.

In *An Innkeeper's Diary* Fothergill describes how he was asked by his nephew if he would lend his name to a new restaurant or inn in London. Here's what he says about it: `Having had here a kitchen staff for seven years composed mainly of half-wits, degenerates, dishonests, drunkards and hystericals, and having done it daily ourselves, I can't conceive lending my name to any establishment where I don't also do it all myself. It's this kitchen business that has knocked the initiative and courage out of me. I

444

suppose everyone who drives his own furrow, especially a romantic one like this, suffers from self-pity at times to compensate for the praise he gets at other times, and for an awful loneliness due to people's not knowing what he has done to do what he has.' Oh, Mr Fothergill, I know exactly what you mean.

18.34 p.m.

Although journalists and broadcasters tend to ignore my books (in that they don't mention them) they do, nevertheless use my work very frequently in their columns and broadcasts. It seems to me that this is unfair to my regular readers. I do not, for example, see why my forecasts should be shared with the rest of the media. I am, therefore, taking the rather unusual step of trying to make sure that my books do not fall into the hands of too many journalists. In future I am not sending out any review copies. In addition, I am no longer making copies available at lower prices for readers to distribute to journalists, politicians and friends.

I've also made a decision not to do any more radio or television interviews. I don't get asked. But just in case someone does ask: I'm not doing any more.

29

14.02 p.m.

I'm still enjoying my Fothergill discoveries. The Great Man tells a story of a friend whom he had asked to write a piece for another book he was preparing called *The Fothergill Omnibus* (what a wonderful title). The friend did nothing and later confessed that `he dared not say he would do it because he was so afraid that he wouldn't, and yet wouldn't say he couldn't because he would so much like to, so he couldn't reply'. I know exactly how Fothergill's friend feels and understand completely. I have lost count of the number of invitations I have accepted and then had to back out of and the number I have avoided and then regretted. I would have never discovered Fothergill's wonderful books without being able to browse in a second-hand bookshop. Local councils who care a jot for the education of their citizens should reduce the rating value of second-hand bookshops and junk shops to zero to help them survive. Without them how else are we ever to discover such joys?

15.06 p.m.

After the print run of 2,000 had almost sold out we sent a few of the remaining copies of my book *2020* to mass market paperbackers, asking them if they would like to produce an edition. I pointed out that we had sold pretty much the entire print of 2,000 copies in two weeks without any sales reps, without any bookshop sales, without any sales on the Internet, without any advertisements and without any promotional interviews. None of the publishers to whom I wrote wanted to know how we had managed this apparent impossibility. Most of the paperback houses just ignored the book and the request but I did receive an undated, pre-printed note from an editorial assistant at Arrow (which had published the paperback edition of my first book *The Medicine Men* in 1976). This is the reply in full: `Thank you for your letter regarding publication of your book. Unfortunately, our policy has changed and we no longer accept unsolicited submissions. May I advise you to consult the *Writers' and Artists' Yearbook*, published every year by A&C Black, with a view to securing a literary agent? The yearbook contains up-to-date information and details of literary agents and publishers and their specialisations.' How quaintly patronising. I bought my first copy of the *Writers and Artists Yearbook* in 1963.

30

22.50 p.m.

We watched the last DVD episode of `John Adams' this evening.

It's a truly excellent television series about the early days of America. Beautifully written, accurate, detailed and exquisite in every way. Oh for a similar series on English history. The trouble is that only the BBC has the money to make such a series and since it is owned by the EU (which is determined to see England disappear) that is extremely unlikely to happen.

31

12.01 p.m.

I wanted to buy two magazines and found myself in a huge queue in W.H.Smith's today. There was only one till open (operated by a rather slow-witted woman) and everyone who reached her seemed to want to pay with a credit card. When a stern looking woman in a dark blue uniform with a name badge on the lapel marched past I gave her a large piece of what is laughingly known as my mind. 'More tills should be opened up,' I told her. 'There are now 15 people in this queue and at this rate it will take us an hour to be served.' The woman looked at me as if I were mad and stalked off. I was furious but could not run after her without losing my place in the queue. As luck would have it she was coming out of the store when I had finally managed to complete my purchases. I started to walk towards her to give her the remainder of my mind but just in time I noticed that the name badge she was wearing carried a Lloyds Bank logo. I felt bad for a moment or two but Lloyds Bank often has long queues too.

16.04 p.m.

I have been self-publishing since 1989. That's pretty close to a quarter of a century. For most of that time I've used Publishing House in Barnstaple as the headquarters for running the business. I've never had an office there myself but have employed people to deal with the storing of books and fulfilling the orders.

To the surprise of many I proved it was possible to earn a living publishing your own books. I published dozens of books, sold scores of foreign rights, sold serial rights to dozens of leading magazines and newspapers, sold large print rights and audio rights in many books and had one novel turned into a major movie.

There were, of course, disappointments.

Despite huge efforts I simply could not persuade bookshops to stock our books. I tried. I really tried. But, although we sold a lot of books through bookshops, almost every single sale was the result of a customer walking into a shop and asking them to order the book. In the last few years we sold over £250,000 worth of books this way. But bookshops (whether large or small) won't take books from small publishers in general. And, contaminated by the prejudices of the trade, they are doubly reluctant to order books which are (whisper it softly) self-published.

Bookshops weren't the only people to be unhelpful.

Reviewers and literary editors refused to look at books from Publishing House. One literary editor openly boasted that he threw my books into a bin without ever looking at them because they were self-published. I discovered that literary editors give most of their space to the big publishers because it is the big publishers who provide them with the crates full of books to sell on Amazon and eBay. It is the big publishers who will publish their little book of memoirs. Or, hope of hopes, the novel they've had in their drawer for ten years.

And libraries have been unhelpful too. Even when people tried to order my books they were frequently lied to and told that they were `unavailable', `out of print' or `impossible to order'.

Several staff members have been with me pretty well since the beginning and when four employees decided that the time had come for them to retire and (deservedly) take life a bit easier I had to rethink the business. I could hardly grumble. One had gone long past normal retirement age. Things were made more critical by the fact that David, my trusted and long-suffering advertising buyer had also retired from the business.

I had two main reasons for taking this opportunity to consider a major restructuring of the way the business is run.

First, threats of various kinds have made it sensible for us to live somewhere difficult to find, and for some years now we've shared our time between our apartment in Paris and our home in Bilbury, where we enjoy our nebulous but rewarding relationships with friends Thumper Robinson, Patchy Fogg et al. For a variety of reasons the regular journey to Barnstaple has become difficult, unpleasant, boring and hazardous.

Second, the small, free-wheeling business I created has grown and been infiltrated by red tape. The stuff is like dry rot. The spores settle somewhere cosy and then spread out and wreak havoc on every conceivable part of the structure.

I never really wanted to be publisher. I'm a writer. I only got into publishing because I found it impossible to find anyone prepared to publish *Alice's Diary* and decided to do it myself. Since the sales of that book alone are now worth close to £750,000 their refusal to consider it tells you everything you need to know about smart London publishers. London publishers also turned down *People Watching* (of which I sold nearly 30,000 copies at £9.99) *Food for Thought* (of which I sold over 40,000 copies at £12.99) and many others including a polemic *Betrayal of Trust* (of which I sold over 5,000 copies at £12.99). After the publishers of *Bodypower* let the book go out of print I had, within a year, sold foreign rights to numerous overseas publishers and had sold several thousand copies in the UK. With the exception of my books on vivisection, every book I've published has sold well enough to at least cover its costs.

In setting up my own publishing business I got rid of the irritation of 17-year-old editors and marketing experts telling me what to write (and how to write it) and gained a considerable amount of freedom. For over two decades I have written whatever books I wanted to write, I have published them myself and I have sold them. I've made enough money to pay my staff (up to around 15 of them at one point), to pay my suppliers, to pay my taxes and to eat, drink and even be merry occasionally. As my own publisher I have kept faith with books that didn't sell well from the start. I have kept books in print and I have sold foreign rights.

To begin with there were, inevitably, a huge variety of problems. There were problems with printing and logistics and advertisements. But these were business problems and it wasn't difficult to find solutions. However, in recent years these structural problems have been overgrown with red tape and with constant interference from bureaucrats and various arms of the establishment. Not all the problems have come from the European Union and the Government. I had to abandon credit card sales because the red tape (and expenses) were just too much to handle. I have had increasing problems with Royal Mail (whose status as a monopoly supplier gives its administrative and executive staff delusions of grandeur). Gradually, my world has been filling up with people who take no risks, no responsibility and no blame but who constantly think up ways to disrupt my business and stop me doing what I do best. For the last few years it seems as though every telephone call, every fax message, every e-mail and every post has brought another problem. And every official is officious. The problems are not presented politely, they are presented with threats. `You will do this or we will do that.' Because I wasn't at Publishing House very often my staff were easily bullied. And ended up gold plating every piece of new legislation. By the middle of 2010 my staff seemed to be spending most of their time responding to instructions, demands and exhortations from various Government departments and quangos. Responding to the bureaucracies had become the driving force, an end in itself.

449

It seemed that the world had become full of people whose role in life was to disrupt my life and to tell me how I should live, how I should spend my time and what I should and should not do. (What particularly annoyed me was that as a taxpayer, and payer of countless fees, I paid these people's salaries, expenses and pensions.)

Gradually, over the years, the dry rot has spread through the business. Slowly, but irresistibly, it has strangled Publishing House and taken over every aspect of the business. For the last year or two the rules have been coming in on a daily basis. Even brand new electrical appliances had to be checked regularly. Fire checks. Employment legislation. Staff training programmes. I was told that, according to the law, staff had to be allowed time off to be trained to do something other than the work I had hired them to do, and which they were already perfectly capable of doing, and so in their absence being trained and collecting diplomas, certificates and, quite possibly, rosettes which would, presumably, enable them to leave and find other work elsewhere, I had to hire temporary staff to do the work they would have done if they hadn't been away being trained to do something that I hadn't hired them to do. This did not seem to me to be an entirely sane way to run a business or the country. Things may change in the future. But if they do I can guarantee that it will be to make things worse, not better. Rules about sick pay. Rules about holidays. Rules about pregnant staff. Rules about pensions. We had to have a designated and trained first aid officer in the building at all times. There was, it seemed, a constant stream of people pouring into Publishing House to check on things. Naturally, there are hefty fees for all these checks and licences. More rules about pensions. Health and safety checks. More health and safety checks. Someone in a suit coming round to check whether the staff had been properly trained in how to use filing cabinets without being crushed. Are all parts of the building the right temperature? Software updates had to be bought. A licence so that staff can listen to the radio if they want to. Publishing House had become a bureaucratic machine. More time and energy were spent satisfying the bureaucrats than on selling books. Indeed, it seemed as though the bureaucrats were actually running the business for their benefit. But I had all the responsibility. And I paid all the bills. Far too much of the business time and money and energy went into training staff how to fill in forms. I felt I was running one business and the staff were running another. It was my fault, of course. I should have been there more often to put a stop to the nonsense.

But I am a writer not a publisher and my foray into publishing has been pretty well brought to an end by EU regulations (which make running a small business which employs people a nightmare), the Royal Mail (which has put up its prices so much that mailing out books has become impossibly expensive), the book trade (which has failed to support small publishers), the media (which is so closely linked to the publishing establishment that it remains determined not to promote self-published books), the libraries (which now buy very few books and which prefer to deal exclusively with the big publishers who give them huge discounts), the supermarkets (which have forced down margins by charging such absurdly low prices), the big publishers (who give massive discounts on their books, cutting their margins to the bone and making it almost impossible for a small publisher to survive) and the Internet (which have made it possible for a bloke on benefits in a bed-sitting room in Leeds to sell back list books for one penny each, making his tiny profit out of the postage charge).

I only became a publisher because the publishing trade only wanted to publish the books they wanted me to write. My efforts did at least prove that publishers are incompetent fools who know nothing about books or readers, but the exercise had exhausted me.

For too long I didn't really make plans or decisions but merely followed fate and my fancies. This is fine for writing (though it isn't the way you are supposed to do it) but not for publishing (which is, after all, a business and which needs short, medium and long-term planning). In the end I had replaced the tyranny of the 17-year-old editor with the tyranny of the 17-year-old bureaucrat.

Damnit, publishing was no longer any fun at all.

It wasn't even my business. The dry rot had taken over.

The bureaucratic monster that Publishing House had become, was sucking the life out of me. The nightmarish mixture of rules, regulations, demands and problems were exacerbated by the fact that in order to make enough money to pay for all the bureaucracy I was under constant pressure to produce what a new short-lived and ineffectual advertisement space buyer insisted on calling `new product' but what I still insisted on regarding as books. I finally realised that I had to close Publishing House when a staff member told me I had been too nasty to the Royal Mail when I'd offered what I had thought were relatively mild criticisms of its gross incompetence and inexcusable stupidity. I needed an income of around £1 million a year to cover all my costs and stand a chance of making a profit. By the time I told British Telecom to turn off the telephone at Publishing House my capacity to cope with crap had dissipated more or less completely.

I really just wanted (and want) to write books; the business of publishing them (and employing a number of people) was beginning to exhaust me. So, I paid off all the staff, closed the telephone lines and pretty well shut down the business. The Princess and I decided that for a few weeks we would deal with the orders which came in ourselves while we decided what to do next. So for a few weeks we have been racing backwards and forwards filling the truck with books and the house with padded bags. The Princess has been putting books into envelopes and I have been sitting on the stairs (at midnight) putting stamps onto the parcels. It has, nevertheless, been far more fun than it was. All communications from Government departments and quangos are returned `Gone Away'.

We realised that we had four choices.

First, I could give up. Retire. Stop writing and stop publishing. This was not really an option.

Second, I could continue to write but just not bother publishing the books. I seriously considered this option but decided that although it would make a useful last resort there might be a better answer.

Third, I could find an outside publisher and allow myself to be patronised by 17-year-olds telling me how to write books.

Fourth, we could start again but keep things under control and put the fun back into the business.

We've chosen the fourth option.

We are going to find new premises and start again. We need a building big enough to hold 60,000 books and to provide us both with an office. Starting again will involve a major restructuring and we know it will pose numerous problems because the bureaucracies which abound seem to delight in making life particularly difficult for anyone trying to run a small business. But we will succeed because we have learned a little.

We have decided not to bother recruiting any permanent staff. There are two reasons for this.

First, it is difficult to find good staff these days. When we advertised for new staff we had an application from a woman who couldn't even spell what she did for a living. Another came into work on day one but on day two she had a migraine and so she stayed at home. On day three she came in and spent most of the day making and receiving private calls and texts and on fourth day she left, saying she could get more money and more interesting work elsewhere. Another applicant wrote saying `I am a very competant person'.

And second the new employment rules make hiring staff a nightmare and firing them an impossibility.

In the future, The Princess and I will do everything ourselves (though we will, of course, hire outside workers and consultants to help with book production).

We aren't going to have a telephone. I don't think we need one and The Princess is happy to put up with this mild eccentricity. Telephones have an innate tendency to ring and to interfere with other things. People who want to get in touch with us can either write or e-mail.

We have also decided to make physically smaller books. Modern books tend to be absurdly oversized. The Victorians and Edwardians published books with over 100,000 words that still fitted into a jacket pocket and were printed in an easily readable type. They did it by choosing good, thin paper that didn't allow any `bleed through'. In future we're going to produce books that fit into a pocket or a bag and which look and feel good and which are easy to read even for those whose eyes aren't as good as they once were. We will sell the stock we have of existing books and then produce smart new editions that fit with our new philosophy. Producing smaller books will help us keep our postage costs down to an acceptable level.

Flaubert advised that a mundane, routine life was best for writing and by golly the old guy was right. Closing Publishing House and starting again has given me hope that publishing can be fun again. I have never had plans. And I don't intend to start having plans. But a little less chaos would be good. Hopefully our new system will produce fewer crises, less drama and less waste.

And more fun, damnit.

November

1
09.03 a.m.
I put the clocks forward last night but got it wrong. All our clocks are now two hours out. I can never remember whether the damned things spring back or fall forward or spring forward and fall back. I had to correct twelve clocks again. And all so that a few Scottish farmers can go out and milk their cows without using torches. Meanwhile millions of English and Welsh schoolchildren have to struggle home in the dark. Lots of them will doubtless die on the roads. Still the EU will have us all on European time soon and that will be the end of that. Meanwhile, we should let the Scots have their own time zone. We would spend less on heat and light, and have fewer accidents. And we wouldn't have to fiddle with our clocks and watches. The saving in energy on that alone would save enough to give every Scotsman a free dram of neat paraquat.

12.17 p.m.
I spent a few minutes making up the most politically incorrect rhymes imaginable. Here are three:
   1.
   A dog is for Christmas
   But just for the day
   Have lots of fun
   Then throw it away
   2.
   Needles are fun
   As long as they're sharp
   But after a year
   You'll be playing a harp
   3.
   Eat lots of burgers
   You'll get a fat belly
   And what's even worse
   You'll also be smelly

I suggested to The Princess that I offer the third to one of the burger chains as an advertising slogan.

16.07 p.m.

I've received a letter from a fellow in Warsaw whose `aim is to be the second largest distributor of Vernon Coleman's books (after English speaking countries) in the world'. He is setting up something called the Health Publishing Company and wants to publish *How To Stop Your Doctor Killing You* and my other health books in Polish. `There is a huge, growing interest on health issues in Poland. To me there is unmet demand. This interest can be met with Vernon Coleman's books.' He is a professional marketer who formerly held managerial posts with major drug companies. I write back suggesting some other books he might start with but I am not over hopeful. Letters like this come in frequently and I usually end up sending off piles of books and never hearing anything else. But we have to keep trying. And somehow I have a good feeling about this guy.

19.12 p.m.

We went to see another house today. We knew as soon as we got there that it wasn't right for us. Usually we drive to a property before arranging a viewing. It's often easy to tell from the outside whether a property is going to be suitable or not. But this time, as luck would have it, we hadn't visited. And this time it was painfully obvious that the house wasn't right for us. It was newer than it looked on the photographs. It had neighbours whose houses and gardens overlooked it and it had a scruffy looking public house next door. The pub had a blackboard outside advertising football matches on Sky television and a large poster promoting a late night karaoke evening on Saturday.

We had been inside the house for less than five minutes when the telephone rang.

`Another appointment for tomorrow?' said the woman. `Certainly. I'll put that in the diary. That's three then for that morning?' She put the telephone down and turned to us. `I'm so sorry about that. Now where was I? Oh, yes the kitchen was hand-built to our design by a firm of German specialists. As you can see...', and she opened and closed cupboard doors as she talked.

After another ten minutes the telephone rang again.

`For tomorrow? It will have to be the afternoon won't it? That's two so far for the afternoon?'

And so it went on. Never before had we visited such a popular house. It seemed as though the whole world wanted to visit, view and buy it.

`Did you believe all that nonsense?' asked The Princess as we left.

`I think it was put on for our benefit,' I said. `Her husband ringing up pretending to be a buyer wanting to make an appointment.'

`Did you notice that she never once confirmed the time of the appointment?' asked The Princess.

`Or the name of the prospective buyers.'

Twenty minutes after we had left my telephone went. It was the estate agent. `What did you think?' she asked. `Do you like the house? Would you like to make an offer?' I said we needed more time to think about it. They rang back three times that day to see if we wanted to make an offer. `Don't worry about the guide price,' said the estate agent. `The vendor is very flexible.'

We are getting desperate. Will we ever find our dream home? Do we still know what we're looking for? Will we know if we find it?

23.50 p.m.

Some years ago I bought an advent calendar for The Princess from Harrods. It is a beautiful thing. The Princess and I saw it together on a trip to London. When we returned home I telephoned the store and arranged for them to deliver it to me. (I wanted it to be a surprise.) It was the only one they had. It is hand carved and hand painted and contains 24 small cupboards into which can be placed all sorts of surprises. Whenever a door is opened a musical roundabout lights up, goes round and plays music. It is delightful. Every year I fill each small box with small toys; pieces of jewellery; polished stones; watercolour paints; shells; bits and pieces suitable for a dolls house; tiny wooden, porcelain and metal animals; small packets of sweets; tiny dolls; Roman coins and whatever else I can find that might entertain or intrigue. I suspect that I get far more joy from it than The Princess does. I always

457

include chocolate money in among the toys and other small surprise gifts. This year I went to buy chocolate coins and could find only chocolate euros. While I was in a newsagent and confectionary shop hunting for chocolate money in sterling I noticed a fat woman on a scooter stuck in the shop. It wasn't easy to miss her since she was complaining very loudly about the lack of turning space. She couldn't reverse and she wasn't a good enough driver to turn her machine round in the narrow space available. She climbed off it and asked for help. I tried to move the machine but it was too heavy for me. I couldn't lift it at all. So the woman, cursing and shaking her head, pushed me out of the way and physically yanked the scooter round so that it was facing the way she wanted it to go, confirming my long held suspicion that many of the people using these things are just fat and lazy rather than genuinely disabled.

2

11.34 a.m.

On the M4, on our way to Cirencester this morning, The Princess who was struggling to find the `play' button for the CD player, accidentally turned on the truck's hazard flashers. Suddenly, a huge stretch of open motorway appeared behind us as the cars behind braked, assuming that I'd spotted an accident ahead. `They shouldn't put the button where passengers can press it,' said The Princess. `They should keep all the driving stuff over your side of the dashboard and all the fun stuff on my side.' I remembered that I was once fined £5 for driving with my hazard flashers on. It happened when I was a GP in Leamington Spa. During a busy evening surgery I received a telephone call from a woman who reported that her husband was having chest pain. I did what I always did in such circumstances. `If you want me to come now I will come now,' I told her. `Otherwise, I will come after I've finished the surgery.' `I'd like you to come now, please,' said the woman. `I think he might be having a heart attack.' I poked my head into the waiting room, explained what was happening and that I would be back as soon as I could, leapt into the car and shot off. It was half past five and the town was packed with `going-home traffic'. To help me ease my way through the traffic I put on my hazard flashers. I was driving a Saab at the time and it didn't take me long to reach the patient's home. Thankfully, it was a false alarm. The patient wasn't having a heart attack. I reassured him and his wife and headed back to finish the surgery. I forgot about the incident until I received a telephone call from the secretary of a high ranking local traffic policeman who had apparently seen me whizzing through the town. I gather he had chased me and failed to catch me. (I bet that really irked him.) I was told that he wanted me in his office at the police station. I declined to go. A few weeks later I found myself in court, charged with driving a motor vehicle while the hazard flashers were switched on. It was, I was told by the counsel hired by the Medical Defence Union, an offence to drive a moving motor vehicle with hazard flashers switched on. Only buses are allowed to do so and then it's to indicate that they are being hijacked. I was eventually fined the grand sum of £5 at the local magistrates court. But it didn't end there. A newspaper erroneously reported that I had claimed that the policeman had tried to browbeat me into making an apology. (It was, in retrospect, probably a fair guess on the newspaper's part. I doubt if Mr Plod wanted me in his office to congratulate me on getting away from him.) With the backing of whichever police union he was in, the copper sued me. His local solicitor was very aggressive. (I remember that during the case (which went on for months) I received an urgent call from a local solicitor whose son was ill. `Can you come as quickly as possible?' he asked anxiously. He was the solicitor representing the police officer who was suing me. It was a nice moment.) I hadn't said what I was reported as having said but this, apparently is no defence. I was sued and I lost. According to the British law of libel you are responsible for anything you are reported as having said even if you haven't said it. My defence union paid my costs and so our respective unions paid the costs of one of the silliest libel suits of the decade. `I would love to have this wretched policeman in court,' said my QC. `But it's really so silly that I suggest you apologise and be done with it.' So I apologised for something I hadn't done and that was that.

In Cirencester, we eventually found a car park which allowed parking for more than three hours. The fee to park for the day was £6.90. How on earth do the people who work in shops and offices in the town manage? There's no mention of a season ticket so five days parking would cost £34.50. And that's before the cost of petrol and so on. It is hardly surprising that more and more people are opting out of work and choosing to take the easy option: staying at home and claiming benefits.

Cirencester is a glorious town. I haven't been there since I had steak and kidney pudding in a restaurant in the town on my ninth birthday. The Princess has never been there before. For a town of less than 20,000 inhabitants it must have the best mix of shops in England. There are some excellent, smart local shops, good examples of the chain stores, a wonderful variety of small shops offering specialist services and well-stocked charity shops. It is a quintessential English market town and seems, thankfully, to be stuck in a 1950s time warp. Perfect.

16.39 p.m.

A man we know has a Range Rover. The back of the vehicle is covered in mud and the number plate is quite indistinguishable. 'I'm likely to get told off if the police stop me,' said our friend. 'But it means the speed cameras can't pick up my number plate details.' I asked him how he'd managed to cover the number plate so completely with mud and he explained that he and a friend had parked their vehicles back to back in a muddy field and then accelerated away as quickly as they could. Both vehicles had thrown up huge amounts of mud which had, he said, done the job very nicely.

3

10.02 a.m.

America plans to print another 600 billion dollars to destroy savings and make life better for debtors and greedy bankers.

How depressing. They call it quantitative easing rather than printing money (in the same newspeak way that when American soldiers kill British soldiers, which they do with such extraordinary efficiency that I am convinced that more of our troops are killed by the Americans than by the people we are supposed to be fighting, it is called friendly fire and not murder or manslaughter). The Bank of England is doing the same so that the American currency will not collapse alone. Obama, just thrashed in mid term elections, is apologising for everything he's done or not done, thought about doing or didn't think about doing. It is as convincing as the pre-election rhetoric. I was right about him in my book *What Happens Next?*

11.45 a.m.

An angry Scotsman has written to complain about my writing a book about my *The 100 Greatest Englishmen and Englishwomen.* He describes this as `racist' though I'm not sure why. There are plenty of books praising great Scotsmen and Scotswomen and I see nothing wrong with those. It is, I suppose, hardly surprising that the Scots (and, indeed, the Welsh) hate the English so violently. They are taught endless lies about England and the English and they see these lies repeated and exaggerated still further in books and films. I sometimes wonder if the whole anti-England industry might not be funded by the European Union, which is, of course, determined to destroy England permanently.

When you ask the more rabid Scots why they hate the English so vehemently those who can think of a reason will usually mention the Massacre of Glencoe. This happened in February 1692 and resulted in the deaths of between 30 and 40 Scots but it has, for romantic rather than logical reasons, become an enduring symbol of Scottish oppression and an everlasting reason to hate the English. Encouraged by absurd Hollywood films (which are as close to history as Bambi on Ice is close to natural history), the slaughter has become a symbol of the English oppression of the Scots.

The best account of what happened is recorded in the excellent small book *The Massacre of Glencoe* by John Buchan.

Buchan was probably the finest, and certainly the most enduring and universally popular, Scottish writer of all time. He is remembered today for novels such as *The Thirty Nine Steps* and *John Macnab* but he was also the author of a number of history books and biographies (among them books about Cromwell and Sir Walter Scott). He spent his final years as Governor-General of Canada, where he was known as Lord Tweedsmuir.

What made the Glencoe massacre particularly notable was the fact that the 120 soldiers who were responsible for the killing were, prior to the massacre, billeted in cottages belonging to the locals. They were, according to Buchan, `mostly Highlanders and Campbells, but there were a few Lowlanders who hung together

461

and talked their own talk, since their lack of Gaelic kept them from much intimacy with the folk of the glen.'

In fact not one Englishman was involved in the planning of the Massacre of Glencoe and the Scots who were massacred at Glencoe weren't killed by English soldiers. The whole hideous operation was planned by Scots and the killing was done by Scots.

Buchan explains in his book that three people were responsible for planning the massacre: John Dalrymple, the Master of Stair (a lowland Scotsman), John Campbell, 1st Earl of Breadalbane and the King (King William III).

None of these was English. (King William III was born in the Hague, Netherlands.)

`The first has the heaviest share (of the blame),' wrote Buchan. `The last the lightest. The guilt varies with the degree of knowledge, and the intimacy of the relationship between the wronged and the wronger. In William, it was a crime against humanity in general, in the Master of Stair against his fellow Scots and in Breadalbane against those who shared with him the blood and traditions of the Gael.'

Of the three ultimately responsible men, one was Dutch and two were Scots.

The men who committed the massacre were Scotsmen too. They were, according to Buchan, `mostly Breadalbane's own people'.

It is clear that if the Scots studied and understood their own history they would understand that the cause of their greatest resentment towards the English is unfounded and is built entirely on an inaccurate representation of history. Perhaps the Scots find it difficult to accept that it was Scotsmen who planned and executed the Massacre of Glencoe.

Buchan's history books are always well researched, well thought through and beautifully written. His book *The Massacre of Glencoe* should be distributed by England to every citizen in Scotland. No one north of the border should be allowed to vote until they've passed a test proving that they've read and digested the contents. American film directors should all be sent copies too.

23.56 p.m.

I spent the evening sorting out more files from Publishing House. I am burning boxes full of paper. The files have not been sorted for over 20 years and have become an impenetrable, multicoloured forest of out of date catalogues, unnecessary letters, bits of accounts, old contracts and all sorts of other administrative debris. It is a Sargasso sea of paperwork that was probably never worth keeping in the first place. But I keep all the accounts stuff. If the taxman wants to see my accounts he will receive as many boxes as we can fit into the truck.

4

11.09 a.m.

Schoolchildren are to be given free iPods so that they can do their schoolwork on them. I would have thought this an April Fool's joke if it hadn't been November. So this is our new world. There is no money to buy schoolbooks so give them all a free iPod. Great. I asked The Princess what an iPod is. She says she thinks it's a sort of electronic device thingy.

12.25 p.m.

Everyone in the mail order business does specific mailings. In other words they sell specific products to a specific group of buyers. And in the world of publishing it is widely accepted that people who buy a novel by an author will not buy a non-fiction book by the same author. (When I first started life as a professional author my agent insisted that I write novels as Edward Vernon and medical books as Vernon Coleman. This led to Pan Books producing paperbacks by two people but then finding out that the books had been written by one person.)

In view of this knowledge I have for some time sent out separate mailings. Readers who had bought my novels would only be sent details of my new novels. Readers who had bought my cat books would only be sent details of new cat books. And readers who had bought medical or political books would be sent details of those.

But, after studying the results of a trial mailshot I have come to the conclusion that all of this is absolute nonsense. Specific mailings really aren't necessary. People who buy a book on politics are quite likely to buy a novel. And vice versa. And why not?

People don't just live in narrow little worlds. We all have a variety of interests. And, after all, if I write several different types of book why shouldn't readers want to read several different types of book?

This discovery is important because our new restructured Publishing House will be much easier to organise if the sales records are simplified. Moreover, I've just heard that the software company we used to employ (which enabled us to keep records of which customer had bought which book and which was, in retrospect, far too clever, far too complex, far too expensive and far too likely to cause problems) is closing down. Maybe we were a more important customer than we'd believed.

So, in future, we will simply keep a list of people who buy our books.

Simple.

I love it when things get simpler.

16.37 p.m.

There are so many keys around for Publishing House that I decided to have the locks changed. I can't even remember how many keys have been made for the old locks. I rang a locksmith who quoted an extraordinary price (the best part of £300 to change two locks) and wanted details of my credit card. They said it had to be a credit card because that was all they took. I don't like using credit cards and so I said I would prefer to pay cash. `We don't take cash,' said the voice at the other end of the telephone. There was a long, long pause while the person at the other end realised they were close to losing the business. `A cheque will do,' said the voice. We agreed that I would pay with a cheque. I've always found that the most potent negotiating ploy is the silence. I learned this as a young freelance writer when the editor of either *Woman* or *Woman's Own* rang me in a spin one day. They needed a cover story for the following week's magazine and wanted me to write something to fit the three pages they had empty. As usual with these things they wanted it yesterday. I said I could provide the copy within 12 hours. There was then the question of my fee to be settled. `I can pay you £1,500,' said the editor. For a few moments I didn't say anything. I was wondering what to write about, how quickly I could write it and when I would able to fax it. `The most I can go to is £2,000,' said the editor. `That's OK,' I agreed. I'd made £500 because I hadn't replied straight away. More importantly I learned the value of the long silence. All negotiations are ultimately all about threats or promises. Without a threat or a promise, a carrot or a stick, a negotiator's position is very weak. And if you have principles then these should be non-negotiable or there is no point in having them.

Incidentally, the reason why doctors tend to get a good deal out of the Department of Health is that they use fairly complex psychology when negotiating. They usually have a `good doc', a `bad doc', a `silent doc' and a `note taker'. There are, of course, many other techniques. When negotiating with racing teams Max Mosley, the motor racing boss, used to favour the technique of asking for something outrageous and then settling for what he wanted. The Japanese technique is to say and do nothing for a long, long time. They know that eventually the person with whom they are negotiating will break and want to start negotiating to make a deal. And there are, of course, female negotiators, who get what they want by wearing revealing and distracting dresses and displaying all the traditional charms.

20.48 p.m.

We have now abandoned our relationship whereby the Royal Mail used to take away our unstamped mail and then send us bills. We aren't selling enough books at the moment to do this. Publishing House is closed a good deal of the time. And I don't trust Royal Mail to bill me properly.

And so we are sticking stamps on all the parcels we send out. The Princess types in all the labels, picks out the books and packs them. I then stick on all the stamps. And together we pile all the books into the back of the truck and take them to the nearest Post Office.

There are many things about the Royal Mail which annoy me.

Why are there such huge jumps between postage bands? If a book weighs 251 grams (and why does a `business' owned by the British Government only publish prices in metric units?) then it is charged the same as a book weighing 499 grams.

Why does Royal Mail still not produce a full range of self-adhesive stamps? Most of its products have to be moistened. I'm surprised they bother to perforate the damned things.

465

And why do they make so few stamps in suitable denominations? The postage cost of sending out a copy of *Alice's Diary* is £1.95 but there is no £1.95 stamp. So instead of just putting one stamp on the envelope we now have to make up the amount with one £1 stamp, and a variety of other stamps. It can take six or more stamps to put the correct postage on a packet. Inevitably, we don't bother. I tend to put two £1 stamps onto a parcel requiring £1.95 in postage. It's quicker and simpler.

They don't make a £2.36 stamp either. Or, indeed, any other stamp that fits their postage chart. So we constantly find that it is easier and quicker to put too many stamps on every packet. It takes so long to sort out all the 1p, 2p, 5p and 10p stamps necessary to make up the price. And since most stamps aren't self-adhesive they all have to be licked.

I worked out that for every 50 copies of *Alice's Diary* I send out I will waste £2.50 and save around 15 minutes. But since the £2.50 I have wasted is tax deductible putting on too many stamps is costing me £6 an hour. So, I will carry on putting too many stamps on the parcels we send out.

How I hate the loathsome Royal Mail.

23.30 p.m.
Selfish BBC staff are striking to retain pensions which take up 7% (and rising fast) of the outrageous BBC licence fee. So, one in 15 licence fees is paid over to former BBC staff members. If nothing is done it won't be long before 100% of all licence fees will be used for the pension fund which apparently has a huge deficit. The BBC is a loathsome institution and its staff are greedy, elitist bastards. Because of their unhappiness at being asked to pay a little towards their pensions they threatened to go on strike and to prevent the transmission of some of the Conservative Party conference in the autumn. That's democracy BBC style. It seems that public sector workers are becoming increasingly dangerous and dictatorial. During the last election, Royal Mail employees refused to deliver leaflets for candidates of whom they did not approve.

There are going to be a good many public sector strikes over pensions. The present pension system is unsustainable but like all greedy people the current lot of employees want to carry on being greedy. They will strike over a wide range of other unsustainable perks too. The Tube workers in London seem particularly enthusiastic about striking and taking days off. I wish their bosses would find some backbone and fire a few hundred of them. What else are the lazy, greedy buggers going to do that will earn them £40,000 for a 35 hour week and a job requiring an IQ of no more than 75?

In the bad old days strikers stopped work because they wanted enough money to be able to eat and to buy shoes occasionally. These days people go on strike for perks or for the right to retire at 50 and enjoy an index-linked pension paid by the next two generations of tax payers. The unions today are just about selfishness and beating everyone else (including the elderly, the poor and the frail) to an economic pulp. Their mantra is 'bugger what happens to everyone else as long as we preserve our better than everyone else privileged position.' Unions strike not because they want to be equal but because they want to be better. Wicked, wicked people. And all strikers deliberately choose times that will cause maximum disruption to other citizens.

I wonder if they will ever realise that we all rely on one another in our complex, modern society. The electricity workers threaten to go on strike during the cold weather, the refuse workers go on strike in hot weather and airline staff go on strike during holiday seasons.

23.47 p.m.
While trying to clear out old drawers I found an old Access credit card and for a moment couldn't remember why I'd kept it. Then it came back to me. When my book *Bodysense* was published by Thames and Hudson they launched it with a huge fuss. My previous book with them, *Bodypower,* had been a massive bestseller and so they'd booked me onto an extensive radio and television tour of Britain and Ireland. The tour, one of the biggest I ever undertook, lasted three weeks and involved five or six interviews every day. I remember very little about that tour. The one thing I remember about the London part of the tour was being interviewed by Pete Murray at LBC Radio in London. Pete Murray had been a hero of mine when I'd been a boy because of his shows on Radio Luxembourg and his appearances on Jukebox Jury and

I'd appeared on his shows a number of times. But that day he was tired and he fell asleep after introducing me. I kept talking for about 15 minutes and he showed no signs of waking up. I had to turn the segment of the show into a monologue, asking myself questions so that I could answer them. And I remember three things about the Irish leg of the tour. First, meeting the seventh son of a seventh son on one radio station there. Second, being interviewed live on television in Dublin by a man whose accent I did not understand while a band played loud music which meant that it didn't really matter what I said. Third, being accompanied by Lizzie Spender, a relative of the poet, who was my PR minder for that stretch of the tour. I travelled light (with just a shoulder bag) to save time and to avoid having to lug large suitcases around. Lizzie travelled with large suitcases which I ended up lugging around for her. I remember going into the BBC in Belfast sweaty and breathless after struggling in and out of cabs with her luggage. Heaven knows what she had with her or why.

During the tour I flew from Birmingham (where I left my car) to Belfast to do television, radio and newspaper interviews there and then took the train down to Dublin to repeat the exercise in Ireland. I then flew back from Dublin to Birmingham. Unfortunately, since this was basically a UK tour, it hadn't occurred to me that I would need a passport to get back into the country and I only realised my problem when I found myself back in Birmingham standing in a customs queue in the middle of a long line of people clutching their passports. The only things I had with me which had my name on were a copy of my own book, *Bodysense*, and an Access card (a brand of credit card which seems to have gone the way of pogo sticks and hula hoops). I didn't think the book would do me much good so when I reached the front of the queue I held up my Access card. To my astonishment and relief the customs officer took it, looked at it, raised an eyebrow a quarter of an inch, handed it back to me and nodded me through. I may have been helped by a small commotion caused by a drug-sniffing Labrador which was furiously attacking a large red suitcase which turned out to contain three veal and ham pies.

5
10.09 a.m.

To my utter astonishment the EU appears to be about to do something good at last. The eurocrats are talking about bringing in new privacy rules which will mean that individuals can force websites to remove information about them. It will be the online right `to be forgotten'. If the legislation is passed then I intend to take full advantage of the offer to disappear from the Web. This is the best piece of news I've ever heard from the EU. The World Wide Web has caused me nothing but misery. It has damaged me and my business of publishing. Newspapers and magazines were far more cautious about printing lies than the anonymous geeks who put material on the Web. There are thousands and thousands of items on the Web about me which are outrageously libellous and/or inaccurate. And many of my books and articles appear free of charge on other people's websites - stolen and used without any offer of compensation. (Internet users who insist on helping themselves to copyright material and who believe they are entitled to steal anything they like are apparently now known as `freetards'.) I do not consider myself the slightest bit famous so I cannot imagine how celebrities cope.

22.46 p.m.

I recently bought The Princess a collection of DVDs of *Cirque de Soleil* shows. We've been watching them for several days but have grown increasingly disappointed. The early shows are brilliant but the later shows are without soul or passion. They are so rehearsed and so pretentious that they are completely without value. Watching them is the visual equivalent of eating cardboard. What a pity. The early shows, raw and exciting, were filled with energy and excitement and more than a whiff of danger. The later shows look as if they have been designed and approved by a committee of superannuated bureaucrats advised by a cadre of Health and Safety experts and political correctness consultants. The DVDs will go into the charity bag.

23.19 p.m.

When the Italian Prime Minister, Mr Berlusconi, was criticised for having had a relationship with a teenage nightclub dancer he said it was better than being gay. (This reminded me of former French President Chirac who, when faced with accusations that he was dishonest, was defended by his supporters with the remark that it was better to be a crook than a fascist.)

23.51 p.m.
My new Polish publisher has sent me an e-mail telling me that he has signed the contract I faxed. He wants to know what he should do now. I tell him that he must print some books and I add: 'But before that you must, I am afraid, send me a cheque.'

23.56 p.m.
We had three book orders today which came without any payment for postage. People make a lot of mistakes with the postage they are supposed to include when ordering books but curiously they always send too little and never too much. It is the same with MPs when they claim their expenses: they never claim too little.

6
09.12 a.m.
The Princess recently wrote to a friend of hers and bared her soul about some of the worrying things that have happened in recent months. Her friend wrote back a letter filled with nonsense such as 'Oh, worse things happen at sea' and 'Onwards and upwards'. She also told The Princess at length about someone she knows whose wife is dying. Neither of us quite understands this 'there is someone worse off than you' mentality. It is patronising rather than comforting. The irony is that The Princess has constantly supported this friend through her own problems and has always provided sympathy, support and encouragement.

14.53 p.m.
We have seen the energy rating on a house we were interested in buying but have decided not to go ahead. The house has a rating of 0 and since the world's oil is now clearly running out (the price is, as I predicted in *Oil Apocalypse*, continuing to rise) I can see the time coming soon when the authorities will either introduce some sort of fuel rationing, or think up some way to punish householders whose homes consume too much energy. In just the same way that motor car owners are punished if their vehicles aren't considered to be sufficiently fuel efficient so home owners will be punished for

living in houses that aren't fuel efficient. There will also be new taxes or higher prices for heating fuels and maybe even some form of rationing. Petrol coupons could come back. And what about oil coupons and gas coupons for home owners? We have to find a house which can be pretty well self-sufficient. It must have at least one and preferably two open fireplaces, enough garden space for the disposal of rubbish and the growing of some vegetables and be within ten miles of a railway station which isn't likely to close at any time in the near future.

It also occurred to me today that if the price of petrol continues to rise it won't be long before many people who commute to work (and have to do so by car) will decide that they would be better off if they stayed at home and allowed the State to pay their bills for them. People have for years demanded that the State deal with all their problems - however trivial those problems might be - and so it is hardly surprising that the State has become bigger and more powerful, and that the number of people demanding their `entitlements' has grown exponentially.

18.32 p.m.
I had a lovely, kind letter from a reader asking why the media doesn't credit me with being the first to draw attention to the cancer risk associated with eating meat and using mobile telephones. The answer, I replied, is that I said it all far too soon and far too plainly. But the genuinely kind and warm-hearted letter from my reader made my day. I do have lovely, kind readers and their warmth and generosity keep us both going.

19.58 p.m.
An old journalist friend has died. Actually he wasn't all that old. D was younger than I am. I remember him for his kindness (hidden behind a very gruff exterior) and his common sense. He had a wonderful way of nipping problems in the bud. I remember being in the offices where he worked when a feature writer had said something outrageously rude about one of the sub editors. There was talk of lawyers and tribunals. D solved the problem quickly and easily by simply forcing an apology out of the sinner. He picked the man up by the lapels and pushed him back against a railing at the top of the stair well. Behind him there was a long

drop into the atrium of the building. The man looked over his shoulder and was clearly terrified. `Apologise,' said D softly. The man apologised. `Louder,' said D. The man apologised again. Everyone heard it. The incident was over. It took less than five minutes.

D died, almost inevitably, of liver disease. Journalists consume alcohol in the way little old ladies consume tea. I remember that when he came to visit me in Devon he bought two bottles of gin and 200 cigarettes for the journey. He was, he told me, worried that there might not be a dining car with a bar. It was D whom I first remember referring to ten pound notes as `brown drinking vouchers'. I remember meeting him in Manchester. He was working there at the time and I stayed in the same hotel while doing some interviews for a book of mine. At around 10 p.m. I tottered across the road to do a live interview on a local radio station and when I got back to the hotel, three quarters of an hour later, D was still in the bar exactly where I'd left him. While I'd been away he'd continued to buy drinks and there were now a dozen double malt whiskies laid out on the table where I'd been sitting.

23.46 p.m.

Newspapers have always been led by advertisements but things are getting worse. For example, *The Financial Times* is forever carrying supplements with absurd titles such as *Commercial Property in Northern Shropshire* (supported, curiously enough, by advertisements for commercial property in northern Shropshire) or *The Growing Telecom Industry in Malawi* supported, again curiously enough, by copious advertisements for growing telecom companies in Malawi. The *FT* even publishes a weekly magazine with the obscene title *How to spend it*. The magazine is clearly intended for bankers desperate to get rid of their taxpayer funded bonuses and is full of absurd articles and advertisements for £400 million yachts and tiny notebooks that cost £400 each. I should feel kindly about the *FT* since the paper was the only one to write a short feature when I resigned from *The People* over its Iraq War policy but I confess I find the writing gruesome and the almost daily attempts at humour childish and embarrassing. I buy the paper for the lists of prices it contains and I suspect most of the other customers do too. I often wonder if anyone actually reads the articles or if they are just there to keep the advertisements apart from one another, and to make the paper look like a newspaper instead of what it really is, a share price listing service.

7

11.09 a.m.

My new Polish publisher sent an e-mail asking for my bank account details. He wants to send me the advance money by electronic transfer. I ask him to send a cheque instead.

12.29 p.m.

An order has come in from a bookshop for a paperback copy of *Mrs Caldicot's Cabbage War* which has been selling for £2.99. The bookshop has given itself a 45% discount. So of the £2.99 cover price I will receive £1.64. When the book is wrapped it will cost £1.95 to post it. I am expected to pay the cost of the posting. And so if I fulfil this order I will lose 0.31 pence before I have included the cost of printing the book, the cost of the packaging and all the other costs involved in running a publishing business. That would be bad enough but the bookshop hasn't enclosed a cheque with its order. They tell me I have to submit an invoice and to post a statement in 60 days. If I am lucky, and they haven't gone bankrupt, they may then pay me. I somehow managed to resist the temptation to put the order on the fire. I sent off the book and made a note to put up the price.

15.57 p.m.

In one week I have deleted, or marked as spam, 87 newsletters sent by quangos, management advisers, financial consultants and marketing experts. Just getting rid of these damned things took ages.

17.38 p.m.

I decided today that I am a bookaholic. A bookaholic is someone whose rooms are lined with bookshelves but where there are also stacks of books piled high on the floor and the stacks grow so high that they topple over in the night and wake everyone up. A bookaholic is someone who cannot go out of the house (even on the simplest journey) without returning with a pile of new books. A bookaholic is someone who owns far more unread books than anyone could ever possibly read. I may write a book about being a bookaholic. Or, perhaps, I could form a charity and get a few grants to help me deal with my problem. Maybe there is an EU agency which would provide me with regular parcels of free books with which to satisfy my craving.

22.40 p.m.

In a pensive mood this evening I found myself wondering where my career went wrong. The Princess is right: I probably attacked too many powerful people. I made the mistake of trying to change things that I thought were wrong. It was, perhaps, hardly surprising that my former agent at Curtis Brown, in despair, described me as `a prophet crying in the wilderness'. There is no room in the modern media world for iconoclasts. Iconoclasts never have been popular, of course. The people who own and worship the icons don't much care for them being smashed. That's only to be expected. The problem these days lies in the fact that the icon owners have all the power and most of the money. They control the politicians, the legislature and the media.

It is, I suppose, difficult to think of anyone in power I haven't annoyed over the last few years. Pretty stupid of me, really. And I haven't helped myself by being a loner; useless at networking and doing the social rounds of London parties. (Not very good! What am I saying? I once went to a reception in Buckingham Palace and spent the whole evening avoiding Margaret Thatcher and Her Majesty and wandering around forbidden corridors.) It's odd that an industry which depends on unsociable loners for its existence should have become an industry of meeters and greeters. But it has. And so the authors who are successful are (with a few notable exceptions) the ones who can do the meeting and greeting without vomiting.

Add to all that the fact that I'm English, white, abrasive rather than smooth, and more of an anarchist than anything else. I suspect that I might have been much more successful (in official terms) if I'd been Jewish, gay and American. Being female would have probably helped, too.

In an era when compromise has become necessary for success I have steadfastly remained glued to impossible principles which have made life difficult going on impossible for decades. On the day I arrived at medical school in the 1960s I was told that I had to become a member of the National Union of Students (a certain Jack Straw was President at the time). It was the default condition. I didn't have anything against the NUS but I knew that if I had to be a member then I didn't want to be a member. This had never happened before and for weeks I had to face enormous pressure from the authorities who seemed to think they faced unsurmountable administrative obstacles. I eventually invoked the United Nations Charter and was eventually allowed to remain a member of the university without being a member of the union. Was there any point to this battle? Probably not. Did winning improve my life? Certainly not. So, why the hell did I bother?

It's too late to change. I'm now elderly as well as everything else and in the world of publishing that's the kiss of death. Publishers and agents are only interested in bright young things who look good on television. As if all that were not enough I am also now so shy and uncertain that I find talking on the telephone a strain. Meeting people is these days so stressful that it is something I avoid as much as possible. Years of orchestrated abuse have shattered whatever small quantity of self-confidence I may have started out with. Sneery reviewers and unsupportive associates have demolished my self-respect, though The Princess constantly tries to repair the damage. Sat in front of a keyboard, or with a pen and a notebook, I am liberated from my fears. The demons do not find me there; they do not enter my private world, the world I share with Mrs Caldicot, Mr Henry Mulligan, Thumper, Patchy, Doc and the other inhabitants of Bilbury, Alice and Thomasina and the rest of my imaginary cast. Only The Princess lives there with me, though readers are welcome to wander in to share the past, the present and the future peace.

8
10.31 a.m.
Today, just a day or two after I decided to sack the wholesalers and abandon attempts to do business with the book trade, we received a large order from a wholesaler. I wasn't tempted. In future, buyers

will only be able to buy our books by writing a cheque, putting it in an envelope and posting it. We will lose bookshop, library and webshop sales but if just half of those frustrated buyers send us a cheque we will be better off.

Since we have stopped dealing with bookshops we have now put this note on the website:

`Please note that Vernon Coleman books are no longer readily available in bookshops (terrestrial or online). This is because shops steadfastly refuse to carry stock (despite years of trying) and seem to prefer to order individual copies from us through wholesalers. If they want six copies they will send in six separate orders. The whole process is so tedious, time consuming and expensive that we have pretty well abandoned it. (The bookshop sends an order to a clearing house which sends the order to a wholesaler who sends the order to us. We then send the book to the wholesaler who then sends it to the bookshop. The buyer pays the bookshop who sometimes pays the wholesaler who then eventually pays us if we send an invoice and at least one or possibly two or more statements.) The environmental cost of all this sending and carrying is phenomenal. Time, energy and money are wasted. And even that isn't the end of it. Wholesalers and bookshops frequently question invoices for orders received long ago, they demand extra copies of invoices and, with increasing frequency, they go bust and don't pay anything. (Bookshops seem to go bust more often than builders, restaurateurs and photographers.) The paperwork is exhausting and often quite pointless. I'm sorry if some readers find this inconvenient but really popping an order and a cheque into the post doesn't take much effort. The easy way to buy Vernon Coleman books is to send a cheque or postal order to Publishing House. Please allow 28 days for delivery. We aim to do much better than this but 28 days allows for the Royal Mail to overcome delays caused by snow, rain, leaves, sunshine and the other entirely unexpected hazards by which it seems to be constantly surprised.'

15.28 p.m.

The Publishing House accounts had become incomprehensible and absurdly overcomplicated. Worse still, the commercial software package we had been using (though allegedly up-to-date) did not

476

match the requirements of the tax form. The result was that the software made life even more difficult.

I tried designing a simple spreadsheet for use on a computer but the words 'simple' and 'computer' don't fit well together these days. I quickly realised that it was going to take forever to fill in a home-made spreadsheet.

And so I have bought myself a large notepad and I'm going to do the accounts by hand. With a pen and a calculator. And I will photocopy the notebook so that I have a copy which I can keep somewhere safe. I have designed my accounts to match the income tax form and I have allowed one page for expenditure which includes VAT and another page for expenditure which doesn't include VAT. It is all breathtakingly simple. And it works brilliantly well. Not for 20 years have I found the accounts as manageable.

I can write. I can add up. I have a spare A4 pad. I have plenty of pen refills and back up pencils. There are no privacy worries. And the accounts are there, easy to read at a glance. (They are, however, in my 'doctor's' handwriting. If anyone wants to investigate them he will need to be determined and patient.) Computers just complicate things unnecessarily.

It all reminds me of when I first started out as an author many years ago. When the VAT man visited and wanted to see my accounts I handed him a small, sixpenny notebook.

'No,' he said gruffly. 'I want to see the complete accounts.'

'You're holding them,' I told him.

18.29 p.m.

Life is full of gambles and buying a new house is quite a big one. The more you are conscious of the problems the more frozen you get. Eventually you have to make a decision, and leap, but it is a scary business. When we buy a car we take it for a spin and read the brochures and the reviews but when we buy a house we tend to do so after one short visit. We have no idea of the problems that lie ahead.

Part of the problem is that I am old enough to have seen just how vendors can cheat and lie when selling houses.

The last time I bought a house the vendors forgot to tell me that the roof leaked in two places; they forgot to mention that the shower ventilation pipe didn't go anywhere except into the loft and that if you used the bath the water emptied through the kitchen ceiling while if you used the shower the water emptied through the hall ceiling (because in both cases the pipes weren't connected up properly). They said that the cellar was good for storage and assured us that it was not damp but when it rained the cellar became a four foot deep swimming pool.

These things rather scar the memory.

When buying a house, we have to look at it with our brains not our emotions. We have to imagine how the rooms will be when they contain our things, instead of the stuff belonging to the people who are leaving, and we have to try to imagine how we will fit into the neighbourhood. What problems will there be with the neighbours? What don't we know about? What problems can we imagine? For example, having an infant or junior school nearby probably won't be a problem as far as the children are concerned. They'll be noisy during playtime and maybe when they leave. But it's the parents who are most likely to cause problems. They will park here, there and everywhere and toot and shout and generally make a nuisance of themselves. Having a pub nearby won't be a problem during the daytime but what about late at night and at weekends? How many neighbours have dogs? How many tinker with motorbikes or cars in their spare time? Are you on a walking route for late night revellers? If you are then they will all be talking, very loudly, on their mobile telephones as they drunkenly make their way home. And they will throw their chip wrappers and their lager cans into your garden. The possibilities for misery are endless.

And, of course, very few people who are selling a house are likely to talk about these problems. `The neighbours? Oh they're all wonderful.' Like hell they are. No one ever formally complains about neighbours these days because if they do then they have to mention it when they sell. So they grit their teeth, keep quiet and sell and move somewhere else in the hope that their new neighbours won't have a son who plays the drums at 3.00 a.m. or a daughter who attracts a swarm of tattooed bikers to the area.

9
15.46 p.m.

We went to Ilfracombe today. What a sad, dull town it is. In Victorian times it must have been a marvellous place. Today it is faded, tawdry and forgotten. Unlike other small seaside towns such as Sidmouth it has allowed itself to fill up with the unemployed. It's easy to understand how it happens. Unemployed youths decide that if they are going to hang around all day doing nothing they might as well do it by the seaside as in Wolverhampton. And so they head south and west. A few hoteliers struggling to cope with long, cold, empty winters decide that they will be better off if they take in long-term residents rather than relying on families coming for two weeks holiday in August. Then when holidaymakers come to the other hotels they are put off by the people they see around them. Hotels are converted into doss houses and flats for people on the dole. Drug addicts abound. The local businessmen running amusement arcades oppose any suggestion that the elderly be encouraged to move into the town because they know well that it is the young, the uneducated and the feckless who patronise their establishments. And gradually the remaining hotels become doss houses, the shops selling plastic windmills and fishing lines close and the decline is inevitable. Locals who are desperate to make a living grasp at public money by opening hostels for drug addicts and ex-prisoners. As the percentage of hoodies and drug addicts increases to the point where their presence becomes noticeable, so decent people move out. The towns become poorer and the downhill slide becomes inexorable. Only the shops and amusement arcades which cater to these very specialised markets thrive. Up-market stores, hotels and cafés close down and are replaced with cheap bars and yet more one armed bandits. Men selling balloons and buckets and spades and wooden cricket sets are replaced by men selling drugs. The Punch and Judy man doesn't come that way anymore. People don't like to go onto the beach because of the risk of stepping on an infected needle.

The only seaside towns in Britain which have survived have been the ones which welcomed elderly residents. Bournemouth and Eastbourne have survived well, as has Sidmouth. Towns such as Ilfracombe and Weston-super-Mare have tattoo parlours, big dogs and nail salons. Bournemouth and so on offer walking sticks, small dogs and hairdressers who specialise in blue rinses. Personally, I prefer the latter.

19.23 p.m.

The Royal Mail has announced that it is going to have another attempt at destroying the mail order industry (and therefore itself) by putting up its prices by 12% next April. The only segment of the mail order business that will survive another mail price hike is the rare stamp business. Their products are small and light and expensive and those will be essential criteria for mail order in the future. Suddenly, I no longer care. There are three reasons to do things. I've given up (temporarily) on changing the world or making money out of books. So it's fun time. And the Royal Mail's idiocy will not interfere with that.

For years I have been trying to fit in by acting like a proper publisher. That hasn't worked. So I am going to make a strength out of a weakness. I am no longer sending out any review copies. And I will no longer sell books through bookshops. I will not supply libraries. There will be no discounts for shops. The only place to buy books is from us.

22.41 p.m.

An independent television producer wanted me to be a consultant on a programme about breast cancer in black women. There was no mention of a fee of course. I explained, honestly, that if my name was attached to the programme it would never be made or aired. The producer seemed miffed and I will probably be reported to a quango somewhere for being sexist or racist or somethingist.

10
10.35 a.m.

In addition to searching for a new home we are also looking for new business premises. And since we are no longer going to live in North Devon we need offices outside Devon. We have found a marvellous old building in Malmesbury. It is several hundred years old and has, in its time been the local council offices and a bank. It looks magnificent. Sadly, there are two problems. First, it is falling to bits. Second, it is Grade II listed and any repairs will have to be done under the eagle eyes of the men and women in cheap suits. One of the problems with listed buildings is that they have to stay as they were when they were listed. Friends of ours who bought a

17th century building wanted to restore it to its original 17th century state but were told by snooty, brain-dead government employees that they had to retain alterations which had been made in the 1950s because those were there when the house was listed.

It occurs to me that one way to ease the pain might be to interest a television company in the restoration project. We can't be the only people to have noticed that when anything is done with television cameras running, problems tend to disappear. We decide that if we do buy the building, and can't get a television company involved, we will hire our own TV crew, form our own production company and make a programme ourselves. The cost of hiring the cameraman and soundman will probably be offset by the savings on the repair bills when the cheap suiters realise that all their decisions are going to be questioned in public. And, with luck, we might have a film we can sell.

Unfortunately, this brilliant idea rather falls apart when the owner refuses our offer which is only a little less than the asking price.

`Hasn't the owner read the papers?' I ask. `Doesn't he know the state of the nation?'

`Please don't,' says the estate agent wearily, with a shrug and a thin smile. The property has been on the market for a considerable time. Thirty people have viewed it. No one has bought it. Our offer is a reasonable one. Actually, it's the only one.

14.15 p.m.

I've been sent a note by someone in a tax office somewhere several hundred miles away telling me that, as an employer, I must, in future, fill in all sorts of forms online. I will be punished if I do not fill them in online. It is already a legal requirement that I fill in my quarterly VAT return online and I find it extraordinary that I am ordered to use a specific communications medium which is unarguably insecure, unreliable, inefficient, expensive and extraordinarily damaging to the environment. The system is an advantage only to the Government because it enables lazy bureaucrats to stop work at 11.00 a.m. instead of having to work on until lunchtime. I wrote back to the anonymous official in East Kilbride to point out that I don't think I can access their site on my iPhone and that if they really insist on my filling in a form online

481

then I will have no choice but to make all my remaining staff redundant. I asked them to let me know as soon as possible if they are going to insist on this new rule so that I can give staff as much notice as possible. I pointed out that I could not see how it helped the country for me to be forced to make people redundant and finished: `I can quite see that you don't want small businesses to exist at all. Maybe the Chancellor will be able to borrow some money from Ireland.' (Two months later I had still received no reply.)

I also sent a note today to the local employment exchange (I know it is called something else now) telling them that I have decided to hire 12 people to work at Publishing House. In line with Government policy the lucky dozen will be invited to work at home and to choose the number of hours they work. They will be allowed to take up to a year off if they become pregnant and to take off as much time as they need to look after their children, spouses or elderly relatives. Finally, in my letter, I have drawn attention to the fact that in return for all these rights my new employees must not expect to be paid any wages.

11
10.01 a.m.
I couldn't help laughing at the news that advertisements for lapdancers, strippers, webcam performers and other sex industry jobs have been banned from Jobcentres. However, adverts for cleaners and administrators working for lap dancing clubs, strip clubs and wherever webcam performers work will continue to be accepted by Jobcentres.

12.34 p.m.
It's good fun having no business telephone. I spoke to someone at HMRC who seemed to have difficulty in believing that I was running a business without a telephone number. (I explained that I was making the call on a borrowed phone.) Eventually I told him that I had got rid of the telephones for environmental reasons. I pointed out that telephone systems require a good deal of plastic and electricity. He accepted this argument quite happily. These days it is possible to explain away any strange behaviour by saying you are doing it to save the planet.

15.06 p.m.

Alice's Diary has now sold over 70,000 copies in hardback. Most years it sells enough copies at Christmas time to be in the fiction bestseller lists. (It never is, of course.) No paperbacker will produce an edition of the book. No one has ever reviewed it. No bookshop has ever stocked a copy on its shelves. There are virtually no copies in public libraries.

18.27 p.m.

I read today that in 1836 the Hon Grantley Berkeley assaulted a Mr Fraser for publishing an attack on him and his family in the guise of a review of his novel *Berkeley Castle*. Mr Berkeley ended up in a court. The judge, Lord Abinger CB, concluded: `I really think that this assault was carried to a very inconsiderate length, and that if an author is to go and give a beating to a publisher who has offended him, two or three blows with a horsewhip ought to be quite enough to satisfy his irritated feelings.'

20.23 p.m.

It struck me today how sad it is that international rugby matches are decided by supplementary referees who sit and watch television replays before deciding whether a try is, or is not, a try. It's sad because, when there is a huge ruck of players on the ground, with the ball somewhere underneath them all, there is one person in the world who really knows whether a try has been scored. And that is the player holding the ball. But the authorities don't (or won't) trust the players to tell the truth. And that's sad. It's the same in cricket, though things used to be so very different. Years ago, at Lords, during an Ashes test match I watched Rodney Marsh, the Australian wicket keeper wave his arms across his body to tell the umpire that what looked like a catch had not, in fact, been a clean catch. The umpire, David Shepherd, who had already given the batsman out, applauded Marsh for his honesty. And so did 20,000 people in the crowd.

22.12 p.m.

We feel that today everything is made in China. But China's share of world exports is now only around 17%. This morning The

Princess pointed out to me that back in the mid to late 19th century, 46% of world trade in manufactured goods had 'Made in England' stamped on them. She's right (of course). Just over a century ago half of Britain worked in manufacturing. Today less than one in seven workers makes things for a living.

23.41 p.m.

An estate agent e-mailed with details of a house that has come on the market. The present owner has lived there for just under two years. `They are down-sizing,' says the agent. `Now that their children have left home they no longer need such a large property.' I do wish that when people lie they would put more effort into it. These people are clearly selling up because they bought a house they can no longer afford.

23.58 p.m.

There has been a tendency in recent years for publishers to produce larger and larger books. A hundred years ago books were quite small but they were still readable. Better, thinner paper and good type made reading easy but enabled readers to carry a book in a pocket. I blame the French and the Americans. Both began producing huge paperbacks some years ago. The French had an excuse (their paperbacks were published in lieu of hardback editions) but the Americans produced big books because they adore anything wasteful and excessive. Huge books are impractical to use but they waste energy in manufacture, transportation and storage.

12

10.19 a.m.

The debate about housing benefits continues. Many commentators are arguing that rules which are being introduced will mean that people on benefits will no longer be able to live in smart London suburbs such as Westminster and Mayfair. They will, say the commentators, have to move. Am I supposed to feel sorry for these people? If so, I don't and simply cannot force myself to. Other than those on benefits only Russian crooks and banking crooks can afford houses in these places. Why should the unemployed and the unemployable be given homes in these ridiculously expensive places? Arguing that they have a right to live there is as absurd as arguing that they should be given free yachts and Bugattis because other people have them.

14.41 p.m.
My new Polish publisher tells me that he has managed to obtain a cheque to send to me. `My bank thought it was very 19th century,' he adds.

15.54 p.m.
A letter arrives from a man living in Barbados. He writes: `I have lived my life in the oil drilling and production industry for 45 years and have enjoyed your book *Oil Apocalypse*, though it has caused me further waking and sleepless pondering. Your book is very alarmist, as it should be. Oil will decline, and it could happen at alarming speed if things go wrong. My beef with your book is at the `All rights reserved', since what I have written has always been given freely to newspapers. You have no right to attempt to stop the spread of what you have written. For mankind's sake, it needs to be spread anyhow it can.' I wrote back: `I don't quite understand your accusation that I am trying to stop the spread of what I have written. Far from it. I would like the world to read my books. I also fail to understand why I should not copyright my work. Your implied suggestion that I should make my books available free to one and all is sweet and has been made by many of my other readers. However, I write for a living and I have a number of bills which have to be paid. If printers, suppliers, utilities, Royal Mail, etc. would all provide their services for free, and I could find staff prepared to work for nothing, then I could sell my books for just enough cash to pay for a little food. Unfortunately, the world ain't quite like that. So, I appreciate your kind comments. But I reject your criticisms. My books are available free in public libraries. But if people want to own them they have to pay for them. Do you know anyone who doesn't expect to be paid for their work? How many doctors, lawyers, architects and businessmen do you know who never charge for their services? Why should an author be different? Am I supposed to starve because I write books?' I was tempted not to put stamps on the envelope on the grounds that the

Royal Mail provides an important service and therefore shouldn't charge for it. But in the end I gave in and put on the stamps.

19.03 p.m.

There is much talk in the newspapers about Britain's libel laws which are so absurd that in the USA, the Great Black Disappointment (as we must now call him) has passed a law protecting American citizens from our laws. (Since America can do what it likes with British citizens, whether or not they have broken any American laws, this is another example of the one-sided `special relationship'.)

The establishment, and the professional writ wranglers, love the current rules which provide great protection for the bad guys and huge amounts of money for the lawyers. It isn't damages which kill people who get involved in the libel business these days - it's the costs.

I've been involved in several truly bizarre incidents over the years. Many years ago, for example, I used a pen name for a magazine for which I was already writing regularly under my own name. I picked the name of a friend. However, a woman doctor with the same name leapt out of the woodwork and suddenly claimed that I had libelled her by using her name. (It was a common name and there were a large number of other people around who might have made the same claim.) The woman doctor claimed, quite falsely, that I had been a student of hers. I'd never heard of the damned woman. The end result was that the Medical Defence Union (which provides and pays for legal advice when its doctor members are sued) represented us both and was paying both lots of legal bills which, as these things do, grew and grew and grew. It was surely one of the dottiest libel cases in a world packed full of dotty libel cases. I can't remember what happened in the end. I rather lost interest. Maybe the MDU is still suing itself in some Dickensian lawsuit that will, like Jarndyce v Jarndyce, go on for ever and ever.

13

14.52 p.m.

There is much talk about something called the `big society'. No one knows what it is but government ministers make it sound very wonderful. From what they say I suspect that they want taxpayers to help government employees do their jobs because the poor dears are so stressed at the very idea that they might have to pay a little more towards their own pensions that they need time off to rest. Another minister claims that the Government wants to have a good relationship with people. If the Government wants us to like it more, and make us feel better disposed towards it, then it should teach its employees (who are, after all, our employees) to learn to be helpful and polite. They don't have to be obsequious. Polite will do nicely. It is very easy for Cameron to talk about a Big Society. I rather suspect that civil servants call him sir and say please and thank you when appropriate. Cameron has always struck me as quite hollow and totally untrustworthy; he seems to me to be an unpatriotic and ignorant buffoon. The man who promised a referendum on the Lisbon Treaty (and austerity) has, in just a few months since choosing the curtains for Number 10, allowed the EU to take control of financial regulation in Britain, handed them hundreds of millions to finance a bigger EU budget and risked tens of billions by participating, quite unnecessarily in the EU bailout of eurozone financial disasters. I am tempted to write a follow up to *Gordon is a Moron* and call it *Cameron is a Cretin*. Or, maybe, *Cameron and Clegg are Cretins.*

Like most people my relationship with society is pretty much one way these days. I give and they take. The big society cannot possibly work because it will depend upon individuals taking over the State's responsibility, while still paying the State to do those things and while the State still has a massive amount of obstructive bureaucracy in place.

The real trouble is that politicians, bankers, businessmen in general are not trusted. One community worker wrote recently about having tried to set up a small community festival in a local park. First he had to fill in a 30-page form to obtain permission to use the public park. Then he was told he needed to give six months notice. And he had to arrange public liability insurance. If children were involved then all volunteers needed to have criminal record checks. The police would need to be asked for help in making sure that everyone was happy. Health and safety rules meant that no food or drink could be served.

In the face of all this overbearing nonsense most people either give up or do it unofficially and quietly and hope they manage to stay out of prison. Cameron's big society is in truth a terrible idea. It's just a way to get services cheap.

What used to be called `society' has broken down under an unrelenting tide of deceit, greed and bureaucratic incompetence. The concept of `Doing the right thing' is now scorned as old-fashioned.

I still believe that `small is beautiful' but if Cameron et al want a friendlier world then they need to set about dismantling some of the State bureaucracy that stifles every good intention before it can be born. Cameron wants the best of both worlds. He wants volunteer labour to help run the State machinery.

14
14.59 p.m.
I have made many mistakes in my career. Setting up as a publisher is definitely high on the list (though a number of the books I have published would never have appeared in any other way). Becoming a self-publisher (and compounding the sin by being a successful self-publisher) has won me regiments of enemies among the publishing and literary establishment. Fighting the medical and scientific establishment has been a mistake from a professional point of view, though from a personal point of view it was never an option. I could go on. I doubt if anyone, with the possible exception of William Cobbett, has done so much to destroy his career. And now I'm going to top the lot by publishing this book. Well, bugger it, it's too damned late to start worrying now about making mistakes.

15
11.52 a.m.
When looking around a house we often ask the vendors: `How can you leave this beautiful home?'. The aim, of course, is to find out why the vendors are selling.

The standard reply, the one we hear more than any other, is: `To be closer to our family'.

This is usually a patent lie.

This morning we visited a house which was full of photographs. The two vendors had told us that they were selling, with great reluctance, so that they could be closer to their children and grandchildren.

As we left The Princess turned to me. `Did you notice that there weren't any photographs of children or grandchildren in the house?'

`I noticed,' I said. `Not one. But there were at least 20 photographs of their pet poodle. The one that followed us round yapping and trying to bite our ankles.'

14.47 p.m.

Because so many books get lost or stolen we no longer send more than three books in one parcel. This costs us more in postage but it also means that we can put the parcels into the local letterbox (which has a wide mouth) instead of queuing at the post office. And if customers have decent sized letterboxes it means that their parcel can be put through their letterbox - saving them the inevitable journey to their local sorting office.

15.50 p.m.

An academic reader writes and tells me that I am very fortunate to be able to publish my own books. It's an extremely rude and offensive letter. I suspect that he has no idea how difficult it is to publish original, iconoclastic work in the UK. I may not be officially banned but in many ways life would be easier if I were. Instead, my books are not reviewed and they are not stocked in shops. Advertisements for them are banned by most publications. And broadcasters dare not interview me. Fortunately, my books do sell abroad. And thanks to a band of loyal readers, I sell more than the vast majority of authors. I don't tell my academic reader any of this. I just write back, return the outline of his proposed book unread, and tell him that, sadly, I am unable to publish his book.

16

12.30 p.m.

We had four huge sacks of books to post off so I drove The Princess and the parcels to the Post Office in Barnstaple. There is nowhere near to park legally so I stopped for a moment or two in the nearby bus stop and helped The Princess with the parcels. As I started to open my door to climb back into the truck, a bus driver who was passing deliberately drove dangerously close to me and crushed me up against side of the truck. 'What do you think you're doing?' he demanded, adding various bits and pieces of abuse to the question. I stared at him in quiet, resigned disbelief. The world is full of officials and Britain is failing at everything except officialdom. There are policemen and traffic wardens about a-plenty but even bus drivers want to be officious too. Without thinking what I was doing I stared at him quizzically and burbled something in what sounded like a bastard mixture of Spanish and Swedish. The bus driver glowered. 'You understand!' he shouted. 'You know what I'm saying!' I shook my head and shrugged and gave him a bit more gibberish. He shouted more abuse, shut his doors and drove off in a furious temper. I smiled and waved and got into the truck. I felt really good. I suppose I should have felt childish and a bit ashamed. But I didn't and I don't. I transferred all my built up anger and frustration to the damned, officious bus driver and he drove away with it. I think I may do this more often.

14.23 p.m.

A reader who forgot to say which books she wanted to buy, forgot to give us her postcode and forgot to include a cheque has remembered to write us a very nasty letter complaining that she hasn't received the books and threatening to report me to someone or other.

18.40 p.m.

A young German called Vettel has won the Formula 1 World Championship at the age of 23. He cried like a little girl when he was told the news. Much has been made about his youth. People forget that Guy Gibson was about the same age when he led the Dam Busters raid. And Hannibal wasn't much older when he took all those elephants over the Alps.

The trouble with sportsmen (and probably women too) these days is that they are one trick ponies; groomed for stardom in some, peculiar backwater of life. They have no depth and so no sense of perspective. And these days young people in their mid 20s are often still referred to as children. 'He's only 25,' say commentators, as though this excuses immature and irresponsible behaviour. I was working as a GP when I was 25 and I don't remember being told not to worry if I made terrible mistakes.

20.30 p.m.

I am so pleased to see that British taxpayers are going to bung container loads of lolly to the Irish bankers. Why doesn't that nasty little popsicle 'Bonio' bail out the sodding Irish banks? We are supporting the Irish banks to help protect the euro. The Irish banks owe around 500 billion pounds or euros (which means it's probably nearer a trillion of whichever) so, instead of simply letting the stupid bankers go bust, the EU is lending the banks another 100 billion. What sort of idiot economist, banker or politician thinks that huge debts can be dealt with by creating more debts? It's sheer lunacy. The lunatics have taken over the banks. (The Irish banks owe money to banks all over Europe. If the Irish banks go under then a hundred fat bankers all over euroland will each have to sell the wife's second Ferrari and no civilised eurostate can possibly allow that.) The result will, of course, be that the Irish banks, which couldn't pay back the 500 billion they owed will now owe 600 billion. To make things easier for everyone the Irish have apparently agreed to lend themselves 17.5 billion to help get themselves out of the hole they've got themselves into. (I didn't make that up. No one could make that up.) I don't know whether this is pounds, euros or potatoes but it really doesn't matter very much. It could be Zimbabwean dollars or even glass beads. A five-year-old with a rudimentary understanding of pocket money logic would be able to tell the idiots doing the lending that someone who can't pay back 500 billion won't be able to pay back 600 billion. But this is called a 'solution' and the politicians expect us to be pleased with them for sorting things out so cleverly.

Osborne is handing the Irish container loads of loot gouged out of British taxpayers because the two useless Scottish banks (RBS and HBOS) stand to go even more bankrupt than they are already if the Irish loans are written off. The figure changes daily. It started that we were lending them about £6 billion, moved quietly up to £9 billion and, the last I saw of it, had soared majestically up to £13 billion. What does Osborne know about billions? What does anyone in Government know about billions? The fact is that we are giving Ireland vastly more than Osborne saved in the Government's much publicised spending review. So Britain's finances are now in a worse state than they were when Gordon the Moron was finally gouged out of office. And to make things worse we are still giving vast amounts of money to China and India, the two fastest growing economies in the world. British taxpayers donate £1 billion a year in aid to India. Has no one in the Government yet noticed that India has nuclear weapons, a space programme and its own international aid programme? We're broke. Why are we giving them money?

Incidentally, I wonder how many people know that Britain exports more to Ireland than to China, Brazil, Russia and India combined. That says more about Britain's export success than about Ireland.

As my long standing prediction about the collapse of the euro (and then the EU) comes true some newspapers (such as the *Economist*) seem incensed by the eurosceptics' joy at the euro's troubles. What the *Economist* doesn't understand is that the collapse of the euro is the best and quickest way for Britain to regain its lost sovereignty and independence. But then, perhaps that isn't something the *Economist* cares much about.

17
11.11 a.m.
One of the most wasteful absurdities of house buying is that every potential buyer has to arrange, and pay for, his or her own survey. Today, we received a survey on a house we visited two weeks ago. We made an offer which was accepted and we are very excited. The Princess opened the surveyor's report with trembling fingers and we read it together.

It would save so much time and money if vendors had a fairly short and simple survey done before offering their home for sale. The survey, done by an independent surveyor, would provide basic information about plumbing, electricity, roof and central heating; it would confirm that these things passed simple basic standards and would certify that the building was free of woodworm and dry rot. The survey would be backed by an insurance company and could then be handed to every prospective buyer. It would save time and money and be better for everyone except surveyors. Copies of the survey could be sold to prospective buyers for say £100. If the house was viewed by a number of prospective purchasers the sellers would eventually cover their costs and buyers would be saved the cost of buying full surveys themselves.

The present system is lunatic. All buyers commission their own survey and vast amounts of money, time and energy are wasted. It is apparently illegal (or, at least, considered so) for one buyer to pass his survey to another. I have known people who have commissioned surveys on five or six houses. By that time most of their deposit money had been spent on surveyors and solicitors. (Actually, it is not surprising that many people walk away from a purchase when they see a full structural survey. Much of a survey is simple observation. `The main walls are of brick and the roof is pitched and covered with slate.' It's the sort of things a child of four would notice. `The house is detached and on such and such a road. It benefits from the provision of gas and electricity.' But the rest of the stuff can be profoundly depressing. No house sounds good when its foibles and frailties are assessed by a professional. And then there are the let-out clauses. `We could not check unexposed or inaccessible parts of the building and have not checked for the presence of hazardous materials in the building.')

The survey we had commissioned made gloomy reading. The house has rotten roof timbers. It has woodworm infestation. The roof is not felted. The loft is not lagged. The window frames need replacing. The house needs rewiring and replumbing. The central heating boiler needs replacing. The floors need to be taken up and replaced. The walls are damp. The glass in the conservatory is plain glass and needs to be replaced with safety glass. The drains are blocked. The water supply is uncertain. The boundaries with two neighbours seem blurred. The roots of a large tree which is close to the house have penetrated the drains and the foundations. It would take a year to put all this right. And cost a fortune. Builders, electricians, plumbers, carpenters, plasterers, glaziers and tree surgeons are all needed. We would be living with builders for a generation. It is a good-looking house but we have enough problems in our lives. We rang our solicitor and the estate agents and backed out as gracefully as we could.

15.25 p.m.

Old people living in their own homes and relying on income from their savings are the new poor. Their interest and dividend income has crashed in recent years and their investments are, on average, worth no more today than they were a decade ago. But because they have worked hard and saved and paid off their mortgages many are not entitled to any benefits. Those who have never worked and never saved are well-looked after by the State. Those who have worked hard, saved and done all the right things are the new poor. Countless thousands are living in penury; unable to afford even the smallest luxury; eking out a miserable existence, often hungry and, in winter, frequently cold.

20.34 p.m.
Kurt Vonnegut argued that reading and writing are in themselves subversive acts because they question the idea that things have to be the way they are, and they question the idea that you are alone, thinking the way you do. The reader is told, argued Vonnegut, that things are more open to questioning than you thought they were, and here it is in black and white. He was right, of course. All great ideas are dangerous because they challenge the status quo, threaten the stability of the establishment and (this worst of all) make people think. I am delighted to say that many years ago, at the start of what might laughingly be called my career, I was fired from a local paper (the *Coventry Evening Telegraph*) which was carrying a syndicated column of mine. I was told by an editor that my trouble was that `I made people think'. Since then I have, I think, been fired by over 40 papers for making people think and upsetting the establishment. On many occasions I have been replaced by a writer employed by the Government, a local authority of a drug company - and offering his services free of charge. I once told The Princess that I would like that (or something like it) on my tombstone. `He made people think.'

18
12.08 p.m.
The Princess has discovered some small but powerful wind up torches. They are excellent; brilliant (in both senses). We have bought a dozen because these are so good that they will doubtless soon be banned. (Lobbyists for the battery industry will produce

evidence showing that they are responsible for causing a case of repetitive strain injury in a six-year-old Greek girl.) Inevitably some brands are better than others. We bought two on Amazon which were broken when they arrived. I doubt if they would ever have worked properly. One of them came in a box which was well worth the purchase price. Here is the blurb from the back of the box: 'Generate electricity the function elucidation of flashlight. Product Characteristics: 1. This product is a new science and technology product and made with high and new science and technology. It can illuminate only placing it in rhythm. 2. No need any power no environmental pollution. Low noise and health. Comparing with common torch, it can be several times on lift. 3. Con stantly using this health torch, it can benefit to your palm, arm and shoulder stretching and blood circulation, so as to let your hands relax and brain clever, hand and brain coor dinate and promote your brain memory and health composition.'

12.16 p.m.
A street light is out and so we sit in a well-lit pool in a field of darkness. I telephoned the council and told an employee in the Department of Street Lighting that drunks might well wander into the road and get run over because of the absence of any light. 'It really won't look good if someone dies because the council couldn't be bothered to change a light bulb,' I said, using my old trick of forcing responsibility onto bureaucrats.

17.19 p.m.
We went to Prinknash in Gloucestershire for an auction. To get there we had to travel along a narrow, winding country road. The road had been dug up and there was a large sign saying: 'Access for residents only. No turning, no reversing, no parking.' So we carried on.

When we arrived we fed the goats and then went in to see what we could bid for. Sadly, much of the good stuff seemed to go to buyers bidding by Internet. This business of allowing bidders to put in bids through the Internet is ruining auctions. It's undoubtedly great for auctioneers, and vendors, but sitting in the auction room while someone in China bids against someone in Pennsylvania isn't a lot of fun. This is another way of life that has been ruined by the

Internet. Traders, small shopkeepers and small town dealers can no longer make a living because big city dealers and collectors around the world can pick and choose from what is available. Auctioneers are of course putting themselves out of business because eventually vendors will do everything on the Internet and save the vast commissions auction houses now demand.

We bought some old ancestors to hang on the walls. We're going to devise strange and wonderful histories for them.

19.50 p.m.

As we drove up to Prinknash (and back) I spent much of the day trying to work out how to plan our new publishing business.

The world is now divided into three roughly equal parts: the shirkers (the ones who deliberately avoid work and who live on benefits of one sort or another), the bureaucrats (the rule makers and enforcers) and the rest of us.

Today, the weight of a huge, intolerant and committed bureaucracy lies behind every order and every form. Every institutional demand, however meaningless and trivial, pointless and wrong-headed in concept, is carved in stone and delivered by truck. There is never room for dissent, discussion or such old-fashioned luxuries as logic and common sense. (Common sense, the most undervalued human quality, and one which has almost vanished, is of course merely applied intelligence. But it is now rarer than mares' nests or hens' teeth.)

I spend far too little time doing what I want to do, or doing what I think I do best. I spend far too much of my life on administrative duties, doing what I have to do if I am to avoid getting into serious trouble. When Publishing House was at its height I employed 15 people. It worked well, I think. But the weight of the bureaucracy ground me down. And as the new rules pour out of Brussels I know that I will never again employ anyone.

There is, unbelievably, a mass of new employment legislation coming into being in the next year or two. Agency workers are to be given the same pay as permanent staff. Staff will have the right to demand time off work for training. Employees will have to be provided with a pension. It is already illegal to ask medical or quasi-medical questions on an application form (so, presumably, it is illegal for people hiring steeplejacks to know whether prospective staff members suffer from fits or diabetes). Anyone who is associated with, or related to someone who is disabled must be given the same rights that they would have if they were disabled themselves. And, of course, the maternity and paternity rights of parents are growing at such a pace that I quite expect couples to be soon given days off work so that they go away and procreate. Indeed, it would not surprise me in the slightest. Why, I can hear the Liberal Democrats demanding, should parents-to-be be denied the chance to create their child at a time of their choice? Why should the employed be denied the joy of afternoon nookie so that they can be exploited by evil, capitalist ironmongers?

The lunacy that is the employment tribunal seems to get worse with each new day. (Staff can sue employees for the most bizarre non-happenings and can be awarded unlimited damages. It is even possible for staff to claim they have been harassed and offended by things they haven't actually seen or heard.) New laws coming in over the next year or two will cost British businesses around £25 billion. Many businesses, particularly small ones, simply won't survive. All this legislation is fine when applied to the bureaucrats in Brussels, London or the local town hall. They don't do any work. They don't have any responsibilities. Everyone benefits when they have time off to shop for baby clothes. But in the real world this constant tinkering with the legislation (most of it then gold-plated by British politicians who have absolutely no experience of the real world) will sound the death knell for entrepreneurs and small businesses. The EU, which is responsible for this barrage of nonsense, believes that businesses should be run for the sake of the employees. You can't run a business that way. The priorities have to be producing something that people want and then making a profit. If a business doesn't do those two things then it won't survive. The problem, of course, is that the vast majority of bureaucrats and politicians have never run a business and so know absolutely nothing about how businesses work. As far as they are concerned the word 'profit' is up there with 'paedophile'.

It is wearing to argue with or to try to fight bureaucrats. There are so many of them and they have unending time and money (our money).

And so, as I restructure Publishing House, and plan for the future, I do so knowing that however it is organised we will not employ anyone again. Everything will be outsourced so that someone else can deal with the latest bits and pieces of employment legislation.

21.34 p.m.

The Government claims that the redundant public sector workers will be hired by private companies hoping to expand. This is laughable nonsense. For one thing very few private companies are going to be hiring for the next few years. And for another, very few private companies will want to hire former civil servants who have been made redundant. The reason is simple: the majority of public sector workers are lazy and incompetent. They have been mollycoddled for so long that they don't know what work is. They're used to huge salaries, vast bonuses, exceptional pension rights (which are, of course, all part of an enormous taxpayer scammed Ponzi scheme), long holidays, short days and as much sick time as they like to take. No company wanting to make a profit is going to hire former civil servants.

23.46 p.m.

I have just noticed that the street light has been repaired. The drunks can now stagger home in safety. And the council staff can sleep comfortably.

19

11.01 a.m.

It is bitterly cold and pouring with rain. We drive past a field in which there are lambs, no more than a few days old. The Princess points to them. I look at her and see that there are tears in her eyes. Neither of us speaks. The lambs will live and die in the cold and wet. They will know no sunshine. How can you gambol in the rain? They just stand there and shiver. These lambs are brought into the world at the behest of greedy farmers who are the same oafish beasts, sanctimonious louts, who will complain when their animals are killed because of a foot and mouth scare. The same money-hungry, inconsiderate bastards who crowd their animals into fields which are too small and who fail to provide any sort of shelter for animals who hate getting wet. We remain silent and in mourning for another 20 miles or so. The rain never stops. If anything it gets harder. We cannot either of us forget that we are warm and dry, comforted by heated seats and an efficient heating system. The lambs will shiver until they die or are big enough to be slaughtered and put onto the menu at some fancy restaurant as out of season lamb.

14.19 p.m.
I bought a DVD of Citizen Kane. On the back of the box there is a promotional blurb which reads: 'If you like Citizen Kane you'll like Spartacus.' Hmm. That's a bit like saying: 'If you like strawberry jam you'll love cheese.'

16.10 p.m.
The Princess has discovered that we lose less parcels if we write 'Contents: Books' on the outside. This is presumably because the thieves who work for Royal Mail don't read books.

17.04 p.m.
As we drive home we sing absurd songs based around the towns and villages we pass. The villages are lit only by the lantern soft light of weak moonbeams and all look quite beautiful. It is extremely difficult to find rhymes for English place names. Suddenly, The Princess changed the subject. `I've been thinking,' she said, `and I've decided that real wealth should be measured not in money but in love. The really wealthy people are those who receive lots of love from the people around them or who have received lots of love from loved-ones who have passed on. The real poor are those who remain unloved. To be genuine, and of real value, the love has to be given freely and unconditionally. And to be of the very best quality it has to be reciprocated.' She is, as usual, absolutely right.

20.56 p.m.
I saw a letter in a paper today from someone who claimed to represent a non-profit organisation. As always the letter writer managed to make this sound as though it put her above the rest of us. But who pays for the electricity, the heating, the rent, the

property taxes, the stamps, the staff and so on? Someone must do. And if someone is paying for all these things and not making a profit then they must have an agenda. They must be lobbying for some cause or some industry. They are in the 'manipulation' business. I'm a For Profit Organisation and proud of it.

20
11.06 a.m.
A reader has sent me a copy of his book arguing that the earth is flat. It looks frighteningly convincing.

14.24 p.m.
I am now abandoning the link to my webshop through Amazon. There is no point in my buying advertisements for books and then sending readers to a webshop run through Amazon when there are always going to be tons of people selling my books at a fraction of the proper price. The problem is that review copies and second-hand copies are now too easily available through webshops such as Amazon. Books of mine have been made available on Amazon before being officially put on sale. We sent out review copies of my book 101 Things I Have Learned to just seven national newspapers. There were no reviews but six of the books were on sale on Amazon within two days. I know it was the review copies that were being sold because the rest of the print run was still sitting in Publishing House. Even the people who work for publishing companies are making a few extra pennies this way. When Mr Henry Mulligan came in from the printers we sent copies to a number of paperback houses (offering paperback rights). Within days of being sent out most of the books were being sold on Amazon for less than the printing costs. I suspect that the people selling the book had not even bothered to read it before selling it. To make matters worse Amazon was listing the book as unavailable. So any potential buyer who wanted to order the book had to order one of the review copies.

The Web is a wonderful way to buy out of print books. But Amazon and similar sites are destroying backlist sales, and backlist sales are an important part of an author's income (and a vital part of the income of a small publisher).

19.01 p.m.

Television viewers are apparently obsessed with a third rate programme called the X-Factor in which the embarrassingly untalented judge the egregiously talentless. I caught half of an X-Factor programme recently and came to the conclusion that it is a vehicle for talentless oafs. The contestants are no better.

21

10.54 a.m.

I am not in the slightest bit surprised to read today that in the 18th century it was believed that the commonest cause of madness was moving into a new home. I firmly believe that the professionals (the estate agents, conveyancing solicitors and so on) are almost entirely responsible for the stress that is caused by moving home.

Estate agents may have a superficial charm but they also have a reputation for being lying, cheating crooks. On the whole, this is entirely fair. No trades people are as consistently, deliberately crooked as estate agents. They have turned deception into an art form and their determination to sell daydreams rather than reality turn what should be an exciting, enjoyable venture into a nightmare. With estate agents you have to learn to read between the lines that aren't there. Not even garages and car dealers can match estate agents. They lie, and then lie again and lie so much that, like politicians, it seems that they no longer recognise the truth. We have seen bedrooms so small that, with the addition of a little plumbing, they could have been turned into toilets for thin people. We have seen garages so narrow that they would be suitable only for racing bicycles with narrow handlebars. We have seen houses, advertised as 'needing some modernisation', which needed knocking down and rebuilding but which were being advertised at the sort of price a buyer might expect to pay for a house in perfect condition. We have visited houses 'requiring some attention' which had rooms we couldn't enter because the stairs or floorboards weren't safe. Estate agents are brilliant at taking photographs which flatter and deceive. Only an estate agent can take photographs of a house sandwiched in between an abattoir and an incinerator plant and make it look as though it is situated right in the heart of the New Forest. Even the text on their brochures is misleading. They hide the fact that the home they are offering for sale is merely a wing of the house pictured on the front of the brochure. Do they really think no one will notice that there's a public footpath through the garden? Reading their brochures becomes an exercise in code reading. We saw one brochure which boasted that the gas fired AGA supplied radiators in all the bathrooms. It wasn't a big move to guess that there weren't any radiators in other parts of the house. Not without good reason do they cover themselves by printing a disclaimer at the end of everything they write. They can't even give decent directions. We received a brochure earlier this week which included the following classic: 'turn left a quarter of a mile before you get to the church'. They sell frustration and disappointment as much as they sell houses. Does their craftiness pay off? Or are they simply so corrupt that they just behave this way naturally? Is deceit their default condition, as it is with politicians? Having discovered the Internet, and e-mail, they send out everything they have to everyone on their list. It costs very little to do this and so they batter prospective buyers with a veritable storm of wildly inappropriate properties.

The Princess has got into the habit of saying to estate agents: 'What's the snag?'

'There is no snag,' they all claim, seemingly offended.

The Princess says nothing for a moment or two and allows the silence to hang in the air. And then the truth pokes its head above the parapet. 'Well, it's next to the recycling centre, but these things are essential for the climate and if you close the windows you hardly notice that it's there. You could put in air-conditioning for the summer months. I can get you a deal on that.'

And their optimism is endless. They are always thinking of ways in which a house can be altered and improved. They never do anything to interfere with their flights of fancy. We looked round one house that had just one very tiny bathroom. 'You could easily turn the master bedroom's dressing room into an additional bathroom,' said one agent of deceit, with a glorious lip-gloss smile. Yes, well, popping in a bath, a lavatory and a basin wouldn't be too difficult. But there was no plumbing or drainage on that side of the house and so to make the bathroom fittings work the mains drains and mains water supply would all have to be diverted. It would have involved digging a huge trench right underneath the house.

The estate agents we see are forever forecasting a rise in house prices. 'We're professionals, we see what is happening, we know that prices are going to soar in a couple of months time.' They're always going up. Never stagnating. Never, ever going down. This unbridled optimism is invariably picked up by the national press who want to please their readers by giving them good news. (House owners are in a majority in Britain so house price rises are regarded in editorial offices as a Good Thing). It is, of course, utterly bizarre that anyone takes any notice of what estate agents say about house prices. Their commission depends upon their pushing up the price of the commodity they are selling. During the boom years, when they made fortunes, they acquired an arrogance which they are finding it difficult to lose now that business is gloomy.

If they listed the upside and the downside for every property they sold they would make life fairer, better and easier for both vendors and buyers. But it would go against the religion of deceit.

'Why don't you tell people about the gasworks/school/incinerator next door?' The Princess asked one estate agent.

'Because people wouldn't go to look at the house if we did!' came back the immediate reply. He didn't seem to realise that if people didn't want to buy the house if they knew what was next door they wouldn't want to buy it when they arrived and had a nasty surprise. Estate agents always want to delay the bad news for as long as possible. They hope that they will wear people down and that their customers will eventually buy just to bring the whole painful process to a temporary end.

The Princess suggests that we should write and publish a *House Buyer's Secret Guide* to explain how to 'read' estate agents and understand their jargon and deceit. It seems a good idea.

17.19 p.m.

In this week's copy of the investment magazine *Investors Chronicle* two writers comment on life expectancy. One tells me that, according to actuaries, a 65-year-old man should live until he is about 88. A few pages further on another tells me that according to the Government Actuary's Department, a man living in the UK who has reached 65 years and is in good or fairly good health is expected to live another 12.9 years.

19.48 p.m.

My book *Oil Apocalypse* has sold over 10,000 copies but the most recent print run is disappearing and I don't think I'll bother printing any more. I don't think the book has been reviewed anywhere though it has been savaged on the Internet by people who didn't bother to read it. `I read part of your book *Oil Apocalypse*,' a reporter for *The Independent* newspaper told me in the nearest thing it came to a review. `But it frightened me so much I couldn't read the rest.' On reflection, I should have charged £10,000 a copy and sold the book as a confidential report. It is no exaggeration to say that the financial advice it contained would have been dirt cheap at that price. It is painful to see the predictions coming true. It is annoying to see other writers coming up with similar predictions (a year or two later) and busily taking all the credit. But at least I took the financial advice I gave in the book. I just wish the Government would start planning for the end of the oil. We need to start building nuclear power stations yesterday. And it would be wise to start re-opening our network of canals. When the oil becomes rare and expensive moving goods about the country by canal will be the preferred way.

22

11.08 a.m.

We took five black bags full of books to a local charity shop. That's 17 bagfuls in the last two weeks. It took a huge effort to part with these books but there is no sign in the house that any books have disappeared. In an attempt to deal with the problem, I purchased only three new books today. This is a new low for me. I was feeling proud of myself. When The Princess came back from the shops she proudly showed me the four new books she had bought. We are not going to win the battle against the books like this.

12.42 p.m.

I have discovered that everyone else in the locality has two green recycling bins we have one. I e-mailed the local council (I could not bear to spend three hours trying to telephone them) and asked for another. They replied telling me that they will send me another but it will take six weeks to deliver it. Six weeks to deliver a small plastic container. Only a public body could get away with this. They must be hand-carved in Guatemala and then brought over by Ellen McCarthy. Six weeks to transport a piece of plastic around two miles. That's 3,520 yards in 1,008 hours. That works out at 10.47 feet per hour. A snail could travel faster - carrying not just a green plastic recycling bin but its whole house. This sounds silly but I happen to know that a snail can travel at around two and a half inches a minute. So in an hour it could travel 150 inches or 12½ feet. So a snail really can move its whole damned house considerably faster than my local council can move a green recycling bin.

17.13 p.m.

Time magazine has an interview with someone called Judd Apatow, a film director whose comment on piracy is: 'It doesn't (bother me) because I can't be the guy who's like Scrooge: 'I must get every nickel of this'. Maybe a lot of people wouldn't watch a movie or listen to music if it weren't free'. Something tells me that Mr Apatow has never yet funded one of his own films. And I may be wrong but I wonder if he perhaps receives a fee for directing films, rather than being dependant on royalties resulting from their sale?

Rupert Murdoch recently announced that 'content is not just king, it is the emperor of all things electronic'. Well, it is as long as people don't just steal it and get away with it.

Most people who run websites don't seem to think that taking words is stealing. They think that owning copyright is old-fashioned. There have always been magazines and publishers around the world who helped themselves to copy. I've had scores of articles and book chapters stolen. But on the Internet thieving is the way things work. Articles are reprinted and if the author receives a mention he is supposed to feel grateful.

The new attitude to copyright has spread into the paper world. I have seen several copies of my books reproduced in two foreign languages without my permission. My name is on the covers but I haven't received a penny in royalties. Nor was I sent any copies of the books. I have no idea how many other books of mine have been stolen this way but I do know that it is now impossible for me to sell my books in those countries.

One critic recently complained that not allowing my books to be distributed free of charge on the Web is akin to refusing to allow my books to be put into libraries or bibliographies. This is nonsense. Apart from the select few libraries which demand free copies of all new books most libraries pay for the books they put on their shelves. And authors receive a small sum when their books are borrowed.

And I'm always honoured to see my books in bibliographies - which do, after all, encourage readers to purchase books. The Web, in contrast, just results in authors being impoverished.

What particularly annoys me is that Internet companies take my copyright (amidst a great deal of baloney about copyright being theft) but then gather together every tiny bit of information they can, guard it jealously and sell it to advertisers. There is no freedom on the Web. Enter your details onto one website and the owners of that website use your information, own your information and sell your information. And, of course, an increasing number of computer companies have stopped selling their work on a disk. They now sell software, which costs them nothing to produce because it has to be downloaded, with a single use licence. You buy one off rights. If you upgrade your computer (or replace it because it has broken down) you have to buy the software again.

20.09 p.m.

I received a letter from an 82-year-old man who has cancer of the bile duct. He wants me to recommend treatment. He is losing weight and visiting an alternative therapist. He has refused chemotherapy. I wrote back saying: `I was so sorry to receive your letter and hear your news. I really do wish I could think of something helpful to say but, as always, I find it impossible to offer specific clinical advice through the post. The problem is simply that all patients vary (even though their problems may be similar) and offering any sort of advice on the basis of a letter would be presumptuous of me and, I fear, dangerous too. I do believe strongly in holistic medicine - taking the best from orthodox and alternative medicine. There are many, many options.

I don't think either orthodox or alternative practitioners have all the answers (whatever the problem). My best suggestion is that you talk to your GP about all the possible ways of improving your health. Hopefully he will be able to help you take advantage of everything available. Meanwhile, please accept my very best wishes for a speedy recovery.' I felt utterly helpless and useless. What else can I do?

23
11.04 a.m.
A wholesaler e-mails, with some urgency, to ask if we have stock of *Alice's Diary* and *Alice's Adventures*. I e-mail back to say `yes, we have thousands of both books in stock'. I hear no more. Another wholesaler sends an e-mail to tell me that it is not their policy to send cheques for the books they buy. I tell them it is not my policy to send out books that have not been paid for. I think they might have noticed that we have a stalemate. I do not expect them to soften their attitude and to start sending me cheques. After all, they have a policy. But I do not intend to soften my attitude. I have a policy too. In future my books will only be available to people who send their name and address and a cheque or a postal order.

15.06 p.m.
My new Polish publisher has sent me, by e-mail, a photograph of the cheque he is sending to buy Polish rights in *How To Stop Your Doctor Killing You*. It's the first time I've ever had a photograph of a cheque sent to me. I hope the cheque arrives in due course.

17.08 p.m.
We met a friend of The Princess's whom she hadn't seen since we married. We had a coffee together. He talked for an hour and a half about himself. He explained how he had become interested in other people and was going to study psychology and become a social worker. At the end of the hour and a half The Princess's friend said: `Well that's it, there isn't anything else to talk about.' He stood up, we shook hands, he left, I paid the bill. He did not ask one question about The Princess or her life.

17.18 p.m.

I believed in global warming when it was opposed by several large and powerful industries. But now that the Big Money supports the idea of man-made global warming it seems clear that it is bound to be a fraudulent notion. The Big Money is always wrong and corrupting.

18.59 p.m.

After we had coffee with The Princess's friend earlier today I bought an old brass toasting fork in a junk shop. I tried it out this evening. It has an extendable handle which enabled me to make toast without burning my fingers. Why does toast made in front of a fire with a toasting fork taste so much better than toast made in a toaster? The two pieces of toast I made were both burnt and both had bits of soot on them, in addition to having three damned great holes where the prongs of the brass toasting fork had pierced the bread. But they tasted wonderful.

23.04 p.m.

This evening I saw The Princess standing on the right hand side of the weighing scales. She was leaning over further than the tower at Piza. `What on earth are you doing?' I asked her. `I've discovered that I weigh two pounds less if I do this,' she said. `And now that I've started doing it I have to keep doing it or else I'll suddenly think I've put on two pounds.'

23.54 p.m.

Now that we are changing the business The Princess and I have decided to change the prices we charge. Everyone in publishing (as in just about all other businesses) agrees that the left digit effect is vital in pricing. So, a book priced at £4.99 will sell better than a book priced at £5. It may seem silly but it is important. Research from Indiana University in the USA has shown that traders in shares are just as irrational. The researchers analysed 100 million trades made on NASDAQ and divided them according to their price point. They discovered that share traders succumb to the power of clever pricing with the result that buy orders outnumbered sell orders to the greatest extent at prices ending in 0.99. They also discovered that sales outweighed buys at prices ending in 0.01. The research also showed that the effect is greatest when the penny brings down the leftmost digit. In other words going from £20 to £19.99 makes more difference than going from £19 to £18.99. (The explanation is presumably that most of us read numbers from left to right.)

The Princess and I have decided that since we do everything else the wrong way we will now do our pricing the wrong way too. Since we have pretty well decided to give up on bookshops (whether sitting on the High Street or wandering around in the ether somewhere) we no longer have to stick to the normal pricing systems. So we are going to sell books at nice even prices. And we're going to try to include the postage and packing charge in with the book price. This should please the small but determined coterie of readers who constantly write and chide me for charging prices that have '99 pence' at the end. Annoyingly, existing books will have to stick with their pricing for a while. If I suddenly change prices to get rid of the '99' pences then there will be chaos because of the number of catalogues still being used. Still, we will be making a move in the right direction.

We did try this sort of pricing with my last book *2020* and it seemed to work well. We charged £20 as long as the order came in within a week or two of the offer being posted out. And we didn't add on any charge towards the cost of postage and packing.

In order to make the offer even more attractive we put the cover price quite high, at £50. Only with the cover price this high could we afford to offer a big discount to readers who ordered quickly.

This system gave us a big unexpected advantage.

When bookshops and wholesalers order books they routinely expect to be given a 45% discount. And we have to pay the cost of posting the books to them. If we charge a high cover price then the discount and postage costs won't hurt us so badly. So, for example, with a £50 cover price the discount and the postage costs will mean that when we sell a book through a bookshop we will make the same sort of return as when we sell a book to a private customer who has ordered directly at the discounted price. I don't see why we should always make considerably less money when selling through a bookshop than we do when selling direct. This also means that webshops like Amazon which offer huge discounts will no longer be able to beat us on price. And since we are no longer going to send out review copies, or copies to other publishers or bookshops, the availability of 'second-hand' books being sold below our price will be dramatically reduced.

24
11.10 a.m.

I read *The Times* on the train to London. It's the only time I ever read it and I can see why they give it away free to travellers. It's a good example of why people in Britain don't read newspapers much any more. (They don't read them much abroad either. In Paris there used to be half a dozen shops within half a mile of our apartment selling a huge variety of newspapers and magazines. Today there are two.) There were five pages on the Ashes series starting in Australia but I could find no mention anywhere of the players involved or the likely teams. The five pages were just fluff, colour, poorly written opinions. I couldn't find any facts, though cricket is a sport which is built upon statistics. People don't buy or read newspapers much any more and most of those who do will not pay for the Internet versions (You can't even light a fire with an Internet newspaper). The result will be that most people won't see any news at all. (Television doesn't 'do' news. It does entertainment.) I dumped the paper and read Nimrod's magnificent book *The Life of John Mytton*. (Nimrod was a penname used by Charles James Apperley, a well-known sporting writer of the times). I have been a fan of Mytton for years and he is included at some length in *England's Glory*, the book I wrote this year with The Princess. Nimrod admits that he wrote the book after Mytton's death to put the record straight and to tell the world that Mytton was not a bad man but was, on the contrary, merely a madman and a drunkard. Fair enough. Mytton was expelled from Westminster and Harrow and knocked down his private tutor. He went to Oxford but left after a day. When he was elected an MP he spent just half an hour in the House of Commons before leaving for good. Nimrod's stories are wonderful. 'He scarcely ever thrashed a man that he did not give him something afterwards as amends,' says Nimrod. Mytton wasn't always so generous however. He expected tradesmen to know their place. When a tradesman in Shrewsbury ventured to call him 'Johnny', Mytton floored the man on the spot. Incidentally, Mytton, like all huntsmen imported foxes to hunt but he did have the decency (unlike today's brood of fox-slaughters) to admit this. One thing I learned from Nimrod was that Mytton was very fond of his children. He apparently showed this by suddenly shouting hunting cries into their ears and by throwing oranges at their heads.

At St Pancras the French customs man studied my passport but didn't bother to look up at me at all. A wonderful old lady in a very smart blue dress was having a hard time with two security employees who were trying to hurry her along. 'I realise you have important work to do, young man,' she said, refusing to be bullied. 'But there is no reason not to perform your work with courtesy and patience.'

We had vegan food on Eurostar and once again it was infinitely better than the vegetarian food they serve. Vegetables and fruit and half-decent bread are much better while travelling than the awful cheese smothered pasta they serve up. The wine is now utterly undrinkable and they seem to have stopped serving champagne (which was acceptable). The coffee has become undrinkable too.

While on the Eurostar train I made a list of ten more things I have learned.

1. People who say they are never frightened are also never brave.

2. The money we use for buying stuff online isn't the same as real money. It is very easy to spend a small fortune on books, just merrily clicking away.

3. When walking downhill lean forward rather than backward. It feels wrong but if you lean back your weight all goes onto your heels and before you know you'll be on your bottom.

4. Never trust a man who wears a ready-made bow tie. If he cheats with his bow tie he will cheat at everything else.

5. Never give advice to friends however much they tell you they will not hold things against you if the advice turns bad.

6. Always tip generously unless the service is bad. But if you intend to go back to the same place always overtip outrageously.

7. Don't sign for registered letters unless you already know what they contain.

8. Don't answer the phone or the door unless you know who it is and you are expecting them.

9. Don't mess with someone who has nothing to lose or who is fighting for something on principle.

10. Don't invest in anything described as `safe'. When I was young I put money into an Equitable Life pension. That largely disappeared through incompetence but Government regulators allowed it to happen so they are responsible. I may receive 22% of my `lost' money in compensation. A little later I invested money in Railtrack, which seemed a solid, blue chip company. That was stolen by the Government. Then there was my investment in Zero Dividend Preference Shares. Again that disappeared because of a mixture of crookery and official incompetence. I received a modest sum in compensation and was forced to pay 40% capital gains tax on it. And then I was foolish enough to put money into Permanent Interest Bearing Shares issued by Bradford & Bingley; as safe and as boring an investment as could be found at the time. The Government took control and is refusing to pay any interest so the shares are virtually worthless.

In Paris, for the second time in succession, we hired a shy and polite Parisian taxi driver. He gave way to everyone and drove so slowly that I wondered if he was ill. He even asked if we minded him having the radio on. He drove so slowly through Paris that we had a chance to do some window shopping on the way. Galeries Lafayette was decorated for Christmas and had a huge display of lights designed to make it look like Notre Dame.

18.27 p.m.

One of the perks of travelling first class on Eurostar is that there's a varied selection of free magazines to choose from at the end of each carriage. I picked up a free copy of the *New Statesman* on Eurostar today. It's an odd little magazine, every bit as twee as *The Lady*, *The Spectator*, *Country Life* and the *Economist*. They are all of them little more than cult newsletters, catering to their own peculiar tribes of prejudiced and bigoted zealots. Apart from the usual barely coherent rubbish the copy I picked up included a supplement entitled *The People's NHS?* The supplement was published `in collaboration with Pfizer'. Now, Pfizer is of course an international pharmaceutical company. Strange bedfellows. I wonder if anyone at the *New Statesman* knows enough about drug companies to have asked themselves why one of them should agree to help pay for a *New Statesman* publication. The back of the supplement explained that Pfizer and the *New Statesman* aimed to bring together leading opinion-formers to explore a range of health issues relevant to policymakers and the electorate alike (are there any health issues not relevant to both?).

We are told that Pfizer sponsors these events and collaborates with the *New Statesman* to determine the discussion topics. I bet it does. There's a bit of text telling readers that the *New Statesman* has sole editorial responsibility for the content of the supplement. Oh how sweet that is. Dare I point out that one of the contributors just happens to be a senior director of Pfizer. What an amazing coincidence that is. If anyone at the *New Statesman* is interested here's the bottom line: Pfizer sponsors the *New Statesman* events (and helps choose the discussion topics) because the drug companies love the NHS more than even the leftist leftie does. Drug companies adore the NHS. It is a cash cow of unprecedented size. Always giving. It is the golden cow that lays an endless row of golden eggs. And I don't mind betting that this merry duo of Pfizer and the *New Statesman* never produce anything questioning the whole existence of the NHS, or the dangers produced by modern drugs or questioning the value of vaccination or vivisection. Drug companies are everywhere these days. It is impossible for two doctors to meet, or a politician and a doctor to discuss health matters or, it seems, a left-wing magazine to produce a supplement without a drug company being involved (and usually paying for the smart lunch or dinner afterwards).

25
08.01 a.m.
We were woken at 7.00 a.m. by workmen doing something at the Embassy across the road. Workmen who are doing things at 7.00 a.m. always do it as noisily as possible. They are, presumably, indignant that the rest of the world should still be asleep. I know that 7.00 a.m. exists. When I was a doctor it was the time when I decided that it wasn't worth going to bed. But these days I think of 7.00 a.m. as the preserve of those pushy businessmen who spend an hour in the gym before heading off to pre-breakfast meetings with their accountants and legal advisors. We put on a CD of Don Williams hoping that his syrupy smooth voice would drown out the

banging and shouting and help us sleep. It didn't work. We found earplugs and tossed and turned in that strange time between sleep and wakefulness.

11.39 a.m.

The electricity and gas companies have been again to read the meters. We missed them again. They do this every month or two, always leaving a note to tell us that they have a legal right to inspect their meters at regular intervals. I rang the number they gave to arrange another appointment but it was, of course, a number that led me into a flow chart of options. I managed to find my way past the first two options but I simply could not understand the third option. Whatever it is they wanted I failed and I was ejected from the system so that I had to go back to the beginning again. Part of the damned system was voice operated. I was expected to give specific words in response to the questions they asked. I told them my name was Sarcozy but it didn't make any difference. I tried pretending to be General de Gaulle come back from the dead with an Australian accent. Nothing worked. It was like a nightmare. Actually, no, it was like one of those damned computer games that takes players from one level to the next. If you get stuck at one level then you stay there, never progressing. Things aren't much different in Britain, of course. The language is English but there's no one to speak to. Ring a government department or utility and work your way through the `press one, press two' sequences and you might end up speaking to a real, live person. But the chances of them being able to provide the answers you need are slim. And the chances of the answers they provide being accurate or reliable are even slimmer.

There are also problems with France Telecom. When we were here last I discovered that one of our phone lines wasn't working. Since we don't really need two lines I thought it would be easier to ask them to cancel the faulty one. But they have, of course, also cancelled the direct debit with which I paid the phone bills so now I have to set up a new one. If there is a way for a utility company (or government department) to screw up they will find it. I should not complain. This is the basic principle of an investment strategy which has over the last decade or so proved extremely profitable. I ring up and set up a new direct debit. But although the woman I speak to tells me that I don't need to write a cheque I decide that I will. I'd rather pay twice then have to go through all the drama of reconnecting a line because it hasn't been paid.

Our building has had new mailboxes fitted. Due to a stroke of luck they are fitted today so we find the key to the new box inside the old box. The old boxes are being taken away tomorrow so it's a good thing we arrived when we did. This is the first bit of luck fate has thrown at us for some while. We grab it with grateful hands. The new boxes cost as much as a small car in India but they are bigger and stronger than the old ones.

12.55 p.m.

While The Princess does some cleaning, I go out to the shops to buy food for lunch. It's freezing cold and the sky is heavy with snow that wants to come down. The noise was apparently caused by a film crew parking its huge lorries in the street outside. The weather in Paris is always like England but more so. If it's warm in England then it's boiling hot in Paris. If it's cold in England then it's always freezing cold. In the taxi from the station last night The Princess worked out that she'd been to Paris over 100 times. That's a lot of Eurostar trips. The street outside is now blocked by huge pantechnicons.

14.32 p.m.

We played a CD of Last Night of the Proms. As the chorus sang 'Britons never never will be slaves' I suddenly remembered the sight of several promenaders at the last Proms concert singing away and waving their EU flags with gusto. The conductor, a well-meaning enough fellow, could hardly speak English. The leading soprano was American - from a country whose cultural history consists of the invention of barbed wire and very little else of significance. (Why the hell do people use barbed wire? Ordinary wire does everything barbed wire does without all the harm.) Don't these idiots realise that in signing away our sovereignty to the EU we have made ourselves slaves? When I published *England Our England*, my first book attacking the EU, I was widely vilified for hating Europe. When I replied that I loved other European countries and the variety they offered but disliked the bureaucracy which wanted to eradicate all those differences I was met with blank, uncomprehending stares. Critics who knew that we spend a good deal of our time on the southern side of the Channel sniggered and accused us of hypocrisy.

15.43 p.m.
We decide to go out and buy a new blanket. Even with the heating on full blast we were cold in the night. And we want to walk to the Rond Point to see the lights on the Champs Elysee. In the Avenue Montaigne the trees are all decorated with red lights, strung in such a way that they make the trees look as though they are wearing party dresses with a full complement of petticoats.

We eventually managed to buy a rather decent blanket. It should be decent. It cost £220 and came with two manuals, its own plastic slipcase and the largest carrier bag ever made. I've never owned a blanket that came with its own instruction manuals before. To the best of my knowledge I've never paid more than £200 for a blanket either. Mind you it's been a while since I bought one here, as in England, and prices rise constantly.

The British Government admits that inflation is running at 3% to 4% but they lie, of course because they exclude boring non-essentials such as food and energy from their figures. The real figure is much higher than that and my guess is that real inflation is running at somewhere between 8% and 10%. Very few people who don't work for Goldman Sachs, or one of Britain's nationalised banks, are increasing their incomes at that sort of rate. High inflation is, of course, exactly what the Bank of England and the Government wants. It will impoverish the middle classes and punish savers. But the bankers, politicians and civil servants all have inflation-proofed index-linked gold-plated pensions to enjoy. They don't give a stuff about what is right or decent. They want plenty of inflation because it's the easiest way to get rid of the nation's debts. And it will, as an aside, rescue the greedy bastards who bought houses they couldn't afford. If house prices just stay stable for the next five years, and inflation carries on at, say, 10% then house prices will effectively more or less halve in that time. And the correction will have taken place without anyone noticing, or feeling poorer. The economy will have been adjusted, at the sole cost of the poor sods who were prudent. Gordon Brown always talked about Prudence. He just didn't mention that he wanted to rape her, slit her throat and dump her in a ditch.

And it isn't just that prices are going up. We invariably get less for our money. Chocolate biscuits get smaller every year. And I read a report this morning showing that each sheet of toilet roll paper is now 25% smaller than it was a decade ago. And there are 15% less sheets on a kitchen roll.

In the blanket shop I thought, for an embarrassing moment, that I didn't have enough cash with me but I then found a small stache of euro notes in an inside pocket of my old Austin Reed jacket. I've had that jacket for nearly 40 years and it will clearly still be going strong when I'm no longer here to fill it, though a small hole has appeared in the lining and next time I am in Regent Street I might pop into the store and let them know.

It occurred to me as I paid that the European bank will never be able to replace the euro notes. There are far too many of them in circulation.

While we were out The Princess and I popped into the Post Office to buy some stamps. The Princess stopped me on the doorstep. `Wait a minute,' she said, rummaging in her handbag. `I can't find my spectacles.' `You don't wear spectacles!' I said, puzzled. `I know,' she agreed. `But I have some with plain glass to wear whenever I go into Post Offices.' I waited while she rummaged. A couple of hours later she produced a spectacle case and took out a pair of very elegant spectacles. `They make me look more intelligent,' she said. `And slightly intimidating. And people treat me better when I'm wearing them.' As we walked in a man in a grey uniform rushed over to ask me what I wanted. I told him I wanted to buy stamps. He nodded and then walked off. Thinking that he was taking me to where the stamps were kept I followed him. But he simply met another bloke in a grey uniform and started chatting. After a couple of minutes of this I went to an empty counter and eventually managed to interrupt a conversation between two more guys in grey uniforms. `I'd like to buy 12 stamps for letters to England,' I told him. He seemed startled but, with some reluctance went to a cupboard and found me 12 stamps. `And 12 stamps for letters within France,' I added. This time he looked as though I'd gone mad. He shook his head wearily, as though tired by the world's strange demands, and then went to another cupboard and took out 12 more stamps. The whole strange expedition reminded me of Post Offices in England. Except that there were no queues.

Back at the apartment I found that the arrondissement magazine had been pushed into our mailbox. It has become a vehicle for promoting the current mayor of the arrondissement. The latest edition contained 14 photographs of her smiling, meeting people and attending things.

26
11.04 a.m.
It's snowing! Huge slowflakes that smother everything within seconds. We go for a walk to the Eiffel Tower and quickly become walking snowmen. Everyone is smiling. Two Frenchmen, arms linked, walk past singing `Jingle Bells' at the top of their voices. Every other person we see is taking photographs on their phones. A Chinese man who looks as though he's never seen snow before is giggling and jumping around like a child. On the way back to the apartment we call into the freezer shop to buy pizzas and ice cream. The assistant who has been there for years, getting fatter month by the month, asks us if it is snowing outside. I tell her no, but that I am walking proof that *Head and Shoulders* does not work for everyone. We also stop at the cake shop next door to buy my favourite confection - a meringue, cream and chocolate confection that used, in less politically correct times, to be known as a Tête du Negre and which is now known as a Rivoli or a meringue au chocolat. I remember that the last time I asked for one by the original name the assistant drew herself up to her full five foot two inches and glowered at me. `We do not call them that in the seventh arrondissement,' she said, implying that it was perfectly acceptable to use the name in less salubrious areas of the city. As we leave the cake shop two cars collide. There is the well-known sound of breaking glass and bending metal. The drivers climb out of their vehicles, snarl at each another for a few moments, look at the damage, shrug and then get back in and drive away. In Paris life is too short to exchange insurance details every time cars collide. Walking around the city it is always nigh on impossible to find a car without a dent. I have long harboured the suspicion that dealers actually sell cars with dents already put in

them so that owners don't feel embarrassed at the newness of their new vehicles.

When we get back to the apartment I turn on the radio and discover that Gordon Brown has earned £60,000 for his first speech since leaving Downing Street. The subject was 'The Global Economic Crisis and how to prevent another one'. Someone paid him £60,000 for this. I assume it was a bank. Only banks are staffed with people idiotic enough to pay Brown for advice on financial matters.

14.50 p.m.
The world is apparently getting warmer but at a slower pace. Yet again this seems to be solid proof that the climate change freaks have got it wrong. The only possible explanation for this is that climate change is natural rather than man-made. If it were man-made then the industrialisation of China et al would mean that the world would be getting hotter and hotter at an increasing pace. The climate freaks miss this obvious point. But then they don't do common sense. And like the AIDS maniacs they have a vested interest in selling the scare that has made so many of them rich and famous.

18.19 p.m.
Ed Miliband, the new Labour leader has returned to work after a fortnight's paternity leave. Being an MP is a part time job as it is. MPs totter home at 5.00 p.m. to prepare tea, feed the babies and prepare for the Archers. What a world of wimps.

20.04 p.m.
Our annual French bill for taxes includes a hefty television licence fee. This is, for France, a relatively new idea but they have quickly caught onto the idea that in order to make sure that the licence is paid it is important to be aggressive about collecting it. The licence fee is, therefore, a default expectation and however often I tell the authorities that we do not have a television licence they always add the fee onto the annual bill. I had some success the first year by writing a letter explaining that in a city as beautiful as Paris a television would be entirely unnecessary. This honest flattery worked once but seems to have lost its zest. So these days I simply

scrawl all over the form, knock off the licence fee and send a cheque for the rest. This little annual problem costs us both some convenience for it means that I cannot pay by direct debit without funding a television service I don't want. Bureaucrats the world over are the same. They send bills for money that isn't owed in the hope that the citizen will eventually be worn down and will pay to get rid of the problem. It is a variation of the old insurance company trick of not paying out on claims and hoping to wear out the claimant with bureaucracy.

22.10 p.m.
A reader has written to me telling me that he has discovered an encryption programme which cannot be broken into. He tells me, with great delight, that not even the authorities can read what has been written in an e-mail if it is sent using this programme. I write back, thank him and tell him that I won't be using the programme. I suspect that anyone who does, and whose e-mails are being read, will be signalling to the authorities that they are hiding something. If the police, Special Branch and MI5 cannot read what has been written they will simply clomp round at 4.00 a.m., hammer down the door (so that there isn't time for a hard drive to be destroyed) and insist that all the mystery material be immediately unencrypted.

23.01 p.m.
Flicking through a pile of mail I discover that I've received yet another invitation to start Forex trading. Any form of trading is gambling and Forex trading is gambling on roller skates. I believe that the only way to make money out of money is by investing for the medium term (because this keeps down the trading costs) and that private investors only have an edge if they can predict macroeconomic factors with some success. A decade ago I decided that huge economic problems were coming and so I put a good chunk of our investment money into gold, silver and oil. As soon as Gordon the Moron started selling the nation's gold I started buying (though, of course, he had considerably more to sell than I could afford to buy). They're all still in our portfolio, and likely to remain there for a little while yet. Economists and politicians all talk about the 2007 financial collapse as though it were a huge

surprise. It seemed to me to be pretty predictable and very avoidable. I'm not a gold bug but I put our money into precious metals simply because it seemed clear that nasty things were going to happen to the economy. When a nation's economy is built on greed and debt and on bizarre financial instruments that no one understands it can only be a matter of time before things go 'bang'. The fact that the price of gold was rising steadily for years before the collapse suggests that I wasn't the only person preparing for the collapse.

23.56 p.m.
I have been reading Robert Vaughan's autobiography. Vaughan was the cool 'Man from U.N.C.L.E' and the gunfighter with dark demons in 'The Magnificent Seven'. Vaughan tells how Brad Dexter, the actor in 'The Magnificent Seven' who is usually forgotten, saved Frank Sinatra from drowning off Malibu. Dexter hardly ever worked again but was on Sinatra's pay roll, usually listed in the movie credits as a producer. At the end of his book Vaughan writes: 'I have come to learn that, like a play, television show or movie, a book is a collaborative effort.' I heartily disagree with him. Although there are notable exceptions (usually in the realms of script writing) writing is not usually a team effort and is best when it isn't.

27
10.50 a.m.
The Publishers Licensing Society has sent me a password for entry to their website. The password entitles me to view financial statements and all sorts of other confidential material. They sent the password to me by e-mail. This is considerably less secure than sending it on a postcard. Still, I don't suppose it matters much. The average Briton has at least 16 passwords. None of us can remember them all. So we write them down and keep them somewhere handy where we (and anyone else) can find them readily.

14.57 p.m.
I am constantly being told about the wonders of the e-book. As a result I now believe that we are approaching the end for big

publishers. Bookshops have little or no future. Wholesalers might as well give up now. Printers who have bought hugely expensive presses might as well call in the bankruptcy people today. Literary agents may struggle on for a while selling e-book rights to people like Amazon but they too will fall by the wayside as soon as authors realise that agents can't get much more for them than the standard e-book rate. Small, niche publishers producing short runs of expensive books will survive. (Digital printing, print on demand, doesn't work for us because it is too expensive to print large quantities of books this way. It really only works for small numbers of very expensive books.) Self-publishers will thrive. Proper books will become far more expensive than they are today. The demand (and price) for second-hand books will collapse for a year or two and then slowly the demand will come back and the prices will go up.

Publishers and authors could have 'killed' the whole e-book trade simply by refusing to permit digital versions of their work to be sold. It would, I believe, have been much easier for book publishers to do this than it was for record companies. The bookselling chains, the publishers and the wholesalers should have fought but instead they committed suicide because they didn't understand the scale or nature of the threat. They misinterpreted the whole situation and the entire publishing industry will now die.

22.19 p.m.
This evening we watched a DVD entitled `The Path To War' with Michael Gambon playing Lyndon B Johnson. Directed by John Frankenheimer. It's a brilliant film about Johnson's administration, also starring Donald Sutherland and Alex Baldwin. The curious thing is that in the film, Johnson talks with tremendous enthusiasm about his plans for a Great Society. It was an excuse for America having no money left after bombing Vietnam. So, David Cameron's one original idea wasn't original after all.

28
11.30 a.m.
Our bank in Paris is threatening to deduct 18% from the interest they pay us if we don't give them all sorts of private details and personal information. It's the usual nonsense from Hitler's

favourite bastard child. They already have my inside leg measurement but it's clearly not enough. I suddenly realised that they don't pay me any interest. So I really don't care. They can deduct 18% from nothing with my blessing. So I ripped up the form and threw it in the rubbish. A similar thing happened in the UK not long ago. A company in which I have an investment threatened to deduct tax from the dividends they pay if I didn't fill in a complex and intrusive form. I wrote and told them to deduct the tax but to make sure they sent me an account of what they had taken. When I fill in my annual tax form I can put down the tax paid and deduct it from what I owe.

15.36 p.m.

The whole world of bookselling is changing rapidly. Figures published today show that four years ago the big chains sold nearly half of all books. Today they sell around a third. The supermarkets have doubled their share of the bookselling market from 5% to 10% and the Internet bookshops have doubled too - from 8% to 16%. Small, independent bookshops (proper bookshops) are clinging on to around 10% of the total. The e-book and the e-book reader are going to change this dramatically. Within another couple of years the chains and the small bookshops will have lost market share dramatically. Many former bookshops will be selling mobile phones or will be charity shops.

22.34 p.m.

I did so little today that my self-winding watch stopped. The Princess and I just sat and read and drew and listened to music and played games. I have been reading Henry David Thoreau's journals, which I bought at Shakespeare and Company, down near Notre Dame. I've had the book on my shelves for years. In his entry for October 28th 1853, Thoreau describes how he had bought 706 remainder copies of his book *A Week on the Concord and Merrimack Rivers*. The books, out of a print run of 1,000, were delivered to Thoreau's home. `They are something more substantial than fame, as my back knows, which has borne them up two flights of stairs...Of the remaining two hundred and ninety and odd, seventy five were given away, the rest sold. I have now a library of nearly nine hundred volumes, over seven hundred of which I wrote myself. Is it not well that the author should behold the fruit of his labour? My works are piled up one side of my chamber half as high as my head, my opera omnia. This is authorship; these are the work of my brain. Nevertheless, in spite of this result, sitting beside the insert mass of my works, I take up my pen tonight to record what thought or experience I may have had, with as much satisfaction as ever. Indeed, I believe that this result is more inspiring and better for me than if a thousand had bought my wares. It affects my privacy less and leaves me freer.'

I understand every word of this and share every one of Thoreau's thoughts. He is, without a doubt, the one American whom I would have liked to have met. He was the quiet revolutionary, caring little for fame and fortune but everything for life, nature and what he saw around him.

29
10.39 a.m.
The postman in Paris is still putting the mail into the old, battered, torn off the wall, smashed open boxes. However, (and I love this example of free enterprise beating the State organisation) the man who delivers publicity material (leaflets, unwanted free magazines, etc.) puts his stuff into the new smart boxes.

I telephoned the agents who look after the building for the freeholders and find it difficult to explain the problem since I do not how to describe a huge collection of mailboxes in English, let alone in French. I am sure the Germans have a word for it. They'll create a word which means: 'thebigcollectionofindividualmailboxeswhichisfixedtothewall'.

The kindly man at the agents tells me that the postman will not put the mail into the new boxes until a bureaucrat from the French post office has come round and given the new boxes the stamp of approval. This means that every morning every resident in the building has to open two boxes (one now leaning loose against the wall and definitely a health and safety hazard). Moreover, the old boxes cannot be taken away and so we must all wriggle past the wrecked old boxes until a French post office bureaucrat can make the effort to totter round and confirm that the newly installed, and extremely expensive, mailboxes are indeed mailboxes and not water buffalo or combine harvesters.

C'est la vie, as someone once said.

15.06 p.m.

It is freezing. We hope it will snow again. The pigeons look really miserable on the roof opposite. I put food out on the window ledge and they fly across immediately. I've bought special food for turtle doves. According to the packet it is full of vitamins and should aid their growth. It's horrifically expensive so I'm sure it must be full of goodness. I don't know whether feeding the birds in Paris is a crime but the locals always get very excited. Last winter a man from downstairs rang our doorbell to remonstrate with me about feeding the birds. (The birds knock bits of bread and seed off the edge and these, being visible on the pavement below, are evidence of our malfeasance.)

17.01 p.m.

I'm delighted to say that it is still possible to buy proper light bulbs in France. The EU may be run for and by the French and the Germans but the French in particular take no notice of the daft laws coming out of Brussels. After buying a bagful of bulbs we went for a walk around the Eiffel Tower. The sky was heavy with unfallen snow. We fed the birds by the lake but the crows grabbed everything. They seemed to be starving. In the park they were pecking at the rubbish bins searching for food. Sadly for them there are no picnickers and therefore no leftover sandwiches. How do they survive?

20.25 p.m.

I told a fellow I know that we were having difficulty finding a country house to buy in England because there is so little on the market. The problem, of course, is that by keeping interest rates absurdly low the Government has enabled people to stay in homes they should not have bought and cannot afford. As we travelled back to England this evening I opened an e-mail from him. `Try the Internet,' he suggested. `It's a really good way to search for property.' I did not dare tell The Princess about his suggestion. For the last six months she has spent at least an hour a day scouring the Internet.

30
11.34 a.m.
I felt sorry for myself this morning. A few months ago I sent out
nearly 200 review copies of *2020*. I prepared special press releases,
drawing attention to items in the book which would, I thought,
interest particular publications. It was my last hoorah. Not one
publication has reviewed or quoted or referred to the book. `You're
beginning to sound like an old star, who is now forgotten and
forlorn,' said The Princess gently. `Like Brando, in On the
Waterfront?' I suggested. 'I could have been a contender.' `I was
thinking more of Gloria Swanson in `Sunset Boulevard,' said The
Princess. I laughed and felt better. The Princess then reminded of
my hero William Cobbett. He fought on and on and on to get his
books and articles published. He fought censorship and
establishment opposition but he never gave up. Remembering
Cobbett and Paine and Defoe and my other heroes I feel a bit of a
wimp and determined not to allow myself to sink into the slough of
self-pity again. Well not until the next time it happens anyway. On
a more practical level I have decided again not to bother sending
out any more review copies of my books. It will save a good deal
of money and help avoid a great deal of disappointment.

14.07 p.m.
I had an e-mail from a fellow wanting to know if I will give a
lecture for a huge American company. They want me to discuss the
future. He wants us to meet to talk and discuss things. Tentatively,
and rather shyly, I broach the subject of money. He writes back
again asking me to ring him so that we can talk. He ignores the
subject of money. I feel bad having to mention money but I have
no agent and I am fed up with people wanting me to travel 300
miles, at my expense, stay in a hotel, at my expense, lose a couple
of days work, and speak (having spent several days preparing what
to say) for nothing. I find this especially grating when the people
organising the event are making money, or using it as some sort of
promotional exercise. I never charge charities but I am getting fed
up with being expected to work free for large international
companies too. I mark his last e-mail as spam in the hope that I
never hear from him again.

15.17 p.m.

A recent survey has shown that 70% of people say they would be happier earning less money and having more time to themselves. The same number say they would be happier earning less and living somewhere more pleasant, with a shorter commute to work. If these people did some sums and a little research they would probably find that they could easily get jobs that paid less and wasted less of their lives. Most people spend a huge percentage of their income on buying season tickets and suitable clothes for work (none of which are tax deductible expenses). They pay vast sums for snack lunches and car parking. In the end many would be better off financially if they took less well-paid, less demanding jobs. The world will change dramatically when people no longer measure themselves by their annual income but, instead, by the quality of their lives.

16.04 p.m.

The cheque has arrived from Poland.

17.23 p.m.

The Government is going to allow farmers and landowners to cull (i.e. kill) badgers at their own expense because of the alleged risks of their cattle contracting TB. There is, of course, no evidence that badgers are a cause of TB in cattle but this new piece of legislation pleases the farmers by allowing them to kill as many badgers as they like and pleases politicians and civil servants by taking the cost away from the Government.

The mass slaughter of entirely innocent badgers is a disgrace. Farmers want to blame badgers when their cattle contract TB so they can claim compensation from the Government (and not take the blame themselves). A cull of farmers would make more sense than a cull of badgers. Their abuse of chemicals and hormones and antibiotics causes much human illness and death. And the high incidence of TB among their animals is simply a result of bad husbandry.

I had a rather acrimonious correspondence with the Bishop of Bath and Wells a few months ago. I wrote pointing out that I was horrified to see that his diocese appeared to be calling for badgers to be killed. I said that as a scientist I was appalled that his branch

527

of the church should appear to be ignoring the scientific evidence which shows conclusively that badgers do not spread tuberculosis to cattle and that as a humanitarian and animal lover I was appalled that his branch of the church should seem to be campaigning for the pointless destruction of God's creatures. I made the point that at a time when our country is falling apart through greed and crookery the church should be devoting effort to raising moral standards not forcing them lower.

Sadly, I don't think my letter did any good.

The sight of farmers ignoring the scientific evidence and blaming badgers for their cows getting TB reminds me of the tobacco industry disclaiming any responsibility for lung cancer. They too insisted on ignoring all the evidence for years.

December

1
09.30 a.m.
A few weeks ago I received a letter from HMRC telling me that in future I, as an employer, must fill in all tax forms online. I wrote back saying that this would be impossible and that if they insisted on it I would have to make my staff redundant. `Would you please let me know as soon as possible if I must give my staff notice. I don't see how it helps the country for me to be forced to make people redundant. I've been running a business for several decades and the rules have become increasingly absurd. I can quite see that you don't want small businesses to exist at all. Maybe the Chancellor will be able to borrow some money from Ireland.' Six weeks after my letter I received a reply from someone in Glasgow telling me that I must use a computer in my local library to complete my PAYE forms. The man in Glasgow obviously didn't know that there is a rumour that our local council is considering closing the local library so that they can sell the building and use the proceeds to pay the pensions of former executives. It is, of course, no surprise that the Government should force employers to use a system which has been proven to be inefficient, costly and disastrously insecure. It's exactly what they would do. As I pointed out in *2020* if the Government and its handmaidens can possibly find a way to screw things up they can be relied upon to find it. And then they can be relied upon to do it. Thanks to the EU (which also follows up the `find a way to screw things up and then turn it into a law' philosophy) electronic invoices will soon be made compulsory by all government departments and large companies. `Most of us already do e-banking, so it should not be too difficult,' says Suvi Linden who is communications minister for somewhere foreign and therefore quite probably in charge of what happens in England.

12.35 p.m.
When I was about 18 the company where my father worked, Crabtree in Walsall, had a Swiss guy over for a few months as a

trainee. I used to play tennis with him occasionally. One late afternoon we were walking back from the courts when he suddenly became agitated and started walking with some urgency. 'What's the problem?' I asked. He looked at his watch and walked still faster. I strode alongside, puzzled and asked him again what was worrying him. 'It is my shoes,' he said, pointing downwards. 'They are brown.' I looked at them. He was right. They were. 'So what's the problem?' 'It is nearly six o'clock,' he said. 'I must change them before six because an English gentleman never wears brown shoes after that time.' It turned out that he had read a rather old-fashioned etiquette book before coming to England. He was a nice fellow, though I've never seen him since. He was the sort of man who carried a furled umbrella but never unfurled it, however hard it rained, because he knew he would never again roll it so that it looked as elegant. And looking elegant was, to him, far more important than keeping dry.

Sir Stirling Moss tells a similar story about former racing driver Rob Walker who raced at Le Mans in the 1930s. At six o'clock, well into the race, Walker would come into the pits and change into black shoes and a suit. He would then go out and drive through the night, properly shod. Those were the days when racers were gentlemen especially if they were English.

15.57 p.m.

There is talk of British companies being forced to have more female directors - whether or not they can find any decent ones. This is a really bad idea. Quotas are always bad. This sort of positive discrimination is sexist and will produce the same sort of disaster that was created when medical schools were forced to increase their intake of female students. Many of the problems with medical care today stem from this absurd piece of legislation. There were never enough good girl applicants applying and so medical schools started taking the dregs in order to fill their quotas. And, today, many female doctors want to work part-time. They don't have the sense of commitment of male doctors. They expect to be home for tea at 5 p.m. and they don't want to work weekends or nights. They want long periods off to have babies. And they don't have the same sense of dedication that has always been a tradition in medicine. Incidentally, it does strike me as rather odd that while medical schools are forced to take in more female students so that there will eventually be equal numbers of female and male doctors there is no pressure on nursing schools to take in vastly more male students. And, as an afterthought, what will be next? Quotas for the army so that we have as many female soldiers as male soldiers? Probably. And what about transsexuals and transvestites? If there are going to be quotas for women then there should also be quotas for transsexuals and transvestites. And quotas for one-legged albinos with hearing problems.

2
09.24 a.m.

We are back in Paris and I am becoming confused. I woke up this morning and took a few minutes to work out where I was.

I rang the Paris taxi company which we have been using for 15 years. They have suddenly decided they won't take bookings between 7.30 and 10.30 a.m. We need a taxi at 10.00 a.m. but we can't book one. We have to ring and take pot luck. So I found the number of another Parisian taxi service. A kindly operator tells me that they won't take bookings before 10.00 a.m. unless I pay them another five euros. `But,' says the operator helpfully, `if you book for 10.05 there is no payment.' `That will do fine,' I tell her. We have our taxi booked and we have a new taxi firm in Paris.

12.46 p.m.

We've been using Eurostar since it started (quickly realising that it was quicker, cheaper and a far more comfortable way to get to Paris than by going to an airport, flying and then getting into Paris from the airport at the other end). But even with train travel the problems seem to be growing. Recently we've been lucky. In the last year or so we have narrowly missed a fire in the tunnel, two major strikes, a broken down train in the tunnel and heaven knows what else. Yesterday we came back on what was apparently one of the last normally running Eurostar trains. And it was an hour late because they had trouble finding someone to clean the carriages in Paris. Still, the French, the most bureaucratic nation on earth, know bureaucratic nonsense when they see it and getting through to the lounge is less troublesome in Paris. Even if nothing goes ping and you aren't selected for a random search it can take ten times as long to pass through the customs area at St Pancras than it does to pass through the equivalent area at Gare du Nord where no traveller has set off a metal detector alarm since 1999 and the customs men are too busy chatting to spare a glance for travellers. On the other hand the British border control people in Paris seem to delight in taking forever studying passports and causing huge queues. Like workmen and policemen on motorways, I can imagine them boasting at teatime about the length of the queues they created.

As we arrived at St Pancras a voice was announcing that Eurostar passengers should only travel if their journey was essential. Snow on the English side of the channel was apparently causing problems. Snow on the French side did not seem to be so troublesome. The Princess and I spent some time trying to decide what would make a journey *essential*. Obviously, all holiday travel is non-essential as is all business travel. Travelling to visit relatives or to go shopping is not essential. What's left? Travelling to see a dying relative or consult the only doctor in the world who can treat your life threatening disorder? We reckon that less than one passenger per train is on a truly essential journey. Incidentally, for the first time, I noticed that at St Pancras there are large pictures of guns up on the walls. Each picture has a red line through it and a notice in four languages (with English last) telling travellers that they aren't allowed to carry guns with them. Johannesburg airport used to have a big sign with models of landmines and rocket launchers with red 'not allowed' signs alongside them. Does the absence of such signs at St Pancras mean that rocket launchers and landmines are allowed there?

15.36 p.m.
The Princess picked up a free copy of *The Lady* magazine on Eurostar. In the magazine's great days I used to write for it quite often (mainly illustrated travel articles and whimsical pieces about things I'd seen) but what a sad little thing it has become. It reminds me of a parish magazine that is being edited by an enthusiastic vicar. This edition includes an interview with Maureen Lipman who has written a book and who is quoted as saying: 'I don't think of myself as a writer but if you can talk you can write.' I feel like writing to Ms Lipman to ask her if the fact that I can talk means

that I can act. What a silly woman. I met her once on one of those Monday morning *Start the Week* programmes I used to do when promoting books. She didn't seem to me to be terribly nice or terribly bright.

15.55 p.m.

A reader writes and tells me he lost both his parents in the last year. He says he no longer feels any ambition. All his drive to succeed came from his urgent desire to please his parents, and make them proud of him. Now that they are both dead they can never tell him how proud they are and so his ambition has left him. He no longer feels driven to prove himself a success. I suspect his experience is not unique.

19.08 p.m.

I see that China lent 68 billion somethings to other governments and private companies during the last 12 months. It's good to know that some of this came out of Britain's overseas aid budget. I'm sure someone in the Government can explain why we still give handouts to China.

21.35 p.m.

I have decided that this diary is going to become a published book and I have been playing with several possible titles. I thought of calling it *Outside Looking Out*. And then fancied *Stumbling in the Dark*. I made a list which I showed to The Princess. The list included *No Compromise, Adventures and Memoirs, Welcome to my World* and *Another Bloody Year*. The Princess looked at my list and then scribbled something on a piece of paper which she handed to me. It said: *Diary of a Disgruntled Man*. It's perfect. She suggests that we add a subtitle: *A year in my life of rants and rages*. That's perfect too. We have a title. Now all I have to do is finish the book.

22.18 p.m.

I am horrified to hear from a private source that the EU is planning more legislation to control the way that private individuals can invest their money. I've been an investor since I was at medical school. I started with money earned by writing articles for magazines and newspapers (I was a drama and book critic for the *Birmingham Post* and the *Times Educational Supplement* and several magazines while I was still studying as a medical student, and a columnist for a variety of newspapers) and I had a very active brokerage account with Dukes and Gilbert throughout my medical school years. I only closed it when I started work as a junior hospital doctor and discovered that with a working week often stretching to 168 hours there was hardly any time left for eating and sleeping, and certainly none at all left for reading the financial pages or making telephone calls to a stockbroker. I was lucky. My years out of the market coincided with the stock market crash of the early 1970s. I began investing more seriously about ten years ago when I realised that a number of my predictions were coming true. Instead of trying to pick shares or specific investments I invest according to macroeconomic judgements.

Over the years I've been ripped off quite enough times to know that the biggest threats to the financial security of the average citizen are not muggers or robbers (who are unlikely to steal more than a few hundred pounds at a time) but bankers, brokers and financial advisers whose larcenous proceeds are never measured in less than thousands at a time. Most private investors lose money because they trust the people in the finance industry - and they know too little to protect themselves. They also lose money because they worry about money in the wrong ways. My parents, bless their hearts, worried about saving pennies on petrol and soap powder, but lost countless thousands through making investments through agents and brokers they thought were 'nice'. Millions of people are just the same. They put enormous effort into saving pennies here and there (thinking that in doing so they are looking after the pounds) while buying a pension plan (which is likely to be their most important and largest purchase) with hardly any thought.

The witless eurocrats seem to believe that investors lose money because they are stupid. What the eurocrats haven't yet worked out (the EU brain being made of such substandard material that it would doubtless fail all quality tests if it were subjected to any) is that investors need protecting from the greed, stupidity and larceny of advisers, bankers and the other riff raff who inhabit the investment world. Ordinary investors need protection not from their own ignorance, nor even from their gullibility, but from crooked investment managers and from incompetent regulators. Bankers and investment advisers are toxic people, inspired by the joy of moral hazard they are thieves and robber barons and anyone without a conscience can do what they do. It is absurd that banks now give so much of their profit to employees who are entirely replaceable. Shareholders provide all the capital and take all the risk and employees grab all the profit for themselves. The Government's economic and financial advisers have made consistently poor judgements based on appalling incompetent analyses; they have made egregious predictions and relied far too much on the past than the present; and the actions they have taken have made everything worse. Sensible investors now assume that the Government will do everything wrong, and will make an endless series of mistakes. Nothing that led us into the recent economic meltdown has changed. And so there will, in due course, be another huge crisis.

Most highly paid bank executives are unimaginative bureaucrats suffering from toxic narcissism. They rise to the top through a mixture of luck, compromise, deceit, hypocrisy and arse licking. They then claim that if they aren't paid millions in salaries, bonuses and expenses they will leave and go elsewhere. It is, of course, a bluff. Any doubt there might have been about the value of bankers disappeared when a man called Peter Gwinnell applied for, and was given, the job of deputy chief executive of a City of London bank. Gwinnell claimed to have gone to Oxford and Harvard and to have spent 20 years working at JP Morgan. He had two interviews with headhunters and with the bank. He did the job for a month, attending a lot of meetings and going on a lot of expensive flights. He wore a banker-style suit and shirt and convinced everyone that he knew what he was talking about. He spoke in banker-speak, saying things he didn't understand in a way that no one else understood but doing it in a convincing and authoritative way. Eventually, the unfortunate Mr Gwinnell was undone by a check which showed that he had never worked at JP Morgan and had never gone to either Oxford or Harvard. He was a conman and ex-con. He was convicted for fraud and put under the supervision of a probation officer. I wonder when they'll put all the other bankers under the supervision of probation officers.

And the EU, I remind myself, is introducing new legislation to protect investors from themselves. Who will protect investors from idiot bankers and idiot investment advisers? The whole damned industry of thieves and intellectual dwarves should be hung, drawn and quartered. And, incidentally, the same is true of the eurocrats themselves. These leeches are drowning in gravy. There are, I discovered this week, 2,558 EU officials who are paid £185,000 or more every year. They pay no tax on these obscene sums and are entitled to between 54 and 60 days holiday a year (which works out, incredibly, at 10-12 weeks a year). They enjoy the best pensions in the known world, are entitled to retire just about whenever they feel like it and work the number of hours per month that the average self-employed businessman puts in per week.

22.46 p.m.

When I first started writing professionally I made a huge mistake. I should have used another name. At first it didn't matter and by the time I had sold a few books it was too late because I had established the beginnings of a reputation. Because I am shy, however, I now feel that I have lost control of my life. If I had chosen to work with a pen name, and had managed to keep my real identity secret, I would have been much better able to separate the two parts of my life. If your reputation is built upon things you care about then you suffer enormously when those things are carelessly and cruelly dismissed. Besides, a writer who uses a pen name never has to worry about personal attacks because the critic (whether professional or amateur) will never know enough to be personal and the writer will never feel that an attack on his alter-ego is an attack on himself.

22.50 p.m.

We have been trying desperately hard to find someone to redo the website www.vernoncoleman.com. The first person we contacted was a website professional who had been sending me e-mails for some time, trying to persuade me to give him the business. I sent him an e-mail but heard nothing back. The next person we tried was very enthusiastic. We drove to meet him and it was immediately clear that he hadn't even bothered to look at the website. He had a laptop with him but struggled to make it work even though there was a perfectly good connection. He didn't know what a zip disk was and seemed to know less than I do about computers and websites. But he seemed enthusiastic and nervously we hired him. A couple of days later we received an e-mail from him saying that he wouldn't be able to do the job because he had suddenly acquired two big commissions which meant that he had no time left for us. I thought this deeply unprofessional until I realised that what had probably happened was that he'd had a small fit when he'd seen how complex and huge the site is and then realised that it was simply beyond him.

I then contacted a large website design company and asked them if they could make some changes. To begin with they sounded very bullish. But it's now a week since I spoke to them and they still haven't sent us an estimate. So The Princess is going to try to update the website herself. We don't even have broadband. If she manages this it will be a feat worthy of an Olympic medal. It will, however, be a joy not to have to deal with computer people. Both the hardware and the software people suffer from the same fault: they all have a massive sense of their own self-importance and skills and invariably think they know more than they do (and their reluctance to admit that they don't know something often leads to problems). Not even lawyers, estate agents, bankers or television presenters are as packed with conceit as IT people.

23.57 p.m.
This evening The Princess and I watched *Joyeux Noel*, an amazing film by Christian Carion about the fraternisation between the trenches in the First World War, when soldiers from Britain, France and Germany emerged from their trenches to drink together, exchange gifts and play football. They also buried each other's dead. This story of humanity and friendship overwhelming political and military stupidity has always fascinated me and the film is fantastic. Afterwards, of course, the soldiers involved were punished. Many were sent to the most dangerous places on the frontline in the hope that they would never return. Others were warned that fraternisation was a terrible sin. The truth about what happened emerged from letters and photos sent home by the

soldiers involved. The British didn't censor their soldiers' mail and the story got through.

3
08.03 a.m.
It is our wedding anniversary.

I wrote a small 'pome' for The Princess:
`*Always*
All ways
Your are my love, my wife
My family, my friend, my life
My very special everyone
You are, and always will be, my other half
Without you I am not, and cannot ever be, whole.'

09.10 a.m.
The cards The Princess and I bought each other (*For my Husband* and *For my Wife* as appropriate) both carried an EU warning on the back which read: `Not Suitable for children under 36 months.' What would we do without the European Union, now best known as `Hitler's bastard love child'. There were of course no small parts on the cards but presumably the EU is worried that husbands and wives under the age of three might eat their cards. EU stupidity gets everywhere these days. Every small toy I see has `Not suitable for children under 36 months' stamped on the label. I wonder what on earth one is allowed to buy a 35-month-old child these days. An incinerator or a set of snow tyres would probably be OK. No small pieces in those.

When The Princess and I married we did so alone. No one turned up. (There was probably something good on television.) The photographer and his wife were our witnesses. Afterwards we sent out about 40 pieces of wedding cake. I don't think we received back any cards or acknowledgements. Today, I gave The Princess a white gold butterfly ring with the butterfly made of different coloured sapphires. We bought the ring from a jewellers in the Rue St Dominique in Paris.

10.04 a.m.

I've been leaked information that Derek Bird, the northern taxi driver who ran amok and killed numerous people with a shotgun, did so because he was being investigated by HMRC. He quite wrongly thought that the tax people were going to send him to prison. If this is true (and I believe it is) I am not in the slightest bit surprised. When I was a boy I remember several well-known people killing themselves because of tax enquiries. The problem these days is that many of the people working for HMRC are little more than intellectual thugs. They assume that everyone is guilty and they treat law-abiding, honest citizens in the same way that they treat crooks. Those who have never been investigated claim smugly that `if you've done nothing wrong then you've nothing to worry about'. Whenever I hear this drivel I always secretly hope that the speaker soon receives an investigation notification. These thuggings go on and on and on and the assumption is always that the taxpayer is hiding something. Nothing you say is believed. I've been done twice now (`just routine' they said) and the two enquiries lasted about a year each. The emotional and economic cost was incredible. On both occasions HMRC ended up giving me money back because I'd paid too much tax but after my experiences I am, to be honest, surprised that not more people run amok. HMRC employees are, in my experience, lying, cheating, discourteous, threatening thugs. If they come after me a third time I intend to begin by taking HMRC straight to court under the Human Rights Act.

10.43 a.m.

We have received our first e-mail Christmas card. Can you think of anything more utterly useless? A complete waste of electricity. People who send e-mail cards are mean and lazy and we have vowed to delete these so-called cards without opening them. We like cards you can put on the mantelpiece and spread around the tree.

10.51 a.m.

There were delays on the motorway again. It seemed that a lorry had done something unsuitable. I suspected that the police had merely created a crisis out of a bump. They love making huge problems out of minor ones, blocking both sides of the motorway, causing tailbacks for eight hours and going for tea while the cost to the nation runs high into the millions.

We turned off the motorway on the way to Barnstaple and watched in utter disbelief as a helicopter flew beneath the wires suspended from electricity pylons. I have never seen anything quite so extraordinary and so dangerous. I have no idea who the pilot was but he was foolhardy and daring. He was also reckless because if his helicopter had touched one of the lines it would have crashed directly onto the road.

15.12 p.m.
I went out to collect our plastic rubbish bins and found that the big green bin, the one we use for our recycling, had disappeared. Without a green bin we are lost. Without an official container for our recycling rubbish the council will not remove our rubbish. Now that councils have become pension fund management organisations, devoted to ensuring that there is enough money coming in each year to pay the vastly inflated pensions which are paid to previous employees, the relationship between council and citizen has changed for ever. Today, the relationship is very simple. We give them money and they harass us and treat us like criminals. It's another example of the big society. It's a DIY world but we pay ever more taxes. I could just see the recycling lorry disappearing down the street so I ran after it as fast as a 64-year-old man with slightly dodgy knees and shoes with untied laces can run. I was shouting and calling to the driver in a way that I knew was utterly pathetic. Eventually the lorry stopped. 'Our green bin has disappeared,' I gasped. A man in an orange plastic jumpsuit smiled at me, surprisingly kindly. 'It must have got put with one of your neighbours' bins,' he told me. I retraced my steps and rummaged guiltily through the empty bins outside the neighbours' back gates. I was terrified that someone would see me and think I was trying to steal their bin. In the end I found our bin. My hands were filthy with the remains of other people's waste. I took the bin back through our gate went indoors and washed my hands in antiseptic. 'I'm 64-years-old,' I said to The Princess. 'I shouldn't be running down the street after bin men.' We have worked hard to buy and own a decent house and to acquire as much freedom as possible but this damned rubbish collecting is ruining our lives. I

swore there and then that within three months we would buy a house with enough land to enable us to burn or bury all our rubbish.

17.10 p.m.

I didn't hear the word 'geopolitics' until around 20 years ago but today I find it difficult to imagine investing without considering geopolitical issues. We live in a world of consequences where a small war in a country few of us could find quickly on a world atlas may have extraordinary consequences for an investment portfolio, a pension fund or house prices in England. An uprising in a small African state, for example, may push up the price of oil. This will push up inflation which will mean that interest rates will have to rise. When interest rates go up house prices go down. People then feel poorer and spend less. When they spend less the economy doesn't grow. Recession is the inevitable consequence. And that leads to unemployment. That's geopolitics.

20.12 p.m.

Using a 200-year-old, creaky, snail powered computer which ought to be in a display case in the Science Museum, half a roll of sticky tape and a handful of drawing pins, and with no experience, without broadband or any official training, The Princess has successfully updated and expanded my website. This is the work of a genius. I celebrated this remarkable feat by pouring myself a large glass of Laphroaig and leaving the water in the tap. I've sent an e-mail to the all-singing, all-boasting professional website designer who, after a week's study, is still trying to work out how best to deal with the huge acreage of my rambling website. 'Please don't worry any more,' I told them. 'My wife sorted it all out yesterday afternoon.' I hope they are duly embarrassed. I did not mention that on one occasion I walked into her study to find her shaking with anxiety. 'I just lost the whole website,' she said. 'It disappeared. I don't know where it went.'

4

15.16 p.m.

At the State opening of Parliament the House of Commons gave, as it always does, a formal first reading to the Outlawries Bill. This tradition goes back to 1588 though the bill has no content and no purpose. The rest of the year will presumably follow suit.

17.01 p.m.

Suspicious trading takes place ahead of nearly a third of takeovers in the UK every year. The boss of the FSA, an organisation which exists to protect investors from this sort of thing, was paid £742,011 for 2009-10. If I had hired a gardener who cut grass like the FSA manages the world of finance I would replace him with some sheep. Isn't the FSA supposed to stop suspicious trading? There are so many crooks in the financial industry that cautious investors must assume that the whole system is crooked.

19.10 p.m.

Reliable sources tell me that the Government may soon issue a warning about meat causing cancer. I have been screaming about this for more than two decades but have, up to now, found it hard going. Despite the fact that I produced a mass of scientific evidence proving that eating red meat is a major cause of cancer the Advertising Standards Authority banned adverts for my book *Food for Thought*. To my utter astonishment the Press Complaints Commission ruled in favour of the meat sellers when they complained about articles I wrote proving the link. I warned both that their indefensible actions would result in thousands of unnecessary deaths. They weren't interested. Even *Private Eye*, gutless little magazine that it has become, refused to accept adverts for *Food for Thought*. Back in the Peter Cook days *Private Eye* had balls. These days it is the *Woman's Realm* for armchair revolutionaries, a comfy magazine for people who like to think they're living on the edge but who would spend a week on the lavatory if they got a parking ticket. I was told that the editor, young Milksop, feared that showing a link between meat and cancer might upset his readers. For some years I had a website called www.meatcausescancer.com. In the end I abandoned it because I just couldn't promote it anywhere. If the Government does have the guts to take on the meat industry I wonder if it will go the whole hog? My guess is that they will confine themselves to warning people of the link and suggesting that they eat less red meat. That would be about as sensible as warning smokers to limit themselves to 20 cigarettes a day. But the meat industry is a tougher proposition than the tobacco industry.

20.12 p.m.

We took a huge pile of unwanted books, DVDs and old videos to the charity shop run by a local hospice this morning. There were over 500 books (many of them first editions). I actually thought this was quite generous of us but the assistant in the shop was rather less delighted than I had expected. She insisted that they would not take video cassettes because there is no call for them. And they have no recycling value. We are handed back a black plastic bag full of them. In the street outside I stuff the videos into a council bin. They fill it. What an awful waste. After the guilt, my first thought is that there should be an agency somewhere providing video players and videos for people who cannot afford the ultra-expensive new stuff. My second thought is that neither social workers nor the modern poor would be prepared to accept videos when DVDs are already considered passé by the Blue Ray generation.

21.30 p.m.

When I was a medical student in Birmingham in the 1960s I ran a nightclub in the city centre. Many of the kids who patronised the discotheque were young, homeless, jobless, penniless and without hope. They had no future. Quite often there were fights in the discotheque as other city gangs would invade the club looking for trouble, anxious to destroy as much as they could.

At the nightclub, called *The Gallows*, I re-learned a lesson I had learned as a Community Service Volunteer in Liverpool the year after I left school. I learned that young single men who have no responsibilities, no commitments and no hope are entirely fearless. I remember, one evening in Birmingham, the nightclub was attacked by a gang from another part of the city. Some of the youths who enjoyed the club actually lived there (probably illegally). They slept in attic rooms and for them it was home. They fought without worry. On the evening of the first fight I watched helpless and amazed as the teenagers around me fought with a ferocity I had never seen before. They carried knives and were not afraid to use them. Several were badly wounded. Others had to go into hiding to avoid the police. I remember standing in the middle of one particularly fierce gang fight trying desperately hard to persuade a boy of 17 or 18 to stop fighting. (I always tried to avoid direct involvement and for some reason never got attacked. This may have had something to do with the fact that I carried, and was known to carry, a swordstick with a three-foot blade.) He had been knifed and had blood pouring from two severe wounds. But he wouldn't stop, none of them would stop, until the intruders had been repulsed. Days later I talked to them about it. 'You could have died,' I said, without exaggeration. 'We had nothing else to lose,' they replied. It was how all of them felt. They had no hopes and no aspirations. There was nothing much to live for. And so they didn't care about dying.

I asked a group of the battered survivors why they had fought so hard to protect something that did not seem to me to be worth dying for.

'We haven't got anything to lose,' said one. 'Except this club.' They weren't frightened of the police because imprisonment was no great threat to them. (They were squatting in a derelict building in awful conditions). They weren't afraid of being injured because that would just mean hospital - clean sheets and regular food. And they weren't even afraid of dying because their lives were so dull, dismal and hopeless that they did not feel that they had much to lose. The only thing they had was the discotheque. And so they fought to protect it.

When I look around Britain (and the rest of the world) I see this now happening on a massive scale. There are revolutions coming. A good many of them. Neither politicians nor army chiefs seem to understand that when you take away the little that people have you leave them with no option but to fight to the death. And they don't much care whether it's your death or their death.

22.30 p.m.

A reader complains that I am a Luddite for opposing the use of computers and the Internet. I disagree strongly. I agree that it is usually a myth that new machinery costs jobs - it usually doesn't. But the Internet really is the exception that proves the rule because it changes the basic rules about how society works. It makes life more complicated, time consuming and exhausting for almost everyone. It does this speedily and probably permanently. Computers and the Internet have been oversold; they promote inefficiency and reduce productivity and encourage people to believe in the impossible - thereby creating almost constant stress and disappointment. Dozens of inventions have been of far more practical value - and have changed our society in a far more positive way. The bicycle, the internal combustion engine, the wireless and even the washing machine all changed the world in a more extensive and far better way than the computer has or the Internet will. I confess I also dislike computers and computer people because the former are inefficient and badly designed and the latter are greedy and stupid. Over the years I have wasted at least £50,000 on software that never did what it was supposed to do. Every software seller I've ever met wanted fees in advance and then disappeared leaving the job half done. I'll never trust any of the bastards again. I'd rather trust a car mechanic or a plumber than a software engineer.

23.40 p.m.

I read that our local council really is very seriously considering closing the local library to save money. I'm not surprised. The local administrators and councillors will not dream of reducing their salaries, expenses or pensions and nor will they do anything to cut the council's existing pension liabilities. As I forecast some years ago, local taxpayers will soon be paying for the privilege of keeping former council employees in the luxury they never deserved to enjoy. I'm not surprised that they are closing the public library (as many other councils are doing) but I am appalled. There have been public libraries in every great civilisation and when ours close it will mark the end of our civilisation. The libraries should be the last things to go; they are more important than schools, roads, fire departments, police forces and everything else the local authority provides. Without a public library we might as well be apes living in trees. The money the bankers stole from our economy (with the encouragement of Gordon the Moron it has to be said) would have paid for ten thousand libraries to be built and maintained.

23.45 p.m.

A reader sends me an e-mail containing his telephone number. He wants me to ring him to discuss the contents of my book *Bloodless Revolution*. To prepare me for the telephone conversation, he has included in his e-mail a list of the 14 most important issues he wishes to discuss. One of them is the importance of ensuring that everyone in the country can afford to purchase boots and shoes. I send an e-mail back suggesting that he write to me and promising that I always respond to readers who send letters.

I've also had an e-mail from a reader suggesting that the world would benefit enormously if car manufacturers were forced to produce only three wheeled cars. He points out that this would save 25% of the expenditure on tyre manufacture. He doesn't seem to have made any allowance for the extra tyre wear or the instability of the vehicles. I thank him politely and suggest that he pass on the idea to the transport ministry. I tell him that my own idea for saving energy is to force racing car teams to run cars operated by pedal power. To satisfy the aficionados who enjoy the noise made by racing cars the drivers could be told that they must make 'brrmm brrmm' noises into their microphones.

5
11.02 a.m.
The BMW wouldn't start today. I needed to take it to the local garage to arrange for its annual MOT but the battery was flat. This is strange because I bought a brand new battery just a month ago. 'It's the clock,' said the mechanic who came to start the car. 'It ticks away day and night and it must have run the battery down.' I find this very strange but don't know enough about cars to be able to question the age of the battery I was sold. I suspect I may have been sold a pup instead of a battery.

14.05 p.m.
The rising price of food is, for most in the UK, a minor inconvenience. But I can't help feeling that it is going to create huge problems in poorer countries where the amount spent on food is a much higher proportion of income. How long before there are revolutions in Africa? Hunger and starvation often trigger explosive behaviour among people who have remained subdued for many years. Suddenly, they don't care whether they live or die

because they know that if they don't do something they will die anyway. There is an argument that the Americans can be blamed for whatever happens. It is certainly their fault that the price of food has risen. By printing huge numbers of dollars they have pushed down the value of their own currency. Since commodities (including food) are priced in food the inevitable result has been a rise in food prices. So, once again, American greed will be the trigger for global problems.

15.55 p.m.

Time magazine has a huge feature entitled `The 50 Best Inventions of the Year'. Their chosen joys include a plastic fur coat which is actually a leather jacket which has 29,000 plastic price tag fasteners sewn onto it. `This is, reports *Time*, `a message about sustainability'. Other selections include a home loan scheme that has been set up by a man who lost $9 billion on bad mortgage bets for Morgan Stanley, an English teaching robot that could eventually phase out flesh and blood foreign English teachers altogether (great for unemployment figures), a piece of software that detects sarcasm, a robot that can send erroneous communications and hide, and a spray on fabric that enables people to spray textiles out of a can. Another winner is a boat made out of discarded soft drink bottles. Finally, when *Time* asked a comedienne I'd never heard of for her thoughts on the best invention in comedy she said someone I had never heard of `lighting up a joint' on a television programme I'd also never heard of. `The doors are wide open now!' she said. I'm in hysterics just thinking about it. I do wish they would stop sending me this wretched magazine. And I wish I could get out of the habit of tearing open the plastic wrapper when it arrives.

17.08 p.m.

Banks and pension companies and investment houses are so insecure these days that it is vitally important to spread savings between three or four different institutions. I now fear that there is a real risk that a major institution will go down, taking with it all the savings of millions of trusting individuals. The Government will not help.

17.10 p.m.

House chains have become a huge problem. Someone trying to sell a £1,000,000 house cannot move because the person to whom they are selling cannot sell their £750,000 house to the person who is selling a £600,000 house because their buyer, who is selling a £500,000 house, cannot sell because the person who wants to buy their house is having difficulty selling their £400,000 house to a keen buyer who can't sell their home. And so on. An estate agent told me that he knows of a housing chain which was broken this week when the person selling the most expensive house, at the top of the chain, bought the cheapest house, at the bottom of the chain, so that all the transactions could go ahead. Everything was being held up because the sellers at the bottom of the chain, who were selling a £90,000 flat, couldn't find a buyer. The story sounds as though it ought to be apocryphal but I believe it to be true. It seems that every estate agent I talk to has a bizarre story to tell. Not long ago I heard of a chain which was being held up because the buyer and seller at the very bottom of the structure were arguing over a refrigerator. The buyer wanted the fridge to be included in the sale price. The seller wanted another £100 for it. And their stalemate was holding up the lives of over two dozen people. That problem was resolved when an agent higher up the chain (with a big commission to lose) bought the refrigerator for £100 and gave it to the person buying the flat.

6

09.01 a.m.

I woke up with symptoms of the flu. `Oh the first two days aren't bad,' said The Princess, who has just recovered from it. `It's only after the third day that it gets *really* bad.' I told her that made me feel much better.

11.05 a.m.

Waterstones are, predictably, closing some branches. The Princess told me about a conversation she had with an assistant worried about losing his job. She told him she thought that Waterstones had been crazy to promote e-book readers. The assistant couldn't understand why. `We need to keep up with what people want,' he told her. I suspect that the clot will soon have more leisure time to contemplate the stupidity of his soon to be former employers. I wonder what they will do with all the Waterstones stores. Turn them into shops selling mobile telephones I suspect.

14.51 p.m.
As the euro crumbles and the EU is threatened with extinction everyone, it seems, is pounding on the hapless eurocrats. What a glorious seasonal delight this is. The pensions industry, the banks, the investment industry and the oil industry all are going berserk at the crass new regulations being brought in by EU bureaucrats who know nothing about anything. Meanwhile there is much annoyance at the fact that while the rest of Europe struggles, EU bureaucrats are paid a fortune. This bastard child of Hitler and Goebbels is doomed. Wonderful.

18.01 p.m.
In America today there are more people receiving food handouts (from the food stamps programme) than there were in the 1930s. The poverty figures in the UK are similar. And still the bankers continue to give themselves huge bonuses.

20.10 p.m.
I found this quote in this week's issue of *Time* magazine. It appeared in an article discussing the decade that is about to end. 'Supposedly, Wikipedia came into existence in early 2001 but we're not exactly sure, mostly because we checked that fact on Wikipedia'. I don't much like *Time* magazine (it is far too American in outlook) but I love this quote.

7
10.02 a.m.
I feel much better today. I think my flu has mysteriously gone. Since we have to catch the train, this is good news.

11.34 a.m.
I have decided not to send out review copies of books until at least a month after the book has gone on sale. This will stop reviewers selling the book before I do. Just about all the books sold as 'new'

or `mint' on Amazon are review copies or books sent offering rights to publishers.

11.36 a.m.

I'd forgotten that I've changed my mind. The Princess reminded me that I decided ages ago not to send out any review copies at all in the future. I could not survive without her memory (or, indeed, any other part of her).

14.01 p.m.

I remember that my parents were thrilled with the telegram they received from the Queen on their 60th wedding anniversary. The envelope in which it arrived was engraved with a stern warning to the Royal Mail that it must be delivered on 18th January and not a day early or a day late. That was years ago, in 2005. Now the Department of Work and Pensions has become involved in the sending of telegrams and inevitably there is a ton of paperwork to fill in. A bureaucrat in a cheap suit calls round to check on the potential recipient to make sure that money is not being wasted sending a card to someone who might not be fully qualified. A spokesman says that they have to save money on unnecessary telegrams in order to pay for the inspectors' wages. I wonder how many fraudulent telegrams have been sent out? My guess is none.

15.58 p.m.

The Princess and I met an old friend of ours who is retired now but who has, over a long career, worked for most of the national newspapers. He was an old-fashioned newspaperman, brought up in the days when young journalists were taught to tell the truth and to leave the readers to make the judgements. He liked to get his facts right. He would not, he agrees, last long in the modern world. He was once arrested in Amsterdam for standing in the street singing `How much is that pussy in the window'. He said we have become a nation of overregulated wimps, frightened to speak up for ourselves and claims that this has happened because it is the way the authorities want us. `Wimps are easier to control,' he said.

We went to a pub nearby and because the car park was full he parked in the street. He reminds me of an old GP I know in that it was difficult to tell which side of the road he had intended to park on. He always was a terrible driver. I remember that he was nearly always right whenever he opened his mouth. This was not because he knew nearly everything but because he only spoke about things he knew. The pub is run by a man who is determinedly politically incorrect. He serves food on plates of two sizes. Men get big plates. Women get small plates. Visitors sometimes complain. We take media people from London to the pub because there is always someone in any small party who will become incandescent with rage.

22.07 p.m.

We had a terrible journey back from London. Our train was delayed and naturally there was no information for quite a while. No one at the station seemed to know anything. Then The Princess had a brainwave. She whipped out her iPhone and looked at the train company's website. To our delight the site contained a wealth of information and even told us when our delayed train would be running. When we eventually got onto our train we found it wasn't going because there was no driver. And then another train load of passengers were put onto our train because their driver hadn't turned up either. So there were passengers sitting everywhere - on the arms of seats and on the floor. It was like the 5.55 p.m. out of Calcutta. Naturally, although we were sitting in a quiet carriage, 90% of the passengers were on the telephone and the racket was deafening. The lady who usually comes round with the drinks trolley wasn't available (she had presumably run off with one of the drivers) and when the train eventually started it crawled along very slowly, as though the driver wasn't entirely sure of the way. (Astonishingly, this does happen. I once got on a train from Bristol to Birmingham which sat for a while in the station at Gloucester while the conductor appealed to passengers for someone who knew the way to Birmingham to go to talk to the driver. He said the driver hadn't done that route before.) The train jerked a lot, too, in the way that cars do when being driven by learner drivers. After we eventually arrived at Bristol our intercity express was put on the line after a slow stopping train (they do this all the time) so we had to stop at every tree and bird's nest.

Eventually, we arrived at our station over an hour late. 'Can we claim compensation?' I asked the train manager. She said that we could but that we had to get a claim form from a station, so we abandoned that idea.

8
10.34 a.m.
There is surprise and panic everywhere. It has snowed. Politicians, quangocrats and journalists have all been warning us for years about climate change and now, suddenly, they are astonished that it is snowing. Councils everywhere are astonished that some of the falling snow has (without even taking the trouble to apply for the appropriate planning permission) landed on their roads. Airports are surprised that the stuff has landed on their runways. Rail companies are dumbfounded that it has landed on railway tracks. All are less well prepared than they would be if Martians arrived. Civil servants have stayed at home in their millions out of respect for the environment. Schools are closed so that teachers can have more days avoiding the work they are paid for but which they so obviously loathe.

14.30 p.m.
We had a new washing machine delivered this morning. It took a man ten minutes to do the necessary plumbing. (Sticking a rubber hose onto another piece of tubing and writing out a bill for £27.50). It took me five seconds to connect it to the electricity supply. It took The Princess a minute to put in the soap powder, fill it with clothes and press a button. And then, hey presto, the machine washes clothes. Why are telephones and computers so ridiculously complicated and user-unfriendly? Why is the Internet so absurdly unreliable? Why is software so complicated that it can only be understood with the aid of a 500-page manual which has to be purchased separately? Why is all the relevant hardware changed with relentless fury when the improvements the manufacturers offer are of such little significance? And why are we all forced to update, and buy unnecessary complicated and unreliable machinery, because there are no ink cartridges or software to fit the old stuff?

16.37 p.m.

The transport minister has suggested that people clear the ice and snow off their local roads themselves. What a good idea. This is, after all, the new big society. We should perhaps also run our own ambulances and take one another to hospital in wheelbarrows. We could all burn our rubbish in the streets and have guns so that we can defend our lives and our property. And naturally we won't pay any more taxes. So all the stupid civil servants and politicians whose fat salaries and pensions we are paying can start looking for proper jobs.

17.10 p.m.
Walking through Barnstaple today I saw a shop I hadn't seen before. Outside there is a large, very smart sign proclaiming: 'Proffesional Body Piercing Studio'. I hope the piercing is more professional than the spelling. And if they branch out into tattooing I hope someone invests in a dictionary.

We arrived at Publishing House to discover that the son of a local bachelor has sprayed black paint graffiti on the white walls. It looks terrible. We will have to buy some white paint and repaint the wall. If you leave graffiti then more will arrive and soon the whole building will look terrible.

9
12.14 p.m.
It is my third day with the flu. The Princess was right. It is now getting *really* bad.

23.26 p.m.
I caught a few minutes of Kelvin Mckenzie on Sky television, discussing the day's newspapers. Kelvin is still the court jester, the genial buffoon. He seems to speak without bothering to think, or without even knowing what he is saying, but the gibberish that comes out is mildly entertaining from time to time, and a pleasant change from the usual, studied, pompous inanities uttered by guests on such programmes. I have a strong suspicion that he himself doesn't know what he is going to say until he's said it and heard what he has to say. Maybe he doesn't even know what he thinks until he's heard himself say it. I was a columnist for *The Sun* during most of Kelvin's years as editor and he had a reputation as a

fearful bully. However, I got the impression he was scared of Rupert Murdoch whom I once upset greatly by writing a column about workaholics which, as an illustration, pretty clearly criticised the paper's working practices. I don't think Kelvin and I ever really got on because I never showed him the right amount of deference. Like a good many former editors he has now managed to carve himself a strange little niche as a media personality. He has survived so long by being politically aware. I remember him ringing me on Boxing Day because one of the company's bosses had broken something fairly serious while skiing. Kelvin, who was presumably planning something, wanted to know how long he'd be out of commission. More memorably I remember walking into the Grill at the Savoy once, to have lunch with the editor of *The People*. I was in a hurry because I was late, having waited for ages in the wrong restaurant. (There were two at the Savoy at the time: the Grill and the River Restaurant. Inevitably, I had picked the wrong one.) There were three cabinet ministers and heaven knows how many other recognisable faces in there. Advertisements for my Telephone Doctor advice lines were running almost daily in just about every national newspaper. Suddenly, Kelvin's unmistakeable roar shattered the relative silence of whispered conversations. 'Hello, it's Vernon Coleman!' he cried. '0898 for advice on oral sex. 0898 for advice on irritable bowel syndrome. 0898 for advice on something else.'

Just about the only real live television we catch is what we see while changing DVDs. For the past week or two we've been watching old television Poirots though we have been careful to watch only the pre 2002 shows. Without Captain Hastings, Miss Lemon and Inspector Japp the programmes are very ordinary, bordering on boring. Indeed the ones made after 2008 are unwatchable. We bought them and then tossed them into the charity bag we keep handy. The problem with the programmes made without the magic trio is that there is no humour in them. The humour was invariably always at Poirot's expense so without the trio there is no one left to make the jokes. Whoever decided to get rid of Hastings, Lemon and Japp made a huge mistake. In the later programmes, David Suchet plays Poirot as insufferably pompous, self-important, worthy, painfully vain and utterly humourless. There is no lightness of touch at all and the

554

programmes are dull. Watching the later Poirots reminded me of watching the later Hancocks. The boy from Cheam destroyed his charm by getting rid of the great actors and writers he had worked with. When he finally got rid of Sid James the graffiti was on the wall. Suchet is good but in my view too precious and not a strong enough actor to hold it all together. He's about as charismatic as the average news reader. Albert Finney could have managed without Hastings, Lemon and Japp but Suchet's Poirot certainly can't.

23.56 p.m.

I found this small ad in an old copy of *Motorsport*. `Mr Scott-Moncrieff will, during August, be chuffing quietly through the canals on a narrow boat, thankful for a month away from motor cars. There will, however, still be a good selection of pre-war Rolls-Royce and Bentley cars on view at Rock Cottage, Basford Hall, Leek. So, by all means, come and have a look. If you see one that you like sufficiently to buy, leave the money (all prices are clearly marked) and take it.' The ad appeared in the August 1960 issue of *Motorsport*.

10

11.31 a.m.

A book order arrives with a request that the book be sent by return of post because it has to be sent out again to arrive at an address in America by the 9th December. The order was posted on the 5th of December. The optimism of the would-be present giver is supplemented by a demand that the book be posted out first class and the fact that they have failed to include any payment whatsoever for postage.

11

11.02 a.m.

There is a campaign to allow dogs into cafés and shops. I hope it fails. Beaches and parks are already ruined by the constant presence of dogs - many of which seem, like their owners, to be borderline rabid. It is impossible to go for a pleasant walk without finding oneself face to face with some slobbering, snarling, heavily fanged beast and his or her canine companion. When I wrote about the fact that the toxocara that dogs leave behind them causes blindness in children an advocate for dogs dismissed this argument for banning dogs from public parks with the comment that no more than 50 children a year are blinded this way. What can you say to someone who dismisses 50 blind children as inconsequential? Allowing dogs into cafés and shops would make life unbearable for the millions who are allergic to dogs or who are (not unreasonably) nervous when they are around. I think maybe I'll start a campaign to ban dogs from all public places – including pavements and parks.

15.38 p.m.

I see that Goldman Sachs has invested in Facebook. Hopefully, that will now be the end of this wretched website. Enthusiasts claim that Facebook is the most valuable company in the world - far more valuable than all the mining companies put together. This is nonsense. First, the next generation will not think something is cool if their mother can be found on it pictured in her bathing suit. Second, now that Goldman Sachs has become involved there will, I suspect, be adverts and intrusive e-mails everywhere as the bankers struggle to make money from their investment. Third, websites are like cafés in Paris. They go in and out of fashion quickly and without warning and for no discernible reason. And finally, Facebook is unbelievably naff. Those who spend their days on Facebook will, like the twats who twitter, soon find other ways to waste time. I have a suspicion that our descendants will look back on families watching TV, and schoolchildren and workers being able to share experiences and opinions about the programmes they have watched separately but at the same time, with the same affection that we look back on our Victorian ancestors sitting around the piano and singing comic songs. In the future people will sit in separate rooms communicating with the best friends they've never even met. But I very much doubt if they'll be using Facebook. That and Twitter will be regarded as embarrassing pieces of social history; about as fashionable as the mangle or the hula hoop. Big international corporations already have rooms full of nerds monitoring and `adjusting' all references to their products on `social media' websites. Those who believe that Facebook will last for ever should ask themselves what happened to `Friendster', `My Space' and `Bebo'. All were highly successful social networks.

20.19 p.m.

In 1914 a gold sovereign was worth £1. Today it is worth several hundred times as much. Sterling has been devalued by well over 99%, thanks to the efforts of bankers and politicians. In the long run paper money is worth little more than the paper it's printed on. The best performing currency in the world in 2010 was the Afghan Afghani (and even that lost value against gold).

21.35 p.m.

It occurs to me that as well as banning dogs from public places we should also ban children under the age of 16. Or maybe we should just ban the parents of children under 16. I suspect that the parents make more noise and cause more trouble than their children. We spent a miserable two hours in a railway carriage this morning. A nanny, travelling with two quiet and pleasant children, insisted on reading them stories all the way. When I gently remonstrated and suggested that if she needed to read out loud in a quiet carriage she might consider lowering her voice she immediately set off in search of the conductor and made a formal complaint.

12

14.22 p.m.

The Princess and I are visited by a friend who lives in Switzerland. He told us that since Christmas Day and Boxing Day fall on a weekend the locals all go back to work on the following Monday. `It's just hard luck if bank holidays fall on a weekend,' he said. The Princess says she thinks that probably explains why the Swiss have all the money and we have all the debts.

21.40 p.m.

Three quarters of all the music tracks downloaded in 2010 were acquired illegally (i.e. they were stolen). Is this going to change? Yes, it's going to get worse. Is it damaging CD sales? Of course it is. Will the same thing happen to books? Obviously. I refuse to provide computer copies of books to foreign publishers and I refuse to sell e-book versions of any more of my books. Modern recording artists are having to go on tour to earn a living. Musicians are using their records (which are downloaded free of charge) as loss leaders because they can no longer prevent or control the thefts. Their income from record sales has collapsed and so now they make their money from concert tickets and T-shirt sales. Some authors will be able to follow this pattern and will give lecture tours (as Dickens, Thackeray and Twain did so successfully in the 19th century). But most won't. And even if I could, I don't really want to. I just want to write books.

22.51 p.m.
Trains on new routes in Italy are not allowed to stop at intermediate stations. If a train starts out from Germany then it must end up in some other country and can't stop in Italy. Brilliant. So wonderful that we have an EU. One country. European countries are being dragged further apart by the consequences of the EU, the euro and the whole fiddle faddle of European bureaucracy. I sometimes think the EU must have a Department of Silly Ideas.

23.44 p.m.
It has become clear that Goldman Sachs asked for American taxpayers' money 212 times between March 2008 and March 2009. But they still managed to claim that they hadn't needed a bailout and they still managed to dole out gazillions to themselves. I still firmly believe that the greatest threat to our civilisation comes not from Muslim fundamentalists but from Goldman Sachs and their ilk. Goldman Sachs reportedly paid a $550 million penalty earlier this year to avoid charges of securities fraud. They reportedly booked $13 billion of deals. Not a bad arrangement. Try shoplifting £100 worth of stuff and then offering the police £4 to let you off and see where it gets you.

23.52 p.m.
I received a letter from a reader who reported that she had been told by several bookshop assistants that *Alice's Diary* is out of print. I get dozens of letters like this every month and have done so for the last 20 years. I wonder how many more copies of *Alice's Diary* we would have sold if the bookshops had bothered to order

copies for their customers. *Alice's Diary* is, like all my books, listed in all the relevant trade directories. There is absolutely no excuse for a bookshop (or library) telling readers that my books are out of print when they are not. I wrote back to tell my reader that she had been given misleading information. 'The fact is,' I wrote, 'that *Alice's Diary* has never been out of print since it was first published over 20 years ago. There are currently well over 2,000 copies of the latest printing in the warehouse.' I have for over 20 years been trying desperately hard to persuade bookshops, libraries and wholesalers to stock my books. Now, I really don't think any of these have much of a future. Bookshops and wholesalers are going to be destroyed by the e-book. And libraries are going to disappear as councils cut their expenditure so that they can continue to pay extortionate salaries and pensions to unnecessary bureaucrats.

23.59 p.m.

I had just finished gnashing my teeth over the Alice letter when I opened one from a publisher wanting permission to print and sell copies of one of my books without paying me a royalty. They are, they tell me, a charity. I receive at least a dozen requests a year like this and I never really know what to do about them. I wonder if surgeons receive requests asking them to perform free operations on Sunday mornings. Or if plumbers constantly receive requests from charities demanding free plumbing work. I always say 'yes' to people wanting to produce audio books or Braille books for the blind though I sometimes wonder about the logic of this. Audio books are available commercially and I sometimes sell the rights. Should I really give away my rights or should I insist on selling them so that I can choose how to spend that portion of my earnings which I want to give to charity? I don't mind sending free books for auctions, or providing drawings for sale, but giving away a portion of my copyright does worry me. This is, after all, what I do for a living.

13

11.31 a.m.

The defunct Bradford and Bingley building society wants to buy back some PIBS (Permanent Interest Bearing Shares) but is offering to pay a little less than a fifth of what I paid for them. This is presumably being done for their benefit. Indeed, in the details of the offer, the wretched company explains, under the heading 'Rationale for the Offers and the Proposal' that: 'The offer aims to generate a profit for B&B'. You bet it does. It's not difficult to make a profit when you arbitrarily stop paying interest and then offer to buy back a bond at a tiny fraction of the price everyone paid for it. They know that most of the people involved are small investors who were daft enough to put their money into (allegedly) safe building society investments. I wrote and complained about the theft of the money I had invested in Bradford & Bingley to both HM Treasury and the Financial Services Authority. I might just as well have sent a letter of complaint to the Manchester United Supporters Club for all the good it did me. This is the fourth time I've had money stolen from me and been unable to do anything about it.

14.15 p.m.
In the last three days I have received four e-mails from printing companies asking me for book printing business. Three were based in England and one in China. It seems likely that the e-book bonanza is already having an adverse effect on printing companies.

17.12 p.m.
I spent much of the day sorting out the old accounts from 1994-5 onwards. I have no idea what I really need to keep. I have huge sackfuls of receipts. Eventually I decided that if the country really needs me to keep train tickets from 1994 then I will give up. But what do I do with it all? I will have to sort through the bagfuls of rubbish and decide what to burn, what to shred and what to dump in the rubbish if the council will agree to take it away. Clearing out the old accounts left me with three huge carrier bags full of used chequebooks and paying in books. I don't want to put them into the rubbish for obvious reasons of security but didn't fancy trying to shred them all. So I burnt them on the fire. And didn't they do well. They provided an excellent and warming blaze for four hours. Tonight and for another week or so we will keep warm with old invoices and receipts.

14

11.01 a.m.

A woman has written asking us to send a book to America by airmail because she wants it to get there by Christmas. She has enclosed £1 towards the postage and packing. The price of sending this parcel by airmail to the USA is over £9 so if I send the book by air I will lose money on the sale. Another reader wants a book sending by airmail to Australia. This customer tells me that staff at Publishing House have been doing this for her for years. I am honestly surprised that I've ever made a profit. I see from the Stanley Gibbons catalogue that the stamp dealer charges £30 to post a book weighing over 500g to Australia if the book costs less than £50. If the book costs more than £50 the postal fee is £45.

15.21 p.m.

The Government, the Bank of England, the nation's economists and the overpaid idiots in the city are apparently all shocked that Britain's inflation figures are rising faster than expected. I've been forecasting rising inflation for years and so this is no surprise. The main reason is one word: China. It seems that the bright financial brains have only just noticed that if the Chinese people want more cars the price of oil will go up, if they want more burgers the price of food will go up and if they want higher wages to pay for these delights then the price of bras, television sets and other ephemera will all go up. It's called geopolitical macroeconomics or common sense. The problem with economists is that they are forever looking backwards without ever looking forwards. They don't even attempt to figure how the past might impinge on the future. Still, their stupidity does at least give the rest of us a chance to beat the markets with our investments. I was sent accounts recently which showed that I've managed 19% a year on my investment portfolio during the last decade - without any gearing whatsoever. So, yah boo sucks to the investment professionals, the hedge fund managers and the economists. I see from today's *Financial Times* that Neil Woodford, described as 'one of the premier fund managers of the last 20 years' has, across all his funds, achieved an annualised total return of 8.6% for the past few years.

Inflation is the new modern opium of the people; it's the trick by which our rulers make people think they are better off, even though they aren't. It's inflation that keeps wages rising (and prices rising). It's inflation (and cheap money) that has for years kept house prices soaring (and stopped them collapsing). It's inflation that keeps taxes rising (and government income rising). And it's inflation that makes people think they're getting richer when they aren't. It's inflation that forces the prudent to subsidise the greedy and the reckless. It's inflation that encourages people to overleverage and to buy houses with fake money, borrowed from banks, rather than to pay at least part of the price with real money that they have worked for with honest toil.

Governments encourage inflation because it helps the indebted (whether a country or someone who has bought a house they can't afford) at the expense of savers. Inflation is an insidious form of taxation. Knowing that inflation will allow house prices to fall without actually going down, the British Government has done everything it possibly can to hold house prices at the current artificial level. The politicians (or, rather, their advisers) know that if food, energy and clothing prices soar as a result of inflation, house prices will, if they remain as they are now, be at a sensible level within five years or so. It's a neat but ultimately damaging piece of deceit which will lead to greater misery for longer. A normal house bubble takes seven years to burst (with prices always going lower than anyone thinks possible) and another seven years to recover. The Government's actions will simply delay the inevitable and extend the unhappiness. Inflation won't push up house prices; it will merely make houses more affordable by making everything else more expensive.

There are losers of course. Pensioners who are not former civil servants find themselves living on shrinking fixed incomes. Savers are discouraged (even though people who save are the backbone of any economy). Inflation destroys the prudent middle classes but benefits the imprudent. The poor are affected more than anyone because commodities (food and fuel) rise when inflation soars and those costs make up a higher percentage of their daily costs. Inflation discourages thrift and encourages recklessness and gambling (although these are the very types of behaviour which cause economic problems). Inflation leads to injustice and desperation and, eventually, a call for more state controls and more fascism. It's no wonder governments and politicians and bureaucrats all love inflation.

Since the banks destroyed the world economy, governments in the USA and the UK have been deliberately supporting policies designed to force people with money to spend it and to push up inflation as fast as they can. We live in a credit hungry economy where people are encouraged to spend money they don't have. Some of the blame for this must lie with Keynes who came up with the good idea of encouraging governments to spend their way out of financial trouble but forgot that wasteful politicians like the wretched Gordon Brown wouldn't have the strength of mind to stop spending other people's money and to save when things were going well. Inflation has also been fuelled by credit cards.

By holding interest rates low (when they should be much higher) governments have forced people to take risks and to invest their money in hazardous projects. The UK (like the USA) desperately needs a correction. People and companies (and the Government) need to deleverage, and pay off their debts. But the Government has done everything it can to prevent the inevitable, healthy correction. In the long run it won't succeed, of course, because the correction is inevitable. But, meanwhile, debtors are rewarded and savers, and the prudent, are punished.

Politicians and bankers lie and claim that printing money won't cause inflation. The Bank of England, in a breathtaking piece of blatant deception, claimed that: 'The Bank sets interest rates to keep inflation low to preserve the value of your money.' What cobblers they talk. If you make a lot of something then the value goes down because its rarity value falls. The Americans in particular are desperate for inflation and so they are creating dollars and will allow their currency to fall. (In reality it doesn't matter a jot whether you actually print all that extra currency or just create it electronically. By and large governments don't actually print money any more, of course. And so from time to time crafty politicians can deny that they are. It's simpler and cheaper than that these days. They now simply credit banks with new money electronically. This means that the banks have money they didn't have. And can lend out a multiple of the new money they've acquired. There is, therefore, vastly more money in circulation. But they're not actually bothering to print more of the stuff.)

The Americans don't give a fig what this will do to the rest of the world. They know that devaluing their currency will produce instability, currency wars, massive widespread unemployment, higher taxes, import controls and impaired competitiveness.

In the medium to long term the Americans will be the losers, of course. The Chinese, if they are as wise as I think they are, will be selling their vast hoard of dollars and buying gold.

I've been screaming for several years now about the coming inflation and it's happening. In late 2010, the Consumer Price Index (the lowest of the Government's fiddled inflation figures) showed that inflation was running at 3.2% a year. The Retail price Index showed a 4.5% annual rise. But these are, of course, figures which exclude non-essentials such as clothing, energy, petrol and railfares. Car insurance is going up at 38% a year. House insurance is rising at 50%. The real inflation figure is currently at least 10% a year. Anyone who has savings and whose investments aren't producing that sort of figure each year (after tax) is becoming poorer and would have been better off just spending their money on scented candles and other fripperies.

Most people are losing money on their investments because of the indecently large fees, bonuses and expenses charged by investment fund managers. These days it has become fashionable for the little bastards to charge huge fees if they actually manage to make a profit. I have noticed that they never take a cut in their standard fee if they make a loss or underperform their peers. It is, of course, a win win situation for them. The whole finance industry needs a drastic overhaul - preferably with a flamethrower. British bankers borrow at 0.5% from the Bank of England and lend to big corporations or foreign bankers at 6%. They can, therefore, make huge, safe profits at the expense of British taxpayers. If they can be bothered to lend to British businesses they charge at least 12%, which is shylocking by anyone's standards.

Many people who now realise (belatedly) that their income is being devastated by poorly performing unit trusts and low interest rates are now investing in high risk bond funds in an attempt to stay ahead of inflation. The result is that, once again, millions of hard working folk are going to see their savings devastated.

We could and should have used the wealth created in the last years of the 20th century on creating a fair society, a decent health service, an effective education system and a host of necessary services that would improve our world. Instead, to the ever lasting shame of the politicians entrusted with the job of managing our world, the money was wasted on quangos, on buying votes from scroungers and zombies and on bizarre pet projects forced upon us by the EU (and which every individual with functioning brain tissue knew were nonsense). Productive jobs have been replaced by zombie jobs, counter productive. Having no experience of the real world (and never having had to run anything, or to create anything) Brown et al, greedy, sleazy and incompetent (how sad that those are the only words we use when talking about politicians these days) believed, in their rank stupidity, that they could create prosperity simply by spending money and by encouraging people to spend. When the money ran out (as it inevitably did) they continued their mad experiment by borrowing (and encouraging the people to borrow). It was a strange sort of massive Ponzi scheme, the sort of fiscal nonsense that in a sane society would result in long prison sentences. In the world created by Brown no one has to pay for anything. Poverty, misery and growing discontent brought on by political correctness and multiculturalism, means-testing and targets, were well matched with a culture of cronyism, dependence, self-indulgence and grasping, well-rewarded incompetence. Bankers, Olympic class incompetence, deception and fraud were massively rewarded. Sleaze and corruption were accepted and went unpunished. 'I'll pay back what I took and it will be OK.' Today, 'public ethics' is as much an oxymoron as 'American culture' or 'military intelligence'.

It is possible to argue (though obviously one would not) that instead of slaughtering Iraqi children and bombing the shit out of wedding parties in Afghanistan, the American and British troops would have been better occupied targeting the bozos at the egregiously greedy Goldman Sachs, RBS and HBOS, and the other bastards who nearly brought the world to ruin and who did bring the rest of us to a state of despair. (Actually, I'd like to keep a few battalions back to deal with the EU headquarters. The EU, Hitler's bastard love child, has done more harm to Britain in general and England in particular, than any other enemy.)

If we rob banks we get sent to prison. If bankers rob us they get bigger bonuses. Bankers caused the world's problems but are today virtually the only ones with sound finances and no financial anxieties. The big banks are our enemies, not the Afghans or the Iraqis. It is the big banks, not some rucksack wearing saddo, who will bring us all down. Nothing is too bad for the blood-sucking bankers. Where the hell are revolutionaries when you really need them?

There is no longer any such thing as a safe investment - or a safe place to put savings. The result? Ninety nine out of a hundred savers are losing money on their savings and investments. Savers are being punished for the excesses of the bankers and the greedy. And the American and British bankers, enjoying by a free guarantee of security from taxpayers, are subsidised by hard working men and women to the tune of £100 billion a year. That's not my figure. That's the Bank of England's official estimate of the value of the subsidy banks receive by having an implicit guarantee that if they get into trouble the Government will bail them out. (The banks' annual tax bill is no more than around a fifth of that so the British taxpayers are paying the banks £80 billion a year just to exist. It's hardly surprising that the bankers can pay themselves even more extravagantly than footballers.) A bank that knows it will not be allowed to fail can take huge risks. If the risks pay off then the bankers give themselves huge bonuses. If the risks don't work the Government steps in and gives the bankers money so that they can give themselves huge bonuses. Moral hazard anyone?

People think they are getting richer by being paid more but they are not because everything they buy costs more so their standard of living falls. And the changes produced by the consequences of inflation and so-called progress mean that their quality of life collapses too.

15
09.34 a.m.
I rang the chimney sweep to fix an appointment. 'What day would you like me to come?' he asked. 'Next Friday would be convenient,' I replied, rather startled. I am more accustomed to

being told by tradesmen when will be convenient for them. 'And what time?' asked the sweep. 'Two o'clock?' I suggested. 'Fine,' he said. I suspect that maybe the sweep business isn't doing too well at the moment. I suppose that in a recession, having the chimney swept is one of the things that gets postponed.

10.02 a.m.
There is going to be a royal wedding next year. As we discussed the forthcoming event (which is bound to be a brilliant piece of English theatre) The Princess suggested that the best commentator for the big day would be Henry Blofeld. It's a brilliantly off the wall suggestion. Blowers, who made his name as a cricket commentator, and who has the plummiest voice on the planet, would be superb. Sadly, I expect the broadcasters will choose a boring newsreader.

11.25 a.m.
The Princess noticed, by chance, a comment on Yahoo that I have been struck off the medical register for providing patients with dangerous advice. This is possibly the worst libel I've ever come across. In fact I suspect it is a criminal libel. Ideally, I would like to find the person who wrote this and punch them on the nose. It would be easier, cheaper, quicker and far more satisfying. But there are problems with this simple solution. First, the chances are that the weedy little liar who wrote this nonsense is either a wimpy little runt or, worse still, a woman and that when it came to it I wouldn't be able to go through with the punching them on the nose idea. Second, if I did sort out the problem in such a civilised way I would doubtless end up doing 30 years inside and paying millions in compensation. So, the first thing is to get a contact e-mail address or telephone number for Yahoo. This is far more difficult than you might think and the Web seems full of people who have tried and failed to find any sort of contact information. But I have a brainwave and enter the words 'Advertising on Yahoo' into the Google search engine. I have a contact telephone number in London within seconds.

The Web is full of stupid, arrogant and incompetent pillocks who delight in sniping and when I told Yahoo that one of them has used their website to announce to the world that I have been struck

567

off the medical register when I haven't (much to my surprise the GMC has never even tried to strike me off) and that I am indeed still a registered and licensed GP principal, this egregious libel turned the writ wranglers at Yahoo a slightly worrying shade of pale. They removed the libel from the Internet before I had properly finished telling them about it. But they will not tell me the identity of the person who wrote it, and will not tell me whether or not they have informed the individual that what they wrote was libellous. So this venomous, hateful, mendacious, spittle-flecked bigot is, presumably, free to repeat their libel endlessly around the Internet. I am always reluctant to take legal action, particularly for libel, but I consulted a libel lawyer who told me that since Yahoo removed the libellous remark there will be very little chance of obtaining any damages. It seems that anyone can write anything they like about anyone on the Internet as long as they remain anonymous. And if the website publisher removes the libel the minute they become aware of it they are effectively safe from prosecution however much damage may have been done. Wonderful. I wonder how Mr Yahoo would like it if I were to spread rumours that he is a paedophile and a terrorist and someone who makes a habit of putting his plastic recycling rubbish in with his general rubbish. The worst bad thing about the Internet is that thanks to the Web every individual will be haunted for ever by the tiniest and most gossipy incident in their lives. Digital technology makes sure that our smallest transgressions (real or imaginary) are recorded, easy to find and well disseminated by our enemies. Even when the allegations are entirely untrue they will still circulate.

The Web has become a dark, shadowy world, populated by dark, shadowy people who seem to wallow in giving gratuitous, purposeless offense. I can understand political opponents attacking one another. But today's bloggers pick on anyone and everyone and seem to take great joy from being nasty for the sake of being nasty. They aren't trying to change the world, or make it a better place, they just seem consumed by a desire to cause mindless pain. Vindictiveness is their driving force. I read recently that when a former model objected to the libellous remarks of a nasty blogger she filed a defamation suit to force Google to identify the blogger. The model subsequently forgave the culprit but the blogger then sued Google for failing to protect her privacy. I understand that some revolutionaries need anonymity (and use pseudonyms) to stay alive. But on the Internet e-mailers, bloggers and reviewers frequently hide behind a pseudonym because they are cowardly and don't want to be sued. The Internet is a mish-mash of misinformation, some deliberate, some commercially inspired, some mischievous, some malicious. I have lost count of the number of reviews of my books I've seen which are libellous. Self-appointed critics make entirely false assumptions and judgements, apparently without any respect for the truth. People who have sued to try to protect their reputations invariably find that it is a full time job. Moreover, the vindictiveness of people who are mostly unemployed and can, therefore, spend all their days simply being annoying means that there is little point in trying to protect your reputation online. Moreover, the worst offenders have no money and so anyone who sues them is likely to end up well out of pocket.

The real problem with the Web is that the nasty, libellous stuff stays around for ever. If someone is maliciously and inaccurately described as a paedophile the item may be removed in theory but it won't be removed in practice. It will be there for ever more for someone to find, repeat and quote. It is dangerously easy for anonymous wierdos to mess with innocent people's lives - just because they can.

Television took a decade or two to reach a point where it satisfied the needs of the lowest common denominator. The Internet didn't wait; it went straight to the bottom. Not bothering to pause to pretend to offer anything honestly educational or of lasting value the World Wide Web headed straight for the cesspit. And, having reached its target it stayed there. The World Wide Web has done more damage to civilisation than any other invention in the history of the world. I would put it above gunpowder, dynamite and television.

As more and more people are ripped off, deceived, cheated, attacked and lied about and as their reputations are savaged and destroyed so they will realise what a dishonest and superficial and untrustworthy medium the Internet is. I look forward to the day when the Internet, like the two-faced gossip of old, will be universally reviled.

I asked The Princess to promise not to look at anything relating to me on the Internet ever again, but she won't promise because she will look because she cares. The EU has talked about introducing legislation which enables individuals to have their names removed from all websites. If such legislation is ever introduced I will take full advantage of it and have my name removed completely from the World Wide Web. I wish devoutly that the damned thing had never been invented. It has caused me endless trouble and never done me any good at all. I have been libelled endlessly and vast quantities of my copyright material has been stolen and spread around by people who make money out of it but never give me a penny. Yahoo pompously refers to its customers as belonging to a `community'. I have never ever felt that I belong to the Internet community or indeed that any community exists. The Internet is a cesspit controlled and largely populated by cowardly thieves and incompetents.

During over 30 years of campaigning I've received more writs and injunctions than I can remember. I've been followed by private detectives and served with sheaves of warning letters. I've been libelled and slandered and lied about. I've been falsely accused of not being a proper doctor. I've received threatening letters from corporate thugs and people have tried to bribe me. I've had books banned around the world and I've been fired by dozens of newspapers and TV and radio companies for upsetting the establishment, annoying governments and being outrageous enough to insist on telling the truth and giving people the facts.

But few things piss me off more royally than the rubbish that appears on the Internet.

16
11.41 a.m.
The Princess failed to warn me that I was about to reverse into a stone wall. She was in the trucky thing with me when I reversed into the wall and, as is widely known, it is always the passenger's responsibility to yell out `mind the wall' on these occasions. This she singularly failed to do. So we now have only three quarters of an offside rear light protector Perspex thing. I e-mailed the garage and asked them to obtain another one so that they can nail it into place. Actually, as something of an expert on these matters, I

suspect they will glue it in place. The Princess said she thinks the wall moved anyway. A small earthquake perhaps.

14.39 p.m.

The official unemployment figures have hit 2,500,000 million but these figures are as honest as a politician's speech (or a BBC news broadcast). There are an additional five million out of work but receiving benefits and most of these are receiving incapacity benefits. Nearly two million people have been too ill to work for five years or more. One in five British adults now relies on government handouts for their fags, booze and gambling. Around half of the millions who claim to be too sick to work claim to be stressed or too mentally ill to do any sort of work that doesn't involve sitting in the pub watching the racing on television or sitting at home playing computer games.

21.52 p.m.

I am delighted to see that publicans in Holland appear to be winning a fight to be allowed to let their patrons smoke. I have been campaigning against smoking for over half a century now. I bought the RCP Report on smoking with my pocket money when I was a kid. I was one of the first doctors to draw attention to the hazards of passive smoking. But the ban on smoking in pubs is nothing to do with health. Indeed, the evidence shows that it causes more ill health than it prevents (by encouraging people to stay at home where they drink and smoke more and by putting bar staff out of work). It is just another example of misguided EU fascism. If people want to smoke in pubs, and people want to work in them, they should be allowed to do so. It is possible to argue that smoking does less damage to our society than alcohol, tranquillisers and anti-depressants. And people who are deprived of one crutch will usually turn to another.

23.44 p.m.

I remember that the rumour that I have been struck off the medical register was started some years ago by a Swiss man called Hans Ruesch. Ruesch claimed to be opposed to vivisection but I was never entirely sure of this. When I was elected President of an organisation called LIMAV (Lega Internazionale Medici per l'Abolizione della Vivisezione) which represented over 1,000 doctors opposed to vivisection he became intensely jealous and rang me up to tell me that he should have been made president instead. (This would not have been possible because the organisation was for doctors and he wasn't medically qualified). He then told me that he was the most important anti-vivisector in the world. Anxious to placate him I immediately assured him that I agreed with this sentiment and would happily give him a letter confirming the approbation. Unfortunately, this didn't work. Ruesch simply became hysterical and incoherent. He was not a pleasant man. He had his bank account details printed on his notepaper so that people could give him money. A misguided reader of mine who was mentally ill sold her house and gave him the proceeds. She didn't have anywhere else to live. I contacted Ruesch and asked him to give her at least some of the money back. He refused, saying it had been given to him and he was keeping it.

23.49 p.m.

After my unhappy experience with Yahoo it occurs to me that the authorities should bring back duelling. It would be a much better way of dealing with disputes than anything else we have at present, far better than litigation or complaints procedures. And what great television it would make. A weekly duelling programme. The health and safety people will never go for it, of course. They are far too wimpy. They prefer to kill people in bits, with red tape, rather than with the sword.

But it's a fine idea.

We should also bring back the stocks. Just think of the fun we could all have throwing old cabbages and rotten tomatoes at Fred Goodwin, Gordon Brown and Tony Blair. We could have stocks built everywhere and fill them with bankers. And we could force supermarkets to give away their rotten eggs and vegetables.

17

08.30 a.m.

When we woke up and pulled back the curtains we had a surprise. There is light snow everywhere. Buses and cars seemed to be running normally but, naturally, there has been no rubbish collection. The big strong binmen down plastic containers the moment a flake of snow hits the road.

09.45 a.m.

The head of a website called Wikileaks is in prison accused of publishing the truth and making rich and important Americans squirm with embarrassment and look as stupid as they are. We live in a humourless, truthless age. Crack a joke to the Gestapo guards at airport security and men with toothbrush moustaches will snap on the handcuffs before you can say: 'Hitler.'

10.18 a.m.

The sweep came. He is a really nice fellow who did an excellent job and made no mess at all. He was here for an hour and charged £35. I give him £40 and he seemed well pleased. He also gave me free advice on how to make our log burner work more efficiently.

12.49 p.m.

The EU is definitely bringing in new laws about annuities which will force insurance companies to pay the same amount of money to men as to women. Even though there is a well-known and well-established difference in life expectation between the two sexes, it will, apparently, be illegal for companies to differentiate between the sexes. The result will be that annuities for men will fall by about 10%. This will, of course, dramatically damage the pension incomes of male citizens. Just about the only people who will not be affected by this utterly absurd and unfair piece of legislation will be those who work for the EU and the Government. Their fat, non-contributory, index-linked pensions will continue as before. The EU seems determined to ape every bad thing the USSR ever did. I wonder how long it will be before the average citizen realises that the EU, Hitler's bastard love child, is the greatest enemy Britain has ever faced. If Mengele and Borman did anything after the end of the Second World War they were surely alive and well in Brussels, planning the downfall of England and furthering the Fuhrer's dream.

16.01 p.m.

We were about to leave the house when The Princess announced that she had lost her mobile phone. I could have rung it to help her find it but she remembered turning it off. After a 15 minute search the phone is found at the bottom of her remarkably capacious handbag. I have travelled on the continent with a smaller bag than the one The Princess carries on her shoulder. If the Nazis lurking in the Eurostar customs sheds ever take it into their heads to search her bag it will take them weeks.

17.23 p.m.

Next year I am 65 and I have to write to tell HMRC because although they must know these things and have them secured in their computer they can't be bothered to notice that I am entitled to a pension and an age related allowance. And so, instead of the computer sorting out these things (and ensuring that I am no longer expected to pay National Insurance contributions) I have to remind them and fill in forms. How convenient for them and how inconvenient for me. The trouble is that I don't know where to write. I receive letters from numerous different tax offices: one in Barnstaple (which is where my offices are), one in Leicester (a city which I have visited only to appear on the local BBC radio station when promoting books), one in Cardiff (which I have visited only to broadcast on the local radio stations), one in Colchester (a town which I am afraid I have never visited) and several in parts of darkest Scotland which even the intrepid Richard Hannay probably never found. When I send HMRC cheques I send them to somewhere in Yorkshire which seems to be where the Government keeps the nation's money, and which is probably a good choice. I compromise by sending letters to two of their many addresses. I will probably have to repeat the exercise in a month or two's time.

21.36 p.m.

I hear that the VAT people are sending me a new password for my account. This will come in the post. 'It will be randomly selected,' said a nice man called Steve. 'That means a mix of letters and numbers that I can't possibly remember?' 'That's right,' he agreed. 'So I'll have to write it down and leave it in a drawer with all the other passwords.' 'Exactly.'

18
12.46 p.m.
While we were out shopping The Princess bought a tin of white paint so that we could cover up the graffiti at Publishing House. I had both arms full with shopping and to the astonishment and awe of the shop assistant The Princess put the tin of paint into her handbag. When we got back home I suggested that she left the paint in the truck so that we wouldn't have to remember to take it to Publishing House. She rummaged in her bag and it took her several minutes to find the paint. I didn't say a word but it seemed astonishing to me that a woman should carry a handbag which is so large that it is possible to lose a can of paint in it.

14.52 p.m.
A judge has decided that Lloyds bank was entirely proper in charging £10,200 for a single premium insurance policy that cost £1,300. The other £8,900 was a commission 'earned' by Lloyds Bank. When the couple complained, a judge said he couldn't see anything wrong. Well, he was probably the only person in the country (apart from bankers) who couldn't. Coincidentally, in the post today I received a note from Lloyds telling me that if I want an overdraft I will have to pay 17.3% interest. Since they currently pay me around 0.5% interest on my deposit account that means that the difference between the rate they pay when borrowing and the rate they charge when lending is 16.8%. Shylock himself would have been proud of that. If the banks didn't pay such obscenely large salaries and bonuses to the half-wits who work in their investment banking departments they really ought to be able to make a profit with margins like that.

16.29 p.m.
The broken rear light on our truck has been mended. It cost £114.23 for a small piece of clear, flimsy plastic that cannot possibly have cost more than ninepence to make.

18.54 p.m.
A man on television, wearing an overcoat and no hat, told us that the weather hasn't been as bad for 25 years. Behind him there is a little snow on the pavement. The cold has apparently disrupted the

country again. Schools are closed. Trains are not running. Airports and council offices are shut. People are advised to stay at home. I suddenly remembered when it snowed when I was a child. It was as cold inside as outside. When still in short trousers I walked two and a half miles to school through snow so deep that it came over the top of my wellington boots and soaked my socks. The kids in my class put their socks on the radiators with the obvious consequences. The snow came but there was little or no disruption. Everyone got to work. Schools remained open. I never missed school because of the weather. We made slides that were longer than a cricket pitch and had snowball fights that lasted until our hands and gloves were frozen solid. What a nation of wimps we have become.

21.43 p.m.

The police are complaining about the cost of looking after protests and demonstrations. Apparently a protest meeting of 1,500 English Defence League supporters needed 1,500 policemen at a cost of £800,000. Even if the policemen were needed for the whole day (and such demonstrations rarely seem to start before lunch or go on after dark) that works out at £533 per policeman per day. Knock off the £33 per head for the cost of wear and tear on truncheons and helmets and you are left with £500 per policeman per day. If the average copper works a five day week and has six weeks holiday that means that they cost £115,000 per year each. Isn't that a bit steep for a bloke with O Level woodwork? I wonder if the police could be complaining about the cost of policing demonstrations as a prelude to demanding tougher laws banning protests? It will not, of course, occur to them or to politicians that if they made an attempt to create a just and democratic society the disenfranchised voters wouldn't feel the need to demonstrate in the streets.

19

10.18 a.m.

While waiting to buy a magazine I stood behind two women in a short queue. 'I spoke to him shortly after he died,' said the shorter of the two women. As soon as I got out of the shop I wrote it down. I can only think that she must have visited a spiritualist. It's a wonderful line, though.

11.02 a.m.

I drove round to the nearest hospice charity shop with another six large black bags full of books. I've been having another of my clearouts and in the last two weeks I've taken them around 30 bags. I have no idea how many books that is. But there are still no spaces on my shelves. All that has happened is that some of the books piled high on the floor have moved onto the spaces on the shelves. When I left the charity shop I reversed the truck into a lamppost and smashed the piece of cheap plastic that I broke a few weeks ago and had repaired this morning at a cost of £114.23. The Princess said I was reversing like a Frenchman: 'Back, Hit, Stop.' I don't think I'll bother mending it this time. The truck really needs a much bigger rear bumper. The one it has is feeble and only comes into action after the taillights have been crushed. When we got home I mended the broken light with eight inches of Sellotape and saved £114.22.

12.45 p.m.

The nation has ground to a halt. We cannot travel to Barnstaple to collect the mail because the road is closed. Football matches carry on (they have underpitch heating) but Heathrow airport is pretty well closed and the would-be travellers are apparently abandoned cold and hungry. I do not understand how it can be so difficult to shovel a little snow off a couple of runways. What a shambles. I half expected to hear that they were leaving the runways closed to save the environment. In fact of course it was all about saving money using health and safety as the excuse (a spokesidiot for the airport said that they couldn't get the army in because soldiers are not trained to shovel snow). What about the health and safety of thousands of highly stressed passengers sleeping on cold floors for night after night? They are apparently not even allowed into the warm terminal for health and safety reasons. Why doesn't the Government do something? Isn't that what they are for? If they want to sell off the infrastructure then they should damned well control the people they sell it to, and ensure they aren't a bunch of skinflints. The airline staff all appeared to have gone home leaving the usual message that says: 'Due to a high volume of calls...' and telling callers to go to the website. Of course, the website tells callers to ring up.

Once again, the odd thing is that the Government spends much of its time (and our money) warning us that the weather is changing but then seems surprised when weather conditions change and we have an unexpected flurry of snow.

18.51 p.m.

I have found out why the European Union issues a 500 euro note. According to a reliable source it is simple. 'The benefits of seigniorage from banknotes held abroad are questionable. For example, the eurozone's decision to issue a 500 euro note made it easier to carry stashes of cash in the single currency than in dollars, whose largest denomination is $100. That enables the block to grab some of the market in cash-for-drugs deals and money laundering.' So, the EU is officially supporting the illegal drug trade and the money-laundering business. The 500 euro note is no longer available in the UK because the Serious Organised Crime Agency reckons that more than 90% of the notes are used or held by criminals. The attraction isn't difficult to understand. £1 million weighs 96% less in 500 euro notes than it does in sterling. It is, apparently, possible to cram 20,000 euros into a cigarette packet if you use 500 euro notes. I must try it.

22.38 p.m.

We watched *22 Bullets* starring Jean Reno. When The Princess bought the film she didn't realise that it was in French, with English subtitles. The makers of DVDs have a naughty tendency to rather hide this information in small print. We have during the past year bought a number of films that looked good but turned out to be in Japanese or some other language neither of us speaks. However, *22 Bullets* is a cracking film and Reno is, as always, enormously watchable. He is a French star in the glorious Gallic tradition; following in the bullet holes of Alain Delon, Jean-Paul Belmondo and Jean Gabin.

23.57 p.m.

The roads are so icy that they sparkle at night.

20

10.01 a.m.

Naturally, we still cannot get to Barnstaple to collect the mail. The North Devon link road, the A361, the death trap road designed for death and disappointment, is closed. Everyone hates the link road except for the policemen armed with speed cameras who love it so much they have even had special hidden lay-bys constructed, at vast expense, to improve their chances of catching motorists rushing around trying to earn a living. There have to date been well over 40 deaths on this damned road. I am not surprised. It is an absurdly dangerous road a hazardous mixture of two and three lanes. It is probably now too late to widen it but it desperately needs some sort of dividing central reservation. Every politician in North Devon should spend every waking minute fighting for some sort of improvement to this death trap. The bizarre thing is that there are many motorways in Britain which are quieter than this road. Building it the way it is undoubtedly saved a small amount of money but the cost in terms of accidents, injuries, deaths and delays must by now be one hundred times as great as the saving. Whoever made the decision to build this road should be put into the stocks for three days and then hung, drawn and quartered.

But now the damned road is closed. Again. North Devon is effectively cut off so we cannot fetch our mail or send out copies of *Alice's Diary* to eager book buyers. We watched the news on TV. It was good to see that there was no snow at all in Downing Street or around the ministries in London. I wonder if the snow was allowed to fall at all or if the Government merely brought in lots of people from Heathrow airport to clear it away. I cannot help feeling that if one of the local North Devon MPs were a Minister of Significance the A361 would be wider and looked after rather more enthusiastically.

21

11.35 a.m.

My Chinese publisher has written wanting to reprint copies of four of my books: *Bodypower*, *Mindpower*, *Spiritpower* and *How To Stop Your Doctor Killing You*. These have, apparently, sold very well and I'm told the first three are considered `classics' in China.

The publishers want me to go to China and to promise to let them see any new book I write before it is published in Britain so that they can bring out their edition at the same time. I don't think I'm too keen on travelling to China (my long legs don't like aeroplanes) but I'll be delighted to let them publish new books. My literary agent in China tells me that two other publishers there are also keen to publish my books and that between them the various publishers want to buy a good many more titles. The Princess made a parcel of 12 books and we posted them to China. The cost of sending the parcel by airmail is so great that it would have probably been cheaper to hire someone to fly to China and to take the books with them in their baggage.

18.22 p.m.
It is obviously the day of the Vernon in China. I receive an e-mail from a newspaper in China asking me if I will write a weekly column for them. They are offering me money, though they want to pay me every six months. I tell them I will accept their offer and allow them to pay me every six months if the editor of the newspaper also gets paid once every six months.

22
11.19 a.m.
The new password for my VAT account has arrived. It consists of a mixture of 12 letters (some upper case and some lower case) and numbers. Naturally, it is impossible to remember. It is so long that I even have difficulty copying it from their letter to my computer. I have to read it several times to check it. Why do computers always ask if you want them to remember the password you have just entered? What is the point of having a password if you allow the computer to store it?

23
14.56 p.m.
Five days after the binmen should have collected our rubbish, they have still not been round. A man from the council has issued a warning that citizens should take their food waste back into their homes for health and safety reasons. Buses are still moving around.

The supermarkets are still delivering groceries. But the binmen are sitting indoors reading the paper and sipping tea.

24
21.55 p.m.
We both spend much of the day wrapping presents and putting them under the Christmas tree. We both enjoy an old-fashioned Victorian-style Christmas.

25
10.30 a.m.
The Princess has spoilt me, as usual, and bought me a huge pile of presents, all carefully and beautifully wrapped. She bought me a solid silver pen, a vast pile of books and DVDs (including just about everything starring the Marx Brothers and everything including Jimmy Stewart that I don't already own), a beautiful pewter model of the Mercedes that Rudolf Caracciola drove in the 1931 Mille Miglia (I already have a similar model of the Mercedes with which Stirling Moss won the 1955 race), a copy of the 1953 edition of the Radio Fun annual and a very old Dandy annual from the days when Desperate Dan was Desperate Dan and not the politically correct wimp he has become. She also bought me the new version of the Seiko Encyclopaedia Britannica and Oxford Dictionary. I have had the old one of these on my desk for years and find it invaluable. It means I can have the essence of both huge books on my desk in something the size of a pocket diary. The new version includes the *Oxford Dictionary of Quotations*, the *Oxford Thesaurus of English, Modern Slang and Abbreviations* and *Fowler's Modern English Usage*. I have all the books, of course, but this piece of technology (which keeps my desk clear and is marvellous for travelling) is good technology. This is real progress. And the batteries fit easily into a neat compartment which doesn't require a screwdriver to open.

I like gadgets but am very picky about them: if they don't work immediately when taken out of the box, without resorting to an hour studying incomprehensible instructions or telephone calls (press 1,2,3, etc. and then pay premium rate money for advice from someone in the Philippines who doesn't speak English) it is a failure and it is their fault not mine. In my considerable experience

99% of modern gadgets are a failure. This one is a thumping success.

Although we had agreed not to buy each other anything which required a plug and the assistance of mains electricity The Princess stretched the rules by buying me a new Senseo coffee making machine. (Christmas is stressful enough but the prospect of having to deal with instruction manuals, batteries and so is too much.) The instructions (clearly written by someone who learned his art writing incomprehensible manuals for DVD players) came on a huge, poster sized sheet of paper (so much more cumbersome than a booklet). There were nine separate instructions for preparing the machine for use, 11 for using it, 11 for cleaning it afterwards, four for flushing it after cleaning it and 10 instructions for descaling (at regular intervals though not everytime). My favourite bit of the poster was the bit headed 'Troubleshooting'. In response to the problem 'I cannot open the lid' the solution is 'Switch off the machine and wait 24 hours'. I began to feel this may have been the one present that was a mistake. I have owned cars that were easier to understand. A new hat might have been a better choice. Hats are so easy. They either fit or they don't. We put away the coffee machine and instead played with some of my new toys. My favourite was the bubble gun which shoots an endless stream of beautiful soap bubbles and lights them up as it does so.

11.50 a.m.

The Princess always buys me a selection of toys as part of my Christmas present. One of my new toys this year required batteries and naturally required the removal of a small plastic cover. I couldn't do this without a very tiny screwdriver. And I couldn't find our very tiny screwdrivers. Not even the smallest screwdriver on my Swiss Army penknife would fit. I was about to break open the plastic cover with the tool for removing stones from horses' hooves when I remembered that there was bound to be a small plastic pouch containing a set of small screwdrivers in one of the crackers we have waiting to be opened. So I fetched The Princess and we pulled a lot of crackers. We found a small, green yo-yo (which works very well), a padlock and key, one of those metal puzzles that drives everyone mad until someone just pulls the two interlocking pieces apart with brute strength, a tiny pack of playing cards that we always put away and think might come in handy when travelling but which we never take with us and so never use, a pen that looks a little like a miniature Mont Blanc if you viewed it through a misted up telescope from a mile or so away but didn't work very well and which came with a notebook half the size of a book of matches, and, finally, at long last, the small pack of very tiny screwdrivers which we knew was hiding in there somewhere. Never before, I suspect, has a small pack of miniature screwdrivers been received more rapturously. Once I'd removed the little battery cover I threw it, and the screws, away. I have started throwing away battery covers and their little screws. There used to be one screw holding these damned things in place. Now the EU has obviously decided that toddlers can operate screwdrivers well enough to remove one or two screws so there are often four and sometimes six screws to unfasten. And then the little battery compartment cover sticks and won't budge even though all the screws are out. The game The Princess bought came with a sheet of instructions which gave me 12 separate pieces of advice about the batteries but had absolutely no instructions about how to play the game. There was boring advice about what to do with exhausted batteries ('lie them down and give them a drink' was The Princess's much more sensible suggestion), the dangers of short-circuiting supply terminals (got me there), the terrifying danger of mixing different types of batteries, the importance of securely screwing the battery cover into place (it is already in the bin, of course), the importance of observing the polarity guide and following the manufacturer's instructions for safe use and disposal of batteries (check with local authority) and a warning that the product isn't suitable for children under 36 months (though they would need a chainsaw to break it into bits suitable to eat) and, penultimately, the inevitable warning 'please retain this packaging for future reference' though they don't say why since it is utterly pointless and so it goes on the fire. Finally, we were advised that for more information about batteries, battery safety and battery disposal we should contact our local authority. The game is excellent fun and involves noise and flashing lights.

14.00 p.m.

The Princess has prepared enough food for a British army expeditionary force. The meal is so big that I don't know whether to eat it or to apply for planning permission for it. I tell The Princess that 17 of the 3,432 visitors she is expecting have had to cancel but that there will still be more than enough food. She looks panicky for a moment. 'How many people are coming?' she asks. 'I thought it was just the two of us.' I reassure her. We eat most of the food but it takes us a long time. It is magnificent. The Princess makes the best Christmas lunch I have ever eaten. Her roast potatoes and roast parsnips are out of this world. I meant to take a photograph to show to people who ask: 'What do vegetarians eat?' But I couldn't drag myself away from the table for long enough to find the camera.

15.48 p.m.
We try to make coffee with the new Senseo machine. The coffee it produces is worse than anything British Rail ever served. It is truly awful and quite undrinkable. I can taste detergent, plastic, nuclear waste, the fetid smell that wafts up through the gratings from the Paris Metro, the dark fluid they serve in seaside hotels and the (to me) disgusting liquid they sell in Starbucks. I couldn't smell anything resembling coffee. I poured myself a triple malt whisky to take away the taste of the Senseo rubbish.

18.17 p.m.
My chess computer beat me. I challenged it to a game of table tennis and won by a walkover.

22.48 p.m.
In the evening we watched, as we always do, Poirot's Christmas. There's a lovely scene at the end of the film when Poirot unwraps a pair of gloves lovingly knitted for him by Inspector Japp's wife. 'Aren't you going to put them on?' asks Japp, proud of his wife's skill. 'Oh no,' says Poirot. 'I will keep them for church on Sundays.'

26
11.34 a.m.

I put the Great Escape DVD into the player and turned it on. I then left it to play. We always do this on Boxing Day. We just wander in occasionally to see how the prisoners are all getting on. And we know the theme music so well that we can wander in to watch our favourite scenes.

13.11 p.m.

I have started reading Oliver Goldsmith's *Vicar of Wakefield* which I discover I have never read before. The Princess has bought me a beautifully bound, century-old, pocket-sized edition. A terrific book to look at, to feel and (most important of all) to read.

22.16 p.m.

We watched a Top Gear programme in which the presenters took the mickey out of Christianity. I'd like to see them try that on Jews or Muslims. In truth, of course, they wouldn't dare.

27

14.55 p.m.

One of my crackers today contained six rather splendid marbles in a small string bag. The bag came with a warning notice which read 'Warning: Not suitable for children under 3-years-old due to small balls.'

16.32 p.m.

Foxes have tipped up the food waste bin across the road. It has been sitting there for weeks since the last collection (health and safety prevented binmen going out with a little light snow in the air). Rotting, stinking food is now spread across the pavement. If the EU bureaucrats are going to force people to put out their food waste for recycling then they really should make sure that they collect the damned stuff.

18.29 p.m.

Obama is quoted as claiming that the American fighting forces are the best in the history of the world which suggests that he has gone back to smoking funny substances. It's nonsense like this which annoys the rest of the world and is, I suspect, one of the reasons why, according to a survey I intend to conduct in the new year,

97% of people outside America think the nation deserves what it is shortly going to get not from terrorists but from Chinese bra and television manufacturers. Lots of Americans are so deluded that they believe they won two World Wars all by themselves. After my books *Rogue Nation* and *Global Bully* were published I received a mass of hate mail 'reminding' me that without the Americans we would now all be speaking German.

28

11.01 a.m.

There is much news in the motoring press about Formula One teams hiring drivers not just because they know how to change gear and steer round corners but because they bring with them millions of pounds in sponsorship. It is clear that only the richest teams can win in Formula One. Only countries with loads of cash have races. They should cut the hypocrisy by getting rid of the races and, instead, have a fortnightly auction for the podium places. The highest bidders would get the cups, the lower bidders would get points and those with not enough money to buy anything would get nothing. This would change absolutely nothing and the same teams and drivers would still win everything. There would be no need for teams to spend a fortune on building cars and then flying them round the world. All the proceeds could, of course, go to Mr Bernie Ecclestone. The whole thing would be a delight for the green campaigners. And the auctions could be weekly. There could be 52 races a year. The BBC could show the auctions which would probably be as exciting as the old-fashioned and now rather passé races.

15.38 p.m.

A former employee wrote to say how sad she was to hear that Publishing House had closed. She had thought and hoped that it would go on for ever. I sent this reply: 'I always hoped that Publishing House would go on for ever too and it was sad to have to close it. Unfortunately, the spirit of the place had changed in recent years and instead of being a fairly carefree publishing enterprise the rules and regulations somehow seemed to become far more important. It seemed to me that a lot of time was spent on staff training, on making sure that various bits of the Government agencies were kept happy and goodness knows what else. I didn't spend enough time managing things and PH lost direction. I just wanted to write books, publish them and help make people think and smile. The last year or two of Publishing House became rather sad and difficult and I felt increasingly isolated from what was going on. I certainly felt very unhappy at the way things had changed. So although it was sad to close it, I also felt relieved. I now have around 30,000 books in stock and no real means of selling them. And I also have a lot of new books in my head to write and publish. So I will clearly have to set up a new version of Publishing House at some point. A new building, a new purpose and new hopes. Publishing House may have reached the end of one life but somewhere, somehow it will be reborn.'

18.42 p.m.

The cracker presents seem slightly better this year, though the paper hats and snaps are worse than ever. The Princess found a whoopee cushion in hers and I found a small water pistol in mine. The Princess commandeered the mini water pistol and had great fun squirting me with it. I did think of seeding the crackers with better toys but in the end I couldn't find anything I could fit into them without tearing them apart and I knew that if I pulled them apart I would never get them back together again. There is no point at all in buying really expensive crackers because they just contain silver plated versions of the things you tend to find in them anyway. There was a tendency last year to put in practical items (nail clippers, shoe horns and absolutely awful egg cups, a compass which pointed north whichever way you held it and a stapler with no staples in it, presumably on health and safety grounds). I don't mind the small screwdrivers because they are useful. I tend to choose the prettiest crackers and buy lots of them.

The Princess's joke this evening was: `What's the difference between a lighthouse keeper, a thief and a pot of glue?' The answer is: `One watches over seas, one seizes watches. And the pot of glue? Ah, that's where you get stuck.' My joke was `What's the difference between a sick horse and a dead bee? One is a seedy beast and the other is a bee deceased.' The people who write this stuff deserve some sort of award though I'm not sure what.

22.58 p.m.

We watched *Mr Blandings Builds his Dream House,* starring Cary Grant and Myrna Loy. What a wonderful film. The two stars buy a house with their hearts rather than their heads. It is so, so much funnier than the Tom Hanks film *The Money Pit* (which also deals with a house purchase). As always with DVDs these days the subtitles were on, and difficult to get rid of, but once we had sorted that and changed the default the film was a delight. We are further encouraged to continue with our house search.

29

11.37 a.m.

Minimum wages in China are soaring by 21%. The Chinese want more money to spend on cars and hamburgers. The result will be that the cost of everything on sale in Britain will also rise. Bras and television sets are going to be more expensive. And since the Chinese will be consuming more the cost of food and oil will soar too. All this was, of course, quite predictable. These days the basic skill investors need is the ability to think globally and to apply geopolitical thinking to every situation. It used to be said that if a butterfly flapped its wings in Brazil it could cause a storm on the other side of the planet. Well, these days, a small political event or a natural disaster in one country can produce massive changes in countries on the other side of the globe.

14.27 p.m.

It is now three weeks since our rubbish was last collected. Food bins are overflowing and stinking. The street is awash with bits of rubbish. The Princess saw three foxes in the garden yesterday. I wonder how long it will be before the rats arrive. I rang the council's rubbish department but there was no answer. I rang the council's main switchboard and my call was answered by a machine. I rang the community health department and got another machine. I rang the complaints department and got a third machine. I was about to ring the `hate incident' line and say that I hate the binmen but I didn't dare. If there are any binmen of ethnic origin I could be in serious trouble. Instead, I tried to ring the trading standards department to complain that I have paid my council tax and am not getting what I paid for. But I got a machine telling me that there was no one available.

18.09 p.m.

There is news today that doctors are complaining that not enough people are being vaccinated. None of the reporters covering the story mention that doctors get paid for giving vaccines and are therefore interested parties.

20.07 p.m.

Over Christmas, the police shot another mentally ill man. Gunmen use tranquilliser darts for dangerous but valuable animals - and they go down immediately - is it really impossible for the police to use tranquillisers? Or tear gas? Or rubber bullets? I realise it probably wouldn't be as much fun but the police in Britain do seem to be trigger-happy these days. The so-called Independent Police Commission will no doubt conduct an independent investigation and independently conclude that the shooting was inevitable, necessary and vital in the fight against global warming.

22.28 p.m.

A reader from Malaysia writes to me about some of my books which are selling there. This is something of a surprise since although a number of my books were published in Malaysia the contracts expired years ago and I currently have no publisher there. It is alarming how many of my books are being published by publishers who have not bought the rights. This is, I fear, the result of the Internet 'no copyright' age. Not only do I get no royalties but it is also impossible to sell rights in a country when this happens.

22.58 p.m.

Some months ago we decided to think about buying a hotel and turning it back into a house. Commercial property prices have fallen far more than residential prices and we really don't want to keep waiting for residential prices to become more sensible. Country hotels are not much sought after at the moment because no one can get commercial loans. Besides, the prices the owners are asking are still entirely unreasonable and most small hotels just don't make sense. A ten bedroom country hotel that costs £1,000,000 to buy would have to charge central London boutique hotel prices to cover its interest costs let alone pay back the capital cover insurance, staff, heating and so on. We saw one hotel priced at £700,000 which had a gross turnover of £30,000 a year. You don't need to be an experienced hotelier to realise that those figures just don't work. It is impossible to see how anyone can buy a hotel or boarding house at current prices and expect to do anything except make a thumping great loss every year. Only an appreciation in the value of the property would give an opportunity to survive financially.

We looked at several possibles and found a hotel that looked perfect. There were woodpeckers in the woods and robins in the garden and swans on the river. It would, we thought, be an adventure. Lots of bedrooms, lots of bathrooms, a little woodland, a beautiful garden and great views. We would turn it back into a house and enjoy it. We showed the pictures to a few friends. Everyone wanted to come and stay.

There are, of course, some advantages to buying a hotel. Massive, thick fire doors protect all the rooms. There are smoke alarms and emergency lighting which comes on if the electricity goes off. All good fun.

There are downsides too. Signs to take down both inside and outside.

And then, today, the whole thing fell through.

The problems just kept mounting. The penultimate straw came when we at last saw the energy efficiency figures and the heating bills. These showed that it would cost us at least £20,000 a year to heat the place. And with no mains gas, we thought there would inevitably be problems keeping the gas tanks filled up. The very thought of it gave us chilly feet. Any attempt to improve the energy efficiency would cost a fortune and take huge amounts of building work. We found this worrying because I have little doubt that within a year or two the Government (urged on by the EU) will penalise owners of low efficiency houses with rationing or vastly increased prices.

The ultimate straw, the one that finally broke the camel's already overladen back, came when we received from the owners a four page list of the items they were prepared to sell us as 'extras'.

The list included the doorkeys, the doorbells, the toilet roll holders, the little wooden wedges that hold open the fire doors, some road cones, the bird nesting boxes, a pile of useful wood, an old door and so on and so on. We were paying a good price for the property and we were being invited to make an offer to buy the keys. We lost all faith in the deal. Our solicitor pointed out that this might be referred to as taking the piss. Another friend said it was killing the golden goose.

I have bought homes where the previous owners have taken the television aerials, the bathroom cabinets and the mirrors but being prepared to take, or sell, the keys is new to me. (I never understand why people take things like bathroom cabinets. The value of such small items is insignificant. Moving them takes time and energy and money. And the replacements never quite fit the holes that are left so the walls have to be redecorated.)

We are devastated. This is a sad end to the year. The search goes on. Our attempts to find new offices are proving equally troublesome. The problem is that in many cases the people who previously occupied the premises we like have gone bust and the banks which have taken over ownership are incredibly slow to make decisions. I suppose the million pound a year guys are simply too nervous to make any sort of decisions - on the grounds that if you don't make any sort of decision you can't make a wrong decision to be blamed for.

23.31 p.m.

More dull news. The French tax authorities are chasing me because I haven't paid my French television licence fee. They are now imposing a penalty. I have written three letters so far explaining that I haven't paid because we don't have a television set in the apartment. I rang the Parisian authorities and explained this. A very nice sounding man sympathised, said I should not have to pay the fee or the penalty, and suggested that I write another letter. So I'll write another letter.

Looking at my investment records I'm delighted to see that for the past decade I had better investment returns than any hedge fund or vampire bank I can find. And I'm proud to say that I did it without borrowing a penny, begging for government aid or cheating thousands of hard-working pensioners out of their savings. I've decided not to reprint my book *Moneypower* when it goes out of print (which won't be long). I'm proud of the book but I made far more money out of following my advice in it than I made out of the book. When the book came out, in a rather handsome hardback edition, we sent copies to every financial magazine, all the nationals and all the regional newspapers. The book received not a single review (though it has been well praised on Amazon).

30
11.01 a.m.
I've received a cheque for £12.25 from BT. This is quite a landmark. Since May I have received a constant barrage of letters, bills and demands from BT. They have asked for quite huge (and seemingly ever increasing and incomprehensible) sums of money for a system I didn't want and had never asked them to provide. They have at long last admitted that I don't owe them any money - but that, on the contrary, they owe me. The complaints procedure was quite unhelpful. It was only when I contacted the Chairman that the company accepted its mistake. I can't begin to imagine how many hours I have wasted on this wretched company. I will do my best to avoid ever having any contact with them again.

13.21 p.m.
A reader who wanted to find a Hungarian publisher for *How To Conquer Health Problems Between Ages 50 and 120* (which I wrote with The Princess) now wants me to publish the Hungarian edition and pay him a commission. He will transport the books to Hungary and to the USA. He does not say where his commission will come from or how I will receive any money for my book. I decline his kind offer.

14.32 p.m.
We received the lawyer's bill for abandoning the purchase of the house we thought we were in love with. I signed a cheque for around £1,200 for not buying a house.

15.26 p.m.

Our rubbish has not been collected for six weeks. After five telephone calls and a mass of e-mails a lorry turned up today and took away some of the rubbish that had accumulated in the street outside. For a moment I felt pathetically happy about this and then, within seconds, I felt pathetically sad that such a small thing should make me so happy.

16.20 p.m.
The Princess's symptoms have improved slightly. We still don't know what caused them, though I have ideas. I will continue to try to heal her with a prescription of love and friendship. And I will continue to try (with only moderate success so far) to shield her from the toxic stresses which are so common these days.

18.39 p.m.
So far, over the holidays, I have built a large plastic Mercedes open tourer, a wooden Grand Prix car and a wooden trebuchet which actually works. I have played a good many games and watched a lot of films. I have read three books and eaten too much.

21.35 p.m.
The oil price is going up. And I believe it is going to keep going up. There will be pull-backs, of course. Nothing goes up in a straight line. But the oil price is going up. I welcome it, not because I have invested a good chunk of our money in oil company shares but because I believe that as people realise just how their lives are being changed by the real environmental disaster (peak oil) so they will be more willing to distrust the politicians and demand some real answers. It is for this reason that I also welcome every daft piece of legislation from the European Union (and the daft stuff has been pouring out of Brussels in recent months). We need a revolution. We need anarchy. The stage is being set.

22.10 p.m.
We bought three different types of coffee to try in the Senseo machine. They are all awful. The coffee the machine makes looks good. But it now tastes of metal, plastic and old shoe.

23.11 p.m.

I had another e-mail from the editor working for the big Chinese newspapers. The editor's boss has apparently read and been impressed by four of my books which are available in Chinese. The newspaper editor asks if I know anyone else who would be qualified to write a column for them. I tell them my wife is very well qualified and would write excellent columns. Only when they agree that this is a fine idea do I tell The Princess. She seems very shocked for a moment but then grins broadly and is clearly excited about the idea of reaching the world's biggest readership. I also receive an e-mail from my new publisher in Poland who tells me that he has bought several domain names (including www.vernoncoleman.pl) to promote my books. He talks of selling hundreds of thousands of books. My future now clearly lies abroad.

23.25 p.m.
A reader sent a very angry e-mail complaining that the book she had ordered had not arrived. She threatened to do all sorts of terrible things, most of them apparently involving defamatory comments on the Internet. I wrote back pointing out that her order had not yet arrived and suggested that she get in touch with her god to see what he could do about it. Alternatively, I suggested that she might blame the Royal Mail for not delivering her letter or the Government for failing to get rid of the snow more efficiently.

23.50 p.m.
Another reader writes to point out that although the bank rate is around 0.5% and savers are lucky if they receive 1% on their savings and mortgages are barely any higher, businessmen wanting to expand must pay around 12% (and possibly even more) to borrow money. He adds that this rate is only available if excellent security is provided. When my bank statement arrived I noticed that my bank is again warning me that if I have an overdraft I will pay 1.34% per month (or 17.3% equivalent annual rate). That is more per month than they pay me on my deposit account per year. The Government owns 40% of my bank.

23.57 p.m.

My wonderful new Polish publisher wants to know if he has to reproduce the cover of the English version of *How To Stop Your Doctor Killing You* or if he can create his own cover. I tell him he can put on whatever cover he likes. He then writes back to ask if the book is the subject of any litigation. This is a little late in the day but I reassure him. A reader sends me a generous and kind e-mail to say that he has 'never been annoyed by a book as much as *Gordon is a Moron* because it hit home just how damaging and negligent this man has been'. And I receive an e-mail from a doctor asking if I would publish his very original and important sounding work in the *British Clinical Journal*. He reminds me that when I was editor of the BCJ in 1973 I published a leading article supporting the work of Oliver Sacks on the relief of the symptoms of post-encephalitic parkinsonism with L-dopa. 'Up to that time, Dr Sacks was unable to publish his work in peer-reviewed journals he sent his paper to, and met universal scepticism of his results, with the exception of the *British Clinical Journal*. Eventually he wrote a book called *The Awakening* which was made into a movie.' I had forgotten just how much good stuff the BCJ published and am saddened to remember that both that journal and the *European Medical Journal* are now defunct. But clearly not forgotten.

31
10.45 a.m.
The 31st is not officially a bank holiday in England but everyone seems to treat it as one. (The Scots have an extra bank holiday at New Year but since very few of them actually ever do any work at all this doesn't make much difference to their dependence on the English economy.) To my surprise however, the binmen arrive. They park their lorry outside and leave it there for one and a half hours. They disappear into a nearby house. They collect nothing. When I ring the council and report this I speak to a man in the rubbish department who says they are very busy. There is now so much rubbish on the pavements that pedestrians are having to walk in the road. Our neighbours have taken their rubbish to the local tip. I hate them for this. If we give in then the council will have won and we will never have our rubbish collected. People like them make it easy for the council to renege on their

responsibilities. When the council does eventually collect the rubbish I don't believe for one second that they will make any attempt to collect the rubbish in categories. Everything will be thrown into one lorry and taken to the dump. I ring the council and am told to visit their website. This apparently has a search facility offering information about rubbish collection. I visited their website, put in our postcode and the full address (why they needed both I cannot imagine) and was taken to a page offering a mealy mouthed, vapid mission statement and a telephone number for me to ring. It is the same telephone number I have just rung; the same number everyone else has been given to ring.

16.40 p.m.
We still haven't found a house. And problems are mounting everywhere. Most importantly of all we still have to sort The Princess's illness.

A few years ago I wrote a book called *Why Everything Is Going To Get Worse Before It Gets Better.*In order to add a touch of optimism I gave the book a subtitle *And What You Can Do About It*. I think the subtitle was rather too optimistic. Much of what is getting worse is now completely out of our hands. The bureaucrats of the European Union run our lives and are rapidly creating chaos and disrupting lives. It is, after all, the EU which is entirely responsible for the rubbish in our streets, queues in our shops, ever declining services and the fact that we are constantly expected to pay more for less. But there's far more to come. Most of our public utilities are now owned by foreigners who have very little interest in maintaining services as long as they continue making huge profits. And if anyone is found prepared to buy the Royal Mail it's a fair bet that people living in rural areas will be told to collect their mail from the nearest sorting office.

17.28 p.m.
A fat man is suing the NHS for allowing him to get fat. If he wins the doors will be open and the nation will go bankrupt. What sort of lawyer takes a case like this?

19.37 p.m.

Two more wonderful pieces of news from the barmy bureaucrats of Brussels. First, thanks to the EU, prisoners will soon have the right to vote and, second, we are going to have elected police chiefs. These fit together so nicely and yet no one seems to have noticed. I wonder who will stand as Police Chief for the Dartmoor region. It could end up being a straight fight between Bert the Bankrobber and Sid the Safecracker, with the winner doubtless promising to ban police patrols, make burglar alarms illegal and introduce new rules making it an offence to lock doors and windows at night. I love these barmy EU laws because in the end people will rebel, we will have a revolution and the EU will be consigned to the dustbin of history. I expect the eurocrats have already negotiated wonderful settlements and pensions for themselves, ready for the day when this happens.

21.58 p.m.

Neither of us can stand those Jools Holland music programmes that appear to celebrate the New Year but which are, as everyone knows, recorded in December. Probably during the afternoon and possibly in a warehouse in North London with blackout on the windows and everyone warned at five minute intervals 'It's New Year, darlings, be enjoying yourselves. And there's real champagne afterwards in the green room for the main guests.' And the fireworks and camera phone waving on the other channel are even more depressing. As midnight approaches we select favourite Sherlock Holmes episodes to connect the two years. From 10.45 p.m. to 11.45 p.m. we will watch the episode called the *Final Solution* in which Jeremy Brett and Eric Porter topple over the Rheichenbach Falls. I will take out a few moments to fill in this diary. And then, after midnight, we will watch the episode called *The Empty House* during which Holmes, pantomime genius, comes back from the dead to delight Watson and Mrs Hudson. A death and a new beginning. We will, as always, wonder if the director had to tell other actors to ignore Jeremy's flamboyance and to restrict themselves to acting. Basil Rathbone was and is the body, mind and soul of Sherlock Holmes but Jeremy Brett gives him magic and makes him fly.

22.47 p.m.

Since it is not their New Year the Chinese are working. The newspaper want to pay me in yuan. They are worried about the fees they will have to pay their bank in order to pay me in American dollars or sterling.

22.56 p.m.

I remembered just in time not to miss the New Year's Day concert that the Vienna Symphony Orchestra always gives. The New Year's Day concert has overtaken in popularity the annual Proms which used to be such a highlight of the year. The BBC has dumbed down the Proms and destroyed most of what was good about them. I find it increasingly difficult to avoid the suspicion that the BBC does everything it can, whenever it can, to destroy, sneer at and belittle England and the English. And it does this with money provided by mostly English licence fee payers. I love seeing promenaders waving their own national flags (I spotted an Iraqi flag this year) but what's the point of waving an EU flag during Britannia rules the waves, Jerusalem, Land of Hope and Glory and other glorious celebrations of England and Britain? Does the EU give a grant for flag wavers? It is also depressing (and I suspect a deliberate policy) that the conductor at the Last Night of the Proms is invariably foreign and often has little command of the English language. I am pleased to see that the conductor of tomorrow morning's concert is a locally born conductor.

23.45 p.m.

Now, here comes the end of another year. I feel exhausted by the torrent of bad news, disappointment and demands, all unleavened by hope or promise.

At the start of the decade there were 857 million people starving or close to it. At the end of the decade there were 925 million people starving. At the start of the decade (in the year 2000) there were 423 terrorist attacks. A decade later, after spending billions and killing millions, there were 10,999 terrorist attacks in the year (nearly half of them in Iraq and Afghanistan). In the year 2000 opium was being grown on 202,626 acres of land in Afghanistan. By the year 2010 the land used for growing opium had almost doubled.

We leave the year with contradictions abounding. There are people who claim to be proud to be English but who see nothing wrong with supporting the EU. There are people who claim to love children but who support vaccination. There are people who claim to want to help the sick but who actively promote vivisection. There are people who are worried about global warming and starvation in Third World countries who still eat meat.

The Government's response to the financial crisis was to force the banks to lend more money (the deal was that they could keep their huge undeserved bonuses if they kept throwing the money around to the undeserving and greedy). It was as though a man whose house was on fire suddenly became aware that his flower border was spoilt by weeds and started digging out the weeds while the fire raged. The real problems remain: a bloated public sector, (where the average male employee now earns 8-10% more than the average private sector employee - and enjoys hugely better benefits) and a seemingly endless queue of greedy and self-serving, hypocritical politicians. They have between them encouraged and endorsed an arrogant, narcissistic society, a society in which reality television has bloomed and where citizens without values, skills or learning may, without work, rise far higher than those who work a society in which the greedy and ruthless are rewarded and the kind-hearted and sympathetic are oppressed, a society in which millions now refuse to take responsibility for their own lives but instead choose positions as State employed slaves. Television is the new opium of the people and like opium it deadens the brain, dulls inquisitiveness, saps the ambition and removes self-respect. Britons are an addictive people and now watch vast amounts of television (four hours a day seems to be the average), plus several more hours spent playing around on the Internet.

So, what does 2011 hold for us? In 2011 our allies will continue to bomb wedding parties wherever there is oil to be found. Animals will be kept in barbaric conditions, pumped full of carcinogens, fed corn that would save millions from starvation so that obese westerners can eat their daily burgers, be carried for days without food or water in two tier lorries designed so that the creatures below are constantly showered with urine and faeces, and, when they eventually reach their destinations, slaughtered in the most inhumane ways imaginable. And the carcasses will be chopped up and eaten with relish by idiots who should know, but don't because they aren't told because the media won't discuss it and doctors don't want to know because it's inconvenient, that the incidence of cancer and heart disease and just about every other killer disease you can think of is far greater among those who eat meat than among those who do not.

My guess is that by the end of the new year the oil price will be higher, there will be more rules and regulations, there will be more taxes, more toll roads, more unemployment. Our rubbish collections will be a bone of contention but nothing will have been done to improve them, indeed council services will have deteriorated noticeably. London will, with New York, still be the joint money laundering capital of the world but anyone wanting to spend their own money will still face absurd regulatory hurdles. The financial system hasn't deleveraged or shown remorse and nothing has changed so there are still more huge shocks to come. Pensions will continue to collapse and politicians will continue to lie and to screw up whenever they possibly can. Even though more and more of them are sent to prison there will still be more thieves and charlatans in the House of Commons and the House of Lords than in any comparably sized building in the country. What an example they all give to the young. Unions and civil servants will whinge and strike when their absurdly cosseted lifestyle is threatened by reality. They will, of course, claim that they are striking to draw attention to the fact that services will be cut back but they will be lying through their teeth. They will be striking to defend their part-time working weeks and their massively unaffordable solid gold pensions. If they really cared about public services they would happily accept a modest reduction in their pension expectations.

When they have two choices to make politicians and regulators will unerringly make the wrong one. White, middle class, middle aged, Christian heterosexuals, the despised vanilla in our multicultural society, will continue to be discriminated against and to have very few rights. White, middle class, elderly, Christian heterosexuals will continue to have no rights at all. The Human Rights Act will apparently continue to apply only to selected groups in our society. EU lawmakers will insist that British prisoners be given the vote they have been denied for more years than most of us can remember. British politicians will complain and protest but they cannot possibly win because our politicians have no power to veto legislation which comes from the EU. The daft law of the week becomes the daft law whatever we say because it comes printed on EU notepaper. We live as an occupied people because successive Prime Ministers, beginning with Heath and to date ending with Brown, have sold our country and paid a hefty price for the privilege. The forecasts in my book *2020* are coming true at a frightening pace far more speedily than I had imagined or feared. Awareness of geopolitical risk is everything because a problem in one country quickly becomes a problem in another. When there is a dispute in America over an oil rig, the resulting high oil price puts up inflation in Britain. And that leads to higher interest rates and lower house prices and reduced growth. Everything is interconnected in a way few people predicted. Will oil pause at $150 a barrel or will it go straight to $200 a barrel? Will there be a pull back or will it then simply carry on soaring until it reaches $250 dollars a barrel? What will happen in Britain when it costs the average motorist £200 to fill the tank of the average motor car? These are serious questions, though I realise that they are questions politicians and journalists don't like to recognise, let alone ask. They are simply too frightening for words. And when the revolutions inspired and fanned by the media (particularly the Internet) really begin to change the nature of the world how keen on the new media will the authorities be?

There is already far more censorship in Britain than most people realise. It's going to get far, far worse. When I wrote *2020* in 2010 I made a number of predictions about how I thought our world would change by the year *2020*. Some of them seemed even to me to be slightly off the wall. But I am now already receiving letters from people pointing out that many of the predictions I made have already come true.

I also believe that we will soon see a revolution within, and against, the European Union. How many predicted the collapse of the Berlin Wall or the fall of the Soviet Union? The world is ready for a revolution. The EU's unelected leadership of corrupt and venal bureaucrats continue to alarm and appal the disenfranchised voters of Europe; injustice and a growing sense of grievance will do the rests. It cannot now be long before there is a pan-European uprising, leading to the collapse of the European Union, the world's most fascist State.

23.56 p.m.
So that's pretty well the end of another 12 months just another year. I'm 65 in 2011. My retirement plan is for The Princess and I to buy our new English dream home, to find new business premises and to start a new publishing company. I also have five books in various stages of being written. And several dozen more in various stages of planning. I have no intention of retiring properly until everyone agrees with me.

23.58 p.m.
At two minutes to midnight, with Sherlock lost in the watery Swiss abyss, we flicked on the television to check the time. The BBC clock on the television tells a different time to our DVD player which has the time sent to it automatically in some mysterious way so we flick around to find a view of Big Ben.

I feel exhausted by the year just gone. 'Let's hope we have a quiet year ahead,' said The Princess, as the clock ticked steadily round to midnight. 'That would be nice,' I agreed.

We say together Sir Jacob Astley's prayer before the Battle of Edgehill: 'O Lord, Thou knowest how busy we must be today, if we forget Thee, do not Thou forget us for Christ's sake. Amen.'

00.01 a.m.
It is a new year. I give The Princess a card on which I have written:
When I am with you I am ready.
When we are apart I am waiting.'

This is the end of Vernon Coleman's first diary. His second diary, 'Just Another Bloody Year' is also available. For a full list of books by Vernon Coleman please visit www.vernoncoleman.com or visit Amazon Author Central.

Technical Acknowledgement

My thanks to The Princess, without whose help I would still be trying to find my pen and work out how to get the electricity into my computer.

Extra 1

The Publishing House Mission Statement (Why We Believe Small Publishers Are The Only Real Publishers Left)

Compared to the big international conglomerates Publishing House is very definitely a `small publisher'.

We don't have a massive sales force (actually, we don't have a sales force at all). We don't have a board of eminent directors (since we're not a limited company we don't have any directors). We don't have offices in a skyscraper (we do have offices but we just have an upstairs and a downstairs). And we don't have a PR department full of bright young things called Hyacinth and Jacoranda. (We don't have a PR department at all).

But we have one enormous advantage over the conglomerates.

We care passionately about books.

They have marketing departments which decide which books will sell. They then commission books that the sales force think they will be able to flog. They won't even consider a book until they've done a marketing feasibility study.

We publish books we believe in. We then try to sell them. Naturally, we try to make a profit. If we didn't we wouldn't last long. We have to pay the printing bills, the electricity bills, the phone bills, the rates, the insurance and so on.

But we've been publishing for 22 years. In that time we've sold over two million books. Our books have been translated into 24 languages and are sold by other publishers (including some big ones) in over 50 countries.

The conglomerates insist that every book should make a profit.

We don't. Some of our books make more money than others. But that's fine with us. We don't mind if the better sellers sometimes subsidise the other books. We don't mind if a book is a little slow to sell. Like good parents we love all our children equally - however successful, or unsuccessful, they might be.

Despite all the talk about the need for each book to stand on its own two feet many big publishers make an overall loss. They are kept alive - effectively as vanity publishers - by other parts of the conglomerate. So, for example, the TV division or the magazine division may help to subsidise the book publishing division.

We believe that book publishing can, and should, be allowed to stand alone. We believe that small publishers are now the only *real* publishers alive.

The big publishers often accept sponsorship from outside companies. We never do. We rely on the sale of books to earn our living and pay our bills. None of our books are sponsored or carry any outside advertising. We believe this helps us to remain truly independent. We publish books which international conglomerates wouldn't dare touch.

Big publishers have lost touch with people's needs. They are slow and unwieldy. It can take them two years to turn a typescript into a finished book! (We can, if pushed, get a book out within a month - while the material is still topical.)

They are too market orientated and derivative. They produce more of what other publishers did well with last year. We look forwards not backwards.

They pay huge amounts as advances to film stars, politicians and young hotshot authors. Much of the time they don't earn back those advances. They don't care because the books are just seen as 'tools' to help other parts of the empire. For example, a conglomerate will publish a politician's dull biography as a way of putting money into the politician's pocket.

Despite their huge marketing departments they are often out of touch with people's needs. If we published as many 'turkeys' as they do we'd be out of business.

They worry enormously about upsetting powerful politicians and other corporations. The big conglomerates need to cooperate with the establishment because they are part of the establishment.

We stand outside the establishment. They don't like us much at all. They often do their best to shut us down.

But we don't give a fig for what politicians or corporate bosses might (or might not) think of us. We're only interested in publishing books that inform and entertain. When they try to shut us down we fight back.

At big publishers there are loads of men and women in suits who slow things down and interfere with the artistic process. Literary originality and integrity have been replaced by marketing convenience.

We have no men or women in suits to tell us what to do. We do what we believe is right.

We publish books the old-fashioned way.

We're a small, independent publishing house. We publish books we believe in, books we want to publish and which we hope that our readers will want to read.

That's what we think publishing is all about.

Extra 2

The Author

Wordsmith Vernon Coleman has always been on the outside looking in, but always without envy. He has always been the sort of person who prefers to stand in the rain, besieged by snakes, scorpions and spiders, throwing rocks at the warm and cosy house wherein complacent and comfortable insiders congratulate themselves on their insight and success. He has always chosen to continue to do this even when he has been invited inside to sup at the groaning table and to warm his frozen fingers. Moreover, he has always done his best to burn both his boats and his bridges and to cut off his nose whenever his face looked as if it was in danger of becoming a little uppity.

His books are usually completely ignored by the media these days, though when he was much younger and knew very little his books were widely reviewed (and usually praised) in the national press. It is probably no coincidence that he was, long ago, classified as a `dangerous iconoclast' - widely disapproved of by the media establishment. `Whenever my books are remarked upon it is usually with a sneer,' he says ruefully. He has far too much imagination and too great a sense of justice to stay out of trouble for more than a few minutes at a time. Unlike most people, who lose their rebelliousness and individuality as they age, he has become increasingly anarchic as the years have passed. 'I was 62 before I realised I couldn't change the world,' he says. 'So the first 62 years of my life were spent in pointless, frustrated agony as I tried the impossible. And, thereafter, I had to endure the pain of knowing that I'd failed and that the world was going to remain the same bleak, miserable place it always had been.'

Most successful authors write the same book time and time again. Vernon Coleman has never wanted to do this. Worse still he has changed direction completely several times. Medical books. Political books. Cat books. It's impossible to build a successful career with this sort of variety. He writes 'feel good' books (such as the Bilbury novels) and 'feel bad' books (such as his political books).

He says that although he has never gone out of his way to challenge the system, he is conscious that the system has most certainly gone out of its way to challenge him. Other writers find that a little fashionable controversy helps their reviews and sales but Vernon Coleman's brand of controversy leads to total bans. He is the most genuinely banned author in Britain.

Although he is the world's leading independent author/publisher, Coleman is also without doubt his own best enemy. All really successful writers these days are part of the establishment. Even the ones who pretend to be rebels always have very nice things to say about the BBC, they creep to agents and publishers, they say lovely things about one anther's books and they turn up to sign autographs and be lionised at literary festivals. Coleman does none of these things; indeed he avoids them with great determination and vigour.

He believes that the independent author has a responsibility to speak for others and is, indeed, one of the few in our society who can. Most people are paid to suppress the truth in one way or another but authors are paid (albeit not very well) to tell the truth and to stick up for people who can't or daren't stick up for themselves. He believes that writers should always strive to avoid respectability and membership of any branch of the establishment. He believes that all writers should be anarchists at heart and should regard all forms of authority with contempt. He is an idealist who, sadly, failed to grow out of hoping to change the world; the only revolutionary anarchist to have had standing ovations both when at an animal rights rally in Trafalgar Square and at a UKIP annual party conference.

He is far too trusting but instinctively wary of administrators. He cannot be bullied or bribed. He is almost incapable of filling in forms correctly. He has been described as an awkward sod and the self-appointed guardian of eccentrics and underdogs. He is congenitally incapable of accepting disrespect from anyone (however much gold braid they have on their uniform). He is obsessive and stubborn and respects conviction and integrity. His default condition is confusion. He has a contempt for the generally accepted and an affection for the imaginative and unusual.

He is a committed anti-fascist, a freedom fighter and self-appointed enemy of bigotry, intolerance, totalitarianism and cruelty. He is constantly screaming to awaken the uncaring, the new dumb, in a world where the activities of Z list celebrities gather more attention from the media than wars and the EU's new brand of superfascism. He is an anti-establishment, revolutionary libertarian, an over-sensitive polemicist, nearly as demanding of others as of himself. He is a cavalier and a roundhead; a traditionalist who rebels; a radical who hates change; a patriot who believes in the values of old England. He loathes social engineering programmes such as means-testing, political correctness and multiculturalism. He is a self-admitted failure who has done everything wrong. Paradoxically, he is one of the biggest selling authors in Britain. He is painfully shy and sensitive to criticism (to a point of being self-destructive). He is unable to compromise and in a world where resentments and grudges are widely nurtured he is far too forgiving.

He is allergic to rules and regulations. Since we live in a world where rules and regulations breed like rabbits this is bound to lead to the occasional confrontation, though these days he tries not to have more than six major confrontations going at the same time and to not have more than three minor confrontations a day. He displays a courtly but obdurate reluctance to accept orders. He suffers from obsessive compulsive disorder and is painfully reclusive.

He is overly sensitive (and therefore too quick to take offence) absurdly self-critical and a workaholic. He is intolerant of intolerance and too firmly idealistic to be pragmatic. He has frequently been described as a Don Quixote but points out that his foes are far from imaginary.

He confesses that he has for the whole of his adult life been paid (often quite handsomely) to develop and air his opinions. He has worked on his existing opinions as a bodybuilder works on his muscles and has regularly welcomed and nurtured new opinions with rare enthusiasm. Most people are rewarded for disguising or even burying their true feelings. Writers are unique in that they are rewarded not for suppressing but for airing their feelings.

As a young man, he worked as a Community Service Volunteer in Liverpool for a year. He then went to Switzerland and worked as a draughtsman for three months. The aim was to learn to speak a foreign language (anything would do) but he was so shy that he didn't speak to a soul and so didn't learn anything. He is the only person in the world to be (or have been) a member of (among other organisations) the MCC, Equity, the Royal Society of Medicine, the BMA, the Desperate Dan Pie Eaters Club, the Beaumont Society and the Vegan Society.

When he worked as a GP he was once fined £5 for speeding on his way to a patient with a suspected heart attack and was sued for libel by a woman doctor he had never heard of who claimed he had stolen her name because he used a pen name the same as hers. He once sued the chief constable of Oxfordshire for a very good reason that is far too complicated to explain. The case was thrown out by an angry judge who seemed to rather miss the point.

He is often melancholic, and suffers from a total lack of self-confidence. Politically he describes himself both as a `libertarian conservative' and a `patriotic anarchist' but admits that if he founded a party there probably wouldn't be many members. He likes malt whisky and champagne (though not in the same glass or even on the same evening) and is obsessively secretive, though he claims that this is merely a question of self-preservation. He has been described as unpredictable, honest, dangerous, iconoclastic and tall and is old enough to remember the distant days when airline passengers were treated with respect and when household rubbish was collected as a regular routine rather than an occasional favour. He remembers when civil servants were civil rather than patronising, obliging rather than obstructive, and when the word 'gentleman' was used as a compliment rather than in a derisory way.

Vernon Coleman was an angry young man for as long as it was decently possible. He then turned into an angry middle-aged man. And now, with no effort whatsoever, he has matured into being an angry old man. He is, he confesses, just as angry as he ever was. Indeed, he may be even angrier because, he says, the more he learns about life the more things he finds to be angry about.

He says you can't be his sort of writer without being angry.

Cruelty, prejudice and injustice are the three things most likely to arouse his well developed sense of ire but he admits that, at a pinch, inefficiency, incompetence and greed will do almost as well. He does not cope well with bossy people, particularly when they are dressed in uniform and attempting to confiscate his Swiss Army penknife. 'Being told I can't do something has always seemed to me sufficient reason to do it,' he says. 'And being told that I must do something has always seemed to me a very good reason not to do it.'

Coleman has an innate dislike of taking orders, a pathological contempt for pomposity, hypocrisy and the sort of unthinking political correctness which attracts support from *Guardian* reading pseudo-intellectuals. He also has a passionate loathing for those in authority who do not understand that unless their authority is tempered with compassion and a sense of responsibility the end result must always be an extremely unpleasant brand of totalitarianism. He believes that multiculturalism on a global scale is perfectly appropriate but that individual countries are best left to be individual. He regards the European Union as the most fascist organisation ever invented and looks forward to its early demise.

Vernon Coleman has written for *The Guardian* (he was a teenager at the time and knew no better), *Daily Telegraph, Sunday Telegraph, Observer, Sunday Times, Daily Mail, Mail on Sunday, Daily Express, Sunday Express, Daily Star, The Sun, News of the World, Daily Mirror, Sunday Mirror, The People, Woman, Woman's Own, Spectator, Punch, The Lady* and hundreds of other leading publications in Britain and around the world. His books have been published by *Thames and Hudson, Sidgwick and*

Jackson, Hamlyn, Macmillan, Robert Hale, Pan, Penguin, Corgi, Arrow and several dozen other publishers in the UK and reproduced by scores of discerning publishers around the world. His self-published novel *Mrs Caldicot's Cabbage War* was made into a film and a number of his other books have been turned into radio or television programmes. Today he publishes his books himself as this allows him to avoid contact with marketing men in silk suits and 19-year-old editorial directors called Fiona. In an earlier life he was the television doctor on breakfast television and in the now long-gone days when producers and editors were less wary of annoying the establishment he was a regular broadcaster on radio and television. He was the first agony uncle on BBC television.

He has never had a proper job (in the sense of working for someone else in regular, paid employment, with a cheque or pay packet at the end of the week or month) but he has had freelance and temporary employment in many forms. He has worked as: magician's assistant, postman, fish delivery van driver, production line worker, chemical laboratory assistant, author, publisher, draughtsman, meals on wheels driver, feature writer, drama critic, book reviewer, columnist, surgeon, police surgeon, landlord, industrial medical officer, social worker, night club operator, property developer, magazine editor, private doctor, television presenter, radio presenter, agony aunt, casualty doctor, care home assistant and investor. He worked as a GP for ten years. He is believed to be the only writer to have had weekly columns in three major British daily newspapers at the same time (not all under the same name). He used to be a practising doctor and therefore tends to be impatient when doing practical things - and to give crisp orders when wanting things passing to him. He has been a medical consultant to a large slimming organisation and the President of LIMAV, an organisation containing over 1,000 doctors opposed to vivisection. For several years he was the Telephone Doctor and his medical advice lines were used by countless thousands. He has been a newsletter writer and publisher, has worked in a Leonard Cheshire home and has lectured at universities and medical schools. Much to his (and probably also to their) surprise, he has given evidence to committees in the House of Commons and the

House of Lords. Whether they took any notice of what he had to say is doubtful. They did not fall asleep.

Today, he likes books, films and writing. He writes, reads and collects books and has a larger library than most towns. He also collects lead soldiers of the Napoleonic era, toy racing cars (from the 1960s and before) hats, lingerie, cigarette cards and postcards.

A list of his favourite authors would require another book. He has never been much of an athlete, though he once won a certificate for swimming a width of the public baths in Walsall (which was, at the time, in Staffordshire but has now, apparently, been moved elsewhere). He no longer cherishes hopes of being called upon to play cricket for England and is resigned to the fact that he will now never drive a Formula 1 racing car in anger.

He doesn't like yappy dogs, big snarly dogs with saliva dripping from their fangs or people who think that wearing a uniform automatically gives them status and rights over everyone else. He likes trains, dislikes planes and used to like cars until idiots invented speed cameras, bus lanes and car parks where the spaces are so narrow that only the slimmest, and tinniest of vehicles will fit in.

He is inordinately fond of cats, likes pens and notebooks and used to enjoy watching cricket until the authorities sold out and allowed people to paint slogans on the grass. His interests and hobbies include animals, books, photography, drawing, chess, backgammon, cinema, philately, billiards, sitting in cafés and on benches and collecting Napoleana. He likes log fires and bonfires, motor racing and music by Beethoven, Mozart and Mahler and dislikes politicians, bureaucrats and cauliflower cheese. He likes videos but loathes DVDs. His favourite 12 people in history include (in no particular order): Daniel Defoe, Che Guevara, Napoleon Bonaparte, W. G. Grace, William Cobbett, Thomas Paine, John Lilburne, Aphra Behn, P. G. Wodehouse, Jerome K. Jerome, Francis Drake and Walter Ralegh all of whom had more than it takes and most of whom were English. Spare heroes include Philippus Aureolus Theophrastus Bombastus von Hohenheim (aka Paracelsus), Ignaz Semmelweiss, Ayn Rand, Henry David Thoreau and Friedrich Nietzsche.

Vernon Coleman, old-fashioned bookwright, lives in the delightful if isolated village of Bilbury in Devon and enjoys toasted muffins and old films. He is devoted to Donna Antoinette who is the kindest, sweetest, most sensitive woman a man could hope to meet and who, as an undeserved but welcome bonus, makes the very best roast parsnips on the planet. He says that gourmands and gourmets would come from far and wide if they knew what they were missing but admits that since he and his pal Thumper Robinson took down the road signs (in order to discourage tourists) the village where he lives has become exceedingly difficult to find.

A catalogue record for this book is available from the British Library.

This is the first of Vernon Coleman's diaries. The second is called `Just Another Bloody Year'. For a full list of books by Vernon Coleman please see Amazon Author Central or visit http://www.vernoncoleman.com/

Printed in Great Britain
by Amazon

35387737R00364